Beyond
the Beauty Strip

Saving What's Left of Our Forests

The Maine Woods between Moosehead and Chesuncook lakes: Before (1977, photo by U.S. Geological Survey) and after (1991, photo by National Aerial Photography Program).

The West Branch of the Penobscot River is visible in the lower right of each picture.
Scale: 1 inch = 0.6 miles. Photo shows 16 square miles, more than 10,000 acres.

Beyond
the Beauty Strip

Saving What's Left of Our Forests

Mitch Lansky

Old Bridge Press
Camden East, Ontario

Published by Old Bridge Press
an imprint of Camden House Publishing, a division of Telemedia Communications
7 Queen Victoria Road
Camden East, Ontario KOK 1JO

Trade distribution by Firefly Books
250 Sparks Avenue
Willowdale, Ontario M2H 2S4

First Printing

Canadian Cataloguing in Publication Data
Lansky, Mitch, 1948-
        Beyond the beauty strip: saving what's left of our forests

        ISBN 0-921820-65-8

        1. Forest management. 2. Forest policy--Economic
        aspects. 3. Sustainable forestry. 4. Forest
        management -- Maine. 5. Forest policy -- Economic
        aspects -- Maine. 6. Sustainable forestry -- Maine.
        I. Title.

        SD144.M2L3 1993   333.75'09741   C92-095577-0

10 9 8 7 6 5 4 3 2 1

Contents

Acknowledgements

I thank the following individuals and groups who helped to make this book possible (but they are in no way responsible for the opinions, conclusions, or errors in this book—for these I take full responsibility):

For faith that I could turn my rough idea into a book, and for patience and guidance as I struggled to do so—Mark Melnicove.

For technical and financial assistance in bringing me into the computer age—Ted and David Lansky.

For financial assistance—anonymous angel.

For flying me over the forest—Susan Meeker-Lowry, members of the Applachian Mountain Club, Alex McLean, and Spike Haible.

For sharing written documents (including their own studies or books), engaging in enlightening discussions, and (in some cases) for reading early drafts of sections of the book—Tom Allen, Phyllis Austin, Eric Bruner, Bob Cummings, Jeff Elliott, Ivan Fernandez, Charles Fitzgerald, Robert Frank, Richard Grossman, Mac Hunter, Lloyd Irland, Alexander Jablanczy, Mike Kellett, Bonnie Lounsbury, David Maass, Maxwell McCormack, Jr., Mark McCullough, Wayne Millen, Steve Miller, Peter Murdoch, Diane Pence, David Orton, Richard and Elizabeth Parker, Charlie Restino, Stephen Salisbury, Jeff Schwartz, Walter Shortle, Gary Schneider, Bob Seymour, Tor Smith, Anne Stewart, Richard Sylvan, Seth Tuler, David Vail, Dirk Van Loon, Michael Vernon, Lissa Widdoff, and Randy Wilson.

For their extraordinary support and interest in the project, for the many documents and newsclippings they sent me, and for their ideas and suggestions—Bill Butler, Jym St. Pierre and Jamie Sayen.

For keeping me involved in the political process—Michael Cline and Karen Tilberg.

For giving moral support to a fellow, struggling author—Cheryl Seal.

For sharing documents and explaining government policy—staff of: Maine Forest Service, Department of Environmental Protection, Bureau of Taxation, Board of Pesticide Control, Bureau of Public Lands, Department of Inland Fisheries and Wildlife, Critical Areas Program, and Department of Labor.

For providing documents, studies, and good discussions from a more industrial point of view—the Paper Industry Information Office, the Cooperative Forestry Research Unit, and some industrial foresters who cared enough to keep a running dialog.

For explaining the realities of timber harvesting—contractors and woodcutters (who shall remain unnamed but whom I thank just the same).

For demonstrating the realities of living in the midst of the industrial forest—the people of Wytopitlock.

For supplying me with numerous books by mail through interlibrary loan—Maine State Library.

For assisting in the design of the book—Edith Allard.

For catching redundancies, repetition, verbosity, wordiness, superfluity, long-windedness, tautologies, circumlocutions, magniloquence, prolixity, as well as inconsistencies, lack of clarity, imprecision, haziness, vagueness, inexactness, laxity, looseness, sloppiness, and obscurity, and for showing me how to rite gooder English—Elizabeth Pierson and Devon Phillips.

For demonstrating that what I wrote in a chapter could be compressed into a couple of pages—Tom Lepisto.

For their faith, support, love, and tolerance—Susan Szwed and Alysha and Jacob Lansky.

For their grace, beauty, shelter, and fiber (without which this book would surely not be possible)—the trees and forests.

Pro-log

I wrote this book in response to years of frustration, not only with industrial management of the Maine woods in which I live but also with industrial management of public opinion. This book is, unapologetically, a polemic. It argues against both the premises and conclusions that guide forestry policy in Maine and elsewhere. In this book I ask for whom does industrial-style forest management work and for how long? Does it work for forest ecosystems? Does it work for local communities? Is it profitable to take ecosystems and communities into account? Is the system sustainable? Turned around, these questions reveal the premises which guide my critique: that forestry policy should be ecologically sound, socially responsible, economically viable and sustainable.

My critique of industrial forestry is based, in part, on direct experience. I am not an outside "expert" studying forest problems this year, and some other problem next. I live here. In 1973, I bought an abandoned farm in Reed Plantation (popularly known as Wytopitlock), a remote town in southern Aroostook County. My land is forty miles from the nearest hospital, police station, shopping center or McDonalds. Most of the land in this and surrounding towns is owned by paper companies. Most of the working men in the town are employed as loggers, truckers or mill workers.

I have found that to survive I, too, have to depend on the forest and the trees. Part of my income has come from cutting in my woodlot (and the woodlots of friends). I have worked as a timber cruiser, forest-fire fighter, sawmill worker and carpenter. My wife and I have gathered balsam fir tips and made Christmas wreaths. One summer we even contracted with a German firm to gather wild forest mushrooms. The forests have provided us with timber for our buildings, firewood for our stove and maple syrup for our pancakes. Every year we like to take time off to canoe on the rivers and lakes in the area, ski over woods trails, and hike in nearby Baxter Park. We have even flown over the region's forests in small airplanes.

I have, therefore, had ample opportunity to observe from inside, outside, and above, the impact of industrial forest management on the forest and local communities. I have also had ample opportunity to examine the arguments by which industrial advocates justify their forest practices and to question state government legitimization of such practices.

My topic, industrial management of second-growth, privately owned forests in a Northeastern state, may seem parochial at a time when national forestry controversies are swirling around the destruction of tropical forests in Brazil, the liquidation of old-growth forests in the Northwest, and the mismanagement of public lands. Maine's forest ecosystems may be unique, but the problems Mainers face are not. In the course of my research, I have corresponded with individuals from different regions who face similar problems despite dissimilar forest types. The problems they face are similar because the multinational timber corporations they face are the same and the global markets in which these companies operate are the same. Although not as exotic a subject as Amazonian rain forests, the forests of northern New York and New England—within a day's drive of seventy millon people—are certainly worthy of attention.

Eighty-five percent of the timber cut in the United States is on private, not public lands. While protecting the small percentage of forests that are still "virgin" is urgent, it is just as urgent to prevent further degradation of non-virgin forests. Indeed, as old-growth controversies are resolved, either by cutting or protection, restoring managed forests will become *the* major forestry issue. Maine, with its long history of logging, represents an appropriate case study.

Finally, there is another compelling reason to look at forest practices on private lands in Maine: because industrial foresters claim they are setting an example for governments to follow. Boise Cascade's 1989 Annual Report states, for example, that ". . . we've joined with other forest products companies in an intensified effort to ensure that the general public and the decision makers in federal and state government understand the importance of managing our nation's forests for multiple uses, including commercial harvest, wildlife, and recreation. We know this kind of balanced approach works, because it's the way we manage our own timberlands." If industrial forest management is the model for the public lands to follow, then Maine, which has the most industry-owned forest land of any state, should have the premier forests in the Nation.

The Industrial Forest
Nearly 90% of the land in Maine (excluding lakes, ponds, rivers, etc.) is forested—the highest proportion of any state. Of that forestland, 97% is "timberlands" (commercial forest rather than wilderness, urban or preserve) and of the timberlands, 96% is privately owned.[1] Even though Maine's forest ranks only seventeenth in size in the nation and contains only 3.5% of all timberlands, it has more than 12% of the forest-industry-owned timberland in the country—more than any other state. With more than 8 million acres of industrially-owned forestland, Maine is far ahead of second-ranked Oregon, which has

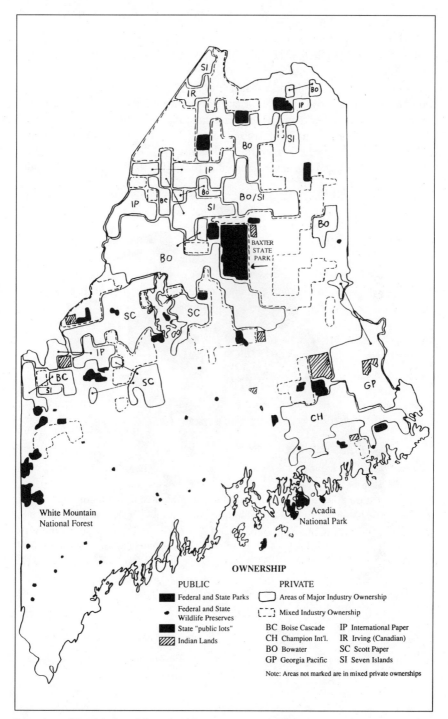

Location of large industrial ownerships. *From Sherman Hasbrouck*, The Forests of Maine *(Orono: Land and Water Resources Center, University of Maine, 1987), p. 9.*

slightly more than 5 million acres.[2]

Most of Maine's industrial forest is located in a vast area with no cities, and with villages and public roads only on the outskirts of hundreds of miles of forest. Although this region of northern and eastern Maine holds more than half the state's landmass, it holds less than 1% of its year-round population. Politically this region is classified as "unorganized territories" whose land use is regulated by the state rather than by local governments. The administering agency, the Land Use Regulation Commission (better known by its ominous sounding acronym, LURC) calls its domain the "wildlands."

LURC, which the legislature created in the early 1970s, did not invent this

UNORGANIZED TOWNSHIPS, TOWNS & PLANTATIONS IN THE JURISDICTION OF THE **LAND USE REGULATION COMMISSION**

Location of unorganized territories regulated by LURC. *Courtesy LURC.*

romantic sounding name. People in Maine have been calling this region the wildlands for centuries. The term implies a region not quite under man's control. There are, for example, thousands of bogs, ponds, lakes and streams that are still "undeveloped." There are rivers, like the Penobscot and Kennebec, with long and turbulent rapids. There are tumbling waterfalls and steep chasms such as Gulf Hagus Gorge. And there is the jagged granite majesty of Mount Katahdin.

The name "wildlands" can also conjure up the sights and sounds of "wildlife"—moose feeding on water lilies in a remote pond, loons calling to one another over a still lake after sunset, or hermit thrushes singing their beautiful flutelike melody in the remote forest. Some of the wildlife—biting, buzzing, tormenting swarms of blackflies, mosquitoes, no-see-ums, deerflies, and mooseflies—create less pleasant images. This is the famed Maine Woods of Henry David Thoreau (minus a few species such as wolves and caribou), a forest as unique and as deeply imbedded in the national consciousness as the Douglas-fir forests of the Pacific Northwest, or the Everglades of Florida.

The wildlands happen to coincide with a spruce-fir/northern-hardwood transition forest (called "Acadian" in the Canadian Maritimes) that is highly prized as a source of fiber for making paper. The land is mostly owned by a handful of paper companies, land-management firms, and ownership consortia (in which many individuals share ownership and management of large tracts).

The term "wildlands" does not conjure up images of mechanical harvesters chewing tens of thousands of acres of forest down to stumps, of helicopters spraying defoliants over vast clearcuts, of aircraft spreading chemical insecticides over millions of acres, or of huge logging trucks negotiating the thousands of miles of private roads that landowners have built to get their timber to the mills. It does not conjure up images of rivers that are dammed and polluted, of air (downwind from pulpmills) that smells like a combination of dead fish and rotten eggs, or of communities that are subject to the blackmail threats of a single dominating company.

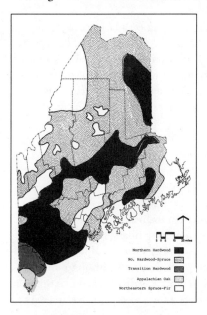

Potential natural vegetation of Maine. *From* The Natural Regions of Maine *(Augusta: Maine Critical Areas Program, 1978), p. 32.*

It also does not conjure up inequities of landownership that one would normally associate with banana republics in Latin America. Ninety percent of the wildlands is owned by only 20 companies. Two-thirds of this land is owned by 9 out-of-state-based paper companies: Bowater (Great Northern) Georgia-Pacific, International Paper, Scott Paper, Boise Cascade, Champion International,

James River, Fraser Paper Ltd., and J.D. Irving, Ltd. Bowater alone, with its 2.1 million acres, owns more than 10% of the state and 20% of the wildlands. In the early 1980s some of the industrial landowners suggested that LURC officially change the name of the wildlands to the "industrial forest." They pointed out that the region is no longer wild; it is a "working forest" that is actively managed for lumber and fiber.

Names have power. They influence how we perceive and relate to that which is named. An "industrial forest" is perceived as a resource that can and should be efficiently exploited. Other values, such as hiking, canoeing, hunting, or fishing, exist by the good graces of the landowners, who inform us they manage their forests for "multiple uses." In an industrial forest we should be grateful that any wildlife survives, that any forest is worth looking at, or that any river is unpolluted and free flowing, since these are not primary considerations.

Although LURC continues to use the term "wildlands," it is the concept of the industrial forest that dominates state forestry policy. Among its forest-resource policies, for example, LURC is supposed to "Discourage development that will interfere unreasonably with continued timber and wood fiber production," and to "Discourage land uses that are not essential to forest management or timber production on highly productive forest lands."[3] Land that is not in "protection zones" (i.e., shorelands and deeryards) is in "management" zones. In management zones, timber companies have been allowed, until recently, to cut every tree in sight until the landscape—i.e. a protection zone— stops them.

Beyond the Beauty Strip

In the mid-1970s, when companies started clearcutting on a large scale, local loggers called the buffers of trees they were leaving around roads and bodies of water, "beauty strips." Beauty strips create the illusion that there really is a forest out there. The buffers do, of course, help to moderate the effects of siltation in streams and do protect some wildlife habitat. To the loggers however, these beauty strips are a sham—they do not protect the forest; they hide forest destruction.

Soon after moving to Wytopitlock in 1973, I discovered that all was not well beyond the beauty strip. I arrived in the area just as companies started clearcutting with mechanical harvesters on a grand scale. The companies claimed that the clearcuts were necessary to "pre-salvage" softwoods that were being attacked by the spruce budworm, a moth larva with a special fondness for the foliage of spruce and balsam fir. The paper companies also have a special fondness for spruce and fir which, because of their long fibers, are superior for making paper. I noticed, however, that along with the spruce and fir, the companies were cutting everything else. One company clearcut right up to my property line. In my own woodlot, I cut some of the fir trees that looked like they were about to die. Fifteen years later, I still have a forest—my corporate neighbor has mostly seedlings and saplings.

In 1975, woodsworkers, including local friends and neighbors, staged a desperate strike against the paper companies. Their organization, the Maine Woodsmen Association (MWA), protested corporate price-fixing, unfair con-

A beauty strip along the Allagash. *Photo by Christopher Ayres.*

Beyond the beauty strip. *Photo by Christopher Ayres.*

tracts, falsified scaling of wood at the mill, and the use of Canadian workers to keep wages low. MWA members also raised some issues normally not associated with labor groups. They claimed the forest was being liquidated, and they opposed the widespread use of clearcuts, mechanized harvesters, and chemical pesticides—issues that the state's large environmental groups were not addressing. The industry accused the woodsmen of being independent businessmen who, by striking, were engaged in antitrust violations. After a Maine court issued an injunction against the strikers to end "economic warfare," the strike fizzled away.

During this same period, Maine was engaged in an enormous spray campaign against the spruce budworm. Sporadically from 1954 to 1970, and every year from 1972 to 1985, airplanes spread chemical toxins over hundreds of thousands or even millions of acres of forest. Although our town is almost totally dependent on the forest industry for its economic survival, 98% of the eligible voters signed a petition, in 1978, to stop the spraying. The state, however, was less moved by an appeal from its citizens seeking to protect their health and their environment, than by appeals from absentee corporate landowners seeking to protect, partly at taxpayers' expense, their economic interests.

On a frosty morning in early June of 1976, three former World War II bombers sprayed my entire farm—fields, gardens, stream, spring, woodlot and house—with chemical insecticides during a budworm search-and-destroy mission. I responded as would any red-blooded American—I sued. I soon discovered, to my amazement, that there was little opposition to what was, at the time, one of the most widespread and long-term spray programs in the United States. That year the State of Maine had sprayed toxic chemicals over 3.5 million acres of forest—an area equivalent in size to Connecticut and Rhode Island put together.

With money from an out-of-court settlement, I helped found a group called PEST—Protect our Environment from Sprayed Toxins. Some of the PEST membership included other spray victims. Since we were being sprayed like pests, we decided we might as well act like them—in particular the resistant ones. Our group's primary focus was the government-subsidized, spruce budworm spray program. We researched, published articles and pamphlets, supplied local groups with information and contacts, attended statewide hearings and conferences, staged protests, issued press releases, confronted spray pilots at airports, and sued the state for faulty environmental impact statements. As the acreage sprayed was reduced, as buffers (pesticide beauty strips) were put into place around populated areas and aquatic regions, as chemicals were replaced by biological controls, as federal and state funding were withdrawn, and as the program finally ended (because the budworm outbreak finally collapsed), PEST slowly faded out too.

PEST members had also been concerned with the the paper industry's growing use of chemical herbicides to "suppress" the "weeds" that "compete" with spruce and fir in large clearcuts. An incident in 1979, however, delayed industry plans for expanding herbicide spray projects. That year, several hundred gardens within twelve miles of a St. Regis Paper Company clearcut in Dennysville, Washington County, were contaminated by herbicide drift. The protests and legal suits that arose from that incident discouraged the paper companies from any large-scale use of herbicides—until the late 1980s, when PEST had ceased to be active. Then, herbicide use came back with a vengeance.

The press and statewide environmental groups expressed no major concern over this trend until 1989, when it was revealed that in the previous year forest landowners sprayed nearly 80,000 acres with herbicides—seven times more acreage than in any other comparable northern state. The next year, landowners sprayed nearly 90,000 acres. The facts were too embarrassing to ignore, but the press did not put the facts into the context of widespread international protests against forestry herbicide use. The beauty strip that hides the dark side of the industrial forest, I learned, does not consist merely in trees.

Industrial Myths

The beauty strip works somewhat like Lewis Carroll's looking glass. To step beyond the beauty strip is to step into a world of distorted priorities, distorted metaphors and distorted logic. If what you see looks degraded and ugly, the fault (according to corporate spokespeople) lies with your vision rather than industry's management. Once you learn the proper attitude, it should all look acceptable, if not admirable.

Beyond the beauty strip, the priorities for the forest are industrial priorities. From the industrial perspective, the forest is not a biological community to which we belong and which we must maintain. It is a resource to exploit.

Beyond the beauty strip, forest and society are described with industrial metaphors that help to justify industrial actions. The forest becomes a pulpwood factory, a fiber farm, or just biomass. It is a commodity to be bought or sold. Rivers become an energy source or (along with air) a pollution sink. Human beings are labor (to avoid), consumers (to entice) or stockholders (to please).

The combination of industrial priorities and metaphors leads to a bizarre form of logic which asserts, for example, that:
- the way to improve forest health is to remove the forest;
- the way to increase wildlife diversity is to fragment and simplify wildlife habitat;
- the way to regulate forest practices is to legitimize what industry is already doing;
- the way to protect forest jobs is to invest in machines and chemicals that replace forest workers;
- the way to prevent timber shortfalls is to accelerate and intensify timber harvest.

I call such statements, for lack of a better term, industrial forest myths. These myths do not exactly endow weed-fighting industrial foresters with the heroic qualities of Hercules battling the Hydra, but they do fulfill one of the functions of mythology suggested by the poet/scholar Robert Graves, i.e., to "justify an existing social system and account for traditional rites and customs."[4] While in traditional societies myths are sacred narratives that provide a foundation for the religious world, in our society myths are considered convenient fictions to support questionable activities. When I use the word "myths" I am referring to this latter usuage.

Industrial forest myths are intended to establish that, by some extraordinarily happy coincidence, whatever industry does in pursuit of growth and profit just happens to be good for the forest and society. For example, to achieve the goal of a cheap supply of wood for the mills, paper companies dominate the markets, exploit workers, fend off regulations, and extract tax breaks. Myths are employed to help convince the public and legislators that such strategies are to their benefit and should be embraced rather than fought.

Those who state these myths are not just representatives of the paper industry—they include former forest-industry employees at the Maine Department of Conservation, legislators receiving industry PAC money, University of Maine professors getting industry-sponsored grants, newspaper reporters relying on industry spokespeople, and even, at times, representatives of some environmental groups that have received industry grants or that have industry managers on their boards, committees, or staff.

Those who expound these myths are not necessarily lying. Many sincerely believe what they say. The myths, after all, are consistent with the entire thought system that dominates our industrial society. What I am describing and criticizing, therefore, is less an organized conspiracy than a shared belief system—a belief system that dominates discussions on forestry policy. As long as this domination continues, policy will continue to serve industrial goals.

Maine's Forest as a Resource for the Paper Industry

If only one person uses a set of myths and metaphors, it is a delusion. If a small group of people shares a set of myths or metaphors, it is a cult. When a majority of society, including prominant leaders, share a set of myths and metaphors, it is reality. Since our society is oriented around markets, and since the Maine market is dominated by the paper industry, it should not be surprising that paper-industry priorities have become accepted as social and ecological priorities by so many people.

The paper industry is proud of its dominance of the state economy. Combined with lumber and wood-product industries (of which the paper industry owns a good share), its impact is even more pronounced, as the following chart indicates:

Economic Importance of Paper Industry[5]
(Census of Maine Manufacturers, 1988)

	State rank of paper industry	Paper industry share of total manufacturers	Percent when combined with lumber manufacturers and wood products
Value of product	1	34.22%	44.2%
Value of exports	1	28.41%	36.4%
Capital expenditures	1	38.68%	45.98%
Gross payroll	1	23.76%	33.86%
Number of employees	1	15.34%	27.64%

Maine's paper industry also has national economic importance. It ranks second in volume of paper production and first in the manufacture of printing and writing papers and in lightweight coated (LWC) papers—papers that rely on the long fibers of spruce and fir.[6]

Multiple Uses
The paper industry is not the only group in Maine that sees the forest as a resource to exploit or that has its own set of myths and metaphors to justify its activities. Other groups interested in the forest as a resource include power companies, the military, mining companies, recreationists, and developers. The paper companies do not see all the activities generated by these groups as threats to the integrity of the forest; some are "multiple uses" which can make their forests more valuable.

Power Companies
To power companies, the forest is a tremendous biomass resource for wood-fuel generators. It is an ideal place for powerline corridors to channel cheap Canadian energy to southern New England. It is a perfect location for hydrodam catchments created from dammed rivers. The forest is also a wasteland, the logical place to locate dumps for toxic incinerator ash or low-level nuclear waste. As I write this, the state is screening wildlands communities as potential dump sites. A few years ago, the U.S. Department of Energy considered (but eventually rejected) the Bottle Lake region, twenty miles away from my home, as a potential site for high-level nuclear waste. Neighboring communities were informed that building such a repository would be an economic boon. It would create jobs. So, I suppose, would a whorehouse.

The paper industry is the biggest consumer of electricity in Maine and one of the biggest producers; most of the state's hydrodams and biomass energy plants are controlled by the industry.

Military

The military likewise sees the forest as a vast, unpopulated hinterland—an ideal training ground for troops, aircraft, or even missiles. Champion International has offered its entire three- quarter million acres of timberlands to the National Guard to create the largest military training area in the country. Air Force bombers routinely fly at high speeds and low altitudes over the forest to practice evading radar. When they fly over my house, it feels as if something nearby has exploded or as if the earth is quaking.

The towns of Monson and Shirley near Moosehead Lake were targeted by the Air Force as a site for GWEN (Ground Wave Emergency Network) relay towers. But local people were not receptive to the idea, especially after they found out that the low-frequency waves the 300-foot-high towers would emit are, according to the National Health Federation, harmful to human health. The towers have not been built.

The Air Force did build, at the cost of about 2 billion dollars, several Back-scatter radar dishes near (ironically) the town of Moscow. These early warning devices have since been abandoned. The Navy has also, against the will of the people (expressed in a referendum), tested the controversial cruise missile over the Maine woods—within site of Mount Katahdin. To support these military activities is to show one's patriotism. To oppose them, however. . . .

Mining

To miners, the forest is an impediment to the real resources underground: gravel (used extensively by paper companies to build woods roads), copper, zinc and other metals and minerals. A Swedish corporation is planning to operate a sizable copper mine at Bald Mountain in Aroostook County. Maine is only just putting together regulations for mining, an activity that has the potential to cause serious long-term groundwater pollution. The Presque Isle Chamber of Commerce and other booster organizations, however, believe that mining will open new opportunities for local industrial development and will create jobs— though the jobs might not last more than ten years.

Recreation

To recreationists, the outdoors itself is a resource. Hunters, fishermen, canoe-ists, and hikers spend hundreds of millions of dollars every year in Maine on equipment, transportation, food, and lodging so they can "consume" scenery, wildlife, and adventure. The economic importance of recreation to the state has led to a multiple-use compromise: where forest management for commercial tree species ends (at the beauty strip), wildlife management for commercial fish and game species begins.

Over the last two decades, since the state banned riverdriving of logs to the mills, forest landowners have built thousands of miles of woods roads. These roads, built to allow landowners to cut formerly remote forests and truck out the timber, have also created access for recreationists in pickups, snowmobiles, and off-road vehicles. The impact on wildlife of thousands of campers or sportsmen trampling the ground, making loud noises, strewing trash, and shooting animals with high-powered rifles can be profound at some sites.

Canoeists and rafters have turned portions of formerly remote rivers into backwoods traffic jams. There have been days when hundreds of hikers, seeking their moment of solitude with nature, have converged at once on the summit of Mount Katahdin. Yet Maine's wildlands are expected to serve even greater numbers of nature-starved urbanites in the coming decades. This is supposed to be a boon to Maine's tourist industry. Our license plate does, after all, read *Vacationland*.

Developers

To developers, forestland near lakes or rivers is a raw, undeveloped commodity. The land is not complete until it has roads, house lots, cottages, or condos. From 1985 to 1988, 150,000 acres of wildlands under LURC's jurisdiction were

Multiple Use Working Forest Algorithm, by Mitch Lanksy.

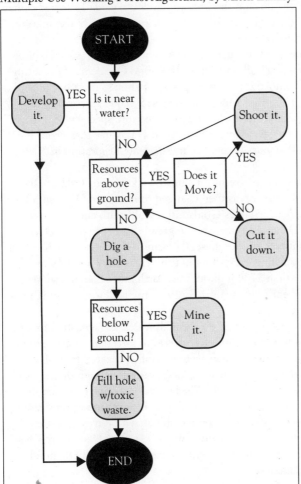

subdivided and thus "improved" by land entrepreneurs.[7] This style of development in Maine helped to fuel the economic boom of the 1980s. When the boom collapsed at the end of the decade, not only developers but banks went bust.

The paper companies have their own real-estate divisions to make profits from their HBU (Highest and Best Use) lands suitable for development. Although the industry is not the only seller of lands for development (the list includes farmers, Indian tribes, and large contractors), as the biggest landowner it has the highest potential to make large and socially disruptive land transactions.

Maine's Forest as a National Issue

Ironically, it was not the threats from logging, power companies, or the military that finally prompted national environmental groups and even the federal government to take notice of Maine's forest—it was the threat from land sales for development. Even though the actual acreage affected has been relatively small, development, because it concentrates in the shorelands, directly assaults the beauty strip. It destroys the illusion that the wildlands are wild. It degrades that aspect of the forest with the highest public value for recreation. It also marginally intrudes into the industrial forest.

The event that finally got the federal government's attention was the offer for sale in 1987-88 of nearly a million acres of Diamond Occidental Forest timberlands in New York and northern New England. Although most of the land in Maine was bought by two other paper companies (560,000 acres by James River and 230,000 by Fraser Paper Ltd.), some of the more spectacular tracts in other states were bought by development firms such as Lassiter Properties Inc. in the Adirondacks, and Rancourt Associates and Patten Corporation in New Hampshire and Vermont.[8]

This massive land sale was the result of a hostile takeover in 1982 of Diamond International (whose name was then changed to Diamond Occidental) by the English corporate raider Sir James Goldsmith. Goldsmith correctly estimated that the assets of Diamond International greatly exceeded its market value. Within eight months of his purchase, Goldsmith had already earned back 90% of his investment by selling everything but the 1.7 million acres of land. The land, valued at more than $700 million, was worth more than his $660 million purchase price of the entire company.[9] By 1988, the land was reaching peak market value.

Despite warnings in 1987 by forest policy analyst Perry Hagenstein that the paper industry was about to unload millions of acres of forestland,[10] conservation groups and state and federal governments were not fully prepared to deal with nearly a million acres at once. They claimed there was not enough money available to purchase such huge tracts of land. The large developers, however, did not hesitate to purchase, and when government and conservation groups came to their senses and discovered that they could come up with the money, they found that some of the purchase prices had gone up. At New Hampshire's Nash Stream Watershed, for example, they were no longer dealing with Diamond, they were dealing with Rancourt.

As a result of the Nash Stream Watershed sale, and amidst predictions that millions of acres of prime wildlands in New York and northern New England could be subdivided, Congress created the Northern Forest Land Study (NFLS) in 1988. The Northern Forest comprises 26 million acres of continuous forest that runs from New York's Adirondacks, across northern Vermont and New Hampshire into the wildlands of Maine. The prime goal of the study was to protect the existing timber-based economy combined with the traditional public access to the woods—in other words, to protect the multiple-use working forest. Senators Patrick Leahy of Vermont and Warren Rudman of New Hampshire clearly expressed this goal when they wrote to the Chief of the Forest Service in October of 1988, stating, "The current land ownership and management patterns have served the people and forests of the region well. We are seeking reinforcement rather than replacement of the patterns of ownership and use that have characterized these lands."[11]

Maine's Commissioner of Conservation, Robert LaBonta (formerly a timberlands manager for Scott Paper Company) was at first wary of federal involvement in Maine forestry affairs. He expressed concern that such involvement would lead to purchases and regulations which would threaten landowner rights. He raised the specter of local forestry policy being dictated by bureaucrats from Washington (as opposed to corporate executives in Georgia, Connecticut, Pennsylvania, or New York). When Maine's paper-industry leaders realized they could not prevent the study, they tried to control its direction (following a strategy that will become familiar to readers of this book). They made sure that the Maine representatives on the decision-making Governors' Task Force, com-

Location of Northern Forest Lands. *From* The Northern Forest Lands: A Strategy for their Future, May 1990, page 1.

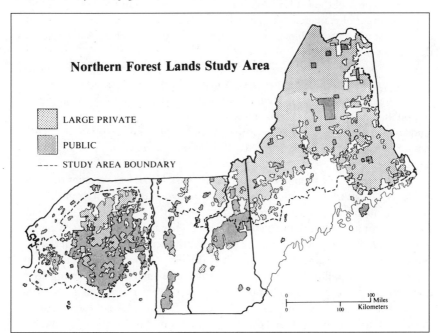

posed of three representatives from each of the four states in the study area, were industry friendly. Indeed, one of the members was Ted Johnston, director of the Maine Forest Products Council, an industry lobby group.

The NFLS final draft, published in April 1990, stated that "The current ownership pattern with its predominance of private ownership has served the region well,"[12] and suggested six general strategies for achieving its goal of a "working landscape":

1) "land use controls and planning for conservation;"
2) "easements and land purchase for conservation;"
3) "maintaining large tracts of private forest land through incentives;"
4) "combining community improvement with land conservation;"
5) "keeping private land open to the public;" and
6) "combining strategies in a coordinated program."[13]

The study's proposed incentives to forest landowners are attractive to the paper industry and include such items as capital-gains deductions on timber, credits for investing in resource-based industry and in forest land, and deductions for timber-management costs.[14] Both conservation easements (another of industry's favored strategies) and some of these incentives come with the promise to continue managing for timber, rather than selling for development, over a specified time period. Companies find such arrangements attractive because only a small percentage, perhaps less than ten percent, of their land is worth developing, but all their land gets the benefit.

Such strategies imply that the forest is protected if it is kept under industrial management. Maine Audubon Society and the Natural Resources Council of Maine, the two largest environmental groups in the state, accepted the premise that the purpose of the NFLS is to deal with the threat of development rather than the threat of management as usual. They felt that the proper forum to address forest practices problems was Maine's new Forest Practices Act, which was then under negotiation.

Some national and regional environmental groups, notably The Wilderness Society, the Sierra Club, and Preserve Appalachian Wilderness, wanted the NFLS to protect forest ecosystem health, not just timber industry prosperity and public access for recreation. They wanted to see large federal purchases of land and large acreages managed primarily for biological diversity rather than just for wood fiber. They advocated a "Greenline Strategy," with all government options being used in a coordinated fashion in a designated area.

The Maine delegation of the Governors' Task Force was resistant to such demands, but after persistent environmental lobbying, the final draft of the NFLS did incorporate the Greenline Strategy as one option and did include information on forest health in an appendix which began by stating that "Changes in landownership and use are not the only factors affecting the future of the Northern Forest. Changes in the health of the forest brought about by harvesting practices, air pollution, acid rain, ozone depletion and global warming are also important issues to a number of people [i.e., the environmental groups who forced the NFLS to cover the issue] who care about the future of the Northern Forest." The section concluded that "It is clear from this overview that there is

"The current land ownership and management patterns have served the people and forests of the region well."—Senators Patrick Leahy and Warren Rudman.
Photo by Christopher Ayres.

not enough data to draw any firm conclusions, and that many important questions about the status of the forest's health remain unanswered. Research efforts are leading in the right direction, but they will not provide immediate answers."[15]

Although the NFLS is over two hundred pages long, the effects of forest practices on forest health merit precisely five paragraphs—most of which describe several research projects. Clearly, the study's emphasis is on maintaining the status quo of landownership and use.

The Status Quo

Traditional patterns of landownership and use, however, have not always served the region well. The status quo has been, and continues to be, the major threat to the forest and the welfare of the people of Maine. In 1958, author Jerome Daviau, writing about Maine's water resources in a book called *Maine's Life Blood*, concluded that Maine's timber industry was part of "an active conspiracy...to deprive the people of Maine of their rights to public waters." "Our troubles," he warned, "are not natural misfortunes visited upon us. They are the result of an industrial group controlling a state's political life for the exploitation of its resources on a scale unique in these United States."[16]

In 1974, William Osborne of the Ralph Nader Study Group wrote *The Paper Plantation*, a book that examined the paper industry's impact on the water, air, workers, forests, and legislature of Maine. In the introduction, Ralph Nader wrote, "The goal of the paper industry is the maximum profitable extraction of pulpwood. And it dominates the state as it pursues this goal, with a tunnel vision unique even for large absentee corporations."[17] "The resulting impact on Maine," wrote Osborne of industry's tactics, "hardly resembles the glowing description offered by paper-company spokesmen. Rather, the industry's narrow economic strategies have created severe and unnecessary burdens on the Maine public."[18]

Some progress has been made at regulating air and water pollution since *The Paper Plantation* was written, but these problems are far from solved. Maine's paper industry continues to be *the* major industrial polluter in the state. The industrial impact on the forest, meanwhile, has definitely become more severe, and until 1989 (with the passage of the Forest Practices Act), there was no progress at regulating forest management. Since 1974 the level of cut and the percentage of clearcuts have risen dramatically. The intensity of removals has increased due to whole-tree logging and whole-tree chipping of hardwoods for biomass markets. And there have been dramatic increases in herbicide spraying and the establishment of softwood monocultures. The one improvement has been the end of the massive chemical war against the spruce budworm—due to the collapse of the infestation in 1985, thirty-one years after the state started spraying.

Maine's Forest as Subject for this Book

The Maine legislature, in honor of its unprecedented determination to pass forestry regulations, declared 1989 to be "The Year of the Forest." Having seen some of the early drafts of forestry bills in 1988, and not having seen any statewide organization with a clear alternative agenda, I suspected that any debate would be dominated by industrial priorities, metaphors and myths. It was this bill which initially spurred me to write this book.

I thought it might be useful to anticipate the myths before they were codified into law and to give a brief refutation. The resulting document, "Forest Practices and Regulations in Maine: Challenging the Myths," catalogued quite accurately the myths that eventually were espoused during the debates, but it, alas, had little influence on the outcome. In the legislature, what is said is not as important as the political power of those who say it. In 1989, the political power of those advocating an ecological/social approach to forestry was not very great.

My effort was not completely in vain. A number of people who read my pamphlet responded enthusiastically. Some people printed it up and distributed it with their own funds. I started getting comments and supportive studies from as far away as Nova Scotia, British Columbia, and Australia. Some friends even urged me to expand the document into book form. I sent "Challenging the Myths" to a publisher friend, Mark Melnicove, who, to my surprise, was enthusiastic enough about the project to offer me a contract.

Time Passes

My ambitions to give the subject the treatment it deserves led to a predictable result: the writing dragged on for more than three times as long as expected. Two inevitable factors contributed—my research continually turned up new information, and the forestry world about which I was writing was rapidly changing.

When I began this book, for example, there was little national awareness of or interest in the problems of Maine's forests. In 1989, however, The Wilderness Society announced its plan for a 2.7-million-acre Maine Woods Reserve surrounding Baxter State Park.[19] Suddenly there was a nationally based environmental group playing in a field that had long been dominated by local interests.

In 1990 the state began to address the long-neglected problems of clearcutting and herbicides. The Maine Forest Service established rules to regulate clearcutting—rules that dispersed, rather than discouraged clearcuts. The state legislature's Energy and Natural Resources Committee established a task force to study the impacts of forest herbicide use. The task force recommended changes in the Board of Pesticide Control—changes that the committee promptly rejected. Thus, despite legislative efforts, the forest-management problems discussed in this book remain.

Also in 1990, the state experienced its first controversy over cutting of old-growth forests. An individual claiming to represent Earth First! allegedly spiked some trees in a 1,700-acre area abutting The Nature Conservancy's Big Reed Preserve, the state's only large, protected old-growth stand. The area in question was slated to be cut by Seven Islands, a land management company responsible for a million acres of forestland in Maine. Representatives of the forest-products industry rose in outrage. The legislature passed an act to make tree spiking (referred to in the press as "ecoterrorism") a criminal offense. While the legislature acted quickly to protect the forest industry from the possibility that an "ecoterrorist" might spike trees in the 5/100 of 1% of Maine's forest that contains old growth, it did not act at all to protect the remaining old growth.

Federal participation in the Northern Forest Lands Study and its followup, the Northern Forest Lands Council, has not only attracted attention from national and regional environmental groups, it has also raised eyebrows amongst property-rights groups such as the Maine Conservation Rights Institute (MECRI) and the John Birch Society, which are hostile to federal land purchases and regulations. These groups assert that the government, under the guise of environmental protection, will either seize citizens' properties (through eminent domain) or cancel their right to use their properties (through regulations). Property-rights groups protested with such vehemence against a proposed Northern Forest Lands Act in 1991 that the legislation quietly died. In their defense of private property, these groups have not differentiated between small, local, family ownerships and large, absentee-owned, multinational-corporate holdings, and thus have become effective defenders of the paper-company status quo.

Perhaps the most dramatic forestry event in Maine since I started writing this book was Georgia-Pacific's hostile takeover of Great Northern Nekoosa Corporation in 1990. This acquisition, which transferred ownership of 2.1 million acres in Maine (11% of the state), sent shock waves through the paper industry, conservationists, and residents of the Millinocket area, where Great Northern had its mills. With this transaction, Georgia-Pacific demonstrated its knack for expanding by acquiring, rather than building, increased capacity and for paying off debts by liquidating newly acquired assets.

Just the threat of the takeover inspired Wall Street speculators to buy 35% of GNN's stock, which went from $40 to $63 a share in 1990.[20] Even if GNN had been able to fend off the takeover bid, it would still have had to buy its shares back at a higher price and thus would have been forced to sell assets to pay debts.

The two companies broke with a long tradition of intra-industry civility by waging an unflattering public-relations war in the media to win over the Maine public and politicians. Great Northern officials claimed to have long-term plans to invest $2.5 billion in new plants and plant improvements.[21] In contrast, they claimed, G-P wanted to dump the Millinocket area mills, which, according to G-P memoranda, were considered "dawgs."[22] Great Northern officials also contrasted the "decentralized style of management" of their CEO, William Laidig, with the "testicle escrow" of G-P's T. Marshall Hahn. "We're all friends," Hahn has stated, "but our managers know they have to perform. I like to say they have one testicle on deposit."[23]

Georgia-Pacific officials responded that despite investing several hundred million dollars in the Millinocket mills in the 5 years preceding the takeover bid, GNN had not invested enough to adequately maintain what it had. The company, G-P claimed, had "starved" the aging mills, and it invested, instead, in its more profitable southern mills. The result was that nearly half the big machines in Millinocket had been shut down and 30% of the labor force laid off. Countering claims that G-P planned to sell off the "dawgs," G-P officials released a

1987 memo from Laidig that showed that GNN was considering selling one or both of the Millinocket mills.[24] Georgia-Pacific officials further claimed that GNN management, which had created a multi-million dollar "golden parachute" of benefits and bonuses for itself, were irresponsible to stockholders. G-P, which controlled a high percentage of GNN stock, prevailed.

Answering concerns expressed by conservationists and state officials that G-P might liquidate its GNN holdings in Maine to pay off its prodigious debt, G-P officials promised not to sell the land for at least two years. Late in 1991, only one year later, however, G-P announced that it was selling an 80% share of the former Great Northern holdings in Maine, which included 2.1 million acres, two paper mills, a sawmill, and an impressive hydro dam complex for only $300 million (far less than market value) to another paper company, Bowater. The remaining 20% was sold to Bowater for $22 million in June 1992.[25] State and local officials, relieved that the land was now in the hands of a company that had a better reputation than G-P for its treatment of local communities and the environment, gratefully ignored G-P's broken promise.

Indeed, despite Bowater officials' claim that Maine has a "bad business climate," the Finance Authority of Maine (FAME) unanimously voted, in January, 1992, to give the company its largest grant ever—$62 million in tax-free bonds—to fund the building of a paper recycling plant in East Millinocket. The grant would save Bowater $2 million a year in taxes.[26] Within a few days of receiving the grant, Bowater announced job layoffs.

In April, the state legislature voted to give owners of older dams exemptions to meeting modern standards for dissolved oxygen and undisturbed fish habitat. Since Bowater now owns the largest private hydro-dam complex in the state (and nation), this was another boon for them at public expense.

The paper industry has historically had boom-bust cycles. It builds capacity during boom periods only to have overcapacity when the boom ends. In the early 1990s industrial overcapacity coincided with a major recession. As the recession deepened, other paper companies in the region besides G-P, such as Scott and James River put some of their mills up for sale and laid off workers. With the increasing instability of the paper industry in the global economy, companies are finding it more difficult to sustain the image of a benign corporate landowner with a long-term commitment to the forest and its communities.

I am sure many more interesting events will occur between now and publication time, but this book is not so much a chronicle of events as an analysis of tactics and a critique of philosophy. In that respect, industrial behavior during the most recent events has been consistent with the thesis which I outlined several years ago. I have incorporated these events in appropriate sections to make sure this book is reasonably up to date, but this process does have limits if a book is ever to come out.

Response to Criticisms
Given the controversial nature of this work, I expect that people who do not share my opinions will come up with a number of criticisms. By responding

here to the mostly likely criticisms, I hope to clarify, for the reader, what I am trying to accomplish.

The author is not qualified.

I am not a professional forester but as forester Gordon Robinson wrote in his book *The Forest and the Trees: A Guide to Excellent Forestry*, "You don't have to be a professional forester to recognize bad forestry any more than you need to be a doctor to recognize ill health. If logging looks bad, it is bad. If a forest appears to be mismanaged, it is mismanaged."[27]

The demand for professional qualifications, ironically, has not extended to foresters who make decisions that should require training as an ecologist, rural sociologist, or pesticide toxicologist. Nor are foresters expected to be experts at resolving conflicts of values. But such conflicts are what this book is really about. Australian writers R. and V. Routley allow that "foresters may be profitably consulted as technical experts in their given areas for factual information and know-how," but insist that "decisions as to how forests are to be zoned and managed should not be left to them. They do not have the right to decide, it is not their role to decide, which forest values should dominate and what the objectives of forest management should be. Decisions on these matters display all the hallmarks of political decisions. . . ."[28]

Since I am not an authority, I have backed up my assertions with references to people who are more qualified than I am. I have referenced all statements of fact. I will be the first to admit, however, that just because a fact is referenced does not make it true. Indeed, in Chapter 5 I discuss a problem I discovered while researching this book: many of the forestry statistics available from the state are inaccurate. No one is accusing the government of over-reporting clearcut acreages or harvest volumes; if these modest figures paint an unflattering picture of industrial impacts on the forest, the real figures would probably paint a far worse picture.

The author is biased.

I *am* biased. I believe that forestry decisions should be ecologically sound, socially responsible, economically viable (taking ecological and social values into account) and sustainable. Industry and government publications, however, are not always as forthcoming about their biases. One is supposed to assume that, in contrast to critics like myself, they are objective—as if the measure of objectivity is the degree to which one can harmonize one's arguments with the dominant political philosophy. Try as one might, one cannot escape putting facts into the context of values.

I also admit that I have not attempted to present my arguments in a "balanced" way (i.e., giving industrial arguments equal weight to my own). While many industrial arguments make sense if one accepts industrial priorities, models, and metaphors, they do not make sense given ecological or social priorities, models, and metaphors. Since I do not give the differing perspectives equal weight, I do not give the respective arguments equal weight. I have, however, attempted to accurately quote the source material I critique.

The state and industrial biases and arguments, being reflections of the dominant ideology of society, are given many forums of expression, whereas many of the concepts found in this book have not been so widely seen or heard. If they were, I would never have felt compelled to write this book. I therefore give much more space to refuting the industrial perspective than to presenting it.

The myths presented in the book are straw men; no one in industry really believes all these myths, each company is different, and many foresters are actually quite concerned about ecological and social issues.
It is true that no one in industry really believes all the myths listed in this book. But they are all myths that I have read or heard. They have been written or stated by someone. Whether those expounding the myths actually believe them is another case altogether.

It is also true that each company is different. But when it comes to defending controversial practices such as clearcutting, budworm spraying, herbicides, government subsidies, sludge spreading, and air and water pollution, they do act like a monolithic entity. They are represented by public relations and lobbyist organizations such as the Paper Industry Information Office or the Maine Forest Products Council. Their size, multi-national status, participation in global markets, and tremendous power over local communities and forest ecosystems are shared characteristics. When I refer to industry in a generic way, I am referring to positions defended by industry lobby groups or to shared characteristics.

It is not the purpose of this book to paint all foresters as evil or to imply that everything they do is wrong. Some of the industrial foresters, government bureaucrats, university researchers, and representatives of environmental groups whom I have criticized in this book actually agree with me on many issues. Indeed, some of them, because of their gracious help, are listed in the acknowledgments of this book. If they have enunciated what I consider to be myths or promote policies that I consider threatening to the forest or my community, I have criticized that particular myth or policy.

Although Maine's environmental groups are often my allies and have done admirable work on many issues, I have at times criticized their efforts. Once again, my criticisms on specific issues should not be seen as blanket condemnations of the groups in question.

In some instances I point out that certain individuals or organizations receive money from industrial landowners. This information is not meant to tar all statements by these individuals or groups as false, but it is pertinent. It implies that the donor does not perceive the receiver as being a major threat, and alerts the reader that there may indeed be a reason for bias.

The book is inaccurate, and therefore should be rejected.
Some of the ideas in the book are controversial, and critics will easily find "experts" who disagree with the "experts" I quote. This does not necessarily mean that the alternative experts possess a higher level of Truth. The debate may be

more over values or interpretations than over facts. Or, the "facts" may not be very conclusive.

Another possibility would be for a critic to take a generalization in the book and find a specific instance where the generalization does not apply and then claim that the whole argument (or book) is therefore invalid. This is arguing by "hasty generalization." It does not prove that the statement is wrong in all circumstances.

Finally, despite my best efforts I may have some genuine errors of fact or interpretation in this book. The question then arises as to whether these errors are equivalent to assuming that the sun orbits around the earth instead of vice versa, or if they are less egregious and do not affect my general conclusions. Readers finding any errors should inform the publisher so that future editions of the book will be more accurate. Since my main thesis, however, is that the assertion of the "happy coincidence" (that whatever the paper industry does for its own economic interest just happens to be good for the forest and society) is a myth, I suggest that critics may not be able to refute my arguments by finding a few factual errors.

The book is unrealistic.

One possible line of attack against this book would be to state that some of the things I say are nice in theory but impractical in the "real world." Such a criticism implies an acceptance of the current political/economic framework as a fixed reality. Unfortunately, it is practical and realistic in this framework to pollute the environment, exploit workers, degrade the present, and write off the future. Minor inconveniences of restraint, conservation, or recycling are impractical or unrealistic, even though without them major inconveniences, such as economic collapse, ecological catastrophes, or destructive wars, become inevitable. When reality is such that it becomes practical to commit cultural and ecological suicide, it is time for people to create a new reality.

References

1. Sherman Hasbrouck and Carl Veazie, eds, *The Forests of Maine: Statistical Supplement* (Center for Research and Advanced Study, University of Southern Maine and Land and Water Resources Center, University of Maine, Orono, 1987), tables 1 and 3.
2. David Field, *Highlights of Maine's Timber Economy* (Orono: University of Maine, Cooperative Forestry Research Unit Information Report 5, 1980), table 2.
3. Maine's Land Use Regulation Commission, *An Action Program for Management of Lakes in Maine's Unorganized Areas* (Augusta: Maine DOC.Maine's Land Use RegulationCommission, 1989), p.4.
4. Robert Graves, in Felix Guirand, ed. *Larousse Encyclopedia of Mythology* (New York: Prometheus Press, 1960), p. v.
5. Maine Department of Labor, Bureau of Labor Statistics, Research and Statistics Division, BLS 623, April 1990.
6. Resource Information Systems, Inc., *Report on the Demand for Forest Products in Maine* (Augusta: Maine Forests for the Future Program, 1987), p. 31.
7. Maine Land Use Regulation Commission, *Report on Large Lot Land Division Activity in Maine for 1989*, (Augusta: LURC, March 15, 1990), p. 2.
8. *Ibid.*, p. 14.
9. Jeff Elliot and Jamie Sayen, *The Ecological Restoration of the Northern Appalachians: An Evolutionary Perspective* (North Stratford, NH: Preserve Appalachian Wilderness, Loose Cannon Publishers, 1990), pp. 36-37.

10. Perry Hagenstein, *A Challenge for New England: Changes in Forest Land Holdings* (Boston: The Fund for New England, 1987).

11. Harper, Falk, and Rankin, *Northern Forest Lands Study*, p. v.

12. *Ibid.*, p. 7.

13. *Ibid.*, p. 39.

14. *Ibid.*, p. 39.

15. *Ibid.*, p. 175.

16. Jerome Daviau, *Maine's Life Blood* (Portland, ME: House of Falmouth, Inc, 1958,) pp. 13 and 139.

17. Ralph Nader in William Osborne, *The Paper Plantation*(New York: Viking Press, 1974), p. ix.

18. *Ibid.*, p. 2.

19. Michael J. Kellet, *A New Maine Woods Reserve* (Boston: The Wilderness Society, 1989).

20. Jeff Elliott and Jamie Sayen, *The Ecological Restoration*, p. 50.

21. *Two Visions for Maine: Georgia-Pacific vs. Great Northern* (Millinocket, Me.: Great Northern Paper Company, January 9, 1990), p. 6.

22. *Ibid.*, p. 5.

23. *Ibid.*, p. 7.

24. Elliot and Sayen, *The Ecological Restoration*, p. 54.

25. Phyllis Austin, "A Rare Deal: Bowater Paid Bargain-basement Prices for Georgia-Pacific's Holdings," *Maine Times* (November 8, 1991).

26. Anon., "FAME approves $62 million in tax-free bonds to fund new Bowater plant," *Bangor Daily News*, January 17, 1992, p. 19.

27. Gordon Robinson, *The Forest and the Trees: A Guide to Excellent Forestry* (Washington, D.C.: Island Press, 1988), p. ix.

28. R. Routley and V. Routley, *The Fight for the Forests: The Takeover of Australian Forests for Pines, Wood Chips and Intensive Forestry* (Canberra: Research School of Social Sciences, Australian National University, 1974), p. 20.

1 Industrial Society

Champion's objective is leadership in the forest products industry. Profitable growth is fundamental to the achievement of that goal and will benefit all to whom we are responsible: shareholders, customers, employees, communities, and society at large.

From "The Champion Way," a 1990 promotional brochure of Champion International

The principal instrument of concentration of economic power and wealth has been the corporate charter with unlimited power—charters which afforded a detour around every principle of fiduciary responsibility; charters which permitted promoters and managers to use the property of others for their own enrichment and to the detriment of the real owners; charters which made possible the violation of law without personal liability; charters which omitted every safeguard of individual and public welfare which common sense and experience alike have taught are necessary.

Temporary National Economic Committee, appointed by Congress, 1941

For unto every one that hath shall be given, and he shall have abundance: but from him that hath not shall be taken away even that which he hath.

Matthew 25: 29

In 1953 when Charles Erwin Wilson, president of General Motors, was asked during his confirmation hearing as Eisenhower's Secretary of Defense whether he could make decisions in the interest of the United States that were adverse to the interests of General Motors shareholders, he replied that he doubted such a conflict could arise: "I cannot conceive of one because for years I thought what was good for our country was good for General Motors, and vice versa. The difference did not exist."[1] As Yale anthropologist Roy Rappaport has observed, ". . . it hardly need be said that this ideology and the process of which it is a part are hardly confined to the automobile industry. The statements of some lumbermen seem to ask us to accept the proposition that what is good for the lumber companies is good for the forests or society or both. . . ."[2]

The thrust of Charles Wilson's (a.k.a, "Engine Charlie") argument is that corporations are run primarily for the benefit of the shareholders who are, after all, just regular Americans. Today's typical stock purchaser, however, is no longer the faithful little old lady who is holding on for the long term. A large percentage of investing is now done by professionals who control vast sums of money from pension, mutual, and insurance funds. These managers are responsible for around 70% of the trading on the New York Stock Exchange.[3] They are quick to shift funds from one corporation to another—a process that has been speeded up by computer trading. And not all of the shareholders are Americans.

In his classic study of corporate society, *The New Industrial State*, John Kenneth Galbraith argued that corporate managers' prime interest isn't even the company shareholders—it is themselves. Managers are not about to work themselves out of a job, even if it means higher profits for the shareholders. They do, of course, have to get acceptable returns for the shareholders, but after that the prime goals (among many) that Galbraith identified are growth of sales and technological innovations.[4] Growth of sales means more jobs with more responsibility and hence more promotion and compensation. Increased technological sophistication requires group planning and specialized knowledge, precisely the attributes that secure the need for, and thus the power of, those in the planning bureaucracy.

Corporate managers can still honestly echo Engine Charlie's sentiment because the goals they have for their corporations are considered sacred goals of society—i.e., growth (as measured by Gross National Product) and progress (new, improved products). When business is booming, society (as measured by these criteria) is booming as well, hence Calvin Coolidge's conclusion that the business of government is business.

This variation on the theme of the "happy coincidence" gets put to the test in this chapter. Does the economic system function according to the perceived free-market model? Does corporate investment translate into regional development? Does the presence of these corporations improve the well-being of local communities? Have the wages, safety, and security of those who work on company lands benefitted from the growth of the companies?

References
1. Quoted in Robert Reich, "Corporation and Nation," *The Atlantic Monthly* (May 1988): 76.
2. Roy Rappaport, "Forests and Man," *The Ecologist*, Vol. 6, No. 7 (1976): 244-245.
3. Robert Reich, "Corporation and Nation," p. 77.
4. John Kenneth Galbraith, *The New Industrial State* (Boston: Houghton-Mifflin Company, 1985), p. 179.

The Market

The paper industry supposedly operates within a free-market system where firms compete to supply what the public demands, at prices consumers can afford and at values that allow company shareholders to reap a reasonable profit. The Invisible Hand of the market is supposed to transform private greed into public good, avoiding the shortages, lines, corruption, and other inefficiencies of centrally-planned economies. The free-market model, however, does not seem to fully correspond to what is actually happening in our economy. Indeed, if you look hard enough in Maine, you can see the Hand that guides our economy.

And it is not uniformly benefitting the populace but rather obeying the Iron Law of Distribution: them that has, gets.

Myth 1
The paper industry competes in the free-market system.

The Free Market ranks with Motherhood, Apple Pie, and the Flag as sacred icons of the American way of life. When attempts are made to regulate industry, a familiar corporate response is that such government intrusion interferes with the workings of the Free Market, thus damaging economic efficiency. For the free market to operate efficiently, there must be competition. A publication of the U. S. Department of Commerce intended to combat "economic illiteracy" made it clear that competition rather than price control is fundamental to the workings of our economic system:

"To the extent that a price is reached by means that are *not* impersonal—to the extent that either the buyer or the seller can dictate or influence the setting of the price—to that extent our system of controlling the efficient use of resources is not working properly."[1]

To this, John Kenneth Galbraith responded: "Since all large firms can dictate or influence prices, this means that wherever they are present, the economy will not work properly. Without being conscious of its action, the Department came up with a massive indictment of the American economy, and had the implications of its assertion been fully understood, its Secretary would have needed impeachment."[2]

Oligopoly
The paper industry exists in an oligopoly—a market dominated by a few sellers who, because of their large market shares, are "price makers." In a high-level oligopoly, which exists for automobiles, steel, or breakfast cereals, the top 4 companies control 50% or more of the total market. The paper industry in the U. S. is not quite as concentrated for most commodities. Few paper companies have more than 25% of the market or production capacity for any one paper grade.[3] Even when 5 to 10 companies control more than 50% of the markets, however, this is still enough power to influence prices.

Since all the companies in an oligopoly are dependent on the success of the same commodity, none can advance without hurting its rivals. Companies compete for market shares not by price cutting, which would have negative consequences for all players, but by advertising and product development. "Each firm, then," wrote economist Robert Dorfman in his textbook *The Price System*, "has the delicate task of advancing its position in the market without igniting an uncontrollable sequence of challenges and retaliations."[4]

Certain rules of behavior are tacitly accepted to prevent mutually destructive competitions. Prices are set by "price leaders" rather than by demand and cost curves. According to Dorfman, "Explicit, carefully drafted agreements among firms would constitute a cartel, which is illegal under American law. Therefore the firms must rely on a vague set of mutual understandings, never directly communicated, and therefore clumsy and unenforceable."[5]

Sometimes these communications are not vague enough. From 1972 to 1978, for example, the major paper companies paid out nearly $535 million in fines and damages for illegally fixing prices on paper bags, plywood, and folding cartons. Among those companies were some that had or now have operations in Maine:

Champion International—$47 million in fines;
Boise Cascade—$26 million;
Diamond International—$11 million
St. Regis Paper—$11 million.[6]

Georgia-Pacific, however, has the worst history of antitrust violations. Indeed, by 1972 it had grown so big, so fast, that an antitrust lawsuit forced it to split in two—and thus was born Louisiana-Pacific. In 1975 the company was convicted of fixing prices of $4.8 billion worth of gypsum board, and it settled out of court in 1980 for $6 million. In 1982 Georgia-Pacific settled a $2 billion price-fixing suit for $165 million. This class-action suit, representing 20,000 lumberyards, charged Georgia-Pacific, Weyerhaeuser, and Willamette Industries with fixing plywood prices.[7]

More recently, Great Northern Nekoosa claimed the potential for antitrust violations when Georgia-Pacific initiated its hostile takeover of that company in 1989.[8] After Georgia-Pacific sold off some of its mills, where potential antitrust "conflicts" might exist (such as controlling 75% of the market for safety paper), regulators saw no problems with Georgia-Pacific's acquisition of a competitor. Under the Reagan and Bush administrations, growth through acquisition has actually been encouraged as a way to allow U. S. corporations to be more competitive in international markets. For oligopolies, "more competitive" means having a higher market share, which means less threat from competition.

According to Galbraith, large corporations, because of their reliance on expensive and complicated technologies, large capital outlays, and planning, *must* indulge, to some degree, in price fixing. They cannot make plans in an atmosphere of wildly fluctuating prices. "It follows that the anti-trust laws, in seeking to preserve the market, are an anachronism in the larger world of industrial planning. They do not preserve the market. They preserve rather the illusion of the market."[9]

Like all general observations (including this one) there are exceptions, but the exceptions prove the rule. Georgia-Pacific's chief executive officer, T. Marshall Hahn, has been viewed by competitors as a "spoiler" because of his willingness (at times) to compete with pricing and to engage in hostile takeovers of competitors. The paper industry normally has had a cooperative atmosphere—companies often swap raw materials to reduce freight costs and are often each others' best customers.[10] "This was a close-knit industry. Now Hahn's kicking over the apple cart," said one competitor. Said another, "They'll reduce the price of paper so much that a printer will leave his old supplier. Then the market will begin to collapse."[11]

Vertical Integration

Another form of price control exerted by large corporations, including paper companies in Maine, is vertical integration. The companies own not only paper mills but also saw mills, forest land to supply the mills, hydrodams or biomass plants to supply some of their power, and even, in some cases, manufacturing plants to supply chemicals used in mill processes.

The paper companies have historically viewed their timberlands as "strategic reserves" to insulate the mill's wood flow from market fluctuations. The companies do not rely totally on the wood from their own timberlands. Since they purchase about 50% (more or less depending on the company) of their wood from others, it is to their advantage to keep the purchase price low, which their reserves help to accomplish. Indeed, they can even lose money on their own timberlands as long as they keep the market flooded with wood, which keeps their purchase prices low.

In the last decade, however, some companies, such as International Paper, which has its lands in a separate corperation, have begun to look at their timberlands as "profit centers" to help fend off unfriendly takeovers. An undervalued forest is a prime target for high-finance predators. The fact that these companies are announcing that their timberlands are now profit centers is a strong clue that previously this was not the case.

Oligopsony

The market for buying pulpwood in Maine constitutes what is known as an oligopsony—the domination of purchase of products by a handful of companies who are considered "price takers."

Oligopsony combined with vertical integration helps ensure that the cost of raw materials for the mills will remain low. Independent logging contractors and small, nonindustrial landowners have few options for finding higher paying markets for their products. Pulp mills all seem to pay a similar price. Oligopsony, like oligopoly, tends to avoid competition through pricing.

The net result of this strategy is that the companies can, according to a number of sources, purchase pulpwood at prices below what it costs to hire woodcutters to work the company forests.[12] Woodlot owners and woodcutters have long complained that timber in Maine is undervalued. Over the last 20 years, the inflation-adjusted, mill-delivered and stumpage prices (the value of wood to landowners after deducting costs for harvest and trucking) of pulpwood have been going steadily down, despite evidence since 1980 that cut has been greater than growth. (See Sidebar, page 32.) Since the revenues from wood sales pay for forest management and labor, these artificially low prices have affected the quality of the forest and the security of workers.

Government Incentives

While corporations may complain that regulations represent government interference in the workings of the free market, they do not seem to be bothered about getting tax breaks and subsidies. Indeed, they often demand such treatment so they can remain "competitive" in a market where other countries or regions are giving away such favors.

The loss of large companies to a region can be so disrupting that some governments will bail out a failing company, as Maine did to Keyes Fiber, a paper company in southern Maine, during the Brennan administration. This is what some economists refer to as "socialized losses." Large corporations such as banks or auto giants can reap profits, but the public has to pay for business failures.

The market also gets distorted when governments sell wood from public lands to wood-processing companies at unrealistically low prices. This is true on many of the national forests in the U. S., on Crown lands in Canada, and on public lands in most other countries of the world. Forest economist Randall O'Toole asserts that these below-cost sales, for the purpose of gaining foreign currency, providing jobs, or enriching political cohorts, are not only a drain to taxpayers but "create a glut of wood on the market, which in turn lowers prices and reduces the incentive for private owners to manage timber on a sustainable basis. The subsidies also lead to logging in environmentally sensitive areas that would not otherwise be touched."[13]

Interlocking Directorship

One interesting phenomenon of the free market is the maintenance of "friendly" ties with related industries through interlocking directorships. Although the directors are not usually the real decision makers in a corporation, they do have more than just a symbolic significance. Jonathan Falk, in his study *Regional Inequality and Rural Development: The Maine Paper Industry*, showed how the directorships of the paper industry interlock with those of utilities, banks, insurance, and transportation. "This does not," said Falk, "demonstrate collusion between the companies, since directors rarely take an active role in management. However it *does* support the contention that the companies have no fundamental disagreements concerning policy matters."[14]

The mix of directors has changed since Falk's study and now seems to emphasize investment, international trade (former diplomats), banks, legal firms, transportation, energy, manufacturing, and academia.

Joint Ventures

Another interesting phenomenon of the paper industry is that some smaller companies are jointly owned by apparent competitors in the world market. James River, for example, has numerous such arrangements in Europe, including a joint venture with an Italian and a Finnish company to form a pan-European tissue and related disposable hygienics operation.[15] In 1988 Scott and Mead corporations sold their joint shares of Brunswick Pulp & Paper Company (in Georgia) to Georgia-Pacific.[16] Before it was bought by Georgia-Pacific, Great Northern Nekoosa was planning a joint venture with a German firm to upgrade the Millinocket mill. After the takeover, Georgia-Pacific explored the possibility of a joint venture in Millinocket with Bowater.

Georgia-Pacific and Bowater did not create the joint venture some people anticipated, however. In October 1991, Georgia-Pacific, still reeling under the enormous debt from its Great Northern buy-out, sold Bowater an 80% share of the mills and land in Maine formerly belonging to Great Northern (at an incredibly cheap price) with the option to purchase the remaining 20% in June 1992.[17]

Owning Competitors

When companies such as Georgia-Pacific initiate a takeover, they buy large blocks of shares of competitors. Georgia-Pacific succeeded in this way to buy Great Northern Nekoosa. But they have owned smaller shares of other competitors. In 1984, for example, Georgia-Pacific bought an 8.5% interest in St. Regis Paper Company, a company that eventually was bought in a "friendly takeover" by Champion International to deter the unfriendly attempts by the likes of Sir James Goldsmith and Rupert Murdoch.[18]

Corporate Cooperation

The paper companies in Maine cooperate not only with other industries but with each other as well. They belong to organizations such as the Paper Industry Information Office, Maine Forest Products Council, Cooperative Forestry Research Unit, and even the Maine Tree Farm Association, which increase the political and economic power of the industry in general. The companies are of course scrupulous in avoiding any discussions in these organizations that could be construed as violating the federal antitrust laws. But within these organizations they lobby for incentives or against regulations that might affect their costs of doing business, they do research involving mechanization and chemicals that reduce labor, and they even look at each others' management plans.

The low costs of labor, raw materials, and forest-land taxes in Maine have been achieved through cooperation, not competition. Had there been true competition, these values would be far higher.

Decline in Real Pulpwood Values

State figures for stumpage and mill-delivered prices show a 20-year downward trend of real value. "$67" refers to inflation-adjusted prices calculated in terms of 1967 dollars according to the Consumer Price Index.

Maine Softwood Pulpwood Stumpage Price[19]

	Nominal $/Cord	Inflation Adjusted $67/Cord
1971-75	5.38	3.90
1976-80	7.84	3.88
1981-85	9.76	3.27
1990	11.70	2.98

Maine Aspen Pulpwood Stumpage Price[20]

	Nominal $/Cord	Inflation Adjusted $67/Cord
1971-75	2.85	2.07
1976-80	4.90	2.42
1981-85	6.15	2.06
1990	6.06	1.55

The authors of the study from which some of this information was extracted noted:

"This weak price performance [for aspen] occurred during a period when overall demand for hardwood pulpwood was expanding and the demand/supply balance for hardwood pulpwood was tightening." They described this as a "seeming independence of hardwood stumpage prices to the underlying demand/supply balance for hardwood fibre."[21]

Maine mill-delivered prices for pulpwood have also not kept up with inflation—even though the state concedes that cut has been exceeding growth since the early 1980s.

Maine Delivered Pulpwood Prices for Softwood and Aspen[22]

| | Nominal $/Cord | | Inflation Adjusted $67/Cord | |
	Softwood	Aspen	Softwood	Aspen
1971-75	27	22	20	17
1976-80	41	33	20	16
1981-85	53	43	18	14
Spring 1990	65	47	17	13

Another telling statistic is the relation of the value of pulpwood input to the value of primary mill product output.

Value of Pulpwood Input to Mill Product Output[23]

	Input/Output
1956	31%
1964	25%
1970	19%
1986	6%

One cannot help but conclude that the mills have been very successful at keeping their costs for purchased wood down even during a period of declining inventory.

References

1. United States Department of Commerce, *Do You Know Your Economic ABC's? Profits and the American Economy* (Washington, D.C.: United States Department of Commerce, 1968), p. 13.
2. John Kenneth Galbraith, *The New Industrial State* (Boston: Houghton-Mifflin Company, 1985), pp. 190-191.
3. Jackey Gold, "Culture Shock: Georgia-Pacific's Hostile Bid for Great Northern Nekoosa Changes the Game," *Financial World* (February 20, 1990): 57.
4. Robert Dorfman, *The Price System* (Englewood Cliffs, N.J.: Prentice-Hall, 1964), p. 99.
5. *Ibid.*, p. 100.
6. Milton Moskowitz, Michael Katz, and Robert Levering, eds., *Everybody's Business: An Almanac. The Irreverent Guide to Corporate America* (San Francisco: Harper & Row, 1980), p. 587.
7. Jim Donahue, "Another Tree Another Dollar: Rampant Expansion at Georgia Pacific," *Multinational Monitor* (October 1990): 30- 31.
8. Jeff Smith, "Antitrust Laws Won't Kill Paper Merger," *Portland Press Herald*, October 16, 1989.
9. John Kenneth Galbraith, *The New Industrial State*, p. 205.
10. Jackey Gold, "Culture Shock," p. 56.
11. Erik Calonius, "America's Toughest Paper Maker," *Fortune* (February 1990): 80.
12. Robert Parlow, *Axes and Taxes: The Taking of Resource and Revenue from the Maine Woods* (Portland, Me.: Allagash Environmental Institute, 1977), p. 25.
13. Randall O'Toole et al., "The Citizens' Guide to the Timber Industry: A Profile of U.S.

Timber Resources," *Forest Watch*, Vol. 12, No. 1 (July 1991): 29.

14. Jonathan Falk, "Regional Inequality and Development: The Maine Paper Industry," senior honors thesis, Harvard University, 1973, p. 44.

15. James River Corporation, *Annual Report 1989/1990* (Richmond, Va.: James River Corporation, 1990), p. 30.

16. Scott Paper Company, *Annual Report* (Philadelphia, Pa.: Scott Paper Company, 1989), p. 46.

17. James C. Hyatt, "Georgia-Pacific to Sell Bowater Interest in Mills," *Wall Street Journal* October 11, 1991, p. B3.

18. "An Especially Welcome White Knight," *Industrial Investor* (January 1985): 218.

19. Keith Balter and Johan Veltkamp, *Report on the Demand for Forest Products in Maine* (Augusta, Me.: Forests for the Future Program, Maine Department of Conservation, 1987), p. 64. Updated with information from Ancyl Thurston, *Annual Report of Stumpage for 1990* (Augusta, Me.: Maine Forest Service, Maine Department of Conservation, 1991).

20. *Ibid.*, p. 64

21. *Ibid.*, p. 67.

22. *Ibid.*, p. 70. Updated with information from Peter Lammert, *Mill Delivered Prices, Spring 1990* (Augusta, Me.: Maine Forest Service, Maine Department of Conservation, Spring 1990).

23. David Vail, *Contract Logging, Chainsaws and Clearcuts: The Human and Environmental Effects of Forest Management Systems in Maine (USA)* (Helsinki, Finland: World Institute for Development Economics Research, United Nations University, May 1986), pp. 31 and 67. Also, William Osborne, *The Paper Plantation* (New York: Viking Press, 1974), p. 217.

Myth 2

Paper industry products and production are dictated by consumer demand.

This myth of Consumer Sovereignty puts the responsibility for industrial actions on those who buy the products, not on those who make the plans. Industry is producing a plethora of disposable diapers, packaging materials, and other instant trash because this is what consumers supposedly "want"—not because foisting this waste on consumers increases sales, which is what management wants. Industry apologists turn social reformers when they add to this argument that consumers also want low costs so that poor people can afford the products of modern industrial civilization. Since consumers demand these products at cheap costs, the argument follows, the public should accept the production consequences, such as exploited workers, stinky air, polluted rivers, clearcut forests, or herbicided clearcuts, that these demands necessitate. Those who decry the proliferation of needless waste are labeled elitists, denying the shopping wisdom of the masses. If it is discovered that the critic indulges in the consumption of the denigrated products, he or she is labeled a hypocrite. Those who oppose local manifestations of offensive industrial practices are labeled NIMBYs (Not In My Back Yard). If they are going to consume the products of industrial technology, they have a Moral Obligation to live with the consequences of this consumption.

If we are to believe this series of myth variations, then we must also believe that industry has no part in creating or magnifying demand through advertising. The planning system of industry, however, requires that an adequate market for products exist to justify the long-term capital and technological expenditures. Demand cannot be left to chance. This is not to say that marketing success is assured. Companies do hedge their bets by diversifying their product lines.

Advertising serves two important functions: to convince consumers they are incomplete without purchasing a given class of products (cars, paper towels, soda, etc.) and to further convince them that when purchasing this class of product, they will be most satisfied if they purchase a particular brand. "Most goods," wrote Galbraith, "serve needs that are discovered to the individual not by the palpable discomfort that accompanies deprivation but by some psychic response to their possession. They give him a sense of personal achievement, accord him a feeling of equality with his neighbors, divert his mind from thought, serve sexual aspiration, promise social acceptability, enhance his subjective feeling of health, well-being or orderly peristalsis, contribute by conventional canons to personal beauty, or are otherwise psychologically rewarding."[1]

Large corporations are fully aware of the susceptibility of the public to psychological manipulation and are not averse to spending enormous amounts of money toward this cause. Some economists dismiss advertising as a wasteful "zero sum game" where the expenditures of one company cancel out those of its competitors;[2] others do not believe that the inane pap that spews from the TV can really induce people to buy. "There is an insistent tendency among solemn social scientists," observed Galbraith, "to think of any institution which features rhymed and singing commercials; provides intense and lachrymose voices urging highly improbable enjoyments; offers caricatures of the human esophagus in normal or impaired operation; and which hints implausibly at means for enhancing the opportunity for effortless and hygienic seduction, as inherently trivial. This is a great mistake."[3]

Perhaps the most important contribution of advertising is, as Galbraith noted, to "help develop the kind of man the goals of the planning system require—one who reliably spends his income and works reliably because he is always in need of more."[4] Because of their need for continued growth of sales, corporate strategy has focused on novelty, obsolescence, and disposability rather than on tradition, durability, and maintenance. Whereas International Paper may have gotten post Earth Day flack in 1970 when it promoted in a 2-page magazine ad "the disposable environment—the kind of fresh thinking we bring to every problem,"[5] we are living in the 1990s with the consequences of this concept.

Advertisements, however, do not inform consumers about the mode of production, the pollution, or the social policies entailed in creating the product. Consumers are not given a choice of paper made from trees grown in ecologically managed forests versus paper made from trees grown in chemicalized fiber farms. Consumers are not consulted as to how to manage forests. That decision belongs to management.

The absurdity of industry's justification of management techniques based on consumer sovereignty becomes even more evident when one realizes that the herbicides being sprayed now are for the benefit of consumers who have yet to be born—the trees being so treated will not be mature enough to harvest for at least half a century. Surely these future consumers have not been consulted as to their preferences.

35   Industrial Society

The invocation of consumer sovereignty is an evasion of morality. By holding that Demand is Sacred and must be met, any means to meet demands become justified. But if projected consumer demands for forest products exceed the carrying capacity of the forests, does this mean that landowners are justified in annihilating their forests?

References

1. John Kenneth Galbraith, *The New Industrial State* (Boston: Houghton-Mifflin Company, 1985), p. 210.
2. Robert Dorfman, *The Price System* (Englewood Cliffs, N.J.: Prentice-Hall, 1964), p. 101.
3. John Kenneth Galbraith, *The New Industrial State*, p. 217.
4. *Ibid.*, p. 219.
5. Milton Moskowitz, Michael Katz, and Robert Levering, eds., *Everybody's Business: An Almanac. The Irreverent Guide to Corporate America* (San Francisco: Harper & Row, 1980), p. 579.

Regional Development

Industrial growth in our society has become synonymous with Development and Progress. Indeed, many politicians have become convinced that for Maine to develop, we will have to create a more favorable business climate in which industry can flourish. When using the word "business," however, these development boosters rarely distinguish what kind, at what scale, owned by whom, or based where. The paper companies are absentee-owned, resource-exporting multinational corporations. Does encouraging them to invest more help develop the state?

Myth 1

A good business climate for the paper industry is good for Maine.

Maine's business climate is a favorite target of paper-industry spokespeople. In September 1990, for example, Pete Correll, a Georgia-Pacific vice president, stated bluntly at a business breakfast, "As many of you have heard me say before, there is no state more difficult in which to do business than the state of Maine."[1] He particularly railed against high property taxes, high workers' compensation costs, and environmental regulations which, he claimed, were stricter than national standards.

"As business leaders," said Correll, "our challenge is to work to create an environment where industry can prosper in today's world marketplace. A survey by the Commission on Maine's Future showed that the majority of Maine people are willing to forego economic growth to enhance the natural environment. If we are to succeed as manufacturers in Maine, we must work to alter that opinion."

In case the public did not catch the gist, he stated his case even more starkly: "All of our locations must compete with other operations for capital money. Competitive disadvantages translate to high cost, which means low returns, which means that the investment goes somewhere else. Economics really works."

University of Maine professors David Field and Robert Forster, in a study titled *Opportunities for Exporting Hardwood Pulpwood Chips from Maine to the Far East*, echoed this negative view of Maine's business climate: "The people of Maine would benefit more from the production of products with high added values from its forest resources than from exports of raw materials, but there is considerable pessimism within the forest products industries about the effects of Maine's regulatory climate on possibilities for establishing new manufacturing facilities."[2]

The same study suggested that even the timber-harvest regulations of the Land Use Regulation Commission (LURC) hurt the business climate. Yet these regulations allow companies to clearcut anywhere they please except within narrow buffer strips around water bodies (where 40% of the wood volume can be cut in a 10-year period). The authors wrote that "In some cases, landowners regard compliance with the regulations to be so burdensome as to eliminate whatever profit margin potential may exist, so they simply remove the forest areas in question from their management plans. This, in effect, eliminates a portion of the physical timber supply from the economic supply."[3]

Toward the end of 1990, a number of business groups, including the Environmental and Economic Council of Maine and the Coalition for a Sound Economy, organized in Maine to lobby for reductions in environmental regulations and worker benefits. These changes would supposedly improve the business climate, reduce companies "competitive disadvantage" in global markets, and aid economic recovery. To get the state to loosen such restrictions, and to leverage more tax "incentives" (i.e., subsidies), companies have the blackmail threat of moving their operations to regions or countries with a more "favorable" climate (see sidebar).

In his study of Maine's forest industry, researcher Jonathan Falk stated, "In general, industries which have located in satellite regions for low wage labor, or for resource exploitation, have a vested interest in the continued backwardness of the region."[4] Falk argued that for such industries, a good business climate would include (if possible): cheap, nonunion labor; minimal regulations; generous governmental infrastructure; governmental incentives; and opportunities to control the political process.

University of Montana economist Thomas Power argues that improving the business climate for such companies is a development strategy that is not necessarily good for communities: "New businesses were supposed to add to the tax base, yet cutting their taxes and funding business subsidies out of other taxpayers' funds can keep them from doing that. If new businesses were supposed to bring high-paying jobs, reducing labor rights and encouraging primarily nonunion, footloose operations to move into the area may do no such thing. New economic activity is supposed to invigorate the community, but the abandonment of zoning, local planning, and environmental protection may simply degrade the community."[5]

Those who claim that community prostration before exploitive industries improves the business climate, leading to community improvement, almost never offer any supporting evidence. Indeed, such claims defy both logic and actual evidence. The idea, for example, that lifting environmental regulations would help end a recession implies that the regulations helped cause the recession. Business in Maine, however, thrived through the economic boom of the late 1980s, despite a regulatory climate that was essentially the same as during the recession of the early 1990s. Most analysts would agree that the

A view of the Allagash River region showing a portion of the physical timber supply eliminated from the economic supply by "burdensome regulations." *Photo by Tor Smith.*

recession is more a correction to overextended greed than to overextended restraint.

Three decades of economic and statistical analysis across the country have revealed little significant relationship between local taxes and economic development. Some studies have even found that higher taxes are associated with development.[6] The reason for the small correlation is that the burden of local taxes to business is relatively small compared to costs for labor, transportation, and raw materials.

To Power, a better business climate, aside from providing transportation and market availability, is one that provides quality: ". . . the quality of the work force given the prevailing wage, the quality and range of commercial services available, the quality of the public infrastructure, the quality of the community as a place to live, the quality of the school system, the quality of the entertainment and recreational opportunities, the quality of the natural environment, and so on. Without making reference to these, one could never explain the geographic distribution of businesses and population location."[7] Since local taxes help fund infrastructure, education, and services, they can be seen as an investment in a better business climate.

The point of development, after all, is not merely to change abstract figures on a chart but to improve the quality of people's lives. "We clearly are not going to compete," argues Power, "by providing stripped and ravaged mountainsides, silted streams and polluted rivers, and noisy dirty plants belching foul smelling gasses into the air."[8]

The Third World—A More Favorable Business Climate?

Phil Pifer, a partner of McKinsey & Company, has suggested that environmentalists should compromise with industry so that increases in harvesting costs are not added while industry is in a downturn. Otherwise, he said, "North American companies will shift production overseas or other people will start building facilities. In fact, I think the more the North American environmental movement resists the harvesting of trees, the more likely it is Third World countries will devastate their natural forests to build plantations."

The major paper companies in Maine are all multinationals. The prime competition offered to U. S. forests and mills is from their Canadian holdings. But many of them, especially International Paper, Georgia-Pacific, Champion International, and Scott, have already started expanding to the Third World.

Third World Paper Company Holdings[9]

Georgia-Pacific:	Indonesia, Brazil, Panama,* and Costa Rica.*
Scott Paper:	Philippines, Thailand, Malaysia, Singapore, Korea, Taiwan, Brazil, Argentina, Columbia, Costa Rica, Honduras, and Mexico.

Champion	
International:	Brazil, Zambia, Ecuador, Nicaragua, and Colombia.
International Paper:	Brazil, Venezuela, Colombia, and South Africa.

*Mills were owned in these countries by Great Northern Nekoosa before the merger. Note: Some of the countries on this list may have been dropped since the list was compiled in 1988-90. This list accounts for companies that were majority-owned, minority-owned, equally-owned or wholly-owned subsidiaries. Some countries may have more than one subsidiary per company.

References

1. "Correll Says G-P's Maine Operation at a Comparative Disadvantage," *Katahdin Times*, September 25, 1990, p. 15.
2. David Field and Robert Forster, *Opportunities for Exporting Hardwood Pulpwood Chips from Maine to the Far East*, Maine Agricultural Experiment Station Miscellaneous Report No. 347 (Orono, Me.: Maine Agricultural Experiment Station, University of Maine, 1990), p. viii.
3. *Ibid.*, p. 53.
4. Jonathan Falk, "Regional Inequality and Development: The Maine Paper Industry," senior honors thesis, Harvard University, 1973, p. 90.
5. Thomas Power, *The Economic Pursuit of Quality* (Armonk, N. Y.: M. E. Sharpe, Inc., 1988), p. 163.
6. *Ibid.*, p. 164.
7. *Ibid.*, p. 128.
8. Thomas Power, "Avoiding the Passive/Helpless Approach to Economic Development," *Forest Watch* (October 1989): 18.
9. "Who's Doing What?, *Earth First!*. (Summer 1989). Also, Scott Paper Company, *1989 Annual Report*; Georgia-Pacific Corporation, 1989 and 1990 *Annual Reports*; Great Northern Nekosoa, 1988 *Annual Report*; and International Paper Company, 1989 *Annual Report*.

Myth 2

Branch plants of resource-based, export-oriented industries, such as the paper industry, provide the foundation for economic development.

At first glance, this myth seems reasonable. It asserts that money comes into a region when that region produces something the rest of the world needs. This export-based income fuels local development. Enticing export-based industries, such as the paper industry, to invest in the region supposedly should be a goal. A corollary to this line of reasoning is that Maine would be an undeveloped hinterland were it not for the paper industry. A 1987 fact sheet from the Paper Industry Information Office estimates that 84% of the jobs in the wood-using industry in Maine are export-oriented (in terms of shipments to other states and countries). By this line of reasoning we must be well on the road to development.

There are a number of problems with this model, however. The first is logical. The whole world cannot export to anyone, but does this mean it cannot develop? "The fact of the matter," writes Thomas Power, "is that improvements in technology, improvements in the quality of the work force, improvements in our knowledge and organization, savings and investment, entrepreneurial spirit, and attitudes toward work and consumption drive economic development.

These are the internal forces that propel economic development. Export markets are not necessary, though they can certainly stimulate the development of these forces."[1]

A second problem is that when we look around the world, we find that some of the best examples of export-based economies are in the Third World. These are hardly stable economies. The exporter has little control over international markets, which, when they fluctuate, create wild economic cycles at home. Local attempts to stabilize the economy can raise operation costs for export-oriented firms—which may threaten to leave. "The more dependent the economy is on exports," writes Power, "the more it is at the mercy of random external events. An export-oriented economy is an underdeveloped economy. It produces little of what it needs itself. 'Colonial' is the word we used to use for such a situation of economic dependence."[2]

The important part of the export/import equation is the imports. This is what a region needs. But money spent on imports benefits economies elsewhere. An economy develops as it produces locally what it once imported. Import substitution leads to the greatest circulation of local wealth. An export-dominated economy can bleed away local wealth. This problem is even worse when the industry is a branch plant of an absentee corporation.

The economic base of a society, asserts Power, "includes the quality of the natural environment, the richness of local culture, the security and stability of the community, the quality of the public services and public-works infrastructure, and the quality of the workforce. None of these are things produced by the commercial economy or produced for export."[3]

These principles are starkly illustrated in the tropical forests of South America, Africa, and Southeast Asia where independent, self-reliant, forest-dwelling tribespeople are being reduced to dependency and serfdom as their forest homes are transformed into export-oriented cattle ranches or coffee, banana, or eucalyptus plantations. The forest resource becomes too valuable to the global market to be wasted on traditional users.[4]

The civilized world ironically calls this process "development" because it gets these people into the market economy—it earns foreign exchange so the "underdeveloped" people can import modern technologies and goods. They now must buy what they once could forage for or grow in the forest. In reality, this "development" is cultural destruction and a war against subsistence.

In *The Paper Plantation*, William Osborne described how the industrial model of export-based "development" in Maine has impoverished rather than enriched the state: "Most people tend to equate the presence of the large paper companies, and the jobs and market for wood products they create, with the very economic survival of the state itself. Naturally, the paper companies do everything they can to encourage this notion of dependence. There is another set of facts, however, which suggests that paper-industry control of Maine's woods economy has not unequivocally benefitted the state, but has also contributed to the relative poverty and stagnation of Maine's economy while fattening the pockets of the out-of-state owners and managers of the large paper companies."[5]

The companies contributed to the stagnation of the economy, Osborne maintained, in part because they deliberately kept it export-based and "discour-aged the development of Maine-based wood-products firms which could utilize existing timber resources and boost local economies."[6]

The worst impact of this strategy is yet to come. The resource upon which this export industry is based has ceased to expand to meet the needs of industry. It is now in decline. According to an overview of forestry issues done for the state in 1987, "the boom years appear to be over. . . . Paper is, to some extent, what economists call a 'commodity,' and commodity markets are softening throughout the world. International competition has grown sharper . . . at a time when the large annual increases in Maine's supply of spruce and fir have ended."[7] Maine faces growing insecurity, rather than security, from this "development" model.

"It is only since the end of the last war," wrote Edward Goldsmith, editor of the British journal *The Ecologist*, "that development has been made out to be a veritable panacea for all the world's ills. The policies that characterise the development process were previously pursued by colonial governments for the avowed purpose of providing them with a source of cheap raw materials and a captive outlet for their manufactured goods. It was rarely suggested that such policies also served the colonies themselves."[8]

References

1. T. Power, *The Economic Pursuit of Quality* (Armonk, N. Y.: M. E. Sharpe, Inc., 1988), p. 114.
2. *Ibid.*, p 125.
3. *Ibid.*, p. 127.
4. Aaron Schneider, *Deforestation and "Development" in Canada and the Tropics: The Impact on People and the Environment* (Sydney, Nova Scotia: Centre for International Studies, University College of Cape Breton, 1989), p. 2.
5. William Osborne, The Paper Plantation (New York: Viking Press, 1974), p. 209.
6. *Ibid.*
7. Sherman Hasbrouck, *The Forests of Maine* (Orono, Me.: Land and Water Resources Center, University of Maine, 1987), p. 7.
8. Edward Goldsmith, "Bankrolling Disaster,"*The Ecologist*, Vol. 15, No. 5/6 (1985): 202.

Myth 3

Large capital investments by the paper industry mean a commitment to sustainable forest management.

Some people see the billions of dollars paper companies have invested in their mills over the last decade as evidence of a commitment to sustainable develop-ment. Surely, industry apologists like to say, the companies would not pour mil-lions of dollars into mill expansions and then cut their forests in a nonsustainable way. It's just not good business. It may not be good business in the long run, but it seems to be good business in the short run.

The cut for both softwoods and hardwoods in Maine in the 1980s was above sustainable limits. State-sponsored supply/demand studies (cited in Chapter 2) predicted shortfalls if this level of cut continued. Yet the *Maine Sunday Telegram* reported on October 28, 1989, that "Maine's paper industry has launched a major expansion in the face of growing evidence that the state will experience a severe wood shortage within the next two decades."

The article listed the following expansions:

1989 Proposed Mill Expansion

Company	Capacity (tons/day)	Capacity (tons/day)	Kind of Wood
Scott Paper, Skowhegan	1,200	1,800	all spruce and fir
Boise Cascade, Rumford	1,460	2,090	mostly spruce and fir
Great Northern, Millinocket	1,900	2,660	all spruce and fir
Madison Paper, Madison	500	1,200	all spruce and fir

Economists quoted in the article argued that it made sense to invest in more efficient manufacturing facilities in the face of a shortfall, because when the shortfall comes it is the efficient machines that will stay on line—the older ones will be shut down. Such an argument implies a deliberate acceleration of resource depletion with the intention of shutting down the least profitable mills when supplies become short. Such a strategy may increase corporate stability, but it hardly contributes to community stability.

Even more telling were the comments by two economists that the payback for the investments would be anywhere from 2 to 5 years—well before any shortfall developed. The article quoted Robert Seymour, a forestry professor at the University of Maine, who summed up the real logic behind the expansions: "Companies expand when they think they can make money by expanding."

If these companies overcut their own lands and force their own mills to shut down, it will not be a unique historical event. Some of these same companies virtually mined their old-growth holdings out west, leading to mill shortages and shutdowns. For example, Champion International managers liquidated all the old growth on the company's 850,000 acres of forest holdings in Montana over a 10-year period. When they were done, less than 1% of their land was fully stocked with trees 9 inches or more in diameter; only 7.1% had medium stocking of trees 9 inches or more.[1] The land is for sale.

The reason for the liquidation was to finance expansions in Michigan, Texas, and the Southeast. The company rationally decided that more money could be made liquidating their forest and investing the revenues elsewhere than in managing the forest for an even flow of wood. Liquidation of old growth on industrial lands has put great pressure on public lands to supply local mills.

Some industrial foresters have argued that the liquidation of sawlog inventory out west is not totally relevant to our pulpwood situation in Maine. Their argument does not hinge on the value of investments in mill improvements but on the value of the mill site. In today's regulatory environment, it would be very difficult to start a new pulp mill on a new site because these mills require so much energy and water and are so polluting. The foresters argue, therefore, that they must sustain their pulpwood supply so they can sustain their valuable existing "rights" to pollute.

A company can cut a local wood supply in a nonsustainable manner and still keep a mill going for a long time, however. As the wood runs out, the company can stretch supplies by importing raw materials. One only has to fly over sections of Maine's industrial forest to see that entire townships have already been stripped of mature timber, without affecting mill stability. We also have the example of Georgia-Pacific in Washington County overcutting its spruce-fir and then switching over its Woodland paper mill from spruce-fir to hardwoods. The mill site was maintained but not the resource. At a time when Maine studies are predicting shortfalls of both quantity and quality, companies not only are expanding their pulp mills, they are building biomass generators and increasing export markets for raw logs and wood chips to the Far East, the Middle East, and Europe. This seems like odd behavior for companies concerned about having a sustainable wood supply. Long-term investments of paper companies have a different time horizon than the long-term interests of communities. One is measured in years; the other in generations.

Reference
1. Dick Manning, "Logging Outstrips Growth: Observers Warn of Effects on Environment, Industry," *Missoulian* (Missoula, Mont.), October 16, 1988.

Myth 4
Paper industry investment and expansion mean more jobs.

One of the major rewards that state and local communities are supposed to reap from improving the business climate is more jobs. Yet despite impressive increases in mill capacity and the level of cut over the last several decades, the level of mill and woods employment has not increased proportionately. In fact, employment, especially in the woods, has decreased. If the estimates of annual average employment in the logging industry from Maine's Department of Labor are accurate,[a] there was a nearly 30% decline in woods employment between 1984 and 1989—a boom period for industry.[1] Paper mill employment has been fairly constant since 1960, but between 1984 and 1990, 1,412 mill jobs were lost.[2] These losses have occurred at a time of increased labor force in the state, so the percentage of paper mill and logging jobs has been declining at an even greater rate relative to all employment.

The paper industry is not investing in jobs when it increases mill capacity; it is investing in machinery. Mechanization likewise explains the loss of jobs in the woods. Chainsaws and cable skidders started replacing bucksaws and horses in the 1950s. Mechanical harvesters, shears, delimbers, slashers, and wood chippers have been replacing chainsaws and skidders since the 1970s.

Between 1952 and 1980, according to forest economist Lloyd Irland, jobs per unit of wood fell by three-fifths for logging and by one-third for paper.[3] A state study on woods labor estimated that before 1965, labor represented 65% of the cost of harvesting wood; now the figure is about 35 to 45%, but it is still the largest single component.[4] Given these trends, unless the level of cut in Maine significantly expands, the level of employment in the wood-products industries in Maine will decline even more, despite (or perhaps because of) impressive investments in mill improvements.

Although governments often focus their hopes, and their tax favors, on large, capital-intensive industries in the hope of creating jobs, research has shown that Fortune 1000 firms create only about 1% (or less) of all new jobs, whereas small businesses create at least 50% of new jobs.[5]

If more new jobs is the goal, then it is clear where government policy should be directed.

Endnote

a. Unfortunately, data from different sources on woods employment are inconsistent, but the significant downward employment trend is generally accepted as fact. Over the same time period, the Northeast Regional Woods Wage Survey from the Maine Department of Labor recorded a 50%, not a 30%, decline in jobs.[6]

References

1. Maine Department of Labor, *Annual Average Employment in the Logging Industry in Maine, 1980-1989,* photocopy (Augusta, Me.: Maine Department of Labor, Bureau of Employment Security, Division of Economic Analysis and Research, 1990).
2. Paper Industry Information Office, *1984 Pulp and Paper Industry in Maine Summary* and *1990 Pulp and Paper Industry in Maine Summary* (Augusta, Me.: Paper Industry Information Office, 1984, 1990).
3. Lloyd Irland, "Future Employment in the Maine Woods: Situation, Forces and Outlook." In *Proceedings, A Forest Based Economy: Carrying a Tradition into the Future, Blaine House Conference on Forestry, December 6-7, 1984* (Augusta, Me.: Maine Department of Conservation, August 1986), p. 85.
4. Richard Donovan and Elizabeth Swain, *Maine Woods Labor Study* (Augusta, Me.: Maine Department of Conservation, 1986).
5. Thomas Power, *The Economic Pursuit of Quality* (Armonk, N. Y.: M. E. Sharpe, Inc., 1988), p. 180.
6. Maine Department of Labor, *Logging and Employment by Class of Worker Based on the Woods Wage Survey, 1980 to 1988,* photocopy (Augusta, Me.: Maine Department of Labor, Bureau of Employment Security, Division of Economic Analysis and Research, 1989).

Myth 5

The paper industry is adding billions of dollars of value to harvested wood. When this money circulates through Maine's economy, it multiplies the number of jobs. Therefore, industry's value to the state economy is far greater than direct tax or employment figures would indicate.

This myth is based on certain truths: paper mills do add enormous value to raw wood (far more than lumber), unionized paper mill workers are comparatively well paid, and money from industry activities and workers' wages does circulate through the economy and create more jobs. Industry has invoked these concepts to attract tax breaks or subsidies (for such activities as budworm spraying, fire control, or investment tax credits) that are larger than would be expected given direct industry values of land or economic activity. It is a myth, however, due to exaggeration; much of the value added to harvested wood does not benefit Maine people.

Exported Profits

The first reason is that virtually all the paper mills and most of the woods are owned by out-of-state companies. The profits garnered from these investments do not get circulated through the state economy—they leave the state and may be reinvested in more profitable company divisions in other regions or nations. Forest economist David Kromm contends that: "Ownership of the forestry activity also influences the quality of the impact multiplier. Proprietary income from stumpage, logging and processing generated under local ownership remains with the regional economy and circulates internally before it leaves. Income from external ownership has no staying power, eliminating the indirect benefits of the multiplier effect which result from local respending."[1]

Imported Machinery and Chemicals

Higher multipliers occur when more industrial inputs are obtained from the local economy. For the paper industry, however, manufacturing and harvest equipment, as well as chemicals and other supplies, are purchased out of state. Indeed, much of the equipment comes from Finland, Germany, Austria, and Japan.[2] This represents export of Maine money to other regional economies or even other countries.

Imported Jobs

A significant percentage of workers employed to harvest wood for mills are not Maine citizens; they are either bonded (imported to work at a specific job) Canadians or Canadians on visas (and thus free to choose amongst jobs). Many of these workers operate in remote locations and return to Canada to spend their money. Thus, a certain proportion of the multiplier effect leaves not only the state but the nation.

The Department of Labor does a 2-week woods worker survey that keeps tabs on domestics, bonds, and visas. It does not necessarily cover all workers or reflect annual averages, but it should show trends. If the trends for the last decade are accurate, Canadians have steadily made up about 30% of the woods work force. Most of them have been commuters who spend their income out of state.

Logging Employment by Class of Worker[3]

Year	Domestics	Bonds	Resident Visas	Commuting Visas	%Canadian
1980	3,430	388	140	1,290	35%
1981	2,860	347	90	990	33%
1982	3,260	244	40	910	27%
1983	3,550	419	60	1,150	31%
1984	3,780	641	50	980	31%
1985	3,560	431	30	910	28%
1986	3,560	441	40	740	20%
1987	3,040	350	30	850	29%
1988	1,847	393	7	470	32%

Exported Logs

Another loss of value added and potential jobs occurs when logs are exported rather than milled in-state. For years Maine has been supplying about 80% of the imported wood for more than 40 saw mills in Quebec. According to Canadian import data, two-thirds of Maine's spruce-fir sawlogs and half of its softwood lumber were exported to Quebec in 1980-85.[a] A study on log exports by forest resource analyst Stephen Blackmer estimated that between 1978 and 1983, an average of 5,638 direct jobs, 3,946 indirect jobs for a total payroll of $76 million (1983 dollars), combined with $134 million in value added were lost to the Maine economy.[4] To add insult to injury, much of the wood milled in Quebec is sold back to New England as lumber, worsening the U. S. trade deficit.

The main reasons large landowners give to explain why they export saw logs to Canada are that the markets are handy ("the natural flow of transportation") and that the prices paid by these mills are better than Maine prices. The Quebec mills lack a local sustainable supply and are willing to pay far more than Maine mills. Researchers have cited other reasons why the Canadian mills can afford the higher prices: the Quebec mills have the advantages of better exchange rates, experienced managers, cheap power, government-sponsored training, state-of-the-art equipment, export assistance, cheap Canadian wood (but shipped in from a distance), lower rates for workers' compensation, and subsidies for new mills or mill expansions.[5]

There are a few more reasons why Maine does not have more sawmills in or near the industrial forest. One is industry's desire to prevent development (and thus an increase in local taxes) in the townships they dominate. Another is to assure control over woods markets. In *The Paper Plantation*, Osborne contended that for decades industrial landowners deliberately discouraged the development of an expanded sawmill industry in northern Maine to prevent competitive

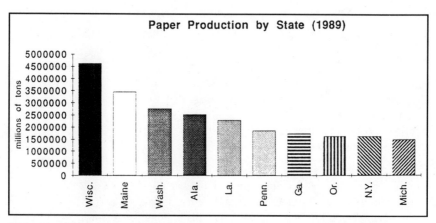

Maine's ranking as paper producer by quantity. *From data supplied by the Paper Industry Information Office.*

Maine's ranking as paper producer by value
Note: Other states are producing less paper than Maine, but have a higher value added to the products. *From PCUSA (1989).*

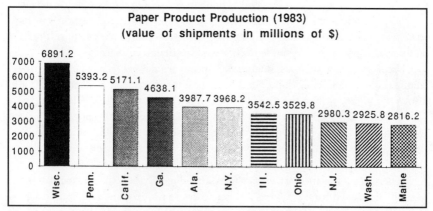

markets. This changed in 1972 when Great Northern acquired the Pinkham Mill in Ashland.[6] By 1980 the 4 largest sawmills in northern Maine were owned by paper companies and accounted for 65% of sawlog production in the region. They obtained only 15% of their wood from nonindustry land.[7] Thus, the area was deprived of significant locally owned industries that could compete for labor and resources with the paper industry.

Forest activist, Bill Butler claims there is yet another reason for this draining of Maine wealth—some of the large Maine landowners, including International Paper, Boise Cascade, and even the so-called nonindustrial Seven Islands, have an interest in the Quebec mills. The companies thus benefit, even if the state and nation do not. It is well known that some of the paper companies get an important percentage of their highest quality fiber from wood chipped from slabs from the Canadian mills. They benefit from the wood both coming and going, even though the state sees little of this benefit.

Logs are also being shipped overseas. During 1989, for example, Georgia-Pacific alone sent 32 barges, each with about 10,000 cords of raw logs (mostly hemlock) to Turkey from Eastport. In 1990, G-P sent out 40 such barges.[8] The only processing of the logs in Maine was to remove the bark. Although G-P argues that exporting hemlock, a species that does not have a big local or regional market, creates jobs, there would be even more jobs if the logs were milled in Maine and the lumber, rather than just raw logs, were exported.

Cost Multipliers

If we consider secondary benefits, we should also consider secondary costs as a result of industry investments. Such costs can include the need for added or improved roads, utilities, social services, and bureaucracies (such as regulatory

Maine logs being loaded onto a Panamanian freighter bound for Japan. *Photo courtesy Bangor Daily News.*

agencies). They can also include the costs of dealing with higher power demands or of sludge and toxic-waste generation. They include the costs of environmental degradation that results from highly disturbing harvest practices or from air and water pollution. They include the costs to human health from high accident rates and from breathing polluted air and drinking polluted water. They also include opportunity costs if the attractiveness of the region for other activities is diminished. The net benefits for the public of exploitive, polluting activities are eventually negative.

Desirable Development

If local communities are to benefit from the economic activities in their region, it makes a difference what type of economic activites are encouraged. The following chart represents an array of development considerations. From this chart, it is clear that much of the paper-industry growth in Maine falls on the wrong side of the chart.

Development: An Array of Considerations

Factors	Less Desirable	More Desirable
Ownership	out of state profits leave state	in state profits reinvested
Resources	imported nonrenewable short-lived strain on other industries	locally obtained renewable sustainable
Markets	international/unstable	local/stable
Value Added	product exported, no further use or processing in state	secondary processing in state
Energy Needs	high/need more power plants	low/conserving
Infrastructure	need more sewers, roads, schools, police; higher taxes	little change; no tax increase
Jobs	low number of jobs per dollar invested imported labor alienated labor; mind-numbing, hazardous work threatened by technological changes	more jobs per investment local labor meaningful, creative, healthful technologically stable

Factors	Less Desirable	More Desirable
Community	rapid demographic changes/instability dominates community neighborhood eyesore	leads to more stability diversifies community benefits area
Environmental	pollutes air/water toxic waste products for which there are no disposal solutions need larger regulatory bureaucracy	little damage or enhances environment
Products	trendy, frivolous, destructive	necessary, beneficial

Endnotes

a. Export figures from Maine and import figures from Quebec do not match. The following table shows the percentage of Maine's harvested logs exported to Quebec based on differing figures from Quebec and Maine.[9]

Percent of Harvested Maine Logs Exported to Quebec: Estimates from Quebec Import Data and Maine Export Data

Species	Quebec 1980	Maine 1980	Quebec 1985	Maine 1985	Maine 1988
Spruce-fir	62%	38%	67%	34%	20%
Pine	13%	4%	14%	1%	2%
Hemlock	4%	1%	9%	11%	1%
Cedar	54%	22%	50%	3%	17%
Weighted Total	46%	27%	53%	25%	13%

If the Quebec figures are correct, and the Maine 1988 figures are as inaccurate as its 1985 figures, then, in 1988, 40% of spruce-fir was exported and 28% of all softwood. Some experts, however, think that even the import figures from Quebec are underestimates. These figures also do not account for shipment of logs across the border to New Brunswick. The level of exports of logs to Canada, therefore, may be significantly higher than the figures reported in the above table.

References

1. William Osborne, The Paper Plantation (New York: Viking Press), p. 219.
2. Ellen Benoit, "Through the Mill: Globalization, Higher Capital Requirements and Renewed Environmental Concern May Lower the Cyclicality of the World's Forest Products Industry," *Financial World* (February 20, 1990): 44.
3. Maine Department of Labor, "Logging and Employment by Class of Worker Based on the Woods Wage Survey, 1980 to 1988," photocopy (Augusta, Me.: Maine Department of Labor, Bureau of Employment Security, Division of Economic Analysis and Research, 1989).
4. Stephen Blackmer, "The Export of Sawlogs from New York and New England to Canada," (Concord, N.H.: SELL-USA, July 1985), Table 18.
5. Jack Aley, *The Export of Maine Sawlogs to Quebec* (Augusta, Me.: Maine Department of Conservation, 1981).

6. William Osborne, *The Paper Plantation* (New York: Viking Press, 1974), p. 215.
7. *Final Programmatic Environmental Impact Statement, Proposed Cooperative 5-year (1981-1985) Spruce Budworm Management Program for Maine* (Broomall, Pa.: United States Forest Service, Northeastern Area, State and Private Forestry, 1981), p. 22.
8. Natalie Springuel, *Corporate Forest Practices in the Maine Woods* (Bar Harbor: College of the Atlantic, Winter and Spring 1991), p. 59.
9. David Field and Robert Forster, *Opportunities for Exporting Softwood Lumber from Maine to the Far East*, Maine Agricultural Experiment Station Miscellaneous Report No. 347 (Orono, Me.: Maine Agricultural Experiment Station, University of Maine, 1990), p. 80.

Community Welfare

On the community level, the dominance of a single industry over a township is complete. Towns are company towns. The companies try to create the image of a paternal, benevolent plantation owner who cares. They point to their support of community projects, their tolerance for public access, their donation of land easements for recreation, and their support of local education.

Great Northern Paper, which was based in Maine before being bought by Nekoosa (and then Georgia-Pacific and Bowater), was once such a corporation. People felt proud to live in Millinocket. But over the last few decades, after multiple changes of ownership, the mill/community relationships have soured. While company participation in the corporate-owned communities has brought benefits, it has also brought costs to the forest, to air and water quality, to human health, and to community stability. When people see companies resist dealing with these costs, they question the true commitment of industry to community welfare.

Myth 1

The industrial landowner makes a good neighbor.

Industrial landowners pride themselves on their responsible management. Since, they assert, they are improving the forest, it follows that they are likewise improving the value of the local communities. Not all the communities that have industrial landowners as neighbors, however, share this optimistic perspective on the benefits of industrial managagement.

Forest Practices

Some citizens have been so displeased with industrial forest management in their townships that they have passed local forest practices ordinances. Large clearcuts can hardly add to the value of neighboring property. It is not just aesthetics, however, that have motivated some towns to try to pass local ordinances. People are concerned that the resource bases of their townships are being liquidated in nonsustainable ways, threatening the viability of future local employment. They are also concerned about the growing use of chemical herbicides on clearcuts.

The towns where these ordinances first got passed were not the vacation retreats of wealthy professionals who were displeased at the scenes from their picture windows; they were small, often relatively poor towns, very much dependent on the cutting of trees for their livelihoods. In 1984, for example, Linneus, a forested town in southern Aroostook County, passed an ordinance that discouraged clearcutting. Several of the selectmen who spearheaded the ordinance were logging contractors who were well aware of the impact of unregulated forestry in surrounding towns. A prime motivation for the people of Linneus was to ensure a sustainable wood supply.

The towns of New Sweden and Stockholm in northern Aroostook County, were shocked by the forest practices of J. D. Irving, a division of a Canadian conglomerate that had bought the forests in the area from International Paper. Irving's standard practice has been to clearcut, spray herbicides, and plant a single species, black spruce. The people in these towns were convinced that such a simplified forestry system was a threat to wildlife and so they passed ordinances.

The people in these towns did not passively accept the insensitivity of their corporate neighbors. In some towns, however, the corporate neighbors pre-vented ordinances with veiled threats. In 1986 the town of Howland, located near two biomass plants as well as a few paper mills, attempted to pass a modest ordinance that would limit clearcuts to 25 acres. This greatly displeased International Paper, which claimed the restrictions would cut into their profits. To make up for these perceived losses from this tiny fraction of one of the largest land bases of any forest company in the world, IP threatened to charge a fee for recreational use of their land.[1]

When citizens tried to pass an ordinance in the town of Dedham, Diamond International threatened to make town officials visit every potential cutting site and check it for every legal detail. The expense, townspeople were informed, would be very high. Diamond also hinted it would gate all access roads and charge admission to recreationists.[2] No ordinance was passed.

The forest industry lobbied hard during the 1989 hearings on forest practices legislation to eliminate local ordinances entirely. They argued that having different ordinances in each town was too confusing for managers who are responsible for many townships, and thus an economic burden. This is somewhat like large real-estate companies arguing that local zoning interferes with their profitability and should be discarded in favor of a single statewide standard. Fortunately the industry did not fully have its way on this issue. Local ordinances still stand (but are being threatened by pending legislation), as long as the terminology in the ordinance is harmonious with state definitions. In the unorganized territories administered by LURC, however, this option does not even exist—yet that is where the bulk of industrial ownership lies.

Taxes

To industrial landowners, the best neighbors are other industrial landowners. Even though the unorganized territories, in which most of the industrial forests lie, have half the land in the state, they have only 1% of the population. In 1846

Henry Thoreau learned one of the major reasons for this phenomenon: "When I asked McCauslin why more settlers did not come in, he answered, that one reason was, they could not buy the land, it belonged to individuals or companies who were afraid that their wild lands would be settled, and so incorporated into towns, and they be taxed for them. . . . "[3]

Industrial landowners do not like to pay taxes, and settled towns with roads, schools, and welfare mean higher taxes. Industrial landowners have preferred to import workers and export raw materials. In 1974 William Osborne observed that "the landowners received the benefit of the communities—the labor and services of local people in tending the forest—without having to pay any of the costs."[4]

In 1972, as an incentive to practice better forestry and to discourage conversion of forestland to developments, Maine initiated the Tree Growth Tax Law, which is a form of present-use valuation. This tax (which I discuss more thoroughly in Chapter 5) is so low that towns with large areas of forest under the tax qualify for reimbursement from the state's general fund. Yet even this tax is too high for some landowners to bear.

In 1991 in Reed Plantation (Wytopitlock), taxes went up, in part because a local contractor moved his business to another town but also because school costs were rising due to loss of federal and state subsidies. The town was forced to cut back on services and nearly had to shut down the school. Fraser Paper, a Canadian corporation that owns most of the land in town, did not like the high taxes and was slow in paying, forcing the town to borrow money, which increased its financial difficulties.

This was not an isolated example. In 1991 Fraser had to pay the state $19 million to settle a tax dispute that was hurting the state's treasury during a time of financial crisis.[5] In 1991, Georgia-Pacific attempted to get a $213 million tax abatement on its Millinocket mill and $171 million on its East Millinocket mill. Scott succeeded in getting a $343,000 tax abatement on its S. D. Warren mill in Westbrook. These towns are now in financial crises, and individual property taxes are going to soar to make up the difference.[6] The message these companies are sending is that the paper industry can no longer have a paternalistic relationship with their mill towns.

"Multiple Use"

There are other ways, aside from brutal forest-management practices, in which companies show their insensitivity to local communities. The "multiple use" idea of the companies seems more like multiple abuse to many citizens.

•Toxic waste. In the 1980s Champion sold some of its land, in a place with the picturesque name of Township 30 in Washington County, to a company called KTI Energy Incorporated. KTI had built a waste-to-energy incinerator in Orrington, and having transformed solid waste into toxic waste, needed a place to dump the ash.

The idea of a toxic waste dump near a wetlands and over the Mopang aquifer, one of the last sizable pure aquifers in the state, greatly displeased many Washington County residents. The Clean Water Coalition that successfully fought the dump (KTI appeared to give up in 1990) did not believe the dump would enhance the region and questioned statements by dump promoters that accepting the dump was somehow akin to economic development.

•Military training. In the fall of 1989, even as debate over the ash dump was still simmering, Champion announced a deal it was making with the Maine National Guard to turn its entire land holdings (730,000 acres) into the largest military training area in the United States. The training area would be used by various branches of the U. S. and Canadian armed services as well as by NATO troops. Champion's timberlands manager Robert Cope claimed in an interview that the military use would create "zero environmental impact."[7]

Part of the landholdings were already being used by the military. At a hearing I attended in Old Town, people testified that the impacts were more than zero. Helicopters were flying low over people's homes at all hours of the day, military convoys were causing traffic jams, and soldiers had even driven their vehicles over commercial blueberry fields.

Champion did not make this deal with the military out of pure patriotism; for its part, the military would build roads and bridges for Champion at taxpayer expense.

Those who oppose intrusions such as large clearcuts, herbicides, toxic dumps, or military training areas are considered selfish NIMBYs. People are insulted first by having their communities threatened, then for daring to defend them.

•Dams. Although the public supposedly owns the rivers and lakes, paper companies control many of them with dams. Bowater's Great Northern Paper division controls the watershed of the West Branch of the Penobscot River with 12 dams and 5 hydroelectric stations that provide the company with $50 million a year of electricity.[8] The dams, however, may conflict with the needs of fishermen for salmon and trout and with recreationists for whitewater. Georgia-Pacific's dams along the St. Croix River have led to conflicts with camp owners because of fluctuating water levels.

When the paper companies try to squeeze out more profits from hydroelectric facilities on public waters at the expense of the public, the public rightfully questions the companies' priorities.

References
1. Mitch Lansky, "Protecting Maine's Forest: Some Towns and Others Want to Regulate Forest Harvesting," *Maine Organic Farmer and Gardener* (September/October 1986).
2. *Ibid.*
3. Henry David Thoreau, *The Maine Woods* (New York: Thomas Y. Crowell Co., 1961), pp. 31-32.
4. William Osborne, *The Paper Plantation* (New York: Viking Press, 1974), p. 182.
5. "Owner Settles Income Tax Dispute," *Bangor Daily News*, September 13, 1991, p. 21.
6. Mark A. Woodward, "Mill Abatements," *Bangor Daily News*, September 22, 1991, p. 10.
7. "Champion's Military Training Has Zero Impact," *Bangor Daily News*, July 2, 1989.
8. Bob Cummings, "Georgia-Pacific Faces Challenge on River Flow," *Maine Sunday Telegram*, September 9, 1990.

Myth 2

Large investments by the paper industry in pollution control show a commitment to a clean environment.

Part of the value "added" to the logs that come from Maine's forests is paper-mill pollution. Pollution can reduce real-estate values, discourage tourism and recreation, harm plants and animals, and make people sick. The biggest air and water polluter in Maine is the paper industry. If you believe paper-company spokespeople, however, you would think their companies are doing the environment and local communities a favor. A typical corporate annual report usually has a section proclaiming the company's commitment to a clean environment and healthy communities, pointing to lavish expenditures on pollution control as evidence.

William Osborne, in *The Paper Plantation*, disputed this commitment: "Like their counterparts in business across the country, pulp and paper mill executives are loathe to spend money on items they feel will not contribute directly to increases in profits or production."[1]

Although it is true that money has been spent on mill cleanup over the years and that air and water pollution have been reduced (indeed, the rivers are no longer prone to catch fire), Osborne argues (and thoroughly documents) that "where progress has been made . . . it has usually been after the most dogged resistance and recalcitrance on the part of industry."[2] Often, Osborne argues, "no distinction is made between expenditures that are actually made for pollution-control devices and those outlays for productive capital equipment that contribute only incidentally to pollution abatement; governmental subsidies or tax write-offs are not deducted; the amount is not compared with what the company could have spent considering its resources or might have spent over past years considering the extent of the damage and cost to the public."[3]

The first line of defense that the companies use against unwanted regulations is, according to Osborne, myth: "By weaving a protective tapestry of myth and fiction around their companies, they attempt to purchase public tolerance of their environmental abuses and postpone imposition of strict controls."[4] Although this was written in 1974, it still applies almost 20 years later.

The Smell of Money

One of the more noticeable effects of having paper-company neighbors is that there is something more than springtime in the air. More than a third of Maine's population lives within the "odor radius" (20 miles, but with the right conditions this increases) of one of the state's half dozen Kraft mills. In the past, industry officials have tried to convince the public that the smell is a sign of progress—it is the smell of money. The environmental director of one mill told Osborne, "The only people who complain are outsiders driving through. The local people don't mind it."[5] Even more telling was the statement of Paul McCann, former director of the Paper Industry Information Office: "They worked to get this air and now they want to keep it. They're proud of this air."[6]

Part of this "pride" is evident in a local bumpersticker that reads "Kiss me where it stinks . . . Lincoln, Maine."

To be fair, it is not easy to get rid of the smell. Scott Paper spent $83 million over 3 1/2 years to put a new state-of-the-art recovery boiler in its S. D. Warren Westbrook mill. This new boiler (whose primary purpose is increased productivity, not environmental improvement) was supposed to reduce total sulfides, including hydrogen sulfide, methyl mercaptan, dimethyl sulfide, and dimethyl disulfide by 75%, which, the company reasoned, would cut odors by 75%.[7] After the improvements, a record number of residents have complained that the odor is still there, only worse. Rather than the odor of rotten eggs or rotten cabbage, to which residents had become accustomed, the smell is now acrid and more akin to that of dead fish. Although total sulfides have been reduced, the percentage of dimethyl sulfide, which can be detected by the nose in smaller amounts, has increased.

As I write this in 1991, Scott has succeeded in getting a tax abatement on this mill and has put the mill up for sale.

Overregulated

Paper-company representatives frequently complain that they are subject to an oppressive regulatory environment in Maine. The reality, however, is that the regulatory atmosphere has historically been lax. In early 1988 the Natural Resources Council of Maine (NRCM) discovered that 8 of Maine's pulp and paper mills were recording at least 1,000 violations of state air-quality laws a year. The Department of Environmental Protection (DEP) had referred none of the violations to the attorney general for enforcement. Smaller industries, however, were routinely assessed fines and penalties or subject to other enforcement.[8]

The smell of money. *Photo by Christopher Ayres.*

The NRCM investigation also concluded that:

•the only violations that reached the DEP were those voluntarily reported by the company—the actual number of violations was probably far higher;

•the major DEP response to the violations consisted of phone calls to the companies urging them to do better;

•the DEP lacked the staff and engineering ability to accurately monitor and enforce violations and had not asked the legislature for the money needed to do so.[9]

Some interesting examples of neglect that the NRCM uncovered were the following:

•Boise-Cascade, Rumford—The mill was continuously violating its air-pollution license because some of the equipment designed to trap dust, dirt, and smoke particles was not operating. The stack had not been tested for 7 years, despite numerous opacity violations.

•Lincoln Pulp and Paper—The mill had been ordered by a superior court to clean up its air-pollution emissions, but the DEP failed to notify the attorney general that violations (such as excessive sulphur emission) were still occurring.

•International Paper, Jay—After receiving complaints about chlorine leaks, an independent consultant discovered that some equipment was being entirely bypassed by the air-pollution-control treatment system and automatic monitors. Large quantities of gases were being vented directly to the atmosphere, without being reported.

•S. D. Warren (Scott Paper), Westbrook—Reported violations of air-pollution standards averaged nearly 4 hours a day for the period looked at, the worst of any mill.

•Georgia-Pacific, Woodland—A stack test had not been done for 8 years. Electrostatic precipitators, designed to capture dust and dirt from smoke, had failed.

•James River, Old Town—Its last stack test was done 10 years previously.

•Great Northern, Millinocket—The existing license was so out of date that there was not even a particulate-emission limit on a chemical recovery boiler.[10]

Despite such information, companies insist they are being overregulated, which creates a bad business climate.

The Right Thing

A Boise Cascade publicity brochure lists a number of examples to demonstrate the company's commitment to improving the community. "Boise Cascade," the brochure tells us, "does all these things for one reason only: they're the right things to do. In the end, the Rumford Mill is more than merely a place where most of the town's residents make their living. It's where they live their lives. And Boise Cascade's resources and commitment to the community have enriched the lives of the people who call Rumford home."

Cancer or respiratory illness hardly enrich people's lives. One local nick-name for the Rumford area is "Cancer Valley." Preliminary results from a survey by the state's Bureau of Health Chronic Disease Surveillance Project showed extraordinarily high incidences of a number of diseases in the region from 1984 to 1988.

•The Rumford area, which includes Mexico, Andover, Byron, Hanover, and Roxbury, had significantly high rates of emphysema, asthma, non-Hodgkins lymphoma, lung cancer, and aplastic anemia, a rare, often-fatal blood disorder.

•The nearby Bethel area, which includes Dixfield, Peru, Woodstock, and 9 smaller communities, had significantly higher-than-average rates of leukemia, lung cancer, and aplastic anemia.

•The Norway area, which includes Otisfield, Oxford, Paris, Waterford, and West Paris, also showed a large number of cases of aplastic anemia.[11]

A 1982 Finnish study found a decrease in blood-forming activity in pulp workers exposed to low levels of hydrogen sulfide and methyl mercaptan, two gases released during the Kraft paper-making process.[12] Researchers wonder if these chemicals may have a role in the abnormally high incidence of the rare type of anemia found in the region.

A study of the respiratory health of Maine paper-mill workers, published in the *Journal of Occupational Medicine*, found that pulp- and paper-mill workers have a high incidence of admittance to hospitals for respiratory infections, bronchitis, asthma, and other respiratory symptoms. The admittance rate was highest for those who worked in Kraft, versus groundwood mills.[13]

Ida Luther, a state representative for the area, stated the general feeling of many area residents when she said, "I don't think the point is to shut the mill. But what is the best they could do with the air emissions? What is the best they could do? Are they making them do that?"[14]

Public Relations Matter

In 1987 workers at the International Paper mill in Jay went on strike. IP subsequently hired 970 replacement workers (i.e., "scabs"). Soon after, a flurry of environmental incidents occurred, including the largest accidental release of wastewater in state history (16.6 million gallons into the Androscoggin River) and the largest evacuation due to an industrial accident in state history (4,000 people).[15]

The evacuation was due to the release of 121,000 gallons of chlorine dioxide when pipe fitters accidentally broke a valve on a 160,000-gallon storage tank. Chlorine dioxide is very unstable and extremely hazardous—more than twice as deadly as the methyl isocyanate that killed thousands of people at Bhopal, India. Fortunately, the temperatures in Jay were below freezing. Had the temperatures been higher than 50° F, most of the chemical would have turned to gas and probably killed townspeople. A gas cloud did form around the plant, however, and some workers and children went to the hospital complaining of respiratory problems.[16]

IP's response to these disasters was to blame the people who reported them. IP safety supervisor Joe Bean complained that the root of the problem was bad public relations, because every time something happened at the mill, it was reported by the media. "It's not just the media," said Bean, "it's the whole goddam town." He accused the strikers of "calling God and anybody else they could find."[17]

IP officials insisted that the working climate had actually improved since scabs took the place of strikers. Said Bean, "I can guarantee this is a far safer place than it was before [the strike was initiated]. If we didn't have all these people watching us run our business, we might have taken care of it without an evacuation."[18] Four days after Bean's remarks, another broken valve released chlorine gas, exposing 10 people to toxic fumes. One worker had to be put in intensive care.[19] If this string of incidents was an improvement on IP's previous record, the previous record was surely nothing to boast about. Indeed, at the time IP was facing millions of dollars in fines for air pollution from its boiler over a 10-year period.[20]

In 1991 IP entered guilty pleas to 5 felony charges in U. S. District Court in Portland for lying to regulators about treatment and disposal of hazardous waste during this same period and was fined $2.2 million, the second-largest corporate environmental fine in U. S. history.[21] Ironically, 3 weeks later, President George Bush named IP's chairman, John Georges, to the president's Commission on Environmental Quality.[22]

Enriched Bread

Maine's rivers are classified from AA to C in terms of water quality. This classification is based only on dissolved oxygen (BOD) and fecal bacteria, not on chemical toxins, odor, or color. There used to be Class D waters, which were legal industrial sewers. Class C waters, though they do legalize some levels of pollution and allow some changes in aquatic life, require that the water body be capable of supporting communities of native aquatic species. The rivers must be swimmable and fishable.

The Androscoggin, however, is so severely polluted that it cannot meet these criteria. In 1991 the DEP agreed to a plan for the biggest polluters (International Paper, Boise Cascade, James River, and Central Maine Power) to pump 27,000 pounds of liquid oxygen into the river each day from July 30 to September 1, in hopes that this will allow fish, such as salmon, to breathe. This approach to pollution control is akin to robbing the nutrients from bread, then adding a few back and calling it "enriched." It is a quick fix, not a permanent one. If the companies were truly concerned about the quality of the river, they would stop polluting it.

Stalling

Citizens made it clear in 1987 that they wanted their rivers cleaned up and upgraded. Early in 1988, in response to such demands, Governor John McKernan had the DEP do a feasibility study for cleaning up the most noticeable pollution effects. Later that year a draft of this study was completed, showing that paper mills were the "major point source contributors of pollutants that preclude people's use of Maine's waters due to excessive color odor and foam."[23]

Pollutants that cause the color problems include cooking liquors and bleachery effluent. The Androscoggin, St. Croix, and Presumpscot are the three most colored rivers in the state, according to the report. Although industry spokespeople implied that color problems are mostly cosmetic, evidence exists that the color cuts available light to aquatic life, binds up metals so they can't be used by stream organisms, may affect fish movements and productivity, and detracts from the water's visual appeal.[24]

The draft recommended legislation that would significantly reduce color, odor, and foam and gave cost estimates for implementation. The technology to do these improvements already exists and is being used in other parts of the country. Dean Marriott, commissioner of the DEP, told the governor in a memo (obtained by NRCM through the Freedom of Information Act) that much of the costs would have to be paid anyway to meet federal guidelines on dioxin discharges. The draft concluded that "many benefits will come from improving water quality. They include new recreational opportunities, increased property values, expanded non-use value and improved economic conditions due to increased income of Maine people."[25]

Oddly enough, this conclusion and the recommended regulations never made it into the final draft. The paper industry, which got to see the original draft, was displeased and apparently was able to convince the governor (whose brother, Robert McKernan, was an American Paper Institute lobbyist in Washington, D.C.) to make some changes. The final draft recommended that each mill study the problem on an individual basis and come up with cost estimates for implementing improvements. It also diverted attention to the raw sewage discharges of towns.

Some people were outraged by what appeared to be stalling tactics and government/industry collusion. Representative John Nutting (D-Leeds) drafted legislation that contained the original recommendations from the suppressed draft report. This legislation passed, but the governor vetoed it. The legislature was unable to override McKernan's veto because the governor did some major arm twisting of Republican legislators. What the public finally got was a 1-year delay while an "expert" studied the problem and a "balanced committee" studied the expert. These delays saved the paper companies money and gave them time to mount a counteroffensive.

Trivializing

A year later, the governor, perhaps sensing the strength of public sentiment, submitted his own bill, which was very similar to Nutting's. In the meantime, the paper industry started a massive lobby campaign against either bill. Industry representatives argued that the bills would mandate expensive changes that would cut into the companies' abilities to compete. For this cost (industry's estimate was nearly 4 times that of the state), they claimed, there would be no real benefits. The problem, they claimed, is cosmetic, not an environmental or health threat. They concluded that the clamor over the bill was a cynical political ploy during an election year (despite the fact that the bill originated a year earlier during a nonelection year).

Job Blackmail

Along with these arguments, the paper industry exerted political pressure on legislators, sometimes in such a heavy-handed manner that they hurt rather than helped their cause. Allan Robinson, a mill manager for S. D. Warren (a Scott subsidiary), wrote an open letter (published in area newspapers) on April 4, 1990, to Senator Judy Kany and Representative Paul Jacques (both Democrats from Waterville and both on the Energy and Natural Resources Committee, which held hearings on the bills) in which he accused these legislators of not being "concerned whether Scott remains in the State of Maine." The color/odor/foam bill, Robinson claimed, was "ill-timed, poorly thought out and not necessary to protect any environmental values of which we are aware."

Harry Vanderweide, in the April 1990 edition of *The Maine Sportsman*, wrote a scathing editorial rebutting industry's attempts at trivializing the issue while threatening jobs: "The paper industry believes it has a divine right to use Maine's best rivers as open sewers. Their campaign is designed to convince us that what our eyes and noses can clearly see and smell doesn't exist. They say you only imagine the colors, odors and foam which come from paper factory outfalls on the Kennebec, Penobscot, Androscoggin and St. Croix Rivers.

"In case that tactic isn't enough, the paper industry has once again stooped to the deplorable device of threatening the jobs of honest Maine working men and women. It seems as though the corporate leaders of the paper industry never tire dragging out the old 'pickerels or payrolls' gambit. . . . Here are the facts the paper companies don't tell you. For their entire history Maine's paper mills have been the major polluters of our rivers. They had no right to desecrate our rivers in the first place and they have no right to continue."

Richard Kazis and Richard Grossman did an exhaustive study of the pickerels-and-payrolls gambit in their book *Fear at Work: Job Blackmail, Labor, and the Environment*, and concluded that companies that indulge in job blackmail have two goals: to make the pursuit of their own interests synonymous with the public interest in employment opportunities, and to scare workers into thinking they have no alternative but to support their employers' demands. They found little evidence that environmental regulations were the "cause" of plant shutdowns: ". . . at worst, environmental protection requirements merely hastened plant closings which were already imminent."[26]

Indeed, they found that environmental protection in some cases actually created jobs—to construct pollution controls, to do clean-ups, for consulting, and for maintenance. It can also save jobs, they suggested: "Fishing, forestry, tourism, agriculture, and the growing leisure and outdoor recreation industries are all important sources of jobs which depend directly upon clean water, clean air, and wilderness for their continuation and growth. Although neither industry nor government has tried to estimate the number of jobs saved as a result of the preservation of environmental quality, it is likely that many jobs would have been eliminated in these industries had the environmental legislation of the past decade not been enacted and enforced."[27]

This time the massive industry lobby campaign did not stop the public's demand for a modest improvement in their rivers. In April 1990, a bill was passed that was, with a few exceptions, very similar to the bill first proposed by Nutting. The bill only regulates color; odor and foam qualities are considered too subjective for specific standards. Companies are given until 1993 to start implementing the needed changes.

Downgrading Dioxin
While state standards require that rivers meet a minimum of Class C, meaning

that rivers must be able to support native fish communities, these standards still do not guarantee that the fish are suitable for eating. Even after color, odor, and foam are reduced and thousands of pounds of liquid oxygen are pumped into the Androscoggin, and salmon, somehow, return in numbers sufficient to support fishing, there still remains a problem—the fish are contaminated with organo-chlorines, including highly toxic dioxins and furans.

The Penobscot, Kennebec, and St. Croix rivers also have dioxin contamina-tion downstream from the Kraft paper mills located on their shores. In 1990 the Department of Human Services recommended that people eat no more than two 8-ounce servings of fish a year from these waters, except in some sections of the Kennebec where the recommended limit is 5 meals. If you happen to be pregnant or a nursing mother, you should not eat any.[28]

The paper-industry response has been to deny that dioxin is a problem (but to reduce levels to appease an "uninformed" public—and state and federal regu-lators). International Paper's 1990 annual report, for example, informs its share-holders that "Considerable recent scientific evidence supports the conclusion that the minute amount of dioxin associated with making bleached paper prod-ucts never posed a danger to humans or the environment." Based on their recent success in reducing (but not eliminating) dioxin and the supposed safety of dioxin to people, the industry is pressuring state regulators to lift the fishing warnings.

Unfortunately, the 3 major studies (conducted by Monsanto) on the toxicity of the most toxic dioxin, TCDD (2,3,7,8-tetrachlordibenzo-p-dioxin) —studies that have been cited to justify the downgrading of dioxin—are fraudu-lent. This fact was uncovered during the longest civil jury trial in U. S. history. Even a mild unscrambling of the doctored data shows significantly higher risks of several diseases, including cancers, nervous disorders, and liver damage, to exposed workers.[29]

Focusing on people, however, misses the point that TCDD is persistent, bioconcentrating, and highly toxic to many wildlife species—including fish and fish-eating raptors such as bald eagles.[30] And TCDD dioxin is only one of, perhaps, a thousand organochlorines, of which only about 300 have been identified.[31] Some of these organochlorines, though not as toxic as TCDD, are still highly toxic. Since they are more abundant in effluent than TCDD, they have a higher toxic equivalency.[32]

Rather than merely regulate these toxins, some countries, such as Sweden and Germany, have been trying to prevent them by eliminating chlorine bleaching processes.[33] Oxygen bleaching, which yields an ivory white rather than a bright white, is a more benign process which yields a product that should be acceptable for most paper needs. What price must local communities pay in health and environmental damage for the sake of whiter paper?

Responsible Corporate Citizens

These corporations, which present themselves as responsible community mem-bers, have polluted community air and water, maimed workers, and lied and cheated to deflect attention from such criminal activity. Sometimes they get caught. Here is just a sampling of some of the more spectacular recent regula-tory problems of the paper companies in Maine:

•Boise Cascade—In 1989 the Labor Department proposed a $1.6 million fine for health and safety violations at the company's Rumford mill. The company settled the case in 1991, agreeing to pay $750,000 in fines and $125,00 as a grant to the Maine Center for Occupational Safety and Health.[34] Maine's DEP fined the company $252,816 for air and water violations in consent agreements in 1989 and 1990.[35]

•Champion International—From December 1988 to October 1990, 60 workers at the Bucksport mill developed documented health problems. Two workers died. One, a nonsmoker and marathon runner, complained of persistent respiratory problems and a burning in his eyes and throat. On April 30, 1989, he told his wife, "I got into something really bad in the mill. My lungs feel like they're on fire. If I drop dead in the next couple of days you'll remember this." He died 7 months later.[36] Champion denies any connection between the health problems and workplace conditions, but they are currently (1991) being investigated by the National Institute for Occupational Safety and Health. In 1989 the company agreed to pay the DEP $20,000 for hazardous materials violations.[37]

•Fraser—In 1991 OSHA fined Fraser $3.9 million in penalties for 313 alleged violations of occupational safety and health rules at its Madawaska paper mill. OSHA inspectors came to the mill after a chlorine release hospitalized 7 employees. Over a 17-year period there have been several crippling accidents and amputations, yet Fraser still had inadequate safety guards with its machinery.[38] Fraser agreed to pay the state $64,650 for water violations in 1986 and $15,000 for hazardous materials violations in 1990.[39]

•Georgia-Pacific—Based on EPA figures, the Citizens Fund has listed Georgia-Pacific as the 21st-largest emitter in the nation of known or suspected carcinogens and the 40th-largest emitter of toxic chemicals known to cause, or suspected of causing, birth defects.[40] The company agreed to pay a total of $109,000 to the state for violations of land, water, and air standards from 1986 to 1989. In 1990 the company agreed to pay a civil penalty of $637,000 for air and water pollution violations since 1986 at its Woodland mill. Some of the episodes included the dumping of 6 million gallons of waste water into the St. Croix River and 6,000 violations of air-pollution discharge limits.[41] In 1991 Georgia-Pacific received a $601,847 fine for air and water violations in the Millinocket area. This included an illegal 500,000-gallon discharge into the Penobscot River and the emission of soot so corrosive it damaged the finish on automobiles.[42]

•International Paper—In 1991, besides the $2.2 million felony charge already discussed, the company agreed to pay the state a $990,000 fine and spend over $4 million to install air-pollution-control equipment at its Androscoggin Mill in Jay.[43] As of 1990, the company was a potentially responsible party for 55 hazardous waste sites in the country.[44]

•James River—In 1990 James River agreed to pay $280,000 in penalties for air and water violations at its Old Town mill.[45] According to figures from the Citizens Fund, from 1988 EPA data, James River was the 20th-largest emitter of toxic chemicals known to cause, or suspected of causing, birth defects. In 1990 the firm decided to sell 28 mills, so its rating should drop. The company is potentially a responsible party at approximately 40 Superfund sites in the country.[46]

•Lincoln Pulp and Paper—In 1990 the company agreed to pay the state a record $1,025,000 for air, water, land, and hazardous waste violations.[47]

•Scott Paper—Scott agreed to pay the state a total of $134,900 in fines for water and hazardous materials violations from 1986 to 1989. The company agreed to pay $250,000 for air violations and $150,000 for water and hazardous materials violations in 1990.[48]

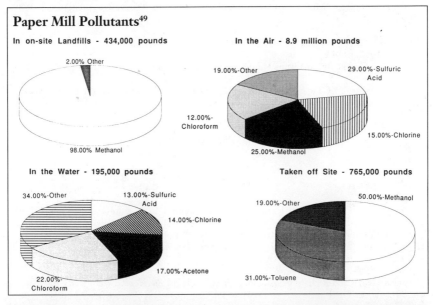

Paper Mill Pollutants[49]

In on-site Landfills - 434,000 pounds
- 2.00% Other
- 98.00% Methanol

In the Air - 8.9 million pounds
- 19.00%-Other
- 29.00%-Sulfuric Acid
- 12.00%-Chloroform
- 15.00%-Chlorine
- 25.00%-Methanol

In the Water - 195,000 pounds
- 34.00%-Other
- 13.00%-Sulfuric Acid
- 14.00%-Chlorine
- 17.00%-Acetone
- 22.00%-Chloroform

Taken off Site - 765,000 pounds
- 50.00%-Methanol
- 19.00%-Other
- 31.00%-Toluene

'89 Maine paper mill pollution (in pounds) [50]

Paper mill	Air	Water	On-site landfill	Taken off site	Total
Georgia Pacific Corp., Woodland	2,368,354	33,780	0	4,900	2,407,034
International Paper, Jay	1,205,600	13,900	175,800	0	1,395,300
James River Paper Co., Old Town	985,085	12,447	0	316,163	1,313,695
Great Northern Paper, Millinocket	1,195,300	24,830	0	25,100	1,245,230
Bolse Cascade Paper, Rumford	1,102,078	27,976	65	105,272	1,235,391
S.D. Warren Co., Westbrook	798,250	6,600	0	230,300	1,035,150
Lincoln Pulp and Paper Co., Lincoln	439,155	5,005	258,207	0	702,367
S.D. Warren Co., Skowhegan	381,840	2,920	0	260	385,020
Champion International, Bucksport	232,404	6,070	0	0	238,474
Eastern Fine Paper, Brewer	126,356	0	0	72,410	198,766
Great Northern Paper, E. Millinocket	100,500	281	0	11,000	111,781
Scott Paper Co., Winslow	9,473	23,187	0	0	32,660
St. Raymond Corp., Pejepscot	750	19,032	0	0	19,782
Fraser Paper LDT, Madawaska	1	18,264	0	0	18,265
Madison Paper Industries, Madison	4,400	250	0	0	4,650
Statler Tissue Co., Augusta	26	146	0	0	172
James River/Otis Div., Jay	0	0	0	0	0
Total	8,949,572	194,688	434,072	765,405	10,343,737
Percent by weight	86.52%	1.88%	4.20%	7.40%	

References

1. William Osborne, *The Paper Plantation* (New York: Viking Press, 1974), p. 51.
2. *Ibid.*, p. 6.
3. *Ibid.*, p. 54.
4. *Ibid.*, p. 52.
5. *Ibid.*, p. 105.
6. *Ibid.*, p. 101.
7. Meredith Goad, "Paper Mill's Neighbors Still Holding Their Noses," *Kennebec Journal*, December 17, 1990, p. 1.
8. Robert Cummings, "Mill Pollution Goes Unchecked," *Maine Sunday Telegram*, April 3, 1988.
9. *Ibid.*
10. *Ibid.*
11. Meredith Goad, "Anger Grows As Illnesses Plague Towns, *Maine Sunday Telegram*, September 16, 1990, p. 14A.
12. Meredith Goad, "Anemia Runs High in Area, *Maine Sunday Telegram*, September 16, 1990, p. 14A.
13. Meredith Goad, "'Cancer Valley' Puzzles Over Causes But Lacks Scientific Proof," *Maine Sunday Telegram*, September 16, 1990, p. 14A.
14. *Ibid.*
15. Scott Allen, "Days of Living Dangerously: IP's Two Poisonous Leaks in Nine Days Put a Town on Edge," *Maine Times* (February 19, 1988): 12.
16. *Ibid.*, p. 13.
17. *Ibid.*, p. 14.
18. *Ibid.*, p. 12.
19. *Ibid.*, p. 12.
20. *Ibid.*, p. 14.
21. United States Attorney, District of Maine, Department of Justice, press release, July 3, 1991.
22. Keith Romig, "CEO of Corporate Felon Appointed to Bush Environmental Panel," United Paperworkers International Union press release, July 29, 1991.
23. Joe Rankin, "Rivers Hearing Set," *Central Maine Morning Sentinel*, April 1, 1989.
24. *Ibid.*
25. *Ibid.*
26. Richard Kazis and Richard Grossman, *Fear at Work: Job Blackmail, Labor and the Environment* (New York: The Pilgrim Press, 1982), p. 19.
27. *Ibid.*, p. 28.
28. "Dioxin Levels Rise in State River Fish: Safe-eating Limits Lowered," *Bangor Daily News*, March 22, 1990.
29. Carol Van Strum and Paul Merrell, "Dioxin Human Health Damage Studies: Damaged Data?," *Journal of Pesticide Reform*, Vol. 10, No. 1 (Spring 1990): 8.
30. Peter Frost, "Bald Eagles on the Columbia River: Threats from Persistent Organochlorines," *Journal of Pesticide Reform*, Vol. 10, No. 2 (Summer 1990): 5-9.
31. Renate Kroesa, *The Greenpeace Guide to Paper* (Vancouver, British Columbia: Greenpeace, 1990), p. 13.
32. Mary O'Brien, "A Crucial Matter of Cumulative Impacts: Toxicity Equivalency Factors, *Journal of Pesticide Reform*, Vol. 10, No. 2 (Summer 1990): 23-27.
33. Renate Kroesa, "Worldwide Roundup on Pulpmills," *Journal of Pesticide Reform*, Vol. 10, No. 2 (Summer 1990): 2-4.
34. Amy Domini, Peter Kinder and Steve Lydenberg, *Boise Cascade* (Boston: Domini Social Index Trust, Kinder, Lydenberg, Domini and Company, January 1991).
35. Brooke E. Barnes, Maine DEP, letter to author, December 27, 1990.
36. Meredith Goad, "Workers Charge Paper Mill With Causing Their Illness," *Maine Sunday Telegram*, October 28, 1990, p. 9A.
37. Brooke E. Barnes, letter to author.
38. Phyllis Austin, "OSHA Penalty $3.9 Million: Another Economic Blow for Fraser Paper," *Maine Times* (September 27, 1991): 11.
39. Brooke E. Barnes, letter to author.
40. Amy Domini, Peter Kinder and Steve Lydenberg, *Georgia-Pacific* (Boston: Domini Social Index Trust, Kinder, Lydenberg, Domini and Company, December 1990).
41. Jim Donahue, "Another Tree, Another Dollar: Rampant Expansion at Georgia-Pacific," *Multinational Monitor* (October 1990): 31.
42. John Hale, "State Fines G-P $601,847: Pollution Penalties Cited Millinocket-area Mills,"

Bangor Daily News, September 26, 1991.
43. Brooke E. Barnes, letter to author.
44. Amy Domini, Peter Kinder and Steve Lydenberg, *International Paper* (Boston: Domini Social Index Trust, Kinder, Lydenberg, Domini and Company, November 1990).
45. Brooke E. Barnes, letter to author.
46. Amy Domini, Peter Kinder and Steve Lydenberg, *James River* (Boston: Domini Social Index Trust, Kinder, Lydenberg, Domini and Company, May 1991).
47. Brooke E. Barnes, letter to author.
48. *Ibid.*
49. Craig Doremus, "New Laws Pushing for a Cleanup at the Mills," *Lewiston Sunday*, April 14, 1991.
50. *Ibid.*

Myth 3

Paper company dominance of a township promotes community stability.

The large paper companies that dominate Maine's landscape are Fortune 500 corporations that perceive themselves as stable entities because of their product diversification. Scott Paper Company's 1989 annual report, for example, proudly proclaims "We are positioned to succeed through economic cycles." If the whole is stable, reason some industry spokespeople, then the parts must be stable. Communities that are dominated by these companies, must therefore be benefitting from corporate growth and stability. The companies do, after all, contribute a secure tax base, and they do have the resources to invest in local communities—an investment that one might assume would be in the companies' best interests. Unfortunately, sometimes corporate stability is achieved not to the benefit but at the expense of community stability.

Ownership Changes
The leveraged takeovers of Diamond and Great Northern have shaken the public's faith in paper-company stability. These acquisitions are not isolated examples. From 1982 to 1987, a third of the nation's pulp and paper productive capacity changed hands.[1] Indeed, in Maine the majority of industry land changed ownership over the last 15 years.

Large Industry Land Ownership Transfers 1976-90[2]

Former Owners	Present Owners	Acreage
Oxford (Ethyl Corp.) &		
Brown (Gulf & Western)	Boise Cascade	640,000
St. Regis	Champion	730,000
Diamond**	Fraser (Noranda)**	230,000
	& James River	285,000*
Great Northern	Georgia-Pacific***	2,100,000
International	Daishawa**	60,000
IP and others	Irving**	250,000+
Boise Cascade	Daaquam**	100,000
Total transfer		4,135,000+
Total industry land		7,700,000
Percent transferred		54%

N.B. This chart does not account for trades of land between companies trying to consolidate holdings.
*According to the 1989-90 James River annual report, this land has been or is being sold to Diamond Occidental Forest which is an approximately 23%-owned affiliate.
**Foreign-owned corporations. Fraser, Irving, and Daaquam are Canadian. Daishawa is Japanese. Diamond has been French (General Occidental) and English (Sir James Goldsmith).
***In 1991 Bowater made an 80% downpayment on the former Great Northern land and mills.

In an attempt to survive in a world of not-always-friendly acquisitions and mergers, companies have been "restructuring." Part of this restructuring has involved selling off "nonessential" mills. As I write this in 1991, for example, James River is trying to unload its 3 New Hampshire mills and Scott has announced that its S. D. Warren Mill in Westbrook is for sale.

Real-estate Development
Companies are also "rationalizing" their forest lands. Rather than view their timberlands only as a strategic wood reserve to insulate the mills from market fluctuations, many companies are treating their timberlands as "profit centers." If land is neither suitable for timber production nor contiguous with other company-owned blocks, and if it is near an active real-estate market, the tendency is to sell. To do otherwise, suggested the Northern Forest Lands Study (NFLS), "would be unfair to company stockholders, who are trusting management to maximize the return on their investment."[3] Some of the companies even have their own real-estate subsidiaries.

Although sales to nontimber interests (for "development") represent a small percentage of the total forested acreage, the local impacts can be profound. Lloyd Irland of the Irland Group estimates that 150,000 acres of the unorganized territories were subdivided from 1985 to 1989.[4] The prime targets seem to be land with lake and river frontage. The purchasers are mostly nonresidents seeking second homes or investment properties.

Although real-estate development may bring some benefits, it also creates many problems, including diminished water quality, decreased access to shorelands, fragmented wildlife habitat, increased demands for utilities and waste disposal, and fewer wilderness opportunities.

Even some of the "benefits," according to the NFLS, are questionable:

" . . . the majority of benefits from the initial construction phase of development do not end up in the community. Some construction materials and equipment are shipped in from elsewhere, and many contractors are from outside the area. Only a quarter to a third of the total outlay will remain in the local economy as wages and other payments. After construction, new residents create increased demand for town services and upkeep as well as food and other living necessities. This may boost local economic activity, but it also creates new government expenses to meet the needs of the growing population. In some places, affordable housing becomes scarce as property values rise and local taxes increase."[5]

Job Security

Another result of corporate restructuring has been cuts in wages, benefits, and even jobs. One result of the call for "concessions" by workers to help the companies be more "competitive" has been long, divisive strikes in the late 1980s against the International Paper mill at Jay and the Boise-Cascade Mill in Rumford. This has hardly improved community relations or community stability.

Colonial Welfare

The Northern Forest Lands Study, written during an economic boom, graphically illustrated the effects of corporate colonization of the forested regions of the Northeast:[6]

Mill workers on strike against Boise Cascade. *Photo by Christopher Ayres.*

•"Population decline is projected for parts of the study area, specifically Aroostook and Washington Counties in Maine. . . . The balance of births and mortality indicates that young people are leaving the area, perhaps attracted by economic opportunities elsewhere."

•"Per capita income in all but one county in the Northern Forest is below the national level of $10,797. . . . All the counties have lower per capita incomes than the averages for their states. Incomes are lowest in Maine, with Hancock County having the lowest per capita income ($6,929) in the area."

•"About half of the study area has more families living below the poverty level than the national average. In contrast to the Northern Forest, fewer families in New England live in poverty than in either the Northeast or the nation."

•"Unemployment in the Northern Forest is high compared to the low rate of unemployment found throughout the rest of New England (3.9 percent). . . . Nationally, the unemployment rate is 7 percent, but two-thirds of counties in the Northern Forest have greater than 7 percent unemployment."

•"The level of education achieved by people living in the Northern Forest varies considerably, but for the most part fewer people have completed high school and college than people in New England as a whole."

•"It is likely that the quality of health care in the Northern Forest is inferior to the quality of care in the rest of the Northeast. . . . "

•"Maine spends generally less than one percent of government expenditures on public welfare [assistance to needy]."

•"The economy and the availability of jobs in the northern forest is heavily influenced by the use of forest resources and the industry it has spawned."

Such statements do not bespeak grand community advantages from corporate domination of the northern forest economy.

References

1. Stephen Harper, Laura Falk, and Edward Rankin, *The Northern Forest Lands Study of New England and New York* (Rutland, Vt.: United States Forest Service, United States Department of Agriculture, 1990), p. 10.
2. Data from Paper Industry Information Office summaries, paper-company annual reports, and personal communications (summer 1991) with Lloyd Irland.
3. Stephen Harper, Laura Falk, and Edward Rankin, *The Northern Forest Lands Study*, p. 11.
4. Lloyd Irland, "Land Ownership in Maine's Exurban-wildland Fringe: Implications for Wilderness in the North Woods." Presentation at Activist Workshop of The Wilderness Society, Bethel, Me., November 10, 1990.
5. Stephen Harper, Laura Falk, and Edward Rankin, *The Northern Forest Lands Study*, p. 20.
6. *Ibid.*, pp. 34-36.

Labor Security

The popular image of loggers is derived from an earlier era—before extensive mechanization. The Bunyanesque lumberjacks of the past were tough men, using bucksaws and axes to cut tall trees in the dead of winter. They yarded the logs with horses or oxen and hauled them on great sleds over icy woods trails.

In the spring they floated the logs down swollen streams and rivers to the mills. It was hard, dangerous, dawn-to-dusk work, and at night, the men slept in crowded, crude, log shelters. The work was seasonal. When the log drives ended, the men would often find summer work on farms.

After World War II (a period that saw such shortages of labor in Maine that German prisoners of war were put to work in the woods), logging technologies and the logger lifestyle changed. The farms that had supplied both the farmboys to cut the wood and the horses to haul it went into decline. Seasonal workers, versed in rural skills, were gradually replaced by full-time industrial workers running and tending complex, expensive equipment.[a]

In the 1950s, chainsaws replaced bucksaws and axes, and in the 1960s, large rubber-tired, articulated-framed, 4-wheel-drive skidders, with cable winches for yarding cut logs, replaced horses and oxen. Also during this period, the river drives were phased out. Companies got wood to the mill over thousands of miles of woods roads in large trucks, loaded by mechanical knuckleboom

The chainsaw is no longer at the cutting edge of logging technology. *Photo courtesy Bangor Daily News.*

loaders. And in the 1970s, mechanical harvesters began replacing men with chainsaws. These introduced technologies have not only been changing the workforce; they have been shaping the forest.

Despite mechanization, modern woodsworkers still have to face extreme cold in winter, ferocious biting insects in summer, fatigue, and danger. Loggers may live in small towns surrounded by trees, but often they do not cut in their own communities, where they might have more of a sense of responsibility and stewardship. Instead, they are more apt to commute long distances—sometimes staying in logging camps far from home. They are cutting for production. It is a job.

Men are not taking such jobs primarily for the romance or the pay—in the hinterlands of Maine, logging is often the only game in town. Women have even fewer opportunities and make up a very small minority of those who work in forest-based industries.[b] Job security is an important issue for those tied to the industrial forests.

Labor policy in the industrial forest is crucial both to the impact of management on forests and on local communities. Researchers or managers may formulate plans for how they would like the woods to be managed, but it is workers, not computers or executives, who actually cut the trees. When those shocked by industrial management demand more restraint, industrial advocates often stress that any restraint would be at the cost of jobs—as if maintaining jobs is a prime industrial concern. Such arguments neatly pit environmentalists against loggers.

Despite the central importance of labor to the forest, Bowdoin economist David Vail concluded that "There is a striking disparity in the extent of knowl-

A "skidder." *Photo courtesy Bangor Daily News.*

edge about Maine's forests and about the loggers who work in them. Entire university departments and government bureaus are devoted to analysis and prescription regarding the trees. Virtually no one in academia or government studies the people."[1] "In contrast to the highly visible, highly political and much studied family farmer," Vail observed," the yeoman logger seems to be lost in the woods—on the fringes both of society and social analysis."[2]

Endnotes

a. There are still many part-time farmer/loggers who work their woodlots only seasonally. These observations are directed more to the industrial forest.

b. There are very few women who actually cut the trees. Women do work as cooks and bookkeepers in logging camps and to some extent in some wood-processing mills. Forest economist Lloyd Irland estimates that of the approximately 25,549 persons employed in 1980 in the primary sector, about 10% were women.[3]

References

1. David Vail, *Contract Logging, Chainsaws and Clearcuts: The Human and Environmental Impacts of Forest Extraction Systems in the State of Maine (USA)* (Helsinki, Finland: United Nations University, World Institute for Development Economic Studies, May 1986), p. 37.
2. *Ibid.*, p. 51.
3. Lloyd Irland, "Future Employment in the Maine Woods: Situation, Forces, and Outlook." In *Proceedings, A Forest Based Economy: Carrying a Tradition into the Future, Blaine House Conference on Forestry, December 6-7, 1984* (Augusta, Me.: Maine Department of Conservation, August 1986), p. 80.

Myth 1

Company lands are cut by company employees.

Most company land is cut by "service jobbers" who are considered independent contractors and technically are not landowner employees. There has been a steady downward trend since World War II in the proportion of company crews. In 1945, 70% of the land cut in Maine was cut by company crews; in 1987 it was only 10%.

In 1986 only 3 companies employed company crews. By 1991 Scott Paper was the last large industrial landowner to have a sizable company woods crew (even though they reduced its size as part of cost cutting). The other companies have decided it is far cheaper to hire "independents." Company crews are unionized and demand more benefits. In contrast, contractors must pay for equipment, insurance, trucking, labor, and sometimes even road building. By getting rid of company crews, companies have washed their hands of responsibilities and saved money at the same time.

Reference

1. David Vail, "How To Tell the Forest from the Trees: Recent Technical Changes in the Forest Industries of Sweden and Maine." In *Harvard University Seminar on Neo-classical Economics* (Cambridge, Mass.: Harvard University, March 1988), p. 18.

Myth 2

Independent contractors are independent.

This myth has legal implications. In 1970 an organization called the Maine Pulpwood Producers Association struck against International Paper's Jay mill in hopes of getting a better price for their wood (IP's price, interestingly enough, was nearly identical to that of every other mill in the state). Judge Webber of the Franklin County Superior Court issued a temporary restraining order against the strikers on the grounds that they were independent businessmen in-

Angry loggers confront Governor James Longley, in 1975, over unfair practices of paper companies. *Photo courtesy Bangor Daily News.*

volved in illegal price fixing and illegal restraint of trade. These marginal pulpcutters were accused of violating the Sherman Anti-Trust Act even though they were striking against oligopsonistic price fixing on the part of the paper industry![1]

The Maine Woodsmen Association (MWA), an association of large and small contractors, wood cutters, and truckers, ran into a similar wall when it attempted a mill boycott in October 1975. The workers had a long list of grievances: the companies' unilateral price setting, arbitrary termination of contracts, falsified scaling of timber at the mills, importation of bonded Canadian workers, lack of a uniform scaling law, and lack of adequate insurance coverage.[2] Costs for pulpwood harvesting had been going up but the price paid by mills hadn't. The strike was a desperate one because the mills had large timber inventories during a period of slack demand, whereas many of the cutters had to make payments on equipment—payments that could hardly be met if the men were not producing. Some mills, however, were actually shut down by the MWA.

Workers were angry. There was an atmosphere of impending violence, and indeed, isolated acts of vandalism and violence (never proven to be by the MWA) did erupt. At one point state police in Old Town spent the day dressed in riot gear to escort pulpwood trucks into the Diamond International plant. Justice Roberts of Maine's superior court issued an injunction (some think this was at the request of Governor Longley) against all the picketing by woodsworkers, calling for an end to "economic warfare." The strike fizzled out not long afterwards.

As with the 1970 strike, industry maintained that the workers were independent businessmen who were violating antitrust laws and engaging in price fixing. This theory, however, was not tested in federal court because of the effective injunction of Justice Roberts. Some observers, such as former MWA vice president Bill Butler, think the workers would have won the right to strike had they taken their case to federal court.[3]

Prior to the MWA uprising, a federal court ruled that a group of contractors from Mississippi and Alabama known as the Gulfcoast Pulpwood Association were, despite their "independent" status, essentially employees of large pulp dealers. The dealers had control over every important aspect of production and exchange. The MWA claimed that its relationship with the paper companies was analogous.[4] During the MWA strike, Butler stated that "We're about as independent as a deer on new ice. They determine our source of raw materials, and where and when, and even if we are going to work."[5]

The contracts these "independent businessmen" sign with paper companies give them little economic power or freedom. There are two types of contracts: the stumpage permit and the pulpwood contract. The stumpage permit specifies that the contractor must pay the landowner a given stumpage price for the wood cut by a given date. Restrictions are placed on how roads are to be laid out and how the wood is to be cut. Some landowners even tell the contractor where to market certain grades and species of logs. The permit often gives the landowner the power to challenge the cutting practices of the operator but offers the operator little protection from the abuse of this power (using this information at a strategic time, instead of informing the operator of abuses as they occur).

The pulpwood contract with the mill also leaves the contractor with few rights. The mills scale the wood that is coming in. They can reduce payment on loads because of defects such as rot or discoloration of wood. Some of the wood that is deducted is still used by the mill. One small contractor I interviewed told me that a mill scaler declared some of his wood unsuitable and made him load it back on the truck and take it back to the woods. When the company forester saw the wood, he declared it good and made the contractor truck it back to the mill. The scaler again rejected the wood, and the forester again told the contractor to bring it back to the mill. Meanwhile, the contractor had to pay for all the loading, trucking, and unloading with no returns for his effort.

In the past some mills used to offer contractors bonuses upon fulfilling parts of the contract. This "incentive" was often the operator's only profit and thus ensured subservience. The mill "tickets" given the operator do not have to have any connection to the operator's stumpage contract. If there is a surplus or shortage, mills can request a halt or speed-up of wood delivery. The contractors can also be adversely affected by loading delays at the mill that cut into scarce and valuable time. If delays or lack of tickets interfere with the operator's contract—too bad.[6]

"The power that the mill woodyards exercise over the production activities of the contractor," wrote William Osborne in *The Paper Plantation*, "illustrate the fiction of his independent status. In reality, he is as dependent on the mill as the mill's own employees; yet, because the companies deal with him at arm's length and callously avoid any responsibility for his welfare, the independent contractor does not even enjoy the minimal benefits and protections of the employment relationship."[5]

References

1. William Osborne, *The Paper Plantation* (New York: Viking Press, 1974), p. 165.
2. David Vail, *Contract Logging, Chainsaws and Clearcuts: The Human and Environmental Impacts of Forest Extraction Systems in the State of Maine (USA)* (Helsinki, Finland: World Institute for Development Economics Research, United Nations University, 1986), p. 55.
3. Bill Butler, personal communication, summer 1990.
4. David Vail, *Contract Logging*, p. 68.
5. Dennis Mills, "Woodsmen's Protest Spreads, 3 Mills Close," *Bangor Daily News*, October 10, 1975, pp. 1-2.
6. Mitch Lansky, interviews with contractors, summer 1990 to winter 1991.
7. William Osborne, *The Paper Plantation*, p. 144.

Myth 3
Workers are paid to manage the forest.

Workers are paid to cut trees, not manage forests. Most contractors follow cutting rules rather than use silvicultural methods. The two most prevalent cutting practices in Maine are commercial clearcuts and diameter-limit cuts. Diameter-limit cuts and commercial clearcuts do not attempt to space trees, remove poor-quality or high-risk trees, or ensure desirable regeneration. They merely establish a minimum diameter of trees per species that the cutter can mine. In the case of the commercial clearcut, whatever the markets will take sets the limit.

Whereas operators of mechanized harvesters may be paid by the hour to remove a forest, most workers using chainsaws are still paid on a piece-rate or per-cord basis. A piece-rate wage has nothing whatsoever to do with management. In fact, as woodsman Mark Hardison so graphically stated, it encourages mismanagement:

"And when you're after that spruce or fir in a thicket, then 9 times out of 10 a dozen trees bite the dust to get 1 or 2. A good selective cut area where a man should reach in with the skidder and pull out one tree at a time ends up being flattened. Why? Because in order to make any kind of a day's pay you must get out and limb 100+ trees a day. Every day. It cannot be done when you have to slow down or do a good careful job. The forests would benefit and so would the health of the workers but that's not the way we cut wood today."[1]

Ironically, though the piece-rate wage is a miner's wage (the more you cut, the faster you cut, the more you make), piece-rate wages for the underground coal miners of Appalachia were abolished in the 1920s.

Reference

1. Mark Hardison, "A Maine Woodcutter Talks About Safety in the Woods." In *Proceedings, A Forest Based Economy: Carrying a Tradition into the Future, Blaine House Conference on Forestry, December 6-7, 1984* (Augusta, Me.: Maine Department of Conservation, August 1986), p. 150.

Myth 4
Worker safety is a top priority for the forest industry.

The same pressures that lead woodsworkers to cut corners to increase productivity also lead them to cut legs and other body parts. Logging has the second-highest accident rate in the nation after anthracite coal mining.[1] In Maine the lost workday rate has been significantly higher than the industrial average.

**Lost Workday Cases per 100 Full-time Employees:
A Comparison Between Logging and All Industries in Maine[2]**

Year	Logging	Industry Average	% Above Average
1978	20.0	5.5	364%
1983	18.6	5.6	332%
1988	18.1	7.4	245%

Woods accidents do not just lead to lost work days; for some men it has led to maiming or even death. In the 1980s more than 50 professional woodsworkers were killed at work. This is a rate of more than 1 death per year per 1,000 workers.[3] In 1987, for 3,885 workers there were 1,042 injuries, including more than 100 broken bones, and 6 deaths.[4] Most deaths in the woods are preventable.

With a piece-rate wage you are paid for quantity. It does not matter what the forest looks like when you are done, just how long it took you to do it. On a hot day with clouds of blackflies and mosquitoes, or on a freezing day with deep snow, a man (there are very few female pulpcutters) must produce if he is to get a decent wage or meet his equipment payments. The faster loggers work, the longer the hours, the more severe the weather . . . the higher the chances of an accident happening. A common woodsworker complaint is that as the day goes on, the saw gets heavier and heavier but quieter and quieter. Hearing loss and back problems come with the job.

One result of the high accident rate has been a steady increase in workers' compensation rates—which at this writing can be more than 45% of a woodsworker's wage. The response to this increased burden for employers has been to blame the victims (for being careless), to mechanize, to have workers subcontract and thus pay for their own insurance costs, or to cheat. These high rates, however, are not completely explained by the high accident rates. Maine has some of the highest workers' comp costs in the nation, but as a study by the Maine Chamber of Commerce and Industry discovered, "Astonishingly, states that offer higher maximum weekly benefits, longer durations for permanent partial incapacity, or cost-of-living adjustments not provided in Maine are experiencing costs well below Maine's costs."[5]

If, as this study implies, the workers are not getting full benefit of such high rates, we can assume the benefits are going instead to doctors, lawyers, and insurance companies. Yet in 1991 the state legislature was involved in a contentious debate on workers' comp where the biggest item on the agenda was to find ways to reduce workers' benefits. The governor used workers' comp as a bargaining chip in political negotiations on state budget deficits and even shut state government down for two weeks in an attempt to force an agreement.

There have been definite improvements over the years in safety equipment, such as safer saws and more protective clothing, and the high insurance rates are causing contractors to take safety more seriously. The average number of deaths per year was far worse in the 1970s, when the number was sometimes as high as 20. But in spite of these efforts, the lost workday rate for logging in Maine is still unacceptably high and has been consistently higher than the national averages.[6]

These high accident rates are not necessary. In Sweden, for example, the accident rate for loggers is on a par with other industries and is a fraction of that in Maine. Sweden used to have high accident rates, but now the majority of workers are on a fixed wage, there are strict safety regulations, the work force is well trained, and equipment is designed with worker safety, not just productivity, in mind.[7]

Since the accident rate in Maine persists above other areas, we can assume that other items come before safety on the industry agenda. A former woodlands manager quoted by Osborne makes it clear why the paper industry keeps its distance from woods safety: "We are discouraged by our attorneys from doing too much in the way of safety, for instance, because of the danger of destroying the independent relationship. If you control their operation you diminish their independence, and the federal government says that they are your employees."[8]

The companies would rather have self-insured, "independent" contractors working on their lands than employees. The exception to this is Scott, which has its own crews, which are mostly mechanized, unionized, and on salary, rather than piece-rate. Scott's accident rate for loggers is half the state average.[9]

The forest products industry has given safety seminars for contractors and has helped fund a Certified Professional Logger training program (taken by more than 100 people in the first half of 1991), which emphasizes safety as well as efficiency.[10] But until the piece-rate wage and the cost/price squeeze (see next myth) are dealt with, the pressures that encourage dangerous practices will still be there. If the companies want professional loggers, they will have to pay professional wages and benefits.

References

1. Occupational Safety and Health Administration, "Occupational Injury and Illness Incidence Rates by Industry, 1982 and 1983," National Database, Table 1, photocopy obtained from Maine Department of Labor, Bureau of Labor Standards, Augusta, Me.
2. "Occupational Injuries and Illness per 100 Full-time Workers—1978, 1983, 1988," photocopies obtained from Maine Department of Labor, Bureau of Labor Standards, Augusta, Me.
3. Randy Wilson and Chip Gavin, "Pulpwood Peonage: Loggers Are the Last Indentured Workers," *Maine Times* (February 2, 1988): 9-15.
4. "Injury Index," *Woodsworker* (June 1988): 1.
5. Andrew Keckas, "Chamber Pushes for Workers' Comp Reform," *Bangor Daily News*, December 27, 1990.
6. David Vail, *Contract Logging, Chainsaws and Clearcuts: The Human and Environmental Impacts of Forest Extraction Systems in the State of Maine (USA)* (Helsinki, Finland: United Nations University, World Institute for Development Economic Studies, May 1986), p. 42.
7. Randy Wilson and Chip Gavin, "Pulpwood Peonage," pp. 9-15.
8. William Osborne, The Paper Plantation (New York: Viking Press, 1974), p. 158.
9. Randy Wilson and Chip Gavin, "Pulpwood Peonage," pp. 9-15.
10. "Maine Loggers Upgrade Skill, Knowledge in Comprehensive Training Program," *Woodsworker* (Spring 1991): 1.

Myth 5

Logging is a high-risk but high-paying profession.

High-risk occupations are often high-paying as well. When an average of 1 logger out of every 1,000 dies from work-related accidents each year, this certainly indicates a high-risk occupation.

Industry spokespeople give the impression that if a logger is not making big bucks, it is because he is lazy. A good logger, they often claim, can make more than $40,000 a year. The 1989 average hourly wage for Maine's logging industry, according to the Maine Department of Labor Woods Wage Survey, was $9.60, and the Census of Maine Manufacturers showed an average annual wage for loggers in 1988 of $18,609 which, though not exactly a poverty wage, certainly is not a high wage for such hazardous work.[1] There is a wide spread around this average, which includes large contractors and machine operators. Some high-production loggers on a piece-rate, given a good "chance" with big, valuable trees that are easy to cut and haul, dry weather, and no accidents or equipment failures can make good money. Others not so fortunate earn far less.

The piece-rate wage is supposedly an incentive for loggers to be more productive. The more they cut, the more they make. Companies fear that a logger on an hourly wage might just sit on a stump and watch the sparkling dew on a delicate spider web or listen to the jewel-like song of a hermit thrush penetrate the darkness of the forest. Productivity would plummet. Operators of mechanical harvesters, however, are paid a salary rather than a piece-rate (and their salaries get factored into the average wage). People on machines apparently are not as likely to be lazy.

Despite these arguments, there is ample evidence to show that loggers generally are not wealthy and that their real income (inflation adjusted) may be declining. If they have more amenities, it is because they have more debt. For example, the reported average hourly wage recorded by the Department of Labor, when adjusted for inflation, showed some improvements in the 1970s but declines in the 1980s.

Average Hourly Wage of Maine Loggers Adjusted for Inflation[2]

Year	Average Hourly Wage	Adjusted to 1967 dollars
1970	$4.00	$3.48
1975	$6.26	$3.88
1980	$9.45	$3.83
1985	$9.04	$2.80
1990	$9.60	$2.47

The average hourly wage, determined by a 2-week woodsworker survey, does not accurately reflect a worker's annual income which may be affected by seasonal unemployment, underemployment, injury, and equipment costs. In 1980, 1 of 5 loggers' households lived in poverty compared to 13% for Maine as a whole and 11% for the U. S.[3] The median earning of loggers was only 25% above the poverty line and was 78% of the average for all manufacturing.[4] Osborne estimated that loggers only work about 200 days a year because of layoffs during mud season, poor weather, equipment breakdown, and injuries.[5] One local logger I interviewed proudly told me that he was working alone (both cutting and skidding) and averaging about 35 cords and almost $350 dollars a week. When I asked him how much this added up to a year, he was not quite as proud—somewhere between $7,000 and $8,000. Bad weather, machinery costs, machinery breakdown, and injuries had taken its toll. This logger is now permanently disabled and living on workers' comp.

The income of loggers, truckers, and contractors is derived from the "spread" between the stumpage and the mill-delivered price. This spread has not always kept pace with inflation, as demonstrated by the following chart:

Logging Cost Squeeze
Spread Between Delivered Logs and Stumpage[6]

Year	Spruce Logs		Pine Logs		Birch Logs		Hardwood Pulp	
	$/MBF*	$67/MBF	$/MBF	$67/MBF	$MBF	$67/MBF	$/cd	$67/cd
1970	36	31	37	32	51	44	16	14
1980	84	34	96	39	91	37	32	13
1984	100	32	·97	31	100	32	43	11
1990	120	31	118	31	118	31	35	9

*$/MBF means dollars per 1,000 board feet; $/cd means dollars per cord. $67 means inflation adjusted to 1967 dollars.

While the spread has not increased above inflation, some expenses have. Loggers on piece-rate are given an "allowance" (compensation per cord, 1,000 board feet, or ton) for the use of their skidders and chainsaws. These allowances have definitely not kept up with inflation. For example, a local logger informed me that in 1974, for his $26,000 skidder he was given $7 per-cord skidder allowance (the allowance depends on the species, market, and whether the tree is limbed, bucked, or piled). In 1990 skidder allowance was about $10 per cord for an $80,000 machine. In 1974, diesel fuel cost $.17 a gallon; in 1990 it soared to over $1.40 a gallon. Costs for insurance, chainsaws, trucks, and other factors in cutting, hauling, and commuting have risen correspondingly.

To make more money, a logger therefore has to produce more. One state study attempted to find out if increased productivity makes up for the declining spread. The study estimated that in 1977 a 2-person crew cutting 12 cords per day, 60 cords per week, would net $303.85 a week per person. A 2-person crew in 1984 cutting 15 cords per day, 75 cords per week, would net $279.93 a week.[7]

If a landowner wants to low-grade (cut only low-value wood to improve the growth and quality of the residual stand), the piece-rate figures for loggers, skidder, and chainsaw allowances suggest that someone is going to lose money:

Costs for Harvest and Delivery of 4-Foot Hardwood Pulpwood
(costs per cord to fell, limb, top, skid tree-length, and pile)[8]

Wage: $15.00
Skidder: $11.07
Chainsaw: $2.94

Cutting cost: $29.01

Trucking $15.00
(approximate, depending on haul distance)

Total cost $44.00
(approximate)

The 1990 spread between mill-delivered price and stumpage for hardwood pulp was only $35 (see page 81). The costs are thus greater than the benefits. Either contractors or landowners are losing money on such operations, or these government-derived figures do not reflect actual prices.

Woodsworkers generally do not get paid overtime (although when the weather is good, they might work 60+ hours a week), they do not normally get paid vacations, and they do not normally expect a smooth and dignified retirement. The median age of loggers is 34.8 years. When they are in their 40s and 50s, they are old. Unlike star athletes, who also have short, demanding careers, woodsworkers cannot spend their declining years doing beer commercials for high pay. The region has few alternate employment opportunities and the worker has few marketable skills. Loggers don't retire, they get injured.

One of the excuses managers give when confronted with workers' demands for higher wages is that wage increases would increase the cost of making paper and make the company uncompetitive. The suggestion here is that the managers are cutting costs for the sake of profits and for the ultimate benefit of shareholders.

The companies do not have the shareholders in mind, however, when giving out salaries and stock options to executives. In 1990 the average compensation (salary plus bonus and stock gains) of top paper company executives was over the million-dollar mark:

Canadian logger expresses solidarity with MWA strikers. *Photo courtesy Bangor Daily News.*

Salaries and Market Value of Stock Holdings of Chief Executive Officers of Paper Companies with Operations in Maine (May 1990)[9]

Company	CEO	Compensation $ (000)	Market value of Stock $(mil)
Boise Cascade	John B. Fery	1,094	2.8
Champion Intl.	Andrew Siegler	1,761	2.8
Georgia-Pacific	T. Marshall Hahn	1,981	5.9
James River	Brenton Halsey	977	16.4
Intl. Paper	John Georges	1,446	6.7
Scott Paper	Philip Lippencott	1,905	1.4

There is clearly a double standard at work here.

References

1. Maine Bureau of Employment Security, *Composite Average Hourly Wage of Cutting Occupation in Maine's Logging Industry, Survey Years 1970-1989*, photocopy (Augusta, Me.: Maine Bureau of Employment Security, Maine Department of Labor, 1990).
2. *Ibid.* Also, Maine Department of Labor, *Consumer Price Index*, photocopy(Augusta, Me.: Maine Department of Labor, 1990).
3. David Vail, *Contract Logging, Chainsaws and Clearcuts: The Human and Environmental Impacts of Forest Extraction Systems in the State of Maine (USA)* (Helsinki, Finland: United Nations University, World Institute for Development Economic Studies, May 1986), p. 66.
4. *Ibid.*
5. William Osborne, *The Paper Plantation* (New York: Viking Press, 1974), p. 151.
6. Lloyd Irland, "Future Employment in the Maine Woods: Situation, Forces and Outlook." In *Proceedings, A Forest Based Economy: Carrying a Tradition into the Future, Blaine House Conference on Forestry, December 6-7, 1984* (Augusta, Me.: Maine Department of Conservation, August 1986), p. 95. Also, Peter Lammert, *Spring 1990 Stumpage and Mill Delivered Prices* (Augusta, Me.: Maine Department of Conservation, Management and Utilization Division, 1990), p. 95.
7. Richard Donovan and Elizabeth Swain, *Maine Woods Labor Study* (Augusta, Me.: Maine Department of Conservation, 1986).
8. Maine Bureau of Employment Security, *Prevailing Wage and Piece Rates for the Pulpwood and Logging Industry Effective May 1, 1990 through April 30, 1991*, photocopy (Augusta, Me.: Maine Bureau of Employment Security, Maine Department of Labor, 1990).
9. "The Power and the Pay," *Forbes* (May 28, 1990).

Myth 6

There is a shortage of labor for woods work.

This myth has legal significance. If woods employers cannot find suitable Maine workers, they are allowed to hire Canadians. The Canadian woodcutters generally come from poor, rural areas of Quebec. They tend to be willing to work longer hours at a lower pay rate than most Maine workers care to. Maine loggers protested the bond program (where Canadian workers are imported for specific jobs) during the MWA strike in 1975 because, the strikers claimed, the Canadians destroyed the Maine workers' bargaining powers. If a Maine worker complains, he can be replaced by a Canadian. If a Canadian complains, he won't be asked to come to Maine again. The bonds are impelled to work longer hours to make their exodus worthwhile. Their productivity helps define the piece-rate wage, which is just enough for loggers to get by. The median age for Canadian bonds in one survey was 30.8 years.[1] They burn out fast.

The number of bonds has declined since the 1950s (from 6,233 in 1956 to 393 in 1988),[2] because of stricter regulations that make the bonds less of a bargain, pressure from groups like the MWA, a phaseout of paper-company woods crews, and a loss in all jobs from mechanization.

Bonds do not work just as pulpcutters. The jobs for which these nonresident workers are recruited include truck drivers, loggers, cooks, bookkeepers, equipment operators and engineers, mechanics, and even logging operation supervisors. The estimated payroll lost to Maine workers in 1984 exceeded $20 million.[3] If one includes income lost to Maine from Canadians on visas, who outnumber bonds by an average of 2 to 1, the effects would be far worse.

There is a problem with the thesis that Canadians are hired because of a shortage of Maine workers; in the regions where this occurs, general wages are low and unemployment and underemployment are high. Researcher Jonathan Falk raises an intriguing point: "If employers were faced with a real shortage of labor, it is likely they would institute training programs on a wider scale, and substantially raise wages to attract workers."[4] This they have not done.

Maine loggers have a catch-22 with Canadian bonded laborers; their presence means that wages will be lower and working conditions inferior, but these prevailing wages and conditions are not acceptable to most Maine workers which means that they will not apply for the jobs—leaving the impression of a shortage of labor that justifies the importation of Canadians. Ironically, although the presence of Canadians helps keep general wages down, because of regulatory requirements, Canadians are more expensive to hire.

References
1. William Osborne, *The Paper Plantation* (New York: Viking Press, 1974), p. 163.
2. Lloyd Irland, "Future Employment in the Maine Woods: Situation, Forces and Outlook." In *Proceedings, A Forest Based Economy: Carrying a Tradition into the Future, Blaine House Conference on Forestry, December 6-7, 1984* (Augusta, Me.: Maine Department of Conservation, August 1986), p. 91.
3. Margaret Wille, "The Threat from Imported Canadian Labor is Alive and Well." In *Proceedings, A Forest Based Economy: Carrying a Tradition into the Future, Blaine House Conference on Forestry, December 6-7, 1984* (Augusta, Me.: Maine Department of Conservation, August 1986), pp. 121-123.
4. Jonathan Falk, *The Organization of Pulpwood Harvesting in Maine*, Yale School of Forestry Working Paper #4 (New Haven, Conn.: Yale School of Forestry, 1977), p. 13.

Myth 7

The use of mechanical harvesters is increasing in Maine because these machines are more efficient for forest management.

The major use of mechanical harvesters is to remove forests, not to manage them. They are becoming more prevalent because they replace labor that is "costly" and "scarce." One contractor told me he would rather make payments on a machine—which eventually he will own—than make payments for workers' compensation, which leaves him nothing. A forester for a big contractor made the point even more clearly. "The advantage of the machines," he said, "is that you don't have to listen to somebody bitch at you all the time. They don't talk back."[1]

Feller forwarder with Koering saw head. One of these mechanical harvesters can cut more in an hour than a chainsaw/skidder crew can cut in a day. *Photo by Christopher Ayres.*

The term "mechanization" covers a lot of ground. After all, chainsaws and skidders are machines that replaced bucksaws and horses. Mechanized alternatives to cable skidders need not be bad for forest management either—skidders can be incredibly destructive in the wrong place with the wrong operator given the wrong motivation for cutting.

In Scandinavia some very sophisticated equipment has been designed for a harvesting system that can select trees without damaging residuals, delimb them on the spot (leaving the slash to enrich the soil), and buck and pile the logs for another machine, called a forwarder, to pick up. The machinery has been designed to meet silvicultural and human needs.[2]

Insurance

In Maine, however, the motives for mechanizing have been different. Delimbers are widely used because limbing trees with a chainsaw is time consuming and has a high accident rate. The use of delimbers in the yard means trees are skidded out branches and all. Whole-tree skidding can increase damage to regeneration and residual trees and removes a vast store of nutrients from the forest ecosystem. To some extent insurance is leading to increased mechanization, and mechanization is leading to a restructuring of the work force and changes in how the forest is managed—thus, insurance companies make forest management decisions.

Markets and Taxes

Whole-tree removals are also becoming the rule for harvesting hardwoods for the new biomass markets. Trees are chipped whole, branches and all, to be used for fuel to power electric generators. The mill developers sometimes have a hand in ensuring the financing of biomass chippers and other expensive equipment for the big contractors who specialize in such markets. The investors, in high tax brackets, get a big write-off on their taxes because biomass, an "alternative energy source," qualifies for tax credits. The benefit from the tax deductions is such that no return on investment is required. Thus, one motivation for mechanization is the tax structure rather than any silvicultural need.

Dog-hair Thickets

Past mismanagement has also led to thick stands of small-diameter softwoods that are unprofitable to cut for hand labor on a piece-rate wage. Large feller forwarders, shears, and other mechanical harvesters have been used to flatten such stands to the ground. Local cutters, however, assure me that mechanical harvesters are not just being reserved for the "dog-hair" spruce-fir stands—they are being used in prime stands that would have given woodcutters with chainsaws, doing a partial cut, a good wage. A few chainsaw workers do benefit from such mechanical operations, however. As "clean-up crew," they go in and cut all the large-diameter trees that the mechanical harvesters could not—ensuring complete utilization and removal of the forest.

Some companies, such as Georgia-Pacific, are using Swedish-style mechanical harvesters to do partial cuts on stands that are not dog-hair thickets. These cuts are not necessarily silviculturally better than those done by crews with chainsaws. In both cases, the trees are cut based on diameter limits rather than on spacing, regeneration, or quality criteria. The major "benefit" of mechanization is simply to reduce jobs.

Contractor Economics

The large machines are quite costly—from $200,000 to $500,000 and upward. The use of such machinery has led not only to a decline in labor but to a shift favoring big-league contractors. Small contractors cannot afford to purchase, let alone maintain, such expensive equipment. Big contractors not only have better purchase and maintenance abilities, they can also get big enough contracts to ensure a constant wood supply to feed the machines' prodigious appetites. Although much of the wood is still cut with chainsaws, the trends stemming from increased mechanization are clear.

Logging Employment, Productivity, and Organization[3]

Year	Number of full-time loggers[*]	Volume[*] harvested (MM cords)	Avg. labor productivity (cords/year)	% harvested by small contractors
1970	6,500	4.61	709	90%
1979	5,300	5.91	1,115	
1984	4,790	6.21	1,297	20-30%
1988	3,660	7.15	1,954	

[*]Although figures for cut and labor are derived from state sources, they may be significantly off. The table should be viewed for its trends rather than its accuracy.

One would think that large contractors controlling large volumes of wood would have a stronger bargaining position with the mills than small contractors. The big contractors generally do get better prices at the mills because they can ensure a reliable supply of wood at crucial times. Local loggers have informed me that large contractors, because of their dependence on expensive machines that require expensive payments, are, however, at the mercy of the paper companies. They cannot afford to threaten mills by holding back on their supplies—they have to operate their machinery full-time to keep up their payments. Management through mechanization may be motivated by insurance companies or tax policies, but it is driven by the banks. Small contractors are beholden to banks as well; skidders are by no means cheap. Forestry activist Bill Butler quipped that loggers are not so much employees as debtors.[4]

It is not clear if the big machines are actually a better bargain than cheap labor. An in-depth series on logging by the *Maine Sunday Telegram* compared interest, capital payments, wages, and operating expenses of a mechanical harvester with conventional 2-person skidder operations. The authors concluded that: 1 harvester operator replaced 6 or 7 conventional loggers; the work was far safer and more comfortable; and the companies could save $3 to $4 per cord—if they could keep the machine going full time.[5] But the same article reported that one large contractor found that owning the giant machines gave marginal benefits and big headaches. They are not operated full time. They need considerable maintenance, and breakdowns can be costly. He said, "We will subcontract out the machines. There is always somebody who thinks they can make money at it. Eventually they will learn they can't. Then somebody else will come along. We will use them up."[6]

Intimidation

The big machines may be marginal or submarginal in their direct economic benefits, but one indirect benefit is that mechanization, according to Jonathan Falk, "intimidates workers who are demanding higher pay and better working conditions."[7] Maine workers are thus kept in their place to accept low wages by the combined threat of Canadian workers and mechanization. Just as Canadian workers may actually cost more than domestics but still keep wages down, mechanized crews get higher wages and safer working conditions than regular skidder crews, but the average wage payments still come out favorably for industry. Most contractors still use some workers with chainsaws, the majority of wood on industrial lands is now cut mechanically.

The motivation for increased mechanization, therefore, is complicated—but the prime consideration is not silvicultural. The loggers who work the mechanical harvesters do get the benefit of safer conditions, higher pay, and higher status than those who cut with chainsaws. A state publication titled *The Forests of Maine* concluded, however, that "Mechanization has made the woods safer for workers but not safer for trees."[8] The study suggested that careless equipment operators can destroy seedlings, cut root systems, create ruts, and cause soil

"Mechanization has made the woods safer for workers but not safer for trees."
Photo by Christopher Ayres.

erosion. Harvesting the limbs and branches takes away shade from seedlings and removes an important nutrient source. The study raised the question of whether such intensive harvesting can be sustained on 50-year cycles.

References

1. Bob Cummings et al., "Hard Times in the Woods: Unemployment Rises as Work in the Woods Changes, *Maine Sunday Telegram*, July 27, 1986, p. 13A.
2. David Vail, "How To Tell the Forest from the Trees: Recent Technical Changes in the Forest Industries of Sweden and Maine." In *Harvard University Seminar on Neo-classical Economics* (Cambridge, Mass.: Harvard University, March 1988), p. 45.
3. *Ibid.*, p. 31. Also, David B. Field and Robert B. Forster, *Opportunities for Exporting Hardwood Pulpwood Chips from Maine to the Far East*, Maine Agricultural Experiment Station Miscellaneous Report 347 (Orono, Me.: Maine Agricultural Experiment Station, University of Maine, June 1990), p. 66, and "Annual Average Employment in the Logging Industry in Maine 1980-1989," photocopy obtained from Maine Department of Labor, Bureau of Employment Security, Division of Economic Analysis and Research.
4. Bill Butler, personal communication, summer 1990.
5. Bob Cummings et al., "Hard Times," p. 14A.
6. Ibid.
7. Jonathan Falk, *The Organization of Pulpwood Harvesting in Maine*, Yale School of Forestry Working Paper #4 (New Haven, Conn.: Yale School of Forestry, 1977), p. 54.
8. Sherman Hasbrouck, *The Forest of Maine* (Orono, Me.: Land and Water Resources Center, University of Maine, 1987), p. 8.

Myth 8

Woods work is honest work.

Cheating is widespread in the woods industry from top to bottom. The paper mills cheat the contractors and small, nonindustrial woodlot owners by keeping wood prices artificially low. They cheat workers by creating the fiction that they are independent and thus not subject to company benefits. They cheat the government by reporting artificially low stumpage for their wood, which becomes the basis for the Tree Growth Tax on their timberlands (see Chapter 5).

Given a small profit margin to work from, the contractors try to squeeze out more from the workers. Cheating on workers' compensation is nearly universal. The contractors pay workers part of their wages in the form of equipment allowances to avoid workers' compensation, or else force the workers to get their own insurance, or else make them subcontract and be responsible for their own insurance. They avoid paying extra for overtime or holiday time by paying workers on a piece-rate. "What these leeches want," said one cutter, "is hot bodies to cut lots and lots of wood."[1]

There are not as many ways for workers to cheat; they are at the bottom. Some cheat by getting "injured" and living off insurance (which of course drives up prices).

The government cheats the public by allowing all the cheating to happen.

Reference

1. Mark Hardison, "A Maine Woodcutter Talks About Safety in the Woods." In *Proceedings, A Forest Based Economy: Carrying a Tradition into the Future, Blaine House Conference on Forestry, December 6-7, 1984* (Augusta, Me.: Maine Department of Conservation, August 1986), p. 150.

2 The Industrial Forest

What is most striking in the Maine wilderness is the continuousness of the forest, with fewer open intervals or glades than you had imagined. Except for the few burnt-lands, the narrow intervals on the rivers, the bare tops of the high mountains, and the lakes and streams, the forest is uninterrupted.
Henry David Thoreau, "Ktaadn," *The Maine Woods*

If you go down in the woods today you're sure of a big surprise. . . .
"Teddy Bears' Picnic," Jimmy Kennedy

. . . the forest is no longer conceived to be a generalized, autonomous, personified ecological system, but to be, simply, one element or sub-element of sub-system in a larger socio-economic system. It is no longer mother and father to us all as it is to the Pygmy, nor an indispensable link in the circle of growth and death as it is to the Maring. It is now a "resource." It has been degraded from the status of the world itself to mere object, an "it," something to be used.
Roy Rappaport, "Forests and Man," *The Ecologist*, August/September 1976

Visitors who step beyond the beauty strip and see industrial management for the first time are often shocked by what appears to be the aftermath of some catastrophe. Industrial foresters, however, view such sights with pride rather than shame. Maine's timberlands, they are quick to explain, are "working forests"—forests managed for economic benefit. The proper way to view forest management is upbeat. Forests are a renewable resource—you can keep cutting them down and growing them back. Foresters haven't destroyed a mature forest when they clearcut—they have regenerated a new, young, healthy forest, or maybe even planted "super trees." Listening to the careful explanations of an industrial guide, a visitor's revulsion should turn to gratitude. These companies are not harming the forest; they are improving it.

Industrial Forest Ecology

For the claims of industrial foresters to be true, working forests must operate under scientific principles unknown to students of biology. I call these principles "industrial ecology." The first law of industrial ecology is that the working forest is a resource, and should be judged by economic, rather than biological, criteria. The second law is that a working forest needs to be managed. Just as a worker "needs" a boss, so a working forest "needs" a manager. If the forest is not managed, it will grow wild; it will get filled with old and decadent trees, or with weeds, insects, and diseases that will threaten other stands. The third law of industrial ecology is that by managing the forests for economic benefit, foresters, by some happy coincidence, are doing the ecosystem a favor.

In this section I examine some of the principles foresters use to justify softwood monocultures, large-scale clearcuts, and short rotations—practices which some industrial foresters claim are perfectly natural. If industrial ecologists are correct about the nature of the Maine woods, we should be able to find supportive evidence from examination of studies of the presettlement forest (the forest before it was cut by European settlers), and existing virgin forests (forests that have never been cut). Evidence from these forests, however, shows industrial forest ecology to be more myth than science.

Myth 1

Because the industrial forest is a spruce-fir, or boreal, forest, paper companies are justified in managing for pure softwood stands.

This myth is frequently raised to justify such practices as establishing softwood plantations on productive sites and spraying herbicides to suppress hardwood "weeds." It is a myth based on a series of logical fallacies.

Fallacy #1: Maine's industrial forest is a spruce-fir forest. A boreal forest is a spruce-fir forest. Therefore, the industrial forest is a boreal forest.
This statement is equivalent to saying that a mouse is a mammal and an elephant is a mammal; therefore, a mouse is an elephant. There is more than one kind of spruce-fir forest.

Boreal forest refers to the vast spruce-fir forest (called "taiga" in Eurasia) found south of the arctic tundra. It is dominated by species such as white and black spruce, balsam fir, tamarack, jack pine, white birch, and aspen that are adapted to the harsh climates and poor soils of a land only recently (in geological terms) evacuated by glaciers.

Except for fir, boreal softwood species have been a minor component of Maine's wildlands, being concentrated primarily in extreme habitats such as the north slopes of mountains, abandoned and depleted fields, and wet soils and bogs. Other softwoods found in Maine, such as red spruce, eastern hemlock, and white and red pine, are not true boreal species; Maine is actually near the northern edge of their ranges. Although red spruce is by far the most abundant of the spruces found in today's Maine woods,[1] paper companies choose white and black spruce for plantations because these species are better adapted to the extreme habitat represented by a clearcut. Red spruce, as a forester once told me, is a child of the forest; it likes to start out in the shade of its mother.[a]

Boreal hardwoods, such as white birch and aspen, are pioneer species that flourish following extreme disturbances, such as forest fires. They are shade intolerant, meaning they do not normally become established in the shade of a mature forest. The most common northern hardwoods—sugar maple, American beech, and yellow birch, which are shade tolerant—are near their northern range in Maine and are only found in the southern fringe of the boreal forest.[2]

Thus, although Maine does have some of the species found in a boreal forest, the majority of trees are not. Calling the Maine forest boreal and managing it as if it were, represents a degradation of both the language and the ecosystem.

Fallacy #2: *The industrial forest is a spruce-fir ecosystem. Hardwoods are neither spruce nor fir. Therefore, hardwoods are weeds.*

The industrial forest is called a spruce-fir ecosystem because spruce and fir make up the plurality of the trees in the region and because they are the most important species for the paper industry. Industrial researchers and even some state-sponsored studies have used this "spruce-fir" label to justify some very bizarre

Map of boreal forest. From *Sherman Hasbrouck,* The Forests of Maine *(Orono: Land and Water Resources Center, University of Maine, 1987), p. 2.*

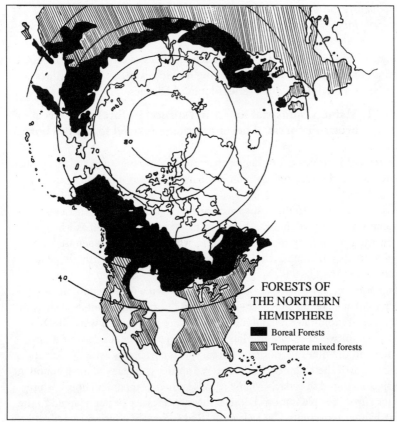

FORESTS OF
THE NORTHERN
HEMISPHERE

■ Boreal Forests
▨ Temperate mixed forests

conclusions. For example, a 1985 state study on silvicultural release (i.e., herbicide spraying) of spruce-fir listed the following trees as "competing species in the spruce-fir ecosystem": aspen, white and gray birch, yellow birch, American beech, white ash, and red and sugar maple.[3] A 1989 state study on herbicides had an even larger list of "competing vegetation," including a few tree species somehow forgotten in the previous study: silver maple, black birch, black ash, black cherry, willow and American basswood.[4] Since these species supposedly compete with the desired trees, managers feel justified in either killing them with herbicides or in cutting them and chipping them whole for biomass markets.

One is supposed to believe that hardwoods are invaders in the pure, natural spruce-fir ecosystem. Few researchers, however, call the whole region a spruce-fir ecosystem. Although there are concentrated areas of spruce and fir, there are also areas of northern hardwoods (American beech, yellow birch, sugar maple, eastern hemlock, and white pine), aspen and birch, cedar swamps, and various mixedwoods (mixtures of hardwoods and softwoods). Canadian foresters call this complicated mix the "Acadian Forest."

Evidence gathered by ecologist Craig Lorimer indicates that hardwoods are not recent invaders to a pure spruce-fir forest—they were an important component of Maine's presettlement forest. Using survey records from 1793 to 1827, Lorimer did an elegant reconstruction of the presettlement forest of northeastern Maine, estimating the species composition of the forest as well as the variability of stand composition by region and by soil quality (see Appendix 4). Nearly half the trees in the entire study area, he found, were hardwoods.[5] The irregular distribution of hardwoods and softwoods leads to the last fallacious argument in this series.

Fallacy #3: It is justifiable to plant pure softwood stands because pure softwood stands are natural.
While it is true that pure spruce-fir stands are natural in specific, limited habitats, planting pure stands in very different habitats that normally are not pure spruce-fir is neither natural nor justified.

Even in the eight million acres that the state declared to be a "Spruce-fir Protection Zone" for the spruce budworm spray program, during the 1970s and 80s only 24% of the area was covered with stands composed of more than 75% softwoods.[6] In his reconstruction of the presettlement forest of northeastern Maine, Lorimer found a clear correlation between the stand type and the soil quality and topography. "Eighty-two percent of the hardwood stands occurred on 1st-rate soil, 57% of the mixed forest on 2nd-rate soil, and 83% of the conifer stands on the 3rd- and 4th-rate soils. . . . However, *hardwoods or conifers did not usually occur in pure stands* [my emphasis], for the conifer type averaged 76% conifers and the hardwood type averaged 65% hardwoods. Thus most of the forest was actually mixed forest with hardwoods or conifers locally achieving partial dominance due to physiographic variation."[7]

The Society of American Foresters (SAF) views the spruce-fir forest type as having two basic subdivisions: (1) primary softwoods (on poorly drained soils, lower slopes, and steep mountain slopes above 3,000 feet) which have less than

25% hardwoods (paper birch, aspen and red maple—which are species adapted to disturbance) and (2) secondary softwood sites (on better drained soils and ridge lands of medium elevation) which have more than 25% hardwoods (beech, sugar maple, and yellow birch—which are shade-tolerant species). "The spruces, balsam fir and associated softwood species," according to an SAF report, "are unable to compete advantageously with the tolerant hardwood associates . . . ; and unless cleanings are undertaken to favor softwoods, they tend to be replaced eventually by the more aggressive American beech and sugar maple."[8]

This information is very important because, in general, management practices such as plantation establishment give much better paybacks on more productive sites, but the more productive sites are not naturally pure softwood stands. Many of the plantations either simplify or convert the natural species mix that would normally occupy the site, reducing wildlife diversity.

Converting a hardwood or mixedwood stand on a rich site to boreal softwood species that are adapted to impoverished soils also can lead to site degradation. The soils under northern hardwoods, generally classified as gray-brown spodosol, or alfisol, have a well-mixed loam, rich in calcium and full of a wide array of soil decomposers such as earthworms, bacteria, slugs, millipedes, and many insect species.

By contrast, the soils under boreal softwoods tend to be true spodosols, or podzols (a Russian word meaning "ash-soil") and are low in calcium, acidic, and have few earthworms or bacteria. The major decomposers are fungi.[9] Conifer needles, unlike hardwood leaves, break down slowly into soil, so there is often a thick layer of raw litter and needles covering the soil. Naturalist Neil Jorgensen describes how this feature of spruce-fir leads to podzolization:

"The humus layer beneath spruces and other conifers is strongly acidic; rainwater seeping through the humus becomes charged with acid. Although this acid is quite dilute, it slowly percolates through the glacial till below, dissolving away all the minerals save the quartz. Hence, the ashy gray layer characteristic of podzols is predominantly quartz. Quartz adds no nutrients to the soil; the leached, sterile layer is of no benefit to the plant life above."[10]

Ironically, despite the desirability of spruce and fir for the mills, and despite these myths that justify conversions to pure softwoods, the acreage that the federal government lists as spruce-fir has been declining while the acreage listed for pioneer hardwoods, especially poplar, has been expanding.[11] The working forest has not been working very well.

Endnote

a. Canadian forest geneticist Stephen Manley states that red spruce are "off site" in a clearcut. What appear to be red spruce in the regeneration are often hybrids of red and black spruce that are more adapted to the moisture, light, and temperature extremes. These hybrids do not have the same characteristics of red spruce in regard to height or longevity.[12]

References

1. D. S. Powell and D. R. Dickson, *Forest Statistics for Maine, 1971 and 1982*, U.S. Department of Agriculture Forest Service Resource Bulletin NE-81 (Broomall, Pa.: United States Forest Service, United States Department of Agriculture, 1984), extrapolated fromTable 17, p. 20.
2. George A. Petrides, *A Field Guide to Eastern Trees: Eastern United States and Canada* (Boston,

Mass.: Houghton Mifflin Company, 1988), see species range maps, pp. 34, 39, 45-47, 71, 131, 156, 162, 165.

3. James R. Hynson, *final Report: Silvicultural Release of Seedling and Sapling Spruce-fir Stands: A Literature Review* (Augusta, Me.: Maine Department of Conservation, 1985), p. 6.

4. James C. Balogh et al., *The Use and Potential Impacts of Forestry Herbicides in Maine* (Augusta, Me.: Forest for the Future Program, Maine Department of Conservation, 1989), p 40.

5. Craig Lorimer, "The Presettlement Forest and Natural Disturbance Cycle of Northeastern Maine," *Ecology*, Vol. 58 (1977): 142.

6. *Final Programmatic Environmental Impact Statement, Proposed Cooperative 5-year (1981-1985) Maine Spruce Budworm Management Program* (Broomall, Pa.: United States Forest Service, United States Department of Agriculture, 1981), p. 13.

7. Craig Lorimer, "The Presettlement Forest," p. 143.

8. Robert Frank et al., "Forest Practices Goals and Standards for the Improvement, Maintenance, and Protection of the Forest Resources of Maine," *The Maine Forest Review*, Vol. 7 (1974): 6.

9. John C. Kricher, *A Field Guide to Eastern Forests of North America* (Boston, Mass.: Houghton Mifflin Company, 1988), pp. 15, 280.

10. Neil Jorgensen, *A Guide to New England's Landscape* (Barre, Mass.: Barre Publishers, 1971), p. 153.

11. D. S. Powell and D. R. Dickson, *Forest Statistics*, pp. 10-11.

12. Stephen Manley, personal communication, Spring, 1992.

Myth 2

The forest is naturally even-aged due to frequent large-scale fires, blowdowns, insect outbreaks, and disease.

This is the Myth of the Catastrophic Forest. While there are many examples in the nineteenth and twentieth centuries of massive fires and insect outbreaks in the Maine woods, industrial ecologists assert that such patterns were the rule, rather than the exception, prior to logging and clearing in the region. Foresters, they claim, are only imitating nature when they subject forests to frequent large-scale clearcuts. Clearcutting, they conclude, is natural and thus justifiable.

There are three false assumptions in this myth:
- that the presettlement forest was mostly even-aged;
- that the "natural catastrophes" that foresters imitate are not human exacerbated; and
- that clearcuts imitate, rather than surpass, the impacts of such disturbances.

Even-aged?
It defies common sense, given the sizes and ages of the trees encountered by the first European settlers and the predominance of shade-tolerant species, to assume that the presettlement forest was mostly even-aged.

Maine's first great forester, Austin Cary, determined the ages of 1,050 spruce logs from all major river systems of Maine during the 1890s and found that 72% of them were between 150 and 250 years old and that less than 5% were under 125 years old.[1]

David Smith, a professor of silviculture at the Yale School of Forestry, has observed of Maine's forests that: ". . . most of the important tree species that we have are adapted to becoming established almost exclusively in varying degrees of shade beneath old stands. There they tend to persist as seedlings, commonly for very long periods, and to retain the capacity to start rapid growth when their parent succumbs. Just as they are not adapted to fire, many of them are also not particularly adapted to severe or sudden exposure to sunlight, desiccation, and that sort of thing. Neither has it been necessary for them to adapt themselves to grow rapidly in height after they germinate. They haven't developed these adaptations because they didn't have to in their natural environment."[2]

In reconstructing the presettlement forest of northeastern Maine, ecologist Craig Lorimer concluded that most of the region supported climax stands (a relatively stable, self-perpetuating association of organisms) that were all-aged or uneven-aged (having three or more age-classes).[3]

Catastrophic?

The "catastrophes" that forest managers imitate were induced or exacerbated to some extent by human intervention, especially land clearing and logging. Nearly 30% of Maine was deforested for crops and pasture by the mid-nineteenth century, but after the Civil War, as many as four million acres of this land were abandoned as settlers moved west for better prospects.[4] These abandoned farms became second-growth forests with very different species ratios and stand structures than the presettlement forest.

Logging came in a series of intersecting waves, each one removing more trees from the forest and causing more disturbance than the last. The first wave swept away the huge "king's pines" that towered above the rest of the forest. These massive trees, marked with the "broad arrow" to serve as lumber for England's royal navy, were nearly all extracted by the time Thoreau visited the Maine woods in the mid-nineteenth century. By then the second logging wave had commenced, carrying off big spruce and hardwoods for sawlogs. At the end of the nineteenth century nearly the whole state had been logged over at least once.[5] By 1909 the sawlog industry peaked and the migratory loggers were moving west for more virgin timber, but the next wave, cutting spruce and fir for the new pulpwood market, had begun. Subsequent waves have included cutting hardwoods for pulp and now literally everything for biomass. The waves now are catastrophic—like a tsunami.

These heavy disturbances have affected the forest's stability, i.e., its resistance to disturbance (or to a magnification of natural disturbance cycles), and, once disturbed, its resilience (its ability to recover its structure, diversity, and productivity). As the forest has become more unstable, cycles of fire and insect and disease problems have become more widespread, intense, and frequent (see sidebar).

Disturbance has also changed the tree-species ratio in Maine's forest. In the presettlement forest reconstructed by Lorimer, balsam fir—the most aggressive softwood recolonizer after severe disturbance—comprised 14% of the forest. Red maple, white birch, and aspen—which also recolonize after heavy cutting—

together comprised 6.7%.

In 1970, according to U.S. Forest Service surveys, 37.5% of all the trees in Maine were balsam fir. By 1980, that figure was reduced to 25% due to an intense spruce-budworm epidemic and heavy cutting, whereas the three disturbance-adapted hardwoods comprised more than 20% of the trees in Maine and more than 55% of the hardwoods.[6] As the trees now regenerating from the heavy cutting that began in the 1970s grow to the minimum diameter used in these surveys (5 inches), the representation of disturbance-adapted species, especially aspen, will become much greater. This is important because these species are shorter lived than the red spruce, hemlock, white pine, or the northern hardwoods that previously dominated Maine's forest. This has shortened disturbance cycles and led to justification for shortened cutting cycles.

Imitate?

Today's intensive, large-scale clearcuts, which remove all the above-ground biomass and compact the soil, do not imitate nature; they are far more destructive and more frequent than natural disturbances. Insect infestations do not kill every tree, let alone remove them. Winds normally blow down isolated, larger trees or small groups, not hundreds of acres of all trees. Even forest fires often leave resistant trees standing, and nutrients from the ash stay on the site. Natural disturbances do not occur in square blocks with straight edges—the results are far more complicated. Furthermore, if unmanaged forests are disturbed, they recover through natural succession. In Maine's forest, however, managers zap successional species with herbicides—a process that hardly imitates nature.

Disturbances: Natural vs. Clearcut

Variable	Natural	Clearcut
Intensity	Residual trees and dead wood remain	All trees removed
Edge	Highly irregular	Straight lines
Landscape pattern	Integrated	Fragmented/roaded
Soil	Undisturbed	Denuded, compacted, dried
Regeneration	Natural succession	Artificial/herbicides
Rotation	Centuries	40-60 years

Catastrophic Disturbance Cycles in the Presettlement Forest

Based on his historical reconstruction work, Craig Lorimer concluded that the intervals between large-scale disturbances in the presettlement forest of northeastern Maine were very long. Other evidence also shows that the presettlement Acadian forest was more resistant to catastrophes than our current forest. Industrial ecologists' predilection for even-aged management is thus not historically justified.

Fire

In some softwood-dominated ecosystems, fire cycles do play an important role in ecosystem regulation. After repeated stands of pure softwoods, the soil becomes more acidic and less productive, litter from branches and dead trees accumulates, and susceptibility to insects and disease increases. Fire or insect infestations followed by broadleaved successional species can rejuvenate such ecosystems by moderating acid soils, recycling nutrients, and increasing wildlife diversity.[7]

Lorimer, however, concludes that such cycles of fire and major disturbance "probably do not apply to the conifer-hardwood forests of northern New England."[7] He estimates that it takes more than 100 years to attain a climax forest after a crown fire. If fires recurred on a given tract at intervals of 100 years, more than half of Lorimer's study area would have been in birch-aspen forests at any one time, as that forest stage lasts approximately 75 years. Based on the distribution of these indicator species, however, Lorimer estimates that fire cycles were more than 800 years apart.[8]

There are several reasons why virgin forests were more resistant than second-growth forests to fire. They include the following:

•The forests were well shaded and very moist. Thoreau noted this phenomenon on his trip to Mount Katahdin: "The primitive wood is always and everywhere damp and mossy, so that I travelled constantly with the impression that I was in a swamp; and only when it was remarked that this or that tract, judging from the quality of the timber on it, would make a profitable clearing, was I reminded, that if the sun were let in it would make a dry field, like the few I had seen, at once. The best shod for the most part travel with wet feet. If the ground was so wet and spongy as this, the driest part of a dry season, what must it be in the spring?"[10]

•Tree trunks rose limb free for dozens of feet, leaving little for fires to burn if they did start on the ground.

•The leafy canopy of northern hardwoods (which provide more moisture and denser shade than coniferous stands) and the tough bark, great height, and clear length of some older trees make them relatively fire resistant.

Fires became a major threat to Maine's forest for a number of reasons:

•Heavy logging dried up the forest floor and created highly flammable slash piles.

•Settlers used fires to clear land. Sometimes these fires went out of control.

•Loggers, camping parties, and railroads often were careless about fires.

•Logging was converting the forest to more fire-susceptible species and stand structures—particularly even-aged fir stands.

In 1904, Maine forest commissioner Edgar Ring, after observing fires in the Rangeley area, had no doubt that logging was the major factor in the increased extent, frequency, and intensity of fires:

"More than anything else, the factor that produced the greatest influence on the direction of the fire in its progress, and consequently on the burned area, was the lumbering operations. Here the fact is brought out, as in no other place studied, that a fire will travel along the lines of lumbering. It is remarkable what a sharp line the fire margin has where it reaches a virgin stand. In not a single case on the entire area in this region did the fire penetrate into a virgin stand for more than 10 rods [165 feet]. In several places it was observed that the fire traveled just far enough into the virgin woods to consume the logs and slash left there in the process of lumbering the adjacent area. Where two strips of lumbered land came to an angle in an unlumbered stand, causing the uncut area to have the shape of a V, it sometimes happened that the fire cut across the narrower part of the V. However, in general, it would be safe to say that fully 95 per cent of the area burned was lumbered land. Where lumbering was most heavy the fire was most intense. On Township D where the trees had been cut to a very small diameter limit the fire burned the land quite clean." [11]

Wind

Hurricanes battered New England forests in 1635, 1815, and 1938. Some researchers hypothesize destructive damage from a storm in 1400.[12] Apparently storms like these did not devastate northeastern Maine, where Lorimer estimates that major windthrow cycles at a given site were more than 1,000 years apart.[13] Research on existing old-growth forests at Big Reed Reserve, Maine's largest old-growth forest, shows that smaller scale windthrow, however, is an important part of forest cycling.

The importance of wind depends on the exposure of the site and the tree species. On more protected sites, winds normally blow down larger, less vigorous trees in isolation or in small groups. Spruce-fir on shallow or rocky soil on the exposed north slopes of large hills or mountains are more prone to windthrow. But even here, according to Lissa Widoff, ecologist for Land for Maine's Future, "these disturbances do not decimate the entire community."[14] Instead, the community type is characteristically a "mosaic of 'disturbance patches,' even within a given forest stand."[15] These patches of disturbed forests in harsh environments hardly justify the industrial practice of flattening hundreds of acres of more diverse forests in more protected environments.

Insects and Disease

Insects and disease are not normally catastrophic unless the forest is composed of pure stands of susceptible species. The presettlement forest, however, was diverse in age and species. Lorimer, in his reconstruction work did not find evidence of massive insect outbreaks such as the spruce budworm. Yet the spruce budworm has been the single most disturbing force in Maine's forest in the twentieth century—except for people. Eighteenth century surveyors noted infestations, but these were less widespread and destructive than those found in the late nineteenth and twentieth centuries.

Part of the reason the outbreaks were less severe is that balsam fir, the most vulnerable species, was less abundant in the presettlement forest, and was more of a subcanopy, rather than a canopy, tree. The removal of big pine and spruce, however, helped turn fir into more of a dominant canopy tree. Fir regeneration responded so impressively to heavy cutting that forest commissioner Edgar Ring wrote in 1906 that fir "should be considered as a weed in our forest garden and eradicated as soon as possible."[16] Foresters obviously did not respond sufficiently to this advice; six years later a major budworm outbreak occurred.

Logging disturbances and the introduction of insects and disease have caused a serious decline in hardwood quality since presettlement times. The last century has seen massive birch diebacks, beeches devastated by nectria-scale complex, the near disappearance of elm due to Dutch elm disease, and attacks on sugar maple from pests such as the saddled prominent moth.[17] The gypsy moth has also invaded as far north as central Maine. Insects and disease may not have been catastrophic in Maine's presettlement forest, but they are tending in that direction today.

References

1. R. S. Seymour, "The Red Spruce-balsam fir Forests of Maine: Evolutions of Silvicultural Practices in Response to Stand Development Patterns and Disturbances." In M. J. Kelty et al., eds., *The Ecology and Silviculture of Mixed-species Forests: A Festshrift Honoring Professor David M. Smith* (Kluwer Publishers, 1991), p. 5.
2. D. M. Smith, "The Forests of Maine Yesterday, Today and Tomorrow." In *Proceedings of the Blaine House Conference on Forestry* (Augusta, Me.: Maine Department of Conservation, 1980).
3. Craig Lorimer, "The Presettlement Forest and Natural Disturbance Cycle of Northeastern Maine," *Ecology*, Vol. 58 (1977): 147.
4. Elaine Tietjen, "The Cycles of Succession," *Habitat* , Vol. 22 (1985).
5. Richard Judd, *Aroostook: A Century of Logging in North Maine* (Orono, Me.: University of Maine Press, 1989).
6. D. S. Powell and D. R. Dickson, Forest Statistics for Maine, 1971 and 1982, U.S. Department of Agriculture Forest Service Resource Bulletin NE-81 (Washington, D.C.: United States Forest Service, United States Department of Agriculture, 1984), p. 20, Table17. Also, D. Gordon Mott, "Spruce Budworm Protection Management in Maine," *The Maine Forest Review*, Vol. 13 (1984): 27.
7. M. L. Heinselman and H. A. Wright, "The Ecological Role of fire in Natural Conifer Forests of Western and Northern North America," *Quaternary Research*, Vol. 3 (1973).
8. Craig Lorimer, "The Presettlement Forest," p. 142.
9. *Ibid.*, p. 147.
10. Henry David Thoreau, *The Maine Woods* (New York: Thomas Y. Crowell Company, 1961), p. 26.
11. Edgar Ring, *Forest Commissioner Report* (Augusta, Me.: State of Maine, 1904), p. 108.
12. Neil Jorgensen, *A Guide to New England's Landscape* (Barre, Mass.: Barre Publishers, 1971), p. 186.
13. Craig Lorimer, "The Presettlement Forest," p. 142.
14. Lissa Widoff, *The Forest Community of Big Reed Pond Preserve, T8 R10, T8 R11, Maine. Results of Field Studies, Summer 1985*, (Topsham, Me.: The Nature Conservancy, 1985), p. 12.
15. *Ibid.*, p. 12.
16. Edgar Ring, *Forest Commissioner Report* (Augusta, Me.: Kennebec Journal Print, 1906), p. 15.
17. Stephen Spurr, *Forest Ecology* (New York: Ronald Press Company, 1973, p. 371.

Myth 3

Old forests are overmature, decadent (harboring destructive insects and diseases), deficient in wildlife, and unhealthy. Corollary: A young forest is a healthy forest.

From these two faulty propositions, industrial ecologists have come up with a faulty conclusion: that the best way to improve an older forest is to cut it down. The propositions are faulty because they are based on misconceptions concerning the nature of old forests and the meaning of forest health.

Old Forests?

To industrial foresters, a forest is old when it passes its economic climax (the period when it is most profitable to cut the trees). This climax varies—depending on the species, quality of the site, and markets for the products—and is measured in several ways. Some managers consider a stand "old" when it passes its peak of average annual growth. In forestry terms, this is the culmination of mean annual increment, which, depending on site, management, and method of measurement, may be anywhere between 30 and 90 years. Others consider a stand "old" when sufficient trees are big enough to cut for a particular market. In general, pulp and biomass get cut on a shorter rotation than quality logs, with some managers planning rotations as short as 35 or 40 years. The maximum expected longevity of Acadian tree species in Maine is much longer: for eastern hemlock, for example, it is 600 years; white pine, 450 years; red spruce, 400 years; American beech, 350 years; and sugar maple, 300 years.[1] What foresters consider to be old age in trees is really only the end of youth and the beginning of maturity.

Balsam fir and aspen, boreal species that are encouraged by heavy cutting, have a maximum expected longevity of 200 years, and a pathological longevity (the age at which trees begin to suffer from serious decay) of 60 to 90 and 40 to 120 years respectively.[2] When these trees make up a sizable proportion of the stand, managers tend to cut everything, including longer lived species. This means that the succeeding stand will have an even larger proportion of short-lived pioneers.

Forest Health

Industrial ecologists, using economic rather than biological criteria, arrive at their definition of forest health through a form of beauty-strip logic:
  •The forest is a resource, an extension of the economy.
  •The economy is healthy when it grows fast.
  •If the economy is to grow fast, then the forest resources that supply it must also grow fast.
  •Therefore, the forest is healthy when it grows at least as fast as the landowner's desired minimum rate of economic return.
  Since young forests grow at a faster *rate* than old forests, they must, by this

reasoning, be healthier. A climax forest, according to this logic, must be unhealthy because its *net growth* (gross growth minus mortality) is close to zero.

This logic is flawed from both ecological and economic perspectives, however. While it is true that the growth rate of seedlings is considerably greater than the growth rate of mature trees, mature trees put on far more fiber per acre per year than do seedlings. Foresters often meet their minimum rate of return by cutting trees faster, not by growing them faster.

In addition to old trees, old forests have other features that bother industrial foresters. Such forests are littered with dead-standing and dead-downed trees and have gaps where trees or groups of trees have fallen. From an economic perspective, it is a terrible waste to allow trees to die and rot. It is no wonder that industrial foresters see such a forest as overmature, decadent, and stagnant; the forest is not working—at least for them.

Ironically, the very characteristics of old growth, which some foresters see as evidence of decrepitude, are the means by which a forest maintains its health (see sidebar). From an ecological perspective, health means stability. If a forest can persist for centuries, it must, quite obviously, be stable. Therefore, the very oldest forests must be the healthiest.

Old-growth characteristics that help maintain forest health (resistance to, and resilience from, disturbance)

Old Trees

Large trees found in old-growth stands have deep, complex canopies that provide more habitats for birds and invertebrates (insects, spiders, etc.) than do young even-aged stands. A study in Oregon found 66 species of invertebrates in an old-growth forest canopy and only 15 in the canopy of a younger forest. Furthermore, few of the species in the young forest were insect predators.[3] This is important because predatory and parasitic species in older forests help check the proliferation of insects that could potentially do widespread damage.

A U.S. Forest Service study that looked at bird predation on spruce budworms in Maine found that young, pure balsam-fir stands "represent some of the poorest bird habitat in Eastern North America."[4] The greatest number of bird breeding pairs in the study occurred in mature spruce and mixedwood stands. Some effective budworm predators (e.g., Cape May, bay-breasted, Blackburnian, and yellow-rumped warblers, golden-crowned kinglets, and red-breasted nuthatches) are associated with mature, rather than young, conifers. The diversity of budworm predators is important because different birds specialize in different tree microhabitats. For example, Cape May warblers feed high in trees, whereas bay-breasteds feed in the middle, near the trunk.[5]

Dead-standing Trees

Dead trees are so important to the functioning of forest ecosystems that Maine wildlife biologist Mac Hunter devoted an entire chapter to the subject in his recent book *Wildlife, Forests, and Forestry: Principles of Managing Forests for Biological Diversity.*[6] He even recommends deliberately killing trees to create standing *snags* where none currently exist. Snags and dead-topped trees create important habitat for many species of birds, insects, and mammals. Cavity-nesting species such as woodpeckers and nuthatches help control insects (e.g., bark beetles) that could cause significant tree mortality if unchecked.[7] Owls and American kestrels, which often live in cavities created by woodpeckers, help control prolific small mammals that could wipe out conifer seeds and severely reduce regeneration.[8] Cavity-nesting birds often comprise 20 to 40% of the birds in a forest and sometimes as much as 66%.[9] According to Hunter, "if we consider cavities in both trees and logs, it is likely that most species of forest-dwelling mammals, reptiles and amphibians seek shelter in cavities at least occasionally."[10]

Estimating tree girth of old white pines at the Hermitage (near Gulf Hagas).
Photo by Mitch Lansky.

Dead-downed Trees

Logs decompose in the shade and moisture of a climax forest, adding important nutrients and organic matter to the soil and serving as seedbeds for species such as red spruce. Insects, millipedes, and other invertebrates, as well as small vertebrates such as mice, and salamanders, invade the logs, opening pathways for fungi. Fungi help rot the logs and break them down into soil. Certain fungi, called *ectomycorrhizae*, form extensions of root tips on trees and other plants, vastly increasing the plants' intake of essential nutrients and water.

Conifers cannot survive without these symbiotic fungi. Each tree has to be inoculated with the fungal spores just as one has to inoculate milk with special bacteria to make yogurt. Chris Maser, a forest researcher in the Pacific Northwest, discovered that mushroom-eating mammals such as deer mice and flying squirrels pass the spores of these fungi (as well as yeasts and nitrogen-fixing bacteria) in their droppings, thus inoculating young seedlings and ensuring the survival of the forest.[11] "A forest," contends Maser, "does not run on dollars; it runs on such things as decomposing wood—large fallen trees—that Nature reinvested in Her forest."[12]

Gaps

It is in the gaps caused by the death (due to wind, insects or disease) of trees, or groups of trees, that old-growth forests demonstrate their resilience. Gaps are also important for wildlife species that require young growth for part of their habitat. Forests with old growth and gaps thus have the widest array of wildlife species because they have the widest array of habitats. Even-aged, managed forests, in contrast, display only a fragment of forest cycles.

What occupies the openings depends on the forest type and the gap size. Hardwood or mixedwood stands normally have smaller gaps and thus a more uneven-aged structure than do softwood stands. As the older trees fall, there is no regeneration lag; there are young trees ready to fill the gap. In the old-growth mixed woods at Big Reed Preserve, for example, the crown closure is approximately 60 to 80% due to windthrow gaps, dying beech, and the ragged nature of the older and larger trees. Yet very little light actually reaches the forest floor because of the abundance of understory trees.[13]

In the most extreme habitats at Big Reed, such as spruce-fir on steep exposed north slopes, the windthrow gaps are larger and can be acres in size, creating a mosaic of openings in the landscape. These openings are quickly covered with a dense mixture of herbaceous growth, including raspberries. According to ecologist Lissa Widoff, who studied the Big Reed forest, "this provides food and cover for wildlife, as well as some shade for the ground, keeping it and the downed trees cool and moist, and decreasing the risk of fire. The shade may also serve to suppress an over abundance of fir seedlings (which normally respond to sunny openings) thus preventing the formation of fir thickets."[14]

Healthy gap dynamics occur where the gap is surrounded by old growth. The gap is assured of regeneration and colonization by the plant, animal, and microorganism species that have become adapted to the forest community over thousands of years. Currently, however, small

Fungi decomposing a dead downed tree at Big Reed. *Photo by Mitch Lansky.*

Dead standing tree in forest gap at Big Reed. Note cavities made by pileated woodpeckers. *Photo by Jeff Schwartz.*

patches of old growth are surrounded by huge gaps and immature forest. There are only about 8,000 or 9,000 acres of old growth (which represents about 5/100 of 1% of the total forest) in Maine.ᵃ Beyond the beauty strip is a widening gap.

Endnote

a. Much of Maine's old growth, except for Big Reed Preserve, which is nearly 5,000 acres, is in stands of 50 acres or less and is thus mostly "edge" to a disturbed forest rather than true interior habitat (see Chapter 4). Even the larger areas do not have some of the species (e.g., wolves, caribou, cougar, wolverine, or lynx) formerly associated with the forest over thousands of years and are thus not truly complete.

While it would be desirable to have more old growth, one cannot create such forests from scratch and expect them to have the same species diversity that larger remnants of presettlement forest had. It is therefore important to protect what little we do have. Unfortunately, as mentioned in the introduction, there are no laws in Maine to protect remaining old growth.

References

1. Lissa Widoff, ed., *Natural Old-Growth Forest Stands in Maine*, Maine Critical Areas Program Planning Report No. 79 (Augusta, Me.: Maine State Planning Office, 1983), p. 13.
2. Malcolm Hunter, Jr., *Wildlife, Forests, and Forestry: Principles of Managing Forest for Biological Diversity* (Englewood Cliffs, N.J.: Prentice-Hall, 1990), p. 63.
3. Tim Schowalter, "Insects and Old Growth," *Forest Planning Canada*, Vol. 5 (1990): 5.
4. H. S. Crawford, "Silvicultural Practice and Bird Predation on Spruce Budworm," *Forest Technique*, Issue 84 (1984):12.
5. John C. Kricher, *A Field Guide to Eastern Forests of North America* (Boston, Mass.: Houghton Mifflin Company, 1988), p. 43.
6. Malcolm Hunter, Jr., *Wildlife, Forests, and Forestry*, Chapter 10.
7. Virgil Scott and David Patten, *Cavity-nesting Birds of Arizona and New Mexico Forests*, USDA General Technical Report RM-10 (Washington, D.C.: United States Forest Service, United States Department of Agriculture, 1975), p. 367.
8. Clarance F. Smith and S. E. Aldous, "The Influence of Mammals and Birds in Retarding Artificial and Natural Reseeding of Coniferous Forests in the United States," *Journal of Forestry* Vol. 45 (1947): 367.
9. Malcolm Hunter, Jr.,*Wildlife, Forests, and Forestry*, p. 162.
10. *Ibid.*, p. 162.
11. Chris Maser, *The Redesigned Forest* (San Pedro, Ca.: R.& E. Miles, 1988), p. 33.
12. *Ibid.*, pp. 97-98.
13. Lissa Widoff, *The Forest Communities of Big Reed Pond Preserve, T8 R10, T8 R11, Maine. Results of Field Studies, Summer 1985* (Topsham, Me.: The Nature Conservancy, 1985), p. 10.
14. *Ibid.*, p. 27.

Management Models

In the city of Bangor, once the busiest lumber port in the nation, is a prominent statue of Paul Bunyan. Paul, as legend has it, started his career in Maine. When he ran out of large white pine and red spruce to mow down with his giant axe here, he moved on to the forests of Michigan, Wisconsin, and Minnesota. After stripping those states of their virgin timber, he moved on to Oregon and Washington to cut the Douglas fir. Today Paul's task is nearly complete. The big trees are nearly all gone, and there are almost no virgin timber stands left to mine in this country.

Despite the honor bestowed on Paul Bunyan in downtown Bangor, this model of migratory forestry, known in Maine as "cut-and-run," is obviously not sustainable. Because of it, the great trees fit for ships' masts have been replaced by lesser trees fit for pulp or biomass. Lumber barons have been replaced by paper companies, which now claim to have a different management model. They are managing for the long term, they say, to ensure a sustainable supply of wood for their mills. They are taming the wild forests to produce a maximum yield of desired species.

The management models most attractive to the paper industry are those that view the forest as an extension of the mills. Seeing the forest as a factory allows the paper companies to emphasize mechanization, economies of scale, worker productivity, and economic efficiency, as if loggers were producing trees on an assembly line rather than removing them from a biological community. Unfortunately, when they clearcut to remove the product (trees) they are also removing the factory (forests).

Myth 1
Industrial forestry is scientific management.

Paper-industry public relations articles and advertisements show us images of professionals using satellite and infrared aerial photography, typing data into a computer, running sophisticated harvest equipment, growing "super trees" in vast greenhouses, and spraying complex chemicals. We are supposed to see such displays of technological virtuosity and exclaim, in awe, "Science!" Some of the results, however, appear more destructive to the forest than anything ever dreamed of in the days of axes and oxen. But paper companies have employed the best scientists money can buy to prove that industrial management, is actually beneficial to the forest, wildlife, and society. Because this "happy coincidence" is enunciated by scientists in their nearly indecipherable jargon, many people believe it must be scientific.

If management is to be scientific, however, it should be based on controlled, long-term experiments on many site, soil, and forest-community types. It should also be based on recognized scientific principles. Industry's version of scientific forestry management miserably fails both tests. It is based not so much on science as on technology harnessed to industrial ideology.

Long-term Experiments
Forest management methods can hardly be considered sustainably productive unless they have been demonstrated over a minimum of three or four rotations. Yet, no forestry experiments have been conducted in Maine using modern chemicals, super trees or whole-tree harvesting techniques for one full rotation, let alone three or four. While industrial researchers may claim that such studies

have been initiated, current management methods are not scientific just because someone is studying them. It is more "shoot first, ask questions later."

Scientific Principles

One would think that in lieu of long-term scientific data, foresters would at least base their management decisions on known scientific principles. Yet foresters routinely ignore principles of ecology:

Stability

Foresters often choose the most disturbing practice, such as whole-tree clearcuts, where a less disturbing one would suffice. By doing so they ignore considerations of stability. Removing a forest stand does not make it more stable.

Resistance.

Foresters favor species for their economic rather than ecological values. Diverse species mixes are replaced by simpler stands. This ignores considerations of resistance, because it reduces the habitats for, and thus the numbers of, predators and parasites that regulate potentially destructive insects.

Resilience

Foresters work against, rather than with, natural succession when they remove whole trees including branches and limbs (which are important nutrient sources) and when they spray herbicides. This ignores considerations of resilience. Some of the species killed by herbicides would normally prevent nutrient leaching and help rebuild organic matter.

Ecological Rotations

Foresters sometimes plan for such short rotations that organic matter and nutrient levels do not have time to recover to preharvest levels, thus ignoring the concept of ecological rotation. If nutrients and organic matter are depleted with each generation, forest productivity will decline.

Biological Legacy

Foresters often do not leave behind old, dead-standing or dead-downed trees. Many clearcuts leave only rocks and stumps, thus ignoring biological legacy (the diversity of species and habitats that survive disturbances and are passed on to subsequent generations). As a consequence, the forest's store of organic matter and its biological diversity become severely simplified.

Despite claims to the contrary, most industrial timber harvesting in Maine is based more on economic expediency than scientific merit. From an economic perspective, less forester supervision and less labor are more important than less destruction of ecological values. Nearly half of the timber harvests reported to the state in 1988 by large industrial landowners, for example, were not even by a legitimate silvicultural system (scientific or otherwise) that purports to manage a forest but were instead by more "traditional" methods such as (1) *diameter-limit cuts,* which remove all trees over a certain diameter (depending on the species); (2) *single-species cuts,* which remove all marketable trees of just one species; and (3) *commercial clearcuts,* which remove all marketable trees.[1] Since these are more rules for extracting trees than methods for managing forests, they do not require much in the way of forester supervision or scientific expertise. Furthermore, the loggers are generally paid by the cord. In such circumstances the first priority is to remove trees as fast as possible, not to ensure a healthy residual stand or un-damaged regeneration.

Neither the new nor traditional forms of forestry management most often employed by industrial landowners are particularly scientific—unless you con-sider short-term economics a science.

Reference
1. Stephen Harper, Laura L. Falk, and Edward W. Rankin, *The Northern Forest Lands Study of New England and New York* (Rutland, Vt.: USDA Forest Service, spring 1990), extrapolated from Table 1, p. 167.

Myth 2
Forestry is an extension of agriculture.

The agriculture metaphor is widely used by foresters. They call the trees they want to cut "crops"; the trees they don't want to cut, "weeds"; and cutting the trees, "harvesting." Most of the big landowners in Maine belong to the Tree Farm organization. The U.S. Forest Service is a division of the Department of Agriculture.

In spite of these metaphors, the reality has not been fiber farming; it has

A northwoods Tree Farm. *Photo by Mitch Lansky.*

mostly been fiber mining. Almost none of the trees now being harvested are from tree plantations. It takes a minimum of four or five decades before plantations are ready to harvest commercially, but the big landowners only started planting on any scale in the late 1970s. Since then, planting has played a minor role. In 1987, for example, only 5% of the clearcuts reported to the state were seeded or planted.[1] Loggers are raping (sic) what they did not sow and not sowing what they rape.

This does not mean that the paper companies are uninterested in growing fiber like farmers grow corn or wheat. The state has projected shortfalls for most commercial species in the coming decades, and state and industrial managers have argued that the only way to prevent such shortfalls is to intensify management. By this they mean to concentrate growth only on commercially desirable species using agricultural techniques such as planting, thinning, weeding, fertilizing, and spraying.

The farmed forest works completely for the industrial boss without wasting precious energy growing superfluous organisms such as mushrooms, orchids, salamanders, and warblers; which have no direct economic value. Paper companies see this as progress, and frequently use the image of mass-produced, fast-growing, high-yielding seedlings in advertisements designed to demonstrate their concern for the future. These public relations efforts have paid off—many people now believe that planting trees is "green." And before you can plant a new crop, you have to harvest (clearcut) the old.

Forest as Commodity

With plantation forestry, the emphasis is on growing a tree crop rather than maintaining a forest ecosystem. The cleavage between these two philosophies of

A new, improved forest. *Photo by Mitch Lansky.*

natural resource management, observed Aldo Leopold in his essay on "The Land Ethic," is profound. "In all of these cleavages," wrote Leopold, "we see repeated the same basic paradoxes: man the conqueror versus man the biotic citizen; science the sharpener of his sword versus science the searchlight on his universe; land the slave and servant versus land the collective organism."[2] As Leopold put it, to "grow trees like cabbages, with cellulose as the basic forest commodity," clearly puts the forester in the conqueror role, a role that Leopold felt is ultimately self-defeating: "Why? Because it is implicit in such a role that the conqueror knows, *ex cathedra*, just what makes the community clock tick, and just what and who is valuable, and what and who is worthless, in community life. It always turns out that he knows neither, and this is why his conquests eventually defeat themselves."[3]

Factory Farms

The metaphorical shift from forest ecosystem to farm crop is drastic enough, but farming itself is subject to Leopold's cleavage, and industrial foresters have chosen the wrong end here as well. The forest industry in Maine is just starting to imitate a form of agriculture rejected by more enlightened agronomists for years. While these agronomists are calling for crop diversity, green manures, composting, interplanting, and biological controls, foresters are embracing an agribusiness approach (exported to the Third World as the "Green Revolution"), which is based on monocultures of high-yield varieties, chemical fertilizers, mechanization, and chemical pesticides. Critics of this approach contend that it has created serious ecological, social, and economic problems worldwide.[4] When the agribusiness model is applied to forestry on a large scale, similar problems occur, but due to the long time necessary to grow tree crops, the problems take on new dimensions.

High-yield Varieties (HYV)

Farms

Green-Revolution crop varieties have higher yields than traditional crop varieties not because they are better adapted to the site but because they are better adapted to high inputs of chemical fertilizers and irrigation. With grains, for example, traditional varieties tend to lodge (fall over) when given extra nitrogen fertilizer. HYVs are often bred to have dwarf characteristics to prevent lodging and allow higher densities. Because the HYVs are hybrids, farmers cannot save seed but must purchase it, thus becoming less self-reliant.

Forest

Forest irrigation and fertilization are expensive and impractical on a large scale. Futhermore, forest fertilization has yielded inconsistent results—sometimes giving little benefit, or worse, sometimes increasing susceptibility to damage from weeds, insects, frost, or snow.[5,6,7] Breeding dwarfing characteristics into trees so that they can accept higher levels of nitrogen without blowing over runs counter to the goal of growing bigger trees faster. Fertilization is more experimental than operational in Maine.

Tree HYVs have not been bred over many generations to adapt to specific local extremes of moisture, temperature, wind, insects, or disease. There is no guarantee that they will outperform local trees in this regard. It is not enough that the trees grow better in greenhouse conditions; they have to survive the worst stresses that are likely to occur over a full rotation. Planted trees, especially those not adapted to the particular characteristics (including nutrients, soil micro-organisms, timing of frosts, or abundance or lack of soil moisture) of the site, are at a disadvantage to locally adapted tree varieties and have sometimes suffered catastrophic failures as a result.[8] Volunteers frequently outgrow the intended crop trees.

Loss of Diversity

Farms

Agribusiness-style agriculture has reduced diversity in two ways: the genetic base for crop varieties has been reduced as farmers have switched to a few seed types, and landscape diversity has been reduced as farmers have become more reliant on single-crop monocultures. The loss of genetic diversity has sometimes had disastrous results, as many of the varieties lost were specifically adapted to local climates and soil types.

Forests

The simpler stand structures of plantations makes them far more susceptible to catastrophic loss than a diverse, natural forest. In some ways, forest monocultures are more vulnerable to pests than agricultural monocultures. Agricultural crops are often quite different from surrounding vegetation and must be recolonized by pests each time a new crop is planted. Plantations, however, are often surrounded by forests with similar types of trees. These trees may harbor potential pests.

While the plantation may provide an ideal habitat for pests, it may not provide sufficient habitat, or adequate alternate hosts, for predators and parasites of the pests. Young plantations lack the deep-crowned, hollow, or dead trees that shelter numerous bird and invertebrate species—ranging from woodpeckers to spiders—that feed on insect pests. Since trees, as opposed to annual farm crops, take many years to mature, pests have plenty of time to find the concentrated food supply plantations offer and to build to epidemic proportions. This double whammy—resource concentration and lack of natural controls—has led to plantation problems worldwide.[9]

Reliance on Pesticides

Farm

The Green Revolution has led to increased use of chemical pesticides for many farmers. Crop monocultures and a small genetic base for crop varieties have increased vulnerability to insect and disease problems. Reliance on chemical pesticides has led to problems of pest flareback (an increase in pests when pest predators are killed), secondary pest infestations (e.g., a formerly innocuous insect becomes a pest because its predators have been killed by pesticides), and resistance (where new generations of plants, insects, or diseases develop resistance to a particular chemical). Increasing pesticide use has led to ecological disruption, human illness, groundwater contamination, and escalating costs.

Forests

Reliance on pesticides starts in tree nurseries, where trees are treated with a witch's brew of chemical insecticides, fungicides, and herbicides. Sometimes, however, nursery problems are not detected or effectively controlled. In New Brunswick, for example, red pines have been attacked by cankers and shoot moths due to nursery contamination.[10]

Herbicides are used routinely for site preparation and crop release (suppressing overtopping vegetation). Insecticides may also be used to protect plantations from catastrophic losses to such defoliators as spruce budworms. While foresters may not spray pesticides on plantations as frequently or in such complicated mixtures as farmers do over some agricultural crops, the foresters' costs, which must be carried for decades, may be more burdensome. Because plantations continue to be vulnerable, foresters must continue monitoring and, if needed, spraying until the trees are harvested.

Attempts to protect stands with pesticides can, as with agricultural crops, lead to unforeseen problems. In New Brunswick, for example, when black spruce plantations were sprayed for spruce budworm, spruce bud-scale problems erupted. The problem subsided when spraying stopped.[11]

Soil Degradation

Farms

Increased reliance on chemical fertilizer and abandonment of crop rotations has led to increased soil erosion, water contamination, depletion of micronutrients (because chemical fertilizers only contribute macronutrients), and depletion of topsoil and organic matter.

Forests

Soil degradation of a plantation starts with clearcutting and site preparation. A site is ideal for planting after all above-ground biomass has been removed, leaving bare soil. This is also an ideal way to encourage nutrient leaching.

Growing softwood plantations on former hardwood or mixedwood sites can further degrade the soil through podzolization. Studies of repeated spruce plantations on former hardwood sites in Germany and Eastern Europe have confirmed this loss of productivity through soil acidification and nutrient leaching.[12] This problem is exacerbated if the plantations are harvested on short rotations, giving the soil inadequate time to replace lost nutrients and organic matter.

Quality

Farms

Although such comparisons are highly subjective, most people would agree that agribusiness' fruits and vegetables simply do not taste as good as those grown in backyard gardens. There is a reason for this: agribusiness produce is bred to survive harvesting, shipping, and handling and still have a good appearance and long shelf life. These criteria are more apt to lead to hard and tasteless rather than soft and juicy tomatoes. Flavor and nutritive values are sacrificed for mass production.

Forests

The primary quality industrial landowners desire from their "super" plantation trees is rapid growth. From an economic standpoint, the sooner landowners can get a return on their investments, the better. The fat growth rings foresters proudly like to display from their fast-growing trees indicate a tradeoff—greater girth for lower density. Unfortunately, these fast-grown, heavily tapered trees make poor, knotty lumber that tends to shrink, warp, and break under stress.[13] The best lumber comes from clear trees, with tighter rings, grown under partial shade.

Plantation-grown softwoods are also no match for old trees as a source for fiber for paper. Young, fast-grown trees have shorter fibers with a higher burst factor and lower tear factor, both undesirable qualities for paper. According to Gordon Robinson, "In view of all factors relating to fiber quality, such as rate of growth and age of trees, it is clear that the highest-quality fiber comes from trees more than 70 years old and from slowly grown and suppressed trees. This implies that chips for pulp should ideally come from slabs of old trees, particularly the butt logs, and from the tops of slowly grown or suppressed trees. This class of material is the product of trees grown on a long rotation, more than 70 years at least, and trees grown in partial shade, characteristic of selection forests."[14]

The young-growth trees harvested from a plantation are also inferior for pulp because they have a high content of extractives (components of wood other than cellulose that must be removed during the pulping process). This waste material adds to production costs, and it creates water-pollution problems at pulp mills.[15]

Burning for site preparation. *Photo by Christopher Ayres.*

Social and Economic Impacts

Farms

Those farmers who can afford the necessary inputs for the Green Revolution have become dependent on agrichemical and farm-machinery corporations. Such farmers tend to grow crops for export, rather than for local consumption. The system is not economically viable without subsidies and price supports or unless the landowner is vertically integrated (owning pesticide and fertilizer plants, farmland, and food-processing plants). In the latter case, corporations can afford to lose money growing crops because their major source of income is from the sale of agrichemical inputs or from food processing.

Small farmers, unable to afford the expensive inputs and ineligible for subsidies, have become displaced, as have workers who have been rendered obsolete by machinery and chemicals. The Green Revolution has not conquered the problems of poverty and hunger; it has sometimes exacerbated them.

Forests

Plantation forestry requires large investments carried over decades. The revenues rarely are captured in the lifetime of the manager who makes the investment. If foresters are to prevent catastrophic losses before final harvest, they must continually monitor the stands and invest in protection (usually pesticides) when needed. Such long-term monitoring and protection require management continuity for at least half a century. Even if all goes well, the stumpage value (the value of wood to the landowner after subtracting costs of harvesting and trucking) of the harvested wood may not compensate for the plantation investments (see discussion in the last section of this chapter).

Because plantation economics are unfavorable in Maine, few clearcuts are replanted. In 1989, Maine forest landowners reported planting only 8,148 acres of trees, or 5.6% of the 145,357 acres they reported clearcutting that year.[16] Plantations in Maine have been almost exclusively the activity of vertically integrated industrial landowners who own mills as well as forests. In 1988, large nonindustrial owners, who clearcut tens of thousands of acres a year, planted a total of 107 acres, mostly in white pine.[17]

In northeastern North America, plantation forestry is only common in Canada, where it is heavily subsidized.[18] When plantation costs are subsidized, the landowners get all the revenues from the final harvest, and the public pays for the costs of management. This is, in effect, a subsidy for clearcutting. Where this occurs, selection cutting, which is not subsidized, becomes less competitive. For its tax contributions, the public gets simplified landscapes, increased water contamination, displaced workers, and diminished wildlife diversity with no guarantee of improved forest productivity or improved forest products.

References

1. Irland Group, *Clearcutting as a Management Practice in Maine Forests* (Augusta, Me.: Maine Department of Conservation, Forest for the Future Program, 1988), Table 2, p. 11.
2. Aldo Leopold, *A Sand County Almanac: With Essays on Conservation from Round River* (New York: Sierra Club/Ballantine, 1966), p. 260.
3. *Ibid.*, p. 240.
4. Vandana Shiva, "The Green Revolution in the Punjab," *Ecologist* , Vol. 21 (March/April 1991): 57-60.
5. David Maass, *Northern Forest Trends, 1985-1988* (Augusta, Me.: The Irland Group, 1989), p. 7.
6. Roy Silen, *Nitrogen, Corn, and Forest Genetics: The Agricultural Yield Strategy—Implications for Douglas Firr Management*, USDA General Technical Report PNW-137 (Portland, Ore.: USDA Forest Service Pacific Northwest Forest and Range Experiment Station, 1982), p. 8.
7. Gordon Robinson, *The Forest and the Trees: A Guide to Excellent Forestry* (Washington, D.C.: Island Press, 1988), p. 133.
8. Roy Silen, *Nitrogen, Corn and Forest Genetics*, p. 8.
9. D. A. Perry and J. Maghembe, "Ecosystem Concepts and Current Trends in Forest Management: Time for Reappraisal," *Forest Ecology and Management*, Vol. 26 (1989): 123-140.
10. B. A. Pendrel and T. R. Renault, "Insects and Diseases in Plantations." In *Reforestation in the Maritimes* (Fredericton, New Brunswick: Maritimes Forest Research Centre, 1984), p. 137.
11. *Ibid.*, p. 140.
12. J. Pelisek, "Conifer Plantations and Soil Deterioration," *The Ecologist*, Vol. 5 (November 1975).
13. Chris Maser, *The Redesigned Forest* (San Pedro, Calif.: R. and E. Miles, 1988), p. 94. Also, Gordon Robinson, *The Forest and the Trees*, p. 74.
14. Gordon Robinson, *The Forest and the Trees*, p. 209.
15. *Ibid.*, p. 74.
16. Maine Forest Service, *Report on Pre-commercial Silvicultural Activities and Harvesting* (Augusta, Me.: Maine Forest Service, Maine Department of Conservation, July 17, 1990).
17. Maine Forest Service, *Silvicultural Practices Report of 1988* (Augusta, Me.: Maine Forest Service, Maine Department of Conservation, 1988).
18. David Maass, *Northern Forest Trends, 1985-1989, North USA and Eastern Canada* (Augusta, Me.: The Irland Group, September 20, 1990), p. 9.

Myth 3
Sweden's forestry system is a good model for Maine.

Sweden seems to be successfully demonstrating that you can farm your forests. Maine's paper companies do not exactly mimic the Swedish example, but they do invoke it as an ideal when defending agricultural-style, even-aged management systems. Although there is certainly much we can learn from Sweden concerning treatment of labor, rights of woodlot owners, and government competence, those who advocate Swedish forest practices for Maine tend to exaggerate the biological applicability, neglect the question of sustainability, and downplay the negative side effects. They also tend to ignore the costs (both financial and political) of such a system to industry.

In 1988 a Maine delegation that included foresters, representatives of large landownerships, an economist, and a journalist visited Sweden and came back with (mostly) glowing reports. Bowdoin College economist David Vail was impressed that in Sweden "forest domestication has reached a point [of] 'fine tuning,'"whereas in Maine the emphasis is still on "mining" trees.[1] Roger

Milliken, president of Baskehegan Lands Company, which owns and manages 100,000 acres of forestland in northeastern Maine, called Sweden's forestry activities "state-of-the-art forest management—an example from which Maine could benefit."[2] *Maine Times* reporter Phyllis Austin described the Swedish forest as the "well-kept forest of Maine's dreams. . . . Beholding it for the first time is like beaming oneself into the future to see the Maine woods the way people—corporation foresters and environmentalists alike—envision."[3]

All three visitors described Sweden's forestry system as being agriculture on a 70 to 140 year rotation. The Swedish system is based on longer rotations than in Maine, partly due to climate—trees grow more slowly in Sweden—but also because the focus is on growing trees suitable for lumber rather than just pulp. Seventy percent of Sweden's forest harvests are clearcuts. The rest are seed-tree cuts, which, like clearcuts, are even-aged. Most of the clearcuts receive site preparation and get planted to commercial species. Young stands are precommercially thinned and "cleaned" (i.e., weeded), which is done mostly with brush saws. (Although at one time up to 150,000 acres a year were sprayed with herbicides, aerial spraying has been prohibited in Sweden since 1972 due to citizen protest.) Chemical fertilizers are spread over 355,000 acres a year, mostly by aircraft. Commercial thinning is done on as many acres as are clearcut, and these thinning operations supply 30% of the timber used by the mills.[4]

Harvests are highly mechanized. Almost 70% of clearcuts and commercial thinning operations are done with highly sophisticated computerized equipment. The machinery has been designed to do specific silvicultural operations and to be safe for labor. Unlike Maine, which uses most of its mechanical harvesters for whole-tree harvesting (which can be highly damaging to the soil and residual stands), Sweden uses its machines for shortwood harvest systems, bucking and sorting the logs at the site to get the most efficient use of each tree.[5]

Here is a forestry system that seems to work. The forest is productive, growing 75% of what experts think is possible, versus 40% in Maine (these productivity figures are based on the assumption that the major purpose of the forest is to produce timber products for industry).[6] It is profitable for industry, labor, and woodlot owners. And it is based on intensive, highly mechanized management—growing trees like farm crops. Does this disprove my previous argument that the farm model is a poor one for forestry in Maine? No. Consider the following:

Applicability
Sweden's forest differs climatically and ecologically from Maine's. The fact that softwoods are economically important in both regions does not mean that management methods should be the same. The softwoods exist in very different contexts—boreal in Sweden, Acadian in Maine:[7]

Maine/Sweden Contrasts

Variable	Maine	Sweden
Latitude	44-47° North	58-66° North
Mean temperature:		
July	70-75° F.	58-62° F.
January	10-15° F.	32° F.
Average rainfall	42 inches	20 inches
Soils	loamy—sandy & gravely	bouldery moraines
Forest type	softwood/hardwood transition; Acadian	mostly boreal
Commercial species	24+	3
Natural regeneration	normally abundant	poor

Sweden has a simpler forest ecosystem than Maine. Alexander Jablanczy, an ecologically minded Canadian forester, now retired, who spent 34 years as a forester in Czechoslovakia and Hungary before coming to Canada, considers it a "myth" that the "Scandinavian silvicultural system, developed for their own simple ecosystems of few species, should be considered imitatable in [Maritime and Maine] forests with dozens of species in vastly variable ecosystems."[8]

In some regions of central Europe, where the climate and forest types are more similar to Maine's than they are to Sweden's, the system of clearcuts followed by monoculture softwood plantations was tried on sites that once supported mixedwoods or hardwoods, and it resulted in soil degradation and declines in subsequent rotations. As a result, various schools of "natural" forestry have developed in Europe whose goal is to keep the forest continually stocked with a mixture of species grown slowly over long rotations to achieve high quality.[9] Unfortunately, the industry, press, and larger environmental groups in Maine have not turned their attention to these examples of more ecologically oriented forestry methods.

Sustainability

Although there are examples in some countries (e.g., Switzerland) of continuous management by selection methods for over 600 years, the Swedish example of intensive plantation forestry does not have the same record of continuity and has not yet passed the test of time—showing continued productivity past the third rotation. Strict Swedish forest-practices regulations were enacted as a result of serious crises in supply. During the nineteenth century, the forest was brutally exploited to meet the growing demands of the Industrial Revolution—a revolution that so strained the land that one out of three Swedes fled the country to seek a better life.[10]

In 1903 a Swedish reforestation act was passed but was not widely obeyed. High-grading (cutting the best and leaving the rest) was still a common practice, but thinning for stand improvement was not. The result was a dip in wood supply that led in 1923 to the banning of clearcuts (because clearcuts remove young trees before they reach their potential). Not until the end of the 1940s did the sustained-yield concept become national policy. In the 1950s, with the creation of new harvesting equipment, clearcutting again gained favor, and the tree-planting boom began. Intensive thinning and longer rotations became policy goals toward the end of the 1960s and early 1970s.[11] Intensive practices such as precommercial thinning with brush saws (which became compulsory in 1979), thinning with computerized mechanical harvesters, and aerial fertilization could hardly have been a major component of Swedish forestry until the technologies were developed to make them possible.

The point of this short, selective history is that the Swedes are still managing the first rotation of the intensive plantation system. Although their approach has certainly increased the commercial productivity of a formerly degraded forest, we do not know what the effects of their emphasis on clearcuts, simplified ecosystems, and chemical fertilizers will be on subsequent rotations.

Negative Side Effects

"Swedish naturalist painters, even those that portray elves and trolls," observed Roger Millikin, "routinely show stumps in the woods. Every forest, including those in the Swedish imagination, is a working forest. My North American sensibilities demanded some untrammeled, uncultivated forest. . . . "[12]

Writer Phyllis Austin reacted in a similar way. "Maine's unmanaged landscape seemed preferable to Sweden's controlled one, if for no other reason than diversity," she wrote. "Tall, nicely spaced trees are pleasing to the eye, but they become boring when that's all you see. It was an unexpected revelation, given my strong sentiments about restoring quality to the Maine woods through intensive management."[13]

The lack of diversity is not just a visual illusion; it is a biological reality. Research by Ingmar Ahlen, an ecology professor at the Swedish University of Agricultural Sciences in Uppsala, suggests that intensive forestry practices, especially since the Forest Act passed in 1980, have had serious impacts. Forty species of vertebrates that feed or reproduce in the forest are seriously endangered, and 50 species of fungi, lichens, and flowering plants are on the verge of extinction, with another 220 species in some danger.[14]

As Sweden's industry and government push to harvest the country's remaining old-growth forests to help stave off an anticipated shortfall, the issue of biodiversity (which will be discussed in Chapter 4) has been intensifying. The controversy has resulted in the establishment of a one-million-acre preserve in which cutting is banned.[15]

Environmentalists have been concerned over other threats to Sweden's working forest:

•the effect of extensive clearcutting on runoff;

•the effect of mechanical harvesting on forest soils and on local employment;

•the introduction of exotic species, such as lodgepole pine, for short-rotation pulpwood;

•water contaminantion from chemical fertilizers;

•air and water pollution by the paper industry; and

•acid rain. Already 15,000 fresh-water lakes are so acidified that sensitive animals and plants can no longer survive in them.[16]

The Costs

Industry foresters in North America who proclaim the benefits of Swedish forestry might not want to live with the economic and political costs. Swedish timber is the most expensive to grow in the world. Strict government regulations mandate that landowners invest in planting, thinning, and cleaning—investments that will not yield marketable lumber in the landowners' lifetimes. These investments in a new forest translate, according to David Vail, to 15% of the cash flow from harvesting the old. In contrast, Vail estimates that Maine companies currently spend only 3% to 5% of harvest revenues on management investments.[17]

The burden of these costs in Sweden is lessened by two major factors. The first is that landowners get much better prices for their wood in Sweden than they do in Maine. Foresters are scrupulous at sorting out harvested timber to send to the highest paying markets. In addition, according to Vail, for similar products, stumpage prices in Sweden average 30% to 50% higher than in Maine.[18] One reason for the higher prices is that half the forestland is owned by nonindustrial landowners who can bargain cooperatively with the mills.

Secondly, direct subsidies (mostly for road building) and tax preferences shift some of the costs to taxpayers. According to Vail, "forest management is one of the most heavily sheltered investments in Sweden."[19] The government, through its tax incentives, buffers investors from some of the risks inherent in establishing forest monocultures that must survive for a century or more. While these incentives lessen the pain of management investments, the investments would not be made at present levels unless they were mandated by government regulations.

Purchased wood for mills is more expensive in Sweden not only because of higher stumpage costs but also because of higher labor costs. Most Swedish loggers are paid a wage (rather than a piece rate as in Maine), and are trained, unionized professionals. The emphasis in Sweden, as compared to Maine, is much more on management than on mining. Loggers are even given bonuses if they do minimal damage to residual stands—a policy that reduced damage rates from 15% to 4%.[20]

That Sweden's forest industries have been able to stay competitive (until recently) in international markets despite such high costs raises serious questions about Maine corporations that claim they cannot pay more for labor or raw materials and still stay competitive. Maine paper-industry proponents who are staunch defenders of the free market would have trouble explaining the ability of Swedish corporations to survive in a regulatory system that dictates what, when, and how to cut, plant, and thin, and even mandates setting aside 10% of corporate profits, during economic booms, to non-interest-bearing accounts for modernization or expansion projects that are government approved.[21]

Without the regulatory framework and the economic incentives for forest landowners and for labor, Swedish plantation-style forestry could not exist at its current scale.[a] The Swedish model does show how an integrated government policy can lead to a working forest that works for a wider range of people, including labor and woodlot owners. But the policy may not be working as well for forest ecosystems. Indeed, British writer Linda Gamlin compares the Swedish government, which has been actively pushing to completely convert forests to industrially desired species, with George Orwell's Ministry of Truth. "This sort of fudging enables the government to preserve the illusion of a caring, responsible attitude to the environment, while it actually pursues highly damaging policies."[22]

Endnote

a. In nearby Nova Scotia, we have a good example of what happens to Swedish forestry without the Swedish political context. Stora Kopparbergs Berlags AB, a Swedish conglomerate, owns a pulp and paper mill in that province and has a 50-year lease on a million and a half acres to cut on Crown (public) lands. The company pays some of the cheapest stumpage prices in North America. Labor is nonunion, on piece rate, and threatened with mechanization. Woodlot owners are forced to compete with cheap Crown wood. The company relies on clearcutting and aerial herbicide spraying (a practice that is banned in Sweden) and claims to be cutting on a 45-year rotation, far shorter than their 100-year rotations in Sweden. Their practices differ little from other exploitive multinationals in the region.[23]

References

1. David Vail, "How to Tell the Forest from the Trees: Recent Technical Changes in the Forest Industries of Sweden and Maine." In *Harvard University Seminar on Neo-classical Economics* (Cambridge, Mass.: Harvard University, 1988): 22.
2. Roger Milliken, "Inspired Forestry," *Habitat*, Vol. 5 (July 1988): 24.
3. Phyllis Austin, "Sweden's Cultivated Forest: How It Evolved and How It Differs from Maine's," *Maine Times* (August 28, 1987): 1B.
4. Phyllis Austin, "Sweden's Cultivated Forest," p. 12B. Also, David Vail, "How To Tell the Forest," pp. 38, 53.
5. David Vail, "How To Tell the Forest," p. 38.
6. Roger Milliken, "Inspired Forestry," pp. 24-25.
7. Phyllis Austin, "Sweden's Cultivated Forest," pp. 12-13B.
8. Alexander Jablanczy, "Message To My Friends Who Care About the Future of Canadian Forests," New Year's, 1984.
9. Alexander Jablanczy, "Message to My Friends." Also, R. Plochman, *Forestry in the Federal Republic of Germany*, Hill Family Foundation Series (Corvallis, Ore.: Oregon State University School of Forestry, 1968).
10. Phyllis Austin, "Sweden's Cultivated Forest," p. 10B.
11. *Ibid.*, pp. 10-11B.
12. Roger Milliken, "Inspired Forestry," p. 24.
13. Phyllis Austin, "How I Earned My Pin and Credit Card," *Maine Times* (August 28, 1987): 23B.
14. Linda Gamlin, "Sweden's Factory Forests," *New Scientist* (January 28, 1988): 41.
15. Phyllis Austin, "Sweden's Cultivated Forest," p. 3B.
16. *Ibid.*, p. 3B.
17. David Vail, "How To Tell the Forest," p. 26.
18. David Vail, personal communication, spring 1990.
19. David Vail, "How To Tell the Forest," p. 51.
20. Phyllis Austin, "Sweden's Cultivated Forest," p. 9B.
21. *Ibid.*, p. 1B.
22. Linda Gamlin, "Sweden's Factory Forests," p. 41.

23. Julia McMahon, "The New Forest in Nova Scotia." In Aaron Schneider, ed., *Deforestation and Development in Canada and the Tropics: The Impact on People and the Environment* (Sydney, Nova Scotia: Centre for International Studies, University College of Cape Breton, 1989), pp. 159-161.

Goals for Sustainable Management

If forest management is not sustainable, it fails the tests of both ecological soundness and social responsibility. Nonsustainable management means that present generations are benefitting at the expense of future generations.

The forest industry in Maine, however, claims its management is sustainable. This may be hard for some observers to believe after seeing the devastated landscapes that lie beyond the beauty strip. Actually, industry foresters assert, there is more wood growing in the forest now than there was 70 years ago. This is true, but it is in spite of, not because of, industrial management. The forest was being overcut around the turn of the century, but it was "saved" by the abandonment (over the past 100 years) of millions of acres of farmland (which grew back as forests), a decline in the sawmill industry after 1909, and the collapse in demand for forest products after the Great Depression. It was not saved by improved management.

In recent years, forest researchers have raised concerns that there may be mill shortfalls within a few decades. Industry foresters claim, however, that on their own lands they are doing a good job—they are following rules for sustainable management leading to forest improvements. The evidence, they insist, is in their dramatic increase in "intensive management" and in data from periodic government forest surveys.

Much of the public is alienated from forestry discussions because of uncomfortability with silvicultural jargon. They end up conceding this realm to the professionals (many of whom are industry employees), restricting their demands to beauty strips suitable for recreation. This concession is unfortunate, howerver, because when one penetrates the jargon, one discovers that what lies beyond the beauty strip is a professional disgrace.

Many of industry's management rules, for example, can be used to justify degradation; they are based on sustaining the flow of fiber to the mills rather than sustaining the ecological values of the forest. And the companies often don't even follow the rules. Close inspection of the surveys reveals a forest inventory that is declining in both volume and quality. The companies seem to be striving harder to sustain the illusion of a forest than the forest itself.

The Maine legislature passed a Forest Practices Act in 1989, leading to the formation in 1990 of rules concerning clearcutting and regeneration. The legislation, a landmark in Maine history, promised to "promote a healthy and sustainable forest." Despite numerous attempts since 1907, the legislature had been unable to pass any statewide regulations governing forest practices (this will be discussed in more detail in Chapter 5). Although the Land Use Regulation Commission established rules in the 1970s to restrict harvesting in the beauty strips around water bodies in the unorganized territories, the 1990 rules were the first directed at practices beyond the beauty strips. Unfortunately, the Forest Practices Act does not prevent industry's unsustainable practices—instead, it legitimizes them.

Myth 1

If wood harvesting is subject to management plans prepared by registered professional foresters, it will be sustainable.

If this myth were true, then industry timber harvesting, almost all of which is subject to management plans prepared by registered professional foresters, would be exemplary. Industry foresters, however, are working to sustain company mills, not a healthy ecosystem. The foresters are under pressure to achieve a rate of financial return demanded by corporate executives, most of whom have little understanding of forestry. At Champion International, for example, only one of 18 executives has forestry training. At Boise Cascade, it is two.[1] Local forest managers often have poor communication with higher level executives on policy issues. According to David Smith, professor of silviculture at Yale, "With some of these outfits, the communication between the top and bottom is about zilch. In fact, there are so many of these foresters accustomed to taking orders from on high that they don't question. They just go on drawing their pay saying it isn't their fault."[2] Some of the forest managers have backgrounds in accounting or engineering rather than forest biology.[3]

Consistently getting desired returns on forestry investments can mean operating in the short term—which can lead to forest liquidation rather than forest improvement. As one company president said, "You have to do something wrong today to make the kind of profits shareholders and Wall Street demand. But you can't sustain it. It's like a pyramid scheme."[4] Or, as a paper company woodlands manager put it, "I can only be as ethical toward the land as economics will allow me."[5]

State lawmakers, undeterred by the industrial example of forester-approved clearcuts that cover 80% of a township, created a requirement, in the Forest Practices Act of 1989, for forester-approved management plans for all clearcuts over 50 acres. This implies that "small" clearcuts (under 50 acres) are no problem, and if larger ones have been approved by a registered professional forester, they must be acceptable.

The minimum requirements for the management plan, however, are not silvicultural. Foresters are not required, for example, to show how they will:
•choose the least disturbing management option suited to the site;
•avoid clearcutting on poor soils or sensitive sites where the forest will not recover well;
•plan for long enough rotations for the soil to recover nutrients and organic

matter to preharvest levels;

•plan for sustainable management within their ownership, township, or district;

•employ methods that will improve the quality, species distribution, and spacing of the trees;

•protect wildlife diversity by avoiding practices that simplify or fragment the forest;

•avoid practices that would be detrimental to local communities.

These considerations, which ought to be the basis of any management decision, can be ignored. Foresters are not held accountable for mismanagement, only for failure to distribute their clearcuts as approved by the Maine Forest Service:

•clearcuts that are 5 to 35 acres must be separated by a 250-foot buffer of trees;

•clearcuts that are 35 to 125 acres require a separation zone 1.5 times the size of the clearcut and at least 250 feet wide; and

•if the clearcut is between 125 and 250 acres, the separation zone must be at least 500 feet wide and twice the size of the clearcut. Landowners can cut up to 40% of the volume of trees in the separation zones, and in 10 years, a clearcut is no longer a clearcut—it can be used as a separation zone.

While such regulations require foresters to pay attention to stand layouts on a map, they do not require foresters to pay much attention to the trees in the forest.

References
1. Phyllis Austin, "Wall Street Rules the Woods," *Forest Watch* (August 1987), p. 9.
2. Phyllis Austin, "Crisis in the Maine Woods," *Forest Watch* (June 1987), p. 22.
3. Phyllis Austin, "Wall Street," p. 10.
4. *Ibid.*, quoting Julius Ingalizeri, president of Elmendof Corporation, p. 12.
5. Phyllis Austin, "Crisis," quoting Robert Hintze, woodlands manager for International Paper Company, p. 19.

Myth 2
The goal of industrial foresters is to have fully stocked stands of desirable trees.

One would think that there could be no more obvious goal of management than to have full stocking of desirable trees. (See sidebar). This would lead to maximum production of products, such as sawlogs, which give the highest stumpage return to the landowner.

Problems with Goal
This goal alone is not sufficient to establish sustainability for forest products because it does not specify the species or age distribution of the trees. Nor does it ensure the sustainability of wildlife species that require the habitats found in

rotten, dead-topped, or dead-standing trees (which can still be present in fully stocked stands). Foresters concerned with sustainability and productivity, however, would certainly have full stocking of desirable trees as one component of their long-term management plans.

Landowner Performance

Forest landowners in Maine, however, either do not share this goal or they have failed miserably to achieve it. Extrapolations from the 1972 forest survey show that if only desirable trees are counted, 0.1% of the commercial forest was fully stocked, 0.2% was medium stocked, 33.9% was poorly stocked, and 65.8% was nonstocked with desirable trees.[1]

What you just read is not a typographical error. Only 1/10 of 1% of the commercial forest was fully stocked with desirable trees. The Maine Chapter of the Society of American Foresters, reacting to those statistics, wrote in 1974 that "The present condition of Maine's timber resource has resulted largely from major emphasis having been placed upon harvesting merchantable timber, with little if any special effort to control the establishment, composition, and stocking of young stands. . . . Consequently, Maine's commercial forest land, commonly characterized by forest stands either too densely or too sparsely stocked and by stands having a sizable proportion of their timber volume in rough and rotten trees, is presently producing wood at a rate considerably below its potential capacity."[2]

In the 1982 U.S. Forest Service survey, the term "desirable trees" is absent. There is a classification of "preferred trees" ("a high quality tree, from a lumber viewpoint, that would be favored in cultural operations . . . "),[3] but no figures are given for stocking of such trees. One chart does give the number of such trees of different species in the forest, and from this one can deduce that only 20% of all trees are "preferred," but 25% are rough, rotten, or dead.[4] Modern forestry practices seem to be better at growing the lowest quality as opposed to the highest quality trees.

The quality of the forest is in decline as evidenced by the following statistics on "unsound" trees from the state's midcycle forest resurvey in 1986:[5]

Forest Quality, 1986

Species	Dead	Rough, Rotten, Cull	Total Unsound
Spruce	8%	9%	17%
Fir	36%	6%	42%
Other softwoods	5%	20%	25%
All softwoods	14%	12%	26%
All hardwoods	8%	35%	43%
All species	12%	21%	33%

Positive Example

The goal of achieving full stocking of good quality trees is not impossible. All the managed stands at the USDA Forest Service's Penobscot Experimental Forest in Bradley attain this ideal. Indeed, in most of these stands, poor-quality trees represent less than 1% of the standing volume.[6] The high percentage of rough, rotten, and dead trees found in Maine's woods is a result of backwards management—where the best-quality trees are removed, and the worst retained.

Lenient Standards

The state's clearcutting standards do not encourage full stocking of desirable trees but rather legitimize poor stocking of poor-quality trees. Landowners who leave behind a poorly stocked stand (but containing more than 30 square feet basal area per acre) of poor-quality trees of any species are exempt from regulations. Such a cut, according to the state, is not a clearcut, even if it removes 85% of the volume of trees originally present. By setting such minimal standards, the state has legalized degradation.

Understanding Stocking and Quality

Stocking refers to the degree of occupancy of land by trees. The USDA Forest Service has established stocking categories that reflect a stand's potential to achieve optimal growth. Stocking is determined by measuring the basal area, which is the area of cross sections of tree stems, measured at breast height (4.5 feet). The U.S. Forest Service compares the density of the stand to a stocking standard (75 square feet per acre) for trees over 5 inches dbh to determine the adequacy of stocking:[1]

Stocking Categories

Category	Percentage of stocking standard
Nonstocked	0-15 %
Poorly stocked	16-59 %
Moderately stocked	60-99 %
Fully stocked	100-129 %
Overstocked	130-160 %

The USDA Forest Service, in 1972, defined "desirable trees" as, "growing-stock trees of commercial species, (a) that have no serious quality defects that limit present or prospective use for timber products, (b) that are of relatively high vigor, and (c) that contain no pathogens that may result in death or serious deterioration before rotation age."[a]

Endnote

a. Although the USDA Forest Service considers a basal area of more than 100 square feet per acre to be "overstocked" (a standard based on hardwoods), the Revised Normal Yield Tables for Nova Scotia Softwoods considers full stocking to occur when there is full canopy closure (the foliage of one tree merges with that of the next). For fully stocked, even-aged stands of ten inch trees, the table estimates that the basal area should be 245 square feet to the acre.[8] The 30-square-foot-basal-area requirement can thus allow landowners to legally remove most of the stand volume with no need for a management plan.

References
1. Robert Frank et al., "Forest Practice Goals and Standards for the Improvement, Maintenance, and Protection of the Forest Resources of Maine," *The Maine Forest Review*, Vol. 7 (1974): 2.
2. *Ibid.*, pp. 2-3.
3. D. S. Powell and D. R. Dickson, "Forest Statistics," p. 187.
4. *Ibid.*, p. 20.
5. Maine Forest Service, *Report of the 1986 Midcycle Resurvey of the Spruce-Fir Forest in Maine* (Augusta, Me.: Maine Department of Conservation, 1988), p. 5.
6. Robert Frank, interview, fall 1990.
7. D. S. Powell and D. R. Dickson, *Forest Statistics for Maine—1971 and 1982*, USDA Forest Service Resource Bulletin NE-81 (Washington, D.C.: United States Forest Service, United States Department of Agriculture, 1984), p. 188.
8. *Revised Normal Yield Tables for Nova Scotia Softwoods*, Forest Research Report No. 22, (Truro, Nova Scotia: Nova Scotia Department of Lands and Forests, 1990), p. 11.
9. R. H. Ferguson and N. P. Kingsley, *The Timber Resources of Maine*, USDA Forest Service Resource Bulletin NE-26 (Washington, D.C.: United States Forest Service, United States Department of Agriculture, 1972), p. 38.

Myth 3
Management is sustainable as long as all harvests are adequately regenerated.

Industrial foresters tell the public not to worry about the large clearcuts that lie beyond the beauty strip. The forest, they say, has just been regenerated—a renewable resource has just been renewed. Every tree cut has been replaced by a seedling. Indeed, these foresters can point to the state's 1986 midcycle forest resurvey, which stated that "On more recently harvested areas, regeneration is 100%."[1] Furthermore, forest-practices rules established by the state in 1990 specify that if harvests do not have adequate regeneration, landowners must plant trees.

Seedlings Do Not a Forest Make
There are serious problems, however, with this simplistic formulation. The myth, for example, implies that as long as you replace mature trees with seedlings (either natural or planted), the forest is sustained. Vast areas of seedlings, however, are not the same for wildlife, aesthetics, or recreation as vast areas of mature trees. And so far, technologists have not found ways to saw two-by-fours out of seedlings. The rate at which the forest is cut and regenerated makes a big difference to the mills. The myth also fails to address the species composition and quality of the regenerating stands, thus allowing stand conversions that are biologically and silviculturally undesirable.

What is Adequate?
The state's definitions of "adequate" (which differ in the 1986 midcycle resurvey and 1990 regeneration and clearcut rules) set standards that would be unacceptable to responsible foresters. What the 1986 resurvey considered "adequate," i.e., finding seedlings on only 4 out of 10 milacre plots (a "milacre" is 1/1000 of an acre, or 43.56 square feet) would be inadequate to any forester trying to establish well-stocked stands. Foresters normally plant from 700 to 1,200

evenly distributed seedlings per acre, which would result in the occupation of 7 to 10 out of 10 milacre plots. The Nova Scotia Department of Lands and Forests considers an even-aged stand of 1-inch-diameter trees to be fully stocked (i.e., have full canopy closure) if there are 30,400 seedlings to the acre.[2] The state's "adequate" regeneration, however, would allow 6 of 10 milacre plots to have no regeneration at all. Judged by a higher standard, regeneration in Maine forests has not been very good.

Percent of Harvested[*] Spruce-Fir Stands Occupied by Regeneration by Species, Quality, and Density—1986[3]

Quality and (Distribution)	All Species	Spruce and Fir	Spruce
All seedlings[**] ("adequate")	100%	92%	40%
Best seedlings[***] ("adequate")	100%	81%	34%
Best seedlings (desirable)[****]	91%	36%	3%

[*]"Harvested" refers to stands in which cutting took place within 20 years of the sampling. The 1986 mid-cycle resurvey estimated the total acreage of harvested spruce-fir at 3,014,000 acres.
[**]"All seedlings" includes any seedling regardless of health or quality.
[***]"Best seedlings" are seedlings found to be free of defects and free to grow (i.e., not severely overtopped). These are seedlings most likely to survive.
[****]"Desirable" distribution occurs when seedlings are found on more than 7 of the 10 milacre plots per acre rather than 4 of 10 for "adequate."

From these state figures (which have very high margins of error because of the small number of samples taken) one can determine that around 19% of harvested spruce-fir stands had inadequate (by state standards) regeneration of best seedlings of spruce-fir. This represents more than 572,660 acres with inadequate regeneration of spruce-fir in harvested spruce-fir stands—surely nothing to crow about. Indeed, these figures show a continuation of the trend discovered by the USDA Forest Service's 1982 forest survey, which showed that 607,800 acres of the spruce-fir type in Maine "disappeared" between 1971 and 1982 (mostly replaced by pioneer hardwoods like aspen and white birch).[4]

Only 36% of harvested spruce-fir acres had the more desirable distribution of spruce and fir seedlings, and only 3% of the stands had a desirable distribution of spruce, the preferred species in the spruce-fir type. Fir seedlings greatly outnumbered spruce—which does not bode well for the future, since fir is shorter lived and more vulnerable to spruce budworm attacks.

Lenient Standards
When the Maine Forest Service created its clearcut and regeneration rules in 1990, it acted as though the definition for "adequate" that it used in 1986 was too strict a standard, even though 100% of harvested areas sampled cleared this already low hurdle. According to the new standards, a harvested stand is "adequately" regenerated if it contains, on average, more than 30 square feet basal

area per acre of "acceptable growing-stock" trees (any commercially used species whether native or exotic) over 1 inch DBH (diameter at breast height). But it allows gaps of up to 5 acres, where this standard is not met. The standards thus allow stand simplification or even conversion to species less suited to the site, with large gaps where no trees grow.

If these minimal standards are not met, then the landowner has up to 5 years to ensure that there are the equivalent of 3 out of 10 milacre plots per acre occupied by at least one tree seedling. In the final draft of the rules, this was changed to an even easier standard—60% of plots that are 1/500 of an acre must have at least one acceptable seedling—with a minimum of one sample plot every two acres. Hardwoods must be 3 feet high, but softwoods only have to have survived one growing season to qualify as "acceptable." And there can be gaps up to 5 acres in size that do not meet this standard. These requirements are far below what prudent foresters would allow to ensure a well-stocked future stand. The landowner can even claim exemption to these standards due to a "natural disaster" (which may actually be a direct result of a very unnatural clearcut) such as a fire or insect and disease problem.

Plantation Fix

Landowners who somehow fail these lenient tests must plant trees. When they plant, landowners can (and usually do) convert a hardwood or mixedwood stand to a single species of softwood—often boreal species, such as white and black spruce, or tamarack. This can lead to site degradation in some cases.

In Maine, natural regeneration is normally so prolific that one almost has to deliberately brutalize the forest to create a regeneration failure. It is a dubious tribute to forest landowners in Maine that they have devised harvest machinery and methods that are capable of achieving this difficult feat. By severely disturbing and compacting the soil, and by creating openings so large that it would take a hurricane to blow heavier tree seeds into the interior, some industrial landowners have succeeded in creating bare spots surrounded by fields of raspberries and pincherries where forests once stood.

Preventing Regeneration Failure

Rather than create low standards to legitimize poor-quality regeneration, the state could have set harvest standards that ensure desirable natural regeneration of trees with heavier seeds. To achieve this goal, the Society of American Foresters in 1974 recommended that foresters limit harvest openings to no more than 2 1/2 times the height of the surrounding seed-bearing trees.[5] In Maine, however, forest openings smaller than 5 acres are not even considered clearcuts, and clearcuts under 50 acres do not require management plans.

References

1. Maine Forest Service, *Report of the 1988 Midcycle Resurvey of the Spruce-Fir Forest in Maine* (Augusta, Me.: Maine Department of Conservation, 1988), p. 14.
2. *Revised Normal Yield Tables for Nova Scotia Softwoods*, Forest Research Report No. 22 (Truro, Nova Scotia: Nova Scotia Department of Lands and Forests, 1990), p. 11.
3. Maine Forest Service, *Report of 1988 Midcycle Resurvey*, p. 28.
4. D. S. Powell and D. R. Dickson, *Forest Statistics for Maine—1971 and 1982*, USDA Forest Service Resource Bulletin NE-81 (Washington, D.C.: United States Forest Service, United

States Department of Agriculture, 1984), p. 16.

5. Robert Frank et al., "Forest Practice Goals and Standards for the Improvement, Maintenance, and Protection of the Forest Resources of Maine," *The Maine Forest Review*, Vol. 7 (1974): 4.

Myth 4

Sustainable forestry means establishing and maintaining a balanced age-class area distribution.

According to Maine's Forest Practices Act of 1989, the way to make the forest healthy and sustainable is to ensure that the forest contains "a balance of age classes necessary for a sustainable timber supply and spatial and compositional diversity." Foresters are concerned with the distribution of trees from age 0 to 9, 10 to 19, 20 to 29, etc., because an imbalanced distribution of age classes can lead to future problems. Suppose, for example, that a mill relies on an abundant supply of trees that are 50 to 70 years old. If there are relatively few trees approximately 30 to 40 years old today, then there will be relatively few 50-to-60-year-old trees 20 years from now. This can lead to mill shortfalls.

There are many problems with the concept of a balanced age-class distribution, however.

Even- versus uneven-age.

Most people who use the concept of balanced age classes envision the trees as existing in even-aged stands. The way to achieve the goal of balanced distribution, therefore, is to have an equal area of the forest in each age class. Forest activist Bill Butler calls these even-aged stands "idiot blocks" because they are so easy for foresters to keep track of from the air and in their computers. While it may make little difference to a computer whether the trees are in uneven-aged forests or in idiot blocks, it makes a big difference to the forest ecosystem.

Landscape.

Reliance on idiot blocks can lead to a situation where one age class is in one township and another in the next. Once again, the size and distribution of the blocks may make little difference to foresters but can make a big difference to the forest creatures that depend on large areas of mature trees for survival.

Range of ages.

Having an equal area of trees in five different even-aged stands (0-9, 10-19, 20-29, 30-39, and 40-50 years old) may be "balance" for a mill that only requires 50-year-old trees to sustain its supply of raw materials, but it is not balance for a forest that can grow 400-year-old trees. Even if all five age classes were in one township, this would mean that most of the area would support seedlings, saplings, and pole-sized trees rather than mature trees.

To cut 60-year-old red spruce in the name of creating a balance of age classes is to impose an abstract, artificial construct on the forest. Certainly such trees are not overmature; they can live for many more decades. These older trees are also preferable for sawtimber over the young, even-aged stands that would replace them.

Landowner Performance

If a balanced age-class structure has been an industry goal, industry has failed to achieve it. An attempt by forest researchers Robert Seymour and Ronald Lemin, Jr., in 1989 to determine the age-class structure of Maine's forest shows that for all forest types looked at, the structure is far from balanced.[1] Seymour and Lemin have used a derived age-class structure as a basis for predicting future timber supply.[a] Their graphs show a dearth of trees in the 5-to-25-year range, which does not bode well for future decades when these stands will represent the supply of mature wood.[b]

Inadequate Regulations

Despite the importance attached to balanced age classes in the Forest Practices Act, the Maine Forest Service did not create regulations that would achieve this goal when it created its regeneration and clearcut rules in 1990. The standards only require a minimum of 3 age classes in townships dominated by one owner. And these age classes do not have to be balanced. With Class I clearcuts (5 to 35 acres), a landowner can clearcut 69% of the township (excluding the required buffer zones around water bodies) in the first 10 years, 30% in the second 10 years, and 1% in the last 10 years, leaving no mature trees. Landowners can now feel assured that their nonsustainable forest practices are regulated and legal.

Endnotes

a. To derive these age-class structures, Seymour and Lemin assumed, based on site quality, that trees of a certain height were a certain age and also that stands were even-aged, even if they were not. If, for example, a stand of 10 acres had 2 age classes, 30% being 50 years old and

Age-class structures for maple/beech/yellow birch and for spuce-fir forest types. Note that there are few good soil sites in either type dominated by trees over 55 years old. From R. S. Seymour and R. C. Lemin, Jr., *Timber Supply Projections for Maine, 1980-2080*, Maine Agricultural Experiment Station Miscellaneous Report (Orono, Me.: Maine Agricultural Experiment Station, University of Maine, 1989), p. 6-7.

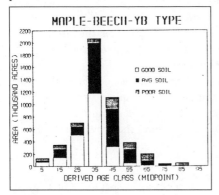 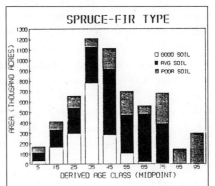

70% being 20 years old, Seymour and Lemin's computer model pretended that instead it was looking at 3 acres of 50-year-old trees and 7 acres of 20-year-old trees.[2]

b. The age structure derived from this attempt came out quite differently from previous attempts (see discussion in Chapter 5, Policy section). Previous attempts assumed more ample representation in younger age classes and less in the 20-to-40 year range. In either case, the forest has been deemed unbalanced, and the solution has been to do more intensive management (starting with clearcuts).

References

1. R. S. Seymour and R. C. Lemin, Jr., *Timber Supply Projections for Maine, 1980-2080*, Maine Agricultural Experiment Station Miscellaneous Report (Orono, Me.: Maine Agricultural Experiment Station, University of Maine, 1989), p. 6-7.

2. *Ibid.*, p. 15.

Myth 5

Sustainable forestry means that cut should be less than or equal to growth.

Problems with Formula

The first question one should ask of this formulation is, The cut *where* equals the growth *where*? The "growth" that the cut is compared to is growth on existing trees on other sites. Unless the question is specified, a manager can justify cutting most of the timber in one township, claiming that such removals are balanced by the growth of trees in another township. Some of the growth that is supposed to balance the cut may even be on trees that are inaccessible or in sensitive areas inappropriate for management.

One should also ask, The cut of *what* equals the growth of *what*? It makes a big difference if you are comparing cut and growth for all species, or for separate species and market types. One can hardly call cutting sustainable if loggers are cutting clear white pine logs, but the growth to which this is compared is on poplar fit for biomass.

Even if landowners are sustaining market values, they still may not be sustaining biological or recreational values. Loggers are not just cutting trees; they are cutting forests. Comparing the volume cut in uneven-aged, diverse forests with volume of growth in even-aged monocultures may make no difference to a computer that tallies up cut and growth statistics, but it makes a big difference to wildlife and people. And if ecological values are to be sustained, then loggers should not take all the annual growth. To do this would be to deprive the ecosystem of valuable habitat, organic matter, and nutrients.

There is also no guarantee that management will be sustainable on the site that is cut. What comes up after a clearcut often differs in quality, species ratio, wildlife habitat, visual qualities, soil fertility, and ecological stability from what was cut. The replacement stand, however, will not enter the growth statistics for decades. It is therefore not even considered.

Current Trends

According to a state study, the total level of cut is already exceeding total growth in Maine, and the total inventory of tree volume is now in decline:[1]

Year	Growing Stock Inventory[*]	Average Annual Growth[*]	Average Annual Removals[*]
1971	21,253	710.8	408.7
1982	22,796	471.587	349.550
1986	20,863	233.8	664.7[**]

[*]Figures represent millions of cubic feet of wood. A cord of pulpwood is approximately 85 cubic feet.

[**]The authors claimed that the removal rate for all species in 1986 was close to 720 million cubic feet, but that this figure is an average estimate with the range being between 645 and 890 million cubic feet of wood.

Declining Forest Inventory. From James F. Connors, *Forest for the Future: A Report on Maine's Forest to the Legislature, the Governor, and the People of Maine* (Augusta, Me.: Maine Department of Conservation, 1988), p. 9.

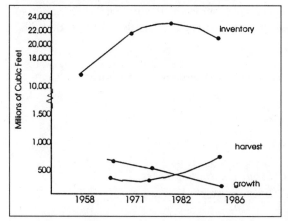

For most species, and for the forest as a whole, the current level of harvest, according to state data, is higher than the estimated sustainable harvest:[2]

Comparison of Sustainable Harvest with Current Harvest Levels
Total Volume (1,000-cord Units)

Species	Sustainable Harvest (After the Year 2000)[*]	Current Harvest[**]
Spruce-fir	2,844	3,346-5,067
Tolerant Hardwood	1,688	1,815-2,285
Aspen-White Birch	1,163	661-994
White Pine	537	736-1,093
Hemlock	392	341-497
TOTAL	**6,624**	**6,899-9,936**

*"Sustainable harvest" is the amount of wood that the state estimates can be consistently removed from the forest on an annual basis without depleting the timber resource. The year 2000 is used as a base year to allow time for establishment of what the state calls the "new forest." The sustainability of this "new forest" (mostly even aged) is challenged in this book.
**Because of uncertainty about current harvest levels, the state gives a range of figures, between which the actual values supposedly lie. Note that for spruce-fir, the higher figure for current harvest is more than 150% of the lower figure. This indicates a fairly large margin of error and demonstrates the unreliability of state statistics.

Inadequate Regulations
If these trends of inventory decline continue, there will be supply shortfalls for some mills within a few decades. Yet the state's Forest Practices Act does nothing to halt such trends. With either clearcuts or partial cuts, a landowner can legally cut the majority of the volume of timber in a township in just one year. And there are no limits to how many townships landowners can cut in at once. If large landowners do not flatten millions of acres in short order, it is due more to economics than to state regulations. A 1988 state study summed this up well: "The demand for forest products is determined by the free-market economy, so harvest levels are usually based on the amount of wood needed to supply the mills."[3]

References
1. James F. Connors, *Forest for the Future: A Report on Maine's Forest to the Legislature, the Governor, and the People of Maine* (Augusta, Me.: Maine Department of Conservation, 1988), p. 9.
2. *Ibid.*, p. 12.
3. *Ibid.*, p. 11.

Myth 6
Sustainable forestry means that cut should be less than or equal to expected future growth.

Mill capacity in Maine has been increasing to levels that require an annual cut greater than current annual growth. One does not need a computer to realize that if this continues, there will eventually be wood shortfalls. To ensure a sustainable level of cut, there are two options—either decrease demand or increase supply. A prudent policy would be to avoid increasing the cut until the annual growth has increased due to improved management. But industrial foresters have added a new twist to the cut/growth equation—the level of cut can be increased *now* in anticipation of greater growth (due to intensive management) *later*. This strategy is called the "Allowable Cut Effect" or the "Accelerated Cut Effect" (ACE).

Accelerated Cut
ACE is a gamble by which today's foresters get the benefits of higher levels of cuts, but future generations get the risks of mill shortfalls if intensive management does not lead to anticipated high yields. The promised high yields from planting, spraying herbicides, and thinning are not immediately realized; landowners must wait 3 or more decades. Foresters don't even know if the methods

will give predicted yields because intensive, even-aged management is relatively new to Maine and there are few long-term response data available.[1]

Rather than discourage such a gamble, state forestry authorities have condoned it. A 1988 state study, *Forest for the Future*, informed us that "landowners have responded to predictions of a wood shortage by increasing their efforts to plant, release and thin stands," and "stands that are intensively managed can grow three times the amount of wood that natural stands can produce."[2]

Forest Improvement: One Step Forward, Three Steps Back

While landowners may have increased their intensive management efforts during the 1980s, they also increased their level of clearcutting so that they were creating more acres of forest that are poorly stocked, overtopped, or overcrowded than were planted, sprayed with herbicides, or thinned.

Intensive Management Practices in Maine:
Average Annual Acreages 1982-1990[3]

Forest Practice	Average Annual Acreage	Percent of Clearcut Acreage
Clearcut*	112,446	100%
Herbicide Release	41,515	37%
Seed and Plant	7,327	6.5%
Precommercial Thin	6,227	5.5%

*The figure for clearcutting is undoubtedly well below the actual figure. These were figures voluntarily reported to the state.

Maine forest landowners did not start the 1980s with a clean slate. Even when all trees (no matter the species or quality) were considered, the USDA Forest Service (using criteria that, as discussed in Myth 2 of this section, are flawed) found 58.5% of the forest to be understocked or overstocked in 1971, and 73% of the forest to be understocked or overstocked in 1982.[4] Foresters would do more for the forest by preventing brush proliferation and unfavorable stocking than by creating such problems but only "fixing" a small percentage of them.

Unfair Comparisons

When foresters claim that intensive management can grow 3 times as much wood as a natural forest, they are neither speaking from experience nor being entirely honest. The figures for intensive management are theoretical. Herbicides alone do not ensure desired stocking of softwoods. The planting and thinning most likely will not be 100% effective due to site degradation, insect and disease problems, weather extremes, or other unanticipated problems.

The "natural" stands used for comparison are certainly not the high-volume, high-quality stands encountered by the first European settlers and loggers. Instead, they are stands that have been repeatedly degraded and are now stocked with low volumes of poor-quality trees. The comparison becomes even more unfair when the growth and volumes of all species except for spruce and fir are ignored.

135 The Industrial Forest

Environmental / Industrial Tradeoff

On the acres where it is practiced, intensive management will not triple the habitat for wildlife requiring mature, minimally disturbed forests. It will also not triple the visual qualities, ecological stability or opportunities for recreation and solitude. The focus is on managing the forest for a single purpose—fiber production.

Intensive management advocates claim that, on the contrary, there is actually no better way to benefit wildlife and recreation than to practice high-yield forestry on productive sites. Robert Seymour and Maxwell McCormack, Jr., researchers for the industry-sponsored Cooperative Forestry Research Unit and professors at the University of Maine's College of Forest Resources, contend that high-yield forestry will so increase spruce-fir productivity (by factors of 3 to 6 times) that less land (anywhere from 29% to 16% of current levels) will be needed to produce the same amount of fiber as is currently being grown; therefore, the surplus land can be used for multiple uses with nontimber values.[5] They emphasize that their approach is "win-win" for environmentalists and industry. "The irony," they write, "is that opponents of intensive forest management criticize the very practices that could free vast areas for their special use and management."[6]

Seymour and McCormack are here comparing the theoretical yields of only spruce-fir (ignoring all other species) on highly productive sites to yields of degraded stands on poor sites. They are also assuming that a balanced age-class structure is already in place. They do not address transition strategies to get to this stage (which would take a minimum of 40 years), but they do confess that "during the transition to this vision, much of the present mature timber may need to be harvested in order to sustain current industrial demands. Thus, the multiple-use forest of the future may have to be grown from young, recently harvested stands, just as the high-yield forest must be."[7]

What this environmental/industrial tradeoff entails, therefore, is for environmentalists to wait 40 years, as the entire forest gets cut over to sustain the mills, before they can recreate on abandoned clearcuts on poor sites. Even this benefit is in doubt, because projections done by Seymour (the same year as his article with McCormack), suggest that there will be no surplus land, not even abandoned clearcuts, on which environmentalists can recreate. He concluded that to avert shortfalls for spruce-fir and tolerant and intolerant hardwoods, landowners may need to increase intensive management acreage by a factor of 7 over current levels.[8] Since such increases in management would mean massive expenditures with no payback, in some cases, for more than 4 decades, it is doubtful shortfalls will be averted, let alone vast areas of land freed for recreation or wildlife.

Far from being a "win-win" stragegy, the environmental/industrial tradeoff would lead to an increase in the very practices people find abhorrent—clearcutting, herbicides, and plantations. The ACE strategy starts with the premise that we must sustain or increase current demand—but such a strategy cannot be continued indefinitely. If we want sustainable forestry or land set aside for wildlife and recreation, we will have to reduce demand. Those who depend on ACE to save us now will put future generations in the hole.

References
1. R. S. Seymour and R. C. Lemin, Jr., *Timber Supply Projections for Maine, 1980-2080*, Maine Agricultural Experiment Station Miscellaneous Report 337 (Orono, Me.: Maine Agricultural Experiment Station, University of Maine, 1988), p. 8.
2. James F. Connors, *Forest for the Future: A Report on Maine's Forest to the Legislature, the Governor, and the People of Maine* (Augusta, Me.: Maine Department of Conservation, 1988), pp. 9-10.
3. Ancyl Thurston, *Silvicultural Practices Report for 1990* (Augusta, Me.: Maine Forest Service, Maine Department of Conservation, 1991).
4. D. S. Powell and D. R. Dickson, *Forest Statistics for Maine—1971 and 1982*, USDA Forest Service Resource Bulletin NE-26 (Washington, D.C.: United States Forest Service, United States Department of Agriculture, 1984), p. 16.
5. Robert S. Seymour and Maxwell McCormack, Jr., "Having Our Forest and Harvesting It Too: The Role of Intensive Silviculture in Resolving Forest Land Use Conflicts." In R. D. Briggs et al., eds., *Forest and Wildlife Management in New England—What Can We Afford? Proceedings of a Joint Meeting of the Maine Division of the New England Society of American Foresters, Maine Chapter of the Wildlife Society, and the Atlantic International Chapter of the American Fisheries Society, March 15-17, 1989, Portland, Maine*, Maine Agricultural Experiment Station Miscellaneous Report 336 (Orono, Me: Maine Agricultural Experiment Station, University of Maine, 1989), p. 209.
6. *Ibid.*, p. 212.
7. *Ibid.*
8. R. S. Seymour and R. C. Lemin, Jr., *Timber Supply Projections*, p. 32.

Industrial Management Choices

In the 1970s industrial landowners started clearcutting to salvage the sizable spruce budworm-induced mortality of fir and spruce. Managers discovered they liked clearcutting so much that often they "salvaged" trees that weren't even dead, or that weren't even spruce or fir. After the budworm left, some companies couldn't stop mowing down every tree in sight—it had become a compulsive habit. They had the equipment, the technique, and the momentum.

The public, however, does not like clearcutting. Rather than stop, some companies decided to prove their responsibility by showing that clearcutting was part of an even-aged management system;[a] they started spraying herbicides, which the public also does not like. To a much smaller degree they also planted and thinned.

Industrial landowners are diverse in their management behavior. Some (such as Scott) clearcut and practice even-aged management more than others (such as Georgia-Pacific, or Fraser). But as a class, large industrial landowners out-clearcut all other landowner groups in Maine, including large nonindustrial landowners.[1]

Clearcut momentum: before (1975—*Photo by U.S. Geological Survey*). . .

and after (1991—*Photo by National Aerial Photography Program*). Scale: 1 inch = 0.7 miles. Photos show 6.3 square miles, more than 4,000 acres.

Reliance on Clearcutting and Even-aged Management*
Large Industrial vs. Large Non-industrial Owners, 1988

Ownership Class	Even-aged as % of Total Annual Harvest[b]	Clearcut as % of Even-aged Annual Harvest	Clearcut as % of Total AnnualHarvest[c]
Large Industrial	74%	81%	60%
Large Non-industrial	38%	39%	15%

*Includes shelterwood and seed-tree methods (see Endnote a).

The 1972 USDA Forest Service survey summed up reasons why companies like even-aged management systems, especially clearcutting: "Many advantages stem from its *suitability for highly mechanized logging*. With these harvesting systems individual *trees do not have to be marked* for cutting and a large volume of wood can be harvested with *less labor* at a *lower per unit cost* than with other harvesting systems."[2] [my emphasis] Another advantage of even-aged systems is the ease of estimating inventory; the landowner merely has to look at a map showing the distribution of even-aged blocks. With uneven-aged stands, the landowner must do periodic cruising to calculate the species, volume, and sizes of standing trees.

The advantages of clearcutting—less forester supervision and labor, higher wood volumes, and more mechanization—are short-term economic, not biological advantages. Industry's strategy has been to convince the public that the two criteria are synonymous. In one respect, industry is right: if a practice is bad biologically, in the long run it will be bad economically. But it does not follow that what is good (in the short run) economically is necessarily good biologically.

Industrial foresters have employed myths concerning the catastrophic forest, the forest as farm, the advantages of balanced age classes (idiot blocks), and the promise of high yields through intensive management to justify their penchant for clearcuts. But this has not been enough. A segment of the public is still shocked by what lies beyond the beauty strip. And they ask the irritating questions, Isn't there a better way to manage a forest than this? Why don't the companies use more selection cutting, which not only yields wood products but also leaves behind an aesthetically pleasing forest more suitable for wildlife and recreation?

Large industrial landowners, who as a group only reported using selection management on 4% of their cuts in 1988,[3] employ myths to convince the public that the choice of management system really is clear-cut. This is achieved by presenting the best case for clearcutting (assuming best management and high yields but somehow forgetting the costs required to establish a new stand) and the worst case for selection (assuming it is improperly done).

During the 1980s, in an effort to fend off regulations, the forest industry vociferously defended the necessity of clearcutting. In 1990, however, after clearcutting "standards" were finally in place, forest landowners reduced their clearcutting (as now defined by the state) by 43% from the previous year,[4] and in 1991 by another 18%. This raises some interesting questions. Should we be happy or sad that the landowners are responding to public concerns and not using what they previously declared was their most efficient form of management? Or, perhaps things have not changed so much. We do not really know how many of the "selection" cuts reported to the state were actually commercial clearcuts that left behind more than 30 square feet of basal area per acre. And many of the companies, due to a slow down in the economy and a dearth of spruce-fir, are cutting less wood.

Endnotes

a. Other even-aged management methods used in Maine include *shelterwood, strip cuts,* and *seed-tree harvesting.* With shelterwood, the overstory is partially cut one or more times to encourage regeneration; then, once regeneration is established, the overstory is completely removed. With stripcutting, foresters remove trees in narrow strips, alternating them with uncut strips. The uncut strips serve as both a shelter and seed source. Once regeneration is established (usually in ten years), the uncut strips are removed, leaving behind what appears as a clearcut. With seed-tree harvesting, which is used primarily for pine rather than spruce and fir (which are not as wind-firm), isolated trees are left after a clearcut to provide a seed source for the new stand.

Uneven-aged management methods include *single-tree selection* and *group selection* (where small clumps of trees, rather than individual trees, are harvested), both of which seek to establish three or more age classes in a stand.

There is a compromise system that falls somewhere between even- and uneven-aged management—*irregular shelterwood*, which maintains a forest with two age classes. With irregular shelterwood, unlike shelterwood, foresters do not cut the overstory after regeneration is established. Thus, there is always some shade, as with selection, but there is also a simplified stand structure as with clearcutting.

b. Some of the management methods not listed as even-aged, such as diameter-limit and single-species cuts, can at times resemble *commercial clearcuts* (in which all merchantable trees are cut) and actually create even-aged or two-aged stands rather than true uneven-aged stands. Therefore, the percentage of acreage cut under even-aged methods is probably higher than that reported to the state.

c. These figures are for acreage. If one looked at the percentage of volume that comes from clearcuts, the figures would be much higher because the volume of wood removed per acre with clearcuts is much higher than the volume removed per acre with partial cuts. If, for example, twice as much wood is cut per acre from a clearcut as from a partial cut, then 75% of the wood volume removed comes from the clearcuts on industrial land, even though the clearcuts comprise only 60% of the area. The total volume of wood that comes from all even-aged methods (including heavy diameter-limit and single-species cuts) on industrial land may be close to 90%.

References

1. Extrapolated from chart in Stephen Harper, Laura Falk, and Edward Rankin, *The Northern Forest Lands Study of New England and New York* (Rutland, Vt.: United States Forest Service, United States Department of Agriculture, spring 1990), p. 167.
2. R. H. Ferguson and N. P. Kingsley, *The Timber Resources of Maine*, USDA Forest Service Resource Bulletin NE-26 (Broomall, Pa.: United States Forest Service, United States Department of Agriculture, 1972), p. 6.
3. Extrapolated from chart in Stephen Harper, Laura Falk, and Edward Rankin, *The Northern Forest*, p. 167. chart in NFLS, p. 167.
4. Ancyl Thurston, *Silvicultural Practices Report for 1990* (Augusta, Me.: Maine Forest Service, Maine Department of Conservation, 1990).

Myth 1
Selection cutting degrades a forest.

Unfortunately, many people assume that any cut that is not a clearcut must be a selection cut. Indeed, the state promulgated this myth in its 1990 silvicultural report by making it appear that most cutting in Maine is by the "selection" method. A nonclearcut, however, should more properly be referred to as a "partial cut." There certainly are many examples of partial cuts in Maine that have led to site degradation, but these are not examples of the selection method. A 1988 state clearcutting study by the Irland Group informed readers that "Despite claims to the contrary, true selection cutting—resulting in multi-aged stands—has been rare in Maine, aside from limited research trials. This is because cutting has almost always been limited to merchantable stems."[1] Historically, loggers have selected the biggest and best trees and left the rest.[a] This is called high-grading and is not the same as the selection method where exactly the opposite takes place—the slow-growing, poor-quality, high-risk trees are removed first and the better trees are left to grow.

Under the selection method, tree quality should therefore improve. And where it has been applied, this has been the case. At the Penobscot Experimental Forest in Bradley, Maine, the U.S. Forest Service has been testing selection harvesting for 40 years with the result that "stand quality has improved most impressively."[2] There is full stocking of desirable trees and almost no culls (trees of poor quality for commercial purposes). Despite the fact that more volume has been cut than was in the original stands, stand volumes have been maintained or increased and average tree diameters have increased.

Foresters who insist they would degrade the forest if forced to selectively cut want the public to believe that, in contrast, they would improve the forest if allowed to clearcut. By admitting they would degrade their forests with selection, they are admitting irresponsibility. We therefore have a right to wonder why changing their management method would suddenly make them responsible. Irresponsible clearcutting can be far more devastating than irresponsible selection. Indeed, the Irland Group's study concluded that most such cuts in Maine were not responsible (i.e., done for stand improvement):

"Many logging operations have no professional forestry involvement; some carry out the worst kinds of commercial clearcuts. Clearcutting in these cases is simply logging and not a planned silvicultural practice. Even where professional supervision is applied, considerations of cost and administrative ease often overrule silvicultural and multiple use considerations. Also, even silviculturally proper applications of clearcutting all too often lack the follow-up that is needed to provide prompt, well-stocked, free-to-grow regeneration. And clearcutting is still being used when much less drastic alternatives might well be suitable."[2]

Endnote
a. If the diameter limits for some species, such as red spruce, are high enough (e.g., 16 inches), cutting only the biggest trees would not constitute high grading.

"Diameter-limit cutting misapplied." *Photo from Forrest Colby*, Forest Protection and Conservation in Maine, (*Augusta, Me: 1919*), *pg. 133*.

Robert Frank, forester at Penobscot Experimental Forest, shows off selection cut forest after seven entries. *Photo by Mitch Lansky*.

References

1. Irland Group, *Clearcutting as a Management Practice in Maine Forests, Report to the Maine Department of Conservation Forests for the Future Program* (Augusta, Me.: Irland Group, 1988), p. 15.
2. United States Forest Service, *Fact Sheet for First 40 Years of Results, C #90, MID-Intensive Selection* (Bradley, Me.: Penobscot Experimental Forest, March 1991).
3. Irland Group, *Clearcutting as a Management Practice*, pp.36-37.

Myth 2

Selection is an inappropriate method for harvesting spruce-fir because spruce-fir is naturally even-aged, is not wind-firm if partially cut, and in uneven-aged stands is more susceptible to spruce-budworm damage.

The industrial even-aged management system is geared, primarily, for growing spruce and fir. It is not used for growing tolerant hardwoods because the favored followup to clearcutting—herbicides—is designed to kill hardwoods. No company has spent money on planting or thinning hardwoods; indeed, industrial landowners have historically avoided managing hardwoods at all (except to convert them to softwood plantations).[a] When spruce and fir are present in a stand, however, industrial foresters have ready myths to justify taking all the trees at once.

Spruce-fir is naturally even-aged?

This myth is an extension of the myth of the catastrophic forest, which implies that the only way to manage spruce-fir is by "imitating" nature with clearcuts. As previously discussed, the catastrophes that managers imitate (or surpass) are partly induced or exacerbated by previous heavy-handed cutting. One only has to look at some of the existing old-growth spruce-fir in Maine to realize that spruce is fully capable of existing in uneven-aged stands. At Basin Pond in Baxter Park, for example, scientists estimate that the larger trees range in age from 111 years to more than 300 years.[1]

In their *Silvicultural Guide for Spruce-Fir in the Northeast*, USDA foresters Robert Frank and John Bjorkbom argue that uneven-aged management for spruce-fir is appropriate:

"Because spruce and fir are usually able to regenerate and grow under overhead shade, truly uneven-aged stands will develop in areas not drastically disturbed by nature or man. Thus the selection method is well adapted to the management of a spruce-fir stand. The periodic harvests maintain a continuous forest cover, and the retention of spruce seed trees can favor the regeneration of this species. These harvests may also increase the proportion of spruce by removing the shorter-lived balsam fir.

"Uneven-aged silviculture has other advantages. The growing space on each acre is more fully utilized in the vertical plane. The environmental conditions are more stable, and the plant and animal populations of the stand are

143 The Industrial Forest

more stable. Fire hazard from slash accumulations is less. In general, there is less chance of losing an entire stand at once through insect attack, infectious disease, or other natural catastrophe. And the area may appear more attractive to the esthetic-conscious public."[2]

Uneven-aged management in Maine's red spruce/balsam fir forests is not just theoretically possible, it has been demonstrated successfully at the Penobscot Experimental Forest in Bradley, Maine. Based on their experience managing such stands, USDA forestry researchers Robert Frank and Barton Blum concluded that "Except in the most degenerate forest stands, the concepts of selection system silviculture can be put into practice in most spruce-fir types. The goals and procedures we have set forth are believed to be both attainable and practical."[3] In contrast, clearcutting spruce-fir can lead to regeneration problems—proliferation of brush and overcrowding—that, unless treated in a timely fashion, can reduce yields and lengthen the time before trees are harvestable.

Spruce-fir is not wind-firm if partially cut?

Some industrial foresters complain that they tried selection cutting in spruce-fir and that many of the residual trees blew over. I encountered this claim at a spruce-budworm researchers' conference and discovered upon further investigation that it was based on attempts to do fir-only cuts during the worst of the latest spruce-budworm outbreak; it had little to do with selection cutting. The stands were even-aged and dominated by fir that were more than 60 years old. Balsam fir, regardless of its age, becomes subject to rot and windthrow when it gets larger. Because the stands had not been previously thinned, the trees, grown under crowded conditions, lacked adequate wind-firmness. A high proportion of the stands (sometimes 40% to 50%) were cut, maximizing the proportion of the forest that could be lost to windfall.[b] Fir-only cuts were a variation of the diameter-limit method and did not ensure that a stand was properly stocked, spaced, or managed for quality.[4]

A better approach would have been to remove a much smaller percentage of the stand at a time (15 to 20% at most), starting with the least wind-firm trees. The Penobscot Experimental Forest, which has many examples of partial cuts ranging from single-tree selection to preparatory shelterwood cuts, has had little problem with blowdowns.[5] Some blowdowns are expected from any silvicultural method, but, if a good road system is in place, it is not too difficult to come back into a stand for salvage a few years after an initial cut. Large clearcuts can create an especially bad blowdown problem along the edges of the cut, because there is nothing to stop the full impact of the wind. Since these edges are often along aquatic buffer strips that would not be harvested anyway, perhaps the industrial foresters do not see this as a loss.

Uneven-aged spruce-fir is more susceptible to spruce budworm damage?

The spruce budworm is the most important disturbance factor (aside from people) in the spruce-fir forests of Maine and eastern Canada. A budworm outbreak covered 200 million acres in the region in the 1970s and early 1980s, causing extensive damage and creating major costs. The budworm will undoubtedly return. Finding the most appropriate silvicultural technique for dealing with this insect is thus of great importance.

Gordon Baskerville, a forestry professor at the University of New Brunswick, has argued that "the natural tendency in the fir-spruce-birch forest is for even-aged stands derived from periodic disturbances by the budworm."[6] Baskerville (who was writing about a white spruce-fir rather than a red spruce-fir forest) argued that selection cutting creates increased susceptibility to attack from spruce budworm by maintaining a continuous mature canopy of "sun-foliage"— a favored budworm food. Indeed, Baskerville once told me that he had never seen a true uneven-aged forest in the region.

A 1988 Maine state publication comments that Baskerville's argument against selection cutting "is largely academic since there are actually very few uneven-aged stands in the state. . . . The cutting practices that were termed 'selection harvesting' in these stands during the 1950's and 1960's were actually partial cuts in even-aged stands, usually based on diameter limits. This harvesting left stands with a single age class, or with an overstory and regeneration, depending on the portion of the stand that was removed. These 'selection' cuts were at worst a euphemism for high-grading, and at best a form of thinning or shelterwood cut that attempted to discriminate against fir through the use of a lower diameter limit."[7]

The idea of actually managing stands to reduce susceptibility to the spruce budworm was tossed around earlier this century, even if few heeded the advice. Marinus Westveld, a USDA forester, addressed the Maine Timberland Owners Committee in Bangor in 1944, suggesting that there was still time for landowners to map their forests to identify susceptible stands and to build roads into them before a predicted epidemic hit in the 1950s. He cautioned that clearcutting such stands might amplify the budworm problem:

"Under the long cutting cycle system, stands are clearcut for merchantable sized spruce and fir, leaving trees ranging from reproduction to six inches d.b.h., with balsam usually the predominant species. Often 40 to 60 years must elapse before the new growth attains sufficient value to justify another cut. This period is of sufficient length, however, to permit considerable numbers of short lived, fast growing balsam to reach maturity and succumb to windfall and decay. . . . The clearcutting system with its attendant long cutting cycle is basically unsuited to the broad objectives of maintaining maximum production in spruce-fir stands. The selection system with its light but relatively frequent cut is the logical answer to these losses."[8]

Westveld pointed out that more frequent entries would capture potential losses, lessen the proportion of fir, increase the vigor of the stand, and also lead to higher yields (he figured double that of clearcutting), ". . . thus offsetting such added costs which may arise through lighter volume removals. . . . The point I've been trying to make," he said, "is that good forest management is good business."[9]

The timberland owners apparently were not moved by Westveld's appeal to "good business." The short-term approach continued to be the long-term strategy. Fortunately, Westveld's approach was tried at the Penobscot Experimental

Forest. After three decades and a major budworm epidemic in the 1970s to test the theory, the preliminary results are promising. A comparison in 1986 of commercially clearcut and selectively managed stands showed that the selection stands had a quarter of the overall mortality in all species. In budworm-susceptible species there was an even more dramatic difference. In the clearcut stand, budworm caused 99% of the mortality; in the managed stands, it caused only 2%.[10] Obviously, Baskerville's sun-foliage was not a problem here.

Endnotes

a. Some hardwood species, especially red maples, that are considered inferior for lumber tend to sprout abundantly after a clearcut. Aspen sends up root sprouts as well as copious seeds. Improving a hardwood stand dominated by numerous stems and sprouts can be very expensive. According to USDA Forest Service researchers Ferguson and Kingsley, "Most of Maine's northern hardwoods have been managed very little, if at all. Most have been harvested by high-grading methods, which removed only the high-value species or the best-quality trees." For managing hardwoods, they recommend the selection system, which "favors the very tolerant species such as sugar maple, beech, hemlock, and red spruce. Where adequate markets for these species are available, or where aesthetic considerations are important, the selection system is the preferred method."[11]

b. According to former U.S. Forest Service researcher Gordon Mott, the percentage of a stand lost to windthrow peaks when approximately half the trees are removed. Cut less and the stand will be more wind-firm. Cut more and a higher percentage of the residual stand will be lost, but the residual stand will be smaller, so the total loss to wind will be less.[12]

References

1. Lissa Widoff, ed., *Natural Old-growth Forest Stands in Maine*, Maine Critical Areas Program Planning Report No. 79 (Augusta, Me.: Maine State Planning Office, 1983), p. 77.
2. Robert Frank and John Bjorkbom, *A Silvicultural Guide for Spruce-Fir in the Northeast*, General Technical Report NE-6 (Orono, Me.: USDA Forest Service, 1973), p. 6.
3. Robert Frank and Barton Blum, *The Selection System of Silviculture in Spruce-Fir Stands—Proceedings and Early Results and Comparisons with Unmanaged Stands*, Research Paper NE-425, (Orono, Me.: USDA Forest Service, 1978), p. 15.
4. Mitch Lansky, "Maine Quits Spray Program: But They're Not Out of the Woods," *Rural Delivery*, Vol. 10 (March 1986): 15.
5. Robert Frank, personal communication, spring 1991.
6. Gordon Baskerville, "Spruce Budworm: The Answer Is Forest Management—Or Is It?" *Forestry Chronicle*, Vol. 51 (1975): 157-160.
7. Lloyd C. Irland, John B. Dimond, Judy L. Stone, Jonathan Falk, and Ellen Baum, *The Spruce Budworm Outbreak in Maine in the 1970's—Assessment and Directions for the Future* (Orono, Me.: Maine Agricultural Experiment Station, University of Maine, October 1988).
8. Marinus Westveld, "There Is Nothing New Under the Sun—Forest Management as a Measure for Controlling the Spruce Budworm," *The Maine Forest Review*, Vol. 13 (1980): 52.
9. *Ibid.*, p. 52.
10. Mitch Lansky, "Budworm Proofing the Forest," *Rural Delivery* (April 1986): 14.
11. R. H. Ferguson and N. P. Kingsley, *The Timber Resources of Maine*, USDA Forest Service Resource Bulletin NE-26 (Broomall, Pa.: United States Forest Service, United States Department of Agriculture, 1972), p. 31.
12. Mitch Lansky, "Maine Quits Spray Program," p. 15.

Myth 3

Clearcutting is superior to selection because it
requires fewer stand entries and fewer roads.

With this myth, clearcut advocates conveniently ignore the follow-up management required for improved yields on short rotations. They are comparing the inconveniences and costs of intensive selection management to the minimal costs involved in cut-and-run. Without frequent entries, yields of even-aged management would be relatively low, because (as pointed out in the last myth) the long cutting cycles would lead to domination by low-quality trees and to significant losses of short-lived trees to mortality. Frequent entries capture potential mortality, remove poor-quality and high-risk trees, and change species ratios to favor longer-lived, higher quality trees. According to U.S. Forest Service researcher Bob Frank, the number of entries into intensely managed even- and uneven-aged stands should be similar.[1] For example, an even-aged unit with a 45-year rotation might require an entry at 15 years for precommercial thinning and another at 30 years for a commercial thinning—thus, once every 15 years, about the same as the cutting cycle for selection cutting.

While it is true that more acres must be cut with selection to get the same amount of wood as from clearcutting, it does not follow that selection requires more roads. Once an area is under management, it needs roads whether it is under even- or uneven-aged management. Since actual even- and uneven-aged management require similar cutting cycles, the need for permanent roads would be the same. The difference would be that the roads required to carry the concentrated loads associated with clearcuts would have to be more substantial than the roads required to handle the lighter cuts per acre associated with selection.

Reference
1. Frank, Robert, personal communication, spring 1991.

Myth 4

Selection is undesirable because it is too labor
intensive compared to clearcutting.

Given its ease of mechanization and simpler management goals, clearcutting requires fewer workers and less skill than selection cutting. It also requires less forester involvement because there is no need to mark trees or do complicated inventory analysis. Requiring skilled labor, however, is not "undesirable" from the perspective of workers or local communities. Indeed, it is an insult to such communities for companies to import expensive machinery and chemicals that force local workers out of jobs. A reduction in labor can only be considered an advantage if workers are unavailable and if the resulting long-term management is more ecologically sound, productive, and economically viable. None of these, however, is the case.

Managers are motivated to do mechanized clearcutting more to avoid labor than to improve forest stands. They cannot completely avoid labor, however, if they want well-stocked stands of quality trees. Even spraying herbicides from helicopters (another way to avoid labor) is not by itself adequate to address unevenness of softwood stocking. Often the result is gaps with too few trees and clumps with too many. If managers are going to harvest fully stocked stands of good-quality trees on a short rotation, as they claim, they will have to employ workers either to plant or thin, or both.

Such seasonal jobs, however, do not always go to local workers. They sometimes go to migrant workers from other states. Indeed, at least one paper company has lowered its planting and thinning costs by hiring Mexican farm workers.[1] Clearcutting, combined with intensive even-aged management, therefore transfers skilled local jobs to workers in machinery and chemical factories in other states or to migrant workers doing repetitive "stoop work."

A major impediment to labor for selection cutting in Maine is the piece-rate payment system where woodcutters are paid by the cord to remove trees rather than by the job or by the hour, day, or week to manage forests. The piece-rate payment system is a disincentive to do careful management. It also leads to a high accident rate, which leads to high insurance rates—another disincentive to use labor. On a piece rate, the highest pay goes to those who cut the biggest and best as fast as possible with no regard for what is left behind. Those workers who remove poor-quality trees and take more time to protect residual trees and advanced regeneration end up making less money. As long as workers are paid on a piece rate, contractors will complain that they cannot afford to do the initial stages of selection (where small volumes of low-quality wood are removed per acre). Hence, landowners can claim that getting labor for selection is impractical. If the landowners can afford to spend money for plantations, herbicides, and precommercial thinning, where there is no immediate return, they should be able to afford to pay workers to do selection management so that these other expenses become unnecessary.

Reference
1. Robert Seymour, personal communication, spring 1991.

Myth 5
Clearcutting on short rotation is more productive than selection cutting.

Until the 1970s, forest productivity was not an issue because paper companies had surplus land that supplied more growth than they needed to cut. The companies spent little money on forest management; loggers cut the trees and more trees grew back. A combination of increased mill capacity and a major spruce budworm outbreak ended this surplus. The forest inventory is now in decline, and companies can no longer rely on abandoned farmland to increase forest acreage in the future. If anything, the commercial forest base may diminish as land is withdrawn for development or wilderness parks. Industrial landowners will have to grow more wood per acre if they wish to keep their mills running at current or increased capacity. Productivity is now a major issue.

To increase productivity, industrial foresters have focused on "intensive," even-aged management, i.e., the planting, herbicide spraying, and precommercial thinning that follow clearcuts. Some foresters claim that they can, with these techniques, get high yields in as little as 35 or 40 years. Unfortunately, discussions on productivity, because they are in forester jargon are beyond the scope of much of the public. It has become a truism in Maine that clearcutting on short rotation is the way to maximize yields. "Younger stands," reasons a 1988 state report, "normally grow faster than old ones, so a given acreage will grow more wood if it is in younger age classes."[1]

This statement, which confuses growth *rate* with *annual increment*, is a poor foundation upon which to base a more productive forest. In an 80 year rotation for an even-aged stand, for example, there is actually more volume and higher quality being grown in the last 40 years than in the first. Short rotations *reduce* productivity in many ways:

Productivity of What?

Industrial foresters view the concept of productivity very narrowly. They look at productivity of spruce-fir fiber for their mills in the short term and not at productivity of quality sawlogs, mature-forest wildlife habitat, soil fertility, or water quality in the long term. They assert that short-rotation forestry is so productive that it indirectly benefits these other values by allowing other lands to be managed primarily for nontimber benefits. The loss of any of these values on intensively managed lands (and many foresters will even deny that this occurs) should be seen as a sacrifice, or tradeoff, for nontimber values elsewhere.

But is intensive, even-aged management the most productive way to grow fiber? Unfortunately, there are insufficient data to verify the long-term productivity of any silvicultural method in Maine, especially intensive, even-aged management. Any comparisons (including this one) thus have to rely on theory and evidence from short-term studies. To be fair, the comparison has to be for the same products on the same site types.

Why Intensive Management?

Without some followup management, clearcutting can lower productivity because the initial clearcut removes trees that are at their growth peak, starting the stand back to zero. The regeneration can be dominated by pioneer species, stump sprouts, and overcrowded clumps of balsam fir. When stands are so crowded, they do not reach a merchantable diameter (depending on site quality) for more than 70 years—long enough to allow considerable loss of trees (and thus potential fiber) to mortality.

Why Short Rotations?

Herbicide spraying, planting, and precommercial thinning are used to concentrate growth on desired softwood species and to space trees so they achieve larger diameters faster. These forms of early stand management require landowners to invest considerable money with payback decades away. Landowners have an incentive to cut the trees sooner rather than later, because the trees do not grow as fast as the interest on their management investment.

Short-rotation Productivity

The wider the spacing, the sooner trees reach a merchantable diameter. The important figure for forest productivity, however, is not the length of rotation, but the average growth per acre per year—the Mean Annual Increment (MAI). Paradoxically, the wider the spacing, the longer the rotations should be to attain maximum productivity, despite the earlier mechantability.

Biologists have postulated a Law of Constant Final Yield, which, according to Roy Silen, a USDA Forest Service researcher in the Pacific Northwest, states that "final yield per unit area is a constant and independent of plant density. At any initial spacing, plants grow rapidly at first to fill out a complete canopy, then individual plant growth slows as competition between plants increases. Finally, competition is so severe that the only additions to yield are from space made available as a plant dies from suppression. This law proposes that this final gross yield is equal or constant at any spacing, and that the difference in spacing only influences the time required to reach the constant final yield. Final yield is approached most quickly at densest spacing."[2]

This principle was dramatically demonstrated by a thinning experiment in Nova Scotia.[3] Fifteen-year-old stands of red spruce were thinned to 4' x 4', 6' x 6', 8' x 8', and 9.5' x 9.5'. Fifteen years later, the control plot (which had not been thinned) had the highest total volume while the 9.5'-x-9.5' spacing had the lowest. Because the average diameter of the trees in the control plot was so small, however, that plot had the lowest merchantable volume. The highest merchantable volume was in the stands thinned to 4' x 4'.

The researchers estimated that the peak of average annual growth (the Culmination of Mean Annual Increment, or CMAI) of all the stands would be the same, about one cord per acre per year, regardless of spacing. This peak, however, would be reached soonest at the closest spacing. Indeed, the CMAI at the closest spacing was estimated to come 25 years earlier than at the widest spacing. Thus, even though the widely spaced stands reached the highest percentage of merchantable volume soonest, cutting these stands before the CMAI is attained would lower productivity, not raise it.

Tree Quality

When comparing productivity, what matters is not just quantity, but quality. One large veneer quality hardwood is worth more to a landowner than an acre of biomass. A University of Maine study published in 1991 compared the volume and quality of black spruce trees grown in 77-year-old unthinned stands versus that of trees grown in 29-year-old stands that had been released (with herbicides) and thinned (to 8' x 8') 10 years previously.[4] Although the average diameters of trees from the two stands were nearly the same, trees from the older stand averaged 18 feet taller and thus had 1.9 times more volume of wood per tree. The researchers did not compare total volumes per acre, but since the unthinned stand was more densely stocked, and each tree had more volume, one can conclude that the unthinned stand had far more volume per acre.

The quality of the wood in the thinned stand was inferior in several ways that would lower its merchantable-yield value. Wood from the unthinned stand, for example, had a 10% higher specific gravity (density) than wood from the thinned stands and would thus have as much as 10% higher yield of pulp per unit of wood from this factor alone.

Pulp yields are also affected by the amount of lignin, a natural glue that holds wood fibers together and must be extracted in the pulping process. Lignin content is higher in juvenile wood (young-growth) than in mature wood. It normally takes 60 years for spruce to put on mature wood. Thus, short-rotation trees are still in the juvenile stage when they are cut.

Trees in the thinned stands also had a high proportion of compression wood (which tends to form on the underside of branches), which also contains a high proportion of lignins. While the living crown (branches with foliage) on the average tree in the unthinned stands occupied 31% of the total height, the crown on the average tree in the thinned stands occupied 94% of the total height. Indeed, the lower branches of the trees in the thinned stands touched the ground. Higher lignin content means lower fiber yields, higher energy and chemical costs, and more mill pollution.

Because of the greater taper, higher proportion of knots, and fatter growth rings (which leads to less strength), the wood from the thinned stands is also inferior for lumber. Each tree would yield fewer boards and the lumber would have to be sold at a lower grade.

Herbicide spraying, which was supposed to increase productivity of spruce-fir by suppressing overtopping hardwoods, actually did little for the spruce-fir but reduced growth of other species. The authors state that "the relatively high pre-release growth rate and the small diameter growth response suggests that many of the trees that presently comprise the stand were experiencing relatively little competition prior to release, either from the overtopping birch and aspen, or from other black spruce."[5] The combination of hardwoods and spruce-fir would create much greater overall yields than the growth of the spruce-fir alone. The hardwoods also might protect the understory spruce-fir from weather extremes and depredation by insects such as the spruce budworm.

Advantages of Selection

Uneven-aged management has productivity advantages over even-aged management even if the even-aged stands are harvested at the CMAI:

Stand Structure

A multispecies, uneven-aged stand makes more efficient use of space, light, and nutrients than does an even-aged stand dominated by one or two species. In the even-aged stands, the trees, which all have the same needs and have roots and crowns at the same levels, are forced to compete with each other for light and nutrients. In uneven-aged stands, shade-tolerant trees of all ages fill spaces in the understory that in an even-aged stand would be empty. The roots of different species have different nutrient needs and occupy different levels in the soil.

After an even-aged stand is clearcut, there is often a time lag as regeneration is established (this is avoided with shelterwood). With uneven-aged stands, there is no lag between harvest and regeneration establishment because shade-tolerant young trees are already growing in the understory. Over many rotations, this should mean a substantial productivity advantage.

Stand Volume

Just as money productivity is a function of capital, interest, and risk, forest productivity is a function of standing volume, tree growth rate, and risk. At a 3% growth rate, a forest with 40 standing cords of wood per acre will put on 1.2 cords per acre per year, but a forest with 15 standing cords of wood per acre (which happens to be the average stand volume for Maine's forests) will put on only 0.45 cords per acre per year (the average prior to the spruce budworm outbreak after the 1970's).

Canadian forester Stephen Manley estimates that on better sites in the presettlement Acadian forest, stand volumes were as high as 50 to 80 cords, with a gross annual increment of up to 2.5 cords per acre per year. He contends, however, that the boreal-type stands of balsam fir and white and black spruce that foresters are encouraging on former mixedwood sites have an upper-yield limit of 1 to 1.5 cords per acre per year.[6]

If foresters follow the conservative practice of focusing cutting on trees that have ceased growing, they can have an annual income while allowing the standing volume of growing trees to increase until it reaches the optimum for the site. Such a strategy would improve long-term productivity better than clearcutting, which removes trees that are still putting on ample growth. It is far more efficient to grow fiber on existing trees than to start growing it on seedlings.

Risk

With diverse, uneven-aged stands, the long-term risk of catastrophic loss is less than with even-aged stands dominated by only one or two species. If insects or disease kill mature trees in the uneven-aged stands, the trees can often be salvaged. If insects or disease kill the trees in a young, even-aged stand where none of the trees have reached merchantable size, the loss can be total.

B. A. Pendrel and T. R. Renault, researchers for the Maritimes Forest Research Centre, have concluded that "the belief that the larger monocultures suffer relatively larger, more intense pest problems seems firmly rooted in reality. Not just monocultures are susceptible, but semi-monocultures and unnatural concentrations that replace the natural diverse forest can be detrimental. These problems arise from the destruction of the former complex community and subsequent reduction in natural enemies of insects or barriers to disease spread. Tree pests remaining in a simplified situation are free to increase in the absence of their normal controls."[7]

Soil Fertility

Clearcutting leads to nutrient losses from removal of biomass and from nutrient leaching in bare soil. Converting a mixedwood or hardwood forest to boreal softwoods tends to degrade the soil further, making it more acidic, leaching out calcium, magnesium, and other alkaline minerals, and impoverishing the communities of soil microorganisms. Landowners have the choice of allowing the site to decline or spending money for fertilizers in the hope of minimizing some of the problems they have caused.

Uneven-aged stands with a hardwood component have a better, more reliable source of fertilizer—the tons of leaves that drop every fall. The difference in soil fertility and thus potential site productivity between the two methods would become pronounced over several rotations.

Products

Per given volume, trees grown under uneven-aged silviculture yield more fiber and lumber of higher quality than trees grown in even-aged stands on a short rotation. And if one looks at productivity of clean water, warblers, salamanders, flying squirrels, or pine martens, there is no contest—short-rotation, even-aged silviculture isn't in the same league.

References

1. James F. Connors, *Forest for the Future: A Report on Maine's Forest to the Legislature, the Governor, and the People of Maine* (Augusta, Me.: Maine Department of Conservation, 1988), p. 6.
2. Roy R. Silen, *Nitrogen, Corn, and Forest Genetics: The Agricultural Yield Strategy Implications for Douglas-Fir Management*, USDA Forest Service, Pacific Northwest Forest and Range Experimental Station General Technical Report PNW-137 (Portland, Ore.: United States Forest Service, Northwest Forest and Range Experimental Station, 1982): p. 5.
3. *Fifteen Year Assessment of Thirty Year Old Red Spruce Stands Cleaned at Various Intensities in Nova Scotia*, Forest Research Report No. 2 (Truro, Nova Scotia: Nova Scotia Department of Lands and Forests, 1988).
4. Robert K. Shepard, James E. Shottafer, and William C. Bragg, *Stand Age and Density Effects on Volume and Specific Gravity of Black Spruce*, Maine Agricultural Experiment Station Technical Bulletin 139 (Orono, Me.: Maine Agricultural Experiment Station, University of Maine, 1991).
5. *Ibid.*, p. 4.
6. Stephen Manley, speech sponsored by the Forest Committee of the Environmental Coalition of Prince Edward Island and the Eastern Woodlands Association, Montague, Prince Edward Island, November 3, 1989.
7. B. A. Pendrel and T. R. Renault,"Insects and Diseases in Plantations." In R. D. Hallett, M. D. Cameron, and T. S. Murray, eds., *Reforestation in the Maritimes* (Fredericton, New Brunswick: Maritimes Research Centre, 1984), p. 138.

Myth 6

Clearcutting is the most cost-effective way to manage forests in Maine. Corollary: Managers cannot afford to use selection.

Concerns over ecological stability, wildlife habitat, watershed protection, and recreation values are all well and good, but the bottom line, as we all know, is money. Some industrial foresters would like us to believe that when it comes to economic returns on forest management, there is simply no contest: clearcutting is the only way to go. Forcing foresters to use any other method, we are told, would be to impose an economic loss. The companies simply cannot afford to selectively cut. Even many environmentalists grow timid when confronted with such a hard-nosed "reality" and are prepared to make the environmental/industrial trade-off.

The key word here, however, is *management*. This means looking at the costs and benefits over at least one rotation, not for just one cut. For a single cut, commercial clearcuts (which the forest industry reported doing on 35% of its harvests in 1989)[1], give the best returns per unit of roads, labor, and equipment. I wish I could demonstrate some economic imperative that would compel landowners to manage for ecological and social benefits, but in our current political/economic context, I cannot. From a strictly short-term economic perspective, it is hard to beat exploitive management for the following reasons:

•*Cut and Sell.* The timber on a forested lot may be worth more than the market value of the land. An entrepreneur need only purchase the land and remove all the timber to make a tidy profit—and then subdivide the land and sell it for development.

•*Devalue Land.* Corporations that have undervalued land can be targets for leveraged takeovers. Clearcutting the forest may be a way to make money and fend off such hostile companies.

•*Pay Off Debt.* Companies that have bought out other companies can clearcut to help pay off the debt incurred by the purchase.

•*Liquidate Assets.* A landowner with good business acumen can liquidate a forest and invest the revenues in more profitable enterprises than growing trees in Maine.

Such cutting strategies hardly qualify, however, as long-term, sustainable management. Assuming that a landowner does want to manage the forest for the long term, then selection seems to have the most advantages:

•Each entry pays for itself, though admittedly, the first one or two cuts, which remove low volumes of poor-quality wood, do not pay very well. The returns on later cuts, which contain high-quality, large-diameter wood, are high.

•Logging costs for large-diameter wood are lower than for small-diameter wood.

Another explanation for clearcutting; attempts to communicate with aliens by use of snail and moth motif? *Photo by Alex MacLean/Landslides.*

•There is more flexibility in management. After cutting selectively, you still have a forest and can apply any other management method later.

•Well-stocked land has a higher market value than denuded land.

•The forest is not subject to the vagaries of a single market. It contains a diversity of products suitable for diverse, often high-paying, markets. Markets can be more specialized and local.

•Local economic stability is greater due to a more stable, highly skilled workforce.

•The value (which cannot be accurately quantified) of the forest for wildlife, recreation, and watersheds is maintained.

After a clearcut, the picture is very different:

•The early stand management that follows does not pay for itself at normal business discount rates and at current values for management and wood (see following examples).

•Loggers cut smaller diameter trees that still have great growth potential. There is an economic as well as biological loss because it is cheaper to grow wood on existing trees than on seedlings.

•There is little flexibility in management once the forest is gone.

•Money invested in early stand management gets tied up for half a century.

•Denuded land has a lower market value than well-stocked forested land.

•Markets for a single-aged, single-species forest are limited. This can be a problem if the trees are due to be cut when the markets are bad. A short rotation does not allow for growth of highest-quality trees for highest-paying markets.

•Mechanization and migrant labor do not lead to as much community stability.

•The market value of land near clearcuts may be diminished. Neighbors may object not only to clearcutting but to herbicide spraying. There may be protests and legal suits.

•The value of denuded land for wildlife, recreation, and watersheds is diminished.

Despite all this, creative economists can manipulate the variables and, by ignoring all values but timber, calculate impressive returns for investments in even-aged management. These cost-benefit analyses, written in jargon alien to the average citizen, create the illusion that for the cold, hard, economic realist, clearcutting and intensive management are the only option. The degree to which these economists must manipulate the variables to show a decent return, however, demonstrates the shakiness of such investments.

Two ways to analyze the economics of early stand management are (1) to look at costs and benefits for a particular site over time and (2) to look at costs and benefits of a management strategy for the entire landholding on an annual basis. I examine examples of each method.

Example 1: Net Present Value

The first example, by David Maass of the Irland Group and Bret Vicary of the

James M. Sewell Company, looks at the costs and benefits of establishing spruce plantations at different spacings, with or without herbicides.[2] Maass and Vicary estimate that planting 800 trees per acre and spraying herbicides once (in the second year) will yield 50 cords of wood in 50 years with a Net Present Value of $237 per acre—a 5.5% return above inflation for a 50-year investment.[a] To accomplish this feat, the authors use low estimates for costs, high estimates for benefits, and a low discount rate.[b] Using more realistic figures for costs, benefits, and discount rates, however, shows the investment to be a loss, not a gain.

Costs

•Plantation establishment. The authors give a figure of $192 per acre for plantation establishment. If site preparation is needed (which it has been on nearly half the plantings in Maine)[3], the figure could be more than $100 dollars higher, and the investment would be a loss.

•Herbicides. The cost of herbicide application varies according to the site and application method. The authors give a figure of $45 per acre for herbicide spraying, a figure that is well below the one I obtained from government sources. The Bureau of Public Lands, for example, estimated in 1989 that applying herbicides would cost $65 per acre (see Chapter 3). The figures can be even higher if more than one application is required. Landowners (according to state timber-harvest reports) have reported that 6% of their herbicide applications are repeats.[4]

•Thinning. The authors assume that spraying herbicides in the second year is the last silvicultural activity until harvest, at year 50. A plantation monitoring report from New Brunswick, however, shows that the average density (of numbers) and height of volunteer softwoods is often greater than the density and height of the crop trees.[5] If the volunteer density is too great, the crop trees may not attain diameters suitable for lumber in 50 years. The cost of thinning varies from less than $100 to more than $300 per acre, depending on tree densities. With precommercial thinning the investment would be a loss.

•Insecticides. The authors assume that over a 50-year period there will be no outbreaks of spruce budworm or other insects that would cause mortality or reduce growth. They assume no costs for monitoring or spraying the stand to protect the original investment. If the spraying must be done early in stand development, the costs must be carried over a longer time period, leading to a loss.

•Land costs. The authors ignore costs of taxes and overhead over the rotation.

Benefits

•Yields. The assumption of high yields on a short rotation is not based on long-term experience. The authors assume no losses or growth reduction from insects, disease, droughts or other factors. They admit that "Real data and better computer models would provide better information."

•Products. The authors assume that in 50 years, with no thinning, pruning, or protection from insects, 60% of the volume of wood will be suitable for sawlogs. The stumpage value they attribute to sawlogs is more than twice the value they attribute to pulpwood. The total future product value is thus 60%

higher than if the wood were used only for pulpwood. With other assumptions remaining the same, if the wood is not suitable for lumber, its NPV would be $61 per acre.

•Future product value. The authors assume that the stumpage values of both sawlogs and pulpwood will increase faster than inflation by 1% a year for the first 20 years and 3% a year for the last 30 years. This, in effect, triples the real value of the wood (accounting for inflation). They assume these values will increase due to an impending wood shortfall.

While such increases would be a boon for nonindustrial landowners, the paper companies, which have leverage over wood purchase prices, will not readily allow such increases. Predicting market values 50 years in the future is wildly speculative. The demand for sawlogs, for example, could diminish if the housing industry slumps (as it recently has). The demand for pulpwood could diminish as the nation aggressively shifts towards recycling and conservation, or as the economy slumps (as it has). Furthermore, the mills can import wood and chips, dampening local supply/demand effects (as they are doing). Ironically, if the supporters of plantation management are correct about high yields, and if enough landowners are convinced to manage intensively, the result might be a wood surplus, with real prices (adjusted for inflation) going down.

If stumpage stays even with inflation, rather than tripling, the Net Present Value would be reduced from a profit $237 per acre to a loss of -$71.61 per acre, assuming all the other variables remain unchanged! If the stumpage values increase as predicted, this would make selection cutting, one alternative to plantation management, even more cost-beneficial.

•Discount rate. The authors use a 4% discount rate (which they call "fairly modest") because "for most industrial landowners there is little risk involved with these types of investments." That risks are low for a 50-year investment in a spruce monoculture is debatable. Even a slight change in the discount can have dramatic effects on the Net Present Value (assuming their other assumptions are valid).

–at 4% discount, NPV per acre = $237
–at 5% discount, NPV per acre = $59.05
–at 6% discount, NPV per acre= -$50.30

Thus, if costs are more realistic, if yields are not as high, if stumpage values do not rise as expected and if the discount rate is closer to industrial standards, investment in plantations would lead to a major net loss. Even if all of Maass and Vicary's happy estimates are correct, a prudent investor might ask, "Why should I spend hundreds of dollars per acre on this denuded land for a speculative return that I will not live to see?" If the goal of the investment is to do future generations a favor, then the altruistic landowner would do better not to clearcut the land in the first place.

Example 2: Annual Costs and Benefits
Maxwell McCormack, Jr., and Robert Seymour have done an analysis which examines the annual costs and benefits for the entire ownership (rather than just the individual stand being managed). They concluded that investment in high-

yield silviculture was more cost-beneficial than "no silviculture" (which is what they call current general practice). McCormack and Seymour pointed out that economists comparing silvicultural options should include the annual costs of owning the land, which they estimated at $2.50 per acre per year for Maine—$1.00 for taxes and $1.50 for overhead (i.e., staff, inventory, road and boundary maintenance, and other costs related to land ownership). They admit that this estimate may be "conservative."

They looked at three scenarios—spraying herbicides over stands that already have good stocking of softwoods, spraying plus planting or thinning (to ensure adequate stocking if there were too few or too many trees), and spraying plus planting genetically improved, fast-growing trees. Since, they reasoned, the high-yield silviculture would grow so much more wood per acre (supposedly from 340% to 630%), managers would need much less land to produce the same volume of wood and thus not have to pay as much in land costs. McCormack and Seymour estimated that to produce 100,000 cords of spruce and fir, the annual costs (assuming that landowners got rid of their surplus land) for three of these scenarios would be as follows.[6]

Land Costs

	No Silviculture	Herbicides	Plant/PCT*
Acres	357,000	104,000	78,000
Cost (at $2.50/acre)	$892,000	$260,000	$195,000

*PCT stands for precommercial thinning

Silviculture Costs

	No Silviculture	Herbicides	Plant/PCT
Cost/acre	0	$50	$200
Annual Acreage Treated	5,100	2,080	1,950
Annual Cost	0	$104,000	$390,000

Total Costs (Land + Silviculture)

No Silviculture	Herbicides	Plant/PCT
$892,000	$364,000	$585,000

McCormack and Seymour reach their optimistic conclusions by incorporating fudge factors wherever possible to inflate benefits and deflate costs.

Fudge Factors

Yields

The high yields are only obtainable on good sites (usually former hardwood sites). The best option (simply spraying herbicides on hardwood sites that, by some good fortune, have regenerated to well-stocked softwood) is not very likely, so McCormack and Seymour admit that planting may be needed. Since best sites are limited, silviculture applied to fair sites would be needed, so the average yield would go down. The yields are highly optimistic and not based on experience or any consideration of risk.

The yields of hardwoods and even other softwoods, such as white pine, are completely ignored for the "no-silviculture" option; McCormack and Seymour are completely fixated on spruce-fir. Other management options, such as selection or even an irregular shelterwood, that would also increase yields above the cut-and-run strategy but at lower investment costs and with far less ecological damage, were not considered.

Costs

As with the previous study, the authors give low estimates for costs for herbicides and for planting and thinning (the planting and thinning costs include the cost of herbicide spraying as well). They ignore costs for site preparation and repeat spraying (which is more likely on natural hardwood sites then on natural softwood sites). They also assume that overhead costs per acre are the same for "no silviculture" as for "intensive management."

Transition.

The authors assume that the system is already in place, so that every acre treated is balanced by an acre of high-volume, high-value softwoods to be harvested. But these high yields will not be obtainable for a minimum of 40 years from the onset of the strategy. This means that for 40 years there will be no surplus land—landowners will have all of the land costs of the no-silviculture strategy in addition to all of the costs for high-yield silviculture. Costs will thus increase for a 40-year period with no improvement in yield.

If the landowner pursues the spray and plant/thin option at a cost of $390,000 dollars a year, this would be added to the land cost of $892,000 a year for a total annual cost of $1,282,000 (1988 price). If the annual cut is still 100,000 cords and the value of spruce-fir pulpwood stumpage is approximately $13.50 (1988 price), then the annual benefit would be $1,350,000 for a total annual profit (before taxes) on 357,000 acres of $68,000, or $0.19 an acre for the next 40 years, assuming their figures are correct. Using more realistic figures for costs or yields would lead to a net loss rather than a profit.

In the meantime, the landowner will have to cut over most of the landholding "to sustain current industrial demands." The landowner, assuming increased future growth from intensive management, may feel justified increasing present cut above current growth rates (the Accelerated Cut Effect, or ACE), thus stripping forests at an even faster pace, based only on computer projections derived from unwarranted assumptions and insubstantial data.

This means that the surplus land, which the landowner can eventually sell for "wilderness" or retain for "multiple use," or for expanding mill capacity will be denuded, low-value softwood stands that industry considers a poor investment opportunity and that would have a low market value.

This annual approach, therefore, does not overcome the cost of time that is dealt with using a discount rate. Instead, it ignores it altogether. Once again, the question arises as to why prudent companies would want to operate at a loss or make very little money for decades based on the promise of high yields after the managers are long dead.

Them That Do
There are a few companies in Maine, most notably Scott Paper Company, that are planting and spraying to an extent that seems to defy the above analyses. I have come up with the following hypotheses to explain this seemingly irrational economic behavior:

•A certain proportion of the silvicultural activities can be deducted from taxes as working expenses and amortized as capital expenses. Their profits, therefore, are higher than they might at first appear.

•Only a fraction of the wood going to Scott's mills comes from its own land. The costs of growing wood this industrial way gets averaged out by the cheaper wood they purchase from other landowners, especially woodlots. The main source of profit for the company is paper, not trees.

•The risks are muted. Losses of timber to natural disaster can be deducted as a noncasualty business loss under Internal Revenue Code Section 165(a). These losses are limited to reforestation processes that will have to be redone.[8] Maine's Tree Growth Tax Law accords a 75% reduction in property taxes to land burned, infested, or made unmerchantable by any natural disaster.[9]

•The corporate executives believe in the paradigm of the forest as farm, a policy that is actually quite profitable in regions (such as Canada) where the practices are highly subsidized. They find it easier to manage in a similar way everywhere. Their policies were formed before the Age of Ecology, and they have too much momentum to rapidly shift to a more benign paradigm.

•Scott managers believe the analysis by Maass and Vicary (Maass used to be a forester for Scott) that anticipates rising value for spruce and fir due to a looming shortfall. The managers want to maximize the softwood stocking on their land as part of a strategy to diversify their investment portfolios, maintaining some low-risk, long-term investments. Although the managers will not live to see the returns, the land, if it is sold, still has value, especially if it is well stocked with spruce and fir that will (they hope) increase in value above inflation. They apparently did not reason that the value of the land would be even higher if it were selectively managed for all forest values—the buyer, which could be the federal government, may be more interested in wildlife and recreation than fiber.

•Scott, which has been clearcutting for more than 20 years, does not have to wait 40 years for the higher returns (if there are any).

•Because much of the public perceives planting trees to be good, Scott's policies have a certain public relations value. Ironically, some of those who live near Scott lands are so offended by the clearcut, plant, and spray policies that they have initiated an international boycott (originated in Nova Scotia) on Scott products. Not all the public relations are good.

Them That Don't
Like the rest of the industrial landowners, Georgia-Pacific did its share of clearcutting during the spruce budworm outbreak. Unlike Scott, however, G-P

greatly reduced its reliance on clearcutting after the mid-1980s. G-P's foresters concluded that the clearcut/plant/spray system was too expensive—not all the plantations grew as promised, and the projected benefits do not justify present costs.[10]

G-P has switched to diameter-limit cutting (mostly with mechanical harvesters) on a 25-year cutting cycle. This is more apt to lead to 2-aged stands than true uneven-aged (3 or more age classes) stands and does not usually lead to optimal spacing or high productivity—especially if the diameter-limits are low (only 8 inches, for example, for spruce).

Productivity is also lower than it could be because loggers on G-P land clear strips 12 feet wide for the mechanical harvesters—thus removing one-third of the forest from production. G-P foresters consider these diameter-limit cuts superior to clearcutting, however, because growth for the next cycle starts on residual trees rather than on seedlings. Regeneration and early growth are already assured. And there is no need to invest in herbicides (G-P does spray its plantations, however).

Despite arguments by other companies that they can't afford not to clearcut, G-P's foresters concluded, purely on economic grounds, that they could not afford to clearcut. The major difference between Scott and G-P that might explain the different cutting strategies is markets. G-P switched its pulp mill in Woodland to use all hardwoods around 1980. G-P, a fully integrated company, has markets for nearly any species that grows. Scott, on the other hand, depends heavily on spruce-fir—hence its attempts at converting "low-quality" hardwood sites to spruce plantations.

When one gets off the industrial lands onto landholdings that rely totally on revenues from stumpage, clearcutting (except by companies specializing in cut-and-run) becomes even less common. It is clearly not in the best economic interest of nonindustrial landowners to cut smaller diameter trees for pulp when these could be sold as lumber in a few decades.

I'm not arguing in this chapter that selection should be the only management choice for all situations, but that it should be the first choice. Managers should choose the least disturbing management practice suitable to a given site. Since we have so little understanding of the long-term sustainability of any management option, the method that maintains the most volume and diversity of trees leaves future managers with the most options.

Endnotes

a. Because plantations do not yield returns for decades, managers must subject such investments to a discount rate—which is the cost of waiting. This money was either borrowed and has to return a minimum yield or it could have been invested elsewhere. When comparing the costs and benefits of long-term investments, economists often convert future costs and future benefits (Future Values, or FV) into Present Value (PV) using the discount rate in the following manner:

$PV = FV/(1 + \text{discount rate})^t$, where t = time in years.

Using the Maass/Vicary example, if the future value of the plantation wood in 50 years is $3347, then its present value, at 4% would be:

$PV = \$3347/(1 + .04)^{50}$ or $470.97.

The costs are likewise discounted. Since the trees are planted in year 0, the discount does not apply. The herbicides used in year 2 would be treated in this way:

PV = $45/(1 + .04)^2$ or $41.61.

The Net Present Value (or NPV) equals the PV of the benefits minus the PV of the costs. In our example we would have:

PV of benefits - PV of costs of plant and spray = NPV

NPV = $470.97   -   ($192 + 41.61)   = $237.36

b. The discount rate is a controversial subject for foresters because at the high levels sometimes used by industry or even by the Office of Management and Budget (10%), the present value of any long-term investment benefits becomes exceedingly small. At a 10% discount rate, for example, a future value of $100 over 40 years has a present value of only $2.21.

The U.S. Forest Service and the Maine Forest Service often use lower rates (4% or 5%) in their benefit/cost analyses. Some economists call these low rates "social discounts," justifiable because there are additional benefits to wildlife, recreation, or watersheds.[11] Critics of such discount rates argue that investments into monoculture forest plantations and herbicides yield social benefits that are highly debatable.

Some economists have argued that a 3% return above inflation on a long-term land-based investment is actually quite good and that for forestry, managers only need to add 1% or 2% to account for risk. Hence, 4% or 5% would be an acceptable long-term discount rate. The degree of risk for plantation forestry on a large scale, however, is an unknown factor. Some paper companies use an "Internal Hurdle Rate" (minimal rate of return—which is their discount rate) of 6% for their forestry investments. Because economics is far from being a science, especially when it comes to anticipating future returns on present investments, some economists calculate returns using high, middle, and low discount rate.

References

1. Maine Forest Service, *Timber Harvest and Silvicultural Practices Report* (Augusta, Me.: Maine Forest Service, Maine Department of Conservation, 1989).
2. David Maas and Bret Vicary, "The Value of Increased Survival and Stocking with Herbicide Treatments." In *Proceedings of Northeastern Weed Science Society Meeting, 1991*, Vol. 45., photocopy.
3. Maine Forest Service, *Timber Harvest and Silvicultural Practices Report*.
4. *Ibid.*
5. R. Speer, "Monitoring Plantation Establishment and Development." In R. D. Hallett, M. D. Cameron, and T. S. Murray, eds., *Reforestation in the Maritimes* (Fredericton, New Brunswick: Maritimes Research Centre, 1984), p. 125.
6. Robert S. Seymour and Maxwell L. McCormack, Jr., "Having Our Forest and Harvesting It Too: The Role of Intensive Silviculture in Resolving Forest Land Use Conflicts." In Russel D. Briggs, William B. Krohn, Joan G. Trial, William D. Ostrofsky, and David B. Field, eds., *Forest and Wildlife Management in New England—What Can We Afford*, proceedings of a joint meeting of the Maine Division of New England Society of American Foresters, Maine Chapter of the Wildlife Society, and the Atlantic International Chapter of the American Fisheries Society, March 15-17, 1989, Portland, Maine, CFRU Information Report 21, Maine Agricultural Experiment Station Miscellaneous Report 336 (Orono, Me.: Maine Agricultural Experiment Station, University of Maine, October 1989), pp. 207-213.
7. S. D. Warren Company, "Northeast Timberlands," Forestry Facts, n.d.
8. David Maass, "Impact of the 1988 Drought on Northern Forests: A Preliminary Review," *National Woodlands* (March-April 1989): 8.
9. Robert Parlow, *Axes and Taxes, The Taking of Resources and Revenues from the Maine Woods* (Portland, Me.: Allagash Environmental Institute, 1977): 30.
10. Lee Stover, forester for G-P, interview with author, January 25, 1992.
11. G. H. Manning, "Evaluating Public Forestry Investments in British Columbia: The Choice of Discount Rates," *The Forestry Chronicle* (June 1977): 155-158.

3 Industrial Forest Fixes

Widespread intensive forest management would bring about a new, unnatural forest that depends on practices such as herbicide and insecticide spraying that many find objectionable. Actually, all interest groups can probably find excuses to avoid the difficult, but essential actions required to shape Maine's forest of the 21st century.
   Robert Seymour, "Where Has All the Spruce-fir Gone?," *Habitat*, October 1985

We shall probably preserve our economic interest in balsam fir by more or less continuous tinkering with the biological system in an attempt to sustain an artificial ecological stability...any action that distorts the system will increase the need of more action for an indefinite period of time.
   Gordon Baskerville, "Spruce Budworm: The Answer is Forest Management;
   Or Is It?," *Forest Chronicles*, 51:25 (1975)

The industrial forest is in trouble. Although the paper industry flourished and expanded in the 1980s, the spruce and fir inventory, upon which this industry is based, declined. Unless industry takes heroic actions to reverse these trends, researchers warn, there will be mill shortfalls within the next few decades. Industrial foresters have identified three biological threats to their spruce-fir resource: poor-quality or low-value hardwoods ("junk" hardwoods) are wasting growing space that could be filled by more valuable spruce and fir; broad-leaved pioneer species and hardwood sprouts ("weeds") are smothering spruce-fir regeneration; and periodic waves of defoliating insects ("pests") especially spruce budworm, are decimating the resource and creating an unbalanced age-class structure.

Experts have warned us, however, not to waste time trying to understand why spruce-fir is declining or who is responsible. University of New Brunswick forestry professor Gordon Baskerville assured Maine's Department of Conservation in 1983 that "Futile arguments about culpability are distinctly counter-productive...."[1]

Robert Seymour, while a researcher for the Cooperative Forestry Research Unit, wrote that "As the debate about Maine's future forest intensifies, we must try to avoid wasting precious energy on retrospective fixing of blame for the present unfortunate situation."[2] And former Maine Audubon Society director Charles Hewett added, "In any crisis, there is a tendency to place blame on others. But in truth, the entire conservation and resource management community has failed in allowing the spruce-fir shortfall to evolve."[3] These gentlemen ask us to ignore the cause of the problem and let the paper industry, the "victim" of any future shortfall, move quickly to treat the symptoms.

Each of the industrial solutions is a quick fix designed to solve a specific problem in isolation. In "solving" the problems, however, these "solutions" create other problems that require their own fixes. Whole-tree clearcutting to get rid of junk hardwoods leads to a proliferation of "weeds." Spraying herbicides to get rid of the weeds leads to even-aged fir stands. Even-aged fir stands are highly susceptible to spruce-budworm invasions, for which landowners spray insecticides. All the while, the paper industry, assuming the fixes will work, increases mill capacity. And to sustain higher harvest levels of spruce and fir, foresters must employ even more fixes.

These three fixes—whole-tree harvesting, herbicide spraying, and insecticide spraying—are the most controversial management practices in the industrial forest. The more controversial a management practice, the greater the volume and complexity of defensive mythology that grows up around it. Forest landowners are not alone in defending these practices; they are joined by biomass energy companies (which burn the whole-tree wood chips), chemical corporations (which sell the herbicides and insecticides), university researchers (who get grants from the chemical, paper, and biomass industries), and government officials. Concerned citizens who oppose spray programs or biomass clearcuts in their communities face formidable opposition.

References

1. Gordon Baskerville, *A Critique and Commentary of the 1983 Supply/Demand Analysis for the Spruce-fir Forest of Maine*, (Augusta, Me.: Maine Department of Conservation, October 1983).
2. Robert Seymour, "Where Has All the Spruce-fir Gone?," *Habitat* (October 1985): 29.
3. Charles Hewett, "Maine: The Forest State—Recognizing the Realities," *Habitat* (October 1985): 3.

Whole-tree Harvesting

Since the 1970s, the spruce-fir type, which the paper industry desires, has declined (losing 781,100 acres, 9.3% of its 1971 area by 1986),[1] but the aspen type, considered low-valued, has rapidly increased (expanding 445,400 acres, 77% of its 1971 area by 1982).[2] Hardwoods in general are in terrible shape and getting worse. Federal and state forest surveys found 32.5% of all hardwoods in 1982 and 43% of all hardwoods in 1986 to be either rough, rotten, or dead.[3]

Industrial foresters view this increase in low-value/low-quality hardwoods as a form of cancer—a malignant growth in their working forest. Because of inadequate markets in the past, these "junk hardwoods" accumulated in the forest. With whole-tree harvesting and whole-tree chipping for biomass, managers can now treat the junk-wood cancer with surgery.

The rapid expansion of biomass electric-generating plants and of whole-tree harvesting during the 1980s excited industry, government, and some environmental groups. There are so many benefits:

•using wood, a renewable resource, rather than fossil fuels for 1/5 of

Maine's electricity needs;

•creating a market for junk hardwoods so that forest quality can be improved;

•creating a market for mill wastes, such as edgings, sawdust, or even paper-mill sludge;

•increasing harvest productivity by using previously wasted material, such as branches;

•clearing a site of low-quality hardwoods in order to plant high-valued softwoods;

•generating wood ash, an inexpensive fertilizer for farms and forests;

•decreasing accidents by switching to mechanical, rather than motor-manual (with chainsaw) limbing;

•creating new jobs; and

•increasing tax revenues and local spending.

To some state officials, biomass has no downside. Richard Anderson, when he was commissioner of the Department of Conservation, was such an enthusiastic biomass booster that in 1986 he won the "National Public Servant of the Year" award from the biomass industry for "his impressive promotion of biomass development in the State."[4] Charles Hewett, then director of the Maine Audubon Society (MAS), stated that Anderson (who also had been a director of MAS), "has done more to promote renewable energy and good forest management than any other single person in the state and probably the region."[5]

Hewett, in an article of his own in MAS's magazine, *Habitat*, wrote that "Whole tree harvesting is the most powerful silvicultural tool now available for managing Maine's forests."[6] After leaving Maine Audubon, Hewett joined Swift River, a company that builds biomass plants.

Originally, whole-tree harvesting was developed to lower the rates of accidents caused by chainsaw limbing of trees in the woods. The whole-tree harvesting solution was to drag out trees with limbs intact, then mechanically delimb them at the wood yard. While biomass markets did not create whole-tree harvesting, they are now used to justify, and potentially intensify it—literally every tree and branch can now be used.

Like all tools, whole-tree harvesting can be misused. Because it can lead to a forest being scraped down to bare soil, it has the potential to be the most powerful silvicultural tool available for damaging Maine's forests. The degraded forests that biomass clearcuts are supposed to fix are the result of former catastrophic management. "Why," asks woods activist Bill Butler, "repair one catastrophe by starting another?"[7]

References

1. Douglas S. Powell and David R. Dickson, *Forest Statistics for Maine*, Resource Bulletin NE-81 (Broomall, Pa.: U.S. Forest Service, U.S. Department of Agriculture, 1984), pp. 10-11. Also, Maine Forest Service, *Report of the 1986 Midcycle Resurvey of the Spruce-fir Forest in Maine* (Augusta, Me.: Maine Department of Conservation, 1988), p. 23.
2. Douglas S. Powell and David R. Dickson, *Forest Statistics*, pp. 10-11.
3. Douglas S. Powell and David R. Dickson, *Forest Statistics*, p. 20. Also, Maine Forest Service, *Report of the 1986 Midcycle Resurvey*, p. 5.
4. "Maine Conservation Commissioner Anderson Named NWEA National Public Servant of the Year," *Biologue*, Vol. 3, No. 6 (December 1986): 3.

5. *Ibid.*

6. Charles Hewett, "Whole Tree Harvesting: The Potential and Pitfalls," *Habitat* (September/October 1985): 38.

7. Jeff Elliott and Jamie Sayen, *The Ecological Restoration of the Northern Appalachians: An Evolutionary Perspective* (North Stratford, N.H.: Preserve Appalachian Wilderness, 1990): 30.

Myth 1

Biomass is a clean, renewable energy resource.

Biomass promoters like to point out that there are enormous amounts of junk wood in the forest—plenty to support their expansion plans, and then some. Biomass is "renewable," however, only if it is derived from ecologically sustainable forestry practices and only if the level of cut stays within the interest and doesn't deplete the forest capital.

A 1989 study of wood supply by Cooperative Forestry Research Unit (CFRU) researchers Robert Seymour and Ronald Lemin, Jr., indicates that the shade-tolerant northern hardwoods (maple, beech, and yellow birch) are already being cut above sustainable levels. Shade-intolerant pioneer hardwoods (white birch and poplar) are expanding but will not be able to meet projected demands from planned mill increases.[1] Maine Watch Institute researchers Ellen Baum, Jonathan Falk, and David Vail came to a similar conclusion:

"Maine's hardwood resource has long been underutilized, but rapid demand growth in the past 10 years has begun to make inroads on the vast inventory of low-quality hardwood. It appears that the current harvest *already* exceeds long-term sustainable yield.... Although a huge inventory of standing, low-quality hardwood will conceal larger forces, in the long run, it is unlikely that the hardwood resource can 'do it all'—substitute for shrinking spruce-fir supplies in paper making and also meet the needs of electrical power and wood products industries, without causing a sharp increase in stumpage and delivered wood prices and threatening long-term timber yields. Because the economic viability of biomass energy generation depends on a cheap fuel stock, most respondents doubt whether this industry will be able to expand at the rate . . . projected."[2]

Looking at local supply, the sustainability of mill increases becomes even more suspect. When biomass entrepreneur Chris Hutchins of Alternative Energy/Beaver Chester announced that he would build a large plant in Haynesville (as of this writing, he has decided to put it 25 miles farther north, in Houlton), he declared that there was an abundant wood supply within a 50-mile radius of the proposed plant. Since I live within that radius, I checked with Maine's Public Utilities Commission to see what other plants have 50-mile radii that intersect that of Haynesville and discovered that West Enfield, Jonesboro, Chester, Greenville, Fort Fairfield, Woodland, and Bucksport all have biomass electric generators on the grid.[3] Others, such as Great Northern (now Bowater) in Millinocket, have a biomass generator that is being used directly by a paper mill, so the electricity is not sold on the grid. The local impact of the combined drain for all these plants, plus cutting for pulp, firewood, and wafer board (there is an aspen wafer-board plant in Houlton), can be profound. One can keep biomass plants going for a long time by cutting smaller and smaller diameter trees and even mining up roots, but sustaining biomass plants is not the same as sustaining the biological integrity of the forest.

Biomass generators do not contribute significant amounts of sulfur dioxide, the acid-rain air pollutant most targeted for regulation. They are, however, a significant source of nitrogen oxides and volatile organic compounds that can be precursors to the formation of ozone.[4] They are not entirely "clean."

References

1. Robert Seymour and Ronald Lemin, Jr., *Timber Supply Projections for Maine, 1980-2080*, CFRU Research Bulletin 7, Maine Agricultural Experiment Station Miscellaneous Report 337 (Orono, Me.: Maine Agricultural Experiment Station, University of Maine, 1989), pp. 22, 27.
2. Ellen Baum, Jonathan Falk, and David Vail, *Maine Forest Economy: Crisis or Opportunity. Vol. 1, Report of Survey Research Finding* (Hallowell, Me.: Mainewatch Institute, October 1988), pp. 11-12.
3. Richard Parker, personal communication, November 1989.
4. Maine Bureau of Air Quality Control, *1988 Emission Rating Report* (Augusta, Me.: Maine Department of Environmental Protection, Bureau of Air Quality Control, 1989).

Myth 2
Biomass is a cheap, local energy source.

Once upon a time there was an oil crisis. Congress decided that it would be a Great Idea to encourage small producers of nonfossil- fuel-generated electricity. The result was the Public Utilities Regulatory Policies Act (PURPA) of 1978, which was supposed to encourage wind turbines, small hydro, solar, and the like. What they got in northern New England were dozens of plans to build fairly substantial biomass plants. Large multinationals such as General Electric, Westinghouse, and Babcock and Wilcox as well as other megabucks investors were drawn to the promise of easy profits and low risk, guaranteed by legislation. The paper industry, which was the biggest single consumer of electric power in Maine became one of the largest producers. Under the leadership of Richard Anderson, Commissioner of the Department of Conservation, the state also actively solicited investors to build biomass plants. Further enticements were Accelerated Investment Credits and Energy Credits, as well as hefty tax write-offs on expensive equipment for investors in high tax brackets.[1] The wood (called "waste" and "junk") was cheap. It was a good deal.

The utilities had to buy the electricity at highest replacement cost. This was such a good deal that some of the first paper mills to get in on it—S.D. Warren (a division of Scott) and Boise Cascade—found that they could swing a healthy profit by selling their electricity to the utility at inflated prices and then buying it back at cheaper rates, rather than consuming their own power. The Public Utilities Commission has since stopped this practice.[2] The electricity produced by these biomass plants is not cheap. It is profitable enough, however, that even some new plants, like that proposed by Chris Hutchins, allow 60% of the energy in the chips to be released into the environment as waste heat. Some plants use cogeneration (where some of the heat is captured and used rather than allowed to dissipate into the atmosphere).[a]

Apologists for biomass admit that it is not cheap for consumers now but promise that in the future, as oil and nuclear power become expensive, it will be a good deal. If the wood is indeed being overcut, and if costs for wood, labor, and equipment go up as expected, then this comparison of present biomass costs with future oil and nuclear costs is misleading. Biomass electricity may be expensive in the future as well.

The electricity is local in that it is produced locally, but it is not necessarily used locally. Some contracts, such as Chris Hutchins's, have the utilities "wheel" the power long distances over the power grid. There are certainly local benefits in terms of taxes and jobs, but there are also regional costs to the community, forest, air, and water that should be considered. These costs may not be compensated for by taxes that accrue to only one town.

Endnote

a. Cogeneration is the best deal of all. In 1982, when state and federal governments were giving out impressive incentives to spur industrial and energy development, the state held a conference in which some of these bonanzas were revealed.[3]

Consultant James Ferry told the audience that investment returns ranged from 40% to 568%! The profits were possible, he said, because of the investment tax credits and tax-exempt industrial bonds. In fact, he said, many companies did not make enough profits to take advantage of all the tax write-offs! Roger Feldman, a Washington lawyer, told the audience that Congress had a solution to this "problem": "The Economic Recovery Taxation Act created such an enormous bonanza that Congress decided to let more people cash in. It allowed sham sales and leases where no cash changes hands, just title to a co-generation facility for tax purposes only."

References

1. United States Department of Energy, *Cogeneration From Biofuels: A Technical Guidebook for Tennessee Valley Authority* (Washington, D.C.: United States Department of Energy, Business Department, 1987). This reference contains more references.
2. Richard Parker, personal communication, November 1989.
3. Robert Cummings, "Cogeneration Urged As Conservation Measure," *Portland Press Herald*, March 5, 1982.

Myth 3

Biomass burners create a market for junk trees and wastewood, thus allowing forest managers to at last profitably do stand improvement.

Junk is a propaganda word that masks the ecological and economic values of hardwoods, justifying abnormally low stumpage rates. The 1990 stumpage report from Maine's Department of Conservation priced softwood chips at $3.16 per cord (2.3 green tons to the cord) and hardwood chips at $5.72 per cord (2.7 green tons per cord) as state averages.[1] These prices hardly reflect the value of the final product—expensive electricity.

Creation of markets for these trees does not necessarily mean that managers will use this as an opportunity for timber stand improvement. Now that there are markets for all trees, it is more profitable than ever to cut all trees (branches, twigs, and all). Clearcuts are more intense. An integrated operation can now sort the wood out to lumber, pulp, and biomass.[a] The next rotation will be for pulp and biomass, or maybe just biomass. Rather than lead to improvement, the biomass market can lead to a forest that is fit only for chips.

Wastewood can refer to sawmill waste (bark, edgings, and sawdust) which, if not burned, can accumulate in huge piles. It also refers to tops and branches that are normally left in the forest as slash or in roadside piles by mechanical delimbers. This material is invaluable to forest ecosystems. It provides shade, moderates soil temperatures, reduces moisture loss, limits animal browsing damage to seedlings, hides seeds from birds, and adds important nutrients and organic matter to the soil.[2] Industry foresters consider wastewood undesirable because it can bury regeneration, create a fire hazard, and look horrible. Whole-tree chipping, rather than careful management of slash, may enrich the biomass contractor but impoverish the ecosystem.

Even if hardwoods are removed in a partial cut, the stand is not necessarily "improved." Skidding out trees with the branches still attached increases damage to advanced regeneration and residual trees. When trees are skidded out whole, their branches scrape anything in the way— including the bark off of standing trees. The heavy equipment used for skidding can damage the fine roots of standing trees, leading either to sickness or death of the tree. Cooperative Forestry Research Unit (CFRU) researchers W. D. Ostrofsky, R. S. Seymour, and R. C. Lemin, Jr., found that "Although the potential for silvicultural and economic gains is great, so is the potential for excessive damage to residual stands and to the site itself. . . .The combination of soil compaction, soil disturbance, tree wounding, and increased solar radiation to residual tree stems and the soil can increase tree stress. Stressed trees are unlikely to benefit from the reduction in competition resulting from the harvest. The primary goal of the thinning will not be realized."[3] Based on the amount of damage these researchers observed, they recommended that biomass thinnings not even be attempted on "high-risk" sites.

Removing hardwoods to create a pure softwood overstory simplifies the ecosystem, leading to consequences already discussed: reduced wildlife diversity, increased susceptibility to spruce budworm and other "pests," and increased soil degradation. Biomass promoters are asking us to accept their technologies based more on the promise than on the actual delivery of improved silvicultural practices.

Endnote

a. Although Department of Conservation officials publicly deny that contractors chip log-quality trees for biomass, loggers and logging contractors have told me that they have either witnessed or participated in the chipping of quality hardwoods in order to finish filling the chip truck. Even more widespread is the chipping of trees that would be suitable for lumber if left to stand for a few more decades. Not all the trees chipped are "junk."

References

1. Ancyl Thurston, "Annual Report of Stumpage Harvested for 1990" (Augusta, Me.: Maine Department of Conservation, October 10, 1991).
2. Maxwell McCormack, Jr., "Interaction of Harvesting and Stand Establishment in Conifers in Northeastern North America." Paper presented at Council on Forest Engineering/International Union of Forest Research Organizations Conference, Fredericton, New Brunswick,

August 17-18, 1984, p. 235.
2. W. D. Ostrofsky, R. S. Seymour, and R. C. Lemin, Jr., "Damage to Northern Hardwoods From Thinning Using Whole-Tree Harvesting Technology," *Canadian Journal of Forestry Research*, Vol. 16 (1986): 1238.

Myth 4

Whole-tree harvests increase forest productivity.

Whole-tree harvests (WTH) certainly can incease the amount of biomass removed per acre. With hardwoods, a conventional stemwood (just the boles, not the branches) clearcut might remove only 50 to 55% of the above-stump biomass, whereas a whole-tree clearcut can remove 96% of this material.[1] A conventional clearcut harvest of spruce-fir could remove 72% of the biomass while a whole -tree clearcut might remove more than 90%.[2] Some forest researchers argue that we must increase the intensity of cutting if we are to prevent a timber shortfall. CFRU researchers Robert Seymour and Ronald Lemin, Jr., estimate that to meet future demands, 43% of all harvests will have to be done with WTH.[3]

More intensive harvests can only be seen as more "productive" if you ignore future growth and focus only on the increased yields per harvest of existing forests. Higher productivity should mean a higher return on biological interest, not a higher rate of capital depletion. There are a number of reasons why whole-tree clearcuts should be seen as ecological capital depletion rather than increased productivity.

Nutrient Depletion

Whereas the trunk of a tree might contain 50 to 75% of the biomass, the branches, twigs, and leaves can have the majority of the nutrients. A study of whole-tree harvesting of spruce-fir found that WTH removed twice the calcium and potassium, three times the magnesium and nitrogen, and four times the phosphorus than would have been removed in a trunk-only harvest.[4]

Some foresters might argue that these nutrient losses are an insignificant percentage (maybe only 3 to 4%) of the total nutrient capital in the soil. When compared to the *available* nutrients (nutrients in a form trees can use) in the soil, however, the removal of nutrients in WTH can be very significant. One study estimated that the number of rotations that would deplete exchangeable (available) soil nutrient reserves without additions of nutrients from other sources is 0.9 for calcium and

Accelerated nutrient depletion from whole-tree logging on short rotations. *From* The Trees Around Us, *Nova Scotia Dept.of Lands and Forests, p. 76.*

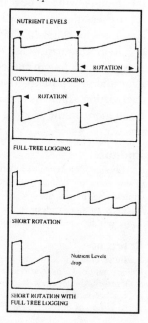

0.8 for potassium. In other words, WTH removes more of these nutrients than are left behind in available form.[5]

Organic Matter Depletion
The biomass removed in WTH is also an important source of organic matter (OM). Organic matter is important for developing soil structure, for air and water holding capacity, for habitat for important soil microorganisms, and for increasing nutrient utilization abilities (cation exchange capacity).[6]

Soil Exposure
WTH exposes the earth to direct sunlight and rain. Soil temperatures become more extreme, which harms soil microlife. Bare soil exposed to heavy rains is more liable to erode. Loss of soil cover can increase damage to seedlings from frost heave.

Leaching
Increased temperature leads to a breakdown of organic matter in the soil and to increased mobilization of nutrients and, with no trees to take up the nutrients, increased leaching. Leaching of nutrients peaks one or two years after harvest and slows as pioneer species revegetate the landscape, taking up the mobile nutrients and storing them in organic matter. These losses can last up to 10 years.[7] In some cases, leaching can remove more nutrients than the initial harvest.[8]

Spraying herbicides, a practice that follows some whole-tree clearcuts, kills the pioneer species that are slowing nutrient losses and thus contributes to increased leaching. This is especially problematic when done within a few years after a clearcut, when leaching potential is at its peak.[9]

Whole-tree chipping may enrich the contractor while impoverishing the soil.
Photo by Christopher Ayres.

Acidification

WTH can lead to a loss in cations (positively charged ions of such minerals as calcium, magnesium, sodium, and potassium, all being alkaline), leading to soil degradation through acidification.[10] Exposure to direct sunlight hastens the breakdown of organic matter. This causes a process called "nitrification," which occurs as organic nitrogen compounds are transformed into inorganic forms (nitrates) that plants can utilize. Nitrification makes the soil even more acidic, exacerbating the effects of acid precipitation (see Chapter 4).

Loss of Nitrogen

WTH, by removing nearly all the biomass, removes a major source of nitrogen—decaying dead wood that is inhabited by nitrogen-fixing bacteria. Indeed, dead branchwood 1 inch in diameter has been identified as one of the few locations in northern hardwood stands where nitrogen is fixed.[11] Nitrogen is an important element for stimulating growth, and unlike mineral nutrients, does not become available over time from weathering of rocks.

Soil Compaction

WTH may disturb more than 90% of the surface soil, cause upwards of 80% of it to be compacted, expose mineral (nonorganic) soil on 18% to 49% of the land, and create extensive wheel ruts. Such disruption can have serious consequences for forest regeneration.[12] Recent research in Maine, at Weymouth Point, by the CFRU has shown slowed growth or even mortality of planted and natural softwood regeneration when in compacted or bare soil.[13]

Reduced Productivity

All of these effects are magnified as rotations get shorter. An ecological rotation

Forest soil compacted and rutted by heavy equipment. *Photo by Christopher Ayres.*

is the time that permits the soil to return to the ecological condition that existed prior to the harvest.[14] If the harvest is more intense, the leaching heavier, the loss of organic matter greater, then the forest ecosystem becomes less resilient and needs a correspondingly longer rotation for recovery. While all these factors speak for longer rotations, company foresters are boasting about shortened rotations. One can only conclude that these foresters have a definition of "sustainability" that goes no further than one cut.

Confidence in the increased productivity of WTH combined with short rotations is certainly not built on any long-term experience. As Canadian forest researcher Alan Gordon commented, "It might be said that the farther away one is from the site on which one's calculations are based, the more feasible the concept for energy from forest residue biomass. . . . Full-tree logging . . . is an entirely new circumstance. . . .This new situation may push ecosystem mechanisms beyond the limits of regulation. This will result in an exaggeration of the disturbance and consequent destabilization. We may not get a forest back as it now stands with the same yield, or, in the worst cases, at all."[15]

If one considers productivity of other values, such as stream quality or wildlife, WTH can cause the most severe impact of any harvest method since it can remove virtually the entire forest.

References

1. James W. Hornbeck and William Kropelin, "Nutrient Removal and Leaching from a Whole-tree Harvest of Northern Hardwoods," *Journal of Environmental Quality*, Vol. 11, No. 2 (1982): 312.
2. C. T. Smith, M. C. McCormack, Jr., J. W. Hornbeck, and C. W. Martin, "Nutrient and Biomass Removals from a Red Spruce-Balsam Fir Whole-tree Harvest," *Canadian Journal of Forestry Research*, Vol. 16 (1986): 382.
3. Robert Seymour and Ronald Lemin, Jr., *Timber Supply Projections for Maine, 1980-2080*, CFRU Research Bulletin 7, Maine Agricultural Experiment Station Miscellaneous Report 337 (Orono, Me.: Maine Agricultural Experiment Station, University of Maine, 1989).
4. Smith et al., "Nutrient and Biomass Removals," p. 384.
5. Maxwell McCormack, Jr., "Interaction of Harvesting and Stand Establishment in Conifers in Northeastern North America." Paper presented at Council on Forest Engineering/International Union of Forest Research Organizations Conference, Fredericton, New Brunswick, August 17-18, 1984, p. 238.
6. C. T. Smith, Jr., *Literature Review and Approaches to Studying the Impacts of Forest Harvesting and Residue Management Practices on Forest Nutrient Cycles*, CFRU Information Report 13 (Ithaca, N.Y.: Cooperative Forestry Research Unit, Cornell University, March 1985).
7. Alan Gordon, "Impacts of Harvesting on Nutrient Capacity in the Boreal Mixedwood Forest." Paper presented at Boreal Mixedwood Symposium, Ontario Ministry of Natural Resources, Sault Ste. Marie, Ontario, April 1981, p. 135.
8. C. T. Smith, Jr., *Literature Review*, p. 1.
9. Alan Gordon, "Impacts of Harvesting," p. 136.
10. M. K. Mahendrappa, G. D. Van Raalte, and S. M. Maliondo, "Forest Biomass and Nutrient Inventories in New Brunswick." In *Proceedings of the 7th Bioenergy Research and Development Seminar*, Energy Mines and Resources Canada, Ottawa, Ontario, April 24-26, 1989.
11. James W. Hornbeck and William Kropelin, "Nutrient Removal and Leaching," p. 312.
12. United States Forest Service, "Results of Recent Research Related to Whole-tree Harvesting for the Northeastern Forest Experiment Station" (Orono, Me.: United States Forest Service, United States Department of Agriculture, November 26, 1985). Also, C. T. Smith, Jr., *Intensive Harvesting Residue Management, Alternatives and Nutrient Cycling in the Spruce-fir Type. The Weymouth Point Study*, CFRU Progress Report 26 (Orono, Me.: Cooperative Forestry Research Unit), p. 25.
13. Maxwell McCormack, Jr., personal communication, winter 1990.
14. J. P. Kimmins, "Sustained Yield, Timber Mining, and the Concept of Ecological Rota-

tion, A British Columbia View," *Forestry Chronicle*, Vol. 50 (1974): 27-31.
15. A. G. Gordon, "Productivity and Nutrient Cycling in Natural Forests," Biomass Strategy Consultation, United Nations Educational, Scientific, and Cultural Organization, Man and Biosphere (February 1979): 34-49.

Myth 5

Nutrient losses from whole-tree harvests can be corrected with fertilizers.

Industrial apologists argue that since the problems resulting from clearcutting with whole-tree harvesting (WTH) could theoretically be mitigated with fertilizers in the *future*, the practice is acceptable *now*. Landowners are now doing whole-tree harvests on a wide-scale basis, but they are doing fertilization only on a limited basis. Trees grow on nutrients, not promises. Fertilization currently is too expensive and the benefits too uncertain for it to be a common practice.

The myth implies that, assuming fertilization does become more practical, the application of fertilizers justifies the complete removal of above-ground biomass from a forest (or what was once a forest). The best fertilizers for a forest, however, happen to be the very items that are removed from the ecosystem by WTH—leaves, branches, and rotting wood. Their benefits extend beyond their contribution of nutrients; they supply organic matter, offer habitats for wildlife, and have important roles in moderating the effects of water and

Blondin sludge spreader. *Photo courtesy Bangor Daily News.*

sunlight on the soil. Looking at the forest as a repository of biomass that can be quantified in tons per acre helps foresters justify replacing these abstract numbers with other abstract numbers—pounds of replacement nutrients.

For those who accept the idea of substituting nutrients for trees, the paper industry has a discovered a great nutrient source—industrial waste. Maine's paper industry annually produces 900,000 tons of sludge (greater than Maine's total annual municipal sludge output of 750,000 tons).[1] Biomass plants also create substantial quantities of ash—up to 25% of the volume of the wood burned. The industry has to get rid of the stuff anyway, and landfilling it is expensive. By calling ash and sludge spreading a "forest management activity," the companies have attempted to disguise the fact that they are actually practicing industrial waste disposal.

If a company's forestry division had to pay for purchasing and spreading the tons of mill waste, the costs would be prohibitive. To the mill division, however, it makes good sense to use the forest as an alternative to scarce landfill space. The forest literally becomes a wasteland. Before spreading sludge and ash, it helps if the site is well prepared, cleared of obstructions that might get in the way of the spreader. This preparation may make the site machinery friendly, but not ecosystem friendly. It ensures a minimum of surviving vegetation on the land and a maximum of disturbance and nutrient loss. But because sludge is added, I suppose the managers see no problem.

Preliminary results on some sludge and ash applications for black spruce plantations are not all that promising—if the goal is actually silvicultural. According to Cooperative Forestry Research Unit researcher Robert K. Shepard, Jr., " . . . field observation from plots treated in May suggest no positive effect on seedling growth and an increase in the amount of herbaceous vegetation as application rates increased."[2] In other words, the sludge and ash were benefitting the "weeds" instead of the crop. Because tree nutrient requirements extend for many decades but fertilization is only good for a matter of years, one forest researcher concluded that "maintaining wood production even at its former level may require soil amelioration beyond our capacity."[3]

While it is understandable that mill managers would like to find alternatives to landfills, such a need does not justify whole-tree clearcutting. The two issues are separate.

The Forest as Wasteland

Industry public relations portrays sludge and ash spreading as "recycling." This buzzword has given mill waste disposal an aura of environmental benignity. However, some of what is added back to the forest did not originate from the trees. Sludge from Kraft mills using the chlorine bleaching process is contaminated with traces of chlorinated hydrocarbons, including dioxins and furans.

The most toxic of these substances is 2,3,7,8-tetrachlorodibenzo-p-dioxin—more commononly known as TCDD or simply dioxin. At extremely low doses, TCDD can trigger cancers and mutations, disrupt the immune and hormonal systems, and cause problems in sexual and brain development.[4] TCDD is fairly stable in the environment and it can bioconcentrate as it moves up the food chain. Controversies have been raging for decades over what levels of this toxin are within regulatory acceptability.

A study in Wisconsin found that dioxin from sludge spread on forests does get into the food chain: residues were detected in wildlife tissues, including bird eggs.[5] Yet the paper industry in Maine convinced the state to allow conditional use of sludge. The Natural Resources Council of Maine, which had initially opposed the use of paper mill sludge as fertilizer, made an agreement not to oppose use of sludge over forestland. Their approval was conditional—the state had to ban mill sludge spreading on farmland and had to conduct a study to look at the dioxin content of the sludge and the effect of the sludge on forest ecosystems.[6]

Maine newspapers did not widely report that while the study was going on, Scott Paper Company, starting in 1989, would be disposing of truckload after truckload of sludge on thousands of acres of clearcuts over a 5-year period.[7] Some local residents, however, have become concerned at the scale of the enterprise. Their unease was increased when, in the winter of 1991, a sludge truck overturned near Monson, spilling some of its contents onto the frozen surface of Spectacle Pond.[8]

Preliminary results from the study have found detectable (in parts per trillion) but "acceptable" levels of TCDD in the tissues of some bird eggs and shrews.[9] The study, because of difficulties in methodology, will be deemed by many critics to be non-conclusive. In the meantime, the dioxins will continue to enter the food chain and higher-level predators will eat the birds and shrews—concentrating the dioxins even more. If, after many years, evidence of harm can be proven, it will be too late to put the proverbial worms back into the can.

Biomass ash can also, at times, be considered a toxic waste. Ash from poplars can have unacceptably high levels of the heavy metal cadmium, which the trees bioconcentrate in their bark.[10] If a biomass plant uses large volumes of poplar, cadmium levels can exceed the Maine Department of Environmental Protection legal limit of 10 parts per million. Some of the ash that does get spread may have cadmium levels close to this limit as evidenced by ash sampling data from some biomass plants.[11]

References

1. "Dioxin: Three-year Truce Declared," *Maine Times* (October 28, 1988): 2.
2. Robert K. Shepard, *Fertilization Project, 1988 Annual Report of the Cooperative Forestry Research Unit*, CFRU Information Report 20 (Orono, Me.: Cooperative Forestry Research Unit, 1988): 30.
3. Alan Gordon, "Impacts of Harvesting on Nutrient Capacity in the Boreal Mixedwood Forest." Paper presented at Boreal Mixedwood Symposium, Ontario Ministry of Natural Resources, Sault Ste. Marie, Ontario, April 1981, pp. 136-137
4. Karen F. Schmidt, "Puzzling over a poison: on closer inspection, the ubiquitous pollutant dioxin appears more dangerous than ever," U.S. News and World Report, April 6, 1992, p. 61.
5. S. G. Martin, D. A. Thiel, J. W. Duncan, and W. R. Lance, "Effects of a Paper Industry Sludge Containing Dioxin on Wildlife in Red Pine Plantations." In *Proceedings of the 1987 TAPPI Environmental Conference* (1987), pp. 363-377.
6. "Dioxin: Three-year Truce Declared," p. 2.
7. An undated Scott Paper Company Fact Sheet on sludge spreading says that the company will

spread sludge on 4,000 acres over a 5- year period.

8. Cheryl Seal, "Dioxin: the invisible killer in Maine's water and soil," *Maine Progressive*, April, 1992, p. 5.

9. Steve Page, Maine DEP, personal communication, April, 1992.

10. Malcolm Hunter, Jr., *Wildlife, Forests, and Forestry: Principles of Managing Forests for Biological Diversity* (Englewood Cliffs, N.J.: Prentice-Hall, 1990), p. 207.

11. For example, the December, 1986 samples analyzed by Northeast Laboratory Services in Waterville for Resource Conservation Services Inc. of ash from the Beaver Wood plant in Chester, Maine showed cadmium levels of 8 parts per million of cadmium.

Myth 6

Whole-tree clearcutting is not a problem because it is only done on a small percentage of the forest each year and the effects can be mitigated.

This is, of course, an admission that there is something wrong, but the idea here is to minimize the problem by showing it in such a large context that it appears small. There is an assumption here that it is okay to damage a forest if it is only "just a little." How many acres have been subjected to whole-tree clearcuts (as opposed to partial cuts) is anybody's guess. The state has no accurate figures on this. The proper question should be, What does WTH do to the forests where it is used? The argument that it is okay to degrade thousands of acres a year because there are millions more is hardly convincing. We are no longer living on the "cutting edge" of a forest resource so abundant we can afford to waste it.

Recommendations for "mitigating" the effects of WTH are rather amusing. Maine Audubon Society's former director, Charles Hewett recommended "less intensive approaches to intensive harvesting [that] leave behind residual vegetation that in turn maintains the uptake of nutrients within the soil water, buffers the acidity of precipitation reaching the soil, and shades the soil to limit increases in decomposition rates.... Planning for an adequate rotation length can ensure that the ecosystem has time to rebuild its productive potential."[1] As I read this, Hewett is saying that the way to mitigate the effects of WTH on short rotations is to avoid complete clearcuts and to cut on long rotations. Right.

Another idea, advocated by Maine Audubon Society as part of their Forest Practices Act of 1989 (but which did not get incorporated in the law), is to have the landowners who do whole-tree clearcuts promise not to do them again for 100 years or 3 rotations of "conventional" clearcuts. I'm sure there are many forest managers who would not hesitate to promise that if you let them biomass/liquidate the forest now, then someone else, a long time from now, won't cut the forest in the same way. Unfortunately, the state does not have the record-keeping ability, nor is there the landowner continuity that would make such a proposal a realistic option—assuming we think it worthy that someone now should get the goldmine and future generations should get the shaft.

Reference

1. Charles Hewett, "Whole Tree Harvesting: The Potential and the Pitfalls," *Habitat* (September/October 1985): 37.

Myth 7

Biomass and other whole-tree harvests are
adequately regulated.

In 1987 a bill to regulate biomass harvesting, Public Law 286, was passed by the state legislature. On the face of it, it seems to require forester supervision and accountability, but in reality the bill is utterly worthless. It requires that a management and regeneration plan be submitted to the State by the mills—after the cut has occurred. The state has no enforcement capabilities and there are no penalties. Since the information is submitted after the cutting has occurred, there is no way to tell if an operation was appropriate to the site and no way to stop an inappropriate operation in progress. Finally, there is a very sizeable loophole—the bill does not apply to members of the Tree Farm Association. The entire landholdings of companies such as Great Northern (now Bowater), Scott, International Paper, and Champion, as well as the lands managed by Seven Islands, are all Tree Farms.

The clearcutting and regeneration standards passed in 1990 also do not address the special problems of whole-tree clearcuts. The standards do not regulate the intensity of harvests nor do they preclude cutting on poor sites that would have difficulty recovering from intensive cutting. There is no reference to appropriate rotation length following WTH. By managing the legislature, the forest landowners have escaped having to manage their forests.

Herbicides

The most prolific and luxuriant plants to recolonize a site following a clearcut are often "noncrop" broad-leaved species rather than the desired spruce and fir. Foresters "treat" this unwanted growth with their own version of chemotherapy—herbicide spraying. Herbicides are used to release the desired crop trees from competing vegetation. During the 1980s, use of this management tool in Maine expanded dramatically:

Estimated Maine Forest Acreage Treated with Herbicides: 1980-1989[1a,b]

Year	Acreage	Year	Acreage
1980	9,000	1985	42,000
1981	10,000	1986	30,000
1982	18,000	1987	56,000
1983	26,000	1988	81,000
1984	25,000	1989	90,000

Note: Approximately three-quarters of these acres were sprayed with Roundup (active ingredient: glyphosate) and much of the rest with Garlon (active ingredient: triclopyr).

Maine's media and larger environmental groups were surprisingly quiet about this trend, even though herbicide controversies were raging in other states and in nearby Canadian provinces. Some Maine citizens, however, especially those who happend to glimpse the browned-out vegetation that lay beyond the beauty strip, were upset. The government response was to study the problem.

In 1985 the Maine Forests Service published a literature review by James Hynson on the use of herbicides for release of spruce-fir.[2] I was concerned that the report might help to justify the trend toward greater herbicide use, so I wrote a critique, published in 1987.[3] Maine's media and larger environmental groups, however, ignored both Hynson's report and my critique.

In 1989, Maine's Forest for the Future Program (which, like the Maine Forest Service, is part of the Department of Conservation) started a study (published in 1990) on forestry herbicide use by Spectrum Research Inc.[4] The Spectrum report, like the Hynson report, has major flaws, but it contains a more comprehensive review of available literature (excluding the extensive literature written by critics of herbicide spraying).

By 1989 Maine forest landowners were spraying herbicides over 11 times more acres than landowners in Minnesota, the northern state with the next most aggressive spray program.[5] The trend could no longer be ignored. Citizens complained that even the forests along the Allagash Wilderness Waterway were being sprayed. In 1989 the legislature passed a bill that declared a one-year moratorium on spraying along the Allagash while a "balanced" commission (of legislators, citizens, and herbicide users)[c] studied the problem (even though

Herbicide spraying along the Allagash. "Target" was mature hardwood ridge. Note that some of spray drifted across river. Herbicided hardwoods appear as light-colored trees in photo. *Photo by Alex McLean/Landslides.*

Forests for the Future Program was also studying it).

In 1990 the commission came up with recommendations for reforming pesticide regulation in Maine, including:

• changing the structure of the Board of Pesticide Control (BPC, the state agency that regulates pesticides) to reduce conflicts of interest;

• posting sprayed areas;

• monitoring for groundwater contamination;

• repealing the sales-tax exemption for pesticide sales;

• funding research for alternatives to pesticides.

The commission members agreed that it should be state policy to ". . . encourage through education and other appropriate means, the reduction of, and alternatives to, pesticide use."[6] A minority report also recommended switching the BPC from the Department of Agriculture to the Department of Environmental Protection. Forestry herbicide use, however, was neither endorsed nor discredited.

Despite the costs, months of study, and negotiations involved in creating these recommendations, and despite the fact that five legislators were on the commission, including Charles Pray, president of the Senate, and John Martin, Speaker of the House, the Energy and Natural Resources Committee of the state legislature quickly killed the commission's bills in response to the busloads of farmers who protested at the legislative hearing. The farmers claimed that the bills jeopardized their way of life and that they had been given no representation on the commission. Some of the legislators running the hearing thought the study was supposed to be about the problems of forestry herbicide spraying

Preparing helicopter for herbicide spray mission against forest "weeds." *Photo courtesy Bangor Daily News.*

and were puzzled about why they were now dealing with angry farmers. Forestry bills in the Maine legislature have a strange pattern of missing their targets.

Endnotes

a. This chart is based on information compiled from various sources by the state Office of Policy and Legal Analysis. For some years, the estimates differed by thousands of acres, depending on the source. I chose the highest estimates from each year.

The acreage for 1990 dropped dramatically, to 33,730 acres, partly due to a reduction in spraying by Georgia-Pacific on land formerly managed by Great Northern (which had the largest spray program in the state), and partly due to a declining economy.

b. The most commonly used forestry herbicides in Maine are Roundup (active ingredient: glyphosate), Garlon (active ingredient: triclopyr), Tordon (active ingredients: picloram and 2,4-D), and Banvil (active ingredient: dicamba, sometimes with 2,4-D).

c. User members included representatives from Georgia-Pacific, Seven Islands (a large nonindustrial forestland manager), the Maine Forest Products Council (an industry lobby group), the Department of Transportation (which sprays along roads), and Central Maine Power (which sprays along power lines).

References

1. Maine Office of Policy and Legal Analysis, *Final Report of the Commission to Study the Use of Herbicides*, State of Maine 114th Legislature, December 1, 1990, p. 25.
2. James R. Hynson, *Final Report on Silvicultural Release of Seedling and Sapling Spruce-fir Stands: A Literature Review* (Augusta, Me.: Maine Forest Service, September 1985).
3. Mitch Lansky, "Questioning the Assumptions, The Use of Herbicides for Short Rotation Conifer Management in Maine," published by author, March 1987.
4. J. C. Balogh, G. A. Gordon, S. R. Murphy, and R. M. Tiettge, *The Use and Potential Impacts of Forestry Herbicides in Maine*, *Report to Department of Conservation's Forest for the Future Program* (Augusta, Me.: Maine Department of Conservation, 1990).
5. David Maass, *Northern Forest Trends, 1985-1989, Northern U.S.A. and Eastern Canada* (Augusta, Me.: The Irland Group, September 20, 1990), p. 7.
6. Maine Office of Policy and Legal Analysis, *Final Report*, Appendix B1.

Myth 1

Herbicides are an essential forestry tool in Maine.

This myth is an example of circular logic: Herbicides are essential to forestry systems designed around herbicides; forestry systems in Maine are designed around herbicides; therefore, herbicides are essential to forestry systems in Maine. The hidden assumption of the "herbicides are essential" argument is that widescale clearcutting is essential. Without widescale clearcutting, there would be little reason for widescale herbicide spraying because there would be no proliferation of brush. Other forest practices, from selection to shelterwood, do not cause such a brush proliferation because they do not provide the intense sunlight and soil disturbance that stimulate its growth.

Even where clearcutting is standard practice, herbicides are still not essential. In Sweden and in national forests in our own Pacific Northwest, aerial herbicide spraying has been banned or severely restricted due to public opposition; yet forest management in these areas has not collapsed due to loss of this "essential" tool. If anything, the bans have clarified what a waste much of the spraying probably was. In the Siuslaw National Forest in Oregon where spraying was once particularly widespread, silviculturalist Thomas Turpin reported that ". . . the necessary site preparation, reforestation, and release treatments are being accomplished . . . . No backlog of work is accumulating.... District silviculturalists have had to hone their remaining tools and learn to treat only the areas that need treatment."[1]

Reference

1. Thomas C. Turpin, "Successful Silvicultural Operations Without Herbicides in a Multiple Use Environment," *Journal of Pesticide Reform* (Fall 1988): 15.

Myth 2

The broad-leaved plants that flourish after clearcuts are "weeds" that "compete" with crop trees.

The targets of herbicide spraying are plant species that foresters call "weeds" and "competitors." The term *weeds* conjures up the image of worthless, rank-growing plants that are out of place in the industrial forest farm. The term *competitors* implies that when the offending species are present, the crop species are harmed and that when the offending species are removed, the crop species benefit. Yet many of the targets of herbicide spraying do not meet these criteria.

Out of place?
Tolerant Hardwoods

The list of competitive species compiled by herbicide researchers includes all shade-tolerant hardwoods (e.g., American beech, sugar maple, and yellow birch). These species do not usually thrive on primary softwood sites but are normally found on northern hardwood and mixedwood sites. Softwoods benefit from their presence in mixed stands because they improve soil quality and increase resistance to fire, blowdowns, insects, and disease.

Ironically, it is on these better sites that foresters feel most justified investing in early stand management for softwoods. To call species that naturally occupy a site "weeds" is to assume that ecological realities are superfluous to industrial intentions.

Pioneer Species

When foresters scrape a forest down to bare stumps, they create habitats more favorable to pioneer species (trees such as pin cherries, aspens, and white and gray birch, and shrubs such as raspberries), than to red spruce and balsam-fir seedlings. The pioneers are adapted to growing under intense light, whereas the spruce and fir are adapted to growing under the canopy of mature trees.

The pioneer species that revegetate a barren landscape play important roles in reestablishing a forest. Because they are so prolific, they can slow the leaching that occurs when organic matter breaks down into soluble nutrients after clearcutting. The pioneers grow fast but are relatively short lived, giving back their nutrients (accumulated in the form of leaves and rotting wood) for the shade-tolerant understory. The pioneers protect the understory seedlings from the harsh extremes of wind, sun, and frost and maintain a greater diversity of

Spruce, fir, and pine growing under shade of birch in stand recovering from a fire 40
years years previously. From *Fifth Report of the Forest Commissioner of the State of
Maine, 1904*, (Augusta: 1904), pg. 67.

predator/parasite complexes to protect the understory from insects. Before the
age of herbicides, foresters referred to the pioneer hardwood overstory as a
"nurse crop."

Red spruce and balsam fir are not normally harmed by growing under such
a nurse crop. Research has shown that conifer seedlings benefit from partial
shade. Conifer height growth tends to be best with shading down to about 45%
of full sunlight. Although weight gain increases with light exposure in some
species, this is not so with shade-tolerant species such as eastern hemlock and
balsam fir, which gain more weight in partial shade.[1,a]

It is inappropriate to call pioneer species "weeds" when they are growing in
the habitats to which they are adapted. As forest ecologist P. L. Marks observed,
"To deny the role of successional species in the maintenance of forest ecosystem
stability is to misunderstand the real significance of stability."[2]

Worthless?

The term "weed" is inappropriate for another reason: hardwoods, both intolerant and tolerant varieties, have economic as well as ecological value. The 1985
Maine Forest Service study concluded that "high value hardwoods (yellow birch,
sugar maple, white ash, paper birch) may be more profitable to manage and
grow than to control, if site conditions are favorable to their production."[3]

Ironically, predictions of timber supply and demand done for the state of Maine in 1989 by Seymour and Lemin show that the worst shortfalls expected after the year 2000 will be for hardwoods, not for spruce and fir. These projections gave the following estimates of expected shortfalls.[4]

Expected Shortfall

Species Group	(cords/year)
Spruce-fir	316,000
Tolerant hardwoods	599,000
Intolerant hardwoods	529,000

If prices respond at all to supply and demand, and if these projections are correct, hardwoods should increase in value and should hardly be considered "weeds."

Competitors?

Like the concept of "weeds," the concept of "competitors" comes from agriculture, where crops that did not evolve on the sites where they have been introduced can be crowded out by volunteer plants better adapted for survival. Agricultural crop plants require some form of protection. Oregon ecologist Phillip Sollins asserts that a forest ecosystem is different:

"Forests...are natural ecosystems, and have evolved over eons. In natural ecosystems, actual competition between species is rare. When two (or more) species compete, that which is better adapted survives; the others become extinct. This is especially true of pioneer species such as brush. Over time, each species evolves such that its requirements are slightly different than those of other species. Instead of competition, we have resource partitioning (or 'niche separation', as it is sometimes called). Resource partitioning occurs when species have evolved so that their requirements are slightly different. Thus, they do not have to compete for exactly the same resource. . . . Intraspecific competition is keener than interspecific competition. It follows that monoculture promotes competition, while species diversity fosters resource partitioning."[5]

If the noncrop species represent competition for light, water, and soil nutrients, we would expect studies to consistently find that the presence of these species leads to growth reductions. In fact, there is no such consistency in the literature. Canadian researcher A. B. Vincent, for example, found that pin cherry may provide valuable shelter for spruce and fir reproduction and does not suppress these crop trees.[6] Another Canadian researcher, R. E. Wall, found little growth suppression of fir under such species as pin cherry, birch, or raspberries. In fact, the greatest growth increase in the fir was during the 3- to 10-year period when cover by noncommercial species was the greatest. According to Wall, "Only under extreme densities, found by searching numerous clearcuts, has measurable growth suppression been demonstrated."[7]

Wall found no obvious correlations between the density of raspberries and the degree of suppression. In some areas, "fir grew significantly better under dense cover than under light cover.... Although the data do not fully clarify effects of cover on fir seedling development, there is little doubt that beneficial effects are as frequent as detrimental ones."[8] One explanation offered by Wall for this apparent lack of suppression is that the tolerant fir and the intolerant pioneer species have different growth strategies that do not lead to total competition for light and other resources.[9]

Wall did find one possible cause of regeneration problems, but it was not competition—it was soil disturbance caused by logging equipment. He found definite correlations between distribution of fir on undisturbed sites and of pin cherry and raspberry on disturbed sites.[10]

Benefit from Removal?

Most herbicide research studies focus on the efficacy of herbicides for suppressing competing vegetation. Few studies have demonstrated long-term beneficial growth responses. Such responses are assumed if the "weeds" are killed. The 1990 Spectrum report mentions that "reviews of vegetation management studies also suggest that despite successful weed suppression, herbicide treatment is not necessarily a guarantee of increased growth of commercially desirable species."[11]

In one example, Canadian herbicide researcher R. F. Sutton used a variety of herbicides to release white spruce and jack pine from brush species such as aspen and pin cherry. The herbicides were quite successful at suppressing the brush, but the crop trees showed no long-term growth increases and were more harmed than benefitted because of damage from frost and browsing animals. Sutton concluded that "vegetation control and coniferous release are not synonymous."[12]

A study by Gordon Baskerville in New Brunswick found that successful suppression of "competing" white birch and pin cherry did not lead to increased growth in "released" spruce-fir over controls. He concluded that these species are not serious competitors of spruce-fir.[13]

Pioneer species and hardwoods do not, just by their presence, compete with softwoods. Rather than blame "weeds" for the problems of establishing softwood regeneration, managers should blame themselves for creating habitats unfavorable to the very species they are trying to grow.

Endnote

a. Pioneer species tend to have multilayered branches. These allow 15 to 45% of sunlight to penetrate beneath them. Shade-tolerant trees tend to have monolayered branches. These allow 5 to 10% of sunlight to penetrate. Shade-tolerant trees are adapted to becoming established under such reduced light.[14]

References

1. Donald Perala, "Early Release—Current Technology and Conifer Response," In *Artificial Regeneration of Conifers, the Upper Great Lakes Region* (Houghton, Mich.: Michigan Technical University, 1982), p. 403.
2. P. L. Marks, "The Role of Pin Cherry (*Prunus pensylvanica L.*) in the Maintenance of Stability in Northern Hardwood Ecosystems," *Ecology Monograph 44* (1976): 86.
3. James R. Hynson, *Final Report on Silvicultural Release of Seedling and Sapling Spruce-fir Stands: A Literature Review* (Augusta, Me.: Maine Forest Service, September 1985), p. 10.
4. Robert Seymour and Ronald Lemin, Jr., *Timber Supply Projections for Maine, 1980-2080*, CFRU Research Bulletin 7, Maine Agricultural Experiment Station Miscellaneous Report 337 (Orono, Me.: Maine Agricultural Experiment Station, University of Maine 1989), p. 30.
5. Phillip Sollins, *Direct Testimony in re: The Dow Chemical Company et al., FIFRA docket no. 415*

et al., Environmental Protection Agency Exhibit No. 2005 (1981), p. 10.

6. A. B. Vincent, *Balsam Fir and White Spruce Reproduction on the Green River Watershed*, Canadian Department of Northern Affairs and Natural Resources, Forest Resources Division Technical Note 40 (1956).

7. R. E. Wall, *Early Stand Development After Clearcutting of the Cape Breton Highlands*, Maritime Forest Research Centre Information Report m-x-143 (Fredericton, New Brunswick: Canadian Forest Service, Department of Environment, 1983), p. 14.

8. *Ibid.*, p.11.

9. *Ibid.*, p.14.

10. *Ibid.*, pp.7-8.

11. J. C. Balogh, G. A. Gordon, S. R. Murphy, and R. M. Tiettge, *The Use and Potential Impacts of Forestry Herbicides in Maine, Report to Department of Conservation's Forest for the Future Program* (Augusta, Me.: Maine Department of Conservation, 1990), p. 44.

12. R. F. Sutton, "Plantation Establishment in the Boreal Forest, Glyphosate, Hexazinone, and Manual Weed Control," *Forestry Chronicle* (October 1984): 283-286.

13. G. L. Baskerville, *White Birch and Pin Cherry May Not Suppress Young Balsam Fir*, Canadian Department of Forestry, Forest Research Branch, 63-M-24 (Fredericton, New Brunswick: Canadian Department of Forestry, 1963).

14. John C. Kricher, *A Field Guide to Eastern Forests of North America* (Boston: Houghton-Mifflin Co., 1988), p. 217.

Myth 3

Managers use scientific criteria to determine the "need" to spray for softwood release.

A report cited by the U.S. General Accounting Office (GAO) stated that foresters often cannot "on a site-by-site basis determine quantitatively and scientifically whether or not weed management treatments are needed."[1] The Hynson report came to a similar conclusion, saying that "disagreement over what species are undesirable, and densities at which they have become undesirable confound the ability to assess individual situations." This lack of methodology has not prevented the annual spraying of tens of thousands of acres. Nor has it discouraged enthusiastic researchers from estimating lavish benefits from such practices.

A 1981 GAO study found that on national forests "standards varied between districts and many decisions are based on 'gut feel' and past practices."[3] Some areas are sprayed "in anticipation" of a problem; others are sprayed only where there is overtopping brush; and still others are sprayed when managers believe that stocking or stocking vigor would be reduced below "accepted standards."

Certainly it is possible to use more specific criteria, but this requires more detailed analysis of each site. Howard Horrowitz, in cooperation with the Cooperative Management Company in Oregon, proposed several guidelines for such analyses, and using these criteria, surveyed and site- mapped several areas that were to be subjected to operational herbicide spray programs. He concluded that "On one site, the target species. . . occupied less than 3% of the treatment area. 42% of the area was understocked and animal damage was severe. On the other site, [target species] occupied 48% of the unit area, but the Douglas fir growing in association with brush had significantly better height and leader growth than those growing in the open."[4] In other words, release in these places was not justified.

Such intensive surveys of site factors are not being done on the tens of thousands of acres sprayed in Maine each year. Managers assume that brush is a problem and that herbicides are the solution. The companies that do major spray projects apparently would rather spend money on chemicals than on foresters.

References

1. United States General Accounting Office, *Better Data Needed to Determine the Extent to Which Herbicides Should Be Used on Forest Lands*, CED 81-46 (Washington, D.C.: United States General Accounting Office, April 17, 1981), p. 39.
2. James R. Hynson, *Final Report on Silvicultural Release of Seedling and Sapling Spruce-fir Stands: A Literature Review* (Augusta, Me.: Maine Forest Service, September 1985), p. 11.
3. United States General Accounting Office, *Better Data Needed*, p. 39.
4. Howard Horrowitz, *An Evaluation of Conifer Growth, Stocking and Associated Vegetation on North Umpqua, BLM Release Sites* (Eugene, Ore.:Hoedads Inc. and Groundwork, Inc., 1980), p.2.

Myth 4

Herbicides increase yields on all acres on which they are sprayed.

If herbicides were not expected to increase yields, why would companies waste money spraying? According to projections of wood supply done by CFRU researchers Robert Seymour and Ronald Lemin, Jr., on acres where herbicides have been sprayed over clearcuts, yields will increase by an average of 147% on good sites and 221% on fair sites.[1] The dramatically increased yields calculated by these researchers to exact-sounding percentages have been used to justify ever higher levels of spraying.[2] The higher levels of spraying will supposedly help mitigate or even prevent future shortfalls (depending on how much spraying is done).

These impressive estimates are not based on long-term, large-scale studies of operational spray programs. Such studies have not been done in Maine. The 1990 Spectrum report admits that "only a few studies have been published in Maine that demonstrate herbicide use for site preparation or release result in increased site productivity. . . . Lack of long-term studies on the relationship of tree growth and site treatment is a serious problem for most of silvicultural sciences."[3] This does not stop the Spectrum report from making an astounding conclusion: "Large scale adoption of herbicide use by the forest industry in Maine confirms the success of chemical management programs."[4]

Predictions of high yields are based on a limited number of mostly short-term studies. Extrapolating these results into operational spray programs is unwarranted when:

•the trees in the study are treated individually (by saw or by herbicides) on small plots rather than aerially sprayed over large acreages;

•the site quality, crop species, brush species, stand densities, and chemical treatments in the study differ significantly from those of operational spray programs (the high yields assumed by Seymour and Lemin, for example, require that the stands sprayed have 90% of full stocking of spruce and fir, which is unlikely);

•the studies are relatively short term and do not take into account possible future problems, such as browsing or insect attacks;

•the growth and volume of hardwoods are ignored in the control plots. Hardwoods do, after all, have economic values. Yet researchers usually look only at the growth of softwoods, as if the hardwoods in the stand did not even exist. According to figures in a New Brunswick forest biomass and nutrient inventory, some of the hardwood species targeted for herbicides actually have greater growth rates than the "crop" trees on the better sites.[a]

The assumption that herbicide spraying will lead to increased yields is also questionable simply because managers rarely do intensive surveys to prove that brush is actually suppressing crop trees. As I showed with the preceding myth, the mere presence of brush is not synonymous with competition. Release is a response to removal of suppression or competition. Herbiciding noncrop species does not always lead to such a response. There is thus no scientific basis to conclude that widescale spray operations will increase yields on every acre sprayed.

Several factors encountered in operational spray programs can reduce yields below figures projected by researchers:

•Terrain, microclimates, and vegetation can vary over large clearcuts that go on for hundreds of acres. Due to economies of scale, many acres get sprayed that may have low levels of brush or low numbers of crop trees.

•The spray may be more effective on some types of brush than on others, leading to inconsistent results. Indeed, some herbicide-resistant brush species can replace the original target species as major crop competitors.[5] Managers may end up spraying more than once (with a different chemical) or may even spray chemical mixtures, which can have more serious environmental consequences.

•Some areas can get skipped (thus receiving no "benefit"), while others receive double swaths of herbicides, creating residues that are toxic even to crop species.

•Poor timing of application can lead to crop damage. Glyphosate and triclopyr, the two most popular herbicides used in Maine, can injure or kill balsam fir and white pine. Glyphosate can also injure red spruce and kill leader growth of hemlock.[6]

•Browsing damage to some species (such as fir or pine) can increase as more preferred species (e.g., striped and red maple, mountain ash, or hobblebush) are killed.

•Risk of frost damage to softwood seedlings can increase after the protective nurse trees are removed.[7]

•Hardwood loss can lead to increased damage from insects such as the pine weevil or spruce budworm.

•Where herbicides are effective at killing brush but softwoods are sparse, the result can be bushy trees with excessive knots and poor form (tree taper).[8]

The impressive yield increases from spraying thousands of acres a year with herbicides may be more easily achieved on a computer screen than in a forest.

Endnote
a. The following chart, extrapolated from New Brunswick data, shows the superior growth of hardwoods on better sites.

Growth of Softwoods and Hardwoods on Different Site Classes[9]

Mean Annual Increment (cords/acre/year)

Species	high	low	Site Class
Black spruce	0.73	0.61	Good
Black spruce	0.70	0.43	Medium
Black Spruce	0.12	0.05	Poor
White spruce	1.14	0.95	Good
White spruce	0.75	0.51	Medium
White spruce	0.51	0.44	Poor
Balsam fir	0.97	0.77	Good
Balsam fir	0.56	0.41	Medium
Balsam fir	0.44	0.37	Poor
	Herbicide Targets		
Aspen	2.65	2.43	Good
Aspen	1.22	1.11	Medium
Aspen	0.41	0.34	Poor
Birch	0.87	0.58	Good
Birch	0.53	0.51	Medium
Birch	0.34	0.32	Poor
Maple	0.75	0.66	Good
Maple	0.53	0.44	Medium
Maple	0.32	0.29	Poor

From this chart we can see that all three hardwood types have better growth rates on good sites than does black spruce, which is the major plantation species in Maine. Intensive management is supposedly concentrated on better sites, yet only on the poor sites were softwoods superior in growth to aspens. On good sites, aspen growth was more than double that of white spruce and nearly 275% that of fir. A two-story stand of poplar and a shade-tolerant softwood such as red spruce or balsam fir would be even more productive. That researchers and paper companies ignore hardwood growth is indicative of a single-minded fixation on spruce and fir.

References
1. Robert Seymour and Ronald Lemin, Jr., *Timber Supply Projections for Maine, 1980-2080*, CFRU Research Bulletin 7, Maine Agricultural Experiment Station Miscellaneous Report 337 (Orono, Me.: Maine Agricultural Experiment Station, University of Maine, 1989), p. 9.
2. J. C. Balogh, G. A. Gordon, S. R. Murphy, and R. M. Tiettge, *The Use and Potential Impacts of Forestry Herbicides in Maine, Report to Department of Conservation's Forest for the Future Program* (Augusta, Me.: Maine Department of Conservation, 1990), p. 7.
3. *Ibid.*, p. 44.
4. *Ibid.*, p. 41.
5. James R. Hynson, *Final Report on Silvicultural Release of Seedling and Sapling Spruce-fir Stands: A Literature Review* (Augusta, Me.: Maine Forest Service, September 1985), p. 26.
6. James R. Hynson, *Final Report*," p. 27. Also, J. C. Balogh et al., *The Use and Potential Im-*

Herbicide-resistant ferns dominate sprayed plantation. *Photo by Christopher Ayres.*

pacts, pp. 43, 46.
7. J. C. Balogh et al., *The Use and Potential Impacts*, pp. 55 (Sutton, 1984) and 59 (Butler-Fastland, 1988).
8. James R. Hynson, *Final Report*, p. 22.
9. Extrapolated from M. K. Mahendrappa, G. P. Van Raalte, and S. M. Maliondo, "Forest Biomass and Nutrient Inventories in New Brunswick." In *Proceedings of the 7th Bioenergy Research and Development Seminar*, Ottawa, Ontario, April 24-26, 1989.

Myth 5
There are no satisfactory alternatives to herbicides.

This myth, like the one that posits that herbicides are "essential," is designed to make us feel that if there were options to herbicides, managers would certainly use them, but such options do not exist. The most obvious option, however, is well proven and quite practical: stop the heavy cutting and soil disturbance that cause brush proliferation. By avoiding such heavy-handed management and relying instead on harvest methods from selection to shelterwood, some large nonindustrial landowners, such as Baskahegan Lands, which owns 100,000 acres, have been able to avoid the "need" for herbicides.[1]

Where brush already exists, a reasonable approach would be to ask if it (1) serves an important ecological function for the site; (2) has economic value and can be managed instead of destroyed; and (3) represents a threat to the establishment of a new forest. If it does not represent a threat, the best alternative is to do nothing.[a]

After taking over Great Northern in 1990, Georgia-Pacific drastically reduced its herbicide spray program from 25,000 acres a year to 2,000 acres. Georgia-Pacific's executive vice president explained that the company is in the forest-products business, not just the paper business; therefore, he claimed, it clearcuts less, grows trees on longer rotations, and uses both softwoods and hardwoods.[2,b] Great Northern had very little use for hardwoods, except for its biomass boilers; its chemical war against hardwoods had more to do with economic markets than biological imperatives.

Manual methods of early stand management, including brush control, have been used for a long time in Europe (where it is called "cleaning") and more recently in the western United States and in the Maritimes. Scandinavia, where aerial spraying has been discontinued, has extensive experience with manual methods and has developed equipment especially suited for it.

Manual release, where appropriate, has several advantages over chemical methods. Aerial spraying does not achieve on its own such basic management functions as removal of poor-quality or high-risk crop trees, salvage of dead or dying trees, or stand spacing for optimal growth. With manual release, all these functions can be combined in one operation.

Endnotes
a. A mediated agreement signed May 24, 1989, resulting from the controversy over the herbicide Environmental Impact Statement of the Pacific Northwest Region, contains a useful outline of priorities and site and economic analyses that would lead to a minimal use of herbicides. The first priority is prevention of brush problems.[3]

b. A more cynical explanation for the reduction in herbicide use is that Georgia-Pacific was not committed to managing Great Northern's forest. Indeed, Georgia-Pacific sold the land to Bowater one year later. On its Washington County lands, however, Georgia-Pacific does clearcut less and uses no herbicides except on its plantations.

References

1. Michael L. Cline, Tim Zorach, Nancy R. Papoulias, and Jody J. Jones, *Pesticide Reduction: A Blueprint for Action* (Falmouth, Me.: Maine Audubon Society, June 1990), p. 38.
2. *Ibid.*, p. 38.
3. *Northwest Coalition for Alternatives to Pesticides et al.*, v. *Richard Lyng and Oregonians for Food and Shelter, Inc.*, Joint Motion to Dissolve Injunction and Dismiss Complaint with Prejudice, United States District Court for the District of Oregon, Civil No. 83-6272-E-BU, May 24, 1989.

Myth 6

Manual release from brush is unacceptable in Maine because it is labor intensive, dangerous, leads to resprouting, damages residual trees, and costs too much.

Assuming that any form of release is justifiable, what should be the first choice? Herbicide advocates argue that the goal of any alternative to spraying chemicals must be to imitate the action of the chemicals, i.e., to kill or set back nearly everthing that isn't a softwood over a wide area and use very little labor to do it. Workers with clearing saws, they argue, are not as good at herbiciding a clearcut as herbicides. The silvicultural goal, however, is to release only trees that are actually suppressed and to do this at a reasonable cost. Killing all brush and releasing softwoods are not necessarily synonymous. Many of these criticisms, therefore, come from misleading comparisons.

a) Labor Intensive

To say that manual conifer release (MCR) is labor intensive is like saying that chemical release is chemical intensive; it is a tautology. Employing people should be viewed as a plus in a region with traditionally high unemployment. If employers pay good wages, they will find workers. A good example of this is the rise of tree-planting crews that contract all over the country. Thomas Turpin, in his summary of the effects of the injunction against herbicides in Oregon's Siuslaw National Forest, found the labor factor a positive one. "Without the use of herbicides," he wrote, "more contracts and jobs are being created, which provides a social benefit. From these jobs, the dollars expended tend to go into more hands and more communities."[1] An estimate from Oregon showed that at a given investment level, MCR provides 34 times more employee days of work than aerial spraying.[2]

b) Dangerous

Opponents of MCR "prove" that it is dangerous by citing national statistics for accident rates in the logging industry. But brush clearing is not the same as other woods work. Statistics from contracts in Oregon and British Columbia show a low rate of accidents from brush clearing (mostly with chainsaws).[3] The clearing saw, which is often more appropriate for early stand management, is also far safer. A Swedish study found 5 1/2 times more accidents from chainsaws than from clearing saws—and in Sweden chainsaws must be used with all safety equipment.[4]

It is difficult to compare the risks of using clearing saws with the risks of spraying herbicides. Bodily injuries are easy to document. It is far more difficult to assign causal factors to cancer, mutations, and neurological and immunological problems that may be associated with chemicals.

c) Resprouting

Many brush species (including hardwoods such as poplar and red maple) tend to sprout prolifically after being cut or topkilled. This is a problem even with herbicides, though some of the most spectacular examples do come from manual cutting. The degree of hardwood and brush resprouting is dependent on such factors as the age of the trees, season and height from the ground at which they are cut, and degree of shade offered by residual trees.

Researchers in the Siuslaw National Forest achieved a 95% success rate using hand cutting with red alder (a species noted for resprouting). The most important factor was the season, with best results coming from cuts in July. Better control was obtained with cuts on older trees (6 to 10 years old) and cuts as close to the ground as possible.[5] An ongoing study of timing with manual cutting of poplar by the Maine Bureau of Public Land has as yet found no such correlations with peak summer months.[6]

It would be unfair to condemn manual release for leading to poor results if those results are due to poor timing technique. Herbicide spraying is just as dependent on timing for results as manual methods. Much more research has been done on timing of herbicide applications than on MCR.

Manual release, in some studies, has led to better results than herbicides. A literature review by forest researcher Donald Perala on conifer release in the Great Lakes Region concluded that ". . . more research is needed to compare growth response of chemically released conifers with those released by hand. The most spectacular release responses in the literature reviewed here are for hand released conifers. We really do not know whether conifer growth is affected by low chronic tissue herbicide concentrations. Indeed, few studies exist on the long term value of chemical release."[7]

d) Crop Damage

Although some studies using inexperienced crews have shown damage to residual stands from manual release, this does not imply that operational programs will lead to the same result. Economist Jan Newton, of Oregon, cautions that "Contract work contains quality and productivity incentives which are not present in studies. There is a direct relationship between quality and quantity of work on the one hand, and earnings on the other. Compliancy must be within 95% of the contract specifications for workers to receive full pay. These pressures for quality and output are absent from research projects."[8]

This assessment is echoed by Tom Dunn in his review of research studies on conifer release: "Because of rigorous specifications and inspection procedures for manual contracts," he writes, "experienced crews rarely damage crop trees. If conifers are damaged, the crew is subject to a fine and the contracts are terminated."[9]

A study summarized in a 1986 GAO report found that in a comparison in Oregon's Coastal Range, manual release led to the least crop-tree mortality. "Significant differences in total tree height have developed since the release treatments were applied. Trees in the manually cut area were taller on the average than trees in the control area. Trees in the area sprayed with glyphosate were no taller than the trees in the control area."[10]

e) Costs

MCR costs are affected by such functions as stem density and height, slope, acreage, logging debris, and accessibility. The price in the northeastern U.S., according to a study cited in the 1990 Spectrum report can vary between $100 and $200 per acre, while herbicide release can vary between $40 and $100 dollars per acre.[11]

These figures are misleading, however, because the costs for herbicides are underestimated and because manual release and herbicide spraying are not equivalent in effect. Indeed, experienced MCR workers consider contracts requiring the cutting of all brush in imitation of herbicides to be absurd. Herbicides do not give optimum spacing of stands, remove high-risk or poor-quality trees, or change species ratios of conifers to favor longer-lived trees (spruce over fir). Simply spraying herbicides, as Robert Seymour stated at the 1984 Blaine House Conference on Forestry, usually is not enough, "because when you're successful, you often end up with far too many trees of the favored species. In this case, if the goal is to achieve maximum production of merchantable timber, it is necessary to carry out thinning or spacing operations. . . . "[12]

Comparisons between the costs per acre of the two methods are also misleading for another reason—herbicides must be sprayed on a large scale to be cost effective, so many acres are treated where there is no need and thus no benefit. For example, after the injunction against herbicides in the Siuslaw National Forest, silviculturalists discovered that even though per-acre costs of MCR were higher than those of herbicides, the overall costs were comparable because, as Turpin observed, "manual treatments can be confined only to acres that actually need treatment."[13]

A 1986 GAO report on conifer release in national forests found that even looking at per-acre costs, herbicides were not always cheaper. On 2 of the 6 forests studied, per-acre costs for MCR were actually lower than costs for herbicides.[14] While MCR may be cost competitive with herbicides in many cases, it is not clear if either method is cost effective at current stumpage prices, except on the best sites for high-value products.

References

1. Thomas C. Turpin, "Successful Silvicultural Operations Without Herbicides in a Multiple Use Environment," *Journal of Pesticide Reform* (Fall 1988): 15.
2. T. Dunn, "From Research Plots to Forest: Losses Along the Way," *NCAP News*, Vol. 4, No. 4 (1985): 7.
3. Michael Conway-Brown, *Alternatives to Herbicides in Forestry* (Powell River, British Colum-

bia: Friends of the Earth, Canada, 1984).

4. *Ibid.*.

5. Thomas Turpin and Dean S. DeBell, "Control of Red Alder by Cutting." Paper presented at the Oregon State Convention of the Society of American Foresters, May 1986. Available from Siuslaw National Forest, Corvallis, Oregon.

6. Tom Morrison, personal communication, winter 1991.

7. Donald Perala, "Early Release—Current Technology and Conifer Response." In *Artificial Regeneration of Conifers, the Upper Great Lakes Region* (Houghton, Mich.: Michigan Technical University, 1982), p. 405.

8. Jan Newton, "An Economic Analysis of Herbicide Use for Intensive Forest Management, Part II: Critical Assessment of Arguments and Data Supporting Herbicide Use," *NCAP Technical Report No. 2* (1979).

9. T. Dunn, "From Research Plots to Forest," p. 7.

10. United States General Accounting Office, *National Forests: Estimated Costs and Results of Alternative Silvicultural Treatments*, GAO/RCED-87-61FS (Washington, D.C.: United States General Accounting Office, December 1986), p. 22.

11. J. C. Balogh, G. A. Gordon, S. R. Murphy, and R. M. Tiettge, *The Use and Potential Impacts of Forestry Herbicides in Maine*, Report to Department of Conservation's Forest for the Future Program (Augusta, Me.: Maine Department of Conservation, 1990), p. 64.

12. Robert Seymour, "Can We Improve Maine's Timber Supply?" In *Proceedings, A Forest Based Economy: Carrying a Tradition into the Future, Blaine House Conference on Forestry, December 6-7, 1984* (Augusta, Me.: Maine Department of Conservation, August 1986), p. 17.

13. Thomas C. Turpin, "Successful Silvicultural Operations," p. 14.

14. United States General Accounting Office, *National Forests*, pp. 10-15.

Myth 7

Herbicides are only harmful to sensitive plant species and represent an acceptable risk to people.

Public debate on herbicides often boils down to comparing the "known" lavish economic benefits of herbicide spraying with the unknown but "insignificant" health risks to humans. When the public starts to make a case that the herbicide in question has risks that are not insignificant, the companies switch chemicals.

Chemical companies have been given the expensive and impossible task of "proving" that their pesticides are not harmful. This is like trying to prove that ghosts do not exist. Proving that the pesticides are harmful should be much easier, but surprisingly it is not. It is very difficult to establish a clear cause-and-effect relationship between a chemical application and a human illness.

The best that can usually be done is to gather evidence from animal studies and from statistics from human exposures. Even when highly suspicious evidence of harm exists, as with the herbicide 2,4,5-T, it may be decades before regulatory action is taken.

In the 1960s and 1970s scientists began to suspect, based on evidence from the U.S. Army's defoliation program in the Vietnam jungles, that 2,4,5-T (an Agent Orange ingredient) and its contaminant, TCDD dioxin, could cause miscarriages, birth defects, and cancer. Indeed, the suspicions were strong enough that, despite an ongoing war, Agent Orange use was suspended in Vietnam. Yet 2,4,5-T was vociferously defended by the manufacturers, Dow and Monsanto, and thousands of acres of forests and farmland were sprayed with the herbicide in the U.S. until the 1980s.

In 1983, activists and journalists uncovered evidence that EPA officials had hidden evidence of harm from 2,4,5-T and its dioxin contaminant in a study of Great Lakes fish. The officials had also concealed evidence that conclusively linked dioxin (from herbicide spraying) to miscarriages in the Alsea region of Oregon. These officials had forbidden EPA scientists from discussing the Alsea project with the public or media. That same year, the EPA withdrew registration for 2,4,5-T. Top officials were fired or resigned.[1]

Industrial forestry advocates (indeed, even manuals for forestry herbicide applicators) are now claiming that the most popular herbicides currently being used in Maine, Roundup and Garlon (the active ingredient of which is one atom different from 2,4,5-T), are safer than aspirin or table salt.[2] These chemicals are "safe" based on a series of industrial "principles" that assert that the chemicals can do no harm and that the public is obligated to accept exposure to them:

The Principle of Product Infallibility asserts that:
    Any tests that support the contention that the chemical is "safe" are valid.
    Any tests that show any possible harm are invalid.
    Since "theoretically" nothing can go wrong, if anyone claims harm, the cause must be something other than the chemical. This argument is based on circular reasoning.

The Principle of Insignificant Quantity asserts that:
    Everything is made of chemicals.
    Anything is toxic in large enough amounts.
    The public is exposed to mind-bogglingly minute quantities of active ingredients (often measured in parts per million).
    Therefore, the chemicals pose no threats.
    Unfortunately, there are some substances that do have toxic, mutagenic, or carcinogenic effects at extremely minute doses. TCDD dioxin, for example, is regulated at parts per trillion, and some scientists think that is not low enough.

The risks are "acceptable" based on the Principle of Universal Victim Guilt:
    Everyone does something risky (e.g., drives a car, smokes, eats peanut butter, takes aspirin).
    Herbicide risks (as established by the Principles of Product Infallibility and Insignificant Quantity) are less than the common risks that people are already taking.
    Therefore, the risks are acceptable.
The above argument declares that since you are already making yourself sick or even risking your life, it shouldn't bother you if a corporation contributes to these existing trends. The fallacy here is that, in the case of herbicides, the exposures are involuntary. Also, people do not normally drive cars or eat peanut butter because they have a death wish.

The risks are "acceptable" based on a fourth principle, the Principle of the Moral Obligation of Contamination:
    Everyone consumes wood and paper products.
    Herbicides are needed to grow wood for these products.

Therefore, the public is obligated to accept the risks entailed in the production of the products they demand and consume.

A corollary to this principle is that anyone who does not accept the Moral Obligation of Contamination is a NIMBY (Not In My Back Yard)—i.e., selfish. The fallacy here is that the risks are not only unwanted but preventable. The paper being produced now in Maine comes from trees that were grown without the use of herbicides, since herbicides have not been in use long enough to have had any effect on present yields. The risks being taken now are for consumers of the future. Neither current nor future consumers have much say over how the forests are to be managed. This is a corporate decision. If consumers had a say, they might want less clearcutting and spraying.

Aside from this flawed logic, the claims of herbicide safety by the forest and chemical industries have been strained by several other factors:

Fraudulent Testing

Herbicides such as atrazine, cacodylic acid, 2,4-D, dicamba, dinoseb, glyphosate, krenite, picloram, silvex, and simazine were registered, in part, from data generated by fraudulent testing by a company called Industrial Biotest (IBT).[3] Industrial Biotest was the nation's largest commercial toxicological testing company until its fraudulent testing was discovered in 1977. Monsanto (manufacturer of Roundup) was IBT's largest customer and was reported to be one of four chemical companies that knew of IBT's fraudulent testing practices. Indeed, one IBT executive, Paul Wright, was employed by Monsanto before and after his tenure at IBT. All of Monsanto's toxicological registration data for Roundup came from IBT. Wright was at IBT while the lab performed fraudulent tests absolving Roundup of causing mutations in mice and tumors in rabbits.[4]

IBT is not an anomaly in the lab-testing world. According to an article by Oregon activist Paul Merrell, "Numerous other laboratories have been found wanting in good lab practices and recordkeeping, with university laboratories generally ranking lowest."[5] The public has no access to the results of much of the testing, as it is confidential.

Data Gaps

The California Department of Food and Agriculture has determined that the following data gaps exist for glyphosate, triclopyr, 2,4-D, picloram, and dicamba. These are the most widely used forestry herbicides in Maine.

CDFA Herbicide Data Gaps[6]

Data Gaps	Glyphosate	Triclopyr	2,4-D	Picloram	Dicamba
Chronic					
Rat	X	X*			X
Dog		X	X	X	X
Oncogenic					
Rat	X	X*			X
Mouse		X	X	X	X
Reproduction					
Rat	X	X		X	X
Teratogenic					
Rat			X	X	
Rabbit		X		X	X
Chromosome			X	X	X
DNA damage	X			X	
Neurotox	NR	NR	NR	NR	NR

*Combined chronic and oncogenic study. No testing was required for neurotoxicity or immunotoxicity.
NR = Study not required

Poor-quality Data

The 1988 Environmental Impact Statement for Managing Unwanted Vegetation in the Pacific Northwest Region assessed the adequacy of the data generated on the herbicides and found very few items for which tests had been adequate.

Quality of Information on Widely Used Forestry Herbicides in Maine[7]

Type of Toxicity	Glyphosate	Triclopyr	2,4-D	Picloram	Dicamba
Systemic	M-I	M-I	A	A	I
Cancer	M	M	M	M	M
Reproductive	M	M	A	M	M
Developmental	A	A	M	M	M
Neurologic	I	I	A	I	I
Immunologic	I	I	M	I	I

Key:
I = Inadequate
M-I = Marginal, with inconsistent results
M = Marginal, more testing may lead to different results
A = Adequate

Lack of Data on Complete Formulations

The estimates of chemical risk are derived from laboratory tests of only the active ingredients. The complete formulations (including inert ingredients and carriers)[a] are not tested, except for acute toxicity. Nor are herbicide mixtures. Nor are chemical metabolites (what the chemicals break down into). Nor are herbicides routinely tested for synergisms (where the effect of the combination is greater than the sum of the parts) with other chemicals, drugs, nutritional deficiencies, or diseases likely to be encountered.[8]

Government Risk Assessment

Whereas chemical or timber companies may claim that currently used herbicides are harmful only to plants, some government agencies have discovered, from animal studies and human exposures, evidence of risk and have even recommended restrictions on use.

In 1988 and 1989, the USDA Forest Service in the Pacific Northwest in its Environmental Impact Statement decided that sufficient evidence of risk exists to warrant restricting the use of 2,4-D (to be used "only as a last resort")[9] and to prohibit female workers from applying 2,4-D, triclopyr, or dicamba with backpack sprayers.[10] The EIS determined that under accidental conditions these chemicals have a high risk of causing adverse effects to the reproductive system.[11]

The EIS considered the carcinogenic risk of 2,4-D, glyphosate, and picloram to be uncertain or controversial.[12] One reason for the severe restrictions on 2,4-D, however, was evidence from several studies (from Kansas and Sweden) linking the chemical to increased risks of a normally rare cancer of the lymph system, non-Hodgkins' lymphoma.[13]

Evidence from the EPA's Pesticide Incident Monitoring System (which was eliminated under the Reagan administration) showed that people exposed to Roundup reported problems with conjunctivitis (inflammation of the eyelid and eyeball mucus membrane), dermatitis (inflammation of the skin), and severe flu-like symptoms.[14] In 1986, Roundup was the fourth-largest cause of pesticide-related illnesses in California out of 143 pesticides.[15] Such risks may be acceptable to the landowners doing the spraying, but they are not acceptable to the spray victims.

Endnotes

a. The active ingredients are combined with inert ingredients to make the formulation. A coalition of Canadian environmental groups demanded in January of 1990 that their country suspend registration of the herbicide Vision (the Canadian version of Roundup) because polyalkoxylated and polyamine inert ingredients contain the chemical 1,4 dioxane (not dioxin), which has been shown to cause liver and kidney damage, cancer, and birth defects in laboratory animals.[16] Inert ingredients are trade secrets, unavailable for public scrutiny.

b. The Northwest Coalition for Alternatives to Pesticides (NCAP) has published a *Glyphosate Information Packet*, prepared by Susan Allen and Mary Ellen McMahon, July 1990, available for $15.50. Write to NCAP, P.O. Box 1393, Eugene, Oregon 97440.

References

1. Joe Thornton and John Hanrahan, "The Dioxin Deception," *Greenpeace* (May/June 1991): 37.
2. R. A. Lautenschlager, "Research Reveals That Herbicidal Spraying Actually Helps Wildlife," *Bangor Daily News*, October 20, 1989, p. 9. Also, Max Williamson and Charles I. Shade, *Safety Training for Forestry Applicators*, USDA Forest Service Fact Sheet 393 (Washington,

D.C.: United States Forest Service, United States Department of Agriculture, February 1986), p. 13.
3. Paul Merrell, "The Industrial Biotest Caper," *NCAP News* (Winter 1981): 5.
4. Anthony Kimery, "Weed Killer," *The Progressive* (July 1987).
5. Paul Merrell, "The Industrial Biotest Caper," p. 4.
6. *Managing Competing and Unwanted Vegetation, Final Environmental Impact Statement* (Portland, Ore.: USDA Forest Service, Pacific Northwest Region, 1988), Appendix D, pp. 3-102 and 3-103.
7. *Ibid.*, "Characterization and Management of Risk," p.42.
8. *Ibid.*, Appendix D, p. 5-58.
9. *Ibid.*, "Summary of Mediated Agreement, May 1989," p.
10. *Ibid.*, "Record of Decision," p. 19.
11. *Ibid.*, "Characterization and Management of Risk," p. 48.
12. *Ibid.*, p. 47.
13. Sheila Hoar et al., "Agricultural Herbicide Use and Risk of Lymphoma and Soft-tissue Sarcoma," *Journal of the American Medical Association* , Vol. 256 (1986): 1141-1147. Also, Lennart Hardell et al., "Malignant Lymphoma and Exposure to Chemicals Especially Organic Solvents, Chlorophenols and Phenoxy Acids: A Case-control Study," *British Journal of Cancer* (1981): 268-269.
14. California Department of Food and Agriculture, *Summary of Illness and Injuries Reported in California by Physicians as Potentially Related to Pesticides, January 1-December 31, 1986* (March 17, 1987).
15. Summary of Reported Pesticide Incidents involving Glyphosate (Isopropylamine Salt) Pesticide Incident Monitoring System Report No. 373, by Health Effects Branch Hazard Evaluation Division Office of Pesticide Programs Environmental Protection Agency, October 1980.
16. Mary O'Brien, "Roundup, Vision, POEA, and 1, 4-Dioxane: Why full formulations are the problem," *Journal of Pesticide Reform* Vol. 9, No. 4, Winter, 1990, p. 14-15.

Myth 8

Herbicides are adequately regulated.

Two basic forms of regulation are prevention and control. Prevention implies a commitment to reduce reliance on chemical pesticides. Maine has not exhibited such a commitment. Reliance on chemical herbicides during the 1980s increased at a rapid rate with government encouragement. The state's Bureau of Public Land even had its own small spray program.

Herbicide applications are regulated by the Board of Pesticide Control (BPC). Of the seven members, four are certified pesticide applicators. Two of these, Andy Berry of Maine Helicopter and Tom Saviello of International Paper Company, have been directly involved in forestry herbicide programs. In 1990, Saviello was elected chairman of the BPC.

The regulations for spraying are not overly restrictive. There are no required buffers. Applicators are allowed to spray in winds up to 15 miles per hour. Notification and posting are voluntary. Drift regulations allow residue levels up to 20% of a direct application to contaminate "sensitive" (within 100 feet of your house) areas of your property, and an unspecified amount beyond that figure for "non-sensitive" portions of your property. At this writing (Spring 1992), no cases of forest herbicide violations have been tried under these lax regulations.

Myth 9

Herbicide release is a cost-effective management technique for spruce-fir forests.

Oregon economist Jan Newton, after a year-long study of more than 8,000 pages of documents on herbicides, came to the following conclusions, which she presented to a Congressional subcommittee during national field hearings on herbicides:

"There does not appear to be a valid economic case for extensive herbicide use in forest management;

"There is no empirical basis for the increased timber yields that are claimed to result from herbicide use;

"The alleged employment impacts [jobs saved in the timber industry by boosting wood production with herbicides] from herbicide use do not exist;

"Forest managers appear to have created a bogus economic analysis for manual methods of forest management, in order to give the impression that there is no cost effective alternative to herbicide use;

"A comprehensive analysis, performed according to accepted scientific procedures, shows that the true costs of herbicide use are many times higher than the published figures and the benefits are a fraction of those claimed."[1] No one at the hearings challenged her findings.

Ironically, even assuming that:
•the company sprays only once;
•the spraying will lead to predicted high yields on every acre sprayed;
•there is no risk involved (such as increased susceptibility to spruce budworm or other insects or diseases);
•hardwoods have no value and can be completely ignored;
•spraying creates no "external" costs to health or the natural environment; and that
•there are no indirect costs, such as public relations, legal costs, etc.,

an economic analysis of herbicide spraying to grow pulpwood on a short rotation (as many companies claim they are doing) comes out with a negative net present value with industrially used discount rates—unless one assumes stumpage values far higher than those currently reported to the state.[a]

In the real world, however, all of the best assumptions of costs and yield are not valid:
•Companies have to spray more than once on a certain percentage of their operations because the brush bounces back too fast or too hard or because some of the brush is resistant to the first herbicide used.
•Herbicides will not always give the predicted yields on every acre; indeed, on many sprayed acres there is no benefit at all.
•Concentrating growth on balsam fir (which dominates many clearcuts) will create stands more susceptible to insects such as the spruce budworm.
•Hardwoods do have economic value and should not be ignored in the calculations. In fact, total volume of wood of all species can be higher without

herbicides when there is an overstory of intolerant hardwoods and an understory of shade-tolerant softwoods.

•Spraying creates external costs because of environmental, social, and health problems. Some of the most significant costs come from the manufacture and disposal of the chemicals—costs that are not incorporated in the product prices.

•Spraying entails indirect costs such as public relations, research, legal suits, regulation, etc.

When all these costs are factored in, spraying, which gives marginal benefits only when you assume higher stumpage values than those reported to the state, is not cost-effective at all. This may explain why nonindustrial landowners who are managing for stumpage rarely use herbicides to grow even-aged, short-rotation pulpwood stands.

In a 1990 Maine Audubon Society policy study on pesticide use in Maine, Michael Cline (formerly a forester for International Paper Company) offered an explanation for why industrial landowners are responsible for the bulk of herbicide spraying in Maine:

"The return on investment from herbicide spraying offers no justification to applying herbicides to grow pulpwood for sale on the open market; however, timber availability drives the paper making process. While it may not make economic sense to manage non-industrial land for pulpwood, a secure and sustainable timber supply is essential to keep multi-million dollar paper machines running. When viewed in this context, the cost of applying herbicides is an inexpensive insurance policy to protect fiber supply [from] the projected softwood supply shortfall for Maine that, according to experts, will occur in 15 to 25 years." [2]

While the companies may have such long-term motivations as suggested by Cline, they also may have some shorter term motivations. Today's corporate forester may be thinking more about current job security than about the well-being of industrial foresters of the future. Spraying herbicides over today's clearcuts, after all, will not do much to alleviate a shortfall that will start in 15 years. Indeed, the wood grown in such a fashion will not become available until 30 or more years after the expected shortfall starts. If anything, the clearcutting itself is exacerbating any imminent shortfall by wiping out medium-sized trees that would be mature when the mills need the wood the most.

One major short-term benefit of herbicide spraying is ACE, the Accelerated Cut Effect. By assuming high future yields from one shot of herbicides, managers can justify high levels of cutting now. Spraying herbicides gives the appearance (from a distance) that the forest manager is actually managing the corporate woodlands rather than simply deciding where the next clearcut should be located.

Herbicide spraying may not be all that profitable for forest landowners, but it is very profitable for chemical companies. They have invested some of their profits into research to find new ways to use their products, and they have contacts in the forestry community (such as the Cooperative Forestry Research

Unit) who are very effective at advising foresters on "effective" ways of dealing with the brush that results from clearcutting. This is analogous to pesticide salespeople advising farmers on pest control. It is simply more profitable to research chemical management methods than more ecologically benign management methods.

Foresters, however, are not so attached to using herbicides that they will keep spending levels on spraying consistent, even during economic downturns. Spraying can be deducted as a working expense and has some tax benefits during economic booms. When times are bad, as in 1990 and 1991, the level of herbicide spraying can drop precipitously.

Endnote

a. A former industrial forester confided to me that herbicide spraying was the only early stand management technique that could meet his company's 6% hurdle rate (minimal return on investment). When I used government figures for herbicide costs and stumpage returns and accepted all optimistic assumptions, however, herbicide spraying did not meet a 6% hurdle rate. It did not even meet a 5% rate of return. The average cost per acre (including contract and administrative) of herbicide release for six national forests in 1983 (before the ban on spraying in national forests) was $94.33.[3] Maine's Bureau of Public Land estimated that a herbicide contract plus administration would cost them $65 per acre for 1988.[4] While a fair middle ground for cost might be $80, I will give the industrial foresters the benefit of the doubt by using the lowest price ($65) in the following analysis.

The benefit of spraying would be the growth that would occur above that expected without spraying. If we use the same figures as those used by Seymour and Lemin in their models projecting benefits from "intensive management" (they assume that such yields will come from spraying, thinning, or planting), we find that on a 50-year rotation, herbicide application will yield a benefit of approximately 31 cords per acre of well-stocked trees whether on a good or a fair site, that is, by some good fortune, 90% stocked with softwood.[3] By using these figures I am not acknowledging their validity but giving the sprayers the benefit of the doubt. Since the average stumpage price for spruce-fir pulp (which is what companies would be managing for on a 50-year rotation if they did no thinning) reported to the state in 1988 was $13.50 per cord, the Future Value of the benefit would be 31 x $13.50, or $418.50 per acre. In the following exercise I compare the present values of the costs and benefits, not at 6% but at 5%.

Net Present Value (NPV) of Herbicide Benefits at 5% Discount

Activity	Year	FV/acre	PV/acre[*]
Benefits: 31 cords at $13.50/cord	50	$418.50	$36.49
Costs: Herbicides	5	$65	$50.93
NPV (benefits minus costs) =			-$14.44

[*]Present Value (PV) is calculated as outlined in Chapter 1, part D.

After reviewing this exercise, you are right to ask how these companies can claim to get a 6% return when spraying doesn't even merit a 5% return. The answer is they probably assume lower costs for spraying and higher values for stumpage or perhaps even estimate higher yields. We can work the PV formula backward to discover what the value of the stumpage is to these companies at a given discount rate and a given value for herbicides. Assuming that spraying does cost $65 per acre, if the investment pays off at 6%, then the stumpage value of the wood can be determined by the following formula:

Stumpage = (PV @ 6% of herbicides ($48.57) x $(1.06)^{50}$)/31 cords.

Thus, the stumpage value of spruce-fir to the company would be $28.86. This is quite a bit higher than the $13.50 figure reported to the state for 1988. The landowner might claim to be managing lumber rather than pulpwood. Spruce-fir lumber had a stumpage value close to $31 a cord in 1988, but it is highly improbable that no management other than herbicides would produce a stand that is 100% suited for lumber in a 50-year period. A good proportion of the wood would be suitable only for pulp. One must conclude, therefore, that the company attributes higher value to pulpwood than does the state.

References

1. Jan Newton, "Herbicides and Economics," *NCAP News* (Fall/Winter 1983-1984): 10.
2. Michael L.Cline, Tim Zorach, Nancy R. Papoulias, and Jody J. Jones, *"Pesticide Reduction: A Blueprint for Action* (Falmouth, Me.: Maine Audubon Society): 38.
3. Extrapolated from United States General Accounting Office, *National Forests: Estimated Costs and Results of Alternative Silvicultural Treatments*, GAO/RCED-87-61FS (Washington, D.C.: United States General Accounting Office, December 1986), pp. 10-15.
4. Tom Morrison, personal communication, spring 1988.

Spruce Budworm Spraying

Being in or near a forest during a major defoliating insect outbreak can be an awesome experience. Millions of caterpillars are climbing up trees and buildings, across roads, and even over parked cars. In the woods, even though it may be a sunny day, it sounds as if it is raining. And it is raining; but what is coming down is not water, it is frass (solid larval insect excrement).

Industry foresters call insects that compete with the mills for desired species "pests." Some forest insect pests in Maine have caused serious economic damage. Hardwoods, for example, have been attacked by gypsy moths, bronze birch borers, saddled prominent moths, and forest tent caterpillars. Softwoods have been ravaged by spruce bark beetles, hemlock loopers, gall midges, woolly aphids, and white pine weevils. But the most devastating bug in the industrial forest program has been the spruce budworm.

The spruce budworm (*Choristoneura fumiferana*) is a plain looking moth whose larvae feed on the needles of fir, spruce, and hemlock. The caterpillars start by feeding on the new growth in the trees' buds, but after a number of years (outbreaks generally last from 5 to 11 years), the defoliation can be severe enough to kill the trees. Balsam fir is the most susceptible species, but in some localities significant quantities of spruce die as well.

During the twentieth century the spruce budworm has been, with one exception (the forest industry), the single greatest disturbance factor in the forests of Maine and eastern Canada. During an outbreak that lasted from 1910 to 1919, the budworm killed an estimated 27.5 million cords of spruce and fir in Maine, and 225 million cords in the whole of northeastern North America.[1] At the time, foresters were powerless to fight the outbreak; they simply had to wait until natural controls—insectivorous birds, reptiles, and other small animals—caught up with the budworm.

In 1919, at the end of the outbreak, Maine Forest Commissioner Forrest

A spruce budworm: the bug in the industrial forest program.
From Maine Forest Review, *Vol. 12, 1980.*

Trees defoliated by the spruce budworm. *Photo by Christopher Ayres.*

Colby wrote: "With poison sprays and sticky paper we may account for a few bugs and flies; but we would soon be overcome without the aid of our many vigilant little allies—the insect hunting birds and many of the smaller animals and reptiles. So we may well give every protection and support to these busy little helpers that render such great assistance in keeping this insect peril in check . . ."[2]

When the next major budworm outbreak started in the late 1940s, foresters were not so passive. They now had squadrons of retired World War II bombers at their command and a new wonder-chemical, DDT. The foresters saw themselves as doctors treating a major forest disease. Their "treatments" in Canada and Maine turned into some of the largest, most persistent aerial spray programs in the world.

New Brunswick started spraying in 1952, and Maine followed in 1954. Unfortunately, budworms were not completely controlled by the spraying, but salmon and eagles nearly were. The Maine Forest Service dropped DDT after 1967 and in the 1970s started using less-persistent organophosphate and carbamate pesticides.

Despite massive annual spray programs during the 1970s the budworm outbreak exploded. By 1976, when spraying peaked, the outbreak covered 200 million acres of Maine and eastern Canada. In that year, Maine sprayed 3.5 million acres of forest with chemical pesticides (this is equal in size to Connecticut and Rhode Island put together) and Quebec and New Brunswick each sprayed more than 9 million acres. Maine sprayed until 1985 (22 times from 1954 to 1985) before the outbreak finally collapsed. New Brunswick's outbreak never completely collapsed—that province is still spraying.

The collapse of the outbreak in Maine, however, is not the end of the budworm story. There will be future outbreaks. No one knows when the next one will occur, but with the interval between the onset of the last two outbreaks (ca. 1950 and 1971) having been only a little more than 20 years, the next one may be as early as early as the mid to late 1990s.

The forest management of yesterday and today will affect the severity of the budworm outbreak of tomorrow. Unfortunately much of yesterday's (since

Extent of spruce budworm defoliation and spraying in 1976. *From* Maine Forest Review, *Vol. 13, 1980, p. 5.*

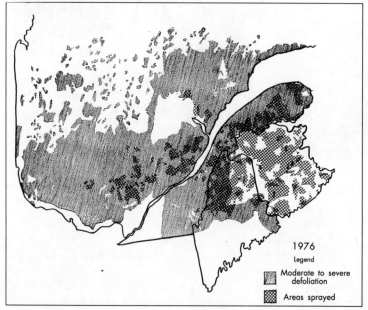

Spruce budworm search and destroy mission. *Photo courtesy Bangor Daily News.*

the 1970s) and today's management is leaving even-aged stands loaded with fir, the budworm's favorite food. The forest industry would like assurance that the government (i.e., the public) will help pay to protect these stands the next time the budworm comes around. From the 1950s through the 1970s the state and federal governments helped subsidize the spray program. In the 1980s the state bowed out, and in 1983 all direct subsidies for spraying were terminated. In 1983, '84, and '85, the spray program was funded entirely by private (i.e., industrial) dollars.

The forest industry was not pleased by these funding withdrawals. During the hearings for the 1989 Forest Practices Act in Maine, a number of industrial representatives suggested that the state should restore government "cooperation" for spray projects. Even as we wait for the budworm to return, other insects, such as the gypsy moth and hemlock looper, are in outbreak condition and are causing mortality and growth losses on hundreds of thousands of acres. The issues raised in this section are not historical curiosities; they are important now.

References
1. Martin Jones, "The Spruce-budworm Disaster: An Integrated Approach," *American Forests*, Vol. 86, No. 6 (June 1980): 19.
2. Forrest Colby, *Forest Protection and Conservation in Maine* (Augusta, Me.: Maine Forestry Department, 1919), p. xxxi.

Myth 1

The spruce budworm is a threat to the spruce-fir forest.

The spruce budworm in all likelihood coevolved with the northeastern forest. Canadian researcher J. R. Blais has found evidence of spruce budworm outbreaks over a period of 250 years,[1] and caterpillar head capsules of the budworm family have been found in pond sediments dating back 10,000 years.[2]

Spruce budworms have important roles in forest succession. In the boreal forest, a fir/white spruce forest that is subjected to a budworm outbreak tends to be followed by fir/white-spruce again, with fir maintaining dominance. According to former USDA Forest Service researcher Gordon Mott, the spruce budworm helps maintain the dominance of red spruce in the Acadian forest of Maine and the Maritimes.[3] Balsam fir regenerates prolifically after a disturbance and could dominate a site, but the spruce budworm tends to "purge" the more vulnerable and shorter lived fir, favoring the more resistant and longer-lived red spruce. Mott hypothesizes that during periods of spruce dominance there would be fewer and less severe budworm outbreaks. During the longer period without severe budworm attacks, disturbances would again favor fir regeneration, until its proportion would be high enough for another budworm purge. A spruce-fir/spruce/spruce-fir cycle would result.

Some industrial managers argue that the budworm is a threat because vast areas of dead forests might burst into flames. There is no conclusive evidence, however, that Acadian forests are more prone to burn after a budworm outbreak. Even after Maine's severe outbreak of 1910-1919, fewer acres burned than in the 1930s and 1940s when presumably there was a young, green forest growing.[4]

Despite the lack of any spraying by Native Americans, the forest was not a devastated wreck when the first European settlers came. Indeed, they marveled at the size of the trees and the extent of relatively unbroken forest. If there is a threat to the forest, it is from forest industries that are competing with the budworm for the same resource. To the degree that industry leaves no fat for the budworm to chew on and encourages a shift to the species that the budworm favors, the budworm becomes a threat to the forest industry.

References

1. J. R. Blais, "Trends in the Frequency, Extent, and Severity of Spruce Budworm Outbreaks in Eastern Canada, " *Canadian Journal of Forestry*, Vol. 13 (1983): 539-547.
2. Lloyd Irland et al., *The Spruce Budworm Outbreak in Maine in the 1970's—Assessment and Directions for the Future*, Bulletin 819 (Orono, Me.: Maine Agricultural Experiment Station, University of Maine, October 1988), p. 10.
3. D. G. Mott, "Spruce Budworm Protection Management in Maine," *The Maine Forest Review*, Vol. 13 (1988): 28.
4. R. H. Ferguson and N. P. Kingsley, *The Timber Resources of Maine*, USDA Forest Service Resource Bulletin NE-26 (Broomall, Pa.: United States Forest Service, United States Department of Agriculture, 1972), p. 35.

Myth 2

Severe spruce budworm outbreaks on short cycles are a natural occurrence. Corollary: Forest management has had minimal impact on budworm cycles.

During the 1970s budworm outbreak, industry foresters insisted that their management had nothing to do with the size, intensity, or frequency of outbreaks. Yet ecologist Craig Lorimer concluded, based on his review of early forest surveys of northeastern Maine, that this region previously experienced only isolated budworm outbreaks and did not have severe, widespread budworm epidemics until the twentieth century.[1]

Area of forest moderately or severely infested with spruce budworms in the twentieth century. *From J. R. Blais, "Trends in the Frequency, Extent, and Severity of Spruce Budworm Outbreaks in Eastern Canada," Canadian Journal of Forest Resources, Vol. 13 (1983), p. 539.*

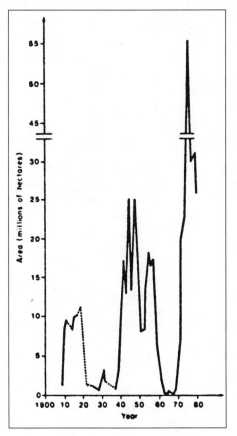

Maine's forest commissioner in 1919, Forrest Colby, mentioned a possible outbreak in the Casco Bay area in 1807 and a fairly severe one in 1878-79 that was confined to the coast and did not penetrate to the northern interior.[2] Quebec researcher Yvon Hardy found that the first 200 years of known budworm history were characterized by regional outbreaks that did not spread to adjacent forests.[3] J. R. Blais's reconstruction of possible outbreaks in the region over a 300-year period found that "earlier infestations were restricted to specific regions, but in the 20th century they have coalesced and increased in size, the outbreaks of 1910, 1940, and 1970 having covered 10, 25, and 55 million [hectares] respectively."[4]

According to Blais this increase in frequency, extent, and severity of outbreaks "appear[s] mostly attributable to changes caused by man, in the forest ecosystem. Clear-cutting of pulpwood stands, fire protection, and the use of pesticides against the budworm favor fir-spruce stands, rendering the forest more prone to budworm attack."[5, a]

Endnote

a. These factors (and others which Blais includes) make the forest more prone to attack in the following ways:

•Clearcutting favors fir regeneration over spruce and makes the forest composition more vulnerable;

•Fire control prevents the formation of a mosaic of spruce-fir and pioneer hardwoods, which would be less susceptible;

•Abandoned farmland has led to large concentrations of white spruce, a species that is less vulnerable than fir but that can support high population levels of budworms;

•Birch diebacks (1930-50) led to higher concentrations of fir, which filled the gaps left by dead birch;

•Insecticide spraying can prolong infestations, as in New Brunswick, which has been spraying for 4 decades, or shorten the intervals between outbreaks, as in the Gaspé region of Quebec, where an infestation ended after 5 years of DDT spraying but then returned in only 21 years.[6]

References

1. Craig Lorimer, "The Presettlement Forest and Natural Disturbance Cycle of North Eastern Maine," *Ecology*, Vol. 58, No. 1 (1977): 145.
2. Forrest Colby, *Forest Protection and Conservation in Maine* (Augusta, Me.: Maine Forestry Department, 1919), p. 143.
3. Yvon J. Hardy, *Dynamics of Spruce Budworm Epidemics* , USDA Forest Service General Technical Report GTR-NE-99 (Washington, D.C.: United States Forest Service, United States Department of Agriculture, 1985), pp. 93-97.
4. J. R. Blais, "Trends in the Frequency, Extent, and Severity of Spruce Budworm Outbreaks in Eastern Canada," *Canadian Journal of Forestry*, Vol. 13(1983): 539.
5. *Ibid.*
6. *Ibid.*, p. 544.

Myth 3

Spruce budworm outbreaks are caused by vast stretches of overmature spruce-fir forests.

Industrial foresters' assumption that vast stretches of overmature spruce-fir cause budworm outbreaks leads to their conclusion that clearcutting spruce-fir on short rotations prevents outbreaks. If past observations and recent theories are correct, however, then both the assumption and conclusion of this myth are wrong—perhaps tragically wrong.

If the myth were true, we would find the most frequent outbreaks in the allegedly most susceptible stands—old-growth spruce-fir. Furthermore, we would expect the most frequent outbreaks to occur in the boreal forest, where vast stretches of spruce-fir are most common. Surely we would not expect to find outbreak centers, or epicenters, in young growth dominated by hardwood. But careful analysis in Quebec, Manitoba, Ontario, New Brunswick, and Maine reveals just that.[1]

Rather than find outbreaks starting in pure boreal spruce-fir forests, Quebec researcher Yvon Hardy found that outbreak epicenters were in mixedwoods or northern hardwoods with a strong maple or yellow birch component.[2] Pure spruce-fir stands were nonexistent in the epicenters. Furthermore, the trees were more often in young age classes than mature. Overmature spruce or fir, according to Hardy, were barely present. Indeed, there was almost no red spruce at all.

Much of these epicenter areas had been logged and had significant levels of such species as poplar, white birch, or red maple, which are indicators of disturbance. Although balsam fir did not make up the majority of such stands, it was usually the single most abundant species, representing anywhere from 9% to 36% of the stand. Hardy concluded that ". . . ecological disturbance is an integral part of the definition of epicenters as they were identified in Quebec. These perturbations initiate the establishment of pioneer species, which in turn facilitate the establishment of transition species, particularly balsam fir. In this way, the spruce budworm is supplied with food and shelter in forest regions normally recognized for their scarcity of fir."[3]

Hardy hypothesizes that these stands are in the "zone of thermal preference" for the spruce budworm. The conifer foliage in these predominantly hardwood and mixedwood stands is more nutritious, causing budworms to grow larger and lay more eggs. Although the boreal forest is full of the spruce budworm's favored food supply, outbreaks have been less common there because the weather is more severe and less favorable to budworm survival. Budworm populations from the hardwood/conifer transition zone epicenters have spilled over to the more vulnerable boreal regions during the latest outbreaks, however, and have caused considerable damage.

Birds and Budworm Control

Recent research by USDA biologists Hewlette Crawford and Daniel Jennings offers fascinating evidence of how birds may help control budworm outbreaks. Although Crawford and Jennings identified numerous predators that feed on budworm at all stages of development, they determined that birds alone are capable of consuming approximately 90% of the budworm at endemic (non-outbreak) levels.[4] Certain species of insectivorous birds (the most important being Blackburnian, Cape May, and bay-breasted warblers) can significantly influence budworm populations and apparently can prevent an upward population swing from becoming an uncontrollable outbreak. Not only do they increase their feeding on budworms as budworm populations increase, but they also increase in number.[a]

In budworm epicenters with a high hardwood component, the common birds such as red-eyed vireos and ovenbirds do not commonly feed on low-density budworm larval or pupal populations. Mature deep-crowned red spruce, which offers the favored habitat for budworm-eating warblers, is absent or negligible. Budworms feeding on the nutritious fir in the zone of thermal preference can increase beyond the regulating threshold of predators and spread out to infest other stands.

Pure fir stands support much lower bird densities than mature spruce stands or mixedwoods, and the warbler species that feed on budworm are few in number here as well. With an ample supply of mature flowering fir and favorable weather conditions,[b] the budworm can escape the restraints of low-level predation.

According to Crawford, Jennings, and R. W. Titterington, "a mature managed forest containing a mix of species and size classes, and scattered openings and patches of regeneration, supports populations of birds that prey effectively on spruce budworm."[5] If birds are indeed as important in controlling budworm outbreaks as these researchers suggest, then it follows that mature forests dominated by spruce, rather than immature forests dominated by fir, should be the goal of forest management. Mature large-crowned spruce is not the problem; it is the solution.

Endnotes

a. There is also evidence that when bird populations are reduced, a budworm outbreak may result. In the springs of 1907 and 1910 in Minnesota, thousands of migrating warblers were killed by late snow and ice storms. Their populations had only recovered to 10% of their former numbers by 1912 when a budworm outbreak occurred in that state.[6]

Recent research by Robbins et al.,[7] has indicated that there has been a significant general decline in many species of North American birds that migrate to the neotropics (Central and South America) since 1978. The researchers compared trends in resident species and temperate-zone migrants to make sure there was no bias in the reporting. Of particular concern for this chapter is evidence that the three most important budworm-feeding warblers are declining over eastern North America. Blackburnian warblers have been declining at 1.1% a year, Cape May warblers at a rate of 2.3% a year, and bay-breasted warblers at a frightening rate of 15.8% a year since 1978.[8] Bird breeding surveys in Maine have also shown a steady decline in bay-breasted warblers. Maine bay-breasted populations in 1989 were 8% of their 1979 levels.[9]

The reason for the decline is habitat degradation in both the tropics and in North America. Robbins et al., end their paper with a chilling prediction: "Given

Blackburnian warbler searching for spruce budworm larvae in fir foliage. *From Daniel T. Jennings and Hewlette S. Crawford, Jr.,* Predators of the Spruce Budworm, *Spruce Budworms Handbook, Agriculture Handbook No. 644 (Washington, D.C.: USDA Forest Service Cooperative State Research Service, 1985), p. 54.*

the patterns of increasing forest destruction and fragmentation in both breeding and wintering areas of neotropical migrant birds, we predict that populations of migratory forest birds will continue to decline.[10]

b. Dry weather, which causes water-stress, increases the concentration of nutrients in the tree needles and decreases the percentage of nonnutrient chemical insect deterrents (such as tannins and turpenes). Budworms grow larger on such food and produce more eggs.[11]

References

1. Russell E. Keenan and Mark C. Maritato, *The Protection of Red Spruce From Spruce Budworm Defoliation: A Literature Review* (Augusta, Me.: Maine Forest Service, 1985), p. 4.
2. Yvon J. Hardy, A. LaFond, and L. Hamel, "The Epidemiology of the Current Spruce Budworm Outbreak in Quebec," *Forest Science*, Vol. 29, No. 4,(1983): 715-725.
3. *Ibid.*, p. 722.
4. Daniel T. Jennings and Hewlette S. Crawford, Jr., *Predators of the Spruce Budworm, Spruce Budworm Handbook*, Agriculture Handbook No. 644 (Washington, D.C.: USDA Forest Service Cooperative State Research Service, 1985), p. 51.
5. H. S. Crawford, R. W. Titterington, and D. T. Jennings, "Bird Predation and Spruce Budworm Populations," *Journal of Forestry*, Vol. 81, No. 7 (July 1983): 435.
6. Daniel T. Jennings and Hewlette S. Crawford, Jr., *Predators of the Spruce Budworm*, p. 51.
7. Chandler S. Robbins, John R. Sauer, Russell S. Greenberg, and Sam Droege, "Population Declines in North American Birds That Migrate to the Neotropics," In *Proceedings of the National Academy of Sciences, USA*, Vol. 86 (October 1989): 7658-7662.
8. *Ibid.*, p. 7659.
9. Office of Migratory Bird Management, Patuxent Wildlife Research Center, *Bird Breeding Survey for Maine* (Laurel, Md.: Office of Migratory Bird Management, Patuxent Wildlife Research Center, 1990).
10. Chandler S. Robbins et al., "Population Declines in North American Birds," pp. 7661-7662.
11. Lloyd Irland et al., *The Spruce Budworm Outbreak in Maine in the 1970's—Assessment and Directions for the Future*, Bulletin 819 (Orono, Me.: Maine Agricultural Experiment Station, University of Maine, October 1988), p. 46.

Myth 4

Maine's spruce budworm spray program was an example of Integrated Pest Management (IPM).

Starting in 1981, Maine's budworm spray program was referred to as Integrated Pest Management (IPM). This was not because it was radically different from previous spray programs that were not called IPM but because it had to be called IPM to qualify for federal funding.[a]

To prove that the spray program was IPM, the authors of the 1981 Final Programmatic Environmental Impact Statement (FPEIS) for Maine's 5-year Budworm Management Program quoted a definition given by President Jimmy Carter from his 1979 Environmental Message to Congress: "IPM uses a systems approach to reduce pest damage to tolerable levels through a variety of techniques, including predators and parasites, genetically resistant hosts, natural environmental modifications and, when necessary and appropriate, chemical pesticides."[1]

Maine, the FPEIS authors claimed, was using a variety of approaches to the budworm, including utilization and marketing of salvaged trees, silviculture, and targeted spraying of chemical and biological pesticides. Thus it was IPM.

The FPEIS, however, deliberately omitted the last sentence in the paragraph from which Jimmy Carter's definition of IPM was taken: "IPM strategies generally rely first upon biological defenses against pests before chemically altering the environment."[2] Carter was making it clear that chemical pesticides should be the last, not the first, choice. Most of the funding for Maine's program, however, was for spraying pesticides. Subsidizing chemical pesticide use is an odd way to encourage a reduced reliance on chemical pesticides. In contrast, the USDA aids farmers getting on IPM programs through research, demonstration programs, and education. It does not pay for farmers' spray costs.[3]

The other components of the state's "integrated" approach were, the FPEIS authors admitted, "largely the responsibilities of private landowners each with their own objectives and constraints."[4] The subsidy for spraying was unconditional—landowners were not obligated to demonstrate that they were practicing responsible silviculture. If they wanted to use destructive, exploitive practices, they could—and often did.

Ironically, much of the pesticide spraying and timber cutting, which were the primary components of Maine's IPM program, harmed rather than enhanced the natural controls of the forest ecosystem.

Pesticide Spraying

During the course of the spray program, the state improved its mapping of forest types and sprayed less hardwood and other nonhost forest types than it previously had. It also attempted to avoid spraying areas that had been clearcut or were about to be. Avoiding some of this obvious waste did not qualify spraying as IPM, however, where chemicals are supposed to be used as a stiletto rather than as a scythe.

"Targeted" Spray

If the target was the spruce budworm, we can safely assume that most of the spray missed the target. The state used a variety of helicopters and planes, the largest of which had a swath width of 1,200 feet with no crosswinds.[5] According to state standards, a 10-MPH crosswind increases the swath width by a factor of 2.2., which means these planes had an effective swath width of 1/2 mile![6] Planes usually flew in formation, making the effective swath even larger. Spray blocks varied in size from 1,000 to 15,000 acres. How targeted could such a spread be over a forest stippled with hardwoods, veined with streams, and dappled with ponds and wetlands?

Natural Controls

Although predators and parasites cannot control the budworm during a severe outbreak, they lessen the impact and, along with diseases, hasten population declines.[7] Broad-spectrum pesticides sprayed repeatedly over thousands of acres hardly enhance natural controls or ecosystem stability. The chemical insecticides used by the state can adversely affect predators and parasites directly by killing or impairing them or indirectly by diminishing their food supply. In either case, pesticides render predators and parasites ecologically redundant—the major control becomes chemical rather than biological, external rather than self-regulated. After spraying, the reduced budworm populations can be more vigorous than before because there is more food per budworm and less predator and parasite controls. Canadian researcher J. R. Blais blames spraying for either prolonging outbreaks or shortening the intervals between them.[8]

Biological Controls

State authorities assumed that if they sprayed the biological pesticide *Bacillus thuringiensis* (Bt) over a minority of the spray blocks, this would justify the use of broad-spectrum chemical pesticides over the majority of the spray blocks and would constitute IPM. Bt certainly has advantages over broad-spectrum chemical insecticides because it does not wipe out bees, aquatic insects, predators, or parasites. It does, however, kill moth and butterfly larvae, many of which are not pests and have important roles in the ecosystem. Just as with chemical insecticides, if the spraying is combined with cutting practices that create a more susceptible forest, the result cannot be considered IPM.

Timber Harvesting

Timber harvesting is clearly the most important factor in influencing the vulnerability of the forest over the long term. The major silvicultural goals for dealing with the spruce budworm are fairly obvious and have been recommended in one form or another since the outbreak of 1911-1919.[9] They include:

1) reducing the percentage of the most susceptible species (balsam fir and white spruce);

2) increasing the percentage of less susceptible or nonhost species (such as red spruce or hardwoods);

3) increasing the health and vigor of the stand; and

4) increasing habitat for budworm predators and parasites.

To create less vulnerable stands, it is not sufficient for landowners to do budworm silviculture only during outbreak conditions; they must do it between outbreaks as well. The federal government, however, did not require evidence of silviculture in the short or long term. Although landowners, as part of their IPM effort, were supposed to have a bias against fir (cutting fir to a lower diameter-limit), this bias did not work. During the outbreak, more spruce than fir was cut.[b] During the outbreak, landowners relied largely on salvage and presalvage (i.e., clearcutting), which the EIS admitted "reduce[s] financial loss but [has] little or no effect on the composition of the succeeding stand."[10] The EIS also admitted that "without advanced regeneration of spruce, and protection of . . . regeneration from damage by heavy harvesting equipment, clearcutting favors the establishment of fir and hardwoods."[11] Though not intentional, this increase in pioneer hardwoods did temporarily reduce susceptibility of some stands, even if it made the forest less stable by converting it to shorter lived trees.

After the outbreak, industrial attempts at early stand management were motivated more by a desire to prevent a spruce-fir shortfall than by a desire to create budworm-resistant stands.[12] Some of these methods actually increase stand vulnerability to budworms (see sidebar).

The EIS did not even list goals for budworm silviculture, but instead listed 6 silvicultural methods for dealing with the spruce budworm, none of which were uneven-aged.[13] Yet uneven-aged techniques (selection or group selection) have many advantages that should make them the first choice for management. A landowner doing partial cuts on 15-year cycles can cover the forest several times over before a landowner relying on clearcuts covers the forest once. With frequent light cuts, a landowner can more aggressively select out the more vulnerable species while retaining the favored habitats of budworm predators and parasites. Selection also preserves large trees for the sawmill industry and protects wildlife and recreational values. It is remarkable that an EIS could have overlooked such an obvious option.

IPM?

Some researchers feel that the Integrated Pest Management concept, which was derived from agriculture, is inappropriate for forestry. A critique of USDA Forest Service IPM programs for controlling the western spruce budworm in New Mexico and Arizona asserted that "IPM perpetuates the focus on individual pests, whereas the focus should be on the forest stand and its complex of pest organisms. The broader term, Integrated Forest Protection (IFP), is suggested."[14] This critique argued that forest management (including spray programs) introduces complexities that were not envisioned in earlier definitions of IPM, and that a broader focus, on the forest ecosystem rather than the pest, is more appropriate.

Rather than attempt to make the forest resistant to the budworm only to discover that it is now susceptible to some other pest, the focus of managers should be to make the forest more ecologically stable in general. Maine's IPM program did not have ecological stability in mind; instead, it was a government-subsidized use of pesticides as shaving cream—keeping the trees standing long enough for them to be shaved down.

Spruce-fir Silviculture and IPM

Since the spruce-budworm outbreak went into decline, industrial landowners have been following apparently contradictory management policies. On the one hand, they are supposed to be managing for a less vulnerable forest, but on the other hand, they are trying to concentrate growth on susceptible species, such as fir, to prevent a spruce-fir shortfall.

Three major systems for increasing spruce-fir yields are planting, herbicide spraying, and whole-tree thinning (to remove hardwoods). All three systems can increase vulnerability to budworm.

Planting

The two species most commonly planted by industrial landowners are white and black spruce. According to Blais, "Should white spruce plantations become common, they will not only be subject to budworm attack, but will also contribute to increasing the severity of outbreaks. It is noteworthy that the only location where budworm populations were maintained at epidemic levels in the mid-1960's in Quebec was situated in the Grand-Mere white spruce plantations, the largest and one of the oldest (established in 1913-1932) in the province."[15] White spruce plantations in New Brunswick are now being sprayed for a different insect, the spruce bud moth.

Many foresters consider black spruce to be budworm resistant. This may explain why black spruce is the species most often planted by industrial landowners in Maine. A study in New Brunswick, however, found all spruce varieties, red, white, black, and red-black hybrids, to be equally vulnerable.[16] Black spruce is normally found on poorly drained, low-fertility sites in Maine. Studies have shown that when black spruce grows on drier sites, it is more vulnerable to budworms. The reason for this is that instead of producing a large quantity of foliage, the tree puts out less but more nutritious foliage.[17] Thus, growing black spruce on better sites or on fertilized poorer sites could create vulnerable stands.

Herbicides

Herbicide spraying to remove brush and hardwoods, according to a USDA study on gypsy moth predators, "often drastically reduce both vertebrate species diversity and the total number of birds and small mammals in the area. The elimination of brush removes the cover necessary for bird species, which occur from the ground to the lower canopy, and eliminates much of the cover necessary for small mammals."[18] Herbicides also remove the protective overstory of hardwoods that would protect softwood regeneration. Blais concluded that herbicide spraying over extensive areas "could render the forest more subject to depredations by [the budworm]."[19]

Whole-tree Thinning

Some landowners, in an effort to increase future yields of spruce and fir, are thinning out hardwoods and chipping the whole trees (branches and all) for biomass. Spruce and fir, however, are far less vulnerable in a mixed stand. Studies at Maine's Baxter State Park found fir mortality in mixedwoods to be one third that in pure softwood stands.[20] The 1988 Irland study summarized some reasons for this phenomenon:[21]

•Budworm eggs are more subject to parasitism by *Trichogramma minutum* wasps due to increased availability of alternate hosts.

•There are more dispersal losses of budworm larvae in mixedwood stands. The larvae have farther to go to get to food and are thus more subject to predation.

•Budworm prefer exposed crowns as sites for laying eggs. Fewer spruce and fir have exposed crowns in mixedwood sites; many are overtopped by hardwoods.

•Hardwood shade reduces cambial respiration of defoliated firs, saving energy.

Chemical Dependence

Some managers believe that encouraging fir isn't such a bad thing since fir is easy to establish, grows fast, and makes good paper. They argue that silviculture will never get rid of the budworm, and since landowners will probably have to spray in any case, they might as well spray fir, which is easier to protect than spruce.[22] But growing even-aged stands on short rotations ensures the worst possible habitat for budworm predator/parasite complexes. This isn't IPM. If anything, it is planning forestry around chemical dependence.

Endnotes

a. In 1979, Rupert Cutler of the USDA Forest Service announced that "I have concluded that it is not appropriate for the Forest Service to continue financial support for large-scale, repeated aerial spray programs designed to maintain a particular forest type in Maine." He funded the program that year anyway because ". . . the abrupt termination of Federal financial assistance at this time would cause a serious hardship on the State and landowners concerned." In 1979, the state, which had been phasing out its spray support, kicked in 35% of costs and the feds paid 6%.

In 1980, the feds did not fund direct costs of spraying chemicals, but rather (according to the 1980 FEIS), "research, pilot testing and demonstration of IPM techniques, monitoring, supply demand analyses and non-industrial landowner assistance." The "demonstration" was the first large spraying of the biological control, Bt.

In 1979, Richard Barringer, then Maine's commissioner of conservation, wrote to Governor Joseph Brennan about the Forest Service's decision:

"This Department has no objection to the principles on which it has been based; in fact, we have reached similar conclusions based on our own experience. In an age of changing pest-management philosophy and tighter budgets, the federal action is hard to fault. . . . We can still maneuver for some funding if we handle it right, so we should be diplomatic at this stage so as not to endanger future aid."[23]

What the state and industry came up with was something that fit into the new pest-management philosophy. In the same letter, Barringer wrote that "[The USDA] does *not* close the door to phased down participation in funding integrated control efforts that rely less heavily on insecticides." State officials argued that the 1981-1985 program, which would marginally reduce use of chemical pesticides over previous years, was IPM. The federal government, under pressure from the timber industry, agreed. In 1983, however, due to budget constraints, federal funding was withdrawn.

b. The FPEIS admitted that in 1979 (when this bias was supposedly in effect) 42% of spruce-fir was used for sawtimber and 58% was used for pulp. Spruce made up 67% of the sawtimber and 43% of the pulp—thus 53% of the spruce-fir cut was spruce.[24] According to the state's 1986 mid-cycle forest survey, between 1980 and 1986, when landowners were supposedly participating in the IPM program, more spruce was cut than fir.[25]

References

1. *Final Programmatic Environmental Impact Statement, USDA-FS-NA-81-01, Proposed 5-Year (1981-1985) Maine Spruce Budworm Management Program* (Broomall, Pa.: United States Forest Service, United States Department of Agriculture, 1981), p. M 19.
2. Council on Environmental Quality, "The President's Environmental Program, Message to the United States Congress," August 2, 1988.
3. Vogelsang, Mohn, Hepp, and Good, *Establishing and Operating Grower-Owner Organizations for Integrated Pest Management*, USDA PA-1180 (Washington, D.C.: Extension Service, United States Department of Agriculture, 1977).
4. *Final Programmatic Environmental Impact Statement*, p. 40.
5. Jan Selser and Richard Dyer, *Spruce Budworm in Maine: The 1981 Cooperative Spruce Budworm Suppression Project* (Augusta, Me.: Maine Forest Service, Maine Department of Conservation, 1981), p. 16.
6. *Ibid.*, p. F-4.
7. Jan Selser and Richard Dyer, *Spruce Budworm in Maine*, p. 16.
8. J. R. Blais, "Trends in the Frequency, Extent, and Severity of Spruce Budworm Outbreaks in Eastern Canada," *Canadian Journal of Forestry*, Vol. 13 (1983).
9. B. B. Blum and D. A. MacLean, "Silviculture, Forest Management, and the Spruce Budworm." In D. M. Schmitt, D. G. Grimble, and J. L. Searcy, technical coordinators, *Managing the Spruce Budworm in Eastern North America*, Agriculture Handbook No. 620 (Washington, D.C.: United States Department of Agriculture, 1984), p. 84.
10. *Final Programmatic Environmental Impact Statement*, p. 39.

11. *Ibid.*
12. Lloyd Irland et al., *The Spruce Budworm Outbreak in Maine in the 1970s—Assessment and Directions for the Future*, Bulletin 819 (Orono, Me.: Maine Agricultural Experiment Station, University of Maine, October 1988), pp. 86-88.
13. *Final Programmatic Environmental Impact Statement*, p. 3.
14. Dave Brown, Samuel M. Hitt, and William Moir, *The Path from Here: Integrated Forest Protection for the Future* (Sante Fe, N.M.: Integrated Pest Management Working Group, 1986): Chapter 2, p. i.
15. J. R. Blais, "Trends," p. 584.
16. Lloyd Irland et al., *The Spruce Budworm Outbreak*, p. 48.
17. *Ibid.*, p. 46.
18. Harry R. Smith and R. A. Lautenschlager, *Predators of the Gypsy Moth*, Agriculture Handbook No. 534 (Washington, D.C.: United States Department of Agriculture, 1978), p. 68.
19. J. R. Blais, "Trends," p. 545.
20. Lloyd Irland et al., *The Spruce Budworm Outbreak*, p. 44.
21. *Ibid.*
22. R. E. Keenan and M. C. Maritato, *Protection of Red Spruce from Spruce Budworm Defoliation* (Augusta, Me.: Maine Forest Service, Maine Department of Conservation, 1985), pp. 47-48.
23. Richard Barringer, interdepartmental memorandum to Governor Joseph Brennan, March 29, 1979.
24. *Final Programmatic Environmental Impact Statement*, p. 20.
25. Maine Forest Service, *Report of the 1986 Midcycle Resurvey of the Spruce-fir Forest in Maine* (Augusta, Me.: Maine Forest Service, Maine Department of Conservation, 1988), figure 10, p. 29.

Myth 5

Chemical sprays for spruce budworm control are designed to be toxic to insects and pose no significant risks to humans.

Government officials in Maine and eastern Canada told this myth to forest residents every year. When those of us on the receiving end of the nozzles succeeded in raising doubts about a particular pesticide, the state and industry in Maine had a wide enough arsenal of chemicals so that another could always be substituted that was not as well studied.

DDT, an organochlorine pesticide that was used in the 1950s and 1960s, was replaced in the 1970s by a number of organophosphate and carbamate insecticides. These chemicals are nerve poisons, not only to insects but to warm-blooded animals.[a] Indeed, in the 1930s, German scientists used organophosphates to make deadly nerve gases for warfare.

The 4 most widely used chemicals in the 1970s and early 1980s were Sevin-4-Oil (which is made with the carbamate carbaryl as active ingredient), Sumithion (also sold as Accothion, which is made with the organophosphate fenitrothion), Dylox (made with the organophosphate, trichlorfon), and Orthene (made with the organophosphate acephate). By 1984 all of these chemicals were dropped in favor of Matacil (made with the carbamate aminocarb), and Zectran (made with the carbamate mexacarbate).

The argument that the risks of spraying are not significant (i.e., they are "acceptable") is based on several questionable assumptions:
• that the health effects should be judged in the narrowest context—i.e., application—and that manufacture and disposal can be ignored;

•that the pesticides are used as directed;

•that human exposure is limited and therefore acceptable;

•that laboratory tests showing negative effects can be explained away;

•that lack of complete testing is not a problem because chemicals, like people, should be considered innocent until proven guilty;

•that chemicals either cause disease or they don't; if spray workers are exposed and do not get ill, the pesticides must be safe;

•that the complete formulations are no more problematic than the active ingredients, because inert ingredients are just that—inert;

•that government efforts to mitigate public exposure through buffer zones and posting make any subsequent exposures acceptable;

•that there is no evidence that budworm pesticide spraying ever harmed anyone; and

•that considering the benefits conferred by spraying, the risks are acceptable.

These assumptions are all myths:

•In judging the safety of pesticides, one should ignore manufacture and disposal and focus only on application?

The fact that the health risks of chemicals extend beyond application to manufacture and disposal was forcefully brought home to Maine during its last spray program. Maine did not switch to a mostly Bt program in 1985 solely out of environmental concerns; the state had actually planned to spray a lower percentage of the forest with Bt and a higher percentage with the carbamate-based chemicals Zectran and Matacil. One of the world's worst industrial accidents, at Bhopal, India, in 1984, changed the state's plans, however.

At Bhopal, Union Carbide was manufacturing methyl isocyanate (MIC), which is a base ingredient for making carbamate insecticides. The explosion of the plant killed 2,500 people within a few weeks, caused tens of thousands of miscarriages within a few months, and blinded, neurologically damaged, or otherwise impaired tens of thousands more people.[1] The explosion also led to short supplies of Maine's desired budworm chemicals, hence the switch to Bt.

•Pesticides are used as directed?

Off Target

In 1976 my entire farm, including my house, was attacked by three World War II bombers spewing Sevin-4-Oil during a budworm spray mission. It was hardly an isolated instance of off-target spraying. Like myself, other victims sued. In one case, an accidentally sprayed farm was nine miles from the intended target area.[2]

Despite computer guidance systems, pilots still ended up spraying outside spray blocks every year. The state employed monitors who flew over spray-plane formations to check on contract violations (i.e., to ensure that the state got its money's worth and the chemicals were deposited on target—these monitors did not have environmental enforcement authority). Monitor reports routinely showed numerous instances where the chemicals were not used as intended. In

1982, for example, monitors reported 58 instances of spraying outside the block, 42 instances of spraying over water, and 11 instances of double application.[3]

Drift

The 1979 monitor reports showed 35 instances of spray rising or hanging instead of settling and 29 instances of spray drifting from the intended target.[4] During one spray program in Newfoundland, the spray drift was so great that some neighboring towns had higher levels of spray deposits than the intended target spray blocks.[5]

Dumping

There were also numerous instances over the years of spray pilots dumping their loads— incidents that occurred from human error, mechanical failure, and forced landings and crashes. In 1979 one plane dumped 1,100 gallons of Sevin before it crashed into Eagle Lake in northern Maine. Another dumped 250 gallons of Orthene over a hardwood ridge.[6] In 1975-76 there were 26 instances of spray dumpings in New Brunswick, averaging 650 gallons per incident.[7]

Pilots dumped their loads in order to gain altitude during emergencies. Because of the toxicity of the chemicals they carried, pilots didn't want to land with a full load.

•Human exposure to pesticides is limited and thus acceptable?

According to the 1980 Final Environmental Impact Statement (FEIS) for Maine's budworm program, "while precautions can be taken to reduce the number of people exposed and the amount to which they are exposed, it is not possible to avoid exposing some people to carbaryl during the spray operation. However, the amount of carbaryl is extremely small."[8] Some people were cer-

Spruce budworm spray plane being towed out of Eagle Lake on the Allagash.
Photo courtesy Bangor Daily News.

tainly exposed to direct applications and heavy drift. Larger numbers of people were exposed to smaller amounts of drift. The number of people exposed to heavy doses of spray may have been a small percentage of the entire population of Maine, but that fact brings little comfort to the spray victims.

•Negative effects can be explained away?

Theoretically safe

The spray program's first step was to use industry calculations to "prove" that theoretically it is not possible for a person to be exposed to harmful levels of pesticides. With carbaryl, for example, calculations in the EIS showed that "theoretically" a person directly sprayed would receive a dose 196 times less than would be needed to become "moderately ill."[9] Since theoretically nothing could go wrong, those who got ill must have gotten ill from some other cause.

Dismiss or ignore

Where scientific literature did indictate that a chemical might cause problems other than acute toxicity, the response was either to ignore such studies or to dismiss them as inconclusive. For example, the Programmatic Environmental Impact Statement for the 1981-85 budworm program completely ignored evidence (which was mentioned in the Carbaryl Decision Document of the Office of Pesticides and Toxic Substances of the EPA, December 1980) that carbaryl can have an effect on germinal tissue leading to male sterility, or that in combination with nitrates in an acid environment (such as the human stomach) it can form nitroso compounds that may be potent carcinogens. Nor was it ever mentioned that organophosphates can have long-term effects on human brain functioning.[10]

Budworm-spray environmental impact statements in Maine acknowledged that in one study pregnant beagles exposed to low doses of carbaryl did miscarry but reassured pregnant women in the spray area that the study is irrelevant because, according to Douglas Campt of the EPA, pregnant women can easily avoid contamination "by remaining indoors or under suitable cover at the time the application is made. Once the spray settles, any further potential for exposure is greatly reduced, and should be no concern."[11]

One finding on carbaryl that was difficult to dismiss was from research published in 1981 by University of Maine scientists Lee Huber Abrahamson and Maryann Jerkofsky, which showed that carbaryl could potentiate (enhance from mild to lethal or near lethal) VZ (chicken pox) viruses by anywhere from 2 to 50 times, with a mean enhancement value of tenfold. The effects were reproducible and dose dependent. The viral enhancement potential of carbaryl is far greater than aspirin, a substance that doctors now routinely warn patients not to use when viruses are present.[12]

The implications of this work were quite controversial because sprayed areas in New Brunswick had what some researchers considered to be an abnormally high number of outbreaks of fatal or near-fatal Reye's Syndrome and encephalitis, both of which start as mild viral infections that somehow get enhanced. In 1979 the state had decided not to use Matacil because it had been shown to enhance viruses in mice.[b] The tests on carbaryl were even more convincing because they involved human cells exposed to a common virus. A Health Advisory Panel made up of American and Canadian health researchers recommended after reviewing the research on carbaryl that there should be "no uninformed, unconsented human exposure during forest spray operations."[13]

Incredibly enough, the same FPEIS that contained the recommendations of the Health Advisory Panel stated that "while precautions can be taken to reduce the number of people exposed and the amount to which they are exposed, it is not possible to avoid exposing some people to carbaryl during the spray operation. However, the amount of carbaryl is extremely small"[14]—thus again asserting the myth of limited exposure.

Accent the positive

Ignoring the fact that there are differing sensitivities among people, especially children and those who are ill, on medication, alcoholic, etc., the 1980 and 1981 Environmental Impact Statements' discussion of carbaryl ended on an upbeat note: Sevin-4-Oil "had an outstanding record" of safety with budworm workers in Maine.[15] Having praised carbaryl, the 1980 EIS tried to whitewash trichlorfon, stating that "the risk to human health posed by trichlorfon seems at least equal to that of carbaryl."[16] This happy though ironic statement was made despite the fact that trichlorfon was at the time on an EPA list of chemicals subject to changes in registration status due to potential associations with tumors, birth defects, mutations, and bone-marrow effects, and despite trichlorfon's ability to degrade into the mutagenic/carcinogenic chemical DDVP. Since then, trichlorfon has been put on Maine's Restricted Use list and will never again be used for budworm spraying.[17]

•Chemicals, like people, should be considered innocent until proven guilty?

The budworm insecticides, like the herbicides discussed earlier, had many data gaps. Some, like carbaryl, were registered before stricter requirements were established. A recent review by the California Department of Food and Agriculture concluded that of 10 studies required for registration in that state, carbaryl had none that were determined adequate.[18] Some of the data gaps for chemicals used later in the program were even worse. A scientific review committee in Newfoundland concluded that for the chemical aminocarb (Matacil), which was also used in Maine, "there is little information available in the literature relating to the possible carcinogenic, teratogenic, mutagenic, neurogenic and other long-term effects of aminocarb on man or other animals."[19]

Some insecticides, including carbaryl, Orthene, and fenitrothion, were registered based on improper testing done by Industrial Biotest.[20] Despite the lack of adequate testing, registration for these chemicals was not revoked, and their use continued as new testing was done.

Even when evidence exists that shows possible harm from a pesticide, the EPA, which is the judge and jury, can act at a snail's pace and has been way behind schedule in assessing chemicals, especially since the Reagan administration considerably reduced the regulatory budget and staff.[21]

•If spray workers are exposed to pesticides and don't get sick, then the pesticides must be safe?

One area of confusion with pesticides has been the concept of specific etiology—where a single cause has a single effect. Human health, however, is less like a simple cause-and-effect machine and more like an ecosystem. An ecological model of human health looks at the body's resistance to and resilience from "insults" just as, on the ecosystem level, health can be seen as resistance to and resilience from disturbances. According to medical writers George Armelagos and Phillip Katz: "An insult can be any physical, chemical, infectious, psychological or social input which adversely affects the individual or population's ability to adjust to the environment. Disease is then defined in terms of the response to insults in which the coping ability of the individual or group is lowered. Health is measured by the ability of the individual or population to rally from insults."[22]

Pesticides represent insults. Some of these insults can act synergistically, with the combined impact being greater than the sum of the separate impacts.

There are also varying degrees of sensitivity to pesticide insults. Children, for example, are far more susceptible than adults to some of the effects of pesticides. In one experiment, 15 out of 16 organophosphates tested were more toxic to young rats than to adults. For some of the compounds, the fatal dose for children was only 1% of the lethal dose for adults.[23] People who are already ill, on medication, or are alcoholic comprise other examples of those who may be more sensitive to pesticide insults.

Unlike laboratory animals, human beings do not live in controlled environments where only one risk is presented at a time. Thus, the finding that a healthy person has been exposed to a pesticide with no observable effects does not prove that the chemical is safe.

•Inert ingredients are inert?

One of the major health concerns of budworm spraying centered around the inert ingredients found in the complete formulations. The concern was first raised in 1974, when an alarming number of children were dying in New Brunswick from Reye's Syndrome, a previously rare disease that starts as a mild virus but then leads to liver damage, brain swelling, vomiting, convulsions, comatose conditions, and even death. Dr. John Crocker, at a hospital in Halifax, Nova Scotia, suspected that since almost all the cases in his hospital were coming from New Brunswick rather than from Nova Scotia, which was not sprayed for budworm, spraying might have something to do with the disease. He began a series of experiments that led to the finding that the carriers and emulsifiers, rather than the active ingredients of the sprays, could potentiate viral effects in test animals. The symptoms were similar to those in humans with Reye's Syndrome.[24]

The EPA does not base its registration of chemicals on tests done with complete formulations, which include inert ingredients. Those ingredients are secret. Indeed, Dr. Crocker and his colleagues obtained the chemicals with great difficulty due to a lack of cooperation from both government and industry.[25]

•Because the government mitigates public exposure, spraying is acceptable?

Only in the late 1970s, after years of public protest, did Maine establish policies for buffer zones, posting, and notification. These policies did reduce the number of problematic spray incidents. But they did not end unwanted, uninformed exposures. It simply proved too difficult to control exposures over millions of acres, eliminate pilot errors, or control spray drift. Mitigating a problem does not necessarily correct it.

•There is no solid evidence that budworm sprays ever harmed anyone?

If budworm sprays were so bad, argued some proponents, where was the evidence, aside from questionable animal studies? Unfortunately, coming up with evidence is not easy because the symptoms of pesticide exposure are so similar to those of other diseases and because pesticides can enhance other diseases. Most doctors are not trained to recognize pesticide-related illness, and many people who were exposed and got ill never went to a doctor.

Spray officials in Maine were well aware, however, from an incident reported in the *Journal of the Maine Medical Association*, that pesticides could make people ill. In 1972 a copilot in Maine's budworm spray program was exposed to Zectran for 110 minutes after a pinhole leak developed in a high-pressure pump line and released a fine aerosol spray into the fuselage. The copilot started experiencing general weakness, a severe headache, stomach cramps, and a metallic taste in the mouth. The pilots put on protective respirators, but the co-pilot's symptoms progressed to drowsiness, blurring of vision, loss of depth perception, and breathing difficulty. After landing, he had no sense of balance and could not walk or stand, his headaches and cramps increased in severity, and he shook uncontrollably. On the way to the hospital his hands and arms became numb and paralyzed and his speech became slurred.[26] Fortunately he was given an antidote and within three days was back at work again.

Most people who became ill subsequent to spray exposure did not even see a doctor. In two cases in Maine, however, the victims sued. The son of Troy and Carol Ramage developed a case of non-fatal encephaltis from chicken pox after exposure to Sevin-4-Oil in 1977 when the local schoolhouse in Greenbush was accidentally sprayed. Retired game warden Don Walker was sprayed with Sevin-4-Oil while fishing from a canoe in 1979 and had immediate acute reactions and persistent long-term neurological and immunological problems. Both the Ramages and Walker sued but eventually settled out of court.[27,28] Large coporations have tremendous financial resources and can delay court decisions almost indefinitely. At some point the plaintiff invariably decides that settling out of court for some money now is better than waiting for possible money a long time from now.

In New Brunswick, the health effects of budworm chemicals were a major source of controversy, with spray opponents alleging that the pesticides were causing many problems with farm animals as well as people. In 1977 a special edition of the *King's County Record*, a weekly newspaper in Sussex, New Brunswick, described case after case of people experiencing metallic taste, dizziness, vomiting, diarrhea, and weakness after exposure to budworm sprays.

A number of studies in New Brunswick suggested that spraying was having adverse effects on children. Drs. Donald Ecobichon and John Crocker in Halifax, Nova Scotia, published a study in 1978 which showed that there was a seasonal fluctuation of the plasma cholinesterase (an enzyme that destroys nerve transmitter chemicals once they are no longer needed) and erythrocyte acetylcholinesterase levels in children near spray zones in New Brunswick, but that similar low levels and fluctuations were not found in children away from spray zones. They concluded that "On the basis of the above results, it is our opinion that the fluctuation in ChE activities in the New Brunswick samples could be due to exposure to the aerial spray [. . .]."[29]

Government response in New Brunswick and Maine to controversial studies was to assume that studies were not valid unless the government did them itself. The Maine Forest Service tried to defuse health concerns in 1982 by releasing two studies that were guaranteed to find nothing. In one, air-monitoring equipment was set up in towns and cities (including Millinocket, Ashland, Houlton, and Fort Kent) "near" spray zones, and the results were compared to those of Bangor, farther away from the spray zones.[30] Surprisingly, even though the nearest of these monitoring stations were miles from any spray block, they detected trace amounts of carbaryl. Some even showed carbaryl in the air before the spraying started![c] Based on these trace amounts, a toxicologist made risk estimates showing that spraying posed little hazard to people.

Another researcher looked at absentee rates of students in elementary schools in cities "near" (i.e., miles from) spray areas and compared this to absentee rates in elementary schools in nonspray areas (Boothbay Harbor, Gouldsboro, Brewer) and found no statistically relevant correlations.[31] This study did not identify whether students had actually been sprayed; if so, at what dose; if so, what percentage of the students were sprayed; and if so, whether those students who were sprayed had a higher absentee rate than other students. Indeed, it is doubtful that the students going to elementary schools in any of these cities were exposed to more than just the trace of drift found in air sampling. The statistics were also just for April, May, and June and did not include those months in which viral infections are more prevalent.

Although the researchers claim no significant differences between "sprayed" and nonsprayed areas, from the 43rd to the 51st day of the study (which were post-spray), the "sprayed" areas had a consistently higher absentee rate than the controls. Indeed, on the 48th and 49th days of the study, the absentee rate of the "sprayed" schools was double that of controls. These studies, because they ignored dose responses, did not disprove the contention that exposure to spray can lead to illness.

•Considering the benefits conferred by spraying, the risks were acceptable?

The state and forest industry kept insisting that the risks involved in spraying were acceptable and were outweighed by the benefits. Pesticide promoters often compare the "miniscule" risks of using their chemicals, which everyone depends on for jobs or consumer products, with the "greater" risks that everyone takes by their own choice. One's definition of "acceptability," however, depends on one's perspective. The public assumed the risks of spraying involuntarily. Alternatives such as use of Bt, reductions in spray blocks, and elimination of spraying would have lessened or eliminated the risks. The paper companies, not the exposed public, garnered the benefits. The risks, therefore, were not acceptable.

Endnotes

a. In her book *Silent Spring*, Rachel Carson described how organophosphates act to poison insects or people:

"They have the ability to destroy enzymes—enzymes that perform necessary functions in the body. Their target is the nervous system, whether the victim is an insect or a warm-blooded animal. Under normal conditions, an impulse passes from nerve to nerve with the aid of a 'chemical transmitter' called acetylcholine, a substance that performs an essential function and then disappears. . . . If the acetylcholine is not destroyed as soon as a nerve impulse has passed, impulses continue to flash across the bridge from nerve to nerve, as the chemical exerts its effects in an ever more intensified manner. . . . A protective enzyme called cholinesterase is at hand to destroy the transmitting chemical once it is no longer needed. By this means a precise balance is struck and the body never builds up a dangerous amount of acetylcholine. But on contact with the organic phosphorus insecticides, the protective enzyme is destroyed, and as the quantity of the enzyme is reduced that of the transmitting chemical builds up. . . . The movements of the whole body become uncoordinated: tremors, muscular spasms, convulsions, and death quickly result."[32]

b. In an interdepartmental memorandum to Maine Forest Service director Kenneth Stratton dated December 11, 1979, Clark Granger, who was reviewing health data on the chemicals, stated, "Assuming the Jerkofsky data is valid, if we stick with our present policy regarding spraying of viral potentiators we should not spray Sevin-4-Oil. It would seem that we must compromise either the policy or the spray project. We can do neither lightly." The state did not cease to use Sevin-4-Oil until 1984, when it switched to Matacil and Zectran, both of which were less expensive.

c. The 1981-1985 FPEIS contained this interesting tidbit about spray drift: "Carbaryl levels detected in the 1980 study 50 to 80 miles from spray blocks and several days after treatment were similar to levels detected one to two miles from spray blocks in 1978 and 1979.[33]

References

1. National Public Radio, "All Things Considered," July 3, 1991.
2. Larry Lack, "Monitoring the Budworm Spray," *Maine Times* (June 22, 1979): 14.
3. Maine Forest Service, *Environmental Monitoring Reports from the 1982 Maine Cooperative Spruce Budworm Suppression Project* (Augusta, Me.: Maine Forest Service, Maine Department of Conservation, 1983).
4. Larry Lack, "Monitoring," p. 14.
5. Dr. William Thurlow, *Matacil Spray Report* (New Foundland: Gander Environmental Group, 1979), p. 59.
6. Larry Lack, "Monitoring," p. 12.
7. Elizabeth May, *Budworm Battles: The Fight to Stop the Aerial Insecticide Spraying of the Forests of Eastern Canada* (Halifax, Nova Scotia: Four East Publications Ltd., 1982), p. 21.
8. *Final Environmental Impact Statement, USDA-FS-NA-80-01, Proposed Cooperative 1980 Maine Spruce Budworm Suppression Project* (Broomall, Pa.: United States Forest Service, United States Department of Agriculture, 1980), p. A-9.
9. *Ibid.*, p. A-3.
10. Frank H. Duffy, James L. Burchfiel, Peter H. Bartels, Maurice Gaon, and Van M. Sim, "Long-Term Effects of an Organophosphate Upon the Human Electroencephalogram," *Toxicology and Applied Pharmacology*, Vol. 47 (1979): 161-176.
11. *Final Environmental Impact Statement*, p. A-4.
12. Lee Huber Abrahamsen and Maryann Jerkofsky, "Enhancement of Varicella-Zoster Virus Replication in Cultured Human Embryonic Lung Cells Treated with the Pesticide Carbaryl,"

Applied and Environmental Microbiology (March 1981): 652-656. Also, A. Wasserman, M. A. Jerkofsky, and A. J. De Siervo, *Effects of Insecticide and Aspirin Treatment on the am Th lipid metabolism of Varicella-Zoster Infected Cells*. Presentation delivered at the Maine Biological and Medical Science Symposium, Farmington, Maine, May 27-28, 1982.

13. *Final Programmatic Environmental Impact Statement, USDA-FS-NA-81-01, Proposed 5-Year Maine Spruce Budworm Managment Program, 1981-1985* (Broomall, Pa.: United States Forest Service, United States Department of Agriculture), p. B-1.

14. *Ibid.*, p. A-9.

15. *Final Environmental Impact Statement, Proposed Cooperative 1980 and 1981 Maine Spruce Budworm Suppression Project* (Broomall, Pa.: United States Forest Service, United States Department of Agriculture, 1980, 1981).

16. *Ibid.*, p. A-10.

17. Bonnie Lounsbury Board of Pesticide Control member, personal communication.

18. Bryan Jay Bashin, "Bug Bomb Fallout," *Harrowsmith* (May/June 1989): 46.

19. Dr. WilliamThurlow, *Matacil*. Spray Report, p.25.

20. From list in *NCAP News* (Winter 1981): 5.

21. Bryan Jay Bashin, "Bug Bomb," p. 46.

22. George Armelagos and Philip Katz, "Technology, Health and Disease in America," *The Ecologist* (August/September 1977): 306.

23. Robin Whyatt, "Intolerable Risk: The Physiological Susceptibility of Children to Pesticides," *Journal of Pesticide Reform*, Vol. 9, No. 3 (Fall 1989): 8.

24. J. F. S. Crocker, K. R. Rozee, R. L. Ozere, S. C. Digout, and O.Huntzinger. "Insecticide and Viral Interaction as a Cause of Fatty Visceral Changes and Encephalopathy in the Mouse," *Lancet* (1974): 22-24. Also, J. F. S. Crocker, R. L.Ozere, S. H.Safe, S. C.Digout, K. R.Rozee, and O. Huntzinger, "Lethal Interaction of Ubiquitous Insecticide Carriers with Virus," *Science* , Vol. 192 (1976): 1351-1253.

25. Elizabeth May, *Budworm Battles*, p. 21.

26. Ernest M. Richardson and Robert I. Batteese, Jr., "An Incident of Zectran Poisoning," *The Journal of the Maine Medical Association*, Vol. 64, No. 7, photocopy, pp. 158-159.

27. David Bright, "Couple Fears Spray Caused Son's Illness," *Bangor Daily News*, May 11, 1979, p. 9.

28. Marie Howard, "Retired Warden Settles Pesticide Trial," *Portland Press Herald*, November 10, 1987).

29. D. J. Ecobichon and J. F. S.Crocker, "Depression of Blood Cholinesterases as a Marker of Spray Exposure," *Chemosphere*, Vol. 7 (1978): 591.

30. Dr. Terry Shehata, *Risk Assessment of Population Exposure to Ambient Carbaryl in the 1982 Spruce Budworm Spray Project* (Augusta, Me.: Maine Forest Service, Maine Department of Conservation, December 1982).

31. Greg Bogden, *Spruce Budworm Spraying Health Evaluation Project: An Assessment of the Association Between School Absenteeism and Spruce Budworm Spraying in Maine* (Augusta, Me.: Maine Forest Service, Maine Department of Conservation, December 1982).

32. Rachel Carson, *Silent Spring* (Boston: Houghton-Mifflin, 1962), p. 27-32.

33. *Final Environmental Impact Statement*, p. A-10.

Myth 6

The spray program was adequately regulated.

The spray program may have been adequately regulated from the perspective of large landowners (who preferred not to be regulated at all), but it was not adequate from the perspective of those who got sprayed. A distinction must be made here between regulations and enforcement. Regulations did exist, but for the most part they were unenforced. Indeed, from 1954 to 1981, no enforcement actions were taken at all, despite hundreds (or perhaps thousands) of violations. Part of the problem was that the State was not sure who had prime enforcement authority—the state's Board of Pesticide Control (BPC), or the federal EPA.

The label

Spraying regulations were intended to protect both people and sensitive areas, such as aquatic ecosystems. Whereas the health effects of the chemicals were debatable, the effects of some of the chemicals on aquatic invertebrates were less so. The labels (with which sprayers must comply) for the two most widely used pesticides in the late 1970s, Sevin and Dylox, were strongly worded to prevent damage to stream, lake, and pond ecosystems. Sevin's label warned users to "avoid contamination" of aquatic areas; Dylox's label warned users to "keep out of" aquatic areas. Drift and runoff make such precautions extremely difficult to follow. The state's compromise for both human and aquatic exposures was to set up no-spray buffer zones.

The spring of 1979 was extremely wet. Much of the lowlands were covered with water. At a BPC meeting, state officials pleaded with an EPA official to give an interpretation of the pesticide labels that would apply to these inconvenient conditions. After the EPA official spoke, there was a long silence; nobody, public or officials, could understand what he had said. This meant that the state would have to make its own interpretation. The BPC voted to halt the use of Dylox in Washington County and came within one vote of halting the use of Sevin altogether. The Department of Conservation, which was represented on the BPC and which also ran the spray program, pressured the BPC into accepting a compromise: unsprayed buffers along waterways. Later in the year the EPA did get a ruling from Washington that whatever went for Dylox also went for Sevin, and vice versa.

Label changes

Events subsequent to the 1979 compromise ensured that the spray program would not be so threatened by regulations again. In 1980 the EPA changed the Sevin label to read "avoid direct application to" (instead of "avoid contamination of") streams, ponds, etc. Now drift and runoff were legal. It may be coincidence, but around this time the former director of the EPA, Russell Train, joined the Board of Directors of Union Carbide, the manufacturer of Sevin.

Contractor license

In 1980 the BPC held a series of hearings on the licensing of the spray contractor, Globe Aircraft of Arizona. The hearings were particularly emotional as spray victims testified to numerous violations. When the board seemed ready to put strong restrictions on Globe's license, the attorney general for the Department of Conservation, Rufus Brown, argued that these restrictions would compromise the state's spray program. Brown threatened that if these restrictions were not changed by 5:00 that afternoon, Globe would leave the state and the spray program would be over. The board buckled under such tactics. Spray opponent Charles Fitzgerald sued, but the only result was that spray pilots had to prove their competence by passing a simple test—a test that did not include questions about navigation or map reading.

New regulations

The next year, the Board of Pesticide Control was changed from an 8-member board with representatives from state agencies (4 user agencies and 4 regulatory agencies) to a new 7-member Citizens' Board, which had 4 user and 3 nonuser members. This new "balanced" board held a series of hearings on regulating some of the more controversial chemicals, including Sevin and Dylox. The board was headed by Bill Ginn, then the director of Maine Audubon, an organization that consistently supported federal subsidies for the spray program. Also on the board were a paper-company forest manager, a helicopter spray pilot, an apple grower, and a University of Maine entomologist who had gotten many contracts to research budworm spray systems. The board decided not to set performance standards within which off-target residues above set limits would be illegal, but rather application guidelines. If someone followed the guidelines and a contamination occurred, it would be no problem.

Evidence from monitors' reports

The public discovered through monitors' reports that plenty of violations were occurring, although there was little in the way of enforcement. In 1981 a helicopter and a plane crashed, several planes experienced engine failures and dumped their loads over hardwood ridges, another plane leaked 114 gallons from a ruptured hose, and 26 other incidents, most of which included overspray or drift into water, were noted by monitors.[1] Although the pilots as much as admitted guilt by paying fines for violations of contract (i.e., wasting the chemicals), the BPC took no enforcement actions.

Board staff, Robert Batteese, explained why no actions were taken:

"In reviewing the above information, there is no doubt but what violations of the label and our guidelines occurred. The problem is in proving it, and this is very difficult since there is frequently a delay before the monitor reports are filed. Even when incidents are immediately reported, it is usually impossible to get to the scene to take samples due to the remoteness of the area where it took place."[2]

There were 42 incidents of water contamination reported by monitors in 1982, 33 in 1983, and 25 in 1984.[3] The declining numbers were perhaps due to smaller spray programs by the state (Irving and International Paper started their own programs), smaller planes flying at lower speeds, and higher proportions of Bt. There were, however, still incidents of double applications, off-target spraying, spray hanging or drifting, and spraying in high wind speeds. The BPC set up its own pre- and post-spray stream-monitoring system and as a result, between 1982 and 1984 a handful of enforcement actions were finally taken; two against Irving and two against Globe.[4]

In 1983 BPC's Robert Batteese explained to the Board:

"You should be aware that as long as you issue aerial applicators licenses for Forest Pest Control there will be streams being hit under the best of conditions. You should also keep in mind that we are operating under a compromise which allows waters not visible at 1,000 feet to receive direct application."[5]

To the extent that regulations allowed frequent, routine violations, this was a subsidy to the sprayers, making spraying artificially cheap and alternatives to spraying less attractive. Since the state both ran and regulated the program, there was a conflict of interest that made it easy to excuse "mistakes" by sprayers who were mostly doing a "good job." This line of thinking does not impress the police when they catch a driver for speeding. Spraying pesticides over aquatic ecosystems, however, is more serious than speeding. It is closer to hit-and-run.

References

1. Robert Batteese, Jr., interdepartmental memorandum, Maine Board of Pesticide Control, November 6, 1981.
2. *Ibid.*
3. Robert Batteese, Jr., interdepartmental memorandum, December 7, 1982; interdepartmental memorandum, August 5, 1983; interdepartmental memorandum, September 11, 1984.
4. Robert Batteese, Jr., personal communication, 1990.
5. Robert Batteese, Jr., interdepartmental memorandum, August 5, 1983.

Myth 7

Maine's spruce budworm spraying was cost effective.

Budworm spraying is done for economic, not biological reasons. The prime economic reason is the demand for and value of the most vulnerable species. If demand for the species is low, as it was for fir during the 1911-1919 spruce-bud-worm outbreak, then the economic consequences of mortality from an insect outbreak are not as serious. To get rid of "junk" trees that are vulnerable to pests, you need a market. But once there is a market, the wood is no longer junk. There is now an incentive to manage for the species (as foresters now do for fir with the use of herbicides). And there is now an incentive to demand subsidies to protect this valuable species because there is no longer a surplus of wood on which the bugs can chew.

To qualify for federal subsidies, spray projects must be "economically efficient." The USDA Forest Service dutifully presented economic analyses in their annual environmental impact statements that showed the benefit/cost ratios calculated to two decimal places at two different discount rates. Every year the methods used, and the assumptions made, differed. Lloyd Irland, who at one time ran the spray program and at another time was the state economist, admitted that "Despite repeated efforts to improve it, economic evaluation has been inadequate. Precise benefit-cost analysis faces severe difficulties."[1]

Much of the analyses were based on educated guesses with wide margins for error. No one knew: how long the outbreak would last, how often spray would be "needed," how many trees would die in nonsprayed and sprayed areas, or how to calculate the social and environmental costs.

Even though Maine's budworm outbreak collapsed after 1985 and some of the uncertainties became certainties, the state has not yet run an economic analysis to judge the cost-effectiveness of its three-decade spray program. While spraying may have been cost-effective on some sites, no one has demonstrated that the program was an economic success over its entire acreage and duration.

Such an analysis, if it is ever done, will not be easy, because even if one knows the facts, one has to determine the context in which to fit them. The statement that the spray program was cost-effective has little meaning by itself. Spraying is cost-effective at accomplishing what, over what time period, for whom, and compared to what alternatives?

Accomplishing What?

A number of theories were entertained in environmental impact statements concerning what the spray program was actually trying to achieve. Some people argued that the goal of spraying was to protect the entire forest industry. For example, in his comments to the 1980 FEIS, Henry Magnuson of the Paper Industry Information Office suggested that the USDA Forest Service was making a grave mistake by not including all the tax revenues generated by the entire spruce-fir forest as the benefit of the spray program. Magnuson argued that the Forest Service should include "federal revenues received from the personal and corporate income taxes and various excises paid by forestland owners, woodcutters, forest product truckers, primary and secondary wood processing mills and their 30,000 wage earners and all of the support industries and businesses whose income derives from providing the forest products industries and their employees with goods and services."

The Maine Forest Service and the USDA Forest Service both rejected this argument, which falsely assumed that not only the entire spruce-fir resource but also any associated industries would collapse with no spraying. Government policy was and is to look only at direct costs and benefits. Secondary or value-added costs and benefits are considered difficult to establish if not misleading, due to possibilities for substitutions, mill changes, utilization changes, changes in management, etc. Furthermore, alternative investments with the same money would also have multiplier effects. Analyses on this level are considered cumbersome, costly, and rarely useful.

EIS economic analyses usually considered the stumpage value of the timber saved as the benefit of the spray program, but there are three major problems with this approach:

1) Not all dead trees are an economic loss for the following reasons:

•Much of the volume lost to the budworm was in small trees that might have died later due to suppression.[2]

•Some of the "loss" was in fir scattered through mixedwood and less vulnerable softwood stands and may have led to growth increases in the surviving trees—a free timber-stand improvement.

•Some of the "loss" was in stands that were inaccessible and even if sprayed would not be cut within 20 years. The 1980 FEIS estimated that 20% of the resource was not accessible or merchantable.[3]

•Some of the "loss" (mortality) was accessible to salvage and thus not lost to the mills. The 1980 FEIS estimated that 25% of the mortality was salvageable.[4]

2) Not all sprayed acres benefitted from spraying for the following reasons:

•Huge blocks were sprayed (for economies of scale) that had areas of hardwoods and spruce where the stands were not very vulnerable and thus did not benefit from spraying.

•Some stands sprayed were not worth cutting due to poor quality, inadequate size, or inaccessibility. The 1980 FEIS estimated that 55% of the spruce-fir resource was inaccessible at the current average acceptable skidding distances.[5]

•Some stands got cut within a few years of being sprayed and thus received no benefit since they could just as well have been cut without being sprayed. For example, of the 80,000 acres sprayed in eastern Maine in 1974, 20,000 were cut by 1976.[6]

•Some stands that got sprayed were later dropped from the program due to high costs, buffers, or other factors. Any benefits claimed for these areas obviously got lost (unless the mortality was salvaged).

•Some areas did not get sprayed due to poor hazard assessment or to weather problems that led to incomplete programs. In 1978, 10.5% of the program was not completed; in 1979, 13.6%.[7] In 1977, 1,000,000 acres near the St. John River were not recommended for spraying and suffered heavy damage. In 1978, 200,000 acres near Telos Lake suffered from the same "mistake."[8] Some of the benefits from previous sprayings were thus lost.

•In 1975, the spray program had to be reduced by 36.2% due, in part, to a worldwide shortage of pesticides.[9] This may have led to some previous benefits being lost.

•Spray effectiveness was reduced in some blocks due to drift, evaporation, or rain. Also, spray concentrations varied greatly within spray blocks due to microclimatic effects. One study found that deposit concentrations within a block varied from 3.5% to 237% of the planned dose.[10]

•Some of the tree mortality was not caused by budworm. In Washington County, for example, much of the fir mortality was due to the balsam woolly aphid.[11] Some of the spruce mortality in Maine was due to the spruce cone worm (which seems to accompany budworms in outbreaks).[12] Other causes of mortality include rot and blowdown. Where trees died from these other causes, one can hardly claim that budworm spraying led to a benefit.

•According to a study done at the end of the outbreak in the Baxter Park Scientific Management Area (SFMA), except in stands with a high volume of fir (where sprayed areas lost considerable volume but unsprayed stands lost even more), the advantage of spraying was marginal. In the SFMA, spruce mortality was actually greater in sprayed stands than in unsprayed stands if less than 20% of the softwood composition was fir. In such stands, the combined loss of spruce and fir was about the same in sprayed and unsprayed areas.[13]

•In some years and some areas, spraying was ineffective. In 1978, for example, some areas sprayed with Orthene were 98% defoliated by the budworm and some areas sprayed by Sevin were 95% defoliated.[14] The pesticides were considered ineffective if they protected less than 35% of the foliage.

•Despite an average of 1,220,000 acres sprayed annually between 1972 and 1985, Maine's fir inventory declined by 43% between 1980 and 1986 (only 58% of the surviving fir was considered sound), and the spruce inventory declined by 14% during the same time period.[15] The Maine Forest Service listed harvesting as the major cause of decline for both species. Some of this harvesting was of dead or dying trees but was reported as harvests rather than mortality, so it may not be possible to know what percentage of the decline was actually caused by spruce budworms.

3) The spray/no-spray difference is not readily recoverable.

Even if one can sort out the difference between how much wood was saved by spraying, considering the stumpage value of the entire difference to be the benefit leads to a problem: this benefit is not recoverable (to pay back the debt incurred in spraying) until the wood is cut. This brings up the question of time.

Over What Time Period?

One year of spraying brings little benefit if the outbreak continues; once you start protecting with chemicals, you have to keep doing so until the wood is harvested, otherwise the investment will be wasted. Most stands, particularly toward the end of the program, were sprayed repeatedly—the average acre in Maine's 5.2-million-acre protection zone got sprayed 3.3 times between 1972 and 1985 (see Endnote a).

Economists subject any costs or benefits considered over time to discount rates to convert all future costs and benefits to present value. The USDA Forest Service calculated all benefit-cost analyses with two discounts—4% (USDA Forest Service standard) and 10% (Office of Management and Budget standard). The higher the discount and the longer the time of accounting, the lower the present value of future returns.

The EISs assumed that accounting should start the year of the particular program and ignored all the costs incurred by previous spray programs. The 1980 FEIS suggested that "a spruce budworm insecticide treatment program may be economically justified in Maine within the discount rates prescribed... only if the duration of the program does not significantly exceed 10 years."[16] Yet spraying lasted 31 years, during the last 14 of which it was heavy and annual.

The environmental impact statements assumed that every stick of wood sprayed and "saved" would be marketed. Yet their analyses were only extended for one or two decades, surely not enough time to capture all the saved wood. With herbicide spraying, thinning, or planting, one usually carries the benefit-cost analysis on until the stands so treated are harvested, yet the USDA Forest Service did not follow this standard economic procedure.

Indeed, the 1981 FPEIS admits that "whether all of the existing timber being protected can be harvested is uncertain. According to a survey of several woodland owners, 21 to 30 years would be needed to harvest only one-half of the mature fir volume at the 1978 rate of harvest and nearly 100 years would be required to harvest 90 percent of this volume, leading to a strong possibility that much of the existing volume would die of old age."[17] Since much of the fir volume being "protected" was either in suppressed trees or trees at the age of pathological rotation (where they are susceptible to rot or blowdown, even without the spruce budworm), the assumption that the sprayed trees would all be harvested was indeed weak.

One serious problem that arises as the time horizon for analysis stretches is that the accounting period starts to include the next budworm outbreak and spray program, which further diminishes any benefits.

Sustainable Harvest

Although the environmental impact statements did not give the concept of sustainable harvest a rigorous economic analysis, they suggested that the long-term advantage of spraying would be that it extended the period over which (the then) current levels of harvest could be maintained. Without spraying, it was argued, the current mill capacity could not be maintained.

There are several problems with this approach:

1) The level of cut is not biologically based. If it were, it would take the budworm, which is a natural part of the ecosystem, into account. Mill capacity was consistently treated as a constant whereas the forest was treated as a variable.

2) The level of cut has not been a constant. From 1954 to 1985, it may have quadrupled.[18]

3) The level of cut of spruce and fir has been nonsustainable since the 1980s despite the spraying and even if there are no more budworm outbreaks over the next 100 years.[19] Yet paper companies expanded mill capacity during the 1980s, ensuring that the level of cut would rise yet higher and that potential shortfalls would be even more severe.

For Whom?

The USDA's benefit-cost analyses did not indicate the distribution of costs and benefits—i.e., who paid and who benefitted. Over the years, tax payers (state and federal governments), nonindustrial landowners (woodlot and large nonindustrials), and industrial landowners paid part of the costs, but the benefits were not evenly distributed.

Public Benefits

Proving significant public benefits (for jobs, local communities, or recreation) from subsidizing budworm spraying proved so difficult that eventually the state and federal governments gave up trying.

The 1980 FEIS authors stated that "In our judgement, the landowner is the primary recipient of the short-term direct benefits derived from the control of the spruce budworm. A significant direct benefit to the general public has not been demonstrated to justify federal financial support for suppression of the Maine spruce budworm infestation.[20]

Nonindustrial Landowners

Most small-woodlot owners did not benefit directly from spraying because their woodlots were not sprayed. Woodlots near homes were in no-spray buffer zones. Many woodlot owners had road systems in place and were able to salvage dead or dying fir. Also, most woodlots comprised mixed stands rather than pure fir; even if some of the fir died, the landowners still had spruce, hemlock, cedar, pines, and hardwoods.

Some large nonindustrials avoided aggressive spraying or spraying altogether. Dead River Company, which owned 150,000 acres and managed an equal acreage for others, withdrew its lands from the spray program in 1980 because it had worked since 1948 to reduce its fir component so that it represented only 11% of all softwoods. It also had an excellent road system in place if there was a need for salvage. Spraying was simply not cost effective.[21]

In 1980, Seven Islands Land Company, which manages nearly a million acres, also opted out of the program. Clifford Swenson, Jr., explained that "Economic reality dictates that it is impractical to invest more in protection and management than is returned from the sale of the wood. To continue the program would necessitate cutting extensive amounts of wood just to pay the costs of spraying and this would ultimately result in the degradation of the forest resource of Maine . . . with the present costs of spraying so high and the results so minimal, spraying is no longer an economically justifiable form of protection for the private non-mill owning forest landowner."[22]

Seven Islands later changed its mind about spray economics and got back into the program. The company reputedly was able to finance its spraying due to a financial arrangement with one of the state's major paper companies. Apparently, it also has special financial arrangements with sawmills in Quebec and may not have been operating under the same stumpage restraints that Mr. Swenson suggested would make spraying such a poor investment.[23]

Nonindustrial landowners did extensive salvage of dead and dying trees. This flooded the market, leading to lower prices for spruce and fir—a phenomenon that was a definite short-term benefit for the mills but not for the landowners dependent on stumpage sales.

Industrial Landowners

The primary beneficiaries of the spray program were the industrial landowners. EISs defined economic analyses around existing mill capacity, not around a sustainable level of cut. Most of the spraying occurred on industrial land holdings. While nonindustrial landowners, depending on revenues from wood sales, may have had trouble financing spray programs, industrial landowners, who make their profits from pulp and paper, could more easily justify such costs to protect their much higher value-added returns.

Although the EISs' economic analyses assumed that the benefit to landowners should be measured in stumpage values, the authors admitted that with industrial landowners it is difficult to calculate such values because the sales of wood to the mills are an internal transaction. One thing is clear, though: the wood is more valuable to the mills than the prices paid to woodlot owners would suggest. Some industrial landowners, such as International Paper and J. D. Irving Ltd., were even able to justify running their own spray programs.

Another reason industrial landowners could more easily justify the cost of spraying is that it was seen as an investment in market leverage that would actually help ensure a flow of low-cost, purchased wood for their mills. Great Northern Paper was one of the most aggressive sprayers. Their mills (now belonging to Bowater) are geared to spruce-fir, not hardwoods. Their stake in the program was so great that they would purchase the chemicals for the state program and get paid back later, after the subsidies came through.[24] A GNP interoffice memo from E. H. Bowling dated July 6, 1987, shows clearly what strategy the company had in mind for its program:

"One of the recommendations of Project 2020 was to reduce the harvest from GNP lands in the near future. The authors of the report speculated in 1981 that, as budworm mortality increased, landowners would rush to cut and salvage timber before it lost value, which would flood the market with low-cost wood. They reasoned that GNP should reduce the harvest on company lands and take advantage of this low-cost fiber. Later, when the epidemic ended and purchased wood became more scarce and expensive, the harvest from company lands would be increased and the dependence on purchased wood reduced. Looking back, this recommendation was right on target."

"Unfortunately," wrote Bowling, "this recommendation was not followed." GNP did increase its cut for a few years, but it cut at a lower rate than the rest of the state and still ended up, Bowling claimed, with more than 20% of Maine's spruce-fir resource. The rate of drain (harvest plus mortality) of spruce and fir during the 1980s was so high that if it continued for 14 years, according to Mr. Bowling's estimate, the entire resource would be depleted. His estimates were based on figures found in the state's 1986 midcycle survey.

Had industrial landowners not sprayed, the short-term effect on nonindustrial landowners would have been more severe, as salvaged wood flooding the market would have been more intense. But after the outbreak collapsed, the demand for purchased wood for the mills would have been higher and the purchase price would have gone up much sooner than with spraying.

Growing more trees is not equivalent to making more money. If, for example, lower wood inventories from no spraying means cutting 25% less wood, but you get 50% more money for the wood cut, you get 12.5% more money than you would with a higher cut but lower stumpage. The long-term benefit (and investment in forest management is a long-term investment) would favor nonindustrial woodland owners.

Industrial landowners gained many benefits from the publicly subsidized, state-run spray program:
•they paid part of the costs but got all the benefits;
•they were partly shielded from liability for spray accidents;
•they could let the state deal with public protest;
•the wood supply for their mills was extended for the short term;
•they gained more short-term leverage over prices of raw materials for their mills; and
•they were able to expand their mill capacities.

If this mill capacity is indeed nonsustainable, then in the long run not only industry but society will pay dearly for these short-term benefits.

What Alternatives?

To prove the benefits of the spray programs, the EISs compared spraying to a no-spray scenario that assumed:
•no attempts at reduction of vulnerability through partial cuts—all harvests would be clearcuts;
•no attempts at conservation, species substitution, or increased efficiency for the mills;
•no attempt to lower cuts to sustainable levels;

•no attempts by the state to reduce raw wood export and increase local secondary wood processing;

•no attempts by the state to prevent the entire resource from being mined to the stump; and

•no effort by society to stop wasteful paper use and initiate more recycling.

The EISs assumed little adaptability on the part of industry or the public. The "no action" alternatives were thus bogus.

Economist Lloyd Irland considers bogus "no-action" options to be a serious flaw in pest management evaluations: "Numerous examples of wildly exaggerated costs of 'no action' exist; it is a responsibility of research to apply liberal doses of exaggeration control. Extreme claims as to the projected direct and secondary impacts of uncontrolled outbreaks have caused considerable damage to the credibility of public pest control programs."[25]

Endnotes

a. The state has not released figures for the entire spray program, but the existing spray summary charts indicate that the spray program was concentrated on about 5.2 million acres, which, divided into the total acreage sprayed since 1954, gives an average of 3.6 times per acre or 3.3 times per acre from 1972 to 1985.[26,27]

The 1980 FEIS, however had a similar chart for 1975-1979, which indicated that the spray zone during that period was 6.6 million acres.[28] I have no explanation for the more than 1-million-acre discrepancy.

References

1. Lloyd C. Irland, "Improving the EIS Process: A Case Study of Spruce Budworm Control." In S. L. Hart et al., eds., *Improving Impact Assessment* (Boulder, Colo.: Westview Press, 1983), p. 382.

2. Lloyd Irland et al., The Spruce Budworm Outbreak in Maine in the 1970's—Assessment and Directions for the Future, Bulletin 819 (Orono, Me.: Maine Agricultural Experiment Station, University of Maine, 1988), p. 94.

3. *Final Environmental Impact Statement, USDA-FS-NA-80-01, Proposed Cooperative 1980 Maine Spruce Budworm Suppression Project* (Broomall, Pa.: United States Forest Service, United States Department of Agriculture, 1980), p. B-6.

4. *Ibid.*

5. *Ibid.*, p. 24.

6. Robert Burke, *Effectiveness of Spray* (Augusta, Me.: Maine Forest Service, Maine Department of Conservation, August 23, 1974), p. 46.

7. *Ibid.*, p. 44.

8. *Ibid.*, p. 32.

9. *Ibid.*, p. 38.

10. J. A. Armstrong, "Relationship Between Rates of Pesticide Application and the Quantity Deposited on the Forest." In *Fenitrothion: The Long Term Effects of Its Use in Forest Ecosystems*, NRCC/CNRC No. 16073 (Ottawa, Ontario: Natural Research Council Canada, April 20-22, 1977), p. 197.

11. Robert Burke, *Effectiveness*, p. 47.

12. R. G. Keenan and M. C. Maritato, *Protection of Red Spruce from Spruce Budworm Defoliation* (Augusta, Me.: Maine Forest Service, Maine Department of Conservation, 1985).

13. Lloyd Irland et al., *The Spruce Budworm*, p. 52.

14. Robert Burke, *Effectiveness*, p. 66.

15. Lloyd Irland et al., *The Spruce Budworm*, p. 39.

16. *Final Environmental Impact Statement*, p. 64.

17. *Final Programmatic Environmental Impact Statement, USDA-FS-NA-81-01, Proposed 5-Year Maine Spruce Budworm Management Program, 1981-1985* (Broomall, Pa.: United States Forest Service, United States Department of Agriculture), p. E-14.

18. Derived from D. Gordon Mott, "Spruce Budworm Protection Management in Maine," *The Maine Forest Review*, Vol. 13 (1980), p. 30, which showed a level of cut of around 1.2 million cords in the mid 1950s along with data from the 1986 midcycle resurvey indicating a level of cut around 5 million cords in the 1980s.
19. Robert S. Seymour and Ronald C. Lemin, Jr., *Timber Supply Project ions for Maine, 1980-2080*, CFRU Research Bulletin 7, Maine Agricultural Experiment Station Miscellaneous Report 337 (Orono, Me.: Maine Agricultural Experiment Station, University of Maine, 1989), p.
20. Seymour and Lemin 1989.
20. *Final Environmental Impact Statement*, p. 85.
21. Reginald Elwell, "Dead River Company and Spruce Budworm: Reflections on Silvicultural Withdrawals," *Maine Forest Review*, Vol. 13 (1980): 7-8.
22. Clifford L. Swenson, Jr., "Spruce Budworm Impact on Lands Managed by Seven Islands LandCo.," *Maine Forest Review* , Vol. 13 (Summer 1980): 9-10.
23. Information from a former government employee who wishes to remain anonymous, and (concerning mills in Quebec) Bill Butler. Both personal communications, 1991.
24. Lloyd Irland, "Improving the EIS Process," p. 382.
25. Lloyd C. Irland, "Management of Insects and Diseases in Forested Environments." In Paul V. Ellefson, ed., *Forest and Resource Economics and Policy Research: Strategic Directions for the Future* (Boulder, Colo.: Westview Press, 1989), p. 333.
26. Lloyd C. Irland, *Notes on Economics of Spruce Budworm Control* , University of Maine Technical Notes 67 (Orono, Me.: University of Maine School of Forest Resources, 1977), p. 5.
27. *Spruce Budworm Environmental Assessment: Proposed Cooperative Spruce Budworm Integrated Pest Management Program, Maine* (Augusta, Me.: Maine Forest Service, Maine Department of Conservation, 1983), p. 42.
28. *Final Environmental Impact Statement*, p. 3.

Myth 8

The public should help pay the costs of large-scale forest protection projects such as the spruce budworm spray program.

Industry, EISs, state officials, and even some environmental groups argued for federal or state subsidies for the spray program because:

•the public benefits from the forest and thus should pay some of the costs;

•the spruce budworm created an emergency situation—without spraying there would be a disaster and public benefits would be lost; and

•without federal participation, there would be no IPM program, making industry spray programs more aggressive.

Although the state and federal governments eventually gave up such arguments, industrial representatives never have. Because the federal and state subsidies led to such wasteful and harmful results, I will review here reasons why, when spruce budworms or other insects start having economically significant effects on the forest, the landowners should not be subsidized to spray the bugs.

Public Benefits

Paying for industrial landowners' spray costs was supposed to make benefits trickle down to the public. In fact, the major item trickling down was pesticide drift. Despite spraying, jobs declined, and despite no spraying along rivers, lakes, streams, and in Baxter State Park, recreation increased.

Industry proponents argue that looking at direct costs and benefits does not take into account value added to the wood through harvest and processing. Taking into account value added to wood, however, should not lead to the public paying the spray bills. Since the mills get most of the revenues from what is added in value to the wood, they, and not the government, should have subsidized the spray program for nonindustrial owners.

Emergency

The claim that the budworm outbreak was an emergency grew hollow over the years. The spruce budworm is not an alien invader like the Gypsy moth. Landowners had known since the 1911-1919 outbreak what the spruce budworm could do. They were warned by entomologists for decades before the big outbreak of the 1970s. Maine had started a limited spray program in 1954 in response to an outbreak that started in 1949. Yet during all this time, landowners, with a few exceptions, managed their forests so that the fir component increased, and paper companies kept increasing their mill capacities.

The argument that if there was no subsidy, the industry would collapse and all the social benefits of jobs would disappear was bogus because it purposely confused no federal or state subsidy with no alternative strategies on the part of the landowners. EISs used to go along with this ploy by implying that "no action" would lead to the companies harvesting as usual without a change in plans—the forests would die and the mills would shut down.

This same argument could be used by potato farmers to get the government to pay for spraying potato bugs. If the farmers were not subsidized to spray, it would be a disaster—the crops would die, the processing plants would shut down, and all the people in Aroostook County would become unemployed. Just as dealing with potato bugs (and one can do this without chemical pesticides) is a normal cost of raising potatoes, so dealing with spruce budworms should be a normal cost of growing spruce and fir for commercial timberland owners.

In 1981 the Draft Programmatic Environmental Impact Statement (DPEIS) finally admitted that "'No action' is not a likely possibility since the State and landowners would carry out a spruce budworm program regardless of Federal financial assistance."[1] Rather than force the public to pay for expected "emergencies" such as budworm outbreaks or fires, landowners should pay for any responses through a dedicated insurance fund.

Integrated Pest Management

Subsidizing spraying did little to encourage landowners to manage for more budworm-resistant stands because the subsidies had no silvicultural strings attached. The argument that subsidies for pesticide use could lead to a reduction in pesticide use is laughable. Several former state budworm officials informed me that when spraying was subsidized, landowners would fight to add more spray blocks to the program. When subsidies were removed and it was pay as you spray, landowners fought to remove spray blocks; they did not want to waste money on spraying if the benefits were questionable.

Twenty years ago IPM researcher R. W. Stark concluded that "The many absurd 'control projects' committed in the name of protection are possible only through government subsidy."[2]

References

1. *Draft Programmatic Environmental Impact Statement, USDA-FS-NA-81-01, Proposed 5-Year Spruce Budworm Management* (Broomall, Pa.: United States Forest Service, United States Department of Agriculture, 1981), p. 58.
2. Quoted in Lloyd.C. Irland, *Notes on Economics of Spruce Budworm Control,* University of Maine Technical Notes 67 (Orono, Me.: University of Maine School of Forest Resources, 1977), p. 9.

4 Industrial Wildlife

The first images conjured up in the minds of most people when they think of wildlife are usually of mammals, such as deer, moose, coyotes, raccoons, or rabbits. Sometimes, however, eagles, ducks, grouse, or even salmon, trout, or bass may come to mind. The images are almost always of animals—usually those exploited as game. But to scientists, wildlife refers to all life forms that are wild, not just economically important vertebrates.[1] Indeed, vertebrates, of which game animals are a small minority, comprise less than 0.2% of all species on earth. Invertebrates, algae, fungi, and microorganisms are far more abundant.[2]

Because Maine's wildlands lie in a transitional zone between northern hardwoods and spruce-fir, and because they are rich with lakes, rivers, streams, bogs, swamps, and mountains, they contain a diversity of genetic types, species, communities, and ecosystems. Scientists call this diversity of life in all its forms and at all levels of organization biological diversity or biodiversity.[3]

The Northern Forest Lands Study (NFLS) declared that "a biologically diverse environment is a healthy environment . . ."[4] but noted that "there is great concern among some of those who commented on the Northern Forest Lands Study that biological diversity is decreasing and will continue to decrease in the Northern Forest if present trends continue. Forest practices, air pollution and global warming were all mentioned as significant threats to biological diversity in the region."[5]

The first priority of the corporations that own most of Maine's wildlands is not preservation of biodiversity but, as stated by International Paper Company forester Thomas Eubanks, ". . . to manage [the company's] timberlands to generate a maximum financial return on [its] investment, consistent with the need to supply its manufacturing plants with appropriate raw material on a sustained yield basis."[6] According to industrial managers, management driven by such motivations just happens to be good for wildlife—despite appearances to the contrary. Indeed, Eubanks stated that his company employs "silvicultural practices that encourage the enhancement of wildlife, soil, air, water, and aesthetic resources."[7]

As evidence of their commitment to protect wildlife, industrial timberlands managers frequently cite their compliance with state wildlife-protection regulations such as the retention of trees in aquatic buffer strips ("beauty strips") or in deeryards. The purpose of these regulations, however, is not to preserve diversity

"A Noble Product of the Maine Woods."
From Forrest Colby, Forest Protection and Conservation in Maine, *(Augusta: 1919), p. 157.*

but to protect species with the greatest economic value—i.e., fish and game.

Game, like wood fiber, is an important economic resource to Maine. Sport fishing alone adds more to the state's economy than such well-known Maine crops as potatoes, blueberries, or lobsters.[8] Wildlife management has traditionally meant maintaining viable regional populations of economically desirable species, especially deer. By following regulations intended to protect exploitable wildlife resources, industrial foresters claim they are practicing "multiple-use" forestry. Multiple use, they claim, is superior to wilderness preservation because it yields timber for industry while providing for wildlife and recreation. Wilderness preservation, in contrast, "locks up" precious resources.

Although industrial foresters may use their compliance with beauty-strip regulations as an example of their commitment to wildlife, they have consistently fought establishment of those regulations, considering them an economic hardship. Indeed, it is not uncommon at hearings to hear industrial foresters suggest they deserve compensation (subsidies) for providing these benefits to the public at industrial expense. This is nothing new. Aldo Leopold wrote in 1949, that "when the private landowner is asked to perform some unprofitable act for the good of the community, he today assents only with the outstretched palm."[9]

References
1. Malcolm Hunter, Jr., *Wildlife, Forests, and Forestry: Principles of Managing Forests for Biological Diversity* (Englewood Cliffs, N.J.: Prentice-Hall, 1990), p. 4.
2. John R. Probst and Thomas R. Crow, "Integrating Biological Diversity and Resource Management: An Essential Approach to Productive, Sustainable Ecosystems," *Journal of Forestry* (February 1991): 13.
3. Malcolm Hunter, Jr., *Wildlife, Forests, and Forestry*, p. 7.
4. Stephen Harper, Laura Falk, and Edward Rankin, *The Northern Forest Lands Study of New England and New York* (Rutland, Vt.: United States Forest Service, United States Department of Agriculture, April 1990), p.24.
5. *Ibid.*
6. Thomas Eubanks, "Industrial Perspective on Integrating Forest and Wildlife Management." In John A. Bissonette, ed., *Is Good Forestry Good Wildlife Management?* (Orono, Me.: Maine Agricultural Experiment Station, University of Maine, April 1986), p. 252.
7. *Ibid.*, p. 253.
8. Phil Andrews, "Remote Ponds and Forest Roads." In John A. Bissonette, ed., *Is Good Forestry Good Wildlife Management?* (Orono, Me.: Maine Agricultural Experiment Station, University of Maine, April 1986), p. 181.
9. Aldo Leopold, *A Sand County Almanac* (New York: Sierra Club/Ballantine, 1966), p. 250.

Clearcuts

Listening to the debate over the impact of clearcutting on wildlife can be confusing. Some environmentalists claim that clearcuts are a disaster for wildlife—destroying habitat, ruining soil, and reducing diversity. Industrial foresters counter that clearcuts are good for wildlife—creating edge and abundant browse. The puzzled listener may wonder if the two sides are talking about the same thing. They are not: the opposing sides use "clearcut" and "wildlife" to mean different things.

The word clearcut, depending on how it is defined, can cover a wide variety of practices. The Irland Group, in its 1988 report on clearcuts for the state's Forests for the Future Program, defined clearcutting as "the practice of cutting virtually all merchantable trees for the purpose of making a complete harvest, preparing a stand for regeneration, or both, creating an opening larger than two tree heights in diameter."[1] Some cuts that would be clearcuts by this definition would not be clearcuts under the state's 1989 Forest Practices Act, which specifies that clearcuts are not clearcuts unless they are over 5 acres in size and retain less than 30 square feet basal area of trees per acre.

Depending on several variables, the effects of clearcutting on wildlife can range from the relatively benign to the catastrophic:

Clearcutting Impacts

Variables	Less Disturbing	More Disturbing
Site	good	poor
Size	small	large
Intensity	residual trees, snags, & slash left	whole-tree/no residual
Distribution	isolated	fragments forest
Slope	flat	steep
Season	winter	spring/early summer
Soil Damage	low	severe
Follow-up	allow natural succession, encourage diversity	create monoculture, use pesticides
Rotation	long	short

Because a less disturbing clearcut is relatively benign does not mean that all clearcuts are benign. Indeed, most are not.

Reference

1. Irland Group, *Clearcutting as a Management Practice in Maine Forests* (Augusta, Me.: Maine Department of Conservation, Forest for the Future Program, 1988), p. 4.

Myth 1

Clearcutting benefits wildlife because it creates abundant browse.

The brush that arises from a clearcut is neither intended nor desired by industrial foresters. But industrial foresters know how to profit from their misfortunes. Brush, they point out, is browse for hare, deer, and moose. By creating browse, foresters are benefitting wildlife.

The browse-eating species that supposedly benefit from clearcutting are habitat generalists. They do not require large clearcuts for their survival; they can live in uneven-aged stands that contain both browse and shelter. Indeed, deer, because they do not like to stray far from shelter, do not even use the interior of large clearcuts. The browse in even-aged stands created by clearcuts is only available for a short time in the stand rotation: on better sites, hares may benefit for only 2 to 3 years, deer for 4 to 6 , and moose for 10 to 12.[2] Afterward, little forage is available until the next harvest or until the stand, through natural disturbance, develops uneven-aged characteristics.

If biodiversity rather than just browse-eating species is a concern, then forest managers must:

•promote less common species that are habitat specialists over more common species that are habitat generalists;

•enhance or expand habitats that are rare over habitats that are common; and

•maintain or enhance ecological stability.

Creating brushfields for the short-term benefit of a few browsing species requires destroying mature forests that offer the following long-term benefits to many species:

Vertical Diversity

Vertical diversity refers to the diversity of vegetation stratification from ground level to the upper canopy. The more varied the layers of vegetation, the more habitats there are for bird and invertebrate wildlife. Vertical diversity is greatest in uneven-aged old-growth stands. Many of the species, such as epiphytic lichens, flying squirrels, and budworm-eating warblers, are habitat specialists that prefer the deep crowns of large, old trees. Clearcutting, which removes such habitat, is particularly disastrous to bird species when conducted in the spring and early summer, during breeding and nesting. USDA Forest Service researchers Robert Frank and Hewlette Crawford state the obvious when they observe that "vertical diversity is almost nonexistent in the early years following clearcutting and increases slowly as the stands develop."[2]

Abundant "browse" resulting from industrial management. The brush pictured here is neither intended nor desired by managers and is often subjected to herbicide spraying. *Photo by Mitch Lansky.*

Structural Diversity

Structural diversity refers to the variety of physical features such as dead, hollow, or downed trees, slash piles, streams, pools, or shorelands. Intensive clearcuts that remove dead, hollow, or downed trees remove a major source of habitat diversity. Dozens of bird and mammal species, including wood ducks, owls, woodpeckers, nuthatches, chickadees, wrens, bats, squirrels, martens, ermines, and weasels, use such structures for part of their life cycles.[3] Even more varieties of invertebrates, fungi, and microorganisms use dead and rotting trees. These species are not expendable—they are vital to normal ecosystem dynamics.

Demes

Demes are genetically distinct plant or animal populations that are adapted to the peculiarities of the local environment. When a forest is clearcut, much of the ground vegetation and associated invertebrate habitats are also destroyed. These shrubs, herbs, ferns, horsetails, mosses, fungi, and lichens are more apt to form demes than are trees, which interbreed more widely. Canadian ecologist E. C. Pielou suggests that "some forest ecologists are ignorant of the ecology of any organism smaller than a tree, and do not realize that herbs ('flowering plants') that reappear in a second-growth forest a few years after the forest is cut are not nearly so genetically diverse as those that were there originally. A plant species may come to reoccupy its original range, but because of the loss of many of its demes it has become genetically impoverished: it has become a species with many of its components missing."[4]

The effects of intense clearcutting on demes and on vertical and structural diversity are so severe that the USDA Forest Service in the Pacific Northwest region is now switching to what it calls "New Forestry" and "New Perspectives" which purport to protect these "biological legacies" that normally survive natural disturbances by preserving a certain proportion of large-living, dead-standing, and dead-downed trees on each acre of a cut.[5,a] This new way of thinking, which incorporates biodiversity concerns, has not yet reached Maine's industrial forest. Maine's 1990 clearcutting rules legalize intensive clearcuts that destroy the biological legacy.

Endnote

a. Unfortunately, in practice this often leads to "sloppy clearcuts" rather than fully-stocked stands with biological legacy intact.

References

1. Hewlette S. Crawford, "Wildlife Management and Changing Forest Practices in the Northeast," *Northern Journal of Applied Forestry*, Vol. 1, No. 1(1984): 13.
2. Hewlette S. Crawford and Robert M. Frank, "Wildlife Habitat Responses to Silvicultural Practices in Spruce-fir Forests." In Richard McCabe, ed.,*Transcript of the 52nd North American Wildlife and Natural Resources Conference*, March 20-25, 1987, Quebec City, Quebec (Washington, D.C.:Wildlife Management Institute, 1987), p. 94.
3. Carl Tubbs and Mariko Yamasaki, "Wildlife Management in New England Northern Hardwood." In John A. Bissonette, ed., *Is Good Forestry Good Wildlife Management?* (Orono, Me.: Maine Agricultural Experiment Station, University of Maine, April 1986), pp. 111-114.
4. E. C. Pielou, "Depletion of Genetic Richness Is Not 'Harmless' Consequence of Clearcutting," *Forest Planning Canada* (July/August 1990): 29.
5. New Forestry is based on the studies of Jerry Franklin with old growth. See, for example, J. F. Franklin, T. Spies, et al., *Modifying Douglas-fir Management Regimes for Non-timber Objectives*

(Portland, Ore.: United States Forest Service, United States Department of Agriculture, 1986). New Perspectives is a Forest Service policy to apply concepts such as New Forestry. See, for example, *Forest Perspectives*, Vol. 1, No. 1 (March 1991).

Myth 2
The effects of clearcuts on wildlife are temporary; the trees will grow back, the habitats will recover, and the wildlife will return.

What grows back after a clearcut is not the same as what was cut—and if subsequent rotations are short enough, the forest will never recover to what it was before. The new forest will either be dominated by disturbance-adapted species, such as raspberries, pin cherries, poplar, white birch, red maple, or balsam fir, or, with planting and herbicide spraying, it will be a simplified stand dominated by a single softwood species.

According to Hewlette Crawford and Robert Frank, vertical diversity on better sites is limited to one-story structures until the stands reach 40 to 50 years of age.[1] If 40 or 50 years is the rotation age, such stands will never develop adequate vertical diversity. On poor sites vertical diversity may take much longer to develop. Consequently, Crawford and Frank consider clearcuts on poor sites to lead to very poor wildlife habitat.[2]

Structural diversity also takes longer to develop than allowed for with shorter rotations. Mariko Yamasaki and Carl Tubbs, USDA Forest Service researchers from New Hampshire, estimate that rotations of 65 to 110 years would produce only marginal amounts of large-diameter cavity-dwelling/foraging habitat in northern hardwoods. Rotations of fewer than 60 years would produce none.[3]

Demes of small plants and animals will not bounce back in 50, 100, or even 500 years. Once exterminated, they are gone forever.

Maine's 1990 clearcut rules allow the shortest possible rotations—an entire township can be clearcut in less than 3 decades. Since any tree that can be used commercially qualifies as acceptable regeneration, new stands can be simplified or even converted to species normally exotic to the site. The destruction of wildlife diversity by these processes is thus perfectly legal.

References
1. Hewlette S. Crawford and Robert M. Frank, "Wildlife Habitat Responses to Silvicultural Practices in Spruce-fir Forests." In Richard McCabe, ed.,*Transcript of the 52nd North American Wildlife and Natural Resources Conference*, March 20-25, 1987, Quebec City, Quebec (Washington, D.C.: Wildlife Management Institute, 1987), p. 94.
2. *Ibid.*, p. 99.
3. Carl Tubbs and Mariko Yamasaki, "Wildlife Management in New England Northern Hardwood." In John A. Bissonette, ed., *Is Good Forestry Good Wildlife Management?* (Orono, Me.: Maine Agricultural Experiment Station, University of Maine, April 1986), p. 120.

Myth 3

Clearcuts are good for wildlife because they create edge.

When wildlife biologists refer to edge, they are describing the intersection between two different ecosystems—an ecotone. Ever since Aldo Leopold noted that "game is a phenomenon of edges" in his 1933 book *Game Management*, wildlife managers (who for the most part are game managers) have accepted the notions that edge is good and the more edge the better. Although some species (notably deer, hare, and grouse) may benefit from edges, not all wildlife do.

Edge Type

The effect of edges on wildlife diversity depends on the type of edge. Inherent edges, based on natural landscape features, are more stable than induced edges, which result from a disturbance (human or natural) and contain plant and animal communities that are often successional. One of the most diverse areas of a forest is the inherent edge between trees and water—the riparian zone. Here the soils are rich and the vegetation lush, attracting both herbivores (plant-eating animals) and their predators. Many forest wildlife species use aquatic areas and associated shorelands for food and drink.

Invasions

When the forest edge is induced by a severely disturbed, human-dominated landscape such as a clearcut, forest interior-adapted wildlife can suffer. Forests near induced edges, for example, may have a higher density but lower diversity of birds than the interior forest. A number of studies have shown increased predation of songbird and quail eggs near forest edges.[1] The predation is worst near developed areas (which might have unnaturally high populations of cats, skunks, foxes, grackles, jays, crows, and cowbirds).[2]

Common weeds from disturbed areas can also invade the interior, causing changes in species composition. Edges are often drier, windier, and more densely vegetated than the forest interior, creating an unfavorable habitat for sensitive small plants such as orchids and even for some trees, such as American beech or sugar maple.[3]

Some of the browsers that benefit from edge habitats can have a devastating impact on the forest interior. Ironically, success at increasing deer herds can mean failure at preserving forest diversity. Research conducted in northern Wisconsin has shown that deer browsing can lead to severe reductions in species such as white cedar, eastern hemlock, or Canada yew as well as in herbaceous species such as showy yellow lady's slipper, blunt-leafed, and purple-fringed orchids, Indian cucumber-root, and large-flowered trillium.[4] Areas subject to intensive browsing in the Great Smoky Mountains National Park lost more than a quarter of their total species numbers compared to a control area.[5] Deer sometimes harbor brainworms, which can be fatal to moose and caribou. The Wisconsin study concluded that "failure to acknowledge these ecological interactions and plans to maintain dense populations of deer by state and federal land stewards work directly against the preservation of these components of natural diversity."[6]

Islands

The negative effects of edge become most insidious in forests that are surrounded by induced edges. The forest then becomes a fragment, an isolated island surrounded by roads, heavy cutting, or forest conversion and development. The smaller the fragment, the higher the ratio of edge to forest—which according to this myth should be a benefit. Yet small fragments tend to lose genetic and species diversity for a number of reasons:

•the forest may be too small to support low-density populations of wide-ranging species (such as lynx);

•residual populations may be too small to reproduce and expand successfully, and there may be no in-migration to make up for losses;

•the genetic base may be so small that inbreeding occurs, leading to populations that cannot adapt to stresses, disturbances, or other changes;

•there may be fewer microhabitats (such as large logs, boulders, streams, or ponds) to support the original diversity;

•the stand may have no true forest interior—the entire area may be subject to invasion from edges. David Wilcove, former biologist for The Wilderness Society, has estimated that edge predators such as the brown-headed cowbird can invade 1,000 to 3,000 feet into interior forest habitat, so that a circular habitat 250 acres in size that is surrounded by edge might not have a true interior.[7]

A "Purina" cut. This checkerboard pattern maximizes "edge" which supposedly benefits wildlife. The result: a fragmented forest. *Photo by Christopher Ayres.*

Fragmentation

Forest fragmentation (where expanses of mature forest are chopped into isolated fragments) is a major threat to biodiversity. In his 1984 book *The Fragmented Forest*, biologist Larry Harris showed how fragmentation has contributed to the decline of many species, including the much-debated spotted owl associated with old-growth forests in the Pacific Northwest.[8] A number of studies have shown a correlation between declines in the diversity of forest-interior bird species (especially those that migrate to the neotropics) and decreases in size of mature forest habitat.[9] One study in Connecticut found that hermit thrushes, black-throated green warblers, and cerulean warblers were absent from all forest tracts smaller than 460 acres.[10] According to former USDA Forest Service wildlife biologist, Hewlette Crawford, bay-breasted warblers, one of the most important budworm feeders, are also habitat sensitive, which may have contributed to their precipitous decline over the last decade.[11]

Maine's 1990 clearcut standards do not require a reduction in total acreage that a landowner may clearcut in a given year. Clearcuts are, however, limited in size and must be spread out over the landscape, separated by a minimum of 250 feet. These standards can thus increase edge effects and accelerate forest fragmentation, favoring common, disturbance-adapted species over more sensitive forest interior species.

References

1. Malcolm Hunter, Jr., *Wildlife, Forests, and Forestry: Principles of Managing Forests for Biological Diversity* (Englewood Cliffs, N.J.: Prentice-Hall, 1990), p. 107.
2. Mary L. Small and M. L. Hunter, Jr., "Forest Fragmentation and Avian Nest Predation in Forest Landscapes," *Oecologia*, Vol. 76 (1988): 62-64.
3. Malcolm Hunter, Jr., *Wildlife, Forests, and Forestry*, p. 107.
4. William S. Alverson, Donald M. Waller, and S. L. Solheim, "Forests Too Deer: Edge Effects in Northern Wisconsin," *Conservation Biology*, Vol. 2, Issue 4 (December 1988): 348-358.
5. *Ibid.*
6. *Ibid.*, p. 357.
7. David S. Wilcove, C. H. McLellan, and A. P. Dobson, "Habitat Fragmentation in the Temperate Zone." In M. E. Soule, ed., *Conservation Biology: The Science of Scarcity and Diversity* (Sunderland, Mass.: Sinauer Associates, 1986), p. 585.
8. Larry D. Harris, *The Fragmented Forest: Island BiogeographyTheory and the Preservation of Biotic Diversity* (Chicago: University of Chicago Press, 1984): p. 211.
9. Chandler S. Robbins, John R. Sauer, Russell S. Greenberg, and Sam Droege, "Population Declines in North American Birds that Migrate to the Neotropics." In *Proceedings of the National Academy of Sciences, USA*, Vol. 86 (October 1989): 7658-7662.
10. John C. Kricher, *A Field Guide to Eastern Forests, North America* (Boston, Mass.: Houghton Mifflin Company, 1988), p. 140.
11. Hewlette S. Crawford, personal communication, summer 1991.

Myth 4

Clearcutting is not a serious problem in the Maine woods because it is only done annually on less than 1% of the entire forest.

This is argument by statistical dilution. According to this myth, any damage to forest wildlife habitat is insignificant when compared to the area left alone.

Clearcuts are not evenly distributed across the state, however. Some townships have had the majority of their timber removed within a 10-year period. Local impacts in such cases are not insignificant.

According to 1989 Maine Forest Service statistics on silviculture and harvesting, 85% of all reported clearcuts were on industry land.[1] If we add industry's reported acreage for clearcuts and shelterwood-removal cuts (which have nearly the same impact on wildlife) and divide by total industry land, we discover that these companies have been clearcutting more than 1.6% of their forests a year—which would mean that all their forests would be cut in slightly more than 60 years.[2] Even this statistic is misleading, because approximately 30% of industry landholdings are cut by non-even-aged systems (such as diameter-limit or selection).[3] Assuming, therefore, that clearcutting will be done on only 70% of the industrial land base, 2.6% of this land base is being clearcut a year, leading to a rotation of less than 39 years.

Not only will the forest be highly fragmented, but the majority of the land will not be allowed to develop any vertical or structural diversity. Mature forests will be scarce. Far from reassuring, the statistics available from the state are alarming.[a]

Endnote

a. As bad as these statistics may seem, the reality may be much worse. These statistics were derived from unverified landowner reports. Matched against other state figures for volume of wood cut, they do not seem credible. The state's 1986 midcycle forest survey, for example, reported an average annual timber harvest of approximately 8.4 million cords per year.[4] The harvested acreage reported to the state is much too small to account for such a high volume of timber—it would mean the average volume removed per acre for all cuts (both even- and uneven-aged) would be 26 cords. This is more than would be expected for clearcuts alone.

References

1,2,3. Ancyl Thurston, *1989 Report on Precommercial Silvicultural Activities and Harvesting* (Augusta, Me.: Maine Forest Service, Maine Department of Conservation, 1990).
4. Calculated from Maine Forest Service, *Report of the Midcycle Resurvey of the Spruce-fir Forest in Maine* (Augusta, Me.: Maine Forest Service, Maine Department of Conservation, 1988), p. 9.

Myth 5

Clearcutting increases forest diversity by creating a mosaic of varied habitat types across the landscape.

Following this myth, we should not be concerned about an apparent reduction in wildlife diversity due to stand simplification, conversion to other species, or fragmentation. Instead, we should look at the diversity of habitat types over the landscape created by management. Most Maine landscapes, argue industrial ecologists, have even-aged stands in a variety of age classes combined with some uneven-aged stands. Even monoculture softwood plantations, by this reasoning, add a different habitat type and thus increase landscape diversity. A diverse landscape, concludes the argument, means diverse wildlife.

Going one step further, wildlife biologist Mac Hunter has argued that forest managers should purposely plan for a diverse landscape by having an equal proportion of their holdings in each of the following categories: large, medium, and small clearcuts, and group and individual-tree selection.[1] Following such a program would result in 60% of a holding being in even-aged stands.

If this myth were true, then it should apply to forest ecosystems everywhere. Thus, people who clearcut tropical forests should be commended for increasing forest diversity by creating a new type of habitat. When applied to tropical forests, this reasoning is obviously flawed. It is equally flawed when applied to the Acadian forest, which in presettlement times was mostly uneven-aged or all-aged rather than 60% even-aged.

Putting degraded and simplified fragments together into a mosaic does not magically compensate for the deficiencies of the constituent parts. A mosaic of relatively young stands does not create habitat for species associated with old growth. A mosaic of stands favorable to common species does not create a larger haven for rare species. A mosaic of fragmented stands does not create habitat for species requiring a more continuous mature forest. A mosaic of unstable stands does not create a more stable forest ecosystem.

Reference
1. Malcolm Hunter, Jr., *Wildlife, Forests, and Forestry: Principles of Managing Forests for Biological Diversity* (Englewood Cliffs, N.J.: Prentice-Hall, 1990), p. 286.

Myth 6
Buffer zones along streams, ponds, rivers, and lakes effectively mitigate the worst effects of clearcuts.

Aquatic buffer zones are supposed to mitigate the following problems caused by clearcutting:

•siltation, which can kill fish and other aquatic life, damage spawning grounds, and contaminate drinking water;
•nutrient runoff, which can lead to algal blooms;
•increased water temperature, which can alter aquatic life; and
•increased peak waterflow.[1]

The buffers are also supposed to serve as animal travel corridors, nesting habitats for riparian species, and deeryards.

The aquatic buffers as administered by the Land Use Regulation Commission (LURC), however, do not adequately protect wildlife diversity for several reasons:

Unprotected areas
LURC buffer regulations do not apply to some significant aquatic ecosystems. These include headwater streams, vernal pools, and wetlands.

Headwater streams. Headwater streams (the sources for larger streams or rivers) are important habitats for spring salamanders not found downstream. The major predators in headwater areas may be shrews rather than larger animals such as mink or otter.[2] Buffers are not required for streams unless they drain more than 300 acres, thus leaving headwaters unprotected.[3]

Vernal pools. Vernal pools (small confined basins that are unconnected to other water bodies and that have water only part of the year) smaller than 3 acres are also unprotected. These are important breeding grounds for salamanders because they have no fish predators. Five species of salamanders in northern New England forests breed only in vernal pools.[4] While salamanders may not be as glamorous as game animals, the average biomass per acre of red-backed salamanders in a healthy Acadian forest is greater than that of deer or moose.[5]

Wetlands. Forested and small open wetlands (land saturated by or covered with water for part of the year and supporting vegetation adapted to saturated soils) are not protected by either LURC or the Department of Environmental Protection (DEP) despite the latter's commitment to the nationwide goal of no net loss of wetlands. The DEP established guidelines to protect wetlands in its 1990 adaption of the Natural Resources Protection Act and Water Quality Certification, but in doing so it excluded wetlands of less than 10 acres and exempted logging from regulation. Landowners not only can cut forested wetlands but can fill open wetlands as they build logging roads.

According to Bill Reid, head of the DOT's location and environmental division, "There's no way to build a logging road without filling wetlands. The paper companies have probably built more new roads per year than DOT [Department of Transportation] has built in my career."[6] Wetlands can be important deme habitats. Approximately 20% of Maine's land surface supports some form of wetlands.[7]

Inadequate Buffers

Streams that drain less than 50 square miles and open wetlands and bogs are required by LURC to have buffers 75 feet from water. Larger ponds, lakes, and rivers must have 250-foot buffers. Landowners are allowed to cut in these buffer zones as long as they leave at least 60% of the trees standing in the first 50 feet of the buffer. Patch cuts are allowed in the outer 200 feet.[8] This allows some rather drastic cutting. In some areas, landowners have gotten permits from LURC (often because the buffer trees were dying from the spruce budworm) to cut more heavily right up to the shoreline. If shorelines are steep, these buffers may not be adequate to halt siltation. Narrow buffers cannot prevent the extreme waterflow fluctuations caused by large clearcuts beyond. As a result, some formerly good trout brooks are now too low in midsummer to support any fish.

Insufficient Habitat

Certain riparian species need forested areas wider than 250 feet. One study showed that of 40 bird species inhabiting riparian forests in Iowa, 9 required riparian strips wider than 300 feet.[9] Waterfowl commonly nest up to 300 feet from the water's edge and may nest up to 1,500 feet away.[10]

Allowing large clearcuts up to the 75- or 250-foot buffer zones means that these areas contain no true forest interiors—the whole strip is a clearcut edge. Such regulations may give minimal protection to aquatic areas, but they give no protection to forest interior species. There is also no protection for species traveling from one aquatic region to the next.

References

1. Jerry Bley, *Forest Clearcutting in Maine: An Assessment of Environmental Impacts and Public Policy Needs* (Augusta, Me.: Natural Resources Council of Maine, 1988), p. 3.
2. Malcolm Hunter, Jr., *Wildlife, Forests, and Forestry: Principles of Managing Forests for Biological Diversity* (Englewood Cliffs, N.J.: Prentice-Hall, 1990), p. 145.
3. "Land Use Districts and Standards: For Areas Within the Jurisdiction of the Maine Land Use Regulation Commission," Chapter 10 of the Commission's Rules and Standards, initially adopted January 12, 1977, revised August 15, 1991, sec. 10.17, Aug 5.
4. Carol R. Foss, *Summary Report on Wildlife Resources for the Northern Forest Lands Study*, a report for the Northern Forest Lands Study, p. 6.
5. Malcolm Hunter, Jr., personal communication, summer 1990.
6. Phyllis Austin, "Disappearing Wetlands: There Are Loopholes Big Enough to Drive a Dumptruck Through," *Maine Times* (July 19, 1991): 4.
7. *Ibid.*, p. 5.
8. "Land Use Districts and Standards."
9. Malcolm Hunter, Jr., *Wildlife, Forests, and Forestry*, p. 148.
10. Carol R. Foss, *Summary Report*, p. 5.

Myth 7

The riparian buffers and the separation zones between clearcuts are adequate travel corridors for wildlife.

Without adequate travel corridors, animal and plant populations become isolated, unable to migrate in response to stress or to have genetic exchanges with other populations.

Buffer zones and separation zones (required by the state's 1990 clearcut-and-regeneration standards) are supposed to suffice as travel corridors for wildlife. Unfortunately, landowners can cut in such a way with Level I clearcuts (limited to 35 acres with a 250-foot separation zone) that the corridors only lead to other corridors. Theoretically, there could be no interior habitat of mature forest for the animals to go to.

Because these buffers and separation zones are all edge, rather than interior habitat, wildlife trying to migrate from one forest interior to another may find traveling along these corridors more like running a gauntlet.

The clearcut standards allow landowners to cut down the separation zone after 10 years. This means that 10-year-old trees become the only shelter in the new separation zone (formed by the previous clearcut). If landowners cut as heavily as standards allow, within a few decades wildlife will have no mature interior habitat to go to. Where do the owls, woodpeckers, bay-breasted warblers, pine martins, or flying squirrels, which all need mature trees for habitat, go? Apparently it doesn't matter.

New Hampshire biologist Jeff Elliott contends that long, thin corridors may be locally useful for individual animals but that animal populations usually migrate by radiating to surrounding ecosystems rather than by "marching single file along a tightrope of unhealthy pathways."[1] Reed Noss, an Oregon-based

Residual strips of trees are often not wide enough, nor continuous enough to serve as effective wildlife corridors. *Photo by Christopher Ayres.*

These buffers between clearcuts along the Allagash are intended as wildlife corridors. Unfortunately the corridors are too thin to be free from the edge effect and they do not lead to mature forest habitat; they only lead to other corridors. *Photo by Tor Smith.*

private consultant in ecology and conservation biology,[a] agrees. To be suitable for population dispersal and migration, corridors, Noss contends, must be wide enough to maintain populations of species sensitive to human disturbance. A corridor suitable for eastern cougar, for example, may need to be miles, rather than several hundred feet, wide. A more suitable strategy for ensuring population mobility and genetic exchange would be to maintain healthy contiguous ecosystems, rather than restrict mature trees to temporary thin bands between clearcuts and along water bodies.

Endnote
a. Conservation biology has been called a "crisis discipline" and involves the application of ecological theory and knowledge to conserving biological diversity.

References
1. Jeff Elliott, personal communication, summer 1991.
2. Reed Noss, personal communication, Jan. 1992.

Herbicides

Industrial foresters, rather than go on the defensive concerning the effects of herbicides on wildlife, have gone on the offensive. They have found researchers who, with perfectly straight faces, will write studies and articles that "prove" that herbicides benefit wildlife. Since it would be difficult to argue that spraying toxins over the forest imitates Nature, industrial forestry advocates have instead argued that herbicides improve Nature by speeding it up. Industrial forestry advocates flatly deny any problems with herbicide spraying, but they are quick to point out that even if there were a problem, it could easily be mitigated. Here we see myth making in its most creative form.

Myth 1
Herbicides are nontoxic to wildlife.

Since plants are a form of wildlife and herbicides kill plants, herbicides do kill wildlife.

Plant destruction indirectly affects many forms of animal wildlife, including insects, mammals and birds. Although changes in plant community structure are the most significant effects of herbicides on animal wildlife, the two most widely used forestry herbicides in Maine—Roundup and Garlon—can directly harm some animal species as well:

Roundup (glyphosate)
Some of the wildlife toxicity studies on Roundup and its active ingredient, glyphosate (and there are not many such studies available for public scrutiny), give seemingly contradictory results. For example, a literature review by Eco-Analysts, Inc. for the Maine Board of Pesticide Control cites 2 studies on the ef-

fect of glyphosate on *Daphnia magna*, a waterflea that is a major component of pond zooplankton.[1] One study (sponsored by the manufacturer of Roundup) found no effect at levels of 500 parts per million (100 times the usual field dose) over a 6-day period; the other study (sponsored by the U.S. Fish and Wildlife Service) found effects at only 3 parts per million over a 2-day period. The latter study also showed toxicity effects on freshwater amphipods and midge larvae.

One possible explanation for the discrepancy is that the manufacturer's test used pure glyphosate and the Fish and Wildlife Service's used the complete Roundup formulation. Tests of pure glyphosate give misleading results since Roundup's complete formulation contains an inert ingredient (the surfactant) that can be more toxic than glyphosate itself. Indeed, one study found that the combined effect of glyphosate with its surfactant on rainbow trout to be "more than additive."[2]

The 1990 Spectrum Report done for Maine's Forest for the Future Program lists $LC_{50}s$ (the concentration of a chemical that is lethal to 50% of a population) for herbicides used in Maine. Some of the wildlife sensitive to Roundup identified in this report were:[3]

Toxicity of Roundup

Species	LC_{50}(milligrams per liter)	Toxicity Class
Green algae	2.0	moderately toxic
Water flea	3.0	moderately toxic
Bluegill sunfish (fingerling)	5.0	moderately toxic
Channel catfish (fry)	3.3	moderately toxic
Fathead minnow (fingerling)	2.3	moderately toxic
Rainbow trout (fingerling)	1.3	moderately toxic

The Spectrum report concluded that "glyphosate and its formulated products do not bioaccumulate in either aquatic or terrestrial species."[4] Yet the 1988 Environmental Impact Statement for herbicides for the Pacific Northwest cited evidence that glyphosate is bioconcentrated in fish, and one reviewer showed that the data revealed a bioconcentration factor of 80 times in rainbow trout.[5]

The Spectrum report cited one study that concluded that the residue levels of glyphosate in the viscera and muscle tissue of game species browsing on sprayed vegetation would be rapidly eliminated and thus no problem. But another paper, using the same data concluded that the residues in the tissues (especially liver and kidneys) of some game animals could exceed the FDA's maximum legal tolerance for commercial livestock.[6]

Garlon (triclopyr)
Garlon 4 is highly toxic to some aquatic organisms:[7]

Sign warning literate wildlife not to feed on herbicide-treated browse. *Photo by Jonathan Carter.*

Toxicity of Garlon

Species	LC$_{50}$ (milligrams per liter)	Toxicity Class
Water flea	1.2	moderately toxic
Bluegill sunfish	0.8	very toxic
Rainbow trout	0.7	very toxic
Sockeye salmon (fry)	1.2	moderately toxic

The Spectrum report describes triclopyr as being "moderately toxic" to mammals, "slightly toxic" to birds, and "mildly fetotoxic" (toxic to a fetus) in mammals.[8] " Highly," "moderately," "slightly," and "mildly" toxic are not the same as nontoxic. The Garlon label states "Do not graze treated areas or feed treated forage," and the U.S. Forest Service indicates that "treated areas should not be grazed for one year following application."[9] While such recommendations may be useful to cattle owners, they are difficult to apply to browsing wildlife. It is impractical to put up elaborate fencing to exclude these species from sprayed areas, and most such creatures are illiterate and would not respond to posted warnings.

References

1. Paul R. Adamus and Charles J. Spies III, *Environmental Risk Assessment of 10 Pesticides Used in Maine* (Augusta, Me.: Maine Board of Pesticide Control, 1985), p. 73.
2. J. Servizi, R. Gordon, and D. Martens, "Acute Toxicity of Garlon 4 and Roundup Herbicides to Salmon, Daphnia, and Trout," *Bulletin of Environmental Contamination and Toxicology*, Vol. 39 (1987): 15-22.
3. J. C. Balogh et al., *The Use and Potential Impacts of Forestry Herbicides in Maine, Report to the Department of Conservation's Forest for the the Future Program* (Augusta, Me.: Maine Department of Conservation, 1990), Table A5.4.
4. *Ibid.*, p. 167.
5. United States Forest Service, Pacific Northwest Region, *Managing Competing and Unwanted Vegetation: Federal Environmental Impact Study* (Portland, Ore.: United States Department of Agriculture, 1988), p. I/B-401.

6. J. C. Balogh, *The Use and Potential Impacts*, p. 167.
7. *Ibid.*, Table A5.8.
8. *Ibid.*, p. 167-168.
9. Mary H. O'Brien, *Triclopyr—A Fact Sheet* (Eugene, Ore.: Northwest Coalition for Alternatives to Pesticides, June 5, 1987).

Myth 2

Herbicides sprayed over clearcuts do not reduce wildlife diversity.

The purpose of herbicides is to simplify a forest stand so that softwoods can dominate the overstory. How can anyone argue that diversity is not reduced? Simple. If species extirpation from the initial clearcut is taken as a given; diversity is defined solely in terms of species richness (the number of species) and evenness (the balance of the proportion of species) is ignored; enough time is allotted for the stand to revegetate; and rare and sensitive plants are ignored, then industrially oriented researchers can claim (as did Michael Newton et al., in a 1989 study)[a] that "To the best of our knowledge, none of these treatments eradicated any plant species."[1]

One industrial forester asserted that, "most of these areas we treat, if left to mother nature, would arrive at the same endpoint of stand composition. All we're doing is moving the succession of the forest along at a faster pace and getting at the same endpoint as would mother nature, except mother nature would take 60-to-65 years and we'll take only 40-to-45 years."[2] These boys ain't hurtin' nothin'; they're just revvin' it up some.

Observers of freshly sprayed clearcuts find such arguments difficult to believe—and with good reason:

Already Simplified Communities

Wildlife communities are drastically altered by the initial clearcut. Species requiring large, old, deep-crowned trees and the shade of a mature forest either die or leave. Species that can survive intense sunlight, temperature extremes, and drier soils flourish. Herbicides are thus applied to species that are already adapted to major disturbances.

Sensitive, sparsely distributed plants and animals that somehow survive the initial clearcut may be eliminated by herbicides. These losses probably would not be statistically significant in a study geared toward observing more commonly distributed species. Indeed, since the study by Newton et al., judged the prespray vegetation by looking at dead stems nearly two years later, the likelihood of noticing sparsely distributed species that had been eradicated probably was very low.[3]

Undeniable Short-term Effects

In the short term, herbicides obviously reduce diversity. They represent yet another disturbance that sets the stand back to harsher conditions. Studies by David Santillo et al. (partly funded by Great Northern Paper Company), found that on sunny days, the surface temperature in sprayed areas was as much as 11° C (nearly 20°F) higher than in unsprayed areas. The climate near the ground was also much drier. Species richness of shrubs and forbs was less on all treated clearcuts compared to controls. There was a drastic reduction in the number of invertebrates. Indeed, much of the invertebrate diversity came from areas inadvertently skipped by sprayers. On one site, 43% of the invertebrates captured came from only 2% of the entire study area, a portion that had been skipped by sprayers. The proportion of insectivorous birds and small mammals and herbivorous small mammals were also reduced.[4,5]

Even-aged young softwood stands already have a poor diversity of insects, with fewer predator and parasite species, compared to older growth.[6] Reducing the bird and mammal populations that specialize in eating insects can have further unwanted consequences on the resistance of forest stands to insect attacks.

Long-term Considerations

The long-term effects of herbicides depend on the size of the spray area, the timing of the spray, the quality of the site, and the species and stocking levels of the softwoods and brush. According to the Spectrum report, the goal of a successful herbicide spraying is to "facilitate conversion of hardwood and brush communities to less complex softwood communities."[7] To the degree that spraying is successful, diversity is obviously reduced.

Herbicides that kill plants before they produce seed may have an impact on species richness in both the current and the next rotation as well.[8]

Endnote

a. Newton et al., were funded by the University of Maine's Cooperative Forestry Research Unit, which gets much of its income from large landowners and chemical companies to do research on "intensive management."

References

1. M. Newton, E. C. Cole, R. A. Lautenschlager, D. E. White, and M. L. McCormack, Jr., "Browse Availability After Conifer Release in Maine's Spruce-fir Forests, *Journal of Wildlife Management*, Vol. 53, No. 3 (1989): 648.
2. Quote from Anthony Filauro of Georgia-Pacific in "Two Views of Herbicides in Maine's Forests," *Communicator* (Maine Board of Pesticide Control), Vol. 1, Issue 2 (February 1990).
3. M. Newton et al., "Browse Availability," p. 648.
4. D. Santillo, P. Brown, and D. Leslie, "Responses of Songbirds to Glyphosate-induced Habitat Changes on Clearcuts," *Journal of Wildlife Management*, Vol. 53, No. 1 (1989): 64-71.
5. D. Santillo, D. Leslie, and P. Brown, "Responses of Small Mammals and Habitat to Glyphosate Application on Clearcuts," *Journal of Wildlife Management*, Vol. 53, No. 1 (1989): 164-172.
6. T. Schowalter, "Insects and Old Growth," *Forest Planning Canada* (July/August 1989): 5-7.
7. J. C. Balogh et al., *The Use and Potential Impacts of Forestry Herbicides in Maine, Report to the Department of Conservation's Forest for the the Future Program* (Augusta, Me.: Maine Department of Conservation, 1990), Table A5.4.
8. Malcolm Hunter, Jr., *Wildlife, Forests, and Forestry: Principles of Managing Forests for Biological Diversity* (Englewood Cliffs, N.J.: Prentice-Hall, 1990), p. 224.

Myth 3
Herbicides, because they lengthen the time that
browse is available, are beneficial to wildlife.

According to Michael Newton's 1989 study, herbicides extend browse availability by killing the taller hardwoods that are out of reach of hare, deer, and moose and replacing them with shrubs and herbs that are more accessible.[1]

Short-term Browse Reduction
The initial effect of herbicide spraying is not beneficial even to these game species, however, because overall browse is reduced. The Santillo study, for example, showed one plot where 99% of all hardwood stems were killed.[2] "The reduction of browse prior to winter," according to the Spectrum report, "may be critical to deer survival, especially when large areas have been treated."[3]

Newton et al., do not list the distribution, abundance, or proportion of the surviving "preferred" browse. Since balsam fir and white cedar (trees that presumably would survive spraying) are listed as "preferred,"[4] an unintended short-term result may be that browsing animals would turn to potential crop trees for a meal—a consequence that certainly would be unappreciated by landowners. If the dominating softwoods are spruce (infrequently browsed), the browsers would be forced to consume plants that are less palatable and less digestible than the plant species that were killed. Thus, the result would be either bad for the landowner or bad for browsing wildlife.

Theoretical versus Actual Benefits
The actual long-term benefits to wildlife from spraying herbicides over large clearcuts are theoretical—Newton et al., did not actually record use by wildlife but only looked at presence of potential browse. It is not clear how much of that potential browse is actually used. Densely stocked, even-aged softwood stands are not easily penetrated by large animals. Indeed, because of "vertical stratification and difficulty of physical access on 336 sample points,"[5] Newton et al., estimated vegetation type, abundance, and size by the "ocular" method (looking at it from a distance). Browse that is located in inaccesible pockets surrounded by dense growth does wildlife little good.

Most herbicide-sprayed clearcuts in Maine have been 300 or more acres in size.[6] University of Maine wildlife biology professor Malcolm Hunter estimates that on a 250-acre clearcut, deer would use only the 20% closest to the edge.[7] In Maine landscapes that have been heavily clearcut for miles, deer lack winter cover and do not benefit from potential browse because they are not there to use it. It is doubtful that spraying herbicides over large clearcuts would suddenly inspire deer to start using such areas. The bulk of the land on which browse will bounce back is more the domain of moose.

Conifer Stocking
The prolonged-browse effect is most likely to occur when softwood stocking is sparse or irregular. If this is the case, however, there is little economic justification for spraying herbicides. Landowners are not spraying to benefit moose;

they are spraying to grow softwoods. If softwoods are well stocked and herbi-cide spraying succeeds in hastening full-crown closure, then there will be no prolonged-browse effect. Indeed, Newton et al., admit that where conifers were well stocked, "conifers prevented low cover from fully responding to release."[8] In other words, the browse did not bounce back.

Newton et al., recommend that plantations can have prolonged browse availability if trees are planted at 3-meter (nearly 10-foot) intervals.[9] Such a wide spacing, however, would be better suited to growing Christmas trees than timber because much of the growth would go into branches rather than stems. The wider the spacing of trees, the longer the wait until the stand reaches the peak of average growth (the culmination of mean annual increment, or CMAI).[10] The longer the rotation, however, the more difficult it becomes to justify the investment in planting and spraying due to the insidious effects of discount rates over time.

References

1. M. Newton, E. C. Cole, R. A. Lautenschlager, D. E. White, and M. L. McCormack, Jr., "Browse Availability After Conifer Release in Maine's Spruce-fir Forests, *Journal of Wildlife Management*, Vol. 53, No. 3 (1989): 648.
2. D. Santillo, P. Brown, and D. Leslie, "Responses of Songbirds to Glyphosate-induced Habi-tat Changes on Clearcuts," *Journal of Wildlife Management*, Vol. 53, No. 1 (1989): 67.
3. J. C. Balogh et al., *The Use and Potential Impacts of Forestry Herbicides in Maine, Report to the Department of Conservation's Forest for the Future Program* (Augusta, Me.: Maine Department of Conservation, 1990), Table A5.4.
4. M. Newton et al., "Browse Availability," p. 648.
5. *Ibid.*
6. J. C. Balogh, *The Use and Potential Impacts*, p. 96.
7. Malcolm Hunter, Jr., *Wildlife, Forests, and Forestry: Principles of Managing Forests for Biological Diversity* (Englewood Cliffs, N.J.: Prentice-Hall, 1990), p. 100.
8. M. Newton et al., "Browse Availability," p. 646.
9. *Ibid.*, p. 647.
10. Nova Scotia Department of Lands and Forests, *Fifteen Year Assessment of Thirty Year Old Red Spruce Stands Cleaned at Various Intensities in Nova Scotia*, Forest Research Report No. 2 (Truro, Nova Scotia: Nova Scotia Department of Lands and Forests, February 1988).

Myth 4

The negative effects of herbicides on wildlife can be acceptably mitigated by intentional "skips" (unsprayed areas) and by spraying large clearcuts in small blocks over a period of years.

Here we have a bit of back pedaling. First the problem was denied; now it exists but can be managed. The recommendation for skips came from a 1989 herbi-cide impact study on small mammals by David Santillo et al. which noted that the unintended skips accounted for much of the variability in vegetation, inver-tebrates, and small mammals.[1] Insect, bird, and mammal abundance and diversity were still reduced, however. The skips only prevented the effects of spraying from being more devastating. The recommendation for staggered spray blocks on large clearcuts came from a 1989 herbicide impact study on birds by Santillo et al., and from a 1989 herbicide impact study on browse by Newton et al.[2,3]

These studies were funded in part by paper and chemical companies. The recommendations for mitigation give the appearance of concern for the environment, but the real motivation seems to be a desire to allow continued spraying. Neither of these forms of mitigation are being intentionally done on any scale now. The possibility that some of the negative effects of herbicides might be mitigated in the future does not justify the thousands of acres that have already been sprayed or are being sprayed now.

Recommendations for mitigation appeal to organizations that view themselves as "responsible" or "reasonable" or willing to compromise. Indeed, the concept of skips is somewhat like the concept of beauty strips. The use of skips and staggered blocks to preserve brush was endorsed by the Spectrum report, which hypothesized that browsing species such as hare, deer and moose would act as "biological controls" for the brush that was left behind.[4] Michael Cline of the Maine Audubon Society, an organization that would like to see less herbicide spraying, also endorsed the idea of skips. "If they are going to spray, I'd love to see them do that. Skips will help in terms of wildlife."[5]

The effect of such a compromise would be that companies would continue to manage for large-scale clearcuts followed by herbicides. Nearly the same acreage would be sprayed. The intentional skips may not be all that different from the unintentional ones. Since wind and temperature differentials are not yet under the control of spray technologists, applicators may have as much trouble missing spots as hitting them.

Yet the concept that wildlife diversity can be enhanced by skips is appealing. Indeed, the bigger the skips, the bigger the benefit to wildlife. The ultimate benefit would occur if the applicators skipped the entire forest.

References

1. D. Santillo, D. Leslie, and P. Brown, "Responses of Small Mammals and Habitat to Glyphosate Application on Clearcuts," *Journal of Wildlife Management*, Vol. 53, No. 1 (1989): 164-171.
2. D. Santillo, P. Brown, and D. Leslie, "Responses of Songbirds to Glyphosate-induced Habitat Changes on Clearcuts," *Journal of Wildlife Management*, Vol. 53, No. 1 (1989): 70.
3. M. Newton, E. C. Cole, R. A. Lautenschlager, D. E. White, and M. L. McCormack, Jr., "Browse Availability After Conifer Release in Maine's Spruce-fir Forests, *Journal of Wildlife Management*, Vol. 53, No. 3 (1989): 648.
4. J.C. Balough et al, *The Use and Potential Impacts of Forestry Herbicides in Maine, Report to the Department of Conservation's Forest for the Future Program* (Augusta, Me: Maine Department of Conservation, 1990), p.180.
5. Paul Gregory, "Two Views of Herbicides in Maine's Forests," *Communicator* (Maine Board of PesticideControl), Vol. 1, Issue 2 (February 9, 1990): 5.

Spruce Budworm Spraying

The chemical insecticides sprayed to control spruce budworms in Maine were not magic bullets that hit only the target insects; they blanketed thousands and eventually millions of acres of forests every year. The state officials who authorized the spraying did not understand enough about how a forest ecosystem works without pesticides to know how it might be harmed with them. Rather than take caution in dealing with this dimly understood but vulnerable community, the state threw caution, and pesticides, to the wind. Indeed, the less they knew, the less precautions they took to protect nontarget organisms. It was a case of shoot first, ask questions later.

State and industry authorities asserted that any problem that spraying inflicted on wildlife was minor compared to the benefit of killing spruce budworms. The stilling of the delicate, shimmering wings of damsel flies on a remote pond was a small price to pay for protecting the wood supply of the paper industry.

The state authorities demonstrated their environmental concern by monitoring rather than preventing environmental damage. Environmental monitoring became a major income source for Maine biologists for over a decade. It was a frustrating experience for some biologists who discovered that areas that were supposed to be sprayed sometimes got missed and that areas that weren't supposed to be sprayed sometimes got hit. In some studies, researchers purposely had streams or ponds sprayed. It is not clear that such sacrifices were justified, however, since the state had no clear guidelines for adjusting spray policy based on the monitoring information.

The willingness of the state to continue using pesticides was exhibited from the start, when the chemical of choice was DDT. Despite national concern raised in 1962 by Rachel Carson in her book *Silent Spring*, Maine continued to use this persistent, bioconcentrating chemical—which proved toxic to eagles and salmon—until 1967.

The carbamate and organophosphate chemicals that replaced DDT are not as prone to bioconcentrate in fish and birds. This does not mean the chemicals were benign, however. Many of the initial monitoring studies of the new chemicals consisted of body counts of animals (mostly invertebrates) killed from a single spray operation. Although interesting, it was not clear if the results were significant. Damaged ecosystems do not stop suddenly like a broken machine—the damage is often subtle.

Because of this subtlety, state and industry authorities who wanted to continue spraying were able to show concern but could express optimism that whatever problems the pesticides caused would be temporary—damaged populations would bounce back. Later studies asked more sophisticated questions and came up with some alarming results, especially concerning the long-term effects of Sevin-4-Oil on pollinators and aquatic invertebrates. Yet Maine continued using Sevin for years, switching only after cheaper, more effective substitutes were found. Authorities were able to defend this continued use by claiming that buffers around aquatic areas mitigated any problems. The buffer zone was a chemical beauty strip, however. In the heart of the industrial forest there was less compromise; ecological concerns came second to economic mandates.

Myth 1

The insecticides used for budworm spraying are safe for wildlife.

The insecticides that were used to battle spruce budworm are broad spectrum chemicals, meaning they kill a wide variety of invertebrate species. Even the biological insecticide Bt is toxic to many species of moth and butterfly caterpillars. Although invertebrates may not win popularity contests among wildlife enthusiasts, these creatures make up the bulk of animal species diversity and play vital roles in nutrient turnover, predator/parasite complexes, and pollination. Invertebrates are also a major food source for many birds, mammals, fish, reptiles, and amphibians.

Most of the data on the impact of spruce budworm chemicals on wildlife are for Sevin-4-Oil (whose active ingredient is carbaryl), the workhorse of the spray program for many years. The data show that for some classes of organisms, budworm pesticides were far from safe:

Terrestrial Invertebrates

Carbaryl is so toxic to so many invertebrates (including springtails, bugs, beetles, flies, wasps, bees, butterflies, moths, and spiders) that a 1985 environmental risk assessment done by Eco-analysts, Inc., for the Maine Board of Pesticide Control gave it a "3" rating, indicative of the most severe effects.[1] Some of the invertebrates it kills, such as spiders, wasps, and beetles, are budworm predators or parasites.

Pollinators

Many insects pollinate flowering plants in the forest. A 1981 state environmental monitoring study on the effects of Sevin-4-Oil on fruitset and wildlife found that many important pollinators, especially solitary bees, were severely reduced by spraying.[2] This led to significant reductions in the number of flowers, percentage of fruitset, or number of seeds per fruit for the plant species studied. A 1978 study showed even more significant effects from spraying in warmer conditions. Sixty-eight species of wild bees were decimated, and fruitset on witherod, a type of shrub, was down 80%.[3] Small fruits play important roles in the diets of 57 species of birds, 13 species of mammals, and 1 species of reptile in Maine. Fruit is especially important to some species of migrating birds.[4] The Eco-analyst report gave carbaryl its most severe rating, "3," for effects on pollinators.[5] A 1983 environmental risk assessment of spruce budworm pesticides done by Stephen Oliveri of the Maine Forest Service rated the other chemical budworm pesticides as "2" (moderate) to "3" (severe) for effects on pollinators and fruitset.[6]

Pond Invertebrates

A 1981 state study found that carbaryl was highly toxic to a number of pond invertebrates, including mayflies, damselflies, dragonflies, and caddisflies, and that it caused "distress" in leeches.[7] The most disturbing effect was a reduction to zero of amphipods, which are small crustaceans. Carbaryl persisted in pond sediments for more than a year. The Eco-Analyst report rated carbaryl as "3" for these effects.[8]

Stream Invertebrates

Sevin-4-Oil caused major reductions in stream invertebrates such as mayflies and caddisflies. In some streams stoneflies were completely wiped out.[9] This result has been confirmed by dozens of studies. Stoneflies are sensitive at levels as low as 1 part per billion.[10] The Eco-Analyst report rated carbaryl as "3" for these effects.[11]

Fish

Budworm chemicals did not affect fish as dramatically as they did invertebrates, but that does not necessarily mean they had no serious effects. Some studies did find evidence of direct toxicity from carbaryl. A 1978 state study noted large numbers of dead juvenile and adult nine-spine sticklebacks in a sprayed shallow pond.[12] Researchers found 50% mortality in caged trout subjected to 121 parts per billion of carbaryl by a 1978 budworm spray program in Washington State.[13]

A bibliography of environmental monitoring done for a joint Canadian/U.S. research effort (CANUSA) listed half a dozen studies showing toxic effects to fish from Matacil and fenitrothion, which were used in both Canada and the U.S.[14] Part of the problem with Matacil was its inert ingredient, nonyl phenol, which is far more toxic to salmon and other fish than its active chemical, aminocarb.[15] For that matter, the breakdown product of carbaryl (1-naphthol) can be more toxic to fish than carbaryl itself, and carbaryl can enhance the effects of other chemicals on trout.[16]

The body-count approach to environmental impact studies is not sufficient to account for more subtle effects. The Eco-Analyst report, for example, lists several studies that show statistically significant depressions of acetyl-cholinesterase, or AChE, in the brains of trout exposed to low levels of carbaryl.[17] Changes in brain chemistry can affect behavior and survival. A 1972 Canadian study on trout predation of salmon exposed to Sumithion (fenitrothion) found that when salmon were exposed to 1 part per million Sumithion, 95% were eaten. Only 50% of unsprayed salmon were eaten. The authors warn that lack of fish mortality after spraying "does not necessarily mean that there has been no impact on fish."[18]

Birds

As with fish, the effects of pesticides on birds include direct toxic effects, changes in AChE that affect behavior, and loss of food, including both insects and small fruits. Direct mortality is not a simple thing to determine because of bird mobility and the difficulty of finding small bodies in the woods.[a] The Eco-Analyst report listed studies that show possible bird mortality (especially of fledglings hatched just before spraying) with carbaryl.[19] Fenitrothion, which is still widely used in New Brunswick, is considered a bird killer and was given the highest risk rating of "3" (significant decrease in reproductive success or direct mortality) by Stephen Oliveri in 1983.[20] One study showed that a reduced insect food supply caused by spraying with Sevin led to altered foraging behavior by warblers and to changes in behavior and growth of fledgling black ducks and chickadees.[21] Both the Eco-Analyst report and Oliveri rated carbaryl as "2" (decreased growth rates of juveniles or decreases in reproductive success).[22]

A 1982 study found that total numbers and species richness of birds on "moribund" plots in Baxter State Park (where budworms in unsprayed forests killed a significant proportion of fir and spruce) were greater than in "healthy" stands in the nearby industrial forest (where fir and spruce had been "protected" with pesticides). The extensive mortality in Baxter State Park created more habitats for species such as woodpeckers and creepers (bark gleaners), white-throated sparrows (early succession), or red-eyed vireos (mixedwoods).[23]

Endnote

a. In the late 1940s C. S. Robbins put out a known number of dead birds on small plots at the Patuxent Wildlife Research Refuge in Maryland and asked people of varying experience to find the dead birds. They were allowed to use any system of search, including going over the ground on hands and knees. Yet very few of the birds were found, even by experienced naturalists.[24] Rather than count bodies, researchers rely on tallies of singing males.

References

1. Paul R. Adamus and Charles J. Spies III, *Environmental Risk Assessment of 10 Pesticides Used in Maine* (Augusta, Me.: Maine Board of Pesticide Control, 1985), p. 46.
2. Richard Hansen, Eben Osgood, and Malcolm Hunter, Jr., "Effects of Spraying with Sevin-4-Oil on Fruit-set and Its Potential Consequences for Wildlife in a Spruce-fir Forest." In *Environmental Monitoring Reports from the 1981 Maine Cooperative Spruce Budworm Suppression Project* (Augusta, Me.: Maine Forest Service, Maine Department of Conservation, 1982), p. 91-122.
3. E. R. Milliczky and E. A. Osgood, *The Effects of Spraying with Sevin-4-Oil on Insect Pollinators and Pollination in a Spruce-fir Forest*, Maine Agricultural Experiment Station Technical Bulletin No. 90 (Orono, Me.: Maine Agricultural Experiment Station, University of Maine, 1979).
4. Richard Hansen, Eben Osgood, and Malcolm Hunter, Jr., "Effects of Spraying," pp.114-116.
5. Paul R. Adamus and Charles J. Spies III, *Environmental Risk Assessment*, p. 38.
6. S. Oliveri, "Assessment of the Environmental Impacts of Spruce Budworm Suppression Operations in Maine and Eastern Canada." In *Transactions of the Northeast Section of the Wildlife Society*, Vol. 40 (1983): 35.
7. K. Elizabeth Gibbs, Terry Mingo, David Courtemanche, and Donald Stairs, "The Effects on Pond Macroinvertebrates from Forest Spraying of Carbaryl (Sevin-4-Oil) and Its Persistence in Water and Sediment." In *Environmental Monitoring Reports from the 1980 Maine Cooperative Spruce Budworm Suppression Project*(Augusta, Me.: Maine Forest Service, Maine Department of Conservation, 1981), pp. 120-147.
8. Paul R. Adamus and Charles J. Spies III, *Environmental Risk Assessment*, p. 40.
9. D. L. Courtemanche and K. E. Gibbs, "Short and Long-term Effects of Forest Spraying of Carbaryl (Sevin-4-Oil) on Stream Invertebrates," *Canadian Entomology*, Vol.112 (1980): 271-276.
10. Paul R. Adamus and Charles J. Spies III, *Environmental Risk Assessment*, p. 41.
11. *Ibid.*, p. 42.
12. D. L. Courtemanche and K. E. Gibbs, "The Effects of Sevin-4-Oil on Lentic Communities." In *Environmental Monitoring of Cooperative Spruce Budworm Control Projects, Maine 1976 and 1977* (Augusta, Me.: Maine Forest Service, Maine Department of Conservation, 1978), pp. 141-150.
13. Paul R. Adamus and Charles J. Spies III, *Environmental Risk Assessment*, p. 43.
14. Jonathan Bart and Laurie Hunter, *Ecological Impacts of Forest Insecticides: An Annotated Bibliography* (Ithaca, N. Y.: New York Cooperative Wildlife Research Unit, Cornell University, 1978), pp. 5, 29, 54, 55, 63, 64.
15. V. D. Zitco, W. McLeese, and D. B. Sargent, "Lethality of Aminocarb and Its Formulation to Juvenile Atlantic Salmon and Marine Invertebrates," photocopy (New Brunswick: Fisheries and Oceans Canada, 1979).
16. Paul R. Adamus and Charles J. Spies III, *Environmental Risk Assessment*, p. 44.
17. *Ibid.*, pp. 43-44.
18. C.T. Hatfield and J.M. Anderson, "Effects of two insecticides on vulnerability of Atlantic

Salmon (*Salmo salar*) parr to brook trout (*Salvelinus fontinalis*) predatios." *Journal of Fish Resources Board Canada*, Vol.29, 1972: 27-29.

19. Paul R. Adamus and Charles J. Spies III, *Environmental Risk Assessment*, pp. 46-47.

20. S. Oliveri, "Assessment of the Environmental Impacts,"p. 35.

21. M. L. Hunter, Jr., and Jack Witham, "Further Studies on the Indirect Effect of Carbaryl on the Behavior of Birds." In *Environmental Monitoring Reports from the 1981 Maine Cooperative Spruce Budworm Suppression Project* (Augusta, Me.: Maine Forest Service, Maine Department of Conservation, 1982), pp. 35-66.

22. S. Oliveri, "Assessment of the Environmental Impacts," p. 35. Also, Paul R. Adamus and Charles J. Spies III, *Environmental Risk Assessment*, p. 49.

23. S. Oliveri and N. Famous, "A Comparison of Bird Populations in Moribund and Healthy Spruce-fir Stands in Maine." In *Environmental Monitoring Reports from the 1982 Maine Cooperative Spruce Budworm Suppression Project* (Augusta, Me.: Maine Forest Service, Maine Department of Conservation, 1983), pp. 93-128.

24. William H. Drury, David Folger, and Garret Conover, "Monitoring the Effects of Spraying for Spruce Budworm on Song Birds in Maine, 1979." In *Environmental Monitoring Reports from the 1979 Maine Cooperative Spruce Budworm Suppression Project* (Augusta, Me.: Maine Forest Service, Maine Department of Conservation, 1980), p. 57.

Myth 2

The effects of budworm chemicals on wildlife are temporary—affected populations quickly bounce back to normal.

While it is true that some species of insects quickly recovered to normal population levels, others did not. For example, biologists monitoring streams and ponds found that amphipod populations had not recovered after 3 years, and stoneflies had not recovered after 4 years.[1,2]

The fact that some species bounce back faster than others can have significant impacts on ecosystem processes such as predator/prey balances. A study on the impact of budworm pesticides on spiders and other predators concluded that "even short-term reductions of spiders and other predatory arthropods at a critical period could act to reduce environmental resistance to budworm moth invasion and reproduction, thus enhancing population flareback."[3] Rachel Carson, in *Silent Spring*, wrote about another possibility of predator knockdowns: secondary pest infestations. When the state of Montana used DDT to fight a spruce-budworm outbreak in 1957, the result was a massive spider-mite infestation.[4]

Ironically, one species that was not wiped out by pesticides was the spruce budworm. Because this insect rebounded so well, most areas got sprayed more than once, some even 6 or more times. The effects of repeated spraying were not well studied, but it is obvious that any species that is slow to recover would have an even worse time recovering from multiple sprayings.

Some researchers have hypothesized that spraying has helped to prolong budworm outbreaks or shorten the time between epidemics.[5] This important shift from normal ecosystem dynamics is indicative of major long-term ecological affects.

References

1. K. E. Gibbs, T. M. Mingo, and D. L. Courtemanche, "Persistence of Carbaryl (Sevin-4-Oil) in Woodland Ponds and Its Effects on Macroinvertebrates Following Forestry Spraying (1980-1983)." In *Environmental Monitoring Reports from the 1983 Maine Spruce Budworm Suppression Project* (Augusta, Me.: Maine Forest Service, Maine Department of Conservation, 1984), p. 37.
2. Joan Trial and Kristin Cree, "The Effectiveness of Upstream Refugia for Promoting Recolonization of Plecoptera Killed by Exposure to Carbaryl." In *Environmental Monitoring Reports from the 1980 Maine Cooperative Spruce Budworm Suppression Project* (Augusta, Me.: Maine Forest Service, Maine Department of Conservation, 1981), p. 56.
3. Susan Hydorn, "The Influence of Pesticides Sprayed for Spruce Budworm Control on Certain Non-target Terrestrial Invertebrates in the Forest." In *Environmental Monitoring Reports, Cooperative Spruce Budworm Control Project, Maine 1978* (Augusta, Me.: Maine Forest Service, Maine Department of Conservation, 1979), p. 50.
4. Rachel Carson, *Silent Spring* (New York: Houghton Mifflin Company, 1962), p. 214.
5. J. R. Blais, "Trends in the Frequency, Extent, and Severity of Spruce Budworm Outbreaks in Eastern Canada," *Canadian Journal of Forestry*, Vol. 13 (1983): 539-547.

Myth 3

The worst effects of budworm chemicals were acceptably mitigated by aquatic buffers.

Until the late 1970s there were few state guidelines in Maine to avoid contaminating streams during budworm spray projects. By the 1980s the strictest aquatic buffers were for Sevin: 250 feet around streams and water bodies visible from 1,000 feet above the terrain for small aircraft; and 500 feet for large aircraft (which had a spray swath width of 1,200 feet with no crosswind).[1] Other chemicals got smaller buffers: 150 feet for small planes and 300 feet for large ones. Legally, vernal pools and small streams not visible from 1,000 feet could be directly sprayed. Rivers, streams, and ponds were still directly sprayed—illegally.

These buffer widths were not based on scientific proof of minimum contamination. Pesticides tend to drift. A study done for the state in 1979 found that when samples were taken downwind and perpendicular to the line of flight, spray deposits declined for about a quarter of a mile. But then they started to climb again until they peaked at 1 3/4 miles out of the spray block, at which point concentrations were 40% of those found at the edge of the spray block![2] The same study concluded that "watershed impact can be expected and is unavoidable. Runoff generated from rainfall will carry pesticides from the watershed into the stream."[3] A 1979 monitoring study by Joan Trial concluded that "smaller buffers, .1 km wide or 'shut off if visible' are not reliable in preventing increased aquatic and terrestrial drift rates. . . . "[4]

Although buffer requirements may have reduced the amount of water contaminated by pesticides, they certainly did not end it. But then, water contamination was not the only problem with spraying. The chemicals did, after all, have very unpleasant effects on pollinators and predator/prey complexes on land. The buffer zones would have been far more acceptable if they had buffered both aquatic and terrestrial ecosystems.

References

1. Maine Department of Conservation, *1983 Spruce Budworm Environmental Assessment* (Augusta, Me.: Maine Department of Conservation, 1983), p. 15.

2. SCS Engineers, "Environmental Monitoring of the 1979 Budworm Suppression Project." In *Environmental Monitoring Reports from the 1979 Maine Cooperative Spruce Budworm Suppression Project* (Augusta, Me.: Maine Forest Service, Maine Department of Conservation, 1980), p. 164.
3. *Ibid.*, p. 186.
4. Joan G. Trial, "The Effectiveness of Unsprayed Buffers in Lessening the Impact of Aerial Application of Carbaryl on Aquatic Insects." In *Environmental Monitoring Reports from the 1979 Maine Cooperative Spruce Budworm Suppression Project* (Augusta, Me.: Maine Forest Service, Maine Department of Conservation, 1980), pp. 129-130.

Air Pollution

Scientists have known since the seventeenth century that air pollution can affect the health of plants as well as people.[1] The role of industrial air pollution in damaging plants has been most obvious near highly polluting point sources such as metal smelters. As a result of mining operations, for example, vegetation at Copper Basin in Tennessee has been subjected to sulfur-dioxide fumes since 1850. After the turn of the century air-pollution damage was so severe that three vegetation zones developed: in the 7,000 acres closest to the mining operations, the land did not revegetate after the forests were cut; the second zone consisted of 17,000 acres of grasslands; the third zone had 30,000 acres of trees and grass. Vegetation damage extended 12 to 15 miles from the smelter, with white pine showing damage up to 20 miles away.[2]

Air-pollution damage has been even more severe near the copper and nickel smelters at Sudbury, Ontario. Local forests have been subjected to sulfur-dioxide fumes, sulfuric-acid mist, acid precipitation, and heavy-metal contamination. Forty square miles around the smelters are virtually barren, 140 square miles have impoverished vegetation, and white pine have been killed over a 700-square-mile area.[3]

In the twentieth century, fossil-fuel use has expanded exponentially, greatly increasing atmospheric carbon dioxide and sulfur dioxide.[4] After World War II, high-compression engines began adding nitrogen oxides and ozone to the air-pollution brew. In an effort to improve local air quality, heavy polluters have built huge smokestacks, such as the 1,250-foot stack at the Copper Gliff Smelter at Sudbury, that have vented contaminants high into the atmosphere. Air-pollution contaminants are now raining down on ecosystems hundreds or even thousands of miles from any immediate sources.

In the 1960s and 1970s scientists and environmentalists became concerned that streams, lakes, and ponds in some regions had become so acidic they could no longer support fish or other aquatic species. In the 1980s scientists in Europe discovered that forests in regions heavily polluted with sulfur dioxide, nitrogen oxides, ozone, and heavy metals were experiencing canopy dieback or even tree death (Waldsterben). Such diebacks, which reduce or eliminate habitat for many plant, animal, and microorganism species, can lead to severe local reductions of biodiversity—especially the rich diversity of life forms that exist in the soil. In the United States the same symptoms have been found in high-altitude forests in the Appalachians. Some environmental groups predicted in the early

1980s that such symptoms were just the beginning of widespread damage from the "rain of death."

Whereas these air-pollution effects are regional, the potential effects of increased carbon dioxide, methane, chlorofluorocarbons, and other greenhouse gasses are global. World climate changes could induce flooding of thousands of miles of populated coastlines, disrupt agriculture and forestry, and reduce biological diversity in natural ecosystems. Transitional ecosystems, such as the Acadian forest of northern New England and eastern Canada, are particularly vulnerable to such changes because many of the flora and fauna are at the northern or southern edges of their ranges and are thus sensitive to climatic shifts. Some environmentalists, reacting to the potential of mass extinctions from global climate change, have contemplated what they call "the end of nature."

Unlike clearcuts, herbicides, and insecticides, air pollution is not an intentional management tool; it is an unwanted by-product of industrial growth based on fossil fuels. With air pollution, foresters cannot buffer sensitive areas such as riparian zones, mountaintops, or wildlife preserves. Where air pollution goes has more to do with the will of the winds than the wills of forest managers. Reducing such pollution means stopping it at its source.

One would think that companies as dependent on productive forests as the paper industry would be the first and loudest protesters against threats to forest health from air pollution. The paper industry, however, has not been a major lobbyist for clean air. Robert Kaufman, director of the air-quality program of the American Paper Institute and National Forest Products Association, asserted in 1988 that, "We do not see conclusive evidence air pollution in general is causing reduced productivity in commercial forests."[5] He also added that industry sees no need for more regulations to curb acid rain but that it does support more research.

The forest industry is likewise skeptical about the role of industrially released greenhouse gasses in changing the world's climate, claiming the models that predict global warming are flawed and the data inadequate.[6] Both forest dieback and global warming are extremely complex, and scientific studies based only on short-term data can hardly be definitive at proving long-term trends. In light of such uncertainty, paper industry lobbyists claim we should be "conservative"—which means giving the benefit of the doubt to industrialism, a relatively new phenomenon in the history of the earth, rather than to forests.

Some forest-industry spokespeople go beyond seeking refuge in complexity—they claim that if there is a problem, by some happy coincidence industrial management, dedicated to short-rotation fiber production, is helping alleviate it. A fact sheet from the Northeastern Loggers' Association stresses these "talking points":

•Trees are nature's most efficient converters of carbon dioxide to oxygen, and young forests take in more carbon dioxide and give off more oxygen than do older forests.

•Genetic tree improvement programs offer the best opportunity to maintain forest productivity if climate changes were to occur. Tree improvement programs match the best adapted species to specific site conditions.

•Intensive forest management practices, such as pest and fire control, thinning and fertilization, result in healthier forests that are more resistant to environmental stress.[7]

Not only are industrial foresters doing the atmosphere a favor by cutting down old growth, they are helping forests resist air-pollution stress by spraying pesticides on their tree monocultures that have been genetically tailored for the climate of the future—which, apparently, foresters have predicted with astonishing accuracy. We should be grateful.

The paper industry, which is a major user of fossil fuels and a source of some of the pollutants that are raining on their own forests, benefits when debate is focused on issues that may not be resolved for decades. If cutting back on burning fossil fuels and polluting the atmosphere is contingent on absolute scientific proof that these pollutants harm the forests, industry may hold the upper hand awhile longer. Such a debate may distract environmentalists from more obvious reasons to kick the fossil-fuel habit, such as depletion of nonrenewable resources, inequities to future generations, destruction of land during drilling and mining, exploitation of workers, creation of oil spills during shipping and toxic waste during refining, waste of tax dollars on military buildup to protect import supplies, and so forth.

Environmentalists' claims of global catastrophe start to ring hollow after a few years to a public expecting instant disaster. Sure we had a hot summer in 1988, but winter cold still cuts to the bone. And sure there seems to be evidence of some air-pollution damage in isolated, sensitive areas. But the bulk of the industrial forest is still green and growing. James Mahoney, director of the 10-year-long study by the congressionally funded National Acid Precipitation Assessment Program (NAPAP) announced reassuringly in 1990 that "the sky is not falling, but there is a problem that needs addressing. . . . Acid rain does cause damage, but the amount of damage is less than we once thought, and it's much less than some of the characterizations we sometimes hear."[8]

The NAPAP study was used by Congress as a basis for the Clean Air Act of 1990. With the air-pollution problem "solved" by Congress, we can now concentrate on the more pressing problem of stimulating greater economic growth—based on deforestation and fossil-fuel consumption.

References

1. Sherman Hasbrouck, *Acid Deposition and Forest Decline* (Orono, Me.: The Land and Water Resources Center, University of Maine, 1984), p. 10.
2. Imants Miller, Daniel S. Shriner, and David Rizzo, *History of Hardwood Decline in Eastern United States*, General Technical Report NE-124 (Washington, D.C.: United States Forest Service, United States Department of Agriculture, 1989), p. 43.
3. *Ibid.*
4. Sherman Hasbrouck, *Acid Deposition*, p. 10.
5. Philip Shabecoff, "Deadly Combination Felling Trees in East," *New York Times*, July 24, 1988, p. 18.
6. David Wheeler, "Scientists Studying 'The Greenhouse Effect' Challenge Fears of Global Warming," *Journal of Forestry* (July 1990): 36.
7. Northeastern Loggers' Association, Inc., *Issue Brief: Global Warming* (Old Forge, N.Y.: Northeastern Loggers' Association, Inc., January 22, 1990).
8. William K. Stevens, "Worst Fears on Acid Rain Unrealized," *New York Times*, February 20, 1990, p. C1.

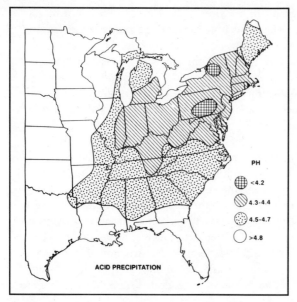

Areas of U. S. affected by acid precipitation. *From Imants Miller, Daniel S. Shriner, and David Rizzo*, History of Hardwood Decline in Eastern United States, *General Technical Report NE-124 (Washington, D.C.: United States Forest Service, United States Department of Agriculture, 1989), p. 48.*

Myth 1

Since scientists have not established definitive proof that acid rain is harming commercial forests, it would be imprudent to create stricter air-pollution standards that would be a financial burden to industries.

This myth demonstrates the paper industry's parochial attitude that it is acceptable for air pollution to damage sensitive lakes, streams, and noncommercial forests elsewhere as long as it does not damage the industrial forest here. The myth also implies that air pollution is not harming the industrial forest.

Sources of Maine Air Pollution

The rain, snow, fog, mist, and some of the dust in Maine, as in much of eastern North America, are acidic.[a] The rain started to become acidic in the 1930s, and the acidity increased markedly in the 1950s with the post-World War II industrial boom.[1] According to a model used by Maine's Department of Environmental Protection (DEP), up to 95% of the sulfur and nitrogen pollutants that acidify Maine's rain comes from out of state (mostly from the Ohio valley, the Midwest, New York, and southern New England) or even from out of country (mostly from Ontario and Quebec).[2]

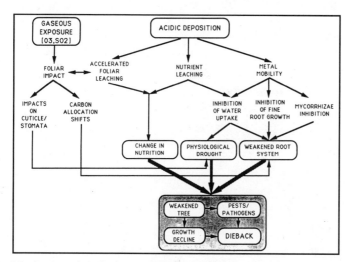

Mechanisms by which atmospheric deposition is thought to contribute to forest dieback, decline, and mortality. *From Imants Miller, Daniel S. Shriner, and David Rizzo,* History of Hardwood Decline in Eastern United States, *General Technical Report NE-124 (Washington: United States Forest Service, United States Department of Agriculture, 1989), p. 41.*

This DEP model assumes that the smoke goes up instead of down and that a gentle wind blows from west to east.[3] When weather conditions do not fit this simplified model, local sources (ranging from power plants to cars and trucks) can make more significant pollution contributions to the immediate surrounding areas. Nine of the top 10 in-state stationary sources of sulfur dioxide, nitrogen oxides, and volatile organic compounds (precursors to ozone) are paper-company power generators or mills.[4] (see Appendix 3).

Damage Elsewhere

The atmospheric pollution generated by the more distant sources does not simply go up in the air and wait until it reaches Maine's industrial forest before it drops onto the trees and into the soil; it rains down on all the points in between. The degree to which the pollution damages aquatic or forest ecosystems depends on the mix of pollutants, the weather patterns, the terrain, the buffering capacity (ability to neutralize acids) of soils or water, the type of vegetation, the season, and other accompanying stresses (e.g., drought, frost, insects, pathogens, and damage from harvesting).

Because of this complexity of combined factors, scientists are reluctant to make categorical statements that a particular pollutant "causes" acidified lakes or tree dieback—the same pollution has been falling on some watersheds and forests without causing easily observable damage. In sensitive areas, however, where pollution has been particularly intense and where the soil lacks adequate buffering capacity, the impacts have been severe. Some of these areas are in or near the Acadian forest.

Damaged Aquatic Ecosystems

Thousands of streams, rivers, ponds, and lakes in eastern North America have become too acidic to support acid-sensitive species (such as salmon) or even to support any fish at all.

Sensitivity of Inland Fish to Acidity[5]

Species	pH at which mortality occurs[*]	Species	pH at which mortality occurs[*]
Yellow perch	4.43	Common shiner	5.27
White sucker	4.65	Atlantic salmon	5.27
Brown bullhead	4.84	Brown trout	6.27
Golden shiner	4.84	Rainbow trout	6.56
Lake chub	5.09		

[*]It makes a difference whether the water is acidic because of organic acids (leached out from vegetation) or from nitric or sulfuric acid from air pollution. In the latter case, soluble aluminum, which is toxic to fish gills, is more apt to be released into the water.

Not only fish but zooplankton, phytoplankton, molluscs, and amphipods have been eliminated or reduced in these water bodies.[6] Reproduction in some frog and salamander species is inhibited by acidity of surface waters.[7] The average pH of a water body can mask toxic seasonal "acid pulses" which occur after snowmelt in the spring or after highly acidic rainfalls. These effects are most profound in smaller headwater streams where much of the water volume may come from rain or snowmelt.

In the southwestern Adirondacks, 51% of the 450 lakes over 10 acres have a pH of 5.5 or less, and 38% of the lakes are so acidic they can no longer support fish.[8] A survey of 234 lakes in Nova Scotia found that one third have a pH under 5.0 and contain no fish. Thirteen rivers in that province have become too acidic to support salmon, and salmon are declining in 18 other rivers.[9]

Maine also has acid lakes, albeit a small proportion. A survey of lakes in Maine's Unorganized Territories did find some with a pH as low as 4.5.[10] A survey of high-elevation lakes by Maine's DEP found 14 of the 90 lakes to be "acidic."[11] Although there are not enough historical records to know what percentage of these lakes have become acidified in recent times, analysis of lake-bottom sediments in Maine reveals that over the last 100 years soil nutrients have been depleted while deposition of heavy metals has increased, and over the last 50 years pH levels of these lakes have declined.[12]

Damaged Hardwoods

A review by the USDA Forest Service of 100 years of hardwood declines in the eastern U.S. concluded that declines have intensified recently in unexplained ways and that pollution might play a role in these events.[13] The authors mapped out areas considered high in acid rain, sulfur dioxide, nitrogen oxides, and ozone, compared them with maps of recent diebacks, and found some correlations with maple, birch, and ash.[14]

Birches have been dying in a 20-mile-wide strip on the northern shore of the Bay of Fundy in New Brunswick. This strip is often bathed in acidic fog.[15] Sugar maples have also been declining and dying in eastern Canada. Young trees that were never even tapped for syrup have lost their tops and died.[16]

Researcher Tom Hutchinson of the University of Ontario found that under dying trees the soil has high levels of soluble aluminum (which can be toxic) and low levels of phosphorus and calcium (important nutrients). He also found evidence of foliar leaching of calcium and magnesium and damage to the important mycorrhizae fungi that help trees increase their intake of nutrients.[17] He collected soils from under healthy and declining trees and found that maple seedlings "do not like growing on the declining soil."[18]

Sugar maples are also declining in parts of Vermont. On Camel's Hump researchers have found reductions in average height, width, and general bulk and a decline of nearly 50% in the number of new trees over the last 25 years.[19] Hubert Vogelmann, a professor at the University of Vermont, has found a correlation between the appearance, starting in the 1950s, of certain heavy metals in tree growth rings and the beginning of decline. He has found evidence that part of the problem is changes in the balance of nutrients in the soil.[20]

Damaged Spruce-fir

Red spruce have been declining during the last 30 years at high altitudes over much of the Appalachians and at low altitudes along coastal areas that are often bathed in acid fog and high levels of ozone.[21,22] Researchers have found extensive damage to spruce on Whiteface Mountain (in the Adirondacks), Camel's Hump (in the Green Mountains), and Mounts Moosilauke and Washington (in the White Mountains).[23]

Two-thirds of the water in the high-elevation regions of the Appalachians comes from cloud/fog moisture. Cloud moisture is more acidic than acid rain and averages around 3.5 pH but can be as low as 2.7 pH (somewhere between vinegar and lemon juice).[24] In the high-mountain regions of the Adirondacks and Green Mountains, ozone concentrations in 1987 were high during14% of the warm-weather season.[25] Researchers in this region also found evidence of foliar leaching in red spruce. Red spruce is more susceptible to winter injury than other species, and experimenters found they could cause similar problems with spruce artificially exposed to acid mist.[26]

Even more serious than the evidence of foliar damage is evidence of long-term, cumulative damage to the acidified soils under declining red spruce. On the peaks where spruce declines have occurred, researchers have found that important nutrients (such as calcium and magnesium) have been leaching out, and aluminum, an element that can have adverse effects on plant growth, has become more available.[27]

Damage to the Industrial Forest

The documented damage to sensitive aquatic and forest ecosystems, as well as to human health, monuments, and buildings, should be reason enough to cut back drastically on polluting emissions. Industrial defenders, however, want the debate to center around the less-clear impacts on commercial forests. To this effect, they have followed two broad strategies:

(1) Deny the role of air pollution in declines.

The first line of defense has been to deny that forest declines have been caused by air pollution. Instead, industrial-pollution defenders can point to evidence of natural causes such as drought, insects, disease, or natural dieback cycles.[28] These "natural" explanations, however, fail to explain the wide geographical area of decline (including Europe), the coincidence that the declines are most intense where pollution stress has been most intense, and the fact that multiple species are affected. Drought, insects, or disease are added stresses to the stress of air pollution. Whether pollution is the primary or secondary cause is a moot point—it is surely doing the forest no good.

The role of air pollution in red-spruce decline has been acknowledged by NAPAP.[29] Forestry/air-pollution experts surveyed by the Society of American Foresters also accepted that acid deposition was harming high-altitude red spruce.[30] Although there is yet no unanimity on how the pollution is damaging high-altitude trees, most scientists accept that pollution is damaging these trees.

(2) Assert that high-altitude forests are a special case.

The next line of defense is to accept that air pollution has been damaging forests in some extreme situations but to deny that these special situations have any relevance to commercial forests. Robert Kaufman of the American Paper Institute stated flatly that "there is no evidence that acid deposition is affecting the soil of commercial forests."[31]

NAPAP concluded that aside from the high-altitude spruce, there is no evidence that acid deposition is causing a decline of American forests. It admitted, however, that there was a "potential" for long-term adverse effects on "sensitive soils in certain areas of the eastern United States in fifty to 100 years, which is within a single rotation for managed eastern forests."[32]

The scientists surveyed by the SAF likewise doubted that acid deposition was damaging low-elevation spruce-fir but still estimated that growth losses caused by air pollution in this forest type are "intermediate" and that the major culprit is probably ozone rather than "acid rain."[33]

Those advocating assessments of no to minimal damage can point to a 1990 forest health monitoring study for New England done by the USDA Forest Service which concluded that "the summary of crown ratings data from open grown, dominant, and codominant trees indicates no pattern of major decline in any species."[34] This study did look at indicator plants, which are especially sensitive to pollution, and found evidence of ozone damage at 9.4% of the locations monitored and of sulfur dioxide damage at 3.1%.[35]

Damage to Soil

Some scientists see the soil imbalances under dying trees at high altitudes as the canary in the coal mine rather than as isolated events with no relevance to commercial forests. Those looking for foliar damage, they claim, are looking in the wrong place. In a 1990 article about the release of the NAPAP study, the *New York Times* reported as "one of the biggest reservations on the forest issue" that "some scientists . . . are convinced that there is no doubt that acid in some soils not only robs the soil of nutrients but also interferes with the ability of trees to absorb them."[36]

In a series of studies with both European and American colleagues, Walter Shortle, a USDA Forest Service researcher at Durham, New Hampshire, has made a compelling case that damage to sensitive soils (such as those found under red spruce) is not just a possibility for the future; it has already happened at many locations. He reached this conclusion after comparing:

•the balance of aluminum to calcium in soils exposed to high versus low levels of acid deposition;[37]

•the calcium concentration in tree rings, formed over many decades, of thousands of trees over a wide geographic area;[38]

•analyses done on forest soils between 1940 and 1988.[39]

In contrast to the NAPAP study, Shortle concluded that "the most sensitive sites appear to have been adversely affected 20 to 40 yr [sic] in the past, and not 50 to 100 yr [sic] in the future. . . . One of the most important impacts of acidic deposition on forests in eastern North America apparently occurred before anybody was looking."[40]

Evidence of Pollution-induced Nutrient Capital Depletion

As soils become more acidic, calcium and other mineral cations (positively charged atoms or groups of atoms) become mobilized and tend to leach out of the soil. At the same time, aluminum becomes more soluble and can compete with calcium at fine root sites, leading to symptoms of calcium deficiency even though there is still calcium in the soil.[41] This aluminum-induced calcium deficiency tends to occur when the ratio of aluminum to calcium is close to or greater than 1.[42] Deficient trees are more vulnerable to insects, disease, cold, and drought. In older trees, which have high calcium requirements, the trees eventually cannot sustain current growth, leading to diebacks in the canopy.[43]

Walter Shortle and his colleagues found that in the soils under dying spruce at high altitudes, the ratio of aluminum to calcium in the fine roots was close to or greater than 1; in soils under healthier-looking spruce at lower altitudes, the ratio was 0.1 to 0.4.[44]

Studying the chemical makeup of tree rings, Shortle found that over a wide geographic area and at all altitudes, and at the same time as the acidification of local aquatic ecosystems, red spruce and nearby trees of other species showed rising calcium concentrations in the 1940s and 1950s but declining levels after the 1970s. The calcium concentrations briefly increased because the heavy load of acid depositions after World War II increased mobilization of cations, which became more available to the trees. But after this period, acid depositions led to lower concentrations in the wood because the prolonged leaching led to reduced calcium availability.[45]

A comprehensive review of past soil studies in the same forest type confirms that available calcium has been declining.[46] In some areas where there has been significant dieback and mortality, the calcium levels are not as low as one might expect. This is because the nutrients from the rotting boles and branches of the fallen dead wood are returning to the soil.[47] If this material were harvested instead of left to rot, the pool of available calcium would be far more depleted.

In the lower-altitude spruce-fir forests, symptoms of soil nutrient changes may not be visible in the foliage for decades, but this does not mean there is no problem. Nutrient imbalance may lead to growth losses or to increased susceptibility to other stresses. If acidic pollution is not drastically reduced, there can be serious long-term problems for soft-woods and hardwoods in soils with low buffering capacity. Mel Tyree, director of the University of Vermont's Proctor Maple Research Center, fears that "we . . . are looking at the early stages of an epidemic problem. We project regionwide decline in forests within the next 50 to 100 years."[48]

Endnote

a. Acidity is measured on the pH scale, which goes from 0 to 14. Anything over 7 (which is considered neutral) is alkaline; anything under 7 is acidic. The pH scale is logarithmic. This means that a reading of 5 is 10 times more acidic than a reading of 6; a reading of 4 is 10 times more acidic than a reading of 5 and 100 times more acidic than a reading of 6. "Normal" rain (unpolluted) is naturally slightly acidic (around 5.6 pH) because of dissolved CO_2 (which creates carbonic acid, H_2CO_3) as well as natural sulfur and nitrogen oxides.

References

1. F. Herbert Bormann, "The Vulnerable Landscape of New England: The Threat from Pollution," *Yale Alumni Magazine*. (April 1982), p. 10.
2. Maine Department of Environmental Protection, *Maine Acid Rain Study* (Augusta, Me.: Maine Department of Environmental Protection, 1987), pp.44-46.
3. *Ibid.*, pp. 20 and 22.
4. Maine Bureau of Air Quality Control, *Emission Rating Report 1988* (Augusta, Me.: Maine Bureau of Air Quality Control, Maine Department of Environmental Protection, 1988).
5. Janice Harvey, *Acid Rain in the East: The Problem and the Polluters* (Fredericton, New Brunswick: New Brunswick Conservation Council, 1988).
6. F. Herbert Bormann, "The Vulnerable Landscape," p. 15.
7. Sherman Hasbrouck, *Acid Deposition and Forest Decline* (Orono, Me.: The Land and Water Resources Center, University of Maine, 1984), p. 11.
8. William K. Stevens, "Worst Fears on Acid Rain Unrealized," *New York Times*, February 20, 1990," p. C4.
9. Janice Harvey, *Acid Rain..*
10. Ellen Baum and James St. Pierre, *Land Use Plan.* (Augusta, Me.: Land Use Regulation Commission, Maine Department of Conservation, 1987), p. 37.
11. Maine Department of Environmental Protection, *High Elevation Lake Monitoring in Maine, 1987 Annual Report to the Legislature*, Executive Summary (Augusta, Me.: Maine Department of Environmental Protection, 1987).
12. Sherman Hasbrouck, *Acid Deposition*, p. 11.
13. Imants Miller, Daniel S. Shriner, and David Rizzo, *History of Hardwood Decline in Eastern United States*, General Technical Report NE-124 (Washington, D.C.: United States Forest Service, United States Department of Agriculture, 1989), p. 1.
14. *Ibid.*, pp. 48-54.
15. Janice Harvey, *Acid Rain..*
16. David Cayley, "From Commons to Catastrophe: The Destruction of the Forests," Part V, transcript (Toronto, Ontario: Canadian Broadcasting Corporation, 1989), p. 36.
17. *Ibid.*, p. 37.
18. *Ibid.*, p. 36.
19. "Sugar Maples Sicken Under Acid Rain's Pall," *New York Times*, May 15, 1991, p. A18.
20. *Ibid.*
21. A. H. Johnson and T. G. Siccama, "Decline of Red Spruce in the Northern Appalachians: Assessing the Possible Role of Acid Deposition," *Journal of the Technical Association of the Pulp*

and Paper Industry, Vol. 67., No. 1 (January 1984): 72.

22. Richard Jagels, "Acid Fog, Ozone and Low Elevation Spruce Decline," *IAWA* (International Association of Wood Anatomy) *Bulletin*, Vol. 7 (1986): 299-307.

23. Philip Shabecoff, "Deadly Combination Felling Trees in East," *New York Times*, July 24, 1988, p. 18.

24. David Cayley, "From Commons to Catastrophe," p. 34.

25. Stephen C. Harper, Laura L. Falk, and Edward W. Rankin, *The Northern Forest Lands Study of New England and New York* (Rutland, Vt.: United States Forest Service, United States Department of Agriculture, 1990), p. 173.

26. *Ibid.*

27. Walter C. Shortle and Kevin T. Smith, "Aluminum-induced Calcium Deficiency Syndrome in Declining Red Spruce," *Science* (May 1988): 1018.

28. A. H. Johnson and T. G. Siccama, "Decline of Red Spruce," p. 297A.

29. William K. Stevens, "Worst Fears," p. C1.

30. J. E. de Steiguer, John M. Pye, and Carolyn S. Love, "Air Pollution Damage to U.S. Forests," *Journal of Forestry* (August 1990): 17-22.

31. Philip Shabecoff, "Deadly Combination," p. 18.

32. John Flynn, "Forest Without Trees: How Congress Was Duped About Acid Rain's Effects," *The Amicus Journal* (Winter 1991): 33.

33. J. E. de Steiguer et al., "Air Pollution Damage," p. 22.

34. Robert T. Brooks, Margaret Miller-Weeks, and William Burkman, *Summary Report: Forest Health Monitoring, New England, 1990*, NE-INF-94-91 (Durham, N.H.: Northeastern Area Association of State Foresters and USDA Forest Service, May 1991), p. 9.

35. *Ibid.*, p. 7.

36. William K. Stevens, "Worst Fears," p. C11.

37. Walter C. Shortle and Ernest A. Bondietti, "Timing, Magnitude, and Impact of Acidic Deposition on Sensitive Forest Sites," draft, *Journal of Water, Air and Soil Pollution* (Vol. 61, 1992): p 262.

38. E. A. Bondietti, N. Momoshima, W. C. Shortle, and K. T. Smith, "A Historical Perspective on Divalent Cation Trends in Red Spruce Stemwood and the Hypothetical Relationship to Acidic Deposition," *Canadian Journal of Forestry Research*, Vol. 20 (1990): 1850-1858.

39. Walter C. Shortle and Ernest A. Bondietti, "Timing," p. 6.

40. *Ibid.*, p. 265.

41. Walter C. Shortle and Kevin T. Smith, "Aluminum-induced Calcium Deficiency," p. 1017.

42. *Ibid.*

43. Walter C. Shortle and Ernest A. Bondietti, "Timing," p. 254.

44. *Ibid.*, p. 264.

45. E. A. Bondietti et al., "A Historical Perspective," p. 1853.

46. Walter C. Shortle and Ernest A. Bondietti, "Timing," p. 258.

47. *Ibid.*, p. 260.

48. "Sugar Maples Sicken," p. A18.

Myth 2

Industrial forest management does not contribute to the effects of acid rain.

Since industrial managers do not take air pollution into consideration in their management plans, this is an assumed rather than stated myth. If managers did take nutrient leaching from acid precipitation seriously, they would:

•use forest practices that minimize soil exposure and nutrient leaching;

•leave harvest residues on site to ensure recycling of nutrients;

•allow adequate time between harvests to recover available nutrients and soil organic matter; and

•encourage tree mixes that include deeper-rooted species that can bring nutrients up from mineral layers.

To the extent that managers emphasize whole-tree clearcuts, herbicides, and short rotations, they are exacerbating the effects of acid precipitation and will hasten any problems caused by soil nutrient imbalance.

A team of researchers from the Northeastern Forest Experiment Station of the USDA Forest Service in Durham, New Hampshire, have made estimates of long-term depletion of calcium and other nutrients from a number of forest types in the eastern U.S., including spruce-fir and northern hardwood. They determined that even if there were no harvesting, forest soils would lose calcium, potassium, and magnesium, with the worst losses being for calcium—a 16%-loss of the total pool over 120 years.[1] The authors commented that "the current input-output imbalances cannot have been maintained for long or the basic elements already would be depleted. Current rates of depletion in the northeastern United States probably are the result of anthropogenic acid precipitation, and the net loss may only have existed over roughly 100 years of the Industrial Age."[2]

Whole-tree harvesting, the researchers estimated, can double the net loss of calcium. They concluded that "the combination of leaching loss and whole-tree harvest at short (40-year) rotations apparently could remove roughly 50% of biomass and soil Ca [calcium] in only 120 years."[3]

This estimate, which suggests a loss in a hundred years of nutrients that took thousands of years to accumulate, is worse than it sounds. It is based on the depletion of the *total* pool of soil calcium, much of which is not in a form available to plants. It also does not take into account the aluminum/calcium balance that would lead to deficiencies well before all the calcium runs out.

If the stand is sprayed with herbicides, the problem could be even worse. Not only are large quantities of biomass nutrients removed during harvest, but after harvest, organic matter in the soil breaks down into soluble nutrients. Since there is no vegetation to take the nutrients back up, they leach out of the soil. Fast-growing pioneer species slow this nutrient leaching over a period of years. When these pioneer species are killed with herbicides, the nutrient leaching resumes.

To the extent that the resulting stand is dominated by shallow-rooted softwoods whose fine roots are concentrated in the humus layer of soil, calcium present in deeper mineral layers of the soil stays unavailable.[4] Some European foresters are starting to mix in hardwoods, such as alders, oak, and beech, with their plantations partly to fight some of the effects of acid rain.[5] Chris Maser, in his book *The Redesigned Forest*, wonders if "the cumulative effects of a century or more of intensive plantation management and use may have strained the forests of Central Europe, and thus predisposed them to the 'Waldsterben syndrome' we see today."[6]

References

1. C. Anthony Federer, James W. Hornbeck, Louise M. Tritton, C. Wayne Martin, Robert S. Pierce, C. Tattersall Smith, "Long-term Depletion of Calcium and Other Nutrients in Eastern U.S. Forests," *Environmental Management*, Vol. 13, No. 5 (1989): 597.
2. *Ibid.*, p. 599.
3. *Ibid.*
4. Walter C. Shortle and Ernest A. Bondietti,"Timing, Magnitude, and Impact of Acidic

Deposition on Sensitive Forest Sites," draft, *Journal of Water, Air and Soil Pollution* (in press): 2.
5. Dean Rhodes, "Alder Could Be Used to Fight Acid Rain, Forestry Experts Say," *Bangor Daily News*, November 1, 1987, p. 12W.
6. Chris Maser, *The Redesigned Forest* (San Pedre, Calif.: R. & E. Miles, 1988), p. 70.

Myth 3

The 1990 Clean Air Act will protect forests from the effects of acid rain.

The 1990 Clean Air Act does not protect forests from acid deposition; it merely legitimizes damage at acceptable levels. The Clean Air Act was supposed to be based on science, but unfortunately the science of the 10-year, $570-million National Acid Precipitation Assessment Program was subject to manipulation by the utility, automobile, and paper industries.[1]

Insufficient Forest Data

The Reagan administration was able to slow forest research for the first half of the 1980s by emphasizing laboratory studies. By the time field research was on track, it was too late. There was not enough time to establish trends in forest-soil changes or to determine the tolerance levels of the most susceptible forest types.[2] Two northeastern sites with the longest record of soil change— Hubbard Brook in New Hampshire and Camel's Hump in Vermont—were excluded from the NAPAP research.[3]

At some sites, such as Mount Mitchell in North Carolina, where there was significant forest damage, NAPAP authorities tended to attribute declines to such causes as insect invasions. This angered some of the researchers who found highly acidic soils (pH as low as 2.7), high levels of aluminum, and low levels of exchangeable calcium.[4] Robert Bruck of North Carolina State University, who has studied the southern mountains for years, protested, "I can take anyone who's interested in climbing Mount Mitchell and my other sites, and show them thousands of dead fir trees that did not have aphids; 65% did not. NAPAP dismissed anything that might have broadened the scope of the problem."[5]

Insufficient Nitrogen Reductions

The 1990 Clean Air Act calls for 40% to 50% reductions in sulfur emissions but only 15% to 25% reductions in nitrogen emissions over the coming decades. This too has upset some researchers in regions where nitrogen pollution has been as serious or worse than sulfur pollution in both forest and aquatic ecosystems.

To some degree, trees in forests with nitrogen-deficient soils can use nitrogen deposition as a fertilizer. But as nitrogen deposition exceeds the biological demand, it becomes a pollutant in soils and water.[6] Some ecosystems, such as the Ohio River basin, are already overloaded.[7] A far wider area, however, can be seasonally harmed by nitrogen deposition caused by pulses of high nitrogen concentrations from storms or spring snowmelt.

During spring high-flow periods in the Catskills, for example, nitrate concentrations in headwater streams approach those of sulfate and play important roles in acidifying these streams.[8] This impact is intensified if the surrounding forests have been harvested and cannot take up the nitrogen compounds that are released as organic matter breaks down or that come from air pollution.[9] Some scientists have recommended nitrogen-emission reductions of 50% to 75% to halt nutrient losses and forest declines.[10]

Pollution Legitimized

Rather than push for prevention of air-pollution problems via increased efficiency, conservation, recycling, mass transit, decentralization, cogeneration, renewable resources, and banning or phasing out toxic or hazardous substances, the 1990 Clean Air Act relies on a quick fix; using the Best Available Control Technologies combined with stricter standards to be put in place over a very generous time scale of decades. The time scale, ironically, is most forgiving for the most polluting industries.[11]

The act hopes to use the market to keep pollution levels at "acceptable levels" once target reductions are achieved. Pollution "rights" would be marketable—those plants that have exceeded emission goals could sell the right to pollute to other power plants, which could then legally pollute more.[12]

Citizens' Rights Diminished

More than 700 pages long, the act is a citizen's nightmare but may be a boon to the careers of lawyers for industry, government, and those environmental groups wealthy enough (probably from corporate donations) to be able to afford an air-pollution legal specialist. Who but a specialist could spend the time wading through such a document? Grassroots activists have been dismayed that the act, which Greenpeace has called "a Bill of Rights for polluters,"[13] reduces rather than increases their power to influence pollution policy.

Richard Grossman, author of *Fear At Work* and publisher of the *Wrenching Debate Gazette*, concluded, while watching the legislation in progress, that, "It appears that all the principal players—the White House, Congress, the polluters, the national environmental organizations—want and need a bill they can call 'clean air' more than they want clean air or an empowered citizenry. As long as they can get the public to believe these bills are about clean air, they will be able to enact antidemocratic and poisoning legislation in the name of the environment."[14]

Some of the regulations that do have teeth are subject to tampering from an organization that meets secretly with no public input or oversight—the Council on Competitiveness. Chaired by Vice President Dan Quayle, this group has already tried to junk some elements of the 1990 Clean Air Act—such as restrictions on burning lead acid batteries—that the members believe will hurt the competitiveness of industry.

While we wait over the decades for the worst polluters to reduce regulated pollutants to politically acceptable levels, the winds will continue to blow and the rains will continue to fall on the rivers, lakes, streams, and forests.

References

1. John Flynn, "Forest Without Trees: How Congress Was Duped About Acid Rain's Effects," *The Amicus Journal* (Winter 1991), p. 31.

2. *Ibid*, p. 30.
3. *Ibid.*
4. *Ibid.*
5. *Ibid.*
6. Gregory B. Lawrence and Ivan J. Fernandez, "Biogeochemical Interactions Between Acidic Deposition and a Low-elevation Spruce-fir Stand in Howland, Maine," *Canadian Journal of Forestry Research*, Vol. 21 (1991): 874.
7. John Flynn, "Forests Without Trees," p. 33.
8. Peter S. Murdoch and John L Stoddard, *The Role of Nitrate in the Acidification of Streams in the Catskill Mountains of New York*, draft (Albany, N.Y.: U.S. Geological Survey, in press), p. 36.
9. *Ibid.*, p. 34.
10. John Flynn, "Forests Without Trees," p. 33.
11. Richard Grossman, "The Song and Dance of the 1990 Clean Air 'Act,'"*New Solutions* (Fall 1990): 6.
12. "Greenpeace Labels Clean Air Act a Bill of Rights for Polluters," *Greenpeace News* (Spring 1990).
13. *Ibid.*
14. Richard Grossman, "Cleaning the Air Gives Way to Protecting Polluters," *In These Times* (April 25-May 1, 1990): 16.

Myth 4

Old trees give off more carbon dioxide than they take up. Young trees take up more carbon dioxide than they give off. Therefore, industrial foresters are doing the global climate a favor by clearcutting older forests and replacing them with young forests.

Although the models for global warming are complex, the concept is fairly simple. The global climate will change as greenhouse gasses, such as carbon dioxide, increase and as carbon sinks, such as forests, decrease. The logical response to prevent or slow human-induced global warming, if it really is happening, is to reduce the production of greenhouse gasses and to increase the area of forests.

The auto, utility, and paper industries, which are all major fossil-fuel consumers, have been enthusiastic supporters of emphasizing the second half of the equation—planting trees. General Motors, which has fought fuel-efficiency standards, now gives out tree seeds with its Geo car. Applied Energy Services (AES), which wants to build a coal-fired powerplant in Bucksport, Maine, promises to offset its carbon-dioxide emissions in Maine by planting trees in Guatamala, as it has done for its powerplant in Uncasville, Connecticut. And the paper industry, through its educational arm, the American Forestry Association, has initiated a highly visible tree-planting campaign called "Global ReLeaf" which has been sponsored by such organizations as Arco Foundation, Conoco, Baltimore Gas and Electric, Edison Electric Institute, Metropolitan Edison, Octane Boost Corporation, Pennsylvania Electric, Texaco, and Keep America Beautiful (the front for the energy-intensive throwaway-container lobby.)[1]

Because the public—which in general has little appreciation of the ecological impacts of exotic or off-site plantings or of replacing forests with monocultures—perceives planting trees as an inherently benign or even spiritual act, these large, polluting corporations have been able to wrap themselves in a mantle of Green—"Plant a tree and cool the globe."

Audubon magazine writer Ted Williams, responding to AES's Guatamalan eucalyptus plantations, commented that ". . . the scheme of planting foreign carbon sinks is so typically *American*. It teaches that the United States—by far the grossest greenhouse polluter on the planet—doesn't need to change its life-style. Instead, it can just pay the Third World to clean up after it."

This "environmental imperialism" is all the worse because research indicates that northern forests are one of the earth's major carbon sinks.[3]

While planting appropriate species of trees on previously forested but now barren ground, where local seed sources of native trees have been extirpated, may benefit the global climate, this myth suggests we can go one step farther and cut down existing mature forests to make room for the young, planted forests that will save the world. This myth is saying we can save the global ecosystem by destroying the local ecosystem—a horrid distortion of the dictum, "Think globally, act locally."

This myth is also saying that not only is clearcutting forests good but that clearcutting old-growth forests is even better. Unfortunately the myth fails to pass the straight-face test. Are we to believe that if all logging ceased, the ice caps would start to melt because the forests of the world would be choked with polluting old trees? Are we to believe that companies are planting trees to stabilize the climate rather than to produce raw materials for their mills, improve their public image, or take advantage of tax incentives?

Several studies by USDA researchers concluded that the myth does not apply to the old-growth forests of the Pacific Northwest. One of the flaws, according to one study, is that the wood, accumulated in the ecosystem over hundreds of years, is cut down and made into products, most of which, like paper, are short lived in use: "Processing, burning, and decaying of these products and associated waste will emit carbon back into the atmosphere. In addition, old growth contains more carbon than young forests, and it takes at least 5–10 years for young forests to begin accumulating carbon. So in both the long and short term, logging of old-growth will lead to a slight increase in atmospheric carbon."[4] The other study stated that "Mass balance calculations indicate that the conversion of 5 million hectares of old-growth forests to younger plantations in western Oregon and Washington in the last 100 years has added 1.5 billion to 1.8 billion megagrams of carbon to the atmosphere."[5]

Applying the logic of this myth to the industrial forests of Maine, where the end products are likely to be paper or biomass fuel, is even more absurd. The whole process of cutting, transporting, processing, manufacturing, shipping, consuming, and disposing of paper, for example, uses enormous quantities of energy—often in the form of fossil fuels. Both paper waste and biomass are rapidly turned into carbon dioxide, but the forests from which these products came take many decades to recover to full oxygen-producing capacity. If anything, paper companies are contributing to global warming, not countering it.

For many more reasons than the potential for global warming, we should be reducing our use of fossil fuels. As for forest management, "A more effective means of greenhouse postponement than planting trees," writes Ted Williams, "is not cutting them—at least when they are very old."[6]

References

1. Ted Williams, "Don't Worry, Plant a Tree: Cluster-bombing the Planet with Seedlings of Whatever Sort are Handiest,"*Audubon* (May 1991): 26.
2. *Ibid.*
3. P. P. Tans, I. Y. Fung, T.Takahashi, "Observational Constraints on the Global Atmospheric CO_2 Budget," *Science.*, Vol. 247 (March 23, 1990): 1431.
4. Paul Alaback and Sherri Richardson, "Logging Old Growth Will Not Help Solve Greenhouse Effect," news release, USDA Forest Service, November 14, 1989.
5. Mark Harmon, William K. Ferrell, and Jerry Franklin, "Effects on Carbon Storage of Conversion of Old-growth Forests to Young Forests," *Science* (February 1990): 699.
6. Ted Williams, "Don't worry," p. 27.

Rare, Threatened, or Endangered Species

The last thing the paper industry in Maine wants is an endangered species to interfere with the exploitation of the forest resource, as the spotted owl has done in the Pacific Northwest. Industry there has used the owl as a symbol of meddling environmentalists who are destroying valuable jobs. Far better for industry that loggers should vent their anger over lost jobs on "environmental preservationists" rather than on overcutting, export of raw logs, mechanization, or corporate greed.

The rarity of the spotted owl is an indicator of the growing rarity of large expanses of old growth that the owl prefers for habitat and that the forest industry prefers for lumber. Even without the spotted owl, limits to this resource will be reached—the old growth will run out. Allowing the owl to become extinct only delays the day of reckoning. Society must decide whether it wants to reach the limits of exploitation with the owl (and associated species) or without it.

In Maine, industry representatives would have us believe we have gone beyond such a choice. The large expanses of virgin forest that might house a spotted owl analog were already logged over a century ago. The forest species that have survived the repeated shearings presumably are adapted to second growth and thus not endangered by further management. The hunting pressures in Maine that led to the overexploitation of game (such as passenger pigeons or caribou) or to the extermination of large predators (such as wolves, cougar,[a] or wolverines) are no longer a threat because hunting and trapping are regulated. Species are endangered, we are supposed to believe, somewhere else.

The forest industry has attempted to appear supportive of endangered-species protection. International Paper Company, for example, helped fund the Maine Critical Areas Program's endangered plant species poster and signed an agreement to protect several hundred acres of critical areas.[1] Although such cooperation is commendable, it gives the impression that protecting a few species on several hundred acres justifies clearcutting and chemically defoliating thousands of acres—that the more drastic examples of modern management are no threat to species in a degraded ecosystem.

Endnote

a. The cougar may not have been completely extirpated in Maine. There have been sightings of cougar from Vermont to Nova Scotia over the last several decades.

Reference

1. "IP Helps Promote Protection of Endangered Plants," *Livermore Falls Advocate.*, May 24, 1980.

Myth 1

Species in the Maine woods are adapted to management and second growth; thus, few species are threatened by further logging.

Much attention has been focused in recent years on the horrifying loss of species due to tropical forest destruction. Every acre of tropical forest seems to have an impressive number of unique wildlife species. If their habitat is destroyed, the species are lost—forever. While Maine wildlife may not be disappearing in the numbers experienced in the Amazon, the percentage of species that are threatened is alarming.

Of Maine's approximately 1,500 native vascular plants, 155, over 10%, are listed by the state's Critical Areas Program as endangered or threatened, and 79 are listed as possibly extirpated.[1] Maine's Natural Heritage Program lists 96 vascular plants that are rare in wooded or forested habitats, and of these, 35 are listed as possibly extirpated.[2] Of the 450 nongame animal species recognized by the state's Department of Inland Fisheries and Wildlife, almost 90, or 20%, are listed as requiring special attention, and 11 are listed as extirpated or extinct.[3] The Maine Natural Heritage Program lists 113 fish, amphibian, reptile, bird, and mammal species that are threatened, rare, of unknown status, or (in the case of 15 species) extirpated.[4]

These lists do not include invertebrates, lower plants, lichens, or fungi and thus are missing classes and orders that have the highest diversity of species. Nor do these lists account for losses of genetic varieties within a species. These lists give only a hint of how serious the problem might be.

The problems are now both local and global. While some species are naturally rare in Maine due to rare habitat requirements or to Maine being the northern or southern edge of their range, other formerly abundant species are declining rapidly over broad areas from multiple causes. Migratory songbirds, for example, are threatened by habitat simplification, conversion, and fragmentation as well as by exposure to pollution and pesticides in both tropical and temperate zones.[5] Amphibians are declining throughout the world. Possible factors include acidification of ephemeral breeding pools, headwater streams, and soil, climatic shifts that dry out the soil, habitat destruction, pollution stress, and habitat fragmentation that prevents population dispersals between aquatic and terrestrial habitats.[6]

The fact that species have survived previous human disturbances does not mean they will survive further human disturbances. Never before have wildlife had to face whole-tree logging, shortened rotations, soil compaction, intensive road building, sludge spreading, and chemical pesticide spraying combined with air pollution, climate change, and development. These multiple stresses are radically converting the environments to which most species are optimally adapted.

References

1. Patricia DeHond, *Maine's Endangered and Threatened Plants* (Augusta, Me.: Maine Critical Areas Program, Maine State Planning Office, 1990), p. 2.
2. "List of Maine's Rare Vascular Plants Found in Wood or Forested Habitats, 1990 (draft) " (Augusta, Me.: Maine Natural Heritage Program, Maine Department of Economic and Community Development, 1990), photocopy.
3. Maine Department of Inland Fisheries and Wildlife, *Research and Management Report* (Augusta, Me.: Maine Department of Inland Fisheries and Wildlife, 1989), p. 29.
4. Maine Natural Heritage Progam, *Natural Diversity Database, Animals* (Augusta, Me.: Maine Natural Heritage Program, Maine Department of Economic and Community Development, 1987).
5. Chandler S. Robbins, John R. Sauer, Russell S. Greenberg, and Sam Droege, "Population Declines in North American Birds That Migrate to the Neotropics." In *Proceedings of the National Academy of Sciences, USA*, Vol. 86 (Ocotober 1989): 7658-7662.
6. Richard L. Wyman, "What's Happening to the Amphibians?," *Conservation Biology*, Vol. 4, No. 4 (December 1990): 350-352.

Myth 2
The Endangered Species Act adequately protects rare and endangered species.

Many industry and government officials have complained that protecting such frivolous-sounding creatures as Furbish's lousewort, snail darter, Mount Graham red squirrel, red-cockaded woodpecker, and spotted owl has become a threat to progress and can hardly be justified considering the loss of projected revenues. In regards to the Mount Graham red squirrel, Interior Secretary Manuel Lujan implied that the Endangered Species Act (ESA) is excessive when he asked in 1990, "Do we have to save (an endangered) species in every locality where it exists?"[1]

Senate majority leader George Mitchell responded that only 1% of the 48,538 biological determinations issued under the act from 1979 to 1986 concluded that a development project would jeopardize an endangered species. "Only about three projects in every 10,000," said Mitchell, "were withdrawn or canceled because of jeopardy options issued under (the act) during that eight-year period."[2] Mr. Mitchell's response leaves one wondering if development is no threat to endangered species or if the ESA is no threat to development.

The ESA requires that all federal agencies protect and conserve species listed by the U.S. Fish and Wildlife Service as threatened or endangered. It also requires that federal agencies identify and protect habitat critical for the survival and recovery of these species. The act's goal is to bring these species to a point of recovery where protection under the ESA is no longer necessary.[3]

Combined with the National Forest Management Act, which mandates protection of genetic, species, and ecosystem diversity and which requires monitoring of Management Indicator Species,[a] the ESA is an important tool for environmentalists who care to spend the money in legal suits to challenge forest practices on federal public land. It has an extremely limited effect on the management of private land in Maine, however.

Limited List

The federal endangered species list includes only 2 species that occur in Maine forests—the bald eagle and peregrine falcon.[4] This does not mean these are the only species endangered in the region. In 1975 Maine passed its own Endangered Species Act. It was not until 1983, however, when funds were made available through the Chickadee Checkoff, a voluntary funding through state income tax for nongame wildlife management, that the state began its own list of rare and endangered species. The list is created by the commissioner of the Department of Inland Fisheries and Wildlife (DIFW), who also has authority to protect and manage endangered species' habitats, to propagate, transplant, or introduce endangered species, and to stop violations of the act and demand restoration (if possible) of an affected area.[5]

The vertebrate list is overseen by the DIFW and has six classifications: endangered, threatened, special concern, indeterminate status, watch list, and extirpated. Only species listed as endangered or threatened are protected by the state law. The list does not include invertebrates (although I am told this will be changed), even though they comprise the majority of animal species.

The plant list is overseen by Maine's Critical Areas Program and has five classifications: endangered, threatened, special concern, watch list, and possibly extirpated. There is no list for mosses, lichens, or fungi. The Natural Heritage Program keeps an unofficial list with classifications that are slightly different from that of the DIFW.

Mostly Voluntary

Protection of rare and endangered plant species on the state endangered species list is mostly voluntary. It is up to the good will of landowners to forgo thousands of dollars of income for the sake of a barely noticeable, fragile little flower. Any state agency dealing with permitting, licensing, or planning, however, must take the existence of endangered species into account. Theoretically, then, an endangered species can halt a threatening project. The applicability of such a tool to forest practices in the Maine woods, however, is marginal. With the exception of some cutting in deeryards and riparian zones, most forest management activities do not require permits. Before commencing massive clearcuts or herbicide spraying, foresters are not required to survey the forest for the existence of any endangered or threatened species.

Endangered Where?

Federal and state ESAs are geared to protect species at a national or state level.

They offer no protection to species endangered only on the local level. There are some townships that have been almost entirely cut over within the last two decades and have no mature forests left. Because the species lost are represented in other parts of the state, local extirpation is legally acceptable.

Genetic Loss

State and federal ESAs offer no protection to a species in rapid decline until the species becomes threatened or endangered. Yet by the time population levels have fallen this low, irreparable damage has been done. As population levels drop, genetic diversity is lost. These genetic types might be well adapted to specific locales or be better equipped to survive climatic extremes and other stresses yet to come.

Ecosystem Loss

Ironically, species may be protected by ESAs while ecosystems are lost. As Professor Bryon Norton observed in his book *Why Preserve Natural Variety? Studies in Moral, Political, and Legal Philosophy*, "Biological diversity is not just constituted by the number of species, subspecies, and populations extant; it is also constituted by the varied associations in which they exist. Viewed through time, a species existing in two different ecosystems can be seen as two different units of diversity. . . . "[7]

Triage

Saving endangered species can be an expensive proposition, and the state has limited funds to spend on such activities. Each year slightly more than 5% of income-tax payers donate less than $4.50 per person to create a Maine Endangered and Nongame Wildlife Fund of little more than $110,000.[8] Funds go mostly to a few well-publicized species such as eagles, peregrine falcons, piping plovers, and whales as well as to monitoring, research, and maintenance of the list.

Bryan Norton suggests that such an approach is not enough—it leads to a form of triage where limited funds compete to save a growing number of threatened species, and hard decisions have to be made as to which to try to save and which to let go. "Attempting to protect genetic diversity through the protection of a few remnant populations ignores the most basic problems and will result only in a continual scramble to save individual species," says Norton. "A true solution would halt the tendency of more and more species to become so severely depleted that they require individual attention. If the deeper problems causing this tendency are not addressed, it can be expected that the effort to protect endangered species in remnant populations will become overwhelming."[9]

Endnote

a. Management Indicator Species include threatened and endangered species, species sensitive to intended management methods, game and commercial species, nongame species of special interest, and ecological indicator species that indicate effects of management on other species.[10]

References

1. "Mitchell Has Harsh Words for Secretary of Interior," *Bangor Daily News*, May 15, 1991.
2. *Ibid.*

3. David S. Wilcove, *National Forests: Policies for the Future*, Vol. 2, *Protecting Biological Diversity* (Washington, D.C.: The Wilderness Society, 1988), p. 5.
4. Maine Department of Inland Fisheries and Wildlife, *Research and Management Report* (Augusta, Me.: Maine Department of Inland Fisheries and Wildlife, 1989), p. 30.
5. Maine Department of Inland Fisheries and Wildlife Laws, 12 MRSA Part 1D, Chapters 701-121, as enacted by Public Law, Chapter 420, Section 1, September 30, 1989.
6. Maine Department of Inland Fisheries and Wildlife, *Research and Management Report*, p. 30.
7. Bryan G. Norton, "Avoiding Triage: An Alternative Approach to Setting Priorities for Saving Species," *Forest Watch* (June 1989): 12.
8. Alan Hutchinson, *1987 Annual Report, Maine Endangered and Non Game Wildlife Fund* (Augusta, Me.: Maine Department of Inland Fisheries and Wildlife, 1987).
9. Bryan G. Norton, "Avoiding Triage," p. 13.
10. Patricia DeHond, *Maine's Endangered and Threatened Plants*, p. 3.

Myth 3
If a species is extirpated from a region, it can always be reintroduced.

According to this myth, local extinctions are not a serious problem as long as representatives of the species are found elsewhere. In New York and New England, governmental and private groups have attempted to reintroduce and manage several species for recovery: woodland caribou in Maine, fishers in Connecticut, martens in Vermont, lynx in the Adirondacks, bald eagles in Maine, New Hampshire, and Massachusetts, peregrine falcons throughout New England, turkeys in Maine and Rhode Island, and Atlantic salmon from the Connecticut to the St. Croix rivers.[1]

Cost
Some of these efforts are extremely expensive. Between 1967 and 1988, for example, salmon restoration in New England cost taxpayers $46 million in federal money, $10 million in states' money, and $55 million in utilities' money (to build fish ladders on hydroelectric dams), courtesy of electricity consumers.[2] Hundreds of thousands of dollars (mostly private donations) were spent to ship caribou from Newfoundland to Maine. After nearly all the caribou died from disease and predation, the project was abandoned.

Politics
Because reintroduction projects are so expensive and funds are limited, decisions on allocating funds become political decisions. Some species are more politically attractive than others. No public or private agency of which I am aware, for example, has plans to fund the reintroduction of timber rattlesnakes to Maine. Nor have there been major efforts on behalf of insects or even plants. In Maine the forest species that the Department of Inland Fisheries and Wildlife has been helping to recover are either potential "working wildlife" (such as caribou and salmon) or noncontroversial. Writer Tony DePaul notes that the bald eagle "poses no threat to the hunting economy and, because it lives near rivers or along the coast, paper companies can continue to level inland forests."[3]

Large predators, on the other hand, are controversial and there are political forces opposed to their reintroduction in Maine. William Vail, commissioner of the DIFW, has strongly opposed a proposal to reintroduce timber wolves to the state. The role of the DIFW, he says, is to manage for maintaining moose, increasing deer, and supporting the reintroduction of caribou. "Any serious considerations to the introduction of timber wolves have repercussions on these management initiatives, both biologically and through the social-political process."[4]

As part of the effort to increase game animals, the DIFW also has a coyote extermination program (an "Animal Damage Control Policy") to "encourage the taking of coyotes during winter, when deer are concentrated in wintering areas and vulnerable to predation. While this activity is compatible with coyote-population biology and our specific management objectives, it would be in direct conflict with a timber wolf recovery effort. It is incomprehensible that the Maine public interest would forego exploitation of coyotes to benefit timber wolves."[5]

Unlike Maine, other northern states have attempted to reintroduce some of the extirpated large carnivores. Wisconsin has introduced a small population of wolves into its northern regions.[6] New York is attempting (not very successfully) to reintroduce lynx into the Adirondack Park,[7] and some biologists are seriously considering reintroducing wolves and cougar in the proposed Bob Marshall Wilderness area of the Adirondacks.[8] These reintroductions face an uphill battle.

Habitat

Just because an extirpated plant or animal once thrived in a given environment does not mean it can be easily reintroduced. The habitat now may be very different from the habitat in which the creature evolved and may contain some of the same features that led to extirpation in the first place. Rivers and lakes may be too polluted or acidic to support sensitive fish. Landscapes may be too fragmented. Other species, such as *Homo rapiens* (sic), may be occupying the habitat. Diseases may interfere with successful reintroductions. Deer, which have invaded the northern part of Maine, harbor the brainworm, which, though relatively harmless to deer, can be fatal to caribou.[9]

Large predators are particularly vulnerable to habitat destruction and fragmentation as well as to overexploitation by zealous hunters and trappers who see these animals as threats to "their" game. New Hampshire biologist Carol Foss writes that "the availability of large areas of undeveloped land connected by travel corridors of undisturbed habitat is critical to maintaining current predator populations and providing future habitat for the reintroduction of currently extirpated species."[10]

Genetics

Reintroduced animals are genetically different from their extirpated relatives. Being from a different habitat, they may have problems adapting to their new environment. Because they have an isolated, small genetic base, introduced creatures may have problems associated with inbreeding. As with the caribou in Maine, they may not be able to sustain a viable breeding population.

Alternatives

It makes more sense to prevent the loss of species and their habitats than to try to bring them back once they are gone. Unfortunately, expensive reintroduction campaigns tie up money that could be going to habitat protection. Jamie Sayen of Preserve Appalachian Wilderness (PAW) has suggested an alternative to the present expensive and questionable practice of trapping animals in one part of the continent and releasing them into habitats that people have altered during their absence. "What we really have to do," he says, "is make a cultural commitment to the recovery of the habitat. We need some wide, wild corridors of land between here and there—'there' being the places where we still have natural populations of cougar, lynx, wolf and wolverine—and just let the animals radiate back here on their own."[11]

References

1. Tony De Paul, "Can They Survive?," *Sunday Journal Magazine* (Providence, Rhode Island), September 17, 1989, p. 8.
2. *Ibid.*, p. 10.
3. *Ibid.*, p. 9.
4. Tom Hennesy, "First It Was Peregrine Falcons, and Now Timber Wolves," *Bangor Daily News*, February 5, 1990, p. 15.
5. *Ibid.*
6. Susan H. Shetterly, "Of Wolves and Maine: Canis Lupus Isn't on Maine's Wildlife Agenda. Should It Be?," *Maine Times* (March 30, 1990): 9.
7. Jeff Elliott and Jamie Sayen, *The Ecological Restoration of the Northern Appalachians: An Evolutionary Perspective* (North Stratford, N.H.: Preserve Appalachian Wilderness, 1990), pp. 65-66.
8. John Mitchell. "A Wild Island of Hope: The Adirondack Park Finds Its Own Set of Problems," *Wilderness* (Fall 1989): 50.
9. Tony De Paul, "Can They Survive?," p. 12.
10. Carol R. Foss, *Summary Report on Wildlife Resources for the Northern Forest Lands Study*, a report for the Northern Forest Lands Study, p. 3.
11. Tony De Paul, "Can They Survive?," p.9.

Myth 4

Hunters are an adequate substitute for large predators.

If this were true, the lack of large predators, or the lack of adequate habitat for large predators, or the lack of reintroduction of large predators would be no problem ecologically even if it still fails the ethical test.

Some Department of Inland Fisheries and Wildlife bureaucrats see large predators as a threat to, rather than an essential factor in, the evolution and health of prey such as deer, moose, and caribou. Carol Foss, in her study of wildlife for the Northern Forest Lands Study, states that "predator populations provide an important indicator of functional health in any natural system."[1]

There are important differences, however, between natural predators, with which game animals coevolved, and modern hunters, even though both kill game. Natural predators hunt all year long. Their primary targets are the young, the sick, the injured, the slow, the foolish, the weak, and the old. They cull herds, leaving behind the strong, the swift, the sharp witted, and the socially cooperative animals. When their favored prey are not available, large predators eat small mammals, birds, or other animals, checking potential overpopulation.

The loss of large predators can affect ecosystems in unexpected ways. Conservation biologists David Wilcove, Charles McLellan, and Andrew Dobson have written that in the eastern U.S. "large predators such as mountain lions, bobcats, and large hawks and owls. . . may regulate populations of smaller, omnivorous species such as raccoons, opossums, squirrels, and blue jays. These omnivores, in turn, prey upon the eggs and nestlings of the forest songbirds. . . . The rate of nest predation in small woodlands is very high, and this may be one reason why songbird populations have declined."[2]

The predator/prey balance can also affect the composition of forest vegetation. According to Stephen Spurr in his book *Forest Ecology*, the disappearance of wolves, bears, cougar, and lynx over much of northern New England (there are still abundant black bear populations in some areas) led to greater browsing of regeneration and understory plants.[3] Heavy selective browsing can significantly affect plant diversity.

Deer hunters, on the other hand, are only (legally) killing for one month of the year. Their target is the big buck with the big set of antlers. They do not normally shoot mice or voles or bag the quantities of snowshoe hare that a lynx, wolf, or cougar might. The conservation ethic of game managers who encourage hunters to "harvest" the bigger deer or fish and protect the young is somewhat akin to diameter-limit harvesting by forest landowners—it leads to high-grading rather than to culling. The loss of large predators is the loss of an important force in the evolution and stability of an ecosystem.

While predators such as coyotes or foxes have proven adaptable to human-dominated landscapes, others such as gray wolves, cougar, lynx, or great gray owls are what conservation biologist David Wilcove calls "wilderness species."[4] These animals now occupy a fraction of their original ranges and are sensitive to logging, roads, and development. Forest ecosystems that evolved with these species are incomplete without them. To allow large predators to fulfill their roles would take major changes in both public attitudes and forest management.

References

1. Carol R. Foss, *Summary Report on Wildlife Resources for the Northern Forest Lands Study*, a report for the Northern Forest Lands Study, p. 3.
2. David S. Wilcove, Charles H. McLellen, and Andrew Dobson, "Habitat Fragmentation in the Temperate Zone." In Michael Soulé, ed., *Conservation Biology* (Sunderland, Mass.: Sinauer, 1986), p. 251-252.
3. Stephen Spurr, *Forest Ecology* (New York: Burten V. Baries, Ronald Press Company, 1973), p. 371.
4. David S. Wilcove, *National Forests: Policies for the Future*, Vol. 2, *Protecting Biological Diversity* (Washington, D.C.: The Wilderness Society, 1988), p. 36.

Myth 5

The extinction of species is a natural process.
Attempting to preserve species on the brink of
extinction is a waste of time, effort, and money since
these creatures will disappear over time regardless
of our efforts.

Those who expound this myth, which is the ultimate excuse for abusive management, are fond of citing the statistic that over 99% of all species that ever lived are now extinct. Mass extinctions, the argument continues, have been occurring for eons, and the result is not an impoverished earth, but an earth that has more species diversity than ever before. When species disappear, it just opens new niches, which are filled by evolutionary innovation. Industrial ecologists argue that we may be doing the planet a favor by letting wimpy species, which are not adapted to industrial management, die off, making room for more competitive creatures that can survive the new habitats that we are continually creating. If the earth has survived collisions with comets or asteroids that wiped out the majority of life forms, surely it can survive western civilization.

The central fallacy of this myth is confusion over scale. While it may be possible that the biosphere will recover from the mass extinctions that humans are causing, the benefits, if there are any, will come millions of years from now—certainly not in our lifetimes. We will experience impoverishment.

Harvard paleontologist Stephen Jay Gould, addressing those who have applied this myth to excuse the destruction of habitat for Arizona's Mount Graham squirrel to make room for a huge telescope, argued that "to say that we would let the squirrels go (at our immediate scale) because all species eventually die (at geological scales) makes about as much sense as arguing that we shouldn't treat an easily curable childhood infection because all humans are ultimately and inevitably mortal. I love geological time—a wondrous and expansive notion that sets the foundation of my chosen profession, but such immensity is not the proper scale of my personal life."[1]

The argument of managers that we should accept the impacts of their activities because the damage is less severe than the "natural" cataclysmic collisions of the earth with extraterrestrial bodies, is far from reassuring.

Reference
1. Stephen Jay Gould, "The Golden Rule—A Proper Scale for Our Environmental Crisis," *Natural History* (September 1990): p. 30.

Myth 6

Forest management is not a threat to biodiversity and endangered species because these resources can be adequately protected in parks and preserves.

The idea here is that the forest is compartmentalized—it is okay for the commercial forest managers to simplify or fragment their segment of the forest because genetic resources are secure in the "preserved" compartment. Some foresters, and even some wildlife biologists and environmentalists, see a direct benefit for the wilderness compartment from an increase in the intensity of management in the industrial compartment—an environmental/industrial trade-off. There is a strange irony in the concept of allowing the vast majority of the forest to rapidly lose diversity through intensive management so that a small fraction of the forest will lose diversity more slowly in isolated preserves. This recalls Thoreau's reference in *Walden* to "the pious slave-breeder devoting the proceeds of every tenth slave to buy a Sunday's liberty for the rest."

One of the shocking facts about Maine's forest is just how little of it is being preserved from logging. Only about 300,000 acres of Maine's forest are managed for "wilderness." Maine forest economist Lloyd Irland calls this 1.5% of Maine's land mass a "trifling proportion."[1] Even these figures are a gross exaggeration of the extent of wilderness in Maine. Parts of Baxter State Park, for example, are accessible to cars and snowmobiles. The park is surrounded by clearcuts and is burdened with overuse during peak season. Much of the Allagash Wilderness Waterway consists of beauty strips surrounded by clearcuts.

A clearcut near Mt. Katahdin in Baxter State Park. *Photo by Alex McLean/Landslides.*

The Allagash Wilderness Waterway as presented to the public by government agencies. *Photo courtesy Maine Department of Conservation.*

The Allagash Wilderness Waterway as seen beyond the beauty strip. *Photo by Christopher Ayres.*

Most of these "wilderness" areas were heavily logged in the past. Less than 0.04% of Maine's forest is in old-growth stands larger than 50 acres, and most of these stands are in fragments too small to have much true interior forest free from edge effects.[2]

This small percentage of unlogged forest does not offer protection to a wide enough sample of forest ecosystem types and associated species to adequately protect biodiversity. The fragments are also too small to support minimum viable populations (MVPs) of animals that need a large range of relatively undisturbed, undeveloped habitat. The more intensive management is in nonpreserved areas, the more isolated preserved fragments become and the less suitable they are for species with large range needs.

Climate change reduces the value of isolated preserves even further. Biologist Robert Peters of the World Wildlife Fund cautions that "habitat destruction in conjunction with climate change sets the stage for an even larger wave of extinction than previously imagined, based upon consideration of human encroachment alone. Small remnant populations of most species . . . would have little chance of reaching new habitat if climate change makes the old unsuitable."[3]

Larry Harris, in his book *The Fragmented Forest*, proposes a practical way to slow species and genetic losses in forests threatened by fragmentation. His strategy calls for preserving old-growth and replacement stands in undisturbed forest core areas (the bigger the better); surrounding these cores with a buffer of forests where low-impact management and recreation can be allowed; and connecting preserves with wildlife corridors.[4] Functional wildlife corridors are not thin beauty strips surrounded by clearcuts but areas of contiguous forest capable of allowing population and genetic flow between core areas. Many wildlife ecologists now endorse variations on this commonsense theme of "multiple-use modules" (MUMs). Most debate is over the size of the reserves and the widths of the corridors rather than the concept itself.[5] According to Harris, the size of preserved core areas and the width of corridors should be directly proportional to the intensity of human use in the surrounding buffer zones and commodity areas. Harris argues that "if it were possible to manage the entire forest landscape in a very low-intensity, long-rotation manner, there would be little if any need for special preservation areas."[6]

USDA Forest Service researcher Jerry Franklin advocates a "New Forestry" which takes biodiversity into account on both the stand and landscape level. "Biological diversity," he asserts, "cannot be dealt with exclusively (or even primarily) through the use of set-asides; maintenance of biological diversity must be integrated into management of commodity lands since they dominate our landscapes."[7]

In the *Journal of Forestry*, ecologists John Probst and Thomas Crow argue that "the challenge of conserving biological diversity is too comprehensive and inclusive to be met on public lands alone. Nor is it realistic to think that conserving biological diversity is nothing more than establishing parks and preserves . . . conserving and enhancing biological diversity must become an integral part of natural-resource management on the 95% of the landscape that sustains a wide variety of human activities and resource uses, including timber harvesting and food production."[8]

Probst and Crow contend that active management rather than passive protectionism is needed to truly protect the viability of all species. "Active management," they claim, "must create landscapes that facilitate movement and dispersal of large mammals. Active management is needed to restore species that are extirpated due to direct or indirect human impact and to reduce the threat of exotics on native species. Active planning will ensure that old-growth forests, with their unique properties, are represented throughout the regional landscape, adding to regional diversity. . . . Active management is vital to providing critical habitats when and where they are needed to ensure that uncommon species do not become threatened or endangered."[9]

This type of active management to protect biodiversity lessens but does not eliminate the need for protected areas. Indeed, Jerry Franklin maintains that preserves "are an important part of any overall forest strategy. But we cannot preserve enough land, and even if we could, changes, such as those threatened under global change, could make our preservation efforts a meaningless exercise."[10]

References

1. Lloyd C. Irland, "Wilderness Redefined: Thoughts on Developing a Definition of Wilderness That Works for Maine," *Habitat* (June/July 1986): 13.
2. Lissa Widoff, ed., *Natural Old-growth Stands in Maine*, Maine Critical Areas Program Planning Report No. 79 (Augusta, Me.: Maine Critical Areas Program, Maine State Planning Office, 1983).
3. Robert L. Peters, "Effects of Global Warming on Biological Diversity," *Forest Watch*, Vol. 10, No. 2 (August 1989): 15.
4. Larry Harris, *The Fragmented Forest* (Chicago, Ill.: University of Chicago Press, 1984).
5. Malcolm Hunter, Jr., *Wildlife, Forests, and Forestry: Principles of Managing Forests for Biological Diversity* (Englewood Cliffs, N.J.: Prentice-Hall, 1990), pp. 123-133.
6. Larry Harris, *The Fragmented Forest*, p. 162.
7. Jerry F. Franklin, "An Ecologist's Perspective on Northeastern Forests in 2010," *Forest Watch*, Vol. 10, No. 2 (February 1989): 8.
8. John R. Probst and Thomas R. Crow, "Integrating Biological Diversity and Resource Management: An Essential Approach to Productive, Sustainable Ecosystems," *Journal of Forestry* (February 1991): 16.
9. *Ibid.*
10. Jerry F. Franklin, "An Ecologist's Perspective," p. 9.

Wilderness

The best way to protect native wildlife species is to protect the environment to which they have adapted over thousands or even millions of years. And the best way to protect that environment is to leave it alone—to let it be wilderness. "A wilderness," according to the National Wilderness Preservation Act of 1964, "is hereby recognized as an area where the earth and its community of life are untrammeled by man, where man himself is a visitor who does not remain."

Managing wilderness consists more of managing people than of managing forests or animals. Trees are allowed to grow and die without forester assistance. Wildlife at all trophic levels, from worms to wolves, are allowed to fulfill their independent (and interdependent) roles. Wilderness, by legal definition, has no roads but may have paths. People may enter on foot, horseback, or canoe but not in motorhomes or all-terrain vehicles.

This concept of wilderness that excludes people (except visitors) is relatively new in human history. It is derived from a people alienated from nature. Wilderness is, after all, not just a biological curiosity to be contained in quaint preserves; it is the environment to which all life, including humans, adapted. "Human culture," Maine essayist Stephen Hyde reminds us, "evolved as a means of helping the species to survive within a wilderness condition, not outside of one."[1] To the Penobscot, Passamaquoddy, Micmac, Maliseets, and their ancestors, what we call wilderness was their hunting and gathering grounds. They were not mere visitors; they had intimate knowledge of and uses for thousands of plant and animal species for food, clothing, medicine, baskets, shelter, tools, and weapons. The forest was home.

The early European settlers, in contrast, viewed this "wilderness" differently. They either hacked it away and replaced it with domesticated species or exploited its resources for financial gain. When the Europeans and their descendants began their quest, their villages and clearings were isolated islands in a sea of wilderness. By the nineteenth century the pattern had reversed—the managed world was dominant and wilderness represented only by isolated fragments.

Society's resounding success at subduing the wilderness aroused a counter-movement to save what was left. Early crusaders such as Henry David Thoreau and John Muir saw contact with wilderness as a tonic for the degenerated, industrialized soul—a contact with the primal essence of life. "Why should not we," asked Thoreau, " . . . have our national preserves . . . in which bear and panther, and some even of the hunter race, may still exist, and not be 'civilized' off the face of the earth?"[2]

By the end of the nineteenth century this dream of protecting the remaining wilderness in parks was becoming a reality in some parts of the country, but not in Maine, where the forest was the domain of the paper industry. In 1894 in New York, the state legislature declared that millions of acres of the Adirondacks would be "forever wild." In the same year, *The Industrial Journal* of Bangor urged that a 900-square-mile state park be created around Mt. Katahdin before the region was destroyed by "lumbermen, fires, and a squatter popula-tion," but the Maine legislature did not respond. Nor did the legislature respond in 1908 after the Maine State Federation of Women's Clubs introduced a bill to create a commission to consider purchasing the Katahdin region for a state park.[3]

Percival Baxter, a legislator who eventually became governor, worked tirelessly for decades to get state park designation for the Katahdin region, but his efforts were thwarted by the Great Northern Paper Company. Finally, in the 1930s he started purchasing the land himself and eventually gave it (much of it had been heavily logged) to the people of Maine as a gift. "This fact," observed forest economist Lloyd Irland, "itself speaks volumes."[4]

References

1. Stephen Hyde, "Something Far Beyond Our Imagining," *Habitat* (June/July 1986): 30.
2. Henry David Thoreau, *The Maine Woods* (New York: Thomas Y. Crowell Company, 1961), p. 205.
3. Elaine Tietjen, "Three Routes to Wilderness: Baxter, Bigelow, and Caribou-Speckled," *Habitat* (June/July 1986): 26.
4. Lloyd C. Irland, "Wilderness Redefined: Thoughts on Developing a Definition of Wilderness That Works for Maine," *Habitat* (June/July 1986), p. 13.

Myth 1

There is already enough wilderness in Maine.

There may be enough wilderness from industry's viewpoint, which is hostile to the concept, but from a biological or social viewpoint, the amount of wilderness in Maine is woefully inadequate. Maine's (and New England's) largest wilderness area, Baxter State Park, comprises only about 200,000 acres (including roaded areas and managed forests)—1/10 that of Yellowstone National Park. Yet a number of studies have determined that Yellowstone and all the other wilderness areas in the lower 48 states are too small to support long-term viable populations of wolves, bears, cougar, or wolverines.[1]

Baxter State Park is also insufficient in size to meet recreation demands. Indeed, the Park Authority has to limit the number of visitors (which averages more than 100,000 visitor-days a year) to prevent severe overuse. Mt. Katahdin, the most popular attraction in the park, is no longer a place to seek solitude. On one day in 1985, 350 people scaled the mountain.[2] Likewise, the Allagash Wilderness Waterway, visited by more than 10,000 visitors a year, is hardly the place to go for a wilderness experience.

In 1982 the World Congress on National Parks recommended in its Bali Action Plan that 10% of a continent's land area (5% at a minimum) be protected as parks to safeguard natural environments.[3] In 1985, according to the International Union for Conservation of Nature and Natural Resources (IUCN), the worldwide average was only 3.2%, with the U.S. having 7% of its land under some protection,[4,a] but only 3% of the lower 48 states in reserves and only 1.8% in designated wilderness.[5] Only 1.5% of Maine's land is considered wilderness. Maine ranks lowest in the Northeast and 47th among the 50 states for percentage of land in public parks.[6]

Even the 10% figure would eventually lead to considerable species loss, especially in tropical forests. The theory of island biogeography (which compares fragmented habitats to isolated islands) suggests that a single reserve containing 10% of the original area of an ecosystem would eventually support only 50% of the original species.[7,b]

Maine's 300,000 acres of "wilderness" would have to be expanded to more than 2 million acres, a nearly seven-fold increase, to come up to the recommended 10% of the Bali Action Plan.

Two million acres may seem like an outrageous figure until one considers that New York State has 6 million acres of public and private land in just the

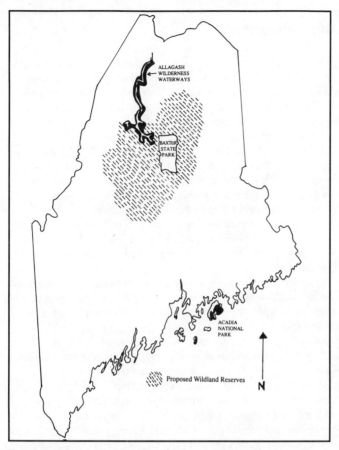

Existing and proposed (by The Wilderness Society) protected
areas in the Northern Forest. *From* Wilderness, *Fall 1989, Vol. 53, No.
186, The Wilderness Society, Washington, D.C., p. 39.*

Adirondack Park—2.6 million of which are considered "wilderness" or "wild
forest" to be kept "forever wild."[8] Maine's unorganized territories are larger and
far less populated than the Adirondack Park, a fact that some national and regional environmental groups have noticed. In 1989, for example, The Wilderness Society proposed a 2.7-million-acre Maine Woods Reserve (not all of
which would be wilderness) in the area surrounding Baxter State Park.[9] In 1990,
PAW (Preserve Appalachian Wilderness) called for an "Evolutionary Preserve"
of 10-15 million acres in the northern forestlands region including Maine.[10]

Although the timber industry traditionally has been antagonistic to proposals for more wilderness, it is their own management, ironically, that creates a
need for dedicated wilderness—a need that is directly proportional to the
intensity and extent of disturbing timber practices. Even The Wilderness
Society's proposal would be too small if the state allowed the rest of the forest to
be cut on short rotations for a pulpwood economy.

The Adirondack Park

Ninety percent of all designated wilderness in the 12 northeastern states is in the Adirondack Park, which has been designated as an International Biosphere Reserve by the United Nations Man and Biosphere Program.[11] The intent of these reserves is to demonstrate the value of conservation and careful use of natural resources to improve human well-being while maintaining biological diversity and ecological integrity.[12]

The Commission on the Adirondacks in the Twenty-First Century is committed to having the Adirondacks support the full range of native diversity, including reintroducing extirpated species. Commission members are aware that this means active management outside as well as within the park. "To maintain and enhance the biological diversity of the Adirondack Park and surrounding areas," states the Commission, "key 'land bridges' should be identified and protected, both in the Park and around it. This will allow the natural dispersion of indigenous plant and animal communities.

"The essential habitats and travel routes of wildland species such as spruce grouse, wolf, cougar, bear, moose, lynx, coyote, deer, fisher, wolverine, otter, and eagles, should be maintained or re-established where biologically feasible."[13]

Achieving the Commission's goal will not be easy. The 6-million-acre park is a politically and biologically complicated mixture of wilderness, wild forests, private timberlands, and populated hamlets. These hamlets, which have a combined year-round population of 130,000 people, are in the midst of, and fragment, the wild areas.[14] Eighty-two percent of the Forest Preserve system is within 3 miles of public roads.[15]

In the 1970s and 1980s population and housing developments grew rapidly in the hamlets. Real estate developers, businesspeople, private-land rights groups, and advocates of motorized recreation have been openly hostile to any expansions of publicly owned wilderness. This hostility has at times erupted into violence.[16] In one incident, the tires of park staff cars were shot. Still, the Adirondack commission is committed to its goal and has recommended adding more than half a million acres of wilderness to the park, including the formation of a Bob Marshall Great Wilderness, which would consist of more than 400,000 acres (some of which is already dedicated wilderness).[17]

In contrast, Maine officials have shown no enthusiasm for expanding wilderness, instead maintaining that Maine's forest is a working forest to be managed for multiple use.

Endnotes

a. Areas that are listed as "protected" by national authorities may not be well protected or adequately managed in practice.

b. Conservation biologist Reed Noss suggests that society should try to preserve 50%, rather than 10%, of the land base as wilderness: "Many people will think that asking for 50 per cent of our land as wilderness is either utopian or insane (or worse). But then again, most people (and nearly all elected officials) believe in infinite economic growth. Few accept the inevitability of catastrophe if we stay on our present course. I rest my case."[18]

References

1. Edward R. Grumbine, "How to Save the National Parks and Forests," *Forest Watch*, Vol. 9, No. 6 (December 1988): 21.
2. "By the Numbers," *Maine Times* (April 10, 1987).
3. Jessica Tuchman Mathews, editor, *A Report by the World Resources Institute and the International Institute for Environment and Development* (New York: Basic Books, Inc., 1986), p. 94.
4. *Ibid.*, p. 282.
5. Reed F. Noss, "Wilderness Recovery: Thinking Big in Restoration Ecology," *The Environmental Professional*, Vol. 13 (1991): 225.
6. "By the Numbers," *Maine Times* (April 10, 1987).
7. Jessica Tuchman Mathews, *A Report*, p. 98.
8. Commission on the Adirondacks in the Twenty-first Century, *The Adirondack Park in the Twenty-first Century* (Albany, N.Y.: State of New York, 1990), p. 2.
9. Michael J. Kellet, "A New Maine Woods Reserve: Options for Protecting Maine's Northern Wildlands (Washington, D.C.: The Wilderness Society, 1989), p. 48.
10. Jeff Elliott and Jamie Sayen, *The Ecological Restoration of the Northern Appalachians; An Evolutionary perspective (North Stratford, NH: Preserve Appalachian Wilderness, 1990).
11. George Davis, *2020 Vision: Fulfilling the Promise of the Adirondack Park*, Vol. 2, *Completing the Adirondack Wilderness System* (Elizabethtown, N.Y.: The Adirondack Council, 1990), p. 6.
12. Stephen C. Harper, Laura L. Falk, Edward W. Rankin, *The Northern Forest Lands Study of New England and New York* (Rutland, Vt.: United States Forest Service, United States Department of Agriculture, 1990), p. 175.
13. Commission on the Adirondacks in the Twenty-first Century, *The Adirondack Park*, p. 83.
14. David Platt, "The Adirondack Park: A Model for Change?," *Maine Times* (August 30, 1991): 19.
15. George Davis, *2020 Vision*, p. 11.
16. Phyllis Austin, "Emotions Are High as Old Adversaries Confront the Northern Forest," *Maine Times* (August 30, 1991): 4.
17. George Davis, *2020 Vision*, p. 7.
18. Reed F. Noss, "Wilderness Recovery," p. 227.

Myth 2

Maine's forest is no longer virgin and thus does not need to be preserved.

The term *virgin forest* tells more about those who use it than it does about the forests. Thousands of years before Europeans settled on this continent, native peoples inhabited the forests, foraging, hunting, even clearing and burning trees. The forest was by no means untouched by humans. Even current stands of old growth are affected by air pollution, human-exacerbated insect and disease problems, forest fragmentation, edge effects, and hunting, fishing, and trapping.

It is certainly true, however, that much of the land that groups such as The Wilderness Society and PAW are considering for reserves or preserves is crisscrossed with logging roads and has been heavily cut, sometimes repeatedly. These areas may bear little resemblance to the region's presettlement forest. Those calling for wilderness in such areas do so not because of the state of the forest now but because of its strategic location and potential for recovery in the future. Conservation biologists now recognize that future wilderness areas in the Northeast will have to be "grown rather than decreed."[1] Roads will have to be closed and habitat and species restored. There are too few "virgin" areas to protect the full range of habitat and species.

Most of the forest in Baxter State Park, for example, was cut before Percival Baxter purchased it. Yet few would dispute the wisdom or vision of Baxter for his trust that natural forces, if left on their own, could recover the land to be suitable habitat for both wildlife and wilderness hikers.

The severe clearcuts of today will take a long time to recover to stable conditions, but this does not mean we should refrain from giving them a chance to recover, especially if they are in prime locations. Those propounding the "virgin" myth argue that if a forest has been cut, even lightly, in the past, it is only suitable for further exploitation. This is like saying that because a woman is no longer a virgin it is acceptable to rape her.

Reference

1. Reed F. Noss, "Wilderness Recovery: Thinking Big in Restoration Ecology," *The Environmental Professional*, Vol. 13 (1991), p. 229.

Myth 3

The industrial forest is managed for multiple use,
taking care of the needs for wildlife and recreation.

There is no need for wilderness, the large landowners argue, because what the public wants—unrestricted access and plentiful wildlife—are to be found in the multiple-use working forest. Multiple-use forests are superior to wilderness, argue these landowners, because they supply needed wood and fiber for society as well as recreation and wildlife.

Multiple use is a vague term. Areas that have been intensively clearcut are hardly ideal for hikers, for those looking for the aesthetic beauty of mature forests, or for those seeking out deep-woods wildlife. The industrial response to this observation is that it is unrealistic to expect all multiple uses to fall on each stand of trees. Their multiple uses are compartmentalized on their holdings— wildlife protection (i.e., deeryards) and public recreation in the beauty strips in riparian areas and timber harvesting everywhere else.

Australian forestry critics R. and V. Routley have numerous objections to industrial concepts of multiple use. "The mere fact that an area has more than one use," they write, "provides no assurance that all relevant or important values have been taken into account and given full weight and that some relevant values have not been omitted. . . .

"It does not follow from the fact that something gets a certain use that that use is considered in the decision-making and is not merely coincidental—in fact the use could occur despite or contrary to planned activities for the area. . . .

"From the fact that something has more than one use it does not follow that the priorities between these uses are properly allocated. . . .

"The terminology rather strongly suggests, what is false, that the value of an area for a particular purpose can be assessed in terms of the volume of overt use. . . .

"Use for more than one purpose as a criterion of adequacy is virtually

A multiple-use industrial forest suitable for timber production, wildlife, and recreation. *Photo by Christopher Ayres.*

vacuous and excludes nothing."[1]

The Routleys suggest that "since the multiple-use terminology has been so eroded and abused by forest interests the best course seems to be to abandon it to them, and to adopt some new terminology which is less open to semantical erosion and misinterpretation and for which conditions are more clearly specified."[2] Their alternative is "multiple values," which would include watershed protection, recreation, wildlife, flora protection, wilderness, scenery, soil fertility, and forest revenue. The object of management, they argue, should be not to maximize one value at the expense of all the others but to optimize values. "Maximizing on wood production variables, particularly through intensive

Roads are a major source of erosion and siltation.
Photo by Christopher Ayres.

management, is not in accord with multiple values and is not good decision making."[3]

Professor Holmes Rolston III and James Coufal, writing in the *Journal of Forestry*, also find fault with the "multiple use" concept. "Multiple use," they maintain, "is a commodity model, treating forests expediently as nothing but a resource. Multiple value is a community model, respecting both human and forest communities and seeking an integrated appreciation and development of values provided by forests. . . . Multiple use asks of a thing, What is it good for?

High altitude aerial photo of forest to west of Baxter Park that is criss-crossed with roads. Even without clearcuts, roads can severely impact some forest wildlife. Within a decade after this photo was taken, however, the whole area was clearcut. 1 inch = 0.4 miles. *Photo courtesy of U.S. Geological Survey, 1975.*

What use does it have? Unsurprisingly, the question is often answered economically, seeking maximum exploitation of resources. . . . Multiple value asks, What values are present intrinsically (in the forests regardless of humans) as well as instrumentally (in forests used as human resources)? How can this richness be optimized?"[4]

Gordon Robinson, in his book *The Forest and the Trees*, contends that even-aged management, which forms the basis for many industrial landholdings, fails at providing these multiple values. "Tree farming," writes Robinson, "in essence, means mass-producing low-quality wood without regard for other values except as they interfere with that objective."[5]

Even if commodity management were for large, old trees in uneven-aged stands, this would still not preclude the need for wilderness, because managed areas are roaded areas. "Probably no single feature of human-dominated landscapes," writes Reed Noss, "is more threatening to biodiversity (aquatic and terrestrial) than roads."[6] Noss lists a number of direct and indirect negative effects of roads, including:

•fragmentation and isolation of populations (especially small vertebrates and invertebrates);
•road kills;
•pollution and sedimentation of streams and wetlands;
•exotic species invasions; and
•influx of people with guns, snares, and traps.

"If Americans," writes Noss, "want the symbols of American wilderness—large carnivores and herds of ungulates . . . then they should be fully informed about roads."[7]

The protected areas in Maine proposed by The Wilderness Society and PAW are, ironically, based on what wildlife ecologist Larry Harris calls "multiple use modules" (MUMs)—i.e., unroaded wilderness cores surrounded by buffers of low-intensity managed areas and connected to other MUMs by wildlife corridors. This concept of multiple use is a far cry from that employed by industrial landowners in Maine.

References

1. R. and V. Routley, *The Fight for the Forests: The Takeover of Australian Forests for Pines, Wood Chips, and Intensive Forestry* (Canberra, Australia: Research School of Social Sciences, Australian National University, 1974), pp. 223-224.
2. *Ibid.*, p. 226.
3. *Ibid.*, p. 229.
4. Holmes Rolston III and James Coufal, "A Forest Ethic and Multivalue Forest Management," *Journal of Forestry* (April 1991): 38.
5. Gordon Robinson, *The Forest and the Trees: A Guide to Excellent Forestry* (Washington, D.C.: Island Press, 1989), p. 69.
6. Reed F. Noss, "Wilderness Recovery: Thinking Big in Restoration Ecology," *The Environmental Professional*, Vol. 13 (1991): 226.
7. *Ibid.*

Myth 4

Wilderness locks up precious resources that society needs, leading to shortfalls and job loss.

Industry's concern over locking up precious resources is selective. As Yale social ecologist William Burch, Jr., observed, "I cannot recall many times when timber industry spokespeople protested the removal of timberlands by highways, condos, ski runs, reservoirs or shopping malls. Of course if you remove something, you certainly don't need to worry about its being locked-up anymore."[1] The same companies who complain about losing timberland to wilderness contribute to timberland loss by selling off HBU (Highest and Best Use) lands from their own real estate divisions.

Wilderness itself is a precious resource that is destroyed by road building and abusive timber harvesting. Those who argue that wilderness deprives society of precious resources (to make such essential goods as disposable diapers, redundant packaging, or junk mail) imply that biodiversity, clean air and water, remote recreation, scientific research, and spiritual renewal have no values.

Citing catastrophic mill consequences that will lead to job losses is a standard and nearly knee-jerk response by the forest industry to regulations or policies it does not like. The paper industry in Maine, however, is clearly not in business to provide social welfare and sustainable employment. If there are timber shortfalls in the state it will not be due to preservationists but to industry policies that have led to nonsustainable mill capacity, overcutting, abusive cutting that degrades the forest, and management-exacerbated budworm outbreaks.

Despite shortfall predictions (which were made before environmental groups announced their goal for more wilderness), some companies are considering increasing mill capacity and expanding exports. We do not have to wait for job losses, they have already occurred—despite increased levels of cutting—due to mechanization.

Lloyd Irland is not concerned about the prospects of imminent industrial collapse due to designation of more wilderness. "I'm comfortable with the guess that we could find ways to designate a good deal more wilderness with nominal sacrifice of commercial values," he says. "Under foreseeable economic conditions, there is simply no need for concern over the impact of Maine's limited current and potential wilderness resource on supplies of wood or other raw materials. If I'm right, the cost of additional wilderness in Maine is nominal from a social standpoint."[2]

Maintaining wilderness implies restraint—restraint from exploiting or destroying every last acre of remaining forest. There are limits to the expansion of exploitive management and forest conversion because there are limits to forests. At some point society must choose if it will live within these limits in a sustainable way or if it will continue expanding its industrial capacity until the resource capacity shrinks to nothing. Allowing the existence of wilderness may mean reaching the limits to growth sooner, but exploiting wilderness does not mean avoiding those limits. A society living within limits and maintaining wilderness would be richer than a society living within limits with no wilderness. As Thoreau once said, "A man is rich in proportion to the number of things he can afford to leave alone."

References

1. William Burch, Jr., "The Rhetoric of Wilderness: Philosophical Paradigm and Real Estate Scams," *Habitat* (June/July 1986): 37.
2. Lloyd C. Irland, "Wilderness Redefined: Thoughts on Developing a Definition of Wilderness That Works for Maine," *Habitat* (June/July 1986): 15.

Myth 5
Wilderness only benefits a privileged minority at the expense of the working classes and disadvantaged.

The image here is of wealthy hikers with their expensive, synthetic, high-tech equipment, cavorting through the woods at their leisure at the expense of the working stiff in the mill or the homeless in the city.

"Here the wilderness opponents," writes William Burch, Jr., "suddenly become social reformers and mutter about elite wilderness types taking things from ordinary working class Americans. But if I were a blue collar employee of Boise Cascade, I might wish they would spend less time worrying in glossy full page ads about us 'Budweiser types' being locked out of our favorite recreation activities by wilderness nuts, and give more attention to our wages, occupational safety and general working conditions. Somehow our corporate executives' bleeding heart concerns about what 'extremist environmentalists' are doing to the lives of their workers does not remain as benign at contract negotiation time or when OSHA infractions are discovered."[1]

The Routleys, responding to the same myth, write that ". . . in fact the argument in question turns the true situation on its head in that those groups which stand to lose most from the impoverishment of public amenities are precisely those with the smallest private resources to provide alternatives, that is less affluent groups. . . . the director of the sand-mining or woodchip company can live in delightful surroundings far from the scene of the crime and take his holidays in Bora Bora, but the less affluent citizens will find their lives and choices far more seriously affected by the results of his company's activities."[2]

An underlying assumption of this myth is that industrial growth, fueled by resource extraction in the region, benefits the poor and disadvantaged. In fact, growth based on exploitive activities leads to greater disparities between the elites and the poor. Unless there are substantial government efforts at income redistribution, the wealth does not always trickle down. Allowing large multinational corporations to dominate and exploit the forest is what really caters to elites.

References

1. William Burch, Jr., "The Rhetoric of Wilderness: Philosophical Paradigm and Real Estate Scams," *Habitat* (June/July 1986): 37.
2. R. and V. Routley, *The Fight for the Forests: The Takeover of Australian Forests for Pines, Wood Chips, and Intensive Forestry* (Canberra, Australia: Research School of Social Sciences, Australian National University, 1974), p. 216.

Myth 6

Increasing dedicated wilderness would change local economies from resource based to service based, catering to outside tourists.

A common tactic of the forest industry is to raise the specter of tourists and wealthy summer people shutting down the ugly forest management or smelly mills on which local people rely for jobs. This myth fails because it assumes an all-or-nothing situation where all forestry activities are shut down and replaced by tourism. The wilderness models suggested for Maine, however, would not exclude forest management or wood processing. Forest management does not have to be ugly, nor do mills have to be polluting at criminal levels.

The myth exaggerates local impacts because most of the land being looked at for wilderness is in a region that currently has no public roads or towns. A substantial proportion of the wood in this region is cut by Canadian workers and sold to Canadian mills, providing little in the way of local benefits.

The myth sets up a false dichotomy, for which many environmentalists unfortunately have fallen, that posits that the only alternative to subservience to companies from away specializing in exploitive management and polluting mills is subservience to tourists from away. University of Montana economist Thomas Power argues that we should not "give away the store to outsiders, whether those outsiders be extractive industry or tourists. . . . Nobody loves a tourist, not even tourists, and no one looks forward to cleaning up after tourists. We do not impress our fellow citizens with talk about putting them to work making motel beds, cleaning toilets, and washing dishes."[1]

Powers argues that many people today choose where they want to live, and they are more apt to choose areas with higher environmental quality and beauty than areas with ravaged forests and polluted air and water. He also argues that most new jobs are being created by small entrepreneurs rather than by large industries. "We must be careful," writes Powers, "not to buy into the vision of ourselves as passive, helpless folks completely dependent upon outside forces."[2]

Any plans for wilderness areas can include plans to ensure the economic stability of nearby communities. The Commission on the Adirondacks in the Twenty-First Century declared that "The people of the state have determined over the last 100 years of Park history that environmental quality within the Park should be more stringently protected than elsewhere. At the same time a thriving Park population is essential, both to maintain the industries and to provide the goods and services required by visitors."[3]

In their plan for the upcoming century, the Adirondack commission gave considerable space to the needs of local communities for jobs, housing, public health, education, and hamlet revitalization. This commission has not fallen for the false dichotomy between wilderness protection and community vitality. Neither should the people of Maine.

References

1. Thomas Power, "Avoiding the Passive/Helpless Approach to Economic Development," *Forest Watch* (October 1989): 18.
2, *Ibid.*
3. Commission on the Adirondacks in the Twenty-first Century, *The Adirondack Park in the Twenty-first Century* (Albany, N. Y.: State of New York, 1990), p. 29.

5 Industrial Government

A 1988 state report on the future of Maine's forest concluded that "The need for sound management to maintain and enhance forest productivity, avoid shortfalls and protect resource values will be met primarily by the private sector. The Maine forest is large and diverse, capable of providing a wide variety of products and supporting many uses, but achieving the desired level of performance demands improved management based upon enlightened self interest."[1]

Unfortunately, the self-interest of absentee corporations has not always benefitted society or the forest. State government has attempted to fill the gaps left by the marketplace through:

•Planning and policy making—to ensure long-term economic, social, and ecological stability;

•Research—to encourage improved forest practices that benefit the forest and society;

•Education—to encourage more responsible management and use of forests and consumption of forest products;

•Taxation/subsidies—to encourage protection of forest values and to discourage irresponsible land use;

•Regulation—to prevent destructive or degrading forest practices; and

•Public land—to demonstrate exemplary management.

In *A Sand County Almanac*, Aldo Leopold suggested that the "gaps" left by industry for government to fill may turn into an abyss: "What is the ultimate magnitude of the enterprise? Will the tax base carry its eventual ramifications? At what point will governmental conservation, like the mastodon, become handicapped by its own dimensions?"[2] Bureaucracies expand to absorb available revenues, and then some. Such growth is encouraged by the bureaucrats who benefit from increased authority, prestige, security, and pay. The problems that they treat, however, never seem to get solved.

For Leopold, the alternative to an unwieldy, expensive expansion of external government controls was to have better internal landowner controls—a land ethic. But, as Eberhard Thiele, a forester and environmental educator, told a meeting of the Society of American Foresters in Maine, "I think it can be safely argued that ethics among company foresters evolve to meet the expectations of employers. . . A job is a precious possession. The fear of losing it and not finding another one is a most potent source of new mindsets and ethics."[3]

There is another consideration even more disturbing than the one raised by Leopold (who was himself a public servant): sometimes government is not filling the ethical gaps but widening them; not restraining industry but serving it; not preventing environmental damage but legitimizing it.

References

1. James F. Connors, *Forest for the Future: A Report on Maine's Forest to the Legislature, the Governor, and the People of Maine* (Augusta, Me.: Maine Department of Conservation, 1988), p. 29.
2. Aldo Leopold, *A Sand County Almanac* (New York: Sierra Club/Ballantine, 1966), p. 250.
3. Eberhard Thiele, "Response to 'Contract Logging, Chainsaws and Clearcuts: The Human and Environmental Effects of Forest Management Systems in Maine, by David Vail.'" Transcript of presentation made at winter meeting, Maine Chapter of the Society of American Foresters, Augusta, Me., April 6, 1987.

Policy

Large industrial corporations, because they must make sizable capital expenditures for projects that take years to develop, must make long-range plans. They cannot afford to have government agencies making unpredictable and perhaps antagonistic decisions that interfere with these plans. Corporations therefore tend to spend considerable effort on the political process to ensure that their plans are harmonious with those the government develops—or vice versa.

In Maine, industry representatives have had roles in nearly all aspects of state forestry policy. Even some of the state's environmental groups, which are supposed to balance industry on various committees and commissions, have not been immune to industrial influence.

Myth 1

State data on the forest and forest practices are accurate and reliable.

State and federal surveys are a major source of information on the amount of wood cut, type of practices used, value of stumpage and mill-delivered prices, and structure and condition of the forest. Taxation, regulations, and planning are based on this information. Yet much of this information is of questionable accuracy. Until passage of the 1989 Forest Practices Act, landowners, though required to supply accurate data on harvest practices, amount of wood cut, and wood prices, often didn't. This can have its problems. Large landowners, for example, have an incentive to report low stumpage prices because their taxes are based on this figure. This information is not checked for accuracy. Some large nonindustrial contractor/landowners refused to send in any information. State data thus have been incomplete, skewed, or misleading.

I have given numerous examples throughout this book of the dubious nature of state figures on cut, stumpage, exports, or employment. Some Maine Forest Service data conflict with data on the same subject from other government sources. For example, 1988 MFS herbicide statistics vary widely from data supplied by the Board of Pesticide Control.

1988 Forestry Herbicide Use[1]

Maine Forest Service:	68,484 acres
Maine Board of Pesticide Control:	81,258 acres
Percent Variance:	18.7%

Maine Forest Service data on harvest levels are even more dubious. For example, the total harvest, as calculated from figures in the Annual Report of Stumpage Harvested for 1986, isn't even in the range of estimates for total harvest for 1986 as derived from the 1986 Midcycle Forest Resurvey:

Total 1986 Harvest[3,4]

1986 Annual Report:	4.781 million cords
Midcycle Forest Resurvey:	8.400 million cords (±16%)
Percent Variance:	76%

(Note: "±16%" means there is a 67% chance that the harvest figure was somewhere between 9.744 and 7.056 million cords. The range of error for the resurvey is 56% of the total figure from the Annual Report!)

There have been other interesting "anomalies" that suggest either that some markets are highly unstable or the state does not have an accurate handle on what is going on. For example, reported volume of stumpage harvested for softwood chips is extremely erratic.

Stumpage Harvested of Softwood for Chips
(measured in thousand cords)[5]

1986	13.464
1987	153.708
1988	22.741
1989	33.026
1990	136.54

Percent change 1986 to 1987	1,142% increase
Percent change 1987 to 1988	85% decrease
Percent change 1989 to 1990	414% increase

Even statistics on forest composition and quality from federal and state forest surveys have large margins of error due to small sample sizes. For example, in the state's 1986 Midcycle Resurvey of the spruce-fir forest, the margin of error for estimates of the volume of balsam fir trees over 15 inches in diameter is + or -46%. This means there was a 67% probability that the exact volume of fir trees of that size lay somewhere between 25.5 and 137.8 million cubic feet.[6] The higher estimate is 5.4 times the lower estimate. Similarly, the state calculated the percent of area of spruce-fir that has 80-100% occupation with "best" spruce seedlings with a ±69% margin of error.[7]

Forestry critic Bill Butler contends that the unreliability of state data goes beyond the small sample size (which averaged 1 plot per every 3,000 acres studied and 1 plot per every 4,000 acres in the heart of the industrial forest). He is concerned about how samples were chosen and how the data were classified and interpreted. One can certainly not accuse the 1986 resurvey planning team of having a bias against the paper industry and its practices since it included a paper industry forester (Roger Greene of Champion International Corporation).[8]

When the data are questionable, complex policy decisions based on the data are also questionable. Computer programmers refer to this truism as GIGO (Garbage In, Garbage Out).

References
1. Ancyl Thurston, *Silvicultural Practices Report of 1988* (Augusta, Me.: Maine Department of Conservation, 1989).
2. James Balogh, *The Use and Potential Impacts of Forestry Herbicides in Maine* (Augusta, Me.: Maine Department of Conservation, 1990), p. 88.
3. Extrapolated from data in Ancyl Thurston, *Annual Report of Stumpage Harvested for 1990* (Augusta, Me.: Maine Forest Service, Maine Department of Conservation, 1991).
4. Extrapolated from data in Maine Forest Service, *Report of the 1986 Midcycle Resurvey of the Spruce-fir Forest in Maine* (Augusta, Me.: Maine Department of Conservation, May 1988), p. 22.
5. Ancyl Thurston, *Annual Report of Stumpage.*
6. Maine Forest Service, *Report of the 1986 Midcycle Resurvey,* p. 19.
7. *Ibid.,* p. 28.
8. *Ibid.,* p. i.

Myth 2

The Maine public has been well informed on forestry issues.

One would think that in a state where forestry is so important, public interest in the subject would be high. Yet the lack of public awareness on forestry issues through the late 1980s was a major motivation for me to write this book.

The news media, especially newspapers, are the public's major source of information on forestry issues.[1] As readers of this book know, forestry issues can be extremely complicated. For a number of reasons, newspapers have trouble rising to the challenge presented by this complexity:

• Because of limited space, articles are often abbreviated and shallow.

• Rather than do independent research, reporters tend to gather information by interviewing "experts," most of whom may be influenced directly or indirectly by industry.

• Simple subjects are more "newsworthy" than complex subjects; car crashes, murders, and rapes are much easier to write about than the incremental degradation of Maine's forest.

• Papers can only cover an issue so long before it grows stale; the public has a short memory. Some editors have discouraged writers from following up on forestry issues.

• Newspapers are made from paper. Some large national papers (e.g., the *New York Times* or the *Washington Post*) or syndicates (e.g., Knight-Ridder), have interests in their own paper mills. Maine newspaper publishers have contracts for some of their paper with in-state paper companies. Some of these papers also get substantial advertising revenues from paper companies. The *Bangor Daily News*, for example has an annual advertising supplement dedicated to the forest-products industry. When material controversial to industry gets published, it is almost always balanced with quotations from industry spokespeople. Industry propaganda, however, is not always balanced by opposing views.

Although I consider some reporters friends, and I have a certain sympathy for the constraints of time and space with which they have to work, nonetheless I have sometimes been appalled and angered by press coverage of events at which I was a witness or participant. Too often a complex issue gets reduced to a few one-liners from a core group of forestry insiders. Further distortion comes from misquotes, statements taken out of context, or omissions of pertinent facts of which the writer is well aware.

There have been some welcome exceptions to this general pattern. In 1986 the *Maine Sunday Telegram* published a 4-part series on forestry that involved extensive research and interviews with a wide range of interests. In the same year the *Maine Times* published a series of articles about the industrial forest. Unfortunately, these efforts were not sufficient to awaken citizen concern over forestry issues. A 1986 poll conducted by the Forests for the Future Program asked Maine people what they considered the 2 most important problems they faced. Only 0.4%—4/10 of 1%—of the respondents "either explicitly used the word 'forests' or its synonyms, or mentioned forest-associated industry in their replies."[2] The authors commented (in surprise), "Apparently, forest-related concerns are not foremost in people's minds. . . ."

The survey found that respondents were concerned about clearcutting, pesticides, acid rain, and other issues, but they were "often poorly informed about the forest." The report illustrated this ignorance (though not intention-ally) when it stated that "the public generally accepts the view that the forest is well managed."

References

1. *Forest of Maine Survey of Public Opinion* (Augusta, Me.: Forest for the Future, Maine Depart-ment of Conservation, 1986).
2. *Ibid.*

Myth 3

Forestry has been a major statewide political issue in Maine.

One would think that in a state like Maine forestry issues would be hotly de-bated by candidates during elections. I would love to cite some of the past stands candidates have taken on such issues during the 1980s but I can't; there is nothing to cite. During the 1986 and 1990 campaigns, no candidate for higher office (governor or Congress) had much to say about forestry matters. Not only were politicians reticent about the subject; the press also failed to force candi-dates to address the issue.

PAC Reminders

This does not mean that candidates do not think about forestry issues or have no forestry agendas. A major reminder to the candidates of the importance of these issues are the large donations they receive from paper companies through Politi-cal Action Committees (PACs). The companies have their own PACs and also are major contributors to other PACs. [1]

Industrial Appointees

John McKernan, elected governor in 1986 and 1990, demonstrated his forestry agenda through his appointments. McKernan, whose brother Robert was a lob-byist for the American Paper Institute in Washington, D.C., chose Robert LaBonta to be his first commissioner of the Department of Conservation. LaBonta had just spent three decades as a timberlands manager for Scott Paper Company. Scott was the first big landowner in Maine to do large-scale mecha-nized clearcuts, and LaBonta was an enthusiastic proponent of following such clearcuts with a generous dousing of herbicides. LaBonta's attitude toward the forest when he worked for Scott was not what most conservationists would call "ecological." In *The Paper Plantation*, LaBonta was quoted as saying, "We [Scott] view our timberlands primarily as a pulpwood factory for our mill."[2]

LaBonta's nomination had to go before the legislature's Energy and Natural Resources Committee for confirmation. Here citizens as well as legislators could speak out. Even though the nomination represented an apparent conflict of interest, only two people—Bill Butler, of Friends of the Maine Woods, and I—testified against LaBonta. The largest environmental groups in the state, Maine Audubon Society, the Natural Resources Council of Maine, and the Sportsman's Alliance of Maine, testified neither for nor against or not at all.

Ronald Usher and Michael Michaud, the two chairmen of the Energy and Natural Resources Committee at the time, were both paper-mill employees. Seven of the 13 committee members had received Scott PAC contributions during the 1986 elections. Nearly all the rest had received paper-company contributions through other PACs.[3] Although some committee members engaged LaBonta in lively dialogue, the confirmation was unanimous.

LaBonta, showing he was not partial to Scott, chose John Cashwell, a former helicopter pilot for Georgia-Pacific, to head the Maine Forest Service. When LaBonta developed cancer in 1988 (he died in 1990), he was replaced as commissioner by Edwin Meadows, a former public-relations director for Seven Islands Land Company.

Industry Agenda?

I am not arguing here that PAC contributions buy candidates. But they do buy candidates' attention. I am also not arguing that because someone worked for a paper company, he or she will pursue an industry agenda in office. Even if an appointee wanted to follow an industry agenda, the pressures from public scrutiny would make such behavior difficult. Such job shifts, however, raise questions about these people's environmental integrity. Either they:

•really were environmentally concerned before and lied to their industrial employees; or

•are still faithful to industry and are pretending to be environmentally concerned in their new positions; or

•went through a radical personality shift after leaving industrial employment; or

•do not see any fundamental difference between what is good for industry and what is good for the state.

Hot Issues

Some readers may object at this point that the Forest Practices Act and the Northern Forest Lands Study were both major political issues in Maine in 1990. I would counter that though these were certainly contentious issues among the "special interest" groups concerned (the forest-products industry and environmental groups), they were not burning issues for the general public. If they were, why weren't they debated in the 1990 election?

Georgia-Pacific's hostile takeover of Great Northern, however, certainly was a major issue for the general public. This transfer of 10% of Maine's landmass rated frequent headlines in the news. The two industry giants also battled for the hearts and minds of Maine people through impressive advertising campaigns. Yet by election time this, too, had become a nonissue. The public memory apparently is very short.

Perhaps one reason for this lack of general excitement over forestry issues (there has been enough local excitement in some towns, however, to pass forest-practices ordinances) is that the majority of industrial holdings are in the unorganized territories which, though comprising half the land in the state, only have 1% of the population.

Change?

While forestry has not been a major issue in Maine during the 1980s, it may well become a major issue in the 1990s. In 1991 the Northern Forest Lands Act (a federal act to continue the NFLS) generated significant oppostion from ultra-conservative groups which alleged that the act opened the door to federal land grabs of private land. The groups are coordinated both regionally and nation-ally. I expect the intense controversy between these groups and the national en-vironmental groups that support federal action, combined with the instability of the paper industry, will be sufficient to finally bring the forest to public con-sciousness.

References

1. Mary Lou Wendell, *Citizens' Guide to the Maine Legislature*. (Portland, Me.: Maine Peoples Resource Center, 1988), pp. 86-88.
2. William Osborne, *The Paper Plantation* (New York: Viking Press, 1974), p. 181.
3. Mary Lou Wendell, *Citizens' Guide*, pp. 86-88, and Scott PAC information filed with the Maine Secretary of State.

Myth 4

Large statewide environmental groups have enunciated clear alternatives to industrial management.

Perhaps one reason the general public was not fired up over forestry issues in the 1980s is because organizations that should have been generating clear critiques of industrial management were not fired up either. If those who are most in-formed about an issue are not gravely upset, why should the public be? The two largest environmental groups in the state, Maine Audubon Society (MAS) and the Natural Resources Council of Maine (NRCM), certainly did not entirely avoid the issues. They attended hearings, published articles and studies, and even initiated legislation, but what did they say?

Budworm Spraying

In the late 1970s and early 1980s the overwhelming forestry issue was spruce-budworm spraying. MAS and the NRCM both were initially in favor of state and federal subsidies for the spray program because they believed government participation would ensure that there would be environmental monitoring. But government subsidies also encouraged more spraying. The NRCM eventually figured this out and became effective critics, but MAS, in comments in environ-mental impact statements, continued to support federal subsidies.

Clearcutting

In September 1985, MAS published a special forestry issue of its magazine, *Habitat*. This could have been an opportunity to print articles critical of controversial industrial practices such as clearcutting, herbicide spraying, and biomass harvesting. Unfortunately, this opportunity was not taken. Wildlife biologist Malcolm Hunter, Jr. had this to say about clearcutting: "Large-scale management, potentially involving clearcuts of hundreds of hectares, is appropriate on the best timber-producing sites."[1] What about the impacts on wildlife? Hunter was philosophical: ". . .there is no question that clearcuts are a visual travesty, and there remain some unanswered questions about soil erosion, nutrient cycling, herbicides, etc. However, clearcutting is not intrinsically good or bad for wildlife; it creates habitat for some species while destroying it for others."

In 1987 the NRCM put out a study, *Forest Clearcutting in Maine: An Assessment of Environmental Impacts and Public Policy Needs*. The study did not look at the impact of clearcuts over space (fragmentation) or time (herbicides, monocultures, short rotations, etc.); it mostly looked at immediate impacts and found that for some of them, such as siltation or increases in water temperature, buffer strips mitigated the problem. The authors declared that much of the public concern over clearcuts was due to the devastating visual impact and mentioned how buffer strips, irregular shapes, and strip cuts minimize these impacts. "If these forest practices were expanded to other sensitive areas, the public clamor over clearcuts would be sure to subside."[2]

Two nearly tautological conclusions of the study were that "clearcuts, if improperly planned and implemented, can have a very destructive impact on the environment," and "If a clearcut is properly conducted, many environmental impacts can be significantly mitigated."[3] But is a clearcut "properly conducted" if there are less drastic actions that could have been taken instead?

Herbicides

In the 1985 special forestry issue of *Habitat*, forest researcher Robert Seymour wrote that "Herbicide application is now regarded as an essential followup to clearcutting on most sites to prevent undesirable conversions to low-value species."[4] Indeed, he suggested that to eliminate such a practice would be "withholding management." If MAS director Charles Hewett had any problems with Seymour's attitude toward herbicides, he did not let on. In the introduction of that issue he wrote that "there is agreement on what needs to be done; the question is getting it done."[a] The NRCM has taken no major initiatives on herbicides.

Biomass

Charles Hewett had an article about biomass harvesting in the same issue of *Habitat*. "Whole tree harvesting," concluded Hewett, "is the most powerful silvicultural tool now available for managing Maine's forests."[5] MAS, as I mentioned in the biomass section of Chapter 3, supported building more biomass plants (even though at the time there were no regulations to prevent the worst abuses).

Northern Forest Lands Study

Both MAS and the NRCM initially accepted industry's premise that the NFLS was to focus on threats to the "working forest" from sales, subdivisions, and conversions rather than on threats to forest ecosystems from management as usual by the current landowners. The forum for addressing forest practices, they claimed, was the Forest Practices Act. Only after intense pressure from nationally and regionally based groups did the NFLS address the issue of forest management (in the appendix of the final draft).

In 1991 the NRCM came up with a proposal that could solve the northern forest problem—if the problem is real estate development. The proposal calls for creation of a NorthWoods Conservation Area (NWCA) using existing-use LURC zoning over the majority of the unorganized territories. Spreading the NWCA over millions of acres creates the illusion that most of the unorganized territories would be "protected."

In reality, developers are targeting their activities on only the fraction of the forest nearest lakes and rivers—i.e., the beauty strips. The sweeping nature of the proposal played into the hands of "landowner-rights" activists who insisted that the imposition of an NWCA amounted to a taking without due compensation because it would take away a landowner's God-given right to subdivide property and build condos.

Both the NRCM and the landowners presented exaggerated positions. Why should industrial landowners be compensated for the loss of the "right" to subdivide and develop the millions of acres of heavily cut industrial forest that are not near accessible, roaded lakes and rivers? Who would want to purchase a condo in a clearcut? In truth, the NWCA would not interfere with the manner in which landowners currently gain their incomes from the land—i.e., exploitive forest management. Calling a zone where landowners can flatten or degrade a forest a "conservation area" certainly stretches the meaning of the word conservation.

Forest Practices Act

In 1989 MAS initiated a Forest Practices Act (FPA), part of which involved the regulation of clearcutting. Both MAS and the NRCM accepted the concept that the way to regulate clearcuts is to set size restrictions and require separation zones between clearcuts. Their debate with industry was over the size of the clearcuts and separation zones. MAS, for example, was ready to accept 200-acre clearcuts before the negotiations even began. Other organizations, however, pointed out that such a strategy, which does not even seek to reduce the total number of acres clearcut, only spreads clearcutting over more acres, leading to more forest fragmentation.

Representatives

Perhaps one reason these groups have not rallied more of the public in opposition to current forestry policy is because some of their spokespeople are from the forest-products community. Michael Cline, policy director at MAS, was a former research forester for International Paper. Roger Milliken, head of the NRCM's forestry committee, is the head of Baskehegan Lands Company, a large forest landowner/manager in Washington County. He has also been active in the Maine Forest Products Council, which was the major industry lobby group trying to turn the Forest Practices Act into a weaker version than MAS originally proposed.

These gentlemen, because of their knowledge and sincerity, make good advisors to their environmental groups. When they are used as representatives in negotiations with the forest industry, however, the public is shielded from the outrage of forest-policy victims. Instead they see a closed group talking to one another, often in alien jargon and moderated tones, about preserving the "working forest."

Industry Influence

One reason a group like MAS would be so cautious on forestry issues might have something to do with its advisory trustees and corporate donors. Prominent among its trustees in the late 1980s were Sherry Huber (of J. M. Huber Corporation, an industrial forest landowner) and Brad Wellman (of the Pingree heirs, one of the largest forest landowners in Maine). In 1984 the president of MAS was David Clements (now an advisory trustee), an official at S. D. Warren (a division of Scott Paper). Among the many corporate donors to MAS have been Scott, Boise Cascade, Seven Islands (the management division of the Pingrees), and International Paper. The IP grant was for a publicity poster for MAS which bore the IP insignia in one corner. IP President Paul O'Neill told *Newspaper* (the newsletter of the Paper Industry Information Office) in early 1987, "As residents of Maine, employees of International Paper all have a vested interest in Maine Audubon's goals."[6]

Class

Despite such "influence," these groups have waged battles with paper companies over issues of mill pollution and hydroelectric dams. Their staff are sincere and committed to working for improvements in the environment. Bowdoin economist David Vail, however, notes that though these organizations have thousands of members, they are not mass-based. The members are recruited largely from what Vail calls "a highly educated socio-economic elite, including numerous representatives of prominent Maine and New England families."[7] Vail also noticed what he called "the 'revolving door' through which some of its prominent leaders have moved into government, consulting positions, and private firms dealing with environmentally sensitive issues."[8]

Vail asserts that the class interests of professional environmentalists are similar to the class interests of professionals in government and industry. This includes support of market competition as the basic mechanism governing relations between people and nature and belief in the promotion of economic growth as the central function of the state. "Ultimately, their project is to find a compromise among competing interests through 'multiple use management.'"[9]

Endnote

a. Although Hewett may have accepted herbicides as a necessary forestry tool at the time, MAS published a study in June 1990, *Pesticide Reduction: A Blueprint for Action*, by Michael Cline, Tim Zorach, Nancy Papoulias, and Jody Jones, that calls for reductions in forestry herbicide use and a preference for alternative management options. After a decade of little action on pesticide issues, MAS took a leading role.

References

1. Malcolm Hunter, Jr., "Forests, Forestry and Fauna," *Habitat* (September 1985).
2. Jerry Bley et al., *Forest Clearcutting in Maine: An Asessment of Environmental Impacts and Public Policy Needs* (Augusta, Me.: Natural Resources Council of Maine, 1987), p. 7.
3. *Ibid.*, p. 12.
4. Robert Seymour, "Where Has All the Spruce-fir Gone? ," *Habitat.* (September 1985).
5. Charles Hewett, "Whole Tree Harvesting: The Potential and Pitfalls," *Habitat.* (September 1985).
6. David Sargent, "International Paper Assists with Maine Audubon Membership Poster," *Newspaper* (April 1987): 2.
7. David Vail, *Contract Logging, Chainsaws and Clearcuts: The Human and Environmental Impacts of Forest Extraction Systems in the State of Maine (USA)* (Helsinki, Finland: United Nations University, World Institute for Development Economics Research, May 1986), p. 77.
8. *Ibid.*
9. *Ibid.*, p. 76.

Myth 5

Policy making should be a balanced process with direct industry input.

The idea that policy is formed by balancing equally legitimate concerns appears to be fair, reasonable and responsible. The industry side, in Maine is certainly well represented. Forest industry representatives sit on nearly all policy-making and regulatory boards and committees concerned with forest practices or the forest industry. These boards and committees, however, rarely have representatives from labor or from local communities that would be directly affected by policy decisions.

In *The Paper Plantation*, William Osborne commented that such a system "gives the paper companies special access to government decision-making and tends to restrain agency action toward them. While such arrangements may have been necessary to placate industry lobbyists in the legislature, this in no way justifies them. Special representation for those who are regulated violates the whole principle of government by impartial citizen commission. . . . The Maine people don't enjoy a 'slot' on the boards of directors of the major paper companies; there is even less reason the companies should have one on Maine public commissions."[1]

Conflict of Interest

When company representatives are on boards that set policy for or regulate their own industries, this certainly seems to be a conflict of interest. The Land Use Regulation Commission (LURC), which regulates forest practices and other activities in the unorganized territories, has several members whose companies are directly regulated by the agency. In 1991, the chairman was Charles Gadzik, a forester for Baskehegan Lands Company.

Four of the 7 members of the Board of Pesticide Control (BPC), the agency that regulates, among other things, forestry budworm and herbicide spraying, are certified pesticide applicators. In 1991, the chairman was Thomas Saviello, a forester who was formerly in charge of International Paper's herbicide spray programs.

An attempt to deal with conflict of interest on the BPC nearly backfired. In 1982, after PEST (Protect our Environment from Sprayed Toxins) repeatedly accused the BPC of having a conflicted structure, the legislature responded with a bill, LD 1723, that attemped to *legalize* conflict of interest on the board.[2] This is not quite what PEST had in mind as a solution. The bill, fortunately, did not pass as written—members with conflicts must excuse themselves from voting. But the state interprets "conflict" in a very narrow sense—when a member votes on an issue that specifically affects that individual or his or her company. Thus, voting on an issue that benefits a member's industry as a whole is not deemed a conflict.

Special Interest?

The balance concept implies that environmentalists advocating clean air and water, healthy wildlife, and forest-ecosystem integrity are a "special interest" in the same class as industrial landowners who would ignore such values in a single-minded pursuit of cheap fiber. Whereas industry's prime motivation is direct financial gain, environmental motivation is often ethical. If preserving the earth for future generations is considered a "special interest," then a logical conclusion is that this is not the "general interest" of society and government.

Compromise

The balance argument rests on the assumption that compromise is always good. But not every issue is amenable to compromise as King Solomon demonstrated by threatening to cut a disputed baby in half. Current policies on clearcuts or herbicides, for example, do nothing to reduce reliance on these practices—at best only mitigation is promised. Compromises that only slow the rate at which problems are increasing hardly solve problems.

Balance

The concept of balance becomes even less credible when one considers that many of the organizations, such as MAS, that are supposed to balance industry receive industry donations and have industry members on their own boards.

J. Mason Morfit, former director of The Nature Conservancy (TNC), for example, was supposed to be the "environmentalist" to balance "industry" representative Edward Johnston (of the Maine Forest Products Council) and "government" representative Edwin Meadows on the Governors' Task Force of the Northern Forest Lands Study. But TNC hardly represents a strong opposing voice.

In response to an article in the *Portland Press Herald* that accused environmental groups of being "antibusiness," Morfit wrote, "I can assure your readers that The Nature Conservancy is not 'arrayed against' any business group; nor do we consider ourselves a 'foe' of the business community. . . .

"Almost half the members of The Nature Conservancy's national board of governors are current or former senior officers of business corporations, many ranked high among the Fortune 500. Similarly, current or former senior officers of Maine-based corporations, including some of the state's largest, make up about half of the membership of the Maine chapter's board of trustees.

"It seems extremely unlikely that these business leaders would work as hard as they do on behalf of The Nature Conservancy if we were, in fact, 'foes' of the corporate sector."[3]

During working sessions on the Forest Practices Act, one of the groups, besides MAS, that was supposed to balance industry representatives was the Small Woodlot Owners Association of Maine (SWOAM). Whereas in Sweden woodlot owners are organized to bargain collectively with the paper industry, in Maine they are not. One of SWOAM's directors at large is Cliff Swenson of Seven Islands (which manages nearly a million acres of forestland in Maine). Another is Fred Knight, director of the industry-funded Cooperative Forestry Research Unit and former dean of the College of Forest Resources. The list of corporate contributors to SWOAM reads like a Who's Who of the paper and lumber industries and includes such familiar names as Boise Cascade, Madison Paper, Great Northern, Diamond Occidental, James River, Seven Islands, and the Paper Industry Information Office.

Rather than acting as a balance to industry, SWOAM is often used by industry to further its own needs. Industry lobbyists, for example, have argued for government tax breaks and subsidies for the woodlot owners. This appears to be a gracious gesture, especially when industrial landowners themselves are excluded from such subsidies. But it would be preferable for industry to pay woodlot owners a decent price for their wood so subsides are unnecessary. The subsidies to woodlot owners are an indirect subsidy to the mills.

Musical Chairs

One problem with Maine's "balanced" government is that it is sometimes hard to identify the players without their hats on. Representatives of environmental groups, industry, and government have been playing musical chairs, switching from one interest group to the next in confusing patterns:[4]

Industry hat off, government hat on:

Who	Former Position	New Position
Robert LaBonta	Scott Paper	Commissioner, DOC
Edwin Meadows	Seven Islands	Head, BPL; commissioner, DOC
John Cashwell	Georgia-Pacific	Head, MFS
Vladek Kolman	J. D. Irving	Forester, MFS, forest management
Thomas Charles	Seven Islands	Forester, BPL
Dean Marriott	E. C. Jordan (engineering firm)	Commissioner, DEP

Environmental hat off, government hat on:

Who	Former Position	New Position
Richard Anderson	Director, MAS	Commissioner, DOC
Robert Gardiner	Director, NRCM	Head, BPL
Dean Marriott	Treasurer, MAS	Commissioner, DEP

Government hat off, industry hat on:

Who	Former Position	New Position
Richard Anderson	Commissioner, DOC	Consultant for developers
Kenneth Stratton	Head, MFS	Consultant for developer
Lloyd Irland	Forest Insect Manager; Head, BPL; State Economist	Consultant, with contracts from paper and chemical companies
Alec Giffen	Head, LURC	Consultant
Thomas Rumpf	Forest Insect Manager	RCS

Environmental hat off, industry hat on:

Who	Former Position	New Position
Richard Anderson	Director, MAS	Consultant
William Ginn	Director, MAS	Head, RCS
Charles Hewett	Director, MAS	Swift River (develops biomass plants)

Initials:
DEP = Department of Environmental Protection
DOC = Department of Conservation
LURC = Land Use Regulation Commission
MAS = Maine Audubon Society
MFS = Maine Forest Service
NRCM = Natural Resources Council of Maine
RCS = Resource Conservation Services (a business that handles paper-industry sludge and ash)
Note: Most of these changes occurred from 1980 to 1989.

Ethics

For those frustrated by apparent conflicts of interest on so many levels with regard to forestry issues, there is always recourse to the state's Commission on Governmental Ethics and Election Practices. Paul McCann, former director of public relations for Great Northern and for the Paper Industry Information Office, was elected chairman in 1990. William Osborne, in *The Paper Plantation*, found McCann so capable of stretching the truth or even outright lying (as exhibited by deliberately misleading the public about the nature of LURC in an attempt to protect the industry from any regulations), that he dubbed McCann the "Minister of Misinformation."[5]

George Orwell's satires become reality in Maine when an industrial forester who sees woodlands as a pulpwood factory becomes head of the Department of Conservation; when an industrial forester who is a specialist on herbicide spraying becomes the chairman of the Board of Pesticide Control; and when a former paper-industry public-relations man, with a history of distortion, becomes head of an ethics commission. Beyond the beauty strip, words like *conservation, regulation, ethics,* and *balance* have an unstated, but implied modifier—*industrial*.

References

1. William Osborne, *The Paper Plantation* (New York: Viking Press, 1974), p. 239.
2. Mitch Lansky, "The Great Leap Backward," *Maine Organic Farmer and Gardener* (June 1982): 17-18.
3. J. Mason Morfit, "Nature Conservancy Not Foe of Business by Any Means," a letter to the editor, *Portland Press Herald,* December 4, 1990.
4. Personal knowledge of individuals listed.
5. William Osborne, *The Paper Plantation* (New York: Viking Press, 1974), p. 247.

Myth 6
State policy should be decided by projecting trends of supply and demand into the future and by developing strategies to meet anticipated demands or to mitigate potential shortfalls.

This myth is a description of the mandate for the Forests for the Future Program (FFP), a Department of Conservation policy-forming structure (currently moribund) which published a number of studies on forestry issues.

History of FFP
How FFP got its mission is instructive. In 1985, in response to citizen complaints about new trends in clearcutting and herbicide spraying, the legislature put together a Forest Practices Committee (a "balanced" committee with industrial membership) to hold hearings and suggest appropriate action. The committee discovered, among other things, that the state lacked adequate information, such as the type and extent of management practices, deemed necessary for setting policy (i.e., we can't act until we "study" the problem more). The forest industry, however, assured the committee that in the unorganized territories under LURC there was no need for further regulations—the companies were doing a responsible job. The problem, they claimed, was in the nonindustrialized forest.[1]

Somehow the committee's attention was focused away from establishing statewide regulations; it went instead toward recommendations to the state on how to manage its public lands and toward dealing with evidence (from computer projections) of possible spruce-fir shortfalls in the coming decades. In response to these dire predictions, the legislature created the Forests for the Future Program and gave it 3 questions to pursue:

1. Can Maine's forests continue to provide all the amenities demanded by society?

2. How can Maine's forests be managed to assure continued availability of resources?

3. What is the state's role in encouraging and promoting conservation of forest resources?

To help address these questions, the governor created a 7-member (2 of whom represented industrial landowners) "balanced" committee, the Citizens' Forestry Advisory Council.[a] This council commissioned more projections that showed possible shortfalls and identified solutions—one of which was "intensive management." The intensified practices, which will supposedly increase supply to help meet future demands, happen to include the very practices citizens were complaining about in the first place—clearcutting and herbicides.

FFP also commissioned "objective" studies on clearcutting and herbicides to help inform the public and policy makers.[2,3] One of the accepted "givens" of both these studies was the belief that we need intensive management to meet the future demands hypothesized by the projections. In response to public concerns over these controversial practices, the authors suggested ways to mitigate the problems through buffers (in the case of clearcuts) and skips (in the case of herbicides).

Is reliance on clearcutting and herbicides really dictated by the future? Is our only option to mitigate the worst excesses of these silvicultural methods? Can researchers peering into computer screens really see the future more accurately than gypsies peering into crystal balls? Is Trend Destiny? Is future demand Sacred? Is it really our task to force the forest to adjust to these projected future demands, no matter how unreasonable?

Chaos

In the last decade, some mathematically oriented scientists playing with computers have discovered they can create models that simulate the "chaos" of complicated events such as weather, fluid motion, or biological cyclic changes. But simulation is far from duplication or prediction. Even using the most sophisticated computers available, researchers cannot accurately predict the weather more than a few days in advance. This class of phenomena, according to "Chaos" theory, is highly sensitive to minute changes that get transmuted into big changes; hence the name "butterfly effect" (where the flapping wings of a butterfly in Africa "causes" a hurricane in Florida).[4]

Supply and demand for Maine forest products over the next 50 years are dependent on many such chaotic and unpredictable forces, some of which are far more significant than the changes in air currents produced by butterfly wings: climate change, wars, recessions/depressions, political upheavals, and industrial catastrophes. To understand just how far off such predictions can go, one need only look back at the predictions for energy demand made just before the 1973 oil embargo. Energy "experts" neither predicted the incredible leap in prices nor the incredible response of conservation.

Valid Models
A number of timber supply/demand projections have been done for Maine. In 1983 the James W. Sewall Company (which consults for paper companies) projected spruce-fir supply/demand to help determine the best strategies—including spraying, forest management, and improved utilization—for dealing with the spruce budworm. The authors (one of whom was Robert Seymour) modestly confessed that "...it must be understood that the future cannot be exactly forecast."[5]

Just to be on the safe side, the DOC hired a consultant, University of New Brunswick forestry professor Gordon Baskerville (who had made computer projections of the spruce-fir resource of his province a few years before), to tell the state if he thought the Sewall model was reliable. "Is the model valid?," asked Baskerville. "In a word, no, but that is not really the issue. Anyone who believes they have a valid model of how the future will unfold believes that the future can be rendered certain. Such people should be prevented from presiding over resource management for they are clearly misguided."[6]

But what he really meant, in a word, was yes—"In general, it would require an enormous error in the initial age class structure to alter the patterns of future development depicted in the Report.... Anyone with experience in the spruce-fir forest will be aware of the current predominance of the 60 and 70 year age classes, and the scarcity of stands in the 20-30 year age range. Thus, one would not expect much sensitivity to any *believable* scale of error in the age structure."[7] Such statements do little to discourage the misguided resource managers.

GIGO
A few years later the 1986 Midcycle Forest Resurvey showed that some basic assumptions of the model concerning the level of cut (186% higher than expected), tree mortality from budworm (also much higher), and the length of the budworm outbreak (which suddenly ended instead of continuing to 1992) were way off the mark.[8] Fortunately for the model makers, some of these effects canceled each other out and the measured levels for the entire spruce-fir inventory were "only" 8% off those predicted 3 years earlier (2.9% for spruce, 16.2% for fir).[9]

As late as 1987 the state was still publishing studies that repeated the "obvious" about the age-class structure of the spruce-fir and the imminent shortfall:

"The spruce-fir shortfall will be in the form of a shortage of older, large-diameter ('log quality') trees. The evidence for the shortfall is in the current age distribution of trees. As the graph below shows, there are now many spruce and fir trees over 50 years of age and many trees under 10 years old. There are relatively few young trees that are 20 to 40 years old now that will reach commercially valuable sizes in 20 to 40 years.

"In other words, the age distribution of spruce and fir trees will shift. The shift will be like a wave moving across the decades. The bottom of the wave now (supply of trees 20 to 40 years old) will move forward to be the shortfall of large trees early in the next century."[10]

To researchers it seemed "obvious" that the budworm outbreak that ended in 1919 would cause a big blip of regeneration, creating a big class of "old" trees now, and that the heavy harvesting of the 1970s and 1980s (to salvage budworm-infested trees) would cause another big blip of young trees.

Two years later, in 1989, Robert Seymour and Ronald Lemin, Jr., of the Co-operative Forestry Research Unit issued another report that showed a very different age structure for the spruce-fir forest. In fact, it is hard to imagine a structure that could have been more different. The chart of the spruce-fir type has very low numbers of trees in the 0-to-10-year-old class and almost no trees over 75 years old on good or average sites; the heaviest abundance of trees is in the 30-to-50-year-old classes—the very classes said to be at the bottom of the wave![11]

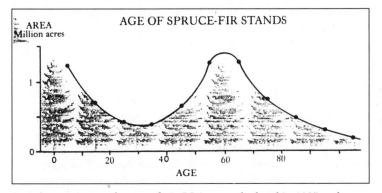

Age class structure of spruce-fir in Maine as calculated in 1987 and 1989. *From Sherman Hasbrouck,* The Forests of Maine, *(top)1987, and Seymour and Lemin,* Timber Supply Projections for Maine, 1980-2080, *(bottom) 1989.*

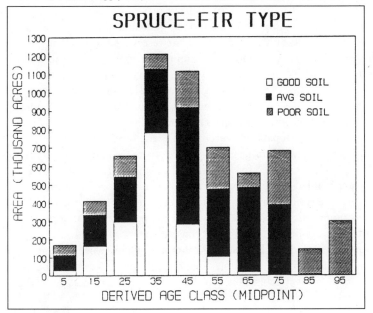

Questionable Assumptions

Besides programming in questionable "facts" about forest inventory and structure or level of cut, those modeling the forest economy also have used questionable assumptions about the frequency, severity, and duration of budworm outbreaks, the growth rate of trees under "intensive management" (i.e., sprayed with herbicides), growth rates of uneven-aged stands (all stands in Seymour's models are assumed to be even-aged), future regulations, future market changes, future economic problems, etc. Multiplying these levels of uncertainty together for a few decades leads to margins of error that make mockery of the impressive point-line graphs generated by the computers.

A report on the demand for Maine forest products done for FFP in 1987 tells us what the gross national product, inflation, interest rates, savings, investments, and labor force productivity will be like through to the twenty-first century.[12] While some of the assumptions based on demographics (e.g., that the housing boom will end) seem reasonable, others are no more than educated guesses that could be disputed by other experts.

Projecting Ideology

Seymour and Lemin projected the uncertain data and questionable assumptions of their timber-supply model 100 years into the future. Ironically, over the next 100 years their model doesn't even show spruce budworm outbreaks. Instead, the "intensive management" that is creating vast stands of even-aged fir will help prevent any imminent severe spruce-fir shortfall (though there will be severe hardwood shortfalls). The fact that Seymour and Lemin promote and justify intensive management (the model assumes that the average increase in yield from just one shot of herbicides on a fair site is 221%)[13] may be related to their employment by the Cooperative Forestry Research Unit which is funded by the forest and chemical industries to research such strategies.

By the time the information from the models gets filtered through the state and media, many of the researchers' qualifiers (the researchers are well aware of the flaws in their models) get dropped and assumptions appear to be realities to be framed into policy. The public learns to accept the vision as though it were inevitable. If the projections are inevitable, however, it is only because government and industry help make it so. These are not so much accurate predictions of the future as projections of present class bias and political/economic ideology. Government is not so much passively accepting a predetermined reality as actively planning to create this future. The future created is in harmony with industrial needs, such as the need for a continued cheap supply of fiber even if these "needs" are fulfilled at the expense of the forest or local communities.

One of the more serious flaws in such long-term projections is the assumption that an economy based on geometric growth can persist for 100 or more years without serious political or ecological consequences or that resources will always be available given enough technological input (i.e., intensive management). If one continues these projections long enough for all commodities, however, the only logical conclusion is that derived nearly 2 decades ago by the Club of Rome in their classic study *The Limits to Growth:*

"If the present growth trends in world population, industrialization, pollution, food production, and resource depletion continue unchanged, the limits to growth on this planet will be reached sometime within the next one hundred years. The most probable result will be a rather sudden and uncontrollable decline in both population and industrial capacity."[14]

By projecting maximum estimates of consumption into the future as if this were the only realistic option, such models do little to encourage conservation and recycling. Yet eliminating waste and encouraging recycling would create far more benefits and options for society—at far less risk—than pursuing a narrowly defined goal of providing cheap fiber for ever-growing industrial needs. It would be better to consider more desirable futures and use our modeling technologies to project backwards ("backcasting") to see how we can best get from here to there.

Endnote

a. The members of the Citizens' Forestry Advisory Council of the Forest for the Future Program were: Howard Specner, Gregory Brown (former dean of the College of Forest Resources at the University of Maine), Donald Hall (Christmas tree farmer and former legislator), Bart Harvey (forest manager for Great Northern Paper Company), Horace Hildreth, Jr. (president of Diversified Communications, Inc., and member of the board of The Nature Conservancy), Michael Robinson (Sherman Lumber Company), and Anee Tara (a consultant for Maine Tomorrow, formerly employed by the DOC).

References

1. Mitch Lansky, "Protecting Maine's Forest: Towns and Others Want to Regulate Forest Harvesting," *Maine Organic Farmer and Gardener* (September/October 1986).
2. James Balogh, *The Use and Potential Impacts of Forestry Herbicides in Maine* (Augusta, Me.: Maine Department of Conservation, 1990).
3. Irland Group, *Clearcutting as a Management Practice in Maine Forests* (Augusta, Me.: Forest for the Future, Maine Department of Conservation, 1988).
4. James Gleik, *Chaos* (New York: Viking, 1987), p. 15.
5. J. W. Sewall Company, *Spruce-fir Wood Supply/demand Analysis* (Augusta, Me.: Maine Department of Conservation, 1983), p. 15.
6. Gordon Baskerville, *A Critique and Commentary on the 1983 Supply/demand Analysis for the Spruce-fir Forest of Maine* (Augusta, Me.: Maine Department of Conservationm 1983), p. 22.
7. *Ibid.*, p. 24.
8. Maine Forest Service, *Preliminary Report of the 1986 Midcycle Resurvey of the Spruce-fir Forest in Maine* (Augusta, Me.: Maine Department of Conservation, 1987), p. 10.
9. *Ibid.*
10. Sherman Hasbrouck,*The Forests of Maine* (Orono, Me.: University of Maine, 1987), p. 10.
11. Robert Seymour and Ronald Lemin, Jr., *Timber Supply Projections for Maine, 1980-2080*, CFRU Research Bulletin 7 (Orono, Me.: Maine Agricultural Experiment Station, University of Maine, 1987), p. 6.
12. Keith Balter and John Veltkamp, *Report on the Demand for Forest Products in Maine* (Augusta, Me.: Forest for the Future Program, Maine Department of Conservation, 1987).
13. Robert Seymour and Ronald Lemin, Jr., *Timber Supply*, p. 9.
14. Donella Meadows, Dennis Meadows, Jorgen Raders, and William Behrens III, *The Limits to Growth* (New York: Universe Books, 1974), p. 24.

Research

Industrial foresters often turn visionary when describing the great "technological innovations" that will bring vast benefits to the forest of the future. These innovations are a result of research going on today. Research, therefore, is a good place to look to get an idea where forestry in Maine could go, or to be more accurate, where those with influence would like it to go.

The major forestry researchers in Maine are the Maine Agricultural Experiment Station (MAES) of the University of Maine, the Cooperative Forestry Research Unit (CFRU, located at the University but mostly privately funded), and the USDA Forest Service's Northeastern Experiment Station and its Penobscot Experimental Forest. Since some of this research is funded by the public through taxpayer dollars, one would assume there would be major benefits to the public from it.

Myth 1

The primary goal of most forestry research in Maine is to benefit the forest and the public.

If this myth were true, we would find that the bulk of research was being done to sustain or improve such forest values as ecological stability, biodiversity, water quality, water flow, aesthetics, recreation, timber productivity and quality, jobs, and local community stability. Much of this research, however, is done to benefit industry, to promote its single-minded need for more fiber—often at the expense of these other factors. There are two reasons for this industrial orientation to research: money and influence. The MAES and especially the CFRU are heavily funded by industry and also have strong industry presence on their research advisory committees.[a]

Using university professors to serve the needs of industry is a nationwide phenomenon. "Universities," states Jack Kloppenburg, a professor at University of Wisconsin, "are becoming, quite literally, marketplaces for knowledge. And as universities become marketplaces, they respond to those who have the deepest pockets. There is plenty of demand within society for different kinds of research, but as economists would point out, it is 'effective demand'—demand backed by dollars—that gets a response. If technological options are going to be established and maintained, then the continued penetration of universities by narrow economic interests cannot be permitted."[1]

The USDA Forest Service's Penobscot Experimental Forest (PEF) in Bradley is not as directly influenced by industry funding and advisors. The land, however, is not federally owned; it is cooperatively owned by Georgia-Pacific, Irving, Champion, Seven Islands, J. M. Huber, James W. Sewall, Prentiss and Carlisle, International Paper, Boise-Cascade, Scott, and Diamond. The owners have a 3-member operating committee which recommends stumpage fees, administers right-of-way leases, and is involved in other aspects of land administration as well as informing owners about PEF activities. Income from sale of stumpage is used to pay property taxes, acquire additional land, and finance research. A decade ago the PEF had an advisory committee (like the other 2 organizations), but the USDA Forest Service outlawed such entities and the landowners have no official input into the direction of research. Thus, with the PEF, money and research priorities are mostly federal.[2]

Industrial Priorities

While the CFRU and MAES do some basic research that would be useful to the general public, much of the research is devoted to forestry techniques that will decrease biological diversity and woods-related jobs. For example, the MAES 1989 Forest Resources Advisory Committee (FRAC) annual report included a report (by three industrial foresters) on "Integrated Research on Forest Productivity and Vegetation Control" which listed for its research agenda such items as herbicide release, herbicide thinning, biomass harvesting, plantation management, and industrial waste application for fertilization.[3] There are even industrially sponsored wildlife studies that attempt to prove, as did a paper by R. A. Lautenschlager and M. L. McCormack, Jr., that "herbicide release may increase plant species diversity."[4]

The CFRU, being more industrially dominated, is even more industrially oriented. These "competitive" paper companies display an astonishing cooperative spirit in funding and running the research. Much of the research is useful for companies who are wondering what to do with the "forest" now that it's

The Cooperative Forestry Research Unit demonstrates how to thin young softwood stands with herbicides. *Photo by Maxwell McCormack, Jr.*

been leveled—i.e., planting monocultures, spraying and thinning with herbicides, and fertilizing with sludge or chemicals. The most highly funded research
activity at the CFRU is finding new ways to use herbicides. CFRU researchers
are also responsible for computer projections (used by the state) of timber supply
which justify the intensive forest practices that the CFRU is paid by industry to
research.[5]

The PEF conducts research on a wide variety of management options, including commercial clearcuts, shelterwood cuts, strip cuts, thinning, and fertili-

USDA Forest Service forester, Robert Frank, shows off a larger
white pine tree in the selection of forests of the Penobscot Experimental Forest in Bradley. *Photo by Mitch Lansky.*

zation. It has never, however, tested herbicides or chemical insecticides. Of great interest to those seeking alternatives to current industry trends are its 4 decades of research on selection cutting. The selection projects began when idealistic USDA foresters thought this method was "intensive" and had major benefits over the commercial clearcuts and diameter-limit cuts of the time. The public is fortunate that somehow these experiments have been allowed to continue, but funding is not at all secure—in fact in 1990 the Orono office of the Northeastern Experiment Station of the USDA Forest Service was almost closed down.

Subsidy

To the extent that any of these organizations use public money to support research that is against the public interest (i.e., it is ecologically or socially regressive), it constitutes not only tacit government approval of industrial goals but subsidization.

Endnote

a. The University gets both public (as MAES) and private funding for research. Industrial influence on research priorities for this public institution is obvious from the 1989 makeup of the Forest Resources Advisory Committee:[6]

Reginald Elwell (Dead River Company, chairman), Anthony Filauro (Georgia-Pacific, vice- chairman), John Cashwell (Maine Forest Service, previously Georgia-Pacific), Michael Cline (Maine Audubon Society, previously International Paper), Peter Ludwig (Champion International), Hewlette Crawford (USDA Forest Service, wildlife), Gary Donovan (Maine Department of Inland Fisheries and Wildlife), Fred Hurley (MDIFW), Jack Hauptman (Acadia National Park), Charles Hewett (Swift River, previously director of Maine Audubon Society), Peter Lawrence (Small Woodlot Owners Association of Maine), David Maass (Irland Group, previously Scott Paper and the Paper Industry Information Office), Edwin Meadows (Department of Conservation, previously Seven Islands), Lawrence Philbrook (Prentiss and Carlisle, which owns and manages forestland), Bradford Wellman (Pingree Associates, also MAS trustee), and Gary Whiting (Wellons Inc., previously J. M. Huber Corporation).

The CFRU is mostly privately funded but does get some state and federal money, and its studies are also published by the MAES of the College of Forest Resources of the University. The list of cooperators and supporters includes major forest landowners, big contractors, wood processors (furniture, lumber, pulp and paper, and biomass), several state and federal agencies (Bureau of Public Land, Forests for the Future, Maine Forest Service, Maine Office of Energy Resources, USDA state and private forestry), and representatives of the 2 other major research organizations—USDA Northeastern Experiment Station and the MAES, chemical companies (Dow, E. I. du Pont, Monsanto, Sandoz), and companies that spread chemicals or sludge.[7]

The CFRU also has an Advisory Committee dominated by industrial landowners (1989):[8]

Michael Coffman, chairman (Champion International), Thomas Colgan, vice-chairman (Scott Paper), Clifford Swenson (Seven Islands Land Company), Thomas Morrison (Maine Bureau of Public Land), Fred Knight (dean of college, director of CFRU), Barton Blum (USDA Forest Service), Edward Chase (Chase Tree Farm), Gilles Couturier (Fraser, Inc., a division of Noranda, Canada's largest paper company), Roger Day (Maine Power Services), Russ Hewett (Pride Manufacturing Company), David Oxley (J. D. Irving, Ltd.), Thomas Saviello (International Paper, also chairman of Board of Pesticide Control), Richard Sirken (Georgia-Pacific), John Stowell (Timberlands, Inc.), Robert Withrow (Boise-Cascade), Robert Wright (Great Northern, bought out by Georgia-Pacific after this list was published; Wright was fired.), and Edwin Meadows (Maine DOC, liason to FRAC, formerly with Seven Islands).

References

1. Jack Kloppenburg, "Biopesticides and Economic Democracy," *Global Pesticide Campaign.*, Vol. 1, No. 2 (January 1991): 5.

2. Robert Frank, personal communication, spring 1990.
3. Forest Resources Advisory Committee, *1989 Annual Report*, Miscellaneous Report 342 (Orono, Me.: Maine Agricultural Experiment Station, University of Maine, February 1990), p. 3.
4. *Ibid.*, p. 12.
5. See, for example, Cooperative Forestry Research Unit, *1987 Annual Report* (Orono, Me.: University of Maine, 1988).
6. Forest Resources Advisory Committee, *1989 Annual Report*.
7. Cooperative Forestry Research Unit, *1989 Annual Report*, CFRU Information Report 22, Miscellaneous Report 343 (Orono, Me.: College of Forest Resources, Maine Agricultural Experiment Station, University of Maine, December 1989), p. 49.
8. *Ibid.* , p. 48.

Education and Training

Just as today's research may be tomorrow's technology or management technique, today's education prepares tomorrow's producers, consumers, and voters. As with research, the forest industry considers it in its best interest to "help" government by providing a forestry curriculum for grades K-12, giving grants, hosting field trips, and allowing training sessions on company land for vocational and forestry college students. Industry, through its generosity and cooperation, presents the image of a benign presence in the community.

Students learn more than the facts formally taught in the classroom, however; they learn attitudes toward forests and forest owners:

•that the forest is a resource for careful exploitation;

•that the degree of corporate control over forests and mills is normal and not to be challenged; and

•that because of the scale of ownership, large-scale approaches to management, such as mechanized clearcutting and aerial herbicide spraying, are acceptable and rational.

Myth 1

It is appropriate for timber corporations to provide a forestry curriculum for public schools.

To schools with limited funds, free educational materials appear attractive, even if the materials subtly (or sometimes not so subtly) promote companies or products. My children, for example, have come home from school with a comic book about how important it is to brush your teeth. This message was conveyed by a superhero who just happened to be a brand of toothpaste (samples of which the children also brought home). In contrast, the forest industry's contribution to public education, Project Learning Tree (PLT), at first glance, seems far more responsible.

PLT, first initiated by the forest industry in the western U.S., has been used in 49 states, 5 Canadian provinces, Finland, and Sweden. From 1978 to 1984,

PLT received only private funding in Maine (the list of donors is a Who's Who of large forest landowners), but then the Maine Forest Service, under the leadership of Kenneth Stratton, polished up its image and pushed to use it statewide. The MFS, in conjunction with industry's American Forest Institute (which also runs the Tree Farm program), put out promotional material in 1984 that advertised PLT as offering "unbiased" and "balanced" "environmental studies."[1]

Even though the major contributors include all the big forestland holders in the state, PLT has been endorsed by various government agencies such as the University of Maine, Cooperative Extension, and Department of Conservation. It has also been endorsed by such groups as the Maine Audubon Society, the Natural Resources Council of Maine, and Small Woodlot Owners Association of Maine.

PLT proves its "balance" by having a team approach to teacher training that includes a forester, an educator, and a conservationist. It uses innovative multidisciplinary teaching techniques that use trees and forests as a basis for learning natural and physical sciences, mathematics, language skills, and social studies. The curriculum includes adopting a tree, going on field trips, learning about predator/prey relationships, and testing overcrowding of plant growth. It has students role play hypothetical situations where trade-offs involving forest values must be made. Students and teachers seem to be enthusiastic about the program. So what's the problem?

When PLT was first promoted for statewide adoption, its major opponent was Bill Butler of Friends of the Maine Woods (FMW). In a November 12, 1984, letter to the state School Board, Butler called PLT "propaganda . . . co-opting unwitting students and corrupting their teachers. . . . The destructive

School children learn benefits of biomass harvesting to forest. *Photo by Christopher Ayres.*

forestry practices which obtain on industry land . . . should be made known to teachers and students. The exploitation of the forest so that it does not afford jobs or tax support to the community should be discussed in our schools; the program now in place is meant to direct us away from such inquiry."

Using industry money for in-school programs, Butler contends, erodes the principle of tax-supported public schools. The state, he argues, should not have to be in a position where it must solicit money and materials. The paper companies, on their extensive landholdings, pay minimal taxes—almost none of which go to education. From the millions the companies save on land taxes, they spend a few thousand on specific education programs that fit their own needs—and for that are considered generous and benign.

The point, however, is not just the content of the industry-sponsored curriculum. Even if the material is superior to what is used in the schools, it corrupts the public education system. Children and teachers tend to associate the "balanced," "unbiased" learning material with the industry that sponsors it. Industry appears as a responsible member of the community (there are no in-depth discussions on the most controversial industrial forest practices) rather than as a force of exploitation and degradation.

Industry sees PLT as a public-relations investment. One can be sure paper companies would not invest in an educational program that would put their practices in a bad light. That educators, state agencies, and environmental groups endorse such a program shows how vulnerable the public education system has become to corporate invasion.

Reference

1. Maine Forest Service, "Project Learning Tree Promotional Pamphlet " (Augusta, Me.: Maine Department of Conservation, ca. 1985).

Myth 2

Maine's technical colleges train workers to manage forests.

Theoretically the technical colleges would be an ideal place to train and certify woodcutters to manage forests carefully, safely, and efficiently. An ideal place for this would be on state lands where foresters would mark trees to improve forest quality and woodcutters would have to meet strict performance guidelines. Landowners interested in managing forests would be able to hire woodcutters who have been certified as competent under such conditions.

In reality woodcutters were being trained for high-production tree removals on company lands. Students at technical colleges were taught important skills in equipment use and maintenance, road layout, wood scaling, work safety, and map and compass use, but the work world they entered when their training was complete was usually oriented to forest removal rather than forest management. This work world was dominated by piece-rate wages, Canadian workers, increasing mechanization, and increasing costs without equivalent increased returns from labor and equipment. These factors were not protested but accepted as normal.

Most telling about the technical college goals was that the "final test" for the students consisted of working for several months in a "corporation logging camp."[1] Once again the corporations showed their generosity and cooperativeness by participating in this government training program. Since corporate forests were the work reality, this seemed to be a logical approach for the technical college to take. But such an approach teaches beginning workers that the exploitive working conditions of the camps are acceptable to government. If the workers have problems, it is their own fault. Joseph Krug, director of the Washington County technical college for logging explained to his students that "Wood harvesting, by its very nature, demands quality employees. Those who have been spoon-fed do not belong in the woods. The job is exact and demanding, and pay is based on ability, nothing else."[2]

If workers complain about undesirable conditions, however, they can be put to work in a "bad chance" where the wood is small in diameter and poor in quality. Even a highly skilled worker cannot make money in such conditions. Companies pay for the quantity removed, not the quality of what is left. If workers do not want to fit in, they quickly learn they are expendable. Why would young people want to enter such an insecure profession?

Although the technical college once had dozens of students in several classes each day, by December 1990 there were only four students enrolled, and by 1991 the program had been shut down. The main culprit, according to former teacher Carl Rollins, was mechanization. The college could not afford the big machines, and no one wanted to train to cut with chainsaws.[3]

References

1. Joseph Krug, "A Condensed Report of Wood Harvesting at the State's VTI's and What Is a Woodsman?" In *Proceedings: A Forest Based Economy: Carrying a Tradition Into the Future, The 1984 Blaine House Conference on Forestry* (Augusta, Me.: Maine Department of Conservation, 1986), p. 127.
2. *Ibid.*, p. 135.
3. Carl Rollins, personal communication, January 1992.

Myth 3
Professors from the College of Forest Resources at the University of Maine are an unbiased source of information on silviculture and wildlife.

University professors are expected to provide unbiased information not only to their students but to government committees and advisory boards on which they participate. Many professors in the College of Forest Resources on the Orono campus, however, get income, directly or indirectly, from the paper industry. The chief researchers, for example, of the Cooperative Forestry Research Unit, which gets most of its income from big landowners and chemical companies, are professors at the college. Indeed, the director of the CFRU until 1990 was Fred

Knight, who was also the dean of the college. Even wildlife professors get industry research grants to study effects of forestry practices on wildlife.

However well-intentioned the professors may be, if they are paid to research activities that seem wrong to their common sense, they will tend to feel a dissonance between their feelings and their actions. To end this dissonance, they can either stop participating in the questionable activities or change their feelings about what they are doing and convince themselves that their decisions are somehow rational and proper. This internal adjustment of one's feelings to end conflicts over difficult decisions is called "cognitive dissonance" by psychologists.[1]

I prefer to think that professors who are advocating or condoning large-scale clearcuts, mechanized harvesting, increased use of herbicides and plantations, or increased subsidy levels for industry are doing so because they have somehow convinced themselves that these actions are actually good, or perhaps necessary. To think that they are aware that the consequences of these trends are disastrous for biodiversity, aesthetics, recreation, watershed values, forest stability, timber quality, community stability, and jobs, and that they prefer to lie and deny for the sake of their financial security, is harder to accept.

For whatever reason, despite the large-scale damage done to forest ecosystems by the big forest landowners, forestry college professors are not in the forefront of those denouncing the perpetrators. They are far more likely to denounce destructive practices on woodlots than on paper-company land. Too often it is college professors who are advocating "solutions" already mentioned in Chapter 3—solutions that are merely extensions of the problems and do not alter the status quo. Since the very same professors are paid by industry to research such "alternatives," it is understandable why they might lose sight of the forest ecosystem for the fiber in the trees.

Reference
1. Leon Festinger, "Cognitive Dissonance," *Scientific American* (October 1962).

Myth 4

Students at the College of Forest Resources at the University of Maine are getting an ecological and community perspective of industrial forest practices.

Despite the fact that the bulk of forest practices in Maine fail to promote the improvement or even maintenance of any of the values people want from a forest, students at the College of Forest Resources are led to accept that industrial practices are rational, excusable, or even benign. This is done in a number of ways.[1] Their professors, who might be receiving industrial research grants, have developed a tolerant attitude toward industry—an attitude that students cannot help but notice. While the professors do teach a range of silvicultural techniques, some of the techniques, such as selection, are considered "theoretical" or "impractical" for industrial landowners and mostly suited for small landowners.

Students learn that practices that are unthinkable on a small scale become desirable on a large scale, as if ecological principles adjust according to ownership. Professors take students out on field tours of industrial holdings where massive clearcuts, herbicide spraying, or monocultural plantations are viewed as examples not of ecological disasters but of the options of "scientific silviculture." First-year students, who may be unaccustomed to such shocking sights, are instructed to pay attention to the positive aspects of abundant regeneration and favorable wildlife edge rather than the loss of a mature forest.

Those students who choose forestry out of a sense of environmental idealism soon learn that they are out of place—the University of Maine's forestry program is oriented toward industrial forestry, not ecological forestry. Indeed, as part of their training, students must participate in a summer program of hands-on timber harvesting—sometimes on industrial forestlands. Many idealists end up transferring to other departments.

It is not sufficient to have a forestry degree to become a certified forester in Maine; an individual must also serve an internship. The most likely employers for such internships are industrial landowners. For many forestry students, therefore, the ultimate goal is not to fight against or reform the large landowners but to work for them.

Reference

1. Conclusions based in part on interviews with students and former students in the Forestry Program at the University of Maine, Orono, spring 1990 to winter 1991.

Taxation/Subsidies

It may be better for the soul to give than to receive, but it is not better for business. Industry has a double standard for government intervention. From the industrial perspective, regulations and taxes are unecessary costs, or even threats to competitiveness in international markets. Subsidies and tax breaks, however, are incentives for better management, or even "compensation" for providing jobs or allowing public access to woods roads. Receiving is not only better, it is deserved. Whereas any public payment of private costs theoretically should be used to encourage private management for the public benefit, in practice this is not always the case—the result often is just cheaper fiber costs and higher profit margins for industry with little to show for ecological or social improvements.

Subsidies can come in many forms:

•direct payments for industrial costs, such as government expenditures on fire control or budworm spraying;

•indirect subsides, such as tax breaks to nonindustrial woodlands owners for management practices or for hiring a forester, thus ensuring lower raw-materials costs to mills;

•tax breaks, such as low land taxes, reduced capital gains taxes, tax credits for mill expansions, and tax breaks on pesticide sales;

•payment of less than fair share for government infrastructure and services, such as roads, sewer and electric utilities, hospitals, schools and police, Land Use Regulation Commission, Board of Pesticide Control, Department of Environmental Protection, Maine Forest Service, Department of Conservation programs such as Forests for the Future, and industry-oriented research and education; and

•external costs (industry-incurred costs that the public ends up paying) such as air and water pollution, aesthetic damage, loss of wildlife, reduction in recreation and property values, road damage, and loss of economic diversity.

The Chinese character for "crisis" also means "opportunity." Industry lobbyists have been able to turn the crisis of impending government controls into an opportunity to extract new cost reductions as "fair compensation" for any regulations industry agrees to accept (and it prefers to accept regulations that allow it to do what it is already doing). During hearings on the Forest Practices Act and the Northern Forest Lands Study, industry lobbyists demonstrated great creativity in trying to obtain "incentives" or "compensation" for a wide array of "just causes" through such treatments as capital gains exclusion to a suggestion (not accepted by the legislature because it is illegal) to tax woods roads as if they were actually forested and thus subject to the low rates of the Tree Growth Tax Law.

The purpose of this section is not to argue that all taxes are good. Nobody (except perhaps empire-building bureaucrats) wants to live with oppressive taxes that go to fund wasteful, inefficient systems. Burdensome taxes, after all, can also create external costs by discouraging public benefits. The high cost of workers' compensation, for example, discourages use of labor in the woods. This leads to higher unemployment and lower state revenues from personal income tax and creates higher costs from social breakdown in communities dependent on logging for employment. The point I am making is that the paper companies do not seem to want to pay their fair share. "Those cheap bastards," said forestry activist Bill Butler, "just don't like to pay taxes."[1]

Reference
1. William Butler, personal communication, winter 1990.

Myth 1

The paper industry is a major source of tax revenues to the state's General Fund.

One would think that the dominant industry in the state would also be a major source of tax revenues. Yet the forest industry has been highly successful at keeping down its taxes.

Property Tax
The unorganized territories, which comprise more than half of Maine's land mass and are mostly owned by 20 large landowners, contribute no money from property taxes to the General Fund. All funds generated, even those listed un-

der General Fund revenues, go to pay for state and county services to the unorganized territories. This is the result of the repeal of the Uniform Property Tax, an effort largely accomplished in 1977 by "housewife" Mary Adams (whose husband, Thatcher, is a tax lawyer).[1]

Of the 10.5 million acres in the unorganized territories, 7.5 million are taxed as commercial forestland under the Tree Growth Tax Law (see next myth). In 1989, of the $10,070,561 raised for state and county services in the unorganized territories, $6,852,519 were collected from taxes on commercial forestland (about $.90 an acre).[2] The balance came primarily from taxes on such items as homes and cottages, dams, and powerlines. This figure, to put it in perspective, is about 1/2 of 1% of the total revenues of the General Fund of state government for that year.

Income Tax

The bulk of revenues coming into the state's General Fund are from individual income tax and various sales taxes. The contribution of income tax from all corporations in the state to the General Fund is not all that great, and the paper industry pays only a minor percentage of that total. Between 1980 and 1990, corporate income tax contributed between 4% and 7% of total state revenues. In 1988 corporate income tax contributed 6.7%. Of that figure, the paper industry contributed approximately 7.4%, which means the corporate-tax contribution of the paper industry was approximately 0.5% (or 1/2 of 1%).[3] This paltry contribution has since declined.

In 1990 corporate contributions plunged to 60% of the previous year's level because of the recession and corporations taking advantage of tax credits.[4] In the late 1980s ample tax revenues were pouring in from sales and income taxes, so state legislators granted corporations tax credits and incentives to encourage them to come to, or stay in, Maine. In 1991 lack of sufficient tax revenues reached such a crisis that the governor shut down state government for 2 weeks while legislators attempted to come to an agreement on the budget.

Tax Incentives

The power of incentives is illustrated by the federal corporate income tax "returns" generated by some paper companies in the early 1980s. As a result of Investment Tax Credits (ITC), Accelerated Cost Recovery System (ACRS), and Capital Gains deductions, some companies actually paid a *negative* tax:

• For the years 1982-85, Great Northern Nekoosa reported profits totaling $427.8 million, yet it received refunds from the U.S. Treasury of $47.2 million for a negative tax rate of minus 11%.

• International Paper reported profits of $581 million during the same period but received refunds totaling nearly $60 million, for a tax rate of minus 10.3%.

• Scott Paper reported profits of $877.8 million for 1982-85 and paid $45 million in taxes for a tax rate of 6.6%.

• Champion International reported profits of $366.5 million for the 4-year period and paid $30.5 million in taxes for a rate of 8.3%. Champion's merger with St. Regis resulted in huge write-offs in 1982. The company received more in tax rebates from the government than it reported in profits: $300,000 in profits and $1.6 million in refunds, for a tax rate of minus 533.3%.[5]

Multinationals

Much of the state of Maine is owned by multinational corporations, some of which are foreign based. Indeed, Maine has the highest proportion of foreign-owned land of any state. Multinational corporations can reduce taxes through creative accounting. Maine currently taxes transnationals based on company profits in the U.S., not worldwide. A company like Irving, Fraser, or Daishawa can legally compute its operations in Maine as a loss and thus evade taxes, even though the parent company is making a profit.[6]

Workers' Contribution

Since the direct paper-industry contributions to the General Fund are so small, industry apologists sometimes argue that one should consider the income taxes contributed by employees and chalk this up as the industry contribution to the General Fund. A rough estimate of the contribution of paper-industry employees to the General Fund from individual income tax is approximately 1.5% (income tax contributes about 37%, the paper industry employs approximately 3% of the work force, but mill wages are higher than average, so I adjusted the figure up),[7] which is approximately 3 times the corporate tax contribution.

If the forest industry wants to count secondary benefits such as workers' income tax contributions, it would be fair enough if we considered secondary costs to the environment and social system. As this book documents, such costs are extraordinarily high. Since it is difficult to know where to draw the line when determining secondary costs and benefits of any policy, government economists find it easier to focus on primary figures. At this primary level, the companies are getting more than they are giving.

References

1. William Butler, personal communication, fall 1991.
2. Information from interview with Rudy Orff of Maine Bureau of Taxation, August 16, 1990.
3. Rough estimates derived from interview with Bill Gardiner of Maine Bureau of Taxation, August 7, 1990.
4. Christine Kukka, "It's Time to Say the T Word, Progressively," *Maine Times* (February 1, 1991): 6.
5. Kim Clark, Dennis Baily, and Robert Cummings, "Industry Casts Wary Eye at Tax Reform," *Maine Sunday Telegram*, August 3, 1986, p. 12A.
6. Christine Kukka, "It's Time," p. 6.
7. Three percent figure from 1989 report of Bureau of Employment Security, Division of Economic Analysis and Records, Maine Department of Labor.

Myth 2

The Tree Growth Tax Law is a method of taxing forestland in a manner that is fair to the public, discourages forestland conversion, and encourages productive management.

This myth is a restatement of the goals of Maine's Tree Growth Tax Law (TGTL). The actual effect of the law, however, seems to be to keep corporate taxes down and to provide a cheap source of raw materials for the mills.

Industry lobbyists presented the TGTL in 1972 in response to a report by attorney/researchers Richard Spencer and Mark Willis, who showed that the previous system of taxing timberlands was inequitable and caused the loss of more than a million dollars a year to the state in potential revenue. Certainly there was need for reform.[1] The industry lobbyists touted the TGTL as the answer. And they claimed that most of the benefits would go to woodlot owners.

The TGTL gives all woodlands a uniformly low assessment instead of taxing for potential development, supposedly taking pressure off woodlot owners to convert their holdings to condominiums. The law also provides for tax penalties should woodlands be converted to other uses. By basing the tax on tree growth rates, the law promised to lead to improvements in forest practices. The lobbyists also promised that this new tax law would increase revenues to the General Fund.

Fairness

In reality the TGTL turned out to be a major subsidy for the big landowners. Valuations did not immediately go up—after passage of the law, they went down. In fact, from 1971, the last year of the old system, to 1973 there was a 13% decline in revenues, a loss of half a million dollars.[2] Despite industry claims that it was fighting for the small woodlot owners (the law applies to woodlands over 10 acres), by 1976 only 4% of acreage under the TGTL was in holdings under 500 acres.[3] By 1976 valuation of woodlands not under the TGTL increased by 500%, whereas valuation of industry land had not quite doubled in the same period.[4]

Because the TGTL leads to large losses in revenues for some organized towns with a high proportion of land under the tax (there are 3.6 million acres of TGTL-assessed lands in the organized townships),[5] the state has reimbursed the towns for 65% of their actual losses—a figure that went up to 90% in 1990.[6] This reimbursement averaged $0.69 an acre, which is more than what large landowners are assessed for their taxes in some townships. (In the northern Aroostook County town of Westmanland, for example, J. D. Irving paid around $0.35 per acre in 1989.[7])

The TGTL is based on three factors:

•estimates of average growth (as determined by federal forest surveys);

•estimates of average stumpage (as determined by annual state stumpage reports);

•and a capitalization rate (which includes an estimate of the risk of investment as determined by state tax assessor). Industrial landowners have been able to reduce their taxes based on all three factors.

Growth

The last federal forest survey, on which growth estimates are based, was conducted in 1982 in the midst of a spruce-budworm outbreak, when growth rates for spruce-fir were low. Growth estimates are based on averaging productive acres with slow-growing, nonproductive acres and diminishing this figure even further to account for rough, rotten, and cull trees. From the 1972 to the 1982 survey, 600,000 acres of spruce-fir were "lost", but low-grade hardwoods (such as poplar) increased. This degradation of the forest was rewarded by lower tax rates because taxes are lower for hardwoods than they are for softwoods.

Stumpage

Of the 3 parts of the TGTL formula, stumpage is the one most subject to manipulation by corporate landowners. The average stumpage prices come from information supplied by landowners to the state, with no check for accuracy. For large industrial landowners, whose timber sales are internal transactions, stumpage rates are less a reflection of the value of the raw material to the mill than of the corporate ability to do creative accounting (see sidebar).

Capitalization

The capitalization rate is based on risks to forest investments. The rate is set by a formula that compares forest investment with other investments, such as AA bonds, and that looks at forestland transactions that do not involve development. The tax only assesses the value of the growth of timber, however; it does not account for the value of the land itself. A change in the capitalization rate of just one percentage point (based, for example, on an exaggerated estimate of risk) can mean a difference of hundreds of thousands of dollars to the state.[a]

Discourages Forest Conversion

Just how much the TGTL has discouraged converting woodlands into development lots is not known. What is known is that when high demands brought land prices up, woodlots got sold, TGTL or no. Most of the big landowners have their own real-estate divisions. Just how much land they are willing to sell is uncertain, since selling off timberland is selling off valuable supplies for their mills. Of the 44% of Diamond Occidental's land that got sold by 1990, for example, 20% went to developers.[8] The seller is not penalized by the tax—the purchaser, the one who changes the use, is. The penalty for conversion is based on a formula that takes into account the value of the higher ("highest or best use," or HBU) tax that would have been imposed over a 5-year period less the taxes already paid times an interest rate. Beyond 5 years, the penalty gradually diminishes. When the market is good (as it was during the land boom of the late 1980s), this penalty is considered an acceptable extra cost to a profitable transaction.[b]

During the debate over the 1989 Forest Practices Act, Edward Johnston, lobbyist for the Maine Forest Products Council, tried to reduce the penalty for withdrawing from the TGTL because, he said, it was discouraging small woodlot owners from taking advantage of the system. If industry was concerned about woodlands being lost to development, this was a strange way to show it.

This is not to argue that timberlands should be taxed according to their development value rather than for current use. The idea of a current use tax is sound; the execution via the TGTL, which grossly undervalues the forest, is not. If the state is serious about discouraging development in especially sensitive areas, however, the best approach is not through taxes; it is through zoning.

Improve Forest Management

The underlying assumption of the TGTL, an assumption that must be fulfilled for the tax to truly fulfill its mandate, is that landowners will manage in a sustainable manner. They will not liquidate their forests and then invest the money in a more profitable venture than growing trees. Timberland owners have long argued that low taxes would mean better, more sustainable forestry. Until passage of the 1989 Forest Practices Law, taxation had been the primary means of "encouraging" good forest practices on most industry land, since LURC regulations only affect the beauty strips. "Unfortunately," wrote Robert Parlow (who researched the TGTL in 1977), "taxation is an ineffective device for compelling good forest management."[9] Indeed, he wrote, "the overriding influence of mill prices upon forest management decisions could . . . be rivaled only if those taxes have increased to an unconscionable level."[10]

Although high taxes might induce forest landowners to overcut to meet payments, one forest economist, quoted in *The Paper Plantation*, argued that high taxes might in some circumstances have the opposite effect: "So far as the difficulty of paying the tax is concerned, its effect upon forestry is not necessarily bad. We hear of owners who resort to some liquidation of timber in order to meet their taxes. But we hear also of owners who, for the same purpose, intensify their timber growing business . . . Perhaps the tax nudges them into seeking more vigorously their best combination, whatever this may be, just as any other type of cost carries with it incentives to economize."[11]

While it is not clear whether higher taxes would encourage better management, it is clear that low forest taxes have not discouraged poor forest management. In *The Paper Plantation*, Osborne argues that the light land tax has been a subsidy to the landowners, allowing them to have a land surplus, which in turn has allowed them to control pulpwood prices and to produce pulpwood with low levels of investment in management.[12]

Besides the positive effect of a low tax rate on management, which is debatable, the TGTL tolerates or even rewards bad management in ways that are less debatable. For example, a landowner can cut a forest so heavily that it is not a forest any more—it is just a field of raspberries. But the land is taxed as though it were still a forest, and the landowner still benefits from cheaper rates. If softwoods are degraded to pioneer hardwoods, the tax rate may go down, as hardwoods are taxed at a lower rate. If the growth rate for the entire state is slowed and the level of culls increases, this, too, leads to lower taxes.

In 1989, as part of the Forest Practices Act, an amendment was added to the

TGTL that requires a management plan signed by a certified forester. Land-owners can take a $200 tax deduction every 10 years to help defray the costs of preparing a management plan. If a management plan meant good forestry, this would be a dramatic improvement; it would be the beginning of the desired integration of governmental tools toward a beneficial end. The paper companies, however, have had management plans for their lands for years, and one result are scars visible from satellites 500 miles above the earth.

What Is Wood Worth?: Capital Gains and Stumpage Prices

Robert Parlow, writing about the TGTL in 1977, when the federal government still offered a tax deduction on capital gains, suggested that the companies might be reporting one set of figures to the IRS, where higher stumpage prices would be rewarded with bigger tax cuts, and another set of figures to the Maine Forest Service, where low stumpage figures would be rewarded with lower taxes under the TGTL. He challenged the companies to disprove his hypothesis, but none responded.[13]

Congress removed the capital gains deduction in 1986, much to the paper industry's displeasure, and industry lobbyists have been fighting to get this tax benefit back ever since, bringing the subject up at every opportunity. One such opportunity was the debate over the Northern Forest Land Study. Industry argued that if it had the capital gains deduction back, its timber operations would be far more profitable and they would

Land taxed under the Tree Growth Tax Law—which supposedly encourages increased productivity. *Photo by Christopher Ayres.*

be less tempted to sell their lands for development. To support this theory, Champion International submitted a study that showed its stump-age returns in Vermont, New Hampshire, and Maine and calculated the difference in the returns on its timber operations if it got the capital gains deduction back again.

The stumpage figures supplied by Champion seem to support Parlow's thesis; they are about twice as high as the figures supplied to the state from Washington County, where some of Champion's land is based. If the Champion figures are accurate, and the state figures are truly the average, other landowners would have to be getting nothing for their wood.[14]

A Comparison of 1988 Stumpage Prices Between Champion's Maine Operations and Average Prices Reported to State from Washington County

Product	Champion	Washington County
Spruce-fir pulpwood	$26/cord	$11.56/cord
Other softwood pulpwood	$16-18/cord	$6.95 (tamarack) $9.64 (white pine) $10.99 (hemlock) $12.10 (cedar)
Spruce-fir logs	$85-100 MBF*	$55.78 MBF
Hardwood fiber	$9/cord	$6.36/cord (includes chips)
Maple sawlogs	$100-120/MBF	$42.35 (hard)- $33.08 (soft)
Birch sawlogs	$110-130/MBF	$63.29 (white) $71.56 (yellow)

*MBF=Thousand Board Feet

State officials could not explain this anomaly to me, and when I offered this information to several newspapers, they declined to pursue the lead. I wrote a brief article on the subject in the *Maine Progressive*, but got no irate responses from industry claiming the figures are wrong.

Endnotes

a. At the time Parlow wrote his critique, the capitalization rate was 10%. According to Parlow, this rate assumed that industry's potential income every year is reduced by almost 40% by weather, fire, insects, or other destructive events.[15] Such an assessment of risk, according to Parlow, is rather extreme. Reducing the capitalization rate by one percentage point, he calculated, would have increased revenues to the state by more than half a million dollars.

Risks to forests are not synonymous with risks to investments. State and federal govern-ments both offer tax cushions for natural catastrophes. The IRS restores to the owner about half the revenues he or she would have received had the lost wood been harvested. The TGTL gives a 75% tax reduction to land burned, infested, or made unmerchantable by any natural disaster. "It is possible, therefore," suggests Parlow, "that the destruction of timber can ultimately result in an economic benefit to the owner."[16] The capitalization rate is now 8.5%, which presumably is more fair than the original rate.

b. In the town of Prentiss, a timber company called Dyer Interests obtained (through a trade with Diamond Occidental) 8,000 acres of woodlands, commercially clearcut it, and then sold it to Patten Corporation, the notorious developer. Patten subdivided the land and sold off the lots. The lots at purchase are still under the TGTL. The purchaser can take a few acres out for the house lot, pay the penalty on that land, and not suffer a major loss, considering the initial purchase price.

References

1. William Osborne, *The Paper Plantation* (New York: Viking Press, 1974), p. 182.
2. *Ibid.*
3. Robert Parlow, *Axes and Taxes: The Taking of Resource and Revenues from the Maine Woods* (Portland, Me.: Allagash Environmental Institute, 1977), p. 34.
4. *Ibid.*, p. 2.
5. Stephen Harper, Laura Falk, and Edward Rankin, *The Northern Forest Lands Study of New England and New York* (Rutland, Vt.: United States Forest Service, United States Department of Agricuture, April 1990), p. 68.
6. *Ibid.*, p. 123.
7. Barbara Miller, tax assessor, Westmanland, personal communication, winter 1990.
8. Stephen Harper, Laura Falk, and Edward Rankin, *The Northern Forest Lands Study*, p. 110.
9. Robert Parlow, *Axes and Taxes*, p. 7.
10. *Ibid.*, p. 8.
11. William Osborne, *The Paper Plantation*, p. 183.
12. *Ibid.*
13. Robert Parlow, *Axes and Taxes*, p. 28.
14. Champion International, New York Region, Timberlands Staff, "Changing the Landowners' Economic Conditions: A New Hampshire/Vermont Case Study of Champion International Corporation." In Clark S. Binkley and Perry R. Hagenstein, eds., *Conserving the North Woods: Issues in Public and Private Ownership of Forested Lands in Northern New England and New York* (New Haven, Conn.: Yale School of Forestry, 1989), p. 106.
15. Robert Parlow, *Axes and Taxes*, p. 31.
16. *Ibid.*, p. 30.

Myth 3

The public should pay a higher share of forest "conservation" costs (protecting the forest from fire or insect damage) on industry land because the public benefits from this land.

The original reason for the creation, around the turn of the century, of the Maine Forest Service was to fight forest fires. Fire control and conservation were synonymous. After the spruce budworm outbreak of 1911-19, protecting trees from insect attack became a major function of the MFS as well. Indeed, in the 1970s and early 1980s the Department of Conservation, of which the MFS is a bureau, had a budget dominated by spruce budworm control projects. This is a "shaving cream" approach to conservation, where the state sprays water or pesticides on the forests to keep them standing long enough for industry to shave them down.

One of the concessions environmental groups made to industry during the negotiations over the Forest Practices Act (FPA) of 1989 was to lessen the burden on large landowners for paying taxes on fire control. Until passage of the FPA, landowners with more than 500 acres were assessed for 50% of the costs of fire control; the rest was paid out of General Fund money. In exchange for minor regulations, industry got a major tax savings. Over a 5-year period commercial forest owners will see a reduction in taxes for fire control until their total contribution is only 25%—the rest to be paid from the General Fund.

Industry representatives argued that they should not have to pay a fire tax in direct proportion to the percentage of forestland they own. Controlling fires, they argued, is a major benefit not just to the landowner but to the public as well. The public, they contended, has access to and use of most commercial forestland. The public, through careless use, is a cause of some of the fires. Forest fires can spread to residential areas. Industry concluded that since the public shares in the benefit of the forests and can suffer the consequences of fires that go out of control, the public should pay a higher share in protection.

This argument directly contradicts the argument the same companies use to fend off regulations. When threatened with regulations, the companies argue that their "tree farms" are their own private land and the public has no right to dictate how to use that land. Farmers, however, do not expect the public to pay for crop protection. If the public is asked to pay part of the costs for protecting tree "crops" from fire or insects, shouldn't the public have some right to demand forest practices that are in the public interest and will make the forest more resistant to fire or insects, thus reducing costs of protection?

Myth 4

Landowners should be given incentives to manage for productivity (i.e., for Timber Stand Improvement).

Both Maine Audubon Society and the forest industry supported additional subsidies for Timber Stand Improvement (TSI) during the debate on the 1989 Forest Practices Act (FPA). I say "additional," because the U.S. Department of Agriculture's Agricultural Stabilization and Conservation Service (ASCS) already offers management subsidies to woodlot owners (the Forestry Incentives Program [FIP], and Agricultural Conservation Program [ACP]). Because of lack of state funds, however, additional incentives (except for tax write-offs for management plans) did not become a part of the FPA.

As with the federal programs, the idea was to give incentives only to "small" woodlot owners, not to large industrial owners. The argument that woodlot owners need to have their management costs subsidized contains hidden assumptions. One assumption is that woodlot owners cannot afford to manage for productivity without incentives. Another assumption (which logically follows the first) is that woodlot owners who do not get the subsidies are probably degrading rather than improving the quality and productivity of their woods—and without a subsidy are justified in doing so. Indeed, the "need" for a subsidy for management was directly connected to the creation of regulations that presumably would require (for the first time) management. These assumptions raise some important questions, the most important of which is, Why can't woodlot owners afford to improve their woodlots without subsidies?

One possible answer is that woodlot owners are not getting sufficient returns on their wood to justify investing in more productive management. If this is true, the fault lies in the mills for not giving adequate compensation for their raw material inputs. Subsidizing woodlot owners is thus an indirect subsidy to mill owners, who continue to pay for artificially cheap wood.

Another possible answer is that some of the subsidies are going for forest practices that are economically inefficient. With even-aged management, the landowner gets all the revenues from the final harvest (a clearcut), but the public is asked to pay part of the costs of plantation establishment, release, and precommercial thinning, all of which have high up-front costs with no returns for decades. At today's stumpage returns, many of these practices have questionable benefits. By subsidizing the follow-up costs to clearcutting, the government is encouraging economic inefficiency. It is also indirectly subsidizing clearcutting.

Incentives that encourage even-aged methods that simplify stand structure (such as purging out hardwoods to put more growth onto more desirable softwoods) may promote "productivity" at the cost of reducing biological diversity and stability. Such a subsidy may promote not only economic inefficiency but biological inefficiency. This once again illustrates the dangers of nonintegrated forestry policy.

Myth 5

Landowners should be subsidized to encourage forest harvesting that promotes wildlife diversity.

This myth contains the hidden assumption that landowners have the right to destroy wildlife habitat and that without a subsidy they would be justified in doing so. Owning a forest entails responsibilities as well as privileges. Forest landowners have no more right to abuse a forest, which is habitat for numerous animals, than they have a right to abuse individual animals, which, if they did so, would surely get them in trouble with the Humane Society. Air, water, and wildlife do not stay within property boundaries. Landowners do not have the right to degrade these transboundary values to the detriment of the community. Unfortunately, because the government has not been consistent in restraining such behavior, landowners have been able to act as though they did have such a right.

That said, there is still a problem: promoting wildlife diversity may entail expenses that give landowners no commensurate returns. A public subsidy supposedly would give the economic incentive that the market currently does not. One major feature (that did not become part of the final bill) of Maine Audubon Society's Forest Practices Act was a "voluntary" program to manage for wildlife diversity. The program required landowners to follow certain planning guidelines which, if met, would result in a per-acre subsidy for all land in the planning unit. The proposal, which was also outlined in Malcolm Hunter's book, *Wildlife, Forests, and Forestry: Principles of Managing Forests for Biological Diversity,*[1] would require an equal proportion of 5 different types of cuts: large, medium, and small even-aged cuts; group selection; and individual tree selection. The plan supposedly would encourage wildlife diversity by promoting habitat diversity. (See pp. 252-253)

It is doubtful such a program could be administered in a meaningful way. Would landowners who phase out of large-scale clearcutting be disqualified because they are not fulfilling their 20% requirement for that category? Do we really need to encourage forest practices that promote disturbed landscapes that are already common? How do you draw the line between what is marginally diverse and what is marginally not diverse? Such an abstract plan invites corruption in execution.

While I consider it totally inappropriate to subsidize paper companies to clearcut in the name of wildlife diversity, I would not be averse to some incentive for landowners to set aside and buffer blocks of land where there is no or very little cutting and to connect such areas with functional corridors. The goal of the subsidy should be to encourage habitats and species that are less common, and one of the least common habitats in Maine is old-growth forests.

Reference

1. Malcolm Hunter, Jr., *Wildlife, Forests, and Forestry: Principles of Managing Forests for Biological Diversity* (Englewood Cliffs, N.J.: Prentice-Hall, 1990), Chapter 15.

Myth 6

Reinstating a favorable capital gains tax for timber would make forest management rewarding enough so that landowners would have less incentive to sell forestland for development.

Of all the tax breaks and subsidies demanded by industry in the Northern Forest Lands Study, the reinstatement of a favorable treatment on capital gains was considered the most important. One letter to the NFLS stated that "Restoration of a capital gains differential is essential to any owner—industrial or non-industrial—who grows trees. The *time and risk factor* unique to timber growing must be recognized in federal tax policy."[1]

From 1944 until 1986, the IRS taxed capital gains at a reduced rate. For individuals the maximum tax rate for high incomes was 50% with a provision for a 60% exclusion of the capital gain from income subject to taxation. The tax rate for corporations was 46% with capital gains taxed at only 28%. This allowed corporations to exclude 40% of capital gains from normal income taxes. The Tax Reform Act of 1986 set the maximum tax rate for corporations at 34% and for individuals at 28%. Thus, though a major tax break was lost, it was accompanied by major tax reductions.[2] Industry certainly has not argued to bring back the previous higher tax rates—it just wants the previous tax breaks.

The forest industry argument is that the change in the capital gains tax means that landowners now have to earn 30% more to achieve the same net income.[3] The lower rate of return, according to industry proponents, means more incentive to sell for development, less incentive to invest in management, and more incentive to cut trees on short rotations for pulpwood, rather than on long rotations for lumber.[4] The NFLS proposed reinstating a discount on capital gains in exchange for a 10-year commitment on the part of the land-owner not to "develop" (i.e., change land use from timber growing).

There are many problems with such a strategy to "save" the northern forests. For one, the favorable tax treatment is applied to all acres, even though only a minority of acres are in areas desirable for development. A tax benefit with "no strings attached" (which was what industry proponents repeatedly demanded) could mean subsidies for forest liquidation with the only benefit being a 10-year wait before desirable tracts, if any, are sold to developers. While the tax break can mean substantial savings to large timberlands landowners (capitalized at $7/acre for a 10% exclusion, $13/acre for a 20% exclusion, and $20/acre for a 30% exclusion),[5] at best it would discourage, but not prevent, lot sales in high-value sites. If the state or federal government is serious about protecting specific areas from conversion, targeted zoning would be a far more successful strategy.

Looking back at forest management in Maine before the tax change, one is hard-pressed to see how the preferential treatment led to any tangible benefits over today's practices. Indeed, some analysts think the capital gains tax exclusions led to highly predatory management. Bill Butler, in his comments to the NFLS, called the capital gains provision:

" . . . the finest tax shelter ever seen. As interpreted, ordinary corporate profits were immunized from taxation. To some of us, it seems more likely that the existence of this shelter hastened the liquidation of the Maine industrial forest rather than preserved it. It may be a tribute to the fiscal foresight of those owners that they converted their trees before the favored treatment was lost. The effect on rural communities was devastating."[6]

Gordon Robinson likewise sees a downside to the capital gains exclusions:

"Ostensibly, the measure was supposed to encourage investment in forest management and encourage people to keep and manage their land. But the impact was quite otherwise. Georgia-Pacific Corporation seized this as an opportunity to acquire smaller companies while maintaining the book value of their timber resources. This enabled Georgia-Pacific to claim capital gains on the difference between the nominal price the original owners had paid for the timber, ranging from $2 to $5 per thousand board feet, and its value as of the first Monday in March in the year Georgia-Pacific cut it, which ranged from $20 to $250 per thousand board feet, depending on the date of the cut. The bulk of that corporation's income, therefore, was taxable at the very favorable rate of 25 percent rather than the standard corporate rate of 50 percent. This money management strategy was copied by a number of firms that were in the process of becoming giant international corporations. They accelerated the rate of cutting, hastily liquidating timber that the acquired companies had been maintaining to provide sustainable yield. As a result, most industry-owned forests were converted to mere tree farms, devoted primarily to production of small trees for pulp and low-quality forest products, if not outright abandoned."[7]

Despite predictions of catastrophic declines in earnings if the tax break were lifted for paper companies, immediately after 1986, paper-company profits soared (I am not implying that the tax changes caused profits to go up but rather that the loss of the tax break did not make profits go down). Indeed, with such ample funds the companies easily could have afforded much more investment in forest management if they had so desired. The demand for tax benefits with "no strings" is an extension of the trickle-down theory, where benefitting the wealthy will somehow benefit the poor. Unfortunately, the results in the forested regions of northern and eastern Maine, which maintain the worst rural poverty in New England, do not confirm this theory.

References

1. Stephen Harper, Laura Falk, and Edward Rankin, *The Northern Forest Lands Study of New England and New York* (Rutland, Vt.: United States Forest Service, United States Department of Agriculture, April 1990), p. 62.
2. *Ibid.*, p. 62.
3. *Ibid.*
4. Malcolm Hunter, Jr., *Wildlife, Forests, and Forestry: Principles of Managing Forests for Biological Diversity* (Englewood Cliffs, N.J.: Prentice-Hall, 1990), p. 284.
5. Stephen Harper, Laura Falk, and Edward Rankin, *Northern Forest Lands Study*, p. 63.
6. William Butler, letter to author, December 13, 1989.
7. Gordon Robinson, *The Forest and the Trees: A Guide to Excellent Forestry* (Washington, D.C.: Island Press, 1988), p. 22.

Regulations

For more than a century Maine people have attempted to reform and regulate forest practices with little success. The late nineteenth century saw a rapacious feeding frenzy in the woods that horrified some observers, incuding even a few in the industry. In 1892 the president of the American Paper Makers Association, William R. Russel, warned his group that "Certainly we shall keep on denuding the forest for as we are turning almost wholly to wood as a fiber...we are drawing on the forest rapidly. I hope that some wiser way of cutting our timber in this country will be devised so that we shall not...see the end of our spruce forests. We must either of our own volition, or by some government control, prevent the destruction. . . ."[1]

Because industry failed to self-regulate, the public demanded that the state regulate forest practices. Since forestry had never been regulated before, in 1907 the legislature requested that the state supreme court rule whether such regulations (in this case setting diameter limits of 12 inches for the harvest of pine and spruce) were legal or were, as some landowners asserted, an illegal taking without compensation.

In 1908 the Maine Supreme Court declared that:

"We think it a settled principle, growing out of the nature of a well-ordered society, that every holder of property, however absolute and unqualified may be his title, holds it under the implied liability that his use of it shall be so regulated that it shall not be injurious to equal enjoyment of others having an equal right to the enjoyment of their property, nor injurious to the rights of the Community.

"While it might restrict the owner of wild and uncultivated lands in the use of them, might delay his anticipated profits, and even thereby cause him some loss of profit, it would nevertheless leave his lands, their product and increase, untouched and without diminution of title, estate or quantity. He would still have large measure of control and large opportunity to realize values. He might suffer delay but not deprivation."[2]

With the legality of regulations clearly established, forest harvesting laws were introduced in 1909, 1911, 1913, and 1915, failing even to make it out of committee each time because of intense efforts by industry lobbyists (who considered the bill to be "freak and viscious legislation").[3] In response to these failures, Senator Sewell of Sagadahoc commented that, "This is as important as any measure which we have had before this legislature...but because it suggests a new idea, a new proposition, it has met with vicissitudes which such measures always meet. It was in advance of the times. It was in advance of the education of the people."[4]

In 1941 the forest commissioner met with owners, operators, and foresters to discuss regulations. They formed a committee to deal with the maintenance of "sufficient growing stock to provide raw material for the industry and to furnish employment to forest communities continuously or without long interruption."[5] The result, according to historian Richard Judd, was that, "To meet these objectives, the board recommended management practices similar to those generally in use."[6]

Not until 1972, when the legislature created the Land Use Regulation Commission (LURC) to regulate the unorganized territories, did the state enact any forestry restrictions. LURC, however, does not so much regulate forest practices as zone them into areas where large clearcuts are acceptable or not.

By the mid 1980s several towns had gotten tired of waiting for the state to come up with meaningful regulations and wrote their own ordinances. These local efforts helped spur statewide activity. Maine Audubon Society began its Environmental/ Industrial Forum in 1986, with a forest practices act in mind. The forest industry, reading the writing on the wall, followed a strategy that ensured that regulation, if it happened, would not threaten their operations.

The first step was to continue the strategy of fending off regulatory efforts through appropriate myths and threats. The second step, upon seeing that some form of regulations was inevitable, was to take control of the regulatory process. The third step was to ensure weak, ineffectual regulations that legitimize current practices and, as a trade-off, extract as many tax favors as possible. That process completed, industry could congratulate itself on being progressive—living within "strict" governmental regulations. The public could turn its gaze elsewhere.

Each of these strategies was accompanied by appropriate myths.

References

1. David Smith, *A History of Lumbering in Maine 1861-1960*, U.S. Studies No. 93 (Orono, Me.: University of Maine Press, 1972), pp. 336-339.
2. Austin Wilkins, "Maine: The Forests Belong to Everyone." In Ralph K. Widner, ed., *Forests and Forestry in the American States: A Reference Anthology Compiled by the National Association of State Foresters* (1968), pp. 120-121.
3. *Ibid.*, p. 121.
4. *Ibid.*
5. Richard Judd, *Aroostook: A Century of Logging in Northern Maine* (Orono, Me.: University of Maine Press, 1989), p. 260.
6. *Ibid.*

1. Myths to Fend Off Regulatory Effects

Myths that fend off regulations range from those that claim all is well to those that threaten dire consequences for a public that dares to restrict industrial practices.

The forest industry is already doing a responsible job and does not need to be regulated. If there are any problems, they are with nonindustrial woodland owners.

Industry proponents expect us to believe that a large clearcut done on industrial land is good management; but done on nonindustrial land (by the very same contractors with the same equipment in the same way) it reflects irresponsible management and unfairly gives industry a bad name.

Industry's claims of responsibility are contradicted by claims that they need to increase the intensity of their management to prevent a shortfall in supply. This "necessity" leads to a dilemma; either the forest has been overcut or it has been undermanaged—neither of which is responsible. Forester demands for forest fixes such as herbicides and biomass harvesting indicate that they themselves perceive the forest to be degraded. Since much of this land has been in industrial ownership for half a century or more, who else is there for foresters to blame for the sad state of affairs but themselves?

Forest practices are already adequately regulated.

LURC regulations are already sufficient, if not overburdensome, according to industrial foresters. Yet LURC regulations limit harvesting in only a fraction of the forest: near water, on steep slopes or high altitudes, and in deeryards. Even in these places landowners can cut 40% of the volume in a 10-year period. The rest of the forest is considered a "management zone" which in effect is unregulated. The myth assumes that it is "adequate" for 90% of forest cutting to be unregulated.

Industry can self-regulate its practices based on voluntary guidelines.

Self-regulation is pretty much all we've had so far. The result is not cause for public confidence.

*Regulation interferes with the free market system. It
takes away the landowners' rights to maximum
financial returns from their land and in effect is taking
of property without due compensation.*

Zoning to protect community values is a long-standing tradition that some large
forest landowners apparently would choose not to recognize. The U.S. Supreme Court has continually said that if a reasonable economic use remains after
application of a state or local restriction to land, then the restrictions do not run
afoul of the "taking" clause of the U.S. Constitution. The purpose of regulations
is not to prevent prudent management but to prevent destructive management.
Preventing destructive practices should hardly be considered "taking" land from
a landowner, but rather preventing the landowner from "taking" the values of
the land from the community or from future generations.

*Regulations are an unfair economic burden which
create a bad business climate and hurt the
competitiveness of industry, causing it to leave the state.*

The financial burden of complying with regulations that prevent forest destruction is not that clear. The cost of wood compared to the total cost of making
paper has steadily declined over the decades. The added cost to paper making,
therefore, from obeying harvest regulations should be extremely marginal. In
any case, the cost of sustainably maintaining the forest should be internalized
into the price paid for the wood. If not, the economic system will make sure
that the forest, and all of its values, are not sustainable. Allowing abuse of the
forest creates an unfair economic burden on other people who depend on the

A forest cut ca. 1989 under LURC regulations. *Photo by Mitch Lansky.*

forests' air, water, or wildlife now, and to people who might rely on forest products and forest jobs later.

2. Myths to Control the Process

Since fending off myths (and threats) were not sufficient to stop the inevitability of regulations, industry initiated the next phase of its strategy: controlling the process. The idea here was to be involved in decision making early on, and to compromise the process to keep the bill as nonthreatening as possible to business-as-usual.

Industry should have input in the formation of regulatory policy by environmental groups.

In 1986 Maine Audubon Society gathered representatives of the forest industry, environmental groups, government agencies, the financial community, and academia for its Environmental/Industrial Forum to help formulate policy that would lead to legislation. From the start, environmentalists had to listen to the concerns of industry and compromise to reach "reasonable," "responsible" regulatory policy. They did not have to listen to the concerns of grassroots environmentalists who actually lived in (rather than recreated in) forest dependent areas. Such representatives were not invited to this Forum. Part of the "reasonable" compromise was to recognize that regulations create industrial costs that should be compensated with tax favors.

Although it makes sense for an environmental group to try to understand industrial concerns, it is another thing altogether to have industry input in putting together policy initiatives. Following such a strategy, an environmental group is less apt to enunciate pointed criticisms of industry practices or to give clear statements of desired alternatives along with the principles behind those desired alternatives. Even before the regulatory battle, stands taken by environmental groups involved in such a process become compromised.

If there are competing bills, the legislature should make a compromise between the bills.

Once MAS came out with its FPA bill, the Maine Forest Products Council came out with a competing bill which had fewer regulations and more subsidies. The Energy and Natural Resource Committee of the legislature decided its job was to make a compromise between an already compromised environmental bill and a thoroughly uncompromised industry bill.

The committee held working sessions that were well attended by industry foresters and lobbyists. The public was not as well represented. It is not always convenient for working people to drive to Augusta during business hours to sit in on committee meetings. During these sessions industry proponents tried to stretch the bill even more in their favor. Were it not for state budget deficits, who knows how many more favors industry could have extracted, such as taxing logging roads as forests instead of roads, lessening the penalties for withdrawing from the TGTL, having the state pay an even higher percentage of fire control costs, or subsidizing woodlot owners' management costs? All of these were on industry's agenda.

The role of government should be to act in the best interests of the state and its people. If there are two competing bills and one of them clearly is not in the state's best interests, this bill should be rejected, not incorporated into a compromise.

Regulatory proposals should be refined by a "balanced" technical committee.

"Regulating forest practices" got transformed by the legislature into clearcut and regeneration rule-making. The object of the rules is not to promote better forest practices but to decide what pattern of clearcuts and buffer strips are acceptable over the landscape. The clearcut and regeneration rule proposals that came out of the legislature got "refined" by a 10-member technical committee that included representatives of two large forest landowners.[a]

Why representatives of the forest industry had to be included in a committee that would formulate regulations for the activities of these same companies is not clear. Certainly industry representatives could testify in front of any committee to make their concerns known. One would think that those writing the regulations—the conservation commissioner (Edwin Meadows, who used to be public-relations director for Seven Islands) and the Maine Forest Service director (John Cashwell, former helicopter pilot for Georgia-Pacific)—would already have been aware of the concerns of large landowners.

3. Myths to Weaken Regulations and Legitimize Current Practices

The rule proposals, after going through the technical committee and being written up by the Maine Forest Service, were aired at hearings. There, paper industry foresters and lobbyists tried to weaken the proposals even further.

The purpose of the rules is not to prevent damage to wildlife habitat but to "address" the problem, and not to promote better management but to set "minimal" standards.

In spite of a mandate from the legislature to "provide a healthy and sustainable forest," and to "address adverse impacts on wildlife habitat," representatives of the Maine Forest Products Council at the rule-making hearings in August 1990 informed MFS officials that their only mandate was to set minimal standards. Addressing adverse impacts on wildlife habitats only meant mentioning the subject, not doing anything about it. Setting minimal standards of course means legalizing practices that meet these standards, which means legitimizing poor forestry practices.

The standards proposed by the MFS allow landowners to clearcut most of a township in a 10-year period if they so desire. In spite of all the wildlife experts on the technical committee, the benefits to wildlife of allowing so much of a township to be leveled in such a short time are difficult to see. Clearly the standards are subminimal (see discussions in Chapters 2 and 4). Industry foresters felt the standards were not minimal enough, however, and argued for bigger clearcuts, smaller buffers, bigger cuts in nonclearcut areas, and shorter waits for a clearcut to no longer be declared a clearcut.

If half of those testifying want to change the rules to be
more strict and half want to make them more lax, then
the rules must be just right.

Since environmentalists were bound to protest the rules, industry foresters' comments to weaken the rules were given to "balance" the environmental comments. For governmental agencies that are more concerned with "balance" than with truth or justice, the result was that little change was needed.

4. Myths of Self-congratulations

With the process complete, the forest industry ended up with regulations that legitimized what they were already doing—most landowners no longer were regularly doing clearcuts over 250 acres. Now they can congratulate themselves on living with strict government regulations. Indeed, Roger Millikin (who played a crucial role in the proceedings because he belonged both to an industry lobby group and an environmental lobby group) in an article in MAS's journal *Habitat* suggested enthusiastically that the creation of these regulations " . . . provides a model of what can happen when we decide as a society to move beyond simplistic divisive rhetoric and address environmental questions as complex, interrelated issues driven by economic forces and social values."[1]

The forest is now regulated. Therefore, it is protected.

Regulation and protection are not synonymous. Bad regulations can be worse than no regulations. The hope of industrial lobbyists is that the public will assume that everything is under control and turn its attention to more pressing problems, such as flag burning.

Endnote

a. The members of the technical committee were Michael Cline (MAS), Robert Seymour (forestry professor, University of Maine), Fred Huntress (consulting forester and SWOAM chapter director), Ray Owen (wildlife professor, University of Maine), Gary Donovan (Inland Fisheries and Wildlife), Mark Stadler (Inland Fisheries and Wildlife), Joe Wiley (Bureau of Public Lands), Tom Charles (Bureau of Public Lands), Mike Dann (Seven Islands), Tom Colgan (Scott Paper).

Reference

1. Roger Millikin, Jr., "Nudging Toward Equilibrium," *Habitat* (June 1990): 48.

Public Forests

Public lands have an advantage over private lands: continuity of ownership. There is no danger that ownership will be abruptly changed by corporate takeovers (although policy can be abruptly changed through politics). State or federal governments have an ideal opportunity to set an example of how they believe the forest ought to be managed for the long term. The three major public forests in Maine are the federally owned White Mountain National Forest, which covers about 49,000 acres (32,000 of which are managed for timber); the

Baxter State Park Scientific Forest Management Area, which is less than 30,000 acres; and the state's Public Reserved Lands, which cover about 452,000 acres. These governmental demonstration areas of multiple-use management make up only about 3% of Maine's forest. Each has a unique history which has led to different management approaches.

White Mountain National Forest (WMNF)

The White Mountain National Forest in Maine is an extension of a much larger unit in New Hampshire and came into being in 1911 with the passage of the Weeks Act which allowed the creation of national forests in the eastern United States.[1] At the time there was much public concern over the effects of exploitive logging, particularly on watersheds. Ironically, some of the biggest protests were coming from the manufacturing industry. As a result of denudation of once forested hillsides, rivers were silting up so badly after heavy rainfalls that the water damaged mill machinery. The first purpose of establishing the WMNF was, therefore, to protect watersheds. The WMNF is also managed for wildlife habitat, recreation, and timber. National Forests are under the control of the U.S. Forest Service and are subject to numerous laws passed by Congress.

Baxter State Park Scientific Forest Management Area (SFMA)

The Baxter State Park Scientific Forest Management Area was also created in response to displeasure with destructive logging. Former Maine governor and philanthropist Percival Baxter personally bought 200,000 acres of land surrounding Katahdin and gave it to the people of Maine with the stipulation that it be kept "forever wild." In 1955 Baxter set aside 30,000 acres in the northwest corner of the park to be used as a demonstration of "scientific management" similar to examples he had seen while touring European forests. His purpose was to set an example of excellent forestry to contrast with the exploitive, destructive practices current in his day. The park is in a trust supervised by the director of the Maine Forest Service, the attorney general, and the commissioner of Inland Fisheries and Wildlife.

Public Reserved Lands (PRL)

Maine's Public Reserved Lands have a very different history, one instructive enough to warrant a brief recounting.[2]

Maine was once a territory of Massachusetts, a state that had the policy of establishing four 320-acre public woodlots (1,280 acres all together) for each new township. The town lot was supposed to provide revenues to support the town minister, church, school, and "courts" (the state). Later this policy was reduced to 3 lots, or 960 acres. When Maine became an independent state in 1820, it continued this policy. In 1832 the courts ruled that there was a problem with using town money to support the church, and thereafter the lots were simply referred to as the "school lots."

Prior to the mid 1800s, Maine had 500,000 acres of such lots, but some of the organized towns sold off their lots. Between 1850 and 1870, the state sold the rights to "cut and carry off" the timber on the lots in the unorganized towns with the remaining 400,000 acres. Over the years, the lots were almost entirely forgotten. In 1947, however, the legislature did an investigation and concluded that by selling the grass and timber rights to the lots, the townships in effect had lost title to the lots. Such a finding is not surprising since the salary of the Maine Forest Service's commissioner was paid in part by the forest industry at the time. A similar study with a similar ruling was made by the MFS in 1963.

This might have spelled the end to public interest in the public lots, but in 1963 White Nichols, whom former newspaper reporter Robert Cummings calls "Maine's first environmentalist," came to Cummings with the latest state study and argued that the MFS's conclusion was wrong. Maine really did have title and right to these lots. Cummings was intrigued by Nichols's arguments but did not get around to writing about the issue until 9 years later. In his first article Cummings asked why the state should be floating bonds to purchase public lands when it already had hundreds of thousands of acres of land held in trust. This land, he argued, could at least be used for recreation, and since the state owned it, the state had the right to regulate forest practices on it.

Bill Caldwell, Cummings's fellow reporter at the Gannett Press, wrote an editorial blaming the public lands fiasco on the Democratic governor, Kenneth Curtis, who had only been in office a few years. To defend his credibility, Curtis did what any self-respecting Maine politician would do—set up a committee to study the issue. Part of the study was done by James Erwin, the state attorney general. Erwin appointed Lee Scheppes, assistant attorney general (newly arrived from Texas), to research the issue of cutting rights. Erwin put a newcomer on the job, perhaps, because he assumed the issue would fade into obscurity. But Scheppes had just researched a similar issue in Texas and concluded that the cutting rights that were sold were only for the trees standing at the time of the sale, not for all future growth into perpetuity. Erwin suppressed Scheppes's report, but Cummings continued writing a series of articles on the subject until, in 1973, Erwin released a summary, and in 1974, the new attorney general, Jon Lund, released the whole document.

In the meantime, several other events were taking place. Some citizen activists, most notably Ed Sprague, lobbied actively for the state to take back its land. Harrison Richardson, a legislator on the Energy and Natural Resources Committee, agitated to create a Grand Plantation system that would create organized townships in which the state could regain cutting rights. Although this scheme failed to materialize, the committee did end up creating the Bureau of Public Lands to oversee the public lots.

In 1973 some of the major landowners filed suit against the state for harassment over cutting rights in the lots. The state filed a countersuit, and in 1982 the Maine Supreme Court ruled that the state did indeed not only own the land but had cutting rights as well. The large landowners had to fork over an additional 50,000 acres in compensation for lost stumpage on 150,000 acres that were still in dispute, bringing total acreage to over 450,000 acres.

Beginning in 1975, conservation commissioner Richard Barringer started a series of swaps with the large landowners to consolidate public lands in choice locations. These swaps were not without controversy (under the leadership of Edwin Meadows they are still going on). In 1985, when the BPL, under Robert Gardiner (former director of the Natural Resources Council of Maine), wrote up its Integrated Resource Policy, 70% of the Public Reserved Lands were in these consolidated units near mountains, lakes, rivers, or other areas desirable for recreation.[3] The BPL's description of these former industrial lands is one of the most vivid condemnations of industrial forestry to be found in a public document:

"Existing forest conditions are characterized by a disproportionate amount of rapidly maturing even-aged timber of diminishing quality. This is due to the combined influence of a variety of elements, including insect and disease infestations, extensive logging for sawlogs, market trends for shorter rotation products such as pulp, and a general lack of past improvement cuttings. . . ."[4]

References
1. Wayne Millen, forester for White Mountain National Forest, interview with author, August 29, 1990.
2. Bob Cummings, interview with author, August 24, 1990.
3. Bureau of Public Lands, *Public Reserved Lands of Maine: Integrated Resource Policy* (Augusta, Me.: Maine Department of Conservation, December 30, 1985).
4. *Ibid.*, p. 17.

Myth 1
Public lands in Maine have served as models of exemplary forest management.

The response to this statement depends on what is meant by "exemplary." For this discussion, I will use a number of criteria: visibility, ecological soundness, social responsibility, and economic viability. The logic behind these criteria becomes clear when one states their converse: management is not exemplary if no one sees it, if it is ecologically unsound, if it is socially irresponsible, and if it is done at an economic loss.

Planning
In order to respond to this myth, I must first briefly discuss how each of the public lands develops its "exemplary" policies. Planning is a process of determining what the forest is like now, envisioning how it should look in the future, and creating and implementing a plan to get from here to there. Without an alternative vision, one can hardly expect alternative management.

Although public lands have a continuity of land ownership that private lands may not, this continuity does not always apply to goals and directions. The goals of the agencies running the public forests can shift with changes in the political climate. The public has reacted to the management blunders they have seen on public forests by demanding more restrictive rules and planning guidelines which in turn have made the planning process more cumbersome.

White Mountain National Forest
WMNF planning is guided by a number of important pieces of federal legislation listed here chronologically:[1]

1891: National forests were first established under control of Gifford Pinchot.

1905: Transfer Act moved national forests from Interior to Agriculture (Forest Service).

1911: Weeks Act established national forests in eastern U.S.

1930: Knutsen-Vandenberg Act set up funding for management activities, including reforestation and thinning. Revenues used for these activities are now referred to as "K-V funds."

1944: Sustained Yield Management Act was established in response to declines of timber harvest on private lands. This act allowed the Forest Service to sell timber to keep mills viable by setting up Sustained Yield Units.

1960: Multiple-Use Sustained-Yield Act established that timber was not the "dominant use" of national forests. Wildlife resources must be considered in management plans, but managers have broad discretion in interpretation.

1964: Wilderness Act was passed in part because the public was dissatisfied with the Forest Service's interpretation of "multiple use." The Act protected millions of acres of undeveloped lands.

1969: National Environmental Policy Act required an environmental impact statement for activities that have significant impacts.

1973: Endangered Species Act required protection of endangered species and their habitats.

1974: Resource Planning Act required national forest plans every 5 years.

1976: National Forest Management Act set limits for the size of clearcuts and required management plans. The Forest Service was required to come up with long-term plans for each national forest. The plans require maintaining viable populations of existing native and desirable non-native species.

The result of all these regulations is a rather ponderous, top-down planning process. Since wildlife habitat protection and recreation are funded from revenues raised through timber harvesting, critics, including forest economist Randal O'Toole, author of *Reforming the Forest Service*, contend that the Forest Service has a built-in bias for timber harvesting. O'Toole feels that the prime motivating force behind bureaucracies like the Forest Service is maximizing their budgets—which timber harvesting accomplishes better than any other activity.[2] Each of the above acts was passed because the public was dissatisfied with the behavior of the Forest Service, but according to O'Toole, as long as the incentives to maximize the budget through timber harvesting exist, the unwanted behavior will persist.

Baxter State Park Scientific Forest Management Area

Originally, management of the SFMA was directed by an MFS silviculturalist under an advisory committee. Ultimate authority to determine if the plans were in harmony with Percival Baxter's vision of a "model forest" rested with the Baxter State Park Authority. Unfortunately this arrangement did not work out well. Even though the SFMA was established in 1955, a plan of action and attempts at management did not commence until the early 1980s under the guidance of MFS silviculturalist Vladek Kolman (a former forester for the Canadian conglomerate J. D. Irving Ltd.).

In 1985 forest activist Bill Butler heard that something was amiss with the cutting and went to check out the 3,000-acre operation. What he saw was a blatant case of exploitive management: loggers simply "cut the best and left the rest." The roads were a disaster zone lined with piles of slash. Wood was being cut during a period of low wood prices, and the best quality logs were being shipped to Canada. There was minimal supervision of logging crews. Butler and environmentalist/businessman Charles Fitzgerald sued to stop the cutting. The result of the suit was a restructuring of decision making and supervision. The SFMA now has its own resource manager, Jensen Bissel, who consults with an advisory committee.[a] The "vision" that Bissel is currently working under is to "show that a working forest can be managed for a variety of values—aesthetic, wildlife, recreational, silvicultural—and still be profitable in the long run."[3]

State Public Reserved Lands
Like the SFMA, the PRL have a short logging history that starts in the early 1980s. The legislature directed the Bureau of Public Lands (BPL) to come up with an "Integrated Resource Policy" by 1985. To develop this policy, BPL director Robert Gardiner put together a number of "balanced" committees representing the major multiple uses for which the forest was to be managed.

Every committee had at least one paper company forester and usually had a representative of large nonindustrial landowners as well.[b] If the BPL was interested in setting out in an alternative direction from the large landowners, it certainly chose odd guides to lead the way.

Having set up the policy, the BPL next set up a Silvicultural Advisory Committee to oversee plans and review management actions. This committee likewise had a paper industry member, Ron Lovaglio of International Paper.[c]

The BPL's "vision" for the PRL came from Maine's legislature which directed "...that the Public Reserved Lands shall be managed under the principles of multiple use and to produce a sustained yield of products and services . . . (that) multiple use shall mean the management of all the various renewable surface resources of the public reserved lots, including outdoor recreation, timber, watershed, fish and wildlife and other public purposes; it means making the most judicious use of the land for some or all of these resources over areas large and diverse enough to provide sufficient latitude for periodic adjustments in use to conform to changing needs and conditions; it means that some land will be used for less than all of the resources; and it means harmonious and coordinated management of the various resources, each with the other, without impairment of the productivity of the land, with consideration being given to the relative values of the various resources, and not necessarily the combination of uses that will give the greatest dollar return or the greatest unit output.

". . . and that such management should be effected by the use of both prudent business practices and the principles of sound planning . . . "[5]

Visibility
The Penobscot Experimental Forest (which is not publicly owned) has signs informing the public of its location, and once there, informational signs about the

management, self-guiding trails, and literature in which management results are summarized over the years. The public lands so far do not have such accessible, up-front information; if they are setting an example, they certainly are not going out of their way to let people know about it.

Although there are signs indicating the presence and location of some of the consolidated public lots, no such information is given for the smaller town lots. The BPL apparently assumes local people know the location, but often this is not true. Once there, there are no informational signs explaining what the BPL is doing. Likewise, there are few such signs at the WMNF or SFMA.

If you want to learn about management objectives, methods, equipment, labor, or costs, you have to do some digging.

Some of the information available to the public is misleading or simply wrong. For instance, there is a chart on page 167 of the Northern Forest Lands Study that allegedly shows the acreage of different types of management practices on all the public lands in the state for 1988. According to this chart, only 1,780 acres were cut out of the 834,000 acres of public land—less than 1%. Of this cut, 659 acres, or 37%, were cut by diameter limit, a practice hardly considered exemplary. I traced these figures to the MFS annual silvicultural report. But in that report, these figures are not labeled "public lands," just "other."

I then called individuals connected with the WMNF, SFMA, and BPL and discovered there were no data that coincided with the figures in the NFLS. At my request, a BPL staffperson sent me copies of the biennial report to the legislature's Energy and Natural Resources Committee. In the 1989 report the BPL declares that in 1988 it harvested timber on 6,277 acres and that "more than 90% of the area cut had been marked (individual tree selection) by Bureau personnel prior to harvest. On the remaining acres, small patch cuts or blocks were laid out for harvest with the largest opening being less than 10 acres."

At last, I thought, official data. After all, this was information sent to the legislature. Individual tree selection, however, is an uneven-aged method, and I had the impression from past conversations with BPL personnel that they did a lot of shelterwood cuts, which is an even-aged method. I finally called Tom Charles, head forester for the BPL, to get my information from the person in charge. Tom informed me that, yes, 6,277 acres were cut, but 2,959 were some form of shelterwood (either preparation, final cut, or commercial thinning—this was not broken down in his figures); 3,108 acres were individual tree selection; 157 acres were clearcut; and 53 acres were blowdown salvage. This means 50%, not 90%, of the acres were in uneven-aged management. Obviously there is some confusion, sometimes within the same department, over not just data but terminology.

Ecological Soundness
Management that is ecologically sound protects or enhances biological diversity and maintains or enhances ecological stability. All 3 public lands have a commitment to protecting wildlife diversity. They have guidelines for leaving behind den trees, potential den trees, and snags. They have guidelines for lighter harvests around riparian areas. They are committed to longer rotations for logs

than is common on industrial lands, and both federal and state forests have guidelines for leaving a certain proportion of older growth behind. The BPL has guidelines for creating at least 4 age classes of trees per square mile. It believes this will ensure both diversity, by increasing habitat edge, and stability, by increasing forest resistance to insects and disease.[5]

While on paper all this sounds wonderful, in the real world there are a few problems. The public lands do not exist in isolation. They exist in a larger context of heavily cut lands. The requirement for both the BPL and WMNF to allow 10% of their forests to have old-growth characteristics seems less than altruistic when one realizes that old-growth currently makes up a fraction of 1% of the entire forest of Maine and that this requirement would add (or protect, if they already are old growth) a whopping 3/10 of 1% to the total.

The BPL's interpretation of "multiple use" is "dominant use." For example, in the riparian areas (which are 330 feet from water edge, 80 feet wider than the required LURC buffer zones) where even-aged management is not permitted, wildlife is a dominant use and timber a secondary use. In the uplands, (which correspond to LURC's "management zone"), timber is a dominant use, wildlife secondary. Since any kind of harvesting creates a habitat for some kind of animal, it is easy to say that wildlife benefits from management and is thus one of several "uses."

Almost all the "old growth" for both the WMNF and BPL is in areas where timber is not dominant—i.e., in the riparian areas or in buffers around trails and campsites. The old-growth definition that the BPL uses is "characterized generally by the presence of tall stems, dbh of 18" or more and age classes exceeding 80 years (up to 150 years for longer-lived species)."[6] This definition is fairly simplistic. Maine's Critical Areas Program, for example, doesn't consider 80-year-old trees as old growth.[7] The value of old growth depends on its size and surroundings as well as its age and lack of human intervention. It also should have a certain proportion of dead standing and dead downed trees and evidence of a replacement stand in the understory.

The BPL definition allows the 10% target to be met with stands that may not have the full value to wildlife, especially if they are in tiny fragments surrounded by disturbed forests in heavily used areas. Some of the wildlife species that would benefit from retention of old growth include bird, mammal, and insect predators of defoliating and sap-sucking insects. Increasing the percentage of true old growth in significant-sized stands would promote resistance to insects and disease and thus promote stability. Present policies fall short of this goal.

Both federal and state wildlife guidelines are from the "old school," which believes that maximizing "edge" of even-aged stands promotes diversity. Both the BPL and WMNF harvest plans rely on even-aged management for about 50% of acres cut.[7] According to the Integrated Resource Policy for the BPL's PRL, up to 20% of a management unit can be "regenerated" (i.e., overstory cut) by even-aged methods in a 10-year period.[8] Whereas shelterwood is the favored technique, clearcutting (up to 20 acres, with a variance up to 150 acres permitted)[9] is allowed, as is the use of herbicides. The WMNF does much of its even-age management with clearcuts—indeed, wildlife biologists tell them they must do so to create habitat for species requiring poplar, even though the industrial landowners in the region are creating plenty of such habitat in surrounding forests and the species so benefitting are already common.[10]

Social Responsibility

Management that is socially responsible benefits rather than harms the local community, creates safe work conditions, offers equitable pay, does not ship away raw materials that could have value added locally, and does not benefit present generations at the expense of future generations. Whereas some of the public lands have attempted to improve their past performances on these issues, they have not yet achieved exemplary status.

Management decisions for the PRL, with the exception of a few towns, are made by the state. There have been instances where local people have not been entirely pleased with these decisions. Cutting was interrupted in two Hancock County lots, one at Duck Lake, the other at Great Pond, because citizens protested the cutting of old-growth pine and hardwoods.[11] The BPL is trying to become more sensitive to local concerns by having public input in the planning process. Advisory committees of 15 to 20 people from or familiar with the management unit are used as a sounding board for management plans. The plans are then presented at a public meeting where further comments can be considered. It must be remembered that the BPL did not wait for these plans to

Not all logging on public lands has been exemplary. A 1985 cut on a public lot in New Sweden. *Photo by Mitch Lansky.*

be formulated before it cut in these townships—cutting went on for years prior to the plans. Indeed, by 1990, 11 of the larger units and all of the smaller lots still had not gone through this planning process.[12]

Contrary to the fears of advocates of total private ownership of the forest-lands, the public lands do contribute some revenues to local governments. The WMNF gives local townships "payment in lieu of taxes" as well as 25% of cutting revenues. While most of the revenues from the original town lots went to the town, the BPL now gives local townships 25% of net revenues from cutting on their lots and 75% of camp leases.

Regional interests could be served even more if raw wood products were milled locally so more money could circulate in the local economy. Contractors cutting on public lands, however, can and have sold logs to mills in Canada or overseas. While the WMNF is near many sawmills in western Maine, it is also near sawmills in Quebec. Local patriotism is often not as good an incentive as higher paying markets. The BPL has established guidelines for when wood can be exported and has set up its contracts in a way that gives preference to contractors who market exclusively in Maine.[13] This mitigates but does not end the problem.

The existence of large public lands represents an opportunity to create safe, stable, local employment toward sound management. Since presumably only legitimate silvicultural practices take place on public lands, this could be an ideal training area for professional woodsworkers. Workers who demonstrate skill and care in their work could be certified, which would be a boon to private landowners who wish to hire workers to manage rather than exploit their lots.

Neither the BPL, WMNF, nor SFMA directly hire workers (and thus become responsible for insurance costs). Instead they hire independent contrac-tors to cut the wood. These contractors normally pay workers on a piece-rate wage. The BPL puts most of its stumpage out for bid. In recent years, it has discovered that large contractors can offer surprisingly higher stumpage rates than one would expect from the annual stumpage figures reported by private landowners to the Maine Forest Service. These large contractors, such as H. C. Haynes, have secured extensive markets and, because they can deliver high volumes of wood at crucial times, they get good prices from the mills. However, these contractors also are prone to hire Canadian woodcutters and have a history of buying large forest plots, cutting off the timber, and selling the land for development.

The BPL has begun to secure its own wood contracts to supply mills, thus allowing them to hire smaller, more local contractors who might not be as good at marketing as the larger outfits. Between 1986 and 1990, the BPL's contracted logging sales, however, only ranged from 2.8% to 13.9% of all sales.[14] The SFMA sells all its own wood in this manner.[15] Ironically, when landowners set up wood sales for independent contractors in such a manner, the fiction of independence becomes even more tenuous. The WMNF sells stumpage to contractors who market the wood themselves.[16]

Economic Viability

With their own land and cutting operations, the state and federal governments have an opportunity to reveal to the public the true costs and benefits of managing forestland in an ecologically and socially responsible manner. These figures should be well publicized. If it is possible to manage in an ethical manner and still make a good return, the public and other landowners should know about it. If the returns are insufficient compensation, then harvesting should cease or the government should help reform the markets. Exemplary management needs good markets. There is no incentive to private landowners to do responsible management at a loss. If markets do not justify responsible management, by inference we can expect irresponsible management instead.

The WMNF operates at a loss. In 1989, expenses (for New Hampshire and Maine) were $1.9 million and revenues were $1.3 million. The net loss was $652,000, or $.19 for every dollar invested.[17] According to a study by Randal O'Toole, national forests are losing money in all but the Pacific Northwest and southeastern regions of the U.S.[18] The Forest Service explains that these losses are due in part to the expensive planning expenditures required by Congress and to expenditures for recreation and wildlife. The "benefits" to wildlife (or rather to biodiversity) from current forest practices are questionable.

The Baxter State Park SFMA is likewise losing money on its sales. Much of the recent cutting is what foresters call *low-grading*. This means cutting only the poor quality wood, leaving a higher quality stand. Due to poor-paying markets, the costs of cutting and shipping products such as hardwood pulp are less than the returns.[19] Another reason for losses is the high cost of building permanent, high-quality logging roads. The SFMA directors consider losses from low-grading and road building less as losses than as investments toward a more productive forest for the future. These losses do not get paid by the public; they are compensated from the trust fund associated with Baxter State Park.

The state's PRL showed a surplus in 1985 and 1986 when the BPL was still doing heavy "salvage" cutting of spruce-fir,[20] losses in 1987 and 1988 due in part to expenses for management plans and to shifting harvest from softwoods to lower-valued hardwoods, and gains in 1989 and 1990 due to better marketing efforts.[22] Like the U.S. Forest Service, the BPL also funds recreation and wildlife from timber revenues. Since the budget for the Bureau comes from cutting revenues, rather than the General Fund, there is an incentive to cut to support the bureaucracy.

Conclusion

Although management on publicly owned forests has not yet achieved exemplary status—and to be fair, most of this land has only been under management for a decade—it still stands out in sharp contrast to management in the industrial forest. Public managers are neither creating clearcuts that roll on for miles nor are they conducting massive herbicide campaigns against invading weeds. Indeed, in 1990, the largest clearcut opening on state-managed forests was less than 2 acres, and herbicides were used on 6 acres.[23] This example suggests that perhaps clearcutting and herbicide spraying are not dictated by biological necessity.

Public forest managers are also paying more heed than their industrial counterparts to the needs of wildlife, recreationists, and local communities. Government agencies not only tolerate public input into their management plans, they sometimes solicit it. To the extent that the public becomes more informed about and committed to their forests, management will improve.

But then, the public forests, which only make up 3% of the timber base of the state, are not currently under severe pressure from industry to sustain their mills. Indeed, all the public land could easily be turned into wilderness without catastrophic economic consequence.

If the majority of the state's timberlands were purchased by the state or federal governments, one can be sure that there would be far more industrial pressure to increase the level of cut. The bureaucracy that directs the forest would be more cumbersome, with those in authority more separated from the forests and local communities that they control. One only has to look at some of the devastated public forests in the West to see what can go wrong. It would take eternal public vigilance to make sure that public foresters do not fall for the industrial myth that large-scale ownership demands large-scale management. This is a good reason to keep management units at a reasonable scale. Forest-management decision making should be site based rather than mill based, and primarily for the benefit of local communities rather than distant, centralized bureaucracies.

Exemplary Management on Public Lands—It Can Be Done

The Maine Department of Inland Fisheries and Wildlife (DIFW) manages 6,500 acres of public lands in the Dover-Foxcroft region of Maine. Mel Ames, a woodlands manager with 45 years experience, has been in charge of 1,800 acres of the DIFW lands for the last 11 years. His workers, though prisoners from the nearby Charleston Correctional Facility, are free from the pressures of working on a piece-rate wage. They are being trained to manage, rather than completely remove, a forest. Ames calculates the cost of their labor on an hourly basis. He is impressed with the quality of their performance.

Ames' priority is to maintain wildlife habitat, which he achieves through selection management. He plans on cutting cycles of 10-15 years, and is currently removing 1/3 of stand volume per cut—mostly in the form of poor-quality or high-risk trees. The residuals are potential log-quality trees.

Much of the wood that is cut gets used locally—logs are milled at the correctional facility, and firewood heats the buildings. Although the top priority is wildlife, the operations have been profitable, with the potential for higher future revenues as tree quality improves.

The location of this public forest is advertised on Route 15, and visitors can follow self-guided tours that help them to understand what they see. Management is thus visible, ecologically sound, socially responsible, and economically viable.

Endnotes

a. The advisory committee consists of Charles Gadzik (Baskehegan Lands), Robert Seymour (University of Maine), Robert Frank (USDA Forest Service), Ted Tryon (J. W. Sewall), Tom Cielinski (Bureau of Parks and Recreation), Jerry Bley (Natural Resources Council of Maine), Mel Ames (forester and woodlot manager), Charles Fitzgerald (citizen), Winston Robbins (citizen), and Dr. Robert Ohler (citizen).

b. The Timber Committee, for example, had 7 members, 2 of them Robert Withrow (Boise Cascade) and Charles Gadzik (Baskehegan Land Company). The Recreation Committee had 6 members, 2 of them Dan Corcoran (Great Northern) and Al Leighton (Seven Islands). The Wildlife Committee had 7 members, 1 of them Tom Hartranft (Champion International).[24]

c. Other membrs included William Leak (U.S. Forest Service), Robert Seymour (forestry professor, University of Maine; researcher for industry-funded Cooperative Forestry Research Unit), Gordon Baskerville (forestry professor, University of New Brunswick; member of Forest Protection Ltd., which runs New Brunswick's spruce-budworm spray program), Malcolm Hunter (wildlife professor, University of Maine), and Michael Cline (Maine Audubon Society, former International Paper forester). The head forester for the BPL, Tom Charles, was formerly employed by Seven Islands Land Company.

References

1. Cascade Holistic Economics Consultants (CHEC), "The Citizens' Guide to Reforming the Forest Service, *Forest Watch*,Vol. 9, No. 3 (September 1988): 4-5. Also, Malcolm Hunter, Jr., *Forests, Forestry, and Wildlife: Principles of Managing Forests for Biological Diversity* (Englewood Cliffs, N.J.: Prentice-Hall, 1990), pp. 291-295.
2. Cascade Holistic Economic Consultants, "The Citizens' Guide," pp. 4-5.
3. John Gerard, "Resurrection of a Forgotten Forest," *American Forests* (July/August 1990): 36.
4. Bureau of Public Lands, *Public Reserved Lands of Maine: Integrated Resource Policy* (Augusta, Me.: Maine Department of Conservation, December 30, 1985), p. 2.
5. *Ibid.*, pp. 18-19.
6. Maine Critical Areas Program, *Natural Old-growth Forest Stands in Maine and Its Relevance to the Critical Areas Program*, Policy Report No. 79. (Augusta, Me.: Maine Critical Areas Program, Maine State Planning Office, October 1983), pp. .2- 3.
7. Thomas Charles, Bureau of Public Lands, interview with author, 1990. Also, Wayne Millen, White Mountain National Forest, interview with author, August 29, 1990.
8. Bureau of Public Lands, *Public Reserved Lands*, pp. 19-20.
9. *Ibid.*, p. 20.
10. Wayne Millen, interview with author, August 29, 1990.
11. William Butler, personal communication, August 1990.
12. Bureau of Public Lands, *Biennial Report to the Energy and Natural Resources Committee* (Augusta, Me.: Maine Department of Conservation, March 21, 1991), p. 3.
13. Bureau of Public Lands, *Biennial Report to the Energy and Natural Resources Committee* (Washington, D.C.: Bureau of Public Lands, 1989), p. 6.
14. Thomas Charles, personal communication, December 16, 1991.
15. Robert Frank, member of Scientific Forest Management Area Advisory Committee, personal communication, August 1990.
16. Wayne Millen, interview with author, August 29, 1990.
17. *Ibid.*
18. Cascade Holistic Economics Consultants, "The Citizen's Guide," p. 9.
19. Robert Frank, conversation with author, August 1991.
20. Bureau of Public Lands, Biennial   1987. p. 8.
21. Bureau of Public Lands, *Biennial Report*, p. 10.
22. Bureau of Public Lands, *Biennial Report to the Energy and Natural Resources Committee* (Augusta, Me.: Maine Department of Conservation, March 25, 1991).
23. *Ibid.*, p. 10.
24. Bureau of Public Lands, *Public Reserved Lands*, p. 37.

6 Changing Directions

In the last chapter of a critique such as this, the author, who has been diligently analyzing the "problem," is supposed to come up with the "solution"—recommendations for new laws, for example, or for better policies. Yet, somehow, these recommendations, even in the most hard-hitting critiques, seem hollow. Something is missing. One wonders how, in today's political climate, the solutions could be implemented, or even if they were, just what problems they would actually solve.

For example, if a bill were passed that banned clearcutting, it would not protect forests from being degraded by legal partial cuts. It would not prevent loggers on a piece-rate wage from being maimed. It would not address the control of the forest and mills by a handful of out-of-state-based multinational corporations. It would not prevent leveraged takeovers of these corporations followed by subdivision and sales of choice locations for development.

If the federal government purchased the Maine woods, this also would not end forestry problems. Indeed, most forestry critiques in the United States are now directed at federal management of national forests.

Even if, by some miracle, landowners adopted more ecologically benign management practices, the health of the forest would still be at risk from air pollution or even from global climate changes accelerated by industrial growth.

The paper companies themselves say that their management actions, employment policies, and prices are driven in part by international market competition. "Solutions" that assume forestry problems to be isolated from this larger political/economic framework will not change our direction, and so we will wind up where we are headed. As long as we assume we must accommodate perpetual global industrial growth, local forests will not be saved.

From this line of reasoning, one can conclude that if we are going to save

"...We will wind up where we are headed." *Photo by Christopher Ayres.*

our local forests, we will have to save the world. We will have to confront the barriers to local solutions imposed by the larger political/economic context.

Distorted Models—Metamyths

Most of the myths discussed in this book are really subsets of larger metamyths—myths so well established that they are generally accepted *a priori* in natural-resource policy discussions. These metamyths are the tenets of the Global Industrial Growth Society ideology (GIGS). The industrial slant to this ideology is so strong that over 99% of prior human culture is now considered "preindustrial" and the majority of people now alive are considered to reside in "underdeveloped" countries.

Within this framework, the beneficiaries of forestry "solutions" (and thus the "owners" of the "problems") are primarily large multinational paper companies. Goals for the "solutions" are defined in industrial terms with industrial priorities. Priorities become inverted; the forest and society are seen as extensions of and dependent on industry rather than the other way around.

These metamyths are extraordinary for two reasons: the degree to which people adhere to them as established truth and the degree to which they are so obviously flawed.

Metamyth 1

The market is the most efficient means to regulate social welfare.

According to economic historian Karl Polanyi, the regulation of social welfare by market forces is a recent development in human history and is an inversion of what was formerly the case; that the economy as a rule was submerged in social relations. The prime motivation for social actions in more traditional societies is not monetary greed but kinship obligations, religion, tradition, social status, etc.[1] Markets, of course, have existed as part of society for thousands of years. They become a problem, however, when they preempt traditional cultural controls.

By the most obvious standards, such as the incidence of crime, violence, suicide, divorce, insanity, alcohol and drug addiction, homelessness, malnutrition, polluted air and water, or blighted landscapes, the market alone does a rather poor job of regulating human welfare. Indeed, by appealing to greed and competition, the market guarantees that there will be big winners and big losers in the economic struggle. If these losers get any benefits from the wealth produced by the market, it is through the nonmarket policies of government welfare systems or charity.

Since social or ecological stability are not major goals of the market system, it is only a happy accident if these attributes are enhanced at all rather than degraded. The claim for the great social benefits of the market can only be made if the "benefits" are measured by industrial criteria (such as growth of the Gross National Product), rather than social and ecological criteria.

Reference
1. Karl Polanyi, "Our Obsolete Market Mentality," *The Ecologist* (July 1974): 213-220.

Metamyth 2

Nature and human beings are market commodities.

In a society treated as a market, nature (land) and human beings (labor) are treated as commodities as if produced for sale. The forest is no longer seen as a source of life and a habitat to live in; it becomes instead the raw material for industry or real estate. It is "rational" to use up this raw material in one township or region if more of it can be found in another township or region.

For a large corporate owner, there is no bond or sense of responsibility to place. There is also no bond to local communities. The bond is to individual or corporate gain instead. It is now rational (in the mind of *Homo economicus*) to leave the land and community to work for $.50 more an hour elsewhere. It is likewise rational for industry to leave a community if, all other things being equal, labor is $.50 less an hour elsewhere. Destruction of ecosystem or community stability is merely an unfortunate side effect of market efficiency.

Metamyth 3

Money is a universal measure of value, even of that which is social or ecological.

"Money," writes anthropologist Roy Rappaport, "has an interesting ecological property: it is a universal solvent. That is to say it tends to dissolve the differences between all things by imposing one simple metric—that of dollars or whatever—upon the marvelous variety of things of which the world is made."[1]

Since the monetary value of an item is its market value rather than its ecological or social value, a forest ecosystem is more valuable if it is simplified to produce mostly tradable goods. For an industrial landowner, the dollar value of a forest is greatest if the forest is turned into a subdivision or pulpwood plantation. Labor, when transmuted into dollars, becomes a cost to be reduced. It is rational for managers to substitute machinery or chemicals for labor if these lead to cost reductions, regardless of the ramifications of such substitutions to the environment or society. Such substitutions lead to higher "productivity" which is a sign of "Progress," even if this progress is accompanied by unemployment, poverty, and polluted watersheds.

Reference
1. Roy A. Rappaport, "Forests and Man," *The Ecologist* (August/September 1976): 244.

Metamyth 4

The bigger the market, the greater the choices of resources and products and the greater the welfare. Growth leads to Progress.

The favorite metaphor of growth promoters is that of the expanding pie. This metaphor is popular partly because it implies that we do not have to worry about uneven distribution of wealth. Since the pie is growing, everyone supposedly benefits.

Benefits and costs from such growth, however, are not always evenly distributed. Often growth benefits a few at the expense of many, or benefits an area in which the wealth is accumulated at the expense of an area from which the wealth was extracted. For some individuals or nations, what is expanding is not the wealth pie but debt.

The wealth pie that is getting bigger does not include natural wealth such as clean air, pure water, and healthy forests. The growth of industrial society is occurring at the expense of living systems and natural resources. A true growth of wealth would imply an increase in capital and interest. What we have instead is a depletion of natural-resource capital. The accelerating rate at which the natural-capital pie is being devoured is being mistaken for growth.

Metamyth 5

The growth of the Gross National Product (GNP) is a measure of social welfare.

With this metamyth, society is seen as an economic organism. When the GNP is booming, the economy is considered healthy. When the GNP is declining, the economy is considered depressed. Consumption, to keep the economy healthy, becomes a moral obligation of citizens, even if it means living in debt. By lowering interest rates to encourage consumer spending, the government even encourages people to go into debt.

Many of the factors that help increase the GNP, however, hardly improve social or ecological welfare. The GNP rises, for example, as nonrenewable resources become depleted and the cost of further extraction increases. It rises as increased ill health requires more health care. It rises as social health deteriorates and money is spent on psychiatrists, prisons, and police. It rises as more people sue each other, creating ample business for lawyers and insurance companies. It rises as the environment becomes polluted and companies get contracts to clean up the mess. It rises as factories produce products that quickly fall apart and must be replaced.

The GNP does not rise as families and communities become more self-reliant. When people live simply, grow their own food, build their own houses, supply their own fuels, entertain themselves and friends, and barter for goods and services, they contribute nothing to the GNP.

The GNP as a measuring stick of social welfare gives no indication of how wealth is distributed. A minority can control the resources and spend the money while others are starving or homeless. The wealth of the minority can grow rapidly while the wealth of the less fortunate remains the same or declines. But this would be masked by the single figure of the GNP. Even if everyone's income grew at the same rate, as implied by the growing-pie analogy, this would actually mean an increasing disparity of wealth. At the same growth rate, large incomes increase quantitatively more than small ones.

Metamyth 6

Free global trade, because it creates the largest possible market with the most players and resources, ensures the greatest benefits.

The reason for creating exports is to pay for imports. To the extent that products are locally produced, the need for imports and exports diminishes. There are many advantages to shortening supply lines. It increases self-reliance, autonomy, and responsibility (because those causing consequences can see and correct them), it captures the production value locally, and it circulates the profits locally. These are not priorities of multinational corporations, however, or of our federal government.

Advocates of free trade say that it creates greater market efficiency because some countries have a "comparative advantage." Certainly the tropics have a comparitive advantage over Maine at producing mangoes. But the advantages of industrial paper production are not as clear. The comparative advantage of lower production costs can be highly misleading due to tax breaks, subsidies, lack of regulations, or exploited labor forces. Communities and nations are forced to compete for industrial jobs based on the lowest common denominator of disadvantages that lead to the lowest production costs for foreign corporations.

Trade between rich and poor nations can exacerbate inequalities. Poor nations borrow enormous sums to pay for infrastructure so they can increase their specialty exports to raise money to pay off debts. Often the result is that farm and forest resources become too important for global markets to be "wasted" in meeting the needs of the rural poor who become, as a result, more impoverished. "The global economy," writes Wendell Berry, "...operates on the superstition that deficiencies or needs or wishes of one place may be safely met by the ruination of another place."[1]

More and more of the world's resources are being controlled by fewer and fewer, but bigger and bigger, transnational corporations that have no allegiance to any community, state, or even nation. On a planetary scale, corrective environmental and social feedback becomes inadequate or nonexistent because responsible individuals are so remote from the problems they are causing that they are often not even aware the problems exist.

Reference
1. Wendell Berry, "Conservation is Good Work," *Wild Earth*, (Spring 1992) :82.

Metamyth 7

There are no limits to industrial growth.

Growth advocates have argued by denial that because limits to growth must not exist, they do not exist. With a religious zeal, economists and politicians in this country have almost universally declared that our salvation from almost any problem—be it balance of trade, budget deficits, poverty, crime, unemployment, or even pollution and resource depletion—is more growth. With a missionary spirit, industrial nations have tried to spread this message to all parts of the globe. All major political ideologies, whether communist, socialist, capitalist, or fascist, assume as first premise the need for industrial growth. The debate is over the best way to achieve this growth.

Sustainable industrial growth on a limited planet, however, is a physical and biological impossibility.[1] There are numerous limits to growth, but they have been masked by the global economy. Countries such as the U.S. and Japan are already living well beyond their own limits and are instead taking resources from (or contributing waste and pollution to) the global "commons." The question is not whether limits exist but which ones will stop us first:

•There are limits to the mining of nonrenewable resources such as fossil fuels and minerals. Easily accessible deposits do not suddenly appear based on increased demand. Further exploitation becomes more expensive, more unpopular, and more risky. The U.S. is a major net importer of oil and most mineral resources. Many of the countries where supplies are located are politically unstable.

•There are biological limits to the exploitation of renewable resources in a given area no matter how intense the management. The U.S. is already a net importer of forest products, vegetables, meat, dairy, and fish products. The world's population and total consumption are rising, but rich topsoil, arable land, healthy fisheries, and quality forests are declining.

•There are limits to how much pollution air and water can take before the climate changes or before people, plants, and animals start getting sick. These limits have already been reached for some regions, as demonstrated by Waldsterben in Europe.

•There are limits to how large infrastructures can become before the maintenance costs become so great that further investment in growth becomes possible only by letting the infrastructure crumble.

•There are limits to how much community disruption society can bear before the costs of external controls such as police, prisons, and welfare become so great that people are left homeless, prisons are overcrowded, and social services are cut back.

•There are limits to how much debt can be incurred to finance growth before the cost of interest payments becomes a disincentive to further growth and those in debt default on payments.

These debts are problematic not just at the international level, but also at national, state, and individual levels.

•There are limits to how much international conflicts can occur over diminishing resources before the costs of military buildup threaten the stability of the civilian world or before countries destroy one another in war.

Sustainable growth is an oxymoron.

Reference
1. See Herman Daly, *Steady State Economics* (San Francisco: W. H. Freeman and Company, 1977).

Distorted Feedback—Mechanisms

The Global Industrial Growth Society (GIGS), according to its advocates, can deal with any social or ecological problems—including apparent limits to growth—through technological innovations, the free market, and government intervention. These mechanisms, according to proponents, are self-regulating. They operate on feedback, somewhat like a thermostat on a furnace. They are capable, the argument goes, of gathering pertinent information and responding with corrective actions to keep society on course. If one of the mechanisms fails to correct a given problem, the others, supposedly, will succeed.

A commonly cited illustration of this argument is Eastern Europe, before the fall of communism. The region lacked these feedback mechanisms—it had backward technologies, a controlled economy, and totalitarian governments—and, as a result, some of the worst environmental problems in the world. In contrast, capitalist democracies seem better off.

Believing in these mechanisms creates an excuse for citizens to take minimal action and represent a formidable barrier to change. The "system" will take care of us they argue. It absolves us of responsibility. Responsibility then goes by default to those with influence over the mechanisms. The further these influential people are from us, however, the more they think about their own interests rather than ours. And their interests are to protect or expand their positions in the existing system—a system that may be causing our problems.

As I have argued throughout this book, from an ecological or social point of view, the current technological, economic, and government solutions to forestry problems are not working. When I say the solutions are not working, I mean that they tend to increase the instability of the forest and society and to decrease the options for future generations. By options, I mean profound options, not frivolous ones. For example, a frivolous option is what to wear to a wedding. A profound option is whether to get married or not. We have all kinds of options regarding consumer products, but we are losing options regarding clean air, pure water, biological diversity, and social stability.

Many now argue that the failure, so far, of our society to solve basic social or ecological problems is due to insufficient application of these mechanisms. We need newer, more complicated technologies, more marketization, or a stonger government, rather than more responsibility over ourselves and our communities.

As long as feedback mechanisms exist in the context of GIGS, however, they will maintain as first priority the course of GIGS. The mechanisms can respond to lower priority goals, such as dealing with environmental or social problems, but these responses are limited to actions that do not disrupt the primary goal, which is maintaining the pace of growth. The result of this hierarchy of priorities is that feedback from the lower priority goals, relating to social and environmental problems, becomes distorted.

Mechanism 1
Technological innovation will save us.

The technological world has proliferated to such a degree that many citizens of industrially advanced nations take it for granted that the manufactured world surrounding them is *the* environment. When they want to describe the less familiar biological world, they do it in the more familiar technological terms. Technology has become a dominant metaphor for describing how nature works. To be "scientific," one has to describe the living world as if it were a machine. This is also called being "objective." As technology has become more sophisticated, so have the models and metaphors.

Treating nature as a mechanism, no matter how sophisticated, helps justify technological solutions. If nature is a mechanism, we need only be its mechanics to make it serve our needs. From this perspective, people are starving, freezing, or naked due to a deficiency of some technology (which is on the verge of being developed) rather than due to social, political, or ecological factors.

Technology, it is argued, will help us solve our problems because it can magnify our ability to sense, gather, process and communicate vital information. Using this information, we supposedly can magnify our ability to control nature to meet our needs. Technology, it is argued, helps us escape limits by increasing productivity of existing resources or by finding substitutes for depleted ones.

Faith in technological solutions is so great that policy makers are willing to create problems (like nuclear waste) for which there are no existing remedies but for which there "surely" will be remedies discovered by future generations. Based on the promise of technological advances like nuclear fusion, superconductivity, genetic engineering, or space colonization, we can consume as much as we like *now* because these technologies will, it is hoped, create unlimited energy and material goods . . . *later*. Future generations are never asked if they want the wonderful opportunity to solve the life-threatening problems that stumped the generation before.

We are living today, however, with the problems caused by yesterday's "miracle" technological solutions. Even though the technologies of today were yesterday's science fiction, they are still not quite advanced enough. We always seem to be on the verge of a technological Utopia, but the dawn of this promise

never quite turns to day. In attempting to solve one problem, these technological solutions seem to create others. Techno-fixes often have side effects. And
even when they do not, their benefits are only temporary—if population and
industrial growth continue apace.

One reason the industrial techno-fixes are not solving social and ecological
problems is that they were not designed to do so. Industry is not developing its
high-tech "solutions"—such as genetically engineered plant varieties that are
resistant to herbicides—to feed the hungry or shelter the homeless; it is developing them to make a profit and to secure the careers of corporate bureaucrats.

Indeed, the industrial priorities for technological development or deploy-
ment are often at odds with the needs of stable social or ecological systems. In
the following chart I compare what best serves industrial or government
bureaucracies with what best serves a stable society:

Technological Innovations

Industrially Appropriate	Socially Appropriate
Expensive, complex, and time-consuming to develop	Easily developed at local level
Ownership and control limited to few	Ownership and control available to many
Increases power of industry	Reduces social inequities
Increases public's dependence on industry	Increases self-reliance of individuals and communities
Professionals needed for maintenance and repair	Maintenance and repair can be done locally by owner
Requires centralized bureaucracy to run and protect technology	Allows decentralized, self-regulating communities
Ecological disruption or pollution OK if within legal limits	Produces little or no ecological disruption or pollution
Increases worker "productivity" (i.e., eliminates jobs)	Improves employment opportunities
Workers become cogs in machine	Enhances worker craftsmanship
Communities must adapt to needs of technology	Technology fits into needs of community
Causes rapid social/ecological change requiring more techno-fixes	Helps maintain social/ecological stability

Rather than act as corrective feedback to resource depletion, pollution, or social inequity, industry-friendly technology has tended to encourage more problems. The reason is simple: it keeps the "solution" in the hands of those who have been causing the problems. Since their goal for unlimited growth and their social and ecological consciences remains unchanged, putting new, more powerful technologies in their control can only lead to new, more serious problems.

The techno-fix in forestry, for example, operates from a narrow focus on fiber production; other values are ignored except as they interfere with this primary goal. Forest practices are now being designed more around the needs of mechanical harvesters, which work best doing clearcuts, than around the needs of forest ecosystems. The forest responds by growing brush rather than the trees desired by industry, so foresters spray herbicides in the hopes of speeding up softwood fiber production. The machines and chemicals, however, will not grow wilderness faster. They will not grow biological diversity faster. As the ecosystem becomes simplified, it loses parts of the nutrient and predator/ prey cycles and thus becomes more unstable. As it becomes more unstable, it "needs" more fixes to continue meeting industrial goals—goals irrelevant to the needs of the forest itself.

The biomass fix, for example, gets higher yields from the forest by increasing industry's ability to use lower quality wood, rather than by increasing the forest's biological productivity. Indeed, as rotations get shorter, the productivity of the soil is decreased. The fix for declining soil fertility is fertilization. But fertilizers, unlike the leaves and rotting wood that they replace, do not supply organic matter and wildlife habitat. Such fixes, from an ecological perspective, are incomplete.

Fixes that improve efficiency and reduce waste, while desirable, only delay the inevitable confrontation with limits—as long as population and economic growth continue. This passes the responsibility for changing direction away from this generation and onto the next.

Rather than liberate us from the constraints of the earth, the sci-fi, mega-tech solutions tend to bind us to the constraints of big industry or big government. We are supposed to believe that such a Faustian bargain will lead to greater security, but as Benjamin Franklin said, "The man who would trade independence for security deserves to wind up with neither."

Mechanism 2
The market will save us.

Market feedback is supposed to optimize human welfare. The belief in the market as a corrective mechanism has grown especially intense with the collapse of communism in eastern Europe. Since centralized planning doesn't work, many people are reasoning, the market must be the only alternative. In this book, however, I described how oligopoly, oligopsony, vertical integration, and subsidies can distort market feedback to prices. The free market is a myth.

The prices paid to small, nonindustrial landowners, for example, do not reflect the value of the wood to the mills. Conversely, industrial landowners can spend amounts of money on planting, thinning, or spraying that do not seem justifiable based on going nonindustrial stumpage rates. And government agencies often grow timber at a net loss.

The market has another serious flaw, "externalities"—costs and benefits not directly accounted for in an activity or transaction. Externalities I have addressed in this book include resource depletion, air and water pollution, habitat destruction, and degradation of community values. They are by no means minor in importance, but they are not accounted for in industry ledger sheets. Industry advertisements do not inform the public about the social and environmental costs of producing, consuming, and disposing of a product. If the market does not account for these externalities, it will not correct them.

Some economists see externalities as a sign that not enough of the world has been marketized. Air, water, and wildlife, they argue, should be privatized rather than be held in common. Such costs are not always easy to quantify, however, especially when the effects are global and irreversible. How, for example, does one, quantify the costs of widening the ozone hole over the Antarctic? On a more local scale, how does one quantify the value of nongame wildlife (which have no market value) that may be adversely affected by timber management? Is managing for the highest return, even if more species are marketized, the same as managing for ecological diversity and stability?

Ironically, even though privatizing and marketing are supposed to "get government off our backs," it would be governments who decide how to privatize such items as air or water. It would then take government regulation and interference to prevent the natural tendency of powerful interests to gain monopoly control over the markets. Often these government roles are subject to corruption.

Due to the scale of forest-products markets and the time it takes to grow trees to maturity, the market is inadequate to protect a forest resource from being depleted. When the market for wood is big enough, as in Maine, whole townships can be flattened with no effect at all on wood prices. Yet such widespread cutting can have drastic effects on local communities and wildlife. By the time mature wood is scarce enough to increase prices at local mills, it is too late; it takes decades to grow a new "crop" of mature wood. Mills will shut down. On a global scale, a nation's forests can be depleted without severely harming international markets. Market feedback is too delayed for price to have a stabilizing effect.

When forests are liquidated, topsoil eroded, or aquifers depleted, the market does not normally find substitutes for these regional scarcities—entrepreneurs move on to seek new resources elsewhere. In this regard, biologist Paul Ehrlich has written:

"Biologists unfamiliar with economic ideas are often shocked when they discover that an industry appears to be deliberately destroying its resource base. The problem first came to my attention when it became clear that the whaling industry was deliberately harvesting whales at a rate that would lead to their extinction. Until then, it had not dawned on me that industries dealing with biological resources were not necessarily concerned with achieving long-term maximum sustainable yields from them (which could be 'uneconomic'), but were only concerned with maximizing the return on their capital. If exterminating the resource (wiping out the whales, clearcutting tropical rainforests, exhausting the soils on industrial farms) brought a maximum return, then the resource would be destroyed."[1]

Reference

1. Paul Ehrlich, "The Limits to Substitution: Meta-resource Depletion and a New Economic-ecological Paradigm," *Ecological Economics*, Vol. 1, No. 1 (1989): 11.

Mechanism 3

Government will save us.

With voter feedback, government is supposed to create the infrastructure that supports the economy and correct flaws in the market. The scale of government activity in this realm—regulating against antitrust to fight the tendencies toward monopolies; manipulating interest rates and public spending to smooth out de-stabilizing economic cycles; creating a safety net to deal with gross social inequities and apalling poverty; setting up safety and environmental regulations to deal with worker exploitation and industrial pollution; and engaging in diplomacy and warfare to deal with the instabilities of international markets—is a clear indication of the quantity and severity of the market flaws that citizens perceive.

As I have argued in this book, there are many problems associated with relying on government as an efficient feedback system on complex issues such as forestry. For democracy to function, the public must be well informed of the issues. But there are many issues competing for the media's attention. The media, which is corporate sponsored and seeks the widest audience, selects the events that are most dramatic and that can be simplified into "sound bites." This affects which issues environmentalists focus on if they wish to make an impact. Groups such as Earth First! or Greenpeace, for example, choose issues that are scandalous and that can be dramatized with a daring symbolic action. Such issues do not reach the wider public attention until they approach a crisis state. Any feedback, therefore, will at best be delayed. This approach hardly leads to stability.

Even when the public is concerned about an issue, voting does not ensure that government will get feedback on that issue. One normally votes for a person or a party rather than for a specific policy on a specific issue. During elections the politicians, who are also competing for sound bites, tend to focus on simple issues that they can be either for or against—flag burning, abortion, crime, or school prayer, for example. Their objective is not so much to have profound analyses and workable policy alternatives—it is to get elected. To get elected for any higher office takes substantial sums of money, which various Political Action Committees are glad to supply. Of those national candidates who wanted to get re-elected in 1990, 96% did.

Citizens are given no choice at all on such crucial issues as limits to indus-

trial growth. Yet the GIGS ideology permeates government actions. Regulation, as I have pointed out, tends to legitimize problems at a level that does not
threaten that higher priority goal. Political parties bicker over how to continue
infinite industrial growth, rather than whether it is advisable to do so.

Government actions, including regulation, can be very expensive. The
countries with the biggest government budgets are the countries that are the
most industrially advanced. From these two premises, political leaders have
come to the bizarre conclusion that the best way to clean up the environment is
to grow bigger, faster. The more industrialized a nation becomes, some
economists argue, the more it can afford to spend to clean up the messes caused
by growing so big and so fast.

Even with nearly universal political support for its policies, a government
cannot prevent the economy from meeting limits to growth, because government itself must meet limits to growth. Government "control" of problems that
are exacerbated by growth does not solve such problems if growth continues.
This means that more controls (both domestic and international) are needed.
Such controls become more and more expensive. Traditionally the federal
government has financed these expenses through debt. But this positive-
feedback approach has limits, government cannot perpetually increase debt to
subsidize growth. At some point (and this has apparently been reached), the cost
of the controls and the level of debt become too great for society to bear. The
public rebels against high taxes, services are cut back, and the infrastructure
supporting growth starts to crumble.

There is another limit to government solutions recognized by Wendell
Berry: "A government undertaking to protect all of nature that is now abused or
threatened would have to take total control of the country. Police and bureaucrats—and opportunities for malfeasance—would be everywhere. To wish only
for a public or political solution to the problem of conservation may wish for a
solution as bad as the problem and still unable to solve it."[1]

References
1. Wendell Berry, "Conservation is Good Work," *Wild Earth* (Spring 1992):82.

Corrective feedback: Metashifts.

When cancer cells grow uncontrollably, the host organism eventually dies.
When the host dies, so do the cancer cells. This is the ultimate feedback to unrestricted growth in a system with limits. Unlike cancer cells, human beings are
able to anticipate the results of their actions. They should also be able to reason
that a societal model that leads to such catastrophic consequences is not an adap-
tive or sustainable one. They should be able to use this information and reasoning to switch to a more appropriate model. This is "metafeedback," where the
correction is not just by the model but to the model.

These metashifts—changes in the dominant societal models—have occurred throughout history. They have been an important mode by which societies have been able to adapt to radical, stressful changes. Scientists call metashifts in the realm of ideas (such as the Copernican or Einsteinian revolutions in physics) "paradigm shifts." Anthropologists call such shifts in the realms of human culture "revitalization movements."

If our society is going to move towards sustainability, it will have to make the following three metashifts:

Metashift 1

We must begin to treat ecosystems not as the content of the economic system but as the context for society.

This metashift requires a change in relationship. It implies treating the forest as a biological community to which we belong rather than as a commodity to exploit for a single-purpose industry. From this perspective, destroying or degrading the forest community (which is part of the community of all ecosystems—the biosphere) would be seen as a form of cultural suicide.

From this new perspective, forest managers would attempt to maintain the multiple values of the forest rather than just mine or farm trees. The management model would be complete ecosystems—containing all stages from regeneration and youth to old age and decay—rather than a factory assembly line. The goal would be ecological stability rather than maximum short-term production. This metashift also implies trying to maintain all the native wildlife, including large predators, through integrating the distribution of managed and reserved forests over the landscape.

Metashift 2

We must recognize that the biological systems upon which we depend have limits, and we must live within those limits (the carrying capacity).

This metashift requires a change in goals. Society has tried to force the industrial growth paradigm onto the forest. This metashift would have society adapt the climax-state paradigm from old-growth forests.

With forests," climax state" refers to reaching a maximum level of biomass and maintaining it. With this shift, society would reach and then maintain an optimal level of population, wealth, and turnover of goods that does not threaten the integrity of the biological systems upon which we depend.

Despite limits to the growth of biomass, mature forests still develop—i.e., they adapt to changes in the environment. A climax state is a dynamic, rather than a stagnant stage of development.

Metashift 3

The scale and organization of society's technology, economy, and government must be changed to be more responsive to corrective environmental and social feedback.

This metashift requires a change in structure. For people to be responsive to the earth and to society, they must be aware of problems and have the power to act. Dependence on complicated, corporate-controlled technologies reduces citizens' abilities to understand the systems on which they depend and their power to change those systems. Dependence on global markets reduces consumers' awareness of the consequences of their consumption. Consumers are not motivated to correct problems of which they are unaware. When industries that are causing the problems dominate the political process, they are hardly motivated to correct the problems from which they profit.

This metashift would help shorten the lines of awareness and responsibility. This implies a transition to more decentralized technological, economic, and political systems. With this metashift, forest management would be designed around smaller-scale technologies that are more affordable, repairable, and environmentally benign than the timber harvesters, delimbers, and pesticides that now dominate.

The products of forests and farms would go to satisfy local and regional needs first. The emphasis on exports would go toward quality and value-added products rather than toward increased quantities of raw materials. This would increase local self-reliance and ensure more market stability, employment, and circulation of local wealth.

Political responsibility for forests would be in local hands rather than in the hands of corporate executives or government bureaucrats far away. Local communities, which live with the consequences of management actions, would have input into management plans.

Corrective feedback: Strategies.

It is time now to come down from the heady world of abstract thought and to grapple with the hardnosed Maine attitude that "You can't get there from here." To be truthful, you probably can't. No society of which I am aware has ever succeeded in following exactly some abstract formula decreeing how people should live. The abstractions are useful, however, as guidelines, indicating the direction to go from here.

In this section I list actions people can take to help stop the destruction of the forests and to start the transition to a more stable and sustainable forest/society relationship. While I have suggested that we may need to save the world to save our forests, a good place to start saving the world is here, in the forests of our own backyard. While I have suggested goals for where we ought to be, the place to start is here, where we are now. This means using the existing structures of our government, media, and market. But this does not preclude reforming these structures or even setting up alternative structures. Transition would be most successful if all these strategies operated at once.

Most of the strategies for action that I discuss here are not new. They are strategies that have already been tried, or are being tried with some degree of success in various regions of the world. To be more effective, however, these strategies need to incorporate the following:

Model—The strategies should operate within a sustainable ecological/social model rather than within the industrial growth model. Issues should not be dealt with in isolation but as symptoms connected to the larger economic/political system.

Coordination—Multiple strategies should be used in a coordinated fashion. Consumers, workers, environmentalists, small woodlot owners, timber framers, mill owners relying on high-quality logs, and forest communities can form powerful political coalitions to get the attention of the media and political leaders.

Linkage—This coalition should extend to other groups dealing with similar problems caused by an ever expanding economy. Toxic waste, energy, transportation, watershed pollution, worker safety, unemployment, welfare, etc. should be viewed as connected to rather than isolated from forestry and dealt with in a more coordinated fashion.

Empowerment—The object is to get those who normally are victims of forestry policy to have a role in decision making.

Strategy 1
Get informed.

The foundation for corrective action is informed awareness of the problems. Much of the information that reaches the public, however, is a variation on the theme of the happy coincidence— that managing industrial forests for short-term profit is benefiting the forest and local communities. While this book is a starting point for countering that myth, I encourage interested readers to go beyond *Beyond the Beauty Strip*.

Strategies:

Experience the forest.
Words or pictures cannot adequately convey how a forest feels. Nothing can substitute for actually being there.

Walk through old growth.
Some old-growth forests in Maine, such as the Hermitage near Gulf Hagas gorge, are accessible from hiking trails. For more information

about old-growth forests in Maine, write to Maine's Critical Areas Program, State Planning Office, State House Station 38, Augusta ME 04333-0038 (phone 207-289-6041).

Hike in a wilderness area.
The best example in the Northeast is the Adirondack Park. Maine's largest example is Baxter State Park. To stay overnight at Baxter, it helps to make reservations because space is limited. Contact Baxter State Park, 64 Balsam Dr., Millinocket, ME 04462 (phone 207-723-5140).

See management options.
While there are management examples on private woodlots and industrial forests scattered throughout the state, a good place to see many examples of management options in one area is at the USDA Forest Service's Penobscot Experimental Forest in Bradley, Maine. Some areas of the experimental forest have been managed selectively for more than 4 decades. For more information. contact Robert Frank. Northeastern Forest Experiment Station, 5 Godfrey Drive, Orono, ME 04473 (phone 207-866-7260).

Fly over clearcuts.
The size and distribution of clearcuts in some parts of Maine can be grasped only from the air. Two pilots who have flown over the the Maine woods for environmental groups at reasonable rates are:
   Rudy Engholm, Environmental Air Force, RR2 2084A, Garnet Road, Brunswick ME 04011 (phone 207-721-0228); and
   Alex McLean, Landslides, 25 Bay State Ave. Boston, MA (phone 617-536-6261).

Meet forest landowners.
To be an effective critic, it helps to understand the viewpoints of all sides of an issue. The following groups can supply literature and even suggest tours of managed lands:
   Paper Industry Information Office, 15 Western Ave., Augusta, ME 04330 (phone 207-622-3166);
   Maine Forest Products Council, 146 State St., Augusta, ME 04330 (phone 207-622-9288);
   Small Woodland Owners Association of Maine, P.O. Box 926, Augusta ME 04330. (phone 207-626-0005).

Read More.
References in this book include numerous books, articles, and studies from all perspectives. Indeed, the number of references can be overwhelming for those who want to read just a few overviews of the subject. For those who just want a condensed list, I recommend the following:
   Although it is dated, *The Paper Plantation* by William Osborne (Viking Press, New York, 1974) is the best analysis of the impact of the paper industry on Maine. I recommend *The Forest and the Trees: A Guide*

to Excellent Forestry by Gordon Robinson (Island Press, Washington, D.C., 1988) for its critique of even-aged management and its promotion of forest practices that consider all forest values. Although I disagree with a few of its conclusions on intensive forest management, I recommend *Wildlife, Forests, and Forestry: Principles of Managing Forests for Biological Diversity* by Malcolm Hunter, Jr. (Prentice-Hall, Englewood Cliffs, N.J., 1990) for its clear exposition of the concepts of conservation biology applied to temperate forests.

For the latest thinking on the impacts of forestry on biodiversity and local communities, two magazines from the Pacific Northwest stand out:

Forest Watch, CHEC, 14417 S.E. Laurie, Oak Grove, Oregon 97267 (phone 503-652-7049);

Forest Planning Canada, P.O. Box 6234, Stn. "C", Victoria, BC V8P 5L5 Canada (phone 604-727-6630).

For an overview of policy options for the northern forest, a must is *The Northern Forest Lands Study of New England and New York* by Stephen Harper, Laura Falk, and Edward Rankin (USDA Forest Service, Rutland, Vermont, 1990), which is obtainable from the Northern Forest Lands Council, 45 Portsmouth Street, Concord, NH 03301 (phone 603-224-6590).

For environmental critiques of the Northern Forest Lands Study, contact the following organizations:

Preserve Appalachian Wilderness (PAW), P.O. Box 52, Groveton, NH 03582 (phone 603-636-2952);

Sierra Club, 85 Washington Street, Saratoga Springs, NY 12866 (phone 518-587-9166);

The Wilderness Society, 7 North Chestnut Street, Augusta, ME 04330 (phone 207-626-5635), or 20 Park Plaza, Suite 536, Boston, MA 02116 (phone 517-350-8866).

For state policy studies and forest practices statistics, contact Maine Forest Service, State HouseStation #22, Augusta, ME 04333 (phone 207-289-2791).

Strategy 2
Get organized.

I encourage individuals to write letters to their congressional delegates, governors, local politicians, or local newspapers, but this alone will not save the forest. The power of individuals is multiplied when they organize into groups.

Strategies:

Citizens' groups.
Citizens groups, which can research, educate the public, lobby legislators, make contact with the media, protest, engage in legal actions, and network with other groups, are essential to get the message across.

Local grassroots.
When I started writing this book, I was concerned over how few local grassroots groups were fighting for forestry reform in Maine, a state that is dominated by forestry interests. Grassroots groups are essential to the forestry debate because the members live where the action is. They directly experience the problems and directly benefit from any solutions. They have the most at stake and usually have the most motivation to succeed. Grassroots campaigns have helped save old-growth forests in the Pacific Northwest, stop clearcutting in national forests in Texas, and cut subsidies for spruce-budworm spraying in Maine. One of the purposes of this book is to serve as a resource for grassroots activists.

Regional networks.
There are a number of forestry-oriented, regional networks that include the Northern Forest region. The Northern Forest Lands Alliance, NFLA (c/o Appalachian Mountain Club, 5 Joy Street, Boston, MA 02108, phone 617-523-0636) is a network of over 20 state, regional, and national conservation organizations interested in the ecological, social, and recreational issues surrounding the forests of northern New York and New England. The Alliance is a major lobbyist of the Northern Forest Lands Council and plans (as of this writing) to put out a publication.

Preserve Appalachian Wilderness, PAW (P.O. Box 52A, Bondville, VT 05340) is a network of activist groups from Georgia to northern New England dedicated to making the Appalachian region into a viable corridor for maintaining biological diversity. PAW has a newsletter, and has published an activists' guide to dealing with National Forests.

Restore: The North Woods (P.O. Box 440, Concord, MA 01742, phone 508-287-0320) is an organization concerned with the ecological and social sustainability of the softwood/hardwood transition forest region that stretches from the Great Lakes to northern New England and the Canadian Maritimes. Restore (which, at this writing, is in the initial stages of organizing), hopes to have newsletters and alerts to keep its members informed and active.

National networks.
Ned Fritz, a grassroots activist who sued to stop clearcutting on national forests in Texas, is coordinator of the Forest Reform Network, a national coalition of forestry groups dedicated to preserving native forests, protecting forest biodiversity, and banning clearcutting. For more information write to Forest Reform Network, 5934 Royal Lane, Suite 223, Dallas, TX 75230 (phone 214-352-8370).

Save America's Forests, SAF, (#4 Library Court, SE, Washington, D.C. 20003, phone 202-544-9219), is a national coalition of groups dedicated to protecting forest ecosystems. SAF is also working to aid displaced workers, families or communities and to create incentives for landowners to manage in ecologically sound ways. Belonging to such a coalition dramatically increases the power of any local group working on forestry issues that involve federal laws. SAF has produced a useful "Citizens' Guide" for activists ($5.00).

Investors.

Those who have money can invest it conscientiously according to ecological and social principles. They can pressure organizations, such as environmental groups, unions, governments, etc. to use environmental criteria in investing surplus funds.

Taking stock.

Stockholders can organize to pressure companies to change socially or environmentally destructive policies. They can divest from irresponsible companies and support more responsible companies. Or better yet, invest money locally, to improve their own communities. This influence can be potent if large institutional investors are influenced to follow such policies. For more information, see *Economics as if the Earth Really Mattered*, by Susan Meeker-Lowry or write to her at Catalyst, P.O. Box 1308, Montpelier, VT 05601, or phone 802-223-7943.

Land trusts.

Land trusts can invest in full ownership or easements for land protection. The trusts oversee management plans or may actively participate in forest management. The Nature Conservancy (122 Main St., Topsham, ME 04086, phone 207-729- 5181), targets lands with special ecosystem values and owns the largest old-growth forest preserve in Maine at Big Reed Pond.

The Mahoosuc Land Trust (Box 981, Bethel, ME 04217, phone 207-665-2577) and the Quoddy Regional Land Trust (Box 49, Whiting, ME 04691, phone 207-733-5509) are protecting forest lands from development and overcutting pressures. Some of the land is being managed for timber products.

For more information about forming land trusts, contact the Maine Coast Heritage Trust, 167 Park Row, Brunswick ME 04011 (phone 207-729-7366).

Producers.

Owners of managed woodlands can organize for community stability and economic justice.

Woodlots co-ops.

Woodlot owners can form cooperatives to collectively bargain with mills for better prices. They can cooperatively purchase equipment and forester services and can even set up their own mills. New Brunswick has an active woodlot organization, The New Brunswick Federation of Woodlot Owners Inc. 88 Prospect St., Fredericton, NB E3B 5P8 Canada (phone 506-459-2990)

Community forests.

Maine towns used to have community woodlots that served the needs of townspeople. Those lots that remain are now managed by the Bureau of Public Lands, which gives the towns a payment in lieu of taxes. They are not really run by the community for the community, though. One town,

Osborne Plantation, does make its own management plans and hires its own loggers (who do not clearcut or use herbicides), but a certain percentage of revenues still go to the Bureau of Public Lands. Towns can lobby to get more control over their lots for their own revenue and benefit, such as firewood for the poor and elderly, and revenues for schools (one of the original reasons for the creation of public lots). Ideally, every community should have a preserved forest. At a minimum, local people can have input into management plans for public lands in their regions. For more information about public lands, contact Bureau of Public Lands, Department of Conservation, State House, Augusta, ME 04333 (phone 207-289-3061).

Workers.

Workers can be, and have been, allies with environmentalists on many issues. Environmentally sound silviculture means sustainable jobs. Fighting pollution means fighting for safe working conditions.

Worker co-ops.

Loggers can start management companies committed to ecologically sound forestry practices. Such companies increase management options for both government and private landowners.

In southern Oregon, a worker/environmentalist alliance has resulted in the creation of two worker-owned companies: the Rogue Sustainable Forestry Company (RSFC), which seeks contracts from public and private landowners, and the Rogue Forest Products Company (RFPC) which processes, markets, and ships products generated by RSFC. These two companies are guided by the nonprofit Rogue Institute for Ecology and Economy (RIEE) which has a 12-member board consisting of three members each from environmental organizations, the woodworkers union, and the two companies. RIEE does research to refine natural selection forestry practices in light of new information and experience and will assist in the development of other environmentally sound business practices. For more information write to Headwaters, P.O. Box 729; Ashland, OR 97250.

Responsible Unions.

Union workers can organize for greater safety and higher environmental standards in logging and paper making. The Pulp, Paper, and Woodworkers of Canada, an independent Canadian union representing 7,000 workers, is tackling the problems of organochlorine pollution created during paper making. They have published an excellent pamphlet on the subject (available for $7.00) written by Barry Reiter. For more information write to Pulp, Paper, and Woodworkers of Canada, 1184 West 6th Avenue, Vancouver, BC V6H 1A4, Canada.

The United Paperworkers International Union (UPIU) has been actively campaigning against paper-mill pollution. A prime target of its campaign has been International Paper Company, which it considers one of the nation's worst polluters. For more information, write to Mark Brooks, special project director, UPIU, 3340 Perimeter Hill Drive, Nashville, TN 37211.

Consumers.

Consumers can organize boycotts of items produced in socially and environmentally unacceptable ways and can demand acceptable alternatives.

Consumer boycotts.

Consumers can boycott environmentally irresponsible companies. As I write this, there are boycotts against International Paper due to union busting, Georgia-Pacific due to trade in tropical lumber and to clearcutting, and Scott Paper due to clearcutting and use of herbicides in Canada. Consumer groups can also be more specific and boycott just the products, such as dioxin-contaminated coffee filters, milk cartons, or toilet paper. For lists of companies being boycotted, write to COOP America, 2100 M Street NW, Suite 310, Washington, DC 20063.

"Green" products.

Consumer and environmental groups can demand the creation of, or stimulate markets for, more environmentally benign products. The Swedish Society for the Conservation of Nature has published a booklet, *Paper and the Environment*, which grades various paper products on "environmental friendliness." By giving consumers a choice, the market, along with political pressure has encouraged an entire line of chlorine-free or low-chlorine products, from sanitary paper products to printing-grade papers. For more information write to the Swedish Society for the Conservation of Nature and the Swedish Federation of Environmental Organizations, Box 4510, 102 65, Stockholm, Sweden.

Renate Kroesa of Greenpeace has put together a more recent document, *The Greenpeace Guide to Paper*, available for $3 from Greenpeace, 4649 Sunnyside Avenue North, Seattle, WA 98103.

Claudia Thompson has authored an authoritative guide, *Recycled Papers: The Essential Guide*, available from MIT Press, 55 Hayward St., Cambridge, MA 02142.

Strategy 3
Work for appropriate technologies.

The goals of appropriate technology strategies are to promote the development of technologies that:

- are easy to produce;
- are affordable;
- maintain or improve rather than degrade or pollute forest ecosystems;
- enhance local employment and community stability rather than displace workers; and
- increase local self-reliance rather than increase corporate dependence.

Strategies:

Watch-dog research.
Forestry activists can serve as watchdogs over government-sponsored research to make sure that public money is going to public and environmental benefits and to expose conflicts of interest where they occur.

Protect jobs.
Labor groups can fight the introduction of technologies that displace workers but do not improve management. In 1983, the California Rural Legal Assistance initiated a precedent-setting suit against the University of California at Davis. The suit charged that this land-grant university was mandated to do research that would benefit small and medium sized farmers but instead was conducting research that benefitted agribusiness to the detriment of labor and small farmers. The suit initially was won, but it was appealed and bounced around to various courts for years until UC Davis was acquitted. The pressure exerted by this suit, though, still had a profound influence and has discouraged the use of public funds for research into perverse technologies.

End government funding.
The Cooperative Forestry Research Unit at the University of Maine in Orono specializes in research on industrial forestry technologies and techniques. Neither state nor federal money, no matter how small, should be contributing to such research if it is done at the expense, rather than benefit, of forest ecosystems and local communities.

Regulate.
Groups can work for limitations of potentially hazardous technologies.

Bans.
Bans are very direct. Managers know that certain technologies are not even options and therefore do not consider them. In Sweden, for example, the aerial application of pesticides over forests is banned.

Informed consent.
Local communities can insist that potentially hazardous activities, such as forestry pesticide application, not occur without the informed consent of those in the community who would most likely be affected. For more information about how this concept has been used in Nova Scotia and other regions, write to David Orton, The Green Web, R.R. 3, Saltsprings, NS, BOK 1PO, Canada.

Ecological standards.
Rather than attack a technology such as biomass or herbicides head on, groups can work to establish ecologically sound standards for forestry in which these technologies simply do not fit.

Set Criteria.
Groups in the Pacific Northwest effectively banned herbicide use over na-

tional forests for 7 years due to a court injunction over the inadequacy of the Environmental Impact Statement. Although the ban has now been lifted, the new regional policy makes preventing vegetation problems its highest priority, making herbicide use a low priority. Any need for treatment must be documented with credible science. For more information write to the Northwest Coalition For Alternatives to Pesticides (NCAP), P.O. Box 1393, Eugene, OR 97440. NCAP publishes the *Journal of Pesticide Reform*, which is an excellent source of both scientific and activist news on pesticide issues.

Incorporate Biodiversity.

The Huron-Manistee National Forest in Michigan has made a commitment to incorporate biodiversity into all aspects of forest planning. Managers will strive to manage for old-growth characteristics as much as possible within their agency's multiple- use mandate. Herbicides are not appropriate for these purposes. Michigan is drafting legislation that would incorporate biodiversity into its resource-management practices. For more information write to Dave Clelend, Huron-Manistee National Forest, 421 S. Mitchell Street, Cadillac, MI 49601

The State of Washington Department of Natural Resources has developed a plan to manage the Olympic Experimental State Forest for both ecological values and commodity protection. Their plan, which would make clearcutting with mechanical harvesters and spraying with herbicides inappropriate, is an excellent example which could be adapted to all the forest. For more information contact Jim Springer, Department of Natural Resources, Olympic Region Office, Route 1, Box 1375, Forks, WA 98331.

Strategy 4

Promote socially and ecologically responsible economics.

The goal of responsible economic strategies is to incorporate ecological and social costs into the price of finished products. This means ending industrial domination of the economy by strengthening the power of workers, consumers, communities, and environmentalists. If ecological and social costs are not incorporated into the price of products, someone else (probably future generations) eventually will have to pick up the bill. This means robbing our descendents of their biological birthrights for the sake of our desire for cheap throwaway paper.

Strategies:

End subsidized destruction.

There are numerous subsidies in forestry and paper manufacturing that shift the costs of environmental and social damage to taxpayers.

Tax breaks.

In Maine, purchasers of herbicides pay no sales tax. There are tax write-offs on biomass plants, which help encourage whole-tree clearcuts. The

Tree Growth Tax Law taxes forest landowners at a low rate but allows them to wipe out their forests.

Direct subsidies.
In New Brunswick, the government subsidizes road building, plantation establishment, thinning, herbicide spraying, and budworm spraying—all of which encourage landowners to clearcut and create chemical-dependent softwood monocultures. Maine forests must compete with these subsidized New Brunswick forests.

Below-cost government sales.
Below-cost government timber sales are destructive both ecologically and economically. They result in cutting of stands where sustainable management is not viable, and they flood markets with artificially cheap wood. Numerous environmental groups throughout the U.S. are fighting this practice.

Labor costs.
Work to ensure that the price of forest products includes the cost of nonexploited labor.

Collective bargaining.
Forest workers can organize for collective bargaining to improve wages and woods safety. While attempts at woodsworker strikes have failed in Maine in the past, organizing is still an option for the future—with Sweden demonstrating the benefits.

End piece-rate wage.
The piece-rate wage has nothing to do with management but a lot to do with high accident rates. Where workers are paid wages, as in Sweden, or even on Scott Paper Company's land in Maine, accident rates have immediately dropped.

Certify eco-professionals.
The forest products industry in Maine has begun sponsoring a Certified Logging Professional program (CLP, P.O. Box 1024, Augusta, ME 04330 (phone 207-626-3002) which emphasizes logging efficiency and safety as well as good business practices. Graduates are eligible for lower insurance rates. A program like this geared to ecological management (training could be on public forests) would protect woodlot owners from unknowingly hiring exploitive loggers. Certified forestry workers would be subject to professional standards and qualify for professional wages.

Stewardship contracts.
In Switzerland, workers have stewardship contracts to assure productive forests rather than harvest contracts to assure rapid wood removal. Stewardship contracts lead to long-term relationships between foresters and workers and a given piece of land.

Hire loggers.

The large companies now maintain the fiction that loggers are independent to avoid insurance and benefits costs. Worker wages, benefits, safety, and security would all be better off if this ruse were ended.

End wage disparity.

The wages of the top managers in the paper companies are greater than the common laborers' by a factor of more than 100, if you include stock options. This is socially obscene and would be unheard of in an industrially competitive country such as Japan. Even limiting the disparity to a factor of 10 would improve wage security for laborers.

Grower costs.

If growers received adequate compensation for their wood, they would not need subsidies to grow it. If growing a new forest is not economically viable, the old forest should not be cut down.

Collective bargaining.

Although woodlot owners are not organized for collective bargaining in Maine, they are in New Brunswick and Sweden. Without collective bargaining, the balance of economic power is grossly lopsided toward industry due to mill oligopsony.

Publicize mill prices.

In Sweden and Florida, mill contract prices are publicly known. Without such disclosure, mills can get away with paying low prices to those without the knowledge or power to confront such inequities.

Diversify markets.

Woodlot organizations in Sweden are powerful enough to create their own markets and even own pulp mills as well as lumber mills. Diversifying markets helps break the blackmail power of industry over prices.

Diversify ownership.

When industry owns the majority of spruce-fir, as it does in Maine, it has leverage over prices. In Sweden, industry is limited by law to owning no more than 25% of the forest land. Fifty percent of the forest is in private woodlots, and the remaining 25% is owned by the government.

Community costs.

Disintegrating communities need not be the inevitable byproduct of producing cheap forest products. Aesthetic, recreational, and economic community values should be accounted for.

Community input.

For large landownerships, whether they be industrial or public, local communities should have input in management plans. The Maine Bureau of Public Lands has set a precedent for this basic gesture of civic decency, but the practice needs to be far more pervasive.

An example from British Columbia shows how this process can both work and not work when applied to a multinational paper company. On the island of Galiano in British Columbia, the community, whose forest land base is owned by MacMillan Bloedel (MB), set up a Forest and Land Use Council to assure that harvest plans would meet the needs of the community as well as the needs of MB. The Council's goals include: long-term planning, selection cutting, protection of sensitive areas, continuation of rural lifestyle, development of small-scale, value-added woods products industries, public input in decision making, and community control of community resources. MB did selection cutting for 3 years and then started selling its forest land for development.

(Source: Gary Moore, Ken Millard, and Geoff Gaylor, "The Betrayal of a Community Involvement Process: Galiano Learns the Meaning of Forest Industry Commitment," *Forest Planning Canada*, May/June 1991, pp. 5-9)

End export of unmilled logs.
Although export markets can have the benefit of giving better stumpage returns to landowners, when the landowner is an absentee corporation that ships raw logs across the border to Quebec, local Maine communities lose both the direct profits from stumpage sales and the value added from milling. To add insult to injury, most of the lumber milled from Maine logs in Quebec is imported back to the United States, thus worsening the balance of trade. Countries such as Malaysia, Thailand, and Indonesia have banned such exports.

Recreation costs.
Access to private lands for recreation is one of the more contentious forestry issues in Maine. Allowing motorized recreationists onto logging roads creates landowner costs that must be accounted for.

User fees.
North Maine Woods (Main Street, Ashland, ME 04732, phone 207-435-6213), a coaltion of industrial, large nonindustrial, and state landowners, is cooperatively managing 2.8 million acres of forestland in northern Maine for recreation, using gates and entrance fees to pay for some of the costs of maintaining roads and campsites. All the roads in this vast region are private. The Fin and Feathers Club of Millinocket has protested that the companies have no right to charge fees because: it denies citizens access to public waters, some of the roads were built with public subsidies, and the companies are paying minimal taxes under the Tree Growth Tax Law.

The concept of user fees as an incentive to maintain the aesthetic and recreational values of a forest is sound. Baxter State Park, for example, relies on fees from out-of-state campers to help pay for expenses. Randal O'Toole recommends that federal forestlands charge some form of user fees as an incentive to cut less and preserve more. Environmental groups such as The Wilderness Society have opposed this. Managing for maximum recreation profits is not always compatible with managing for wilderness or biodiversity. Limited use of the concept, however, could benefit some sites where use is heavy.

Non-game wildlife diversity costs.

Companies that own land primarily for fiber consider planning and managing for wildlife diversity to be a major extra cost. This "extra cost" is based on the assumption that the forest is primarily a commodity and that even-aged management is the most cost-effective method for exploiting it. I have argued in this book that the economic benefits of even-aged management are a myth. Managing for long-term productivy is to some extent synonymous with managing for ecological diversity and stability. Land ownership entails both rights and responsibilities. One of the responsibilities is to maintain rather than flatten or degrade the ecosystem.

Subsidies with strings.

Because biological diversity is a public good, some form of public incentive for landowners to protect that resource could be justified. The landowners, however, are already getting substantial subsidies, in the form of low taxes, to keep the land forested. Such subsidies, if they are to continue, should have strings attached—if the landowners do not manage according to ecological standards, they do not qualify for further tax breaks.

Wilderness costs.

Land taken out of production for wilderness reduces the timber base. To the extent that landowers degrade, simplify, and fragment their forests, environmentalists will be justified in demanding larger wilderness areas to protect wildlife diversity and primitive recreation. Thus mismanagement has an indirect wildlife cost attached to it. The size of proposed wilderness areas can be used as leverage for more ecologically sound management.

Global market costs.

Industrial landowners will object to all the previous proposals by arguing that the added costs will make them uncompetitive in the global market. They will have to shut down and move elsewhere. Sweden incorporates many of these costs (except ecological costs) and until lately has been able to remain competititve. A global market that forces companies to degrade forests and exploit workers is ripe for reform.

Fight GATT.

Groups can fight the imposition of international trade policies (such as GATT, the General Agreement on Trade and Tariffs) that penalize regions that have more restrictive labor or environmental policies. One possible alternative is the creation of social and environmental tariffs, where a tax is put on goods that are imported from countries that lack similar environmental or labor policies. For more information on GATT, write for a copy of *Trading Away Our Environment: Special Report on Proposals for the Global "Harmonization" of Pesticide Regulations and other Environmental Protection Measures at the General Agreement on Tariffs and Trade,* from the Institute for Agricultural and Trade Policy, 212 3rd Avenue North, Suite 301, Minneapolis, MN 55401, and send $5.

Reduce demand.

Buying "green" products, such as unbleached paper, is not sufficient to stop the destruction of the forests. We must reduce demand for forest products. As environmental and social costs are included in the product prices, increased expenses will certainly be an incentive to reduce demand—but activists can push for more.

Government purchases.
The state can take the lead in reducing waste, recycling all its paper and creating markets for recycled and unbleached products. Maine has a Waste Management Agency (State House Station 154, Augusta, ME 04333, which has taken tentative steps in that direction, and which can help towns make the shift.

Reduce use.
Recycling, though important, has limits—paper can only be recycled so many times before the fiber quality is unacceptable for many products. Our society must address overconsumption and waste. Consumer and environmental groups can demand an end to wasteful packaging and advertising throwaways. A tax can be put on environmentally frivolous, non-recyclable, uses of paper to pay for costs of resource depletion, waste disposal, and environmental damage. Such a tax would lead consumers to choose products with minimal packaging.

Strategy 5
Push for environmentally and socially responsive government.

The goals of responsive government strategies are to end the industrial domination of the political process, to harmonize government tools toward environmental and social goals, and to decentralize political power and put more of it in the hands of local communities.

Strategies:

Set goals.
Goals educate the public about the failures of current policy (to the extent, for example, that it is not ecologically sound, socially responsible, or economically viable) and set an agenda for future action. It is far superior if a group is for something that government or industry is failing to achieve than if it is simply against something.

Sustainable communities.
The British Columbia Round Table on Environment and Economy, a committee set up in response to the United Nation's Bruntland Report on sus-

tainable development, has put together its agenda, a set of principles for achieving sustainable forest-based communities. Committee members range from enviromentalists to a paper company executive. The Round Table clearly recognizes that society must live within the limits of the carrying capcity of the forest; that biological diversity must be preserved; that depletion of nonrenewable resources must be minimized, that development must be based on limited resources and should emphasize efficiency and high-value rather than high-volume products; that the measure of economic performance should include the costs of environmental damage and resource depletion; that the benefits and costs of resource use and environmental protection should be fairly distributed; and that sustainability should be held as a moral good.

Needless to say, the British Columbia forestry commissioner told the Round Table to keep out of forestry affairs—but such a vision cannot be suppresed. For further details, contact British Columbia Round Table on Environment and Economy, Suite 229, 560 Johnson St., Victoria, BC V8W 3C6, Canada (phone 604-387-5422).

Development Training.
The Rocky Mountain Institute (1739 Snowmass Creek Road, Snowmass, CO 81654-9199; phone 303-927-3851) holds Economic Renewal Training Seminars aimed at helping communities chart their own course toward diversity and stability. They emphasize four major principles:
1) plug the unnecessary leak of dollars from the community,
2) support existing business,
3) encourage new local business, and
4) recruit business that is compatible with the community.
Such an approach is an alternative to prostration before absentee-owned, export-oriented branch plants of exploitive corporations.

Make maps.
Using maps, communities can help identify areas needing special attention and protection. People can symbolically draw the line. Mapping is also essential to locate the damage. Just how much of an area has been clearcut? Statistics alone cannot tell the whole story because they do not show how cutting is distributed over the landscape and where it is located.

Mapping owls.
In the Pacific Northwest, groups such as The Wilderness Society, National Audubon Society, and Headwaters made detailed maps showing locations of old-growth forests and spotted owl habitat. These groups used different techniques for drawing their maps, ranging from satellite photos and computers to aerial photos and trained volunteers on foot. The process of mapping not only helped to save many old-growth stands but also helped get many citizens involved in the issue.

Satellites and computers.
The forestry school at the University of Maine at Orono and the State Department of Conservation have sophisticated computer system called Geo-

graphic Information Systems (or GIS) that use satellite photos that can be viewed in a variety of colors to reveal details of vegetation and land use. GIS will be used by the state to assist in monitoring forest practices for the Forest Practices Act. If local communities could have access to such photos and maps, the result could be powerful.

High Altitude Aerial Photography
Individuals, groups, or communities can purchase reasonably priced high altitude aerial photos (either in black and white or color) from Sioux Falls-ESIC (Earth Science Information Center), U.S. Geological Survery, Sioux Falls, SD 57198 (phone 1-800-USA-MAPS for more details). These photos can clearly show what areas of a township have been clearcut, and can be a basis for map making.

Local ordinances.
The best way for local communities in Maine to have a say in management is to have their own regulations. There have been many industry attempt to pass bills in the legislature to preempt local regulations (one is before the legislature as I write this). So far these attempts have failed.

Forest practices ordinances.
In the early 1980s, officials of the small Aroostook County town of Linneus grew alarmed at the massive clearcuts by out-of-state landowners that were devastating surrounding towns. In 1984 the town passed a local harvesting ordinance that effectively banned clearcutting except for special circumstances. This ordinance still stands, and now a few dozen other towns in the state have created their own ordinances. For examples of local ordinances, write to Maine Forest Service, Department of Conservation, State House, Augusta, ME 04333 (phone 207-289-2791).

Environmental ordinances.
Soon after International Paper Company started hiring scabs during a long and divisive strike at Jay, Maine, serious environmental incidents, such as chlorine leaks, increased. Frustrated at the lack of adequate state response to these incidents, the townspeople voted to establish their own environmental ordinance and hired former state Department of Environmental Protection official David Tudor to be their enforcement officer. For more information, write to Town of Jay, Jay, ME 04239.

Regional regulation.
The next step, which has not yet been taken in Maine, is for clusters of towns to hire foresters and enforcement officers. This would be the beginning of a regional people-directed forestry agency rather than the industry-dominated bureau that currently is wielding (or not wielding) power.

Santa Cruz rules.
The central coast of California has strict forest practices regulations that ban clearcutting, allow timber companies to harvest no more than once per decade on any site, and that have tough standards to control erosion and preserve soil fertility. According to the book *Saving Our Ancient For-*

ests by Seth Zukerman (The Wilderness Society, Living Planet Press, Los Angeles, 1991), one forester for an industrial landowner calls the resulting practices "pretty forestry" and credits the rules with keeping the "environmental monkey off our backs."

Fight blackmail.
Large landowners should be stopped from exerting job blackmail when communities or the state enact reasonable regulations and taxation standards that the companies don't like. Environmentalists can form coalitions with labor to study options and to prevent disasters.

For information on labor/environmental cooperation in dealing with attempted job blackmail by Champion International at a North Carolina pulpmill, write to the Clean Water Fund of North Carolina, 138 East Chestnut Street, Asheville, NC 28801. Send $3.

State laws.
This book has documented the insufficiencies of current attempts to protect forests with zoning and regulations. Adequate state laws will not be put in place until a well organized public demands it. The public must understand, however, that although regulations may prevent the worst management abuses, they do not necessarily force the best management practices. These come from ethics, education, example, assistance, and incentives.

Zoning.
Maine's Land Use Regulation Commission could, if it had the will, protect lakes and rivers from development pressures. The public has to supply that will to stop the incremental defilement of shorelands. The Natural Resources Council of Maine (271 State Street, Augusta, ME 04330, phone 207-622-3101) has recommended that much of the unorganized territories (not just shorelands) be zoned for present use (forestry) to prevent subdivisions and development. Such blanket zoning, however, would prevent those who work the forest from living near it.

Regulations.
Current forest practices regulations represent a nuisance to landowners with little or no public benefit—except for better data gathering. The public and the forest lose when clearcutting and herbicide spraying are considered an acceptable first management choice. An organized public could work for regulations that would reduce or end clearcutting (especially whole-tree clearcuts), rather than just spread it out. An organized public could work to reduce or end herbicide spraying rather than just hope for skips and buffers. Rather than allow most of a township to be cut over in as little as 20 years, an organized public could set as a goal that each township should have substantial proportion of forests that contain trees over 150 years old.

Perhaps one reason why industry lobbyists have been trying to get rid of local ordinances is that these examples are demonstrating that landowners can live with regulations that prevent the worst abuses.

Referendums.

When the "proper political channels" fail to execute the will of the people, citizens can initiate referendums to bypass the legislature and go directly to the voter. The referendums should be clearly worded, easily understood, and easily defended.

In the 1990 election, California voters had two major referendums to vote on that would have affected forestry policy: "Big Green" which would have had major effects on pesticide use and agriculture, and "Forests Forever," which would have set strict forest practices regulations, including restricting clearcuts to a fraction of an acre. Both referendums lost. Besides the massive industrial lobbying against the referendums, these efforts lost votes due to overcomplexity (they tried to be too comprehensive), and due to high estimated costs at a time of recession.

Public example.

In a state dominated by "working forests," Maine does not need yet another example of a bogus form of "dominant use"—where people can recreate in the beauty strips and loggers can cut beyond the beauty strips.

Public Lands.

Some state forestland, however, could be used to demonstrate forest practices that are ecologically sound, socially responsible, and economically viable. If the state can manage in an ecologically sound manner and make a decent return, then industrial landowners should be able to do the same. If the state cannot do so, then the public should be alerted that the system needs to be reformed so that sustainable forestry can be made economically viable. In either case, forestry on public lands should be made highly visible and should be closely scrutinized.

Assistance.

Many more woodlot owners would do ecologically sound silviculture if they had access to ecologically minded foresters and loggers. The first step is for the government to accept that model and then train individuals.

Sue government and industry.

Although expensive, the courts offer one remedy for government and corporate misdeeds. Legal suits have been used to ensure that government agencies follow their own laws concerning Environmental Impact Statements, the Endangered Species Act, or even diversions from stated policy.

Legal Suits.

Bill Butler and Charles Fitzgerald, long-time forestry critics, were appalled by the cutting they saw in Baxter State Park's Scientific Forest Management Area back in 1985. When park authorities refused to cease their operation, the two men sued. The suit led to an immediate end to cutting and a restructuring of the management process. For more information write to Bill Butler, Friends of the Maine Woods, Aurora, ME 04408 (phone 207-584-5311).

Whistle blowing and internal reform.

Conscientious individuals in industry or government can act as whistle-blowers when the political or economic process is corrupted. They can work from within to reform their organization and to maintain more open communication with groups interested in reform.

Internal Ethics.

Jeff Debonis, a U.S. Forest Service employee in Oregon, found that his conscience bothered him. Was the purpose of the Forest Service to serve the industry or to serve the forest and the public? He decided he was there to serve the forest and the public. He wrote a letter to the Forest Service chief about his concerns, started an organization called The Association of Forest Service Employees for Environmental Ethics (AFSEEE), and in 1989 began publishing a newsletter called *Inner Voice*, to give voice to those in the system with desires for change. He got national media attention. For more information write to AFSEEE, P.O. Box 11615, Eugene, OR 97440 (phone 503-484-2692).

Coordinated approaches.

A combination of state, federal, and local governments can help establish large biodiversity preserves either through direct purchase or through coordinating government strategies. Certainly citizens should strive to ensure that current government policies do not contradict one another but instead work together to accomplish goals.

Government purchases.

Millions of acres of Maine forest are currently available for purchase if the offered price is right. Because of cost, a multimillion-acre purchase would have to have federal government involvement. Government purchase, in one swift move, prevents forests from falling into the hands of developers and speculators. But coupled with government control would have to be government reform. The land use would have to meet ecological and social guidelines and not be a new supply of subsidized stumpage. There would have to be local input, not control by distant, unresponsive bureaucracies.

Federal Reform.

National forest reform coalitions are working on a number of bills that could lead to major changes in forest practices across the country. The most important such bill at this writing is H.R. 1969, the Forest Biodiversity and Clearcutting Prohibition Bill, sponsored by Representative John Bryant (D-TX). This bill would end clearcut logging on national forests and mandate federal agencies to restore native biodiveristy. For more information, contact the Forest Reform Netowrk, or Save America's Forest (addresses listed previously in this section).

Greenlining.

Greenlining is a strategy used in the Adirondacks of New York, the Pine Barrens of New Jersey, and the Columbia Gorge of Washington which consists of identifying an area to be protected and then applying a combination of strategies, such as outright purchase, taxation, regulation, zoning, and purchase of easements, to achieve desired protection goals.

An array of government strategy options are listed in the Northern Forest Lands Study. Individuals and groups can write to the Northern Forest Lands Council (45 Portsmouth Street, Concord, NH 03301, phone 603-224-6590) and their legislators to choose the combined strategies that will actually solve problems, rather than just reinforce the status quo.

Greenlining has become the most controversial suggestion of the NFLS, because private landowner rights groups perceive it as the ultimate in government intrusion. They see greenlining as an attempt by manipulative government agencies, which are not accountable to the people in the region, to direct local people's lives for the sake of out-of-state tourists. One of the more vocal groups in Maine is the Maine Conservation Rights Institute (MERCRI), Box 220, Lubec, ME 04652 (phone 207-733-5593).

Based on government performance in the past, these groups have some basis for their fears. The greenlining that environmental groups have been promoting for Maine, however, would be for areas that are almost completely dominated by a few large, corporate, absentee landowners, and have few, if any, settlements. Any agency would have to be accountable to the public. Direct purchase of large blocks of land from willing sellers, however, is certainly an easier strategy for creating preserves.

Just say "no!"

Communities and individuals do not always have regulatory or legal options to protect their forests. When they are up against the wall, people can stop environmentally destructive events before they happen by just saying No! to the building of unwanted mills, the initiation of unwanted logging in sensitive ecological or cultural areas, the spreading of dioxin- contaminated sludge, or the spraying of herbicides over clearcuts.

No! to unwanted logging.
The Haida Indians of South Moresby, British Columbia, did not want their old-growth forests ruined by an impending logging operation. They began a series of blockades and protests that attracted world attention and eventually saved their forests. The Canadian Ministry of the Environment declared South Moresby a national park.

No! to unwanted mills.
Citizens have recently halted or slowed plans for the construction of Kraft paper mills (which create dioxins and furans as byproducts) in Alberta, Canada, and at the mouth of the Columbia River in Oregon. Particularly significant in these cases was testimony on the problems of dealing with the accumulation and bioconcentration of organochlorines. For more information see the special issue on "Organochlorines, Pulp Mills, and Change" of the *Journal of Pesticide Reform*, Summer 1990, Vol. 10, No. 2.

No! to herbicides.

Even an individual taking a stand can make a difference. Michael Vernon lives on land surrounded by Scott Paper Company in Brighton Plantation, Maine. In September of 1990, a crew of herbicide applicators trying to enter a Scott clearcut via a road through Vernon's land discovered that Vernon had blocked the road with his pickup truck. He insisted that he would not allow a truck full of poison to cross his property. Even after the Scott crew came back with the local sheriff, Vernon refused to budge. The crew was able to spray, however, by approaching the clearcut from another road.

That was not the end of the story, however. Scott is suing Vernon. Vernon, who is also trying to pass a local ordinance to ban herbicide spraying and restrict the maximum size of clearcuts to five acres, has suffered for daring to confront Scott. In January 1992 his house was burned. Vernon's address is RFD 1, Box 4025, Solon, ME 04979.

Political Reform.

The politicians and the system in which they operate have to become more accountable to the public, rather than to absentee special interests. The subject deserves major rethinking, and the system needs major restructuring.

Conflict of interest.

The board that regulates pesticide spraying in Maine is dominated by those who spray pesticides. The commission that regulates forestry practices in the unorganized territories is dominated by those with forestry interests. The committees which set forestry policy are also dominated by forestry interests. These interests, of course, have the right to testify before and advise such boards, commissions or committees. But they should not have decision-making positions on these governmental bodies.

Accountable candidates.

From 1974-1990 forestry was not debated by candidates for higher office in Maine. Obviously, they will not debate this issue unless the public makes them. Once again, this can only be accomplished through organization. The political process does not respond as well to reason as it does to power.

Delete PACS.

Big Money distorts elections. Political Action Committees are not exactly buying candidates, but they are surely influencing them. Without Big Money, it is difficult to get elected. Campaign spending limits are necessary. The public gets what it deserves when it votes for officials based on saturation sound-byte advertising that has no real content. Common Cause, 335 Water Street, Augusta, 04330 (phone 207-622-5798), and the Maine People's Alliance (MPA), 20 Danforth Street, Portland (phone 207-761-4400) are two groups working for electoral reform. The MPA has published, *Citizen's Guide to the Legislature*, which lists the state candidates' backgrounds, voting records, and sources of contributions.

Building Coalition

Rather than rely on politicians to solve forestry disputes from the top down, local stakeholders with a common interest in sustainability can build coalitions where consensus is reached towards mutually satisfactory solutions.

Maine's Forest Practices Act was developed in advance by an Environmental/Industrial Forum that consisted mostly of professional environmentalists (who did not live in or near the industrial forest) and representatives of absentee-based industrial ownerships. Major grassroots stakeholders from forest-based communities were left out of the debate until the forestry bill was already crafted. The result was a bill that allowed cutting that can be non-sustainable for timber, wildlife, and local jobs.

In contrast, in British Columbia, the Tin Wis Coalition included representatives of labor, local communities, Native American tribes, and grassroots environmentalists. Despite years of antagonisms, these groups recognized that sustainable, local-based forestry could benefit all. They hammered out a Forest Stewardship Act (not yet passed as of Winter, 1991-1992) that would allow local input into management plans, respect for Native culture, preservation of work opportunities, with an emphasis on local value-added products, rather than export of raw materials. For more informaiton contact the Tin Wis Coalition, c/-12 N. Delta Avenue, Burnaby B.C. V5B 1E6 (phone 604-299-9532).

Epilog

If my analysis of Maine's forest is correct, we are facing some serious problems. Most people, understandably, would prefer simple solutions—a button to push, a product to buy, or a vote to cast—to make forestry problems go away without inconveniencing their lives. But I have suggested in this book that we will need major changes in the way we think and live if we are to have a healthy forest or a stable society for our descendents. These changes will require efforts to reform both what industry is doing beyond the beauty strip and what consumers are doing in their homes. Many people, looking at the immensity of the problems facing us, have decided that the situation is hopeless, that the difficult struggles required are not worth the effort.

The prospects are indeed discouraging, and for many reasons:

Existing damage.

Some people who are familiar with the region are puzzled at why I would bother to write a book about saving Maine's forest. "It is too late," they insist. "The forest has already been ruined." Much of the forest has been severely high-graded, simplified, and fragmented. Soil nutrients that were built up over thousands of years are being depleted in a few hundred. It will take many generations for the forest to recover, and even then, it will never be the same, because key species have been lost. The cost to society of restoring these degraded forests will be substantial.

Momentum.

Society is designed around growth without limits. Even if there were no resistance to change and everyone agreed to create a more sustainable society, it would take decades to change the technological, economic, and political infrastructures. It also takes time to to re-educate people to a new way of thinking about nature and society. The idea of sustainability is so foreign to our political system that there are currently no major political parties that even discuss, let alone advocate, a shift in that direction. Momentum assures that despite our best intentions, severe ecological/social disruptions will continue and that the situation will become even more unstable before it gets more stable.

Resistance.

Those who have power will not relinquish it willingly. They will continue to overwhelm the population with propaganda, myths, information overload, biased laws, blackmail, or appeals to patriotism. Some companies will fund bogus "citizens'" groups that promote the industrial agenda. Paper companies are already attempting to co-opt environmentalism by claiming to sell "green" products. A government that sees its prime business as the promotion of big corporations will use its police force to harass and imprison environmentalists who appear to threaten business. The more people try to reform the system, the more industry will resist and the more desperate the situation will become.

Burnout.

The burden of these actions will go to a relatively few overworked activists. This has always been the case. Unfortunately, the number of issues is increasing. Each larger issue has many factions who agree there is a problem but disagree over the solution. Those who want to set up an alternative system, for example, will be enraged by those who wish to reform the current one. Warring between these factions over correct ideology can be just as intense as warring of these factions against industrial management. There are those in industry and government who are well aware of such conflicts and who will not hesitate to take actions to encourage them. Activists tend to burn out.

Change itself.

Assuming activists are successful in initiating change, there is yet another problem: change itself. By definition, one cannot rapidly change to a stable structure because rapid change itself is destabilizing. Furthermore, we have no good examples of any society that has deliberately deindustrialized before. Mistakes will be made. Many of the strategies for change will lead to unanticipated problems. Public doubts over the new direction will grow. There will be movements to return to the good old days of industrialism. The scale of problems and the seeming futility of action can lead to a sense of helplessness and hopelessness.

Escapism.

For those with an overwhelming sense of hopelessness, our society offers various avenues of escape: alcohol, drugs, computer games, television, withdrawal, violence, or even accelerated shopping. These regressive responses can further the rate of ecological and social breakdown. As the social trends become more intolerable, as more paper companies swallow one another in leveraged buy-outs, as landowners continue to liquidate their forests to invest the revenues into commodities with higher returns, as mill shortfalls loom nearer, as more jobs are lost to mechanization, as wildlife diversity continues to decline, as more forests are reduced to brush fields, more people will become convinced that the stress entailed in trying to replace the current system couldn't be worse than the stress entailed in continuing to accept it.

Vision.
By the time the majority of people are ready to junk a disfunctional system and work for (or accept) a new one, there are usually a number of alternative options vying for public support (or acquiescence). The alternative that wins the competition is usually one that not only promises to address the issues the previous model failed to correct but that also is conspicuous and has well-organized supporters. As has been demonstrated throughout history, not all the new societal models accepted lead to results that are sustainable, or even desirable.

When I began this book, the vision of the future of Maine's forest that was most conspicuous and had the most organized support was the vision coming from industry. It was a vision that promised to turn the most productive sites (often hardwood or mixedwood) into short-rotation softwood plantations. It was a vision that promised more clearcutting and herbicides in the spruce-fir forests. It was a vision that declared that the bulk of the forest was an industrial commodity first but that the public could recreate on industry roads, on the lakes and rivers (surrounded by beauty strips that give the illusion of mature forests), and in isolated public parks. It was a vision that promised that local communities would benefit best from a continuation of the status quo of ownership and control.

The established environmental groups in the state were not questioning the larger issue of industrial control. Their response to the industrial vision of a working forest was to modify rather than replace it. They were willing to regulate rather than stop destructive industrial management activities. They were willing to compromise with industry over what could go on beyond the beauty strip, as long as the beauty strip remained intact for recreation.

While I appreciate that there are times when the most responsible action is to compromise, this is not such a time. The environmental/industrial trade-off is not comprehensive enough. It does not account for the social needs of local communities and the biological needs of forests. I wrote this book to set out an alternative vision that was more comprehensive in scope. The book is based on the premise that forest management should be ecologically sound, socially responsible, economically viable, and sustainable. I have tried to demonstrate that from this perspective, not only current but promised future industrial management practices fall short of the mark. I have also tried to show that forestry problems are not isolated from the bigger world and that the problems of industrial forestry can not be solved without dealing with the problems of our industrial economy and philosophy.

In the course of researching this book I have discovered that numerous people around the world have independently come to similar conclusions. I have also been heartened to see that the number of people in the United States who share this alternative vision is growing rapidly. There are public forests in some states where some of the ecological principles are already being applied, and there are groups pushing for these principles to be applied on all national forests. Even some industrial landowners in Maine, especially Fraser, are experimenting with lighter cuts that leave more of the forest intact. These could be the examples that would increase the visibility of the new forestry paradigms for when the public is ready for change.

Part of the reason this new forestry paradigm is spreading so fast is that it is so sensible. One nation that is in the process of making the switch is Germany. Germany was a pioneer in imposing a mechanical order on natural forests. But the old paradigm of the forest as commodity created severe problems. According to the late Richard Plochman, former professor of forest policy at the University of Munich, previous forestry practices based on short-rotation softwood monocultures led to extinctions of and threats to numerous plant and animal species. The water table was getting polluted from pesticides and fertilizers. The quality of lumber was declining, and low-quality industrial wood was becoming noncompetitive in the world market.

According to Plochman, the shift toward natural selection forestry—based on long life cycles, natural regeneration, retention of dead timber, and low input of energy, fertilizers, or pesticides—is leading to obvious benefits for recreation, water resources, landscape stability, wildlfe diversity, and even for forest landowners. In this regard, wrote Plochman, "What needs to be achieved, is not the highest volume, but the highest value per unit area per year."[1] This means managing for large diameters and clear boles on older trees.

Unfortunately, this sensible approach is not enough. German forests, which are fragmented by farms and development and which lack large predators, have excessive deer populations that are causing severe damage in some areas. Forest health is declining in some heavily polluted regions due to the mysterious Waldsterben. The shift to natural regeneration has been difficult because so much of the existing forest is composed of planted exotics—the natural diversity of plant species has been severely reduced. And despite a conspicuous Green party, the German government is still firmly committed to continued industrial growth in a global-based economy, rather than to sustainable development in a community-based economy.

I told an economist friend who is interested in world forestry issues about these changes in German forestry. We discussed the potential of adopting similar ecologically based practices in Maine, where development, monocultures, and air pollution are much less severe. Being an economist, he could not help asking, "But is that kind of forestry economically viable?"

Such a question has great irony, because the social and ecological values destroyed by massive clearcuts exceed the stumpage value of the wood "harvested." And the followups to clearcutting are often not economically viable without government subsidies.

While the question was a rational one within the current economic/political context—where much of the forest is a resource for absentee, multinational corporations that need to maintain adequate returns to shareholders—it reveals how irrational that context is. Our technological, economic, and political systems are supposed to serve people, not enslave them. If it becomes impractical within these systems to have healthy forests and stable communities, if it becomes impractical to ensure the passing of biological wealth to future generations, then there is obviously something wrong with these systems. Rather than degrade forests and communities to adjust to the needs of these systems, we should adjust the systems to the needs of forests and communities. This change will not happen, however, until people who have an interest take an interest.

Reference

1. Richard Plochman, "The Forests of Central Europe: A Changing View,*Forest Planning Canada*, Vol. 7, No. 1 (1991): 40.

Appendix 1
Scientific Names of Tree Species Mentioned in Beyond the Beauty Strip

American basswood (linden): *Tilia americana* L.
American beech: *Fagus grandifolia* Ehrh.
American elm: *Ulmus americana* L.
aspens (poplars) (several species): *Populus* spp.
balsam fir: *Abies basamea* (L.) Mill.
black ash: see brown ash
black birch: *Betula lenta* L.
black cherry: *Prunus serotina* Ehrh.
black spruce: *Picea mariana* (Mill.) B. S. P.
brown ash: *Fraxinus nigra* Marsh.
chokecherry: *Prunus virgiana* L.
eastern hemlock: *Tsuga canadensis* (L.)
eastern hop-hornbeam (ironwood): *Ostrya virginiana* (Mill.) K. Koch
eastern white pine: *Pinus strobus* L.
gray birch: *Betula populifolia* Marsh.
hard maple: see sugar maple
jack pine: *Pinus banksiana* Lamb.
larch: see tamarack
moose maple: see striped maple
northern red oak: *Quercus rubra* L.
northern white-cedar: *Thuja occidentalis* L.
paper birch: see white birch
pin cherry: *Prunus pensylvanica* L. f.
poplars: see aspens
red maple (soft maple, swamp maple, white maple): *Acer rubrum* L.
red pine (Norway pine): *Pinus resinosa* Alt.
red spruce: *Picea rubens* Sarg.
rock maple: see sugar maple
silver maple: *Acer saccharinum* L.
soft maple: see red maple
speckled alder: *Alnus rugosa* (Du Roi)
striped maple (moose maple): *Acer pensylvanicum* L.
sugar maple (hard maple, rock maple): *Acer saccharum* Marsh.
tamarack (eastern larch, hackmatack, juniper): *Larix larcina* (Du Roi) K. Koch
white ash: *Fraxinus americana* L.
white birch (paper birch, canoe birch): *Betula papyrifera* Marsh.
white maple: see red maple
white spruce: *Picea glauca* (Moench) Voss
willows (many species): *Salix* spp.
yellow birch: *Betula alleghaniensis* Britton

Appendix 2:
Whose Woods These Are (January, 1992)

Large Corporate Landowners in Maine
Company: Boise Cascade Corporation
Maine Timberlands: 670,000 acres
Management Style: Boise Cascade, which has only owned its forests in Western Maine for a decade and a half, has contributed some of the largest clearcuts in the region. The company uses a variety of cutting methods—from diameter-limit and shelterwood to large clearcuts—depending on forest type. It also uses some herbicides.
Mill Location: Rumford
Products: Commercial printing, peridical publishing, book, converting papers, market pulp
Capacity—Tons/day:
    Groundwood pulp—180
    Kraft pulp—1,100
    Paper—1,500
Paper Machines: 9
Employees: 1,650
Maine Headquarters: Rumford, ME 04276 (phone 207-364-4521)
Corporate Headquarters: Boise Cascade Corporation, One Jefferson Square, P.O. Box 50, Boise, Idaho 83728-0001 (phone 208-384-6161)
Chief Executive Officer: John B. Fery
Major Owners: State Street Bank and Trust Co. (preferred stock), 6.6 million shares; State Street Bank and Trust Co., 2.4 million shares of common stock, or 6.50 percent of the company; Dodge & Cox of San Francisco, 2.2 million shares, or 5.83 percent; Sanford Bernstein & Co. Inc. of New York, 3.2 million shares, or 8.60 percent; State Farm Mutual Automobile Insurance of Bloomington, 1.9 million shares, or 5.20 percent.

Company: Bowater Incorporated
Maine Timberlands: 2,088,432 acres
Management Style: Before it was bought out by Georgia-Pacific, Great Northern Nekoosa created some of the largest clearcuts and sprayed the most herbicides in the state. It is too early to tell what management methods Bowater (which bought Great Northern from G-P in 1991-92) will emphasize.
Mill Location: East Millinocket
Products: Newsprint, directory paper
Capacity—Tons/day:
    Groundwood pulp—720
    Paper—932
Paper Machines: 3
Mill Location: Millinocket
Products: Uncoated and coated specialty groundwood papers
Capacity—Tons/day:
    Groundwood pulp—550
    Refiner groundwood—110

Sulfite pulp—480
Paper—950
Paper Machines: 6
Other Mills:
Ashland (Pinkham Lumber)
Chips—97,500 cords/year
Lumber—97,350,000 board feet/year
Other Holdings: Owns the largest private hydroelectric dam complex in the United States along the Penobscot River.
Employees: 2,184
Maine Headquarters: Great Northern Paper, Millinocket, ME 04462 (phone 207-723-5131)
Corporate Headquarters: Bowater Inc., One Parklands Drive, P.O. Box 4012, Darien, CT 06820-1412 (Phone—203-656-7200)
Chief Executive Officer: Anthony P. Gammie
Major owners: American Express 3,817,856 shares, or 10.59 percent of the company; Delaware Management Co. Inc. of Philadelphia, 2,829,700 shares, or 7.67 percent; and Wisconsin Investment Board of Madison, 2,603,729 shares, or 7.06 percentof the company.

Company: Champion International Corporation
Timberlands: 730,000 acres
Management Style: In the late 1970s and most of the 1980s, St. Regis, and then Champion (which bought St. Regis), made some of the largest clearcuts in eastern Maine. Because of a spray drift accident in 1979, St. Regis, and then Champion, delayed getting into heavy herbicide spraying. In the early 1990s, Champion has been doing more partial cuts, but still clearcuts. It has reduced cutting on its own lands.
Mill Location: Bucksport
Products: Coated printing papers for magazine and catalogue publishers, wood products
Capacity—Tons/day:
Groundwood pulp—325
TMP (thermo-mechanical pulp)—150
Paper—1,117
Paper Machines: 4
Other Mills:
Costigan
Studs—75,000,000 board feet/year
Chips—45,000 cunits/year
Maine Headquarters: Champion International Corporation, P. O. Box 1200, Bucksport, ME 04416 (phone 207-469-1700)
Corporate Headquarters: Champion International Corporation, One Champion Plaza, Stamford, CT 06921 (phone 203-358-7000)
Chief Executive Officer: Andrew Sigler
Major owners: Loews Corp. of New York, 15.1 million shares, or 16.28 percent of the stock outstanding; Berkshire Hathaway Inc. of Omaha, 3000,000 shares of preference stock convertible into 7.8 percent of the company's common stock.

Company: Fraser Paper, Limited (Fraser is a division of Noranda Inc., a Canadian conglomerate that owns interests in mining, energy, manufacturing, as well as forest products)

Timberlands: 230,000 acres

Management Style: Fraser, which bought its lands from Diamond Occidental, has been setting an example of how an industrial landowner can manage without an emphasis on clearcutting. Fraser uses a variety of cutting methods, including selection, depending on the site.

Mill Location: Madawaska

Products: Bond, books, coated fine, directories, publication, catalogues, specialty papers

Capacity—Tons/day:
    Paper—1,250

Paper Machines: 8

Employees: 1,100

Maine Headquarters: Fraser Paper, LTD, Bridge Street Madawaska, ME 04756 (phone 207-728-3321)

Corporate Headquarters: Noranda Inc., P.O. Box 45, Commerce Court West, Toronto, Ontaria, M5L 1B6, Canada (Phone 416-982-7111)

Chief Executive Officer: Alfred Powis (Adam H. Zimmerman is chairman of Noranda Forest)

Company: Geogia-Pacific Corporation

Timberlands: 486,035 acres

Mill Location: Woodland

Management Style: In the early 1980s, G-P's clearcuts were as vast as any other company's. In the late 1980s, however, G-P primarily shifted to mechanized partial cuts. It has reduced cutting on its own lands.

Products: Market pulp, specialty and fine paper, xerographic papers, building products

Capacity—Tons/day
    Kraft pulp—1,030
    Paper—318
    Cut size—128
    Studs—66,000,000 board feet/year
    OSB (oriented strandboard)—198,000,000 square feet/year

Paper Machines: 1

Employees: 680

Maine Headquarters: Woodland, ME 04756 (phone 207-427-3311)

Corporate Headquarters: 133 Peachtree Street, N.E., Atlanta, Georgia 30303

Chief Executive Officer: T. Marshall Hahn, Jr.

Major owners: No person or entity owns more than five percent of the outstanding shares. As of March 1, 1992, directors and officers of G-P owned a total of 2.2 million shares of common stock, approximately 2.5 percent of the outstanding shares.

Company: International Paper Company

Timberlands: 980,891

Management Style: In the late 1970s and early 1980s, IP made some of the most extensive clearcuts in the state in the Allagash region. It now (early 1990s) does smaller clearcuts and strip cuts for softwood and diameter cuts for hardwoods. It clearcuts, sprays, and plants some hardwood sites to convert them to softwoods.

Mill Location: Jay

Products: Bond papers,tablet, business forms, machine coated publication, envelope papers, specialty papers, wood products
Capacity—Tons/day:
    Paper—1,500
Paper Machines: 5
Other Mills:
Presque Isle—container facility
Lisbon Falls—insulation board
Employees: 1,878
Maine Headquarters: International Paper Company, P.O. Box 547, Jay, ME 04239 (phone 207-897-3432)
International Paper Woodlands, 9 Green Street, Augusta, ME 04330 (phone 623-2931)
Corporate Headquarters: International Paper, Two Manhattanville Road, Purchase, NY 10577 (phone 914-397-1500)
Major owners: Bankers Trust Company, 10.8 million shares, or 7.66 percent of the total common stock outstanding.

Company: James River Corporation
Timberlands: (joint venture with Diamond Occidental Forest Inc.) 526,000 acres.
Management Style: James River has not had its land very long. Diamond and James River are not currently noted as big clearcutters (Diamond did do some heavy budworm salvaging during the early 1980's, however), but instead favor diameter-limit cuts which, at times, may be heavy.
Mill Location: Old Town
Products: Market pulp, tissue products
Capacity—Tons/day:
    Kraft pulp—600
    Paper—190
Paper Machines: 2
Other Mills:
Milo
    Chips—94,000 cords/year
Houlton
    Chips—52,000 cords/year
Costigan
    Chips—52,000 cords/year
Employees: 918
(also owns Otis Specialty Papers in Jay, Maine which manufactures conductive copy base, carbonizing bond, specialty coating base, carbonless base, relase base paper—employs 301)
Maine Headquarters: James River Corporation, P. O. Box 547, Old Town, ME 04468 (phone 207-827-7711)
Diamond Occidental Forest Inc., Old Town, ME 04468 (phone 207-827-4471)
Corporate Headquarters: James River Corporation, P. O. Box 2218, Richmond, VA 23217 (phone 804-644-5411)
Chief Executive Officer: Brenton S. Halsey
Major owners: C & S Sovran Corp of Atlanta, 11.5 million shares, or 14.2 percent; INVESCO MIM PLC of London, 7.4 million shares, or 9.2 percent; The Capital Group Inc. of Los Angeles, 7 million shares, or 8.6 percent; Sanford C. Bernstein &

Co. Inc. of New York, 5 million shares, or 6.4 percent.

Company: Scott Paper Company
Timberlands: 480,000 acres
Management Style: Scott has the distinction of being the first company (starting in the late 1960s) to do extensive, mechanized clearcuts in the state. Scott has set the standard for clearcutting, herbicide spraying, planting, and precommercial thinning in Maine. Nine-tenths of their cuts are clearcuts. Scott was the last company to retain a company crew (mostly for mechanized operations).
Mill Locations:
Scott Wordwide—Winslow
S. D. Warren—Skowhegan and Westbrook
Products:
Scott Worldwide—wax base paper, rolled towels, C-fold, M-fold, hard roll, sanitary tissue
S. D. Warren—book, coated cover, commercial printing, converting graphic, specialty papers
Capacity—Tons/day:
Winslow
    Paper—400
Skowhegan
    Kraft pulp—1,000
    Paper—1,800
Westbrook
    Kraft pulp—300
    Paper—600
Paper Machines: 13 (total, all 3 mills)
Maine Headquarters: Scott Paper Company, Winslow, ME 04902 (phone 207-877-5000
S. D. Warren Company, RFD #3, Skowhegan, ME 04976 (phone 207-453-9301)
S. D. Warren Company, 89 Cumberland Street, Westbrook, ME 04098 (phone 207-856-4000)
Northeast Timberlands, Fairfield, ME 04937 (phone 207-453-2527)
Corporate Headquarters: Scott Paper Company, Scott Plaza, Philadelphia, Pennsylvania 19113 (215-522-5907)
Chief Executive Officer: Phillip E. Lippincott
Major owners: Newbold's Asset Management of Bryn Mawr, 4.2 million shares or 5.7 percent of the company.

Other Large Landownerships
Industrial
Company: J. D. Irving, Ltd.
Timberlands: 561,000 acres
Based: New Brunswick, Canada
Comments: Irving is a family-owned Canadian conglomerate with paper mills, chemical plants, mining, and oil refineries in New Brunswick and oil and gas dealerships throughout Eastern Canada and Maine. Irving prides itself on being the "tree planting company." Its style has been to clearcut, plant black spruce, and spray herbicides. Some towns in Aroostook County passed ordinances in response to

Irving's brutal plantation style. It appears that Irving is starting to rely more on natural regeneration.

Company: J. M. Huber Corporation
Timberlands: 405,000 acres
Based: Edison, New Jersey
Maine Office: J. M. Huber Corporation, 900 Main Street, Old Town, ME 04468 (phone 207-827-7195)
Comments: J. M. Huber is a family-based company with holdings and mills from the South to Maine. Because its only mill in Maine is a wafer-board plant in Easton, it behaves more like a large nonindustrial than a large industrial landowner. Huber family members have been prominant in Maine government and environmental groups.

Company: Kruger-Daquaam
Timberlands: 100,000 acres (approximate)
Based: Quebec, Canada
Comments: Daquaam's land in Maine supplies its sawmills in Quebec.

Company: Daishawa Forest Products
Timberlands: 60,000 acres
Based: Tokyo, Japan
Comments: Daishawa, a multinational paper company, bought the Maine land as a supply of chip wood for its Canadian mills.

Nonindustrial
Company: Prentiss and Carlisle Management Company
Timberlands: 975,000 acres (approximate)
Maine Office: Prentiss and Carlisle Management Company, 107 Court Street, Bangor, ME 04401 (phone 207-942-8295)
Comments: Prentiss and Carlisle is a management company that cuts on the lands of the Griswald Heirs, Webber Timberlands, Lydia Godsoe, McCrillis Timberlands, and Moulton Timberlands. Prentiss and Carlisle cutting can be very "agressive" at times.

Company: Seven Islands Land Company
Timberlands: 1,011,000 acres
Maine Office: Seven Islands Land Company, 304 Hancock Street, Bangor, ME 04401 (phone 207-947-0541)
Comments: Seven Islands manages the land of the Pingree Heirs and other landowners. Pingree and Seven Islands representatives have been involved in the Maine Forest Products Council (industry group), Maine Audubon Society (environmental group), and Land Use Regulation Commission (government agency).

Company: Baskehegan Lands Company
Timberlands: 100,000 acres (approximate)
Maine Office: Baskehegan Company, Route 1, Brookton, ME (phone 207-448-2224)

Comments: Baskehegan manages the lands of the Millikens (a family-based textiles manufacturer). The company is considered to be one of the more responsible forest managers among the large nonindustrials. Most of its cuts, however, are even-aged (shelterwood). Representatives of Baskehegan have played prominant roles in the Maine Forest Products Councl (industrial group), Natural Resources Council of Maine (environmental group), and Land Use Regulation Commission (government agency).

Company: Dunn Timberlands
Timberlands: 171,000 acres
Maine Office: Dunn Timberlands Inc., Garfield Road, Ashland, ME 04732 (phone 435-8024)
Comments: Dunn Timberlands manages the lands of the Dunn Heirs.

Company: Penobscot Nation
Timberlands: 150,000 acres (approximately)
Maine Office: Penobscot Indian Reservation, Indian Island, Old Town, ME 04468 (phone 207-827-7776)
Comments: The Penobscot Tribe's forestlands were acquired through a settlement in the early 1980s.

Company: Passamaquoddy Forestry
Timberlands: 90,000 acres (approximate)
Maine Office: Passamaquoddy Forestry Department, Peter Dana Point, Princeton, ME 04668 (phone 207-796-5100)
Comments: The Passamaquoddy Tribe's forestlands were acquired through a settlement in the early 1980s.

Total (approximate) acreage for these 18 large landowners
10.2 million acres

Total (approximate) including the 450,000 acres of Public Reserved Lands
10.6 million acres

Area of Maine's Unorganized Territories (where most of these large holdings are located)
10.5 million acres

Note: There are other large land ownerships not listed here that may be as large a′ some of those listed.

References
Paper Industry Information Office, *Maine Times, Bangor Daily News*

Appendix 3
Stationary Pollution Sources in Maine

Stationary Sources of Sulfur Dioxide in Maine

Company *Tons/Year*	*State Rank*	
International Paper	1	9,736
Great Northern	2	8,696
Boise Cascade	3	5,487
Central Maine Power*	4	4,583
S.D. Warren (Scott)	5	4,058
James River	6	3,240
Georgia-Pacific	7	2,776
S.D. Warren (Scott)	8	2,719
Lincoln Pulp and Paper	9	2,438
Champion International	10	2,015

Stationary Sources of Nitrogen Oxides in Maine

Central Maine Power*	1	2,452
S.D. Warren (Scott)	2	2,251
"	3	1,899
Boise Cascade	4	1,733
Great Northern	5	1,618
International Paper	6	1,613
Champion International	7	1,553
G-P (wafer board)	8	1,447
Georgia-Pacific	9	901
Great Northern Paper	10	828

Stationary Sources of Volatile Organic Compounds in Maine

G-P (wafer board)	1	3,101
Wood Fiber Industries (IP)	2	1,872
S.D. Warren (Scott)	3	784
"	4	739
Georgia-Pacific	5	605
Texaco Refining*	6	439
International Paper	7	429
Boise Cascade	8	403
Champion	9	347
Great Northern (G-P)	10	261

*Not a paper company
Source: Maine Department of Environmental Protection, Bureau of Air Quality Control, Emmission Rating Report 1988.

Appendix 4:
Presettlement Forest Composition

Forest ecologist Craig Lorimer did an elegant reconstruction of the presettlement forest of northeastern Maine using survey records of 1793-1827. The surveyors listed the species of every "witness tree" (one witness tree per measured mile). From this data, Lorimer was able to estimate the species composition of the forest, as well as the variability of stand composition by region and by soil quality. For the entire tract he studied, he found the following percentages of tree species (I include figures from a 1971 forest survey—right before last big spruce budworm outbreak occurred—for contrast):

Softwood Species	Lorimer's percent	1971 percent
Spruce spp.	20.7	27.1
Balsam fir	14.1	36.5
Cedar	11.9	8.6
Hemlock	4.2	3.2
Pine spp.	1.3	1.4
Larch	1.0	
Total softwoods	53.2	

Hardwood Species	Lorimer's percent	1971 percent
Birch spp.	17.0	5.1
Yellow birch	10.3	
White birch	2.6	
Unspecified	4.1	
Beech	14.9	3.4
Maple spp.	8.1	9.4
Sugar maple	4.4	
White maple	1.8	
Unspecified	1.9	
Ash spp.	2.6	
Black ash	1.9	
Yellow ash	0.1	
Unspecified	0.6	
Poplar spp.	2.3	3.3
Moosewood	0.8	
Hornbeam	0.3	
Alder	0.3	
Willow	0.3	
Cherry	0.1	
Total hardwoods	46.7	

Note: These figures refer to number of trees, not to relative volume.

One can see from this data that by 1971 the percentage of budworm-susceptible species (especially balsam fir) had greatly increased, but that high-quality hardwoods had decreased. The decline in beech and birch (yellow) occurred because of cutting and disease. The increase in maple was for the disturbance-adapted red maples.

Lorimer points out that a large proportion of the white birch and poplar trees were found on an area that had been burned in 1803. If this area were excluded, the percentage of these pioneer species would have been much lower.

Source: Craig Lorimer, "The presettlement forest and natural disturbance cycle of northeastern Maine," *Ecology*, December, 1977, pp. 139-148 and R. H. Ferguson and N. P. Kingsley, *The Timber Resources of Maine*, USDA Forest Service Resource Bulletin NE-26, Broomall, Pennsylvania, 1972, p. 51.

Glossary

Acadian forest: The mixed red spruce-fir/northern hardwood forest of northern New England and eastern Canada.

age-classes: The distribution of trees by age (usually in 10-year increments).

allowable (or accelerated) **cut effect (ACE)**: Justifying high levels of present cut based on the promise of high future yields from intensive management.

balanced age-classes: Having an equal proportion of trees in desired age classes.

basal area: The measurement at breast height (4.5 feet) of the area of cross section of tree stems per acre.

bioconcentrate: When a chemical or heavy metal becomes more concentrated as it moves up the food chain.

biodiversity: *Biological diversity.*

biological diversity: The diversity of life in all its forms and at all levels of organization.

biological legacy: The legacy of structural features and biodiversity that gets passed to succeeding generations of forest despite disturbances.

biomass: The weight of all producers, consumers, and reducers that exist in an ecosystem at a particular time. For forestry, biomass is woodchips (used for energy) from all sources, including sawmill waste; branches, and tops.

boreal forest: The "spruce-moose" forest, sometimes called taiga, found below the tundra. It is dominated by white and black spruce, fir, and jack pine with poplar and birch growing in disturbed areas.

broad spectrum pesticide: A pesticide that is toxic to a wide variety of organisms besides the target "pest."

canopy, closed: A canopy (tree foliage) that shuts off direct sunlight to the understory.

canopy, open: A canopy that allows direct sunlight to reach the understory.

clearcut: The removal of all merchantable trees in an area larger than 2 tree lenghts in diameter (Irland Group Definition). A tree harvest over 5 acres that leaves less than 30 square feet *basal area* of residual trees per acre (state definition).

climax forest: Stage of forest development which is relatively stable and self perpetuating. The climax stage is also called a shifting mosaic or steady state. Because it is continually changing with time, it is dynamic rather than stagnant.

CMAI: *Culmination of mean annual increment.*

commercial clearcut: A clearcut in which all marketable trees are removed, but trees that are non-marketable (either due to size, quality, or species) are left behind. A mining operation.

conifers: Trees whose fruiting bodies are cones; *softwoods*.

culmination of mean annual increment (CMAI): Age at which the *mean annual* *increment (MAI)* of a stand peaks.

deme: An endemic population of plants or animals that may be genetically distinct.

diameter-limit cut: A logging operation in which the logger is told to cut all trees of given species over a certain diameter.

disturbance: Any factor, such as wind, fire, insects, diseases, or timber harvesting, that alters a forest landscape. When the disturbance is severe, it sets a forest back to an earlier successional stage.

ecological rotation: A *rotation* which permits soil nutrients and organic matter to return to preharvest conditions.

ecological stability: *Resistance* to and *resilience* from disturbances.

ecosystem diversity: The variety of ecological communities that occur over a landscape.

ecotone: The border between two types of ecosystems or habitats (also called *edge*).

ectomycorrhizal: See *mycorrhizae*.

edge: The intersection between two habitat types (Also called an *ecotone*).

epicenter: A "hot spot" of insect or disease activity from which an outbreak spreads.

even-aged: Comprising only one or two age classes.

eveness: See species, eveness.

extirpate: To eliminate a species or genetic type locally but not nationally or worldwide.

extractives: Substances other than cellulose removed from wood chips in the pulping process.

fragment: To create islands of habitat that are too small to support viable populations of some species.

frass: Solid larval insect excrement.

gaps: Openings in the forest *canopy*.

genetic diversity: the variety of genetic types within a species.

group selection: The removal of small groups of trees to ensure regeneration while maintaining an *uneven-aged* stand structure.

hardwoods: Broad-leaved trees; Stands containing 75% or more hardwoods.

headwater streams: Streams at the sources of a river.

herbaceous: Characterized by soft-stemmed plant growth.

induced edge: An *edge* induced by *disturbance*.

inert ingredients: "Non-active" (i.e., not intended to be toxic) additives (including spreader-stickers and emulsifiers) to pesticide formulations. Some inert ingredients are toxic.

inherent edge: An *edge* on a stable landscape feature, such as a stream, marsh, or stone outcropping.

integrated pest management (IPM): The integration of cultural, biological, and (as a last resort) chemical methods to bring pest problems to acceptable levels.

intolerant: Unable to grow under the shade of a closed *canopy*.

IPM: *Integrated pest management.*

irregular shelterwood: A variation of *shelterwood* in which the *overstory* is not removed after regeneration is established, thus leading to a forest with two *age classes*.

junk wood: Wood from poor-quality trees.

juvenile wood: The relatively younger growth of wood that tends to have lower density, and higher *lignin* than more mature wood.

LC50s: The concentration of a chemical that can kill 50% of a population.

lignins: Natural glues that hold wood fibers together. These *extractives*, which are removed in the pulping process, are more concentrated in *juvenile wood*.

manual conifer release: The use of chainsaws or clearing saws to remove vegetation that overtops desired *conifers*.

mean annual increment (MAI): The average growth per acre per year of a stand over a *rotation*.

mixed woods: Stands that contain both *softwoods* and *hardwoods*, but where neither constitutes more than 75%.

mor: Rich forest soils, full of leaf mold, found mostly under *hardwoods*.

multiple use management: Managing a forest for a range of resource uses—such as recreation, grazing, or mining—rather than for just timber.

multiple use modules (MUMs): Core preserved areas surrounded by buffers (where low-intensity management is allowed) and connected to other preserved areas with corridors.

MVP: Minimum viable population; the population level required for species continued survival in a given area.

mycorrhizae (or ectomycorrhizae): Fungi that form a symbiotic relationship with tree (or other plant) roots, often playing important roles in increasing water and nutrient intake.

net present value (NPV): A calculation of net value of an investment that discounts future net revenues to reflect current values.

NIMBY: Not in my back yard.

northern hardwoods: Forest communities dominated by sugar maple, American beech, and yellow birch (but may also contain conifers such as red spruce, white pine, and hemlock).

old growth: *Climax* (with the exception of pines) forest stands that have had minimal or no harvesting and that have old (120+ years), dead-standing, and dead downed trees.

oligopoly: The domination of selling markets by a few large companies that can act as price makers.

oligopsony: The domination of buying markets by a few large companies that can act as price takers.

overstory: The trees that make up the upper *canopy* of a forest.

pathological rotation: The average age at which the trees begin to suffer from serious decay.

pioneer species: Fast-growing, early *successional* plant species (often shade-intolerant) that dominate disturbed areas.

podzol (or spodzol): A Russion word for "ash soil." A gray, acidic soil found mostly under cool, moist, spruce-fir forests.

podzoliztion: The transformation of richer soil types to *podzols*.

precommercial thinning: Thinning of a young stand before the trees reach merchantable size.

presettlement forest: The forest as it was before European settlement.

release: Removing vegetation that overtops desired tree species.

resilience: The ability of a forest ecosytem to recover from *disturbance*.

resistance: The ability of a forest ecosystem to resist *disturbance*.

richness: See *species, richness*.

riparian zone: The distinct habitat found near the edge of water bodies, especially within the floodplain.

rotation: The time allowed between *even-aged* harvests of a forest stand.

seed tree harvest: The removal of nearly all marketable trees—except for a small number of desirable seed bearers to provide for natural regeneration—in one cut. In Maine, this is done only with pine, as most other softwoods are not as windfirm.

shelterwood harvest: The removal of marketable trees in a series of cuts to allow regeneration of a new stand under the partial shade of older trees which are removed later. A one-stage shelterwood cut is a clearcut with advanced regeneration. With an irregular shelterwood cut, the overstory is not removed, resulting in a forest with two age classes.

single-species cut: A cutting operation in which only one species is removed.

single-tree selection: the removal of individual trees to create an *uneven-aged* stand.

skid: To drag out trees with a cable, or behind a skidder, tractor, crawler, or horse.

skidder: A large, rubber-tired, articulated framed tractor with a cable winch, or grapple, and a blade used for piling logs.

snags: Dead standing trees.

softwoods: *Coniferous* trees; stands containing 75% or more softwoods.

species diversity: the variety of species types.

species eveness: The degree of proportionate representation of species.

species richness: the number of species.

spruce-fir: Stands containing 75% or more spruce and fir; spruce and/or fir as a resource for mills.

stability: The *resistance* to and/or *resilience* from disturbances.

stocking: The degree of occupancy of land by trees.

strip cuts: A series of *clearcuts* thin enough to assure natural seeding and minimal windfall.

structural diversity: The variety of special features in a forest landscape, such as dead, hollow, or downed trees, slash piles, streams, pools, or shorelands.

stumpage: The value of wood to landowner after subtracting costs of harvest and trucking.

succession: The change in dominant species of vegetation over time. Usually refers to the recovery of forest communities toward *climax* following a severe *disturbance*.

synergism: Where the combined impact is greater than the sum of the impacts of the parts; with toxic chemicals, also called potentiation.

tolerant: Able to grow in the shade of a *closed canopy*.

twitch: The bundle of logs that a *skidder* pulls from the woods to the yard.

understory: The smaller trees and shrubs beneath the *canopy*.

uneven-aged: Having three or more *age classes*.

vernal pools: Small, confined basins that are unconnected to other water bodies and that have water only part of the year.

vertical diversity: The diversity of *canopy* layers in a forest.

vertically integrated: When a company controls successive stages of the production process—such as managing forests, trucking wood to the mill, manufacturing pulp, and manufacturing paper.

virgin forest: A forest that has not been cut. It is not necessarily *old growth*, however, because it may have been subject to major disturbances such as fire.

waste wood: Wood from slash, tops, and mill waste (bark, edgings, and sawdust).

wetlands: Lands saturated or covered with water for part of the year and supporting vegetation adapted to staturated soils.

whole-tree harvest (WTH): The removal of trees with limbs and branches intact.

wildlife: Living organisms that are neither human nor domesticated.

yard: The area where logs are cut to length, sorted, piled, and loaded.

Government Acronyms

BEP: Maine Board of Environmental Protection

BPC: Maine Board of Pesticide Control

BPL: Maine Bureau of Public Lands

CFRU: Cooperative Forestry Research Unit (at the University of Maine)

DEP: Maine Department of Environmental Protection

DIFW: Maine Department of Inland Fisheries and Wildlife

EIS: Environmental Impact Statement

EPA: Environmental Protection Agency

DOC: Maine Department of Conservation

ESA: Endangered Species Act

FDA: Food and Drug Administration

FEIS: Final Environmental Impact Statement

FPA: Forest Practice Act

FPEIS: Final Programmatic Environmental Impact Statement

MFS: Maine Forest Service

NWCA: North Woods Conservation Area

NFLC: Northern Forest Lands Council

NFLS: Northern Forest Lands Study

NFMA: National Forest Management Act

PEIS: Programmatic Enviromental Impact Statement

PRL: Maine's Public Reserved Lands

PUC: Maine Public Utilities Commission

PURPA: Public Utilities Regulatory Policies Act

SFMA: Scientific Forest Management Area

TGTL: Tree Growth Tax Law

USDA: United States Department of Agriculture

WMNF: White Mountain National Forest

Index

People

Organizations

United States Navy, 12
United States Supreme Court, 362
University of California at Davis, 401
University of Maine (*see also* College of
    Forest Resources), 10, 43, 136,
    150, 230, 345, 408
Washington Department of Natural
    Resources, 402
Washington Post, 319
Westinghouse, 167
Weyerhauser, 29
Willamette Industries, 29
World Congress on National Parks, 302
World Wildlife Fund, 299

Places

Adirondack State Park, New York, 15,
    277, 292, 293, 303, 304, 395, 412
Alabama, 75
Allagash Wilderness Waterway, 179,
    297, 302
Alsea, Oregon, 196
Amazon River, 2
Andover, Maine, 59
Androscoggin River, 60, 62
Argentina, 39
Arizona, 216, 229
Ashland, Maine, 49, 226
Australia, 19
Austria, 46
Bald Mountain, 12
Bangor, Maine, 106, 226
Baxter State Park, 2, 143, 239, 268, 297,
    302, 306, 395, 405
Bay of Fundy, 277
Bethel, Maine, 59
Bhopal, India, 59, 220
Big Reed Preserve, 19, 99, 104
Bob Marshall Great Wilderness,
    Adirondacks, 304
Boothbay Harbor, Maine, 226
Bottle Lake, 11
Brazil, 2, 39, 40
Brewer, Maine, 226
Bryon, Maine, 59
Bucksport, Maine, 64, 166, 285

California, 199, 411
Camel's Hump, Vermont, 277, 283
Canada (*see* subject index or individual
    provinces)
Catskill Mountains, New York, 283
Chester, Maine, 166
Columbia, 39, 40
Columbia Gorge, Washington, 412, 413
Connecticut, 8, 15, 188, 206, 251, 292
Copper Basin, Tennessee, 271
Copper Gliff Smelter, Sudbury, Ontario,
    271
Costa Rica, 39
Czechoslovakia, 118
Dedham, Maine, 53
Dennysville, Maine, 8
Dixfield, Maine, 59
Dover-Foxcroft, Maine, 376
Durham, New Hampshire, 282
Eagle Lake (on Allagash), 221
East Millinocket, Maine, 54
Eastport, Maine, 49
Ecuador, 40
Everglades, 5
Finland, 46, 340
Florida, 404
Fort Fairfield, Maine, 166
Fort Kent, Maine, 226
Galiano, British Columbia, 405
Georgia, 15
Germany, 46, 63, 113, 219, 419-420
Gouldsboro, Maine, 226
Great Pond, Maine, 373
Green Mountains, Vermont, 277
Greenville, Maine, 16
Guatamala, 285
Gulf Hagas Gorge, 5, 394
Hancock County, Maine, 70, 373
Hanover, Maine, 59
Haynesville, Maine, 166
Hondurus, 39
Houlton, Maine, 166, 226
Howland, Maine, 53
Hubbard Brook, New Hampshire, 283
Hungary, 118
Huron-Manistee National Forest,
    Michigan, 402
Indonesia, 39, 405
Iowa, 254
Japan, 46, 404

Animals

peregrine falcons, 292
pine martens, 247, 255, 292
quail, 249
rabbits, 242
raccoons, 242, 295
rainbow trout, 258, 259, 276
red-backed salamanders, 254
red-breasted nuthatches, 102
red-cockaded woodpeckers, 289
red-eyed vireos, 211
reptiles, 288
saddled prominent moths, 204
salamanders, 153, 254
shoot moths, 113
shrews, 253
skunks, 249
snail darters, 289
sockeye salmon, 259
spiders, 102, 266
spotted owls, 251, 287, 289
spruce bark beetles, 204
spruce budworms (*see* subject index)
squirrels, 247, 295
sticklebacks, 267
stoneflies, 267
Trichogramma minutum (wasp), 217
turkeys, 292
warblers (*see also* individual species), 153, 246
wasps, 266
waterfleas, 258, 259
weasels, 247
white pine weevils, 204
white sucker, 276
woolly aphids, 204
wolverines, 106, 287, 294, 302
wolves, 106, 287, 293, 294, 295, 302
wood ducks, 247
woodland caribou (*see also* caribou), 292
woodpeckers, 103, 247, 255
wrens, 247
yellow perch, 276
yellow-rumped warblers, 102
zooplankton, 276

Plants

algae, 258
American basswood, 93
American beech, 92, 93, 94, 100, 101, 166, 192, 249
aspen, 91, 92, 93, 94, 96-97, 98, 101, 128, 164, 166, 176, 182, 211, 148
balsam fir (*see also* spruce-fir in subject index), 91, 94, 100, 101, 102, 105, 149, 152, 183, 184-185, 208, 211, 248, 262
black ash. 93
black birch, 93
black cherry, 93
black spruce, 53, 91, 113, 152, 217
Douglas fir, 186
eucalyptus, 41
ferns, 247
Furbish's lousewort, 289
gray birch, 93, 182
hobble bush, 188
horsetails, 247
indian cucumber-root, 249
jack pine, 185
large-flowered trillium, 209
lichens, 246, 247, 288
mosses, 247
mountain ash, 188
mycorrhizae fungi, 104
orchids, 249
phytoplankton, 276
pincherries, 182, 184-185, 248
poplar (*see* aspen)
purple-fringed orchids, 249
raspberries, 182, 184-185, 248
red maple, 93, 94, 96, 188, 211, 248
red pine, 91, 113
red spruce (*see also* subject index for spruce-fir), 91, 97, 101, 135, 145, 183, 208, 217, 277, 279
showy lady's slipper, 249
silver maple, 93, 94
striped maple, 188
sugar maple, 92, 93, 101, 166, 182, 249, 276
tamarack, 91
water lilies, 5

white ash, 93
white birch, 91, 92, 93, 94, 96, 98, 128, 182, 184, 248, 277
white cedar, 93, 249, 262
white pine, 91, 93, 97, 101, 159, 271
white spruce, 91, 145, 185, 216
willow, 93
yellow birch, 92, 93, 94, 166, 182, 210

Subject

1992 photo of author Mitch Lansky standing in the same spruce tree plantation photographed in 1985 that appears on page 110. Note scarcity of spruce, despite herbicide "treatment" several years previously. *Photograph by Jym St. Pierre.*

Mitch Lansky

In 1976 Mitch Lansky was drenched with pesticides in his own backyard by modified WWII bombers targeting the spruce budworm. He consequently founded P.E.S.T. (Protect our Environment from Spray Toxins), an organization that investigated environmentally dangerous forestry practices. Lansky lives with his wife and two children in Wytopitlock, Maine, where he has worked as a carpenter, construction worker, woodsman, saw-mill worker, timber-cruiser, environmental activist, and writer.

Beyond the Beauty Strip

Beyond the Beauty Strip was designed on Crummet Mountain by Edith Allard.
Editorial and production assistance: Devon Phillips, Elizabeth Pierson, Angela Colwell, Kelly Beekman
Layout: Nina Medina
Imagesetting: High Resolutions, Inc., Camden, Maine
Cover and jacket printing: Western Maine Graphics, Norway, Maine
Printing (text) and binding: Maple-Vail, Binghamton, New York
Printed on Cross Pointe's Heritage Book, a recycled paper, with soy-based ink.